CELEBRATE!

FIRST CENTURY MOSAIC FLOOR FOUND IN JERUSALEM

CELEBRATE!

The Complete Jewish Holidays Handbook

Written and Illustrated
by
LESLI KOPPELMAN ROSS

JASON ARONSON INC.
Northvale, New Jersey
London

This book was set in 10 pt. Palatino by Alpha Graphics of Pittsfield, New Hampshire, and printed by Haddon Craftsmen in Scranton, Pennsylvania.

Library of Congress Cataloging-in-Publication Data
Ross, Lesli Koppelman.
    Celebrate! : the complete Jewish holidays handbook / Lesli
Koppelman Ross.
        p.   cm.
    Includes bibliographical references and index.
    ISBN 1-56821-154-6
    1. Fasts and feasts—Judaism. 2. Judaism—Customs and practices.
I. Title.
BM690.R565 1994
296.4'3—dc20   94-1940

Manufactured in the United States of America. Jason Aronson Inc. offers books and cassettes. For information and catalog write to Jason Aronson Inc., 230 Livingston Street, Northvale, New Jersey 07647.

For my grandparents and parents, who gave me the past,

For Beth and Ariel, who are the future, and

For Jordon, who makes the present special.
May we have much to celebrate *ad maya v'esrim*.

CONTENTS

CONTENTS

CONTENTS

A NOTE ON TRANSLITERATION

The English rendition of a Hebrew word can take a variety of forms (a good example is the candle-lighting holiday Chanukah (or Channukah, Hanukkah, Khanukah). The "ch" combination, used to represent the back-of-the-throat rasping sound of the Hebrew letters *khaf* (כ) and *khet* (ח), is particularly problematic, because someone unfamiliar with Hebrew would, on seeing it spelled Cheshvan, pronounce the first syllable of the name of the month like the first syllable of Cheshire Cat.

Some printed materials indicate the guttural sounds by using an "H" with a dot placed under it. I have chosen instead to use a combination of letters that seems to be gaining wider usage and approximates the sound of the Hebrew, "kh." This does have the effect of making some familiar words look odd (like *Khabad*, *khasid*, *khayim*) but gives a more accurate guide to how a word is said. (For consistency I use the *kh* combination throughout the text, even for recognized names such as those above. The only place alternate spellings appear is in bibliographic references, where I give names and titles as they are printed in the books cited.)

There are also differences in rendering the Hebrew letters *bet* (ב), which has either a "b" or "v" sound depending on whether or not there is a dot in the middle of it, and the *tof* (ת), which in the same way has either an "s" or a "t" sound. *Ashkenazi* liturgical pronunciation prefers the former in both cases (*Akiba, Abot, Sukkos, Shabbos*), which gives a Yiddish sound to words, while the *Sephardim* and modern Hebrew prefer the latter (*Akiva, Avot, Sukkot, Shabbat*). The latter is the system I use in the text.

On the introductory page for each chapter, the Hebrew pronunciation of the holiday is indicated, and in some cases its Yiddish pronunciation is also given. We may think of the Yiddish as the anglicized version; it is the one you are probably more familiar with because it is the version introduced here by Yiddish-speaking immigrants from Europe.

I have tried to be faithful to the plural and adjectival forms of words in the Hebrew (*sedarim* rather than *seders*, *Sephardi* rather than Sephardic). All transliteration is phonetic; full pronunciation guidance (with syllable accents) is included in the glossary listings.

THANKS

Like any writer, I now face the impossible task of expressing appreciation to all the people who have contributed, directly and indirectly, to this book. So many have shared themselves, their knowledge, and their wisdom. They have been my teachers, formal and informal, known to me and anonymous. Each has had an impact, whether through a connection that lasted over time or through the briefest contact. I thank all those who have imparted specific bodies of information and all those who have inspired—with even a brief word—new ways of thinking that led to better understanding and unexpected insights.

As with good Jewish education and meaningful holiday celebration, I have to start with family and home. I am fortunate that my paternal grandparents, Max and Madelyn Koppelman, of blessed memory, who lived the humility and *khesed* integral to the *yom tov* mind-set, and my maternal grandparents, Jack and Irene Lowinger, of blessed memory, around whose gracious hospitality so many holiday celebrations in our family took place, safeguarded Jewish tradition so that I was able to experience it as a child. Every day I feel their influence and embrace and am immensely grateful.

I wish to lovingly thank my parents, Lee and Connie Koppelman, for whom being Jewish was always a matter of pride. They also gave me a strong connection with Israel, which has resulted in a lifelong love affair with the country. In their home I first learned to chant the "*Mah Nishtanah*" (from transliterated words my father wrote out for me when I was three or four years old), arranged—in a carefully chosen colorful array—and lit Khanukah candles in a musicbox *menorah* that played "*Maoz Tzur*," and was costumed, in my mother's satin dressing gown and mother-of-pearl Palestine beads, as Queen Esther.

I will always associate the beginning of my adult Jewish education with Rabbi Dr. Jay Goldburg, whose explanations at a Sukkot holiday talk for the employees of The Jewish Hospital of St. Louis made me realize that my values and ideals meshed beautifully with the Judaism from which I had drifted since college, and that drawing closer to it again would not be as difficult as I had sometimes anticipated. Rabbi Dov Heller, whom I think of fondly and with gratitude, patiently guided me during the first years of my learning. Thanks also have to be extended to Rabbi Elazar Grunberger and Mrs. Shelley List, with whom I subsequently learned, and who, along with numerous other friends in St. Louis' University City, opened their homes to me for Shabbat and *yom tov* celebrations that are among my sweetest memories.

At the top of that list are two very special people, not only to me, but in their own right. Both have contributed immeasurably to this book. HaRav Sholom Rivkin, Av Bet Din and Chief Rabbi of St. Louis, clarified matters of *halakhah*, identified sources, and, by sharing insights and information, helped me refine my thinking for certain parts of the text. Rebbetzin Paula Rivkin, in reviewing the entire manuscript, offered invaluable comments and suggestions that again helped clarify my thinking and also resulted in a better book. (It should go without saying that the fault for any errors that remain in the text lies entirely with me.) Above and beyond what they have added to this work, which as I've noted is considerable, is their continual encouragement, love and support, and simply their being who they are. Through their scholarship, *ahavat Yisrael*, humanitarian concerns, open-mindedness, and even-handedness, they exemplify what Judaism and being Jewish are really all about. They will always be an inspiration.

I also want to thank the faculty of the Wexner Heritage Foundation with whom I have been privileged to study, especially Rabbi Nathan Laufer, Rabbi David Silber, Dr. Bernard Steinberg, and Rabbi Joseph Telushkin, who have opened worlds of scripture, commentary, history, and Jewish value in stimulating and insightful ways. Among the many other superb lecturers I've had the opportunity to hear over the years and who have influenced my thinking, the following come to mind: Mrs. Tzipporah Heller and Rabbi Nathan T. Lopes Cardozo of Neve Yerushalayim College, Rabbi Motti Berger of Aish Hatorah, Rabbi Shlomo Riskin of Ohr Torah Institutions, and Avraham Infeld, of Melitz Centers for Jewish-Zionist Education. All merit my grateful appreciation for contributing to my comprehension and experience of Judaism and Jewish holidays.

Thanks are also extended to the staff of the library at Chicago's Spertus College of Judaica, and in particular to Dan Sharon, reference librarian *extraordinaire*. He assisted me not only by helping locate materials and expertly answering questions but by anticipating my needs and making me aware of resources he thought I could use. He made my job considerably easier, and for that and his expertise, I am tremendously grateful. Barbara Raznik, head librarian at the Saul Brodsky Jewish Community Library in St. Louis, also gave freely of her time and efforts during the brief time I spent researching there, and I appreciate her help as well.

In addition, thanks go to Jane Jordan Browne, my agent, for her belief in this project from the start and her guidance through its early stages, and to the many friends, relatives, and acquaintances who were always excited and encouraging about this book. My dear sister Laurel Heard deserves recognition for training her educator's eyes on the manuscript and offering valuable reactions and suggestions. I also want to gratefully acknowledge Tom Silverstein, a family member and friend, who helped me through all sorts of computer problems. And I am especially thankful for my wonderful husband, Jordon, for his constant support and unfailing good humor, even through missed dinners, solitary evenings, late late nights, and other interruptions of marital bliss.

SPECIAL WAYS FOR SPECIAL DAYS

Nothing, in the memories of my childhood years, shines so clearly and so lovingly as this evening of the Passover. The luminous shadows of it have been cast forever across my life, and the magic does not decrease with the years. For on that evening the house was a palace, my father was a king and all of us were members of a royal family, queen and princes and princesses. Even the poorest guest that sat at table with us was an ambassador. My joy was too full to be contained; it spilled over, and poured itself through the room and over the people in it. I wanted the older people to tell me wonderful stories, and I wanted to tell others in return. I was full of the glorious exodus from the land of Egypt, and I lived, in my own way, through all the acts of that greatest of world-dramas.*

Perhaps you can conjure the sensations of similar scenes—the intimate glow of Khanukah candles and the aroma, rising above the crackle of oil, of *latkes* browning to crispness; or the pine-scented embrace of pleasantly cool autumn air, the *sukkah*, providing the perfect setting for a meal of pound cake, grape juice and a Macintosh apple so fresh it sends sweet nectar running down your chin; or the melody of laughter, bells and popping balloons dancing like colored streamers around you, costumed for Purim from Mom's closet of old clothes and a toy chest of props.

If you are fortunate enough to have such recollections, they probably provide the strongest and most positive foundations of your Jewish identity. But not having experienced the holidays with this mixture of awe and excitement, sensory stimulation and family warmth does not mean you cannot create these kinds of memories in your own home. One thing Judaism teaches is that it is *never* too late to learn and to do.

The holidays have always occupied a special place within Jewish consciousness. Initially, they helped forge the nation, establish its relationship with God,

and define its purpose. During the Commonwealth, they promoted unity and served as a reminder of communal goals. Throughout our long exile, they provided relief from a dark existence and reinforced belief in a better future. No matter how oppressed, Jews celebrated freedom; no matter how sad, they rejoiced with abandon; no matter how dreary their present, they anticipated a glorious tomorrow.

Sadly, considering the longevity, wealth, and beauty of our tradition, we are living at a time when many Jewish children are growing up with little or no exposure to it at all. This is not the first time in our history that large numbers of Jews have abandoned Jewish practice, often because they no longer understood it or the depth of what was behind it.

In previous periods, we had King Josiah, who rediscovered a discarded scroll of the Law during a renovation of the Temple, and Ezra and Nehemiah, who reintroduced the people to what they had forgotten before and during the Babylonian exile. Medieval rabbis devised engaging customs to strengthen the resolve of a persecuted people, and mystics injected spirituality into every aspect of Jewish life. Later the *khusidim* emphasized joy in worship over dour intellectual pursuit. In such ways our leaders always managed to reinvigorate Jewish practice and increase commitment to Jewish ideals.

Their emphasis in doing so, like similar efforts today, often focused on family observance. They knew that the family, as the teacher of value, is the seat of Jewish identity, and the home, as the transmitter of memory, is the key to Jewish continuity. At the center of home observance have always been the holidays—with their special smells, sounds, tastes, and rituals, with their rational underpinnings, historic connections, and humane values. This is the stuff of both positive emotional experience and inspiring intellectual appeal that fosters lasting meaningfulness.

The problem for many of us today is that we did not have much exposure to the holidays, and often our Jewish education, if we had any, ended in childhood. That means we never progressed beyond simplistic Sunday school explanations, truncated—often

---

*Shmarya Levin, *Childhood in Exile*, trans. by Maurice Samuel (New York: Harcourt, Brace & World, 1929), pp. 170–171.

fairy tale—history, or superficial glimpses of what Judaism, a religion as intricately layered and beautifully adorned as an ornamented Torah scroll—encompasses. This deficit impedes our ability to comfortably teach others about the celebrations of a way of life designed to elevate the spirit, stimulate the mind, and satisfy the body. But there is no reason our Jewish education cannot begin, or continue, now.

Encompassing numerous dimensions, the holidays open the entire spectrum of Jewish life and thought to us. Through the progress of the Jewish year, we are exposed to who we are as individuals and what we are as a nation. We see what happened to us, how we are supposed to behave, and the long-term reasons behind our actions. The full cycle runs the gamut of emotion and style of celebration. Within a context of recurring themes (exile and redemption, today's reality and tomorrow's perfect world, creating justice and ensuring continuity), each holiday presents its own history lesson, moral message, and opportunity for personal growth. In enjoyable and engaging ways, the Jewish year encases the treasured legacy that is your and your children's rightful inheritance.

This book is designed to help you use that legacy to enrich your life and your family's life today and to bequeath it to your descendants for tomorrow—as your ancestors did for you. In previous generations it was the Jewish, not the universal Gregorian, calendar that defined the passage of a Jew's life. According to it a Jew would sow and reap, rejoice and weep. Public events were set on Hebrew dates, birthdays and anniversaries remembered in reference to them ("she was born on the fifth candle of Khanukah," for example). Through the rhythm of the Jewish year, our grandparents and great-grandparents and their forebears learned to live as Jews. If you observe a year of holidays, you will also know what it means and how to be Jewish. So come. Let's celebrate!

DEAR READER

This is the book on holidays I was looking for when I began, as an adult, to reconnect with my heritage—one that synthesized material I could get only from a variety of sources, went beyond the superficial to embrace the richness and depth of our tradition, and, with a full range of information on why and how to celebrate, provided a foundation for both knowledge and action.

The purpose of *Celebrate!* is to help you do just that: introduce or enhance holiday tradition in your own home. While ostensibly directed at people with little previous Jewish experience, this book, because of its range of information, can be useful to many different groups of people: the first-time celebrant and the veteran of many holidays; those who want to follow tradition to the letter as well as those who want to increase their understanding of some aspect of observance; those looking for an authentic folk custom and those needing inspiration for new ways to celebrate. Of course, trying to accommodate readers from diverse Jewish backgrounds, Jewish educational levels, and philosophical orientations toward Jewish practice poses a number of inherent dilemmas.

If you are looking for a general overview of a holiday, you might think there is more here than you need to know or want to undertake. Not necessarily. This book is comprehensive so that it will remain a valuable resource in your library as your interests—and your children's ages—change. It allows you to make personal connections with the holidays from different angles and levels according to your own situation. (Religious importance not important to you? Perhaps you can more easily relate to historical development. Or maybe you are fascinated by folklore or have an interest in holiday cuisine.) Sections like those on *halakhah* may not be of any concern to you. So skip them. They are here as reference material, when and if you need them.

In fact, the book is arranged so that you do not have to wade through material you do not want in order to find what you need. It can be read in portions, consulted to find answers to questions (yours and your children's), or used to guide you through steps of preparation or execution. Notations throughout refer you to other sections or chapters so that you can easily find needed background explanations that will enhance your understanding of particular points.

There was another reason for being comprehensive: Since Jewish culture is so rich, sometimes different aspects may seem to be in conflict. I wanted to avoid setting up contradictions based on omission. Having a full explanation can give you a better appreciation for why we do certain things and insights into how they can be incorporated into your own celebrations.

On the other hand, if you come from a more observant vantage point, you might question the inclusion of theories drawn from nonreligious literature of how certain thoughts or practices evolved. Raising these points—which are not new to anyone who takes a secular view of Judaism—allows for them to be lifted out of the realm of easily dismissed superstition and placed within Judaism's rational moral and spiritual framework. In the text, I have indicated views that are considered to be outside of classic Jewish thought.

The overall approach is decidedly a traditional one. (The point of this book, after all, is to support a renewal or enhancement of traditional holiday observance.) However, this does not mean "Orthodox," as opposed to Conservative, Reform, or Reconstructionist practices (divisions that did not even exist for most of Jewish history and that you still will not find in most countries where there are Jewish communities today). I do indicate differences, where they occur, in the specific holiday practices of the various movements.

In past generations, choices of what and how to observe were more likely to be made from a position of awareness and understanding than is often the case today. And since most of us try to make any worthwhile decisions in life out of knowledge rather than ignorance, I wanted to present what is recognized as classic Jewish thought in all its depth and variety (which is not necessarily in conflict with liberal interpretations). How you define yourself as a Jew, what *mitzvot* you choose to follow, and the holiday observances you want to keep are entirely up to you. But at least you will have exposure to the basis of all Jewish interpretation, literal or liberal.

Jewish text has never been "the last word" but the beginning of analysis and action. I hope you will use this book in the same way, as a resource and impetus.

NOTES ON ORGANIZATION

Each chapter consists of two main sections. "Why We Celebrate" presents the factual basis for understanding the holiday and its development, along with its significance within Jewish life. "How We Celebrate" gives you all the practical information you need in order to follow the traditional observances connected with the holiday.

The following outlines what you will find in each subsection and provides additional guidance to help you get the most out of this book.

WHY WE CELEBRATE

Historic Foundation

This section explains the origin and development of the holiday. Part of the purpose is to show that the holidays, like Judaism and the Jewish people, are not monolithic or static. Rather, they are filled with diversity and dynamism. Over time they have been shaped by changing needs and circumstances, but always with faithfulness to the original spiritual values. We may continue to make the holidays relevant to our lives today—as long as we do so within the framework of the tradition. If you want to get an overview of Jewish history, you might want to read this section in each chapter.

Religious Importance

This section shows how the holiday promotes certain principles, values, and philosophies of Judaism. If you read all the "Religious Importance" sections, you will gain an understanding of what Judaism is all about. One thing you will notice is that you cannot talk about our religion without mentioning God. Belief in God is the number one commandment and number one principle of faith on which Judaism is built.

Classically, that was no problem. And for those of us who embrace God in our everyday lives—feeling comfortable acknowledging Him, talking about and to Him, consciously and actively working to obey Him—that is still no problem. But for people not used to thinking about God, or even spirituality, the subject may be strange and discomforting. If you have difficulty relating to it, perhaps substituting your own concepts (nature, community, goodness, conscience, social action) will help you better deal with the basic principle.

While recognizing that there are different opinions as to how to understand God, as there have been throughout our history, I have chosen to present the tradition of Jewish thought passed down for three thousand years, a tradition still widely adhered to—despite the so-called advancements of civilization. Jewish religious beliefs reflect human nature, psychological, emotional, and even scientific truths, and are as applicable today as ever.

Personal Meaning

One reason adherence to the holiday calendar has lasted over such a long period of time is that our festivals reflect much more than isolated points on our national timeline. In addition to marking our progress as a people through history, and as a community through the year, with their recurrent themes and moral messages, the holidays present opportunities for personal introspection and growth. The combination of the warm familiarity of a holiday that comes year after year and the fact that you are different each time you celebrate it helps keep observance perennially new.

Here you will find explanations of how and why the ancient commemorations have meaning today. Included are questions, to ask yourself and your children, that will highlight the holidays' significance for you and help you achieve new levels of understanding and commitment.

HOW WE CELEBRATE

Many people who find ritual irrelevant or bothersome do so simply because they do not understand what they are doing or what is being done around them and why. Discomfort and reluctance connected with going into a synagogue or someone else's home when "strange things" will be happening is understandable. (The feeling is captured in an amusing song written by a newly observant man, "I Got the I Don't Know What Page We're On in the Prayer Book Blues.")

The second part of each chapter is meant to remedy that. It provides the practical information you need in order to observe the holiday and/or to understand how it is being observed by others. You may not want to do everything that is explained; you do not have to. I'm giving you the full palette of the rainbow so you can see how all the colors coordinate. If you can accommodate only select hues in your home, choose those.

Ritual Items

For many of the holidays, special items are used, either in the home or synagogue, as part of celebration. (If you visit a Jewish museum, you are likely to see a collection of this Judaica, often works of great artistry and artistic creativity, from different parts of the world and different eras.) Any ceremonial supplies you need or are likely to encounter are described and explained. (You do not have to incur a great expense for them; many of the ritual items are provided by synagogues for their members to use during services, and those required for home use can all be made at little or no cost.) For those who want to purchase any of the items and do not have local access through synagogue shops or Jewish book/supply stores, mail-order services are listed in the Appendix.

Observance

This section details what we do on the holiday at home, in synagogue, and/or in other public settings. The rituals we follow are a combination of those specifically commanded in Torah, the rites and liturgies developed by the rabbis to substitute for celebration no longer possible after we lost the Temple, and customs so widely accepted through common practice that over time they became incorporated into holiday celebration. The why's of observance have been included along with the how's.

Preparation

Like any special event in life, meaningful observance of a holiday does not just happen: There are things we do to get ready, psychologically, spiritually, and physically. During the period of preparation, which might be as short as a few days or as long as forty, we have a great opportunity to build joyful anticipation and excitement for the holiday within the family.

Halakhah

The word, which means Jewish law (plural: *halakhot*, laws), comes from the same root as the words *holeikh* (go, as in "I go down the road") and *halikhot* (ways). It is the body of statutes, ordinances, and rules that govern every aspect of the Jewish way of life—personal and civil, public and private, spiritual and ethical. We can credit adherence to it for keeping the Jews a distinct people despite our lengthy sojourn among alien nations.

The original source for the *halakhah* is the Torah with its 613 commandments (*mitzvot*) regulating the relationship between individuals and between wo/man and God. In the twelfth century, the brilliant scholar Moses ben Maimon (popularly known as Maimonides or by the acronym Rambam; 1135–1204) codified the law in his fourteen-volume *Mishneh* (Second) *Torah*, a commentary on the laws of the Bible based on talmudic interpretation and his own philosophy. Three centuries later, the eminent *Sephardi* Rabbi Joseph Karo (1488–1575) wrote the *Shulkhan Arukh* ("Set Table"), the last great code of rabbinic Judaism. The latter is considered the authority on issues of *halakhah* and the source for Jewish law followed today, although Maimonides, on whose work Karo based his, is also consulted.

I have included *halakhah* for the holidays for two reasons. One is the obvious: so that readers who want to follow the Jewish calendar fully in accordance with our tradition will have the legal guidance at their fingertips. In addition, the *halakhah* often provides lovely insights into the Jewish value system, the evaluative process of the rabbis, the situation of Jews in different times and places, and the evolution of practices connected with the holidays. This comes through in what was permitted, where exceptions to the rule were written into law, what was given precedence in situations of conflict, and how interpretations of law changed over time and in the particular circumstances of a community.

In general, I have included only those *halakhot* that are most relevant in modern circumstances, and refer readers to more detailed resources for less likely or highly specific situations. Laws that are standard for all festivals are covered in the first chapter, on Pesakh, the first festival. Notations in subsequent chapters refer you back to laws you need for the other holidays.

Customs

Different communities at different times developed holiday rituals based on their own particular interpretations of scripture and local circumstances. Sometimes they were the result of a tremendous blow to a community, when an infusion of spirituality or renewed optimism was needed. At others they were in response to economic conditions or the relationship with the non-Jewish community—with whom practices were sometimes shared. Often quaint, they add tremendous color to the tapestry of Jewish life and show us something of our history among the nations. You might see some of these things done in the homes of people who come from different cultural backgrounds than your own. Just as Jews borrowed customs from local populations and, by giving them a Jewish slant, made them their own, or introduced innovative practices that enhanced a holiday's meaning for them, there is no reason you cannot adapt any of these folk customs to add meaning, interest, and fun to your family's celebration.

Traditional Foods

We eat certain foods on the holidays because they are directly commanded (such as *matzah* on Pesakh), represent some aspect of the event behind the holiday (like pancakes fried in oil for Khanukah's miracle of the oil), or symbolize a value of the holiday (honey on Rosh Hashanah for a sweet year). Some of them were chosen because, while meeting a symbolic or halakhic dictate, they also happened to be within the physical reach and budget of the majority of Jews in a particular region at a given time. Cookbooks containing appropriate holiday recipes are listed in the Appendix.

Songs to Sing

Since there are songbooks as well as numerous recordings and a growing library of music videos that are much more comprehensive than a book like this could ever be, you won't find full refrains and notation staffs for holiday songs. Instead, I have suggested songs that are traditionally sung for an occasion or would be most appropriate. In special cases, background or explanation is also provided. Armed with the names, you have your pick of collections of sheet music and recordings that include them. Sources for printed and recorded selections are included in the Appendix.

Stories to Read

While the classic designation for us, "people of the book," comes from our adherence to Torah, we also have the reputation, because of our stress on education, of being voracious readers—and our library keeps growing to prove it. That makes it difficult to keep up with everything that is available.

The materials I have chosen to list—suggestions to get you started—are those that contribute to understanding and appreciation of a holiday. They include traditional folktales (which are sometimes included to provide a glimpse of Jewish life in other eras), story books, young adult novels, and, occasionally, fiction for adults. I have tried to cover a range of settings

and styles, ancient and modern, mystical and matter-of-fact, and works that connect with a theme or message of a holiday in an elucidating and/or inspiring way. Collectively the listings include books produced by all major movements in Judaism; all conform to a traditional Jewish view and are in accordance with the standards of *halakhah*.

The age ranges designated for children's books were provided by professional educators and/or publishers. You may find that your younger children will enjoy some of the books suggested for older ones when they are read aloud. I have not included the picture and board books for very young children, simply because there is not much to recommend one over another and new versions are continually being produced. But if you have an infant or toddler, know that such resources do exist and that my failure to include them in no way indicates their unsuitability. On the contrary, the first three years are critical for Jewish education, and such books are very helpful in introducing the basic concepts of holiday observance to children.

Many of the books listed are available through local libraries, Jewish and sometimes general public facilities as well. Do not overlook the possibility of finding them in synagogues or Jewish center or other Jewish organization libraries, or ordering them through inter-library loan. Any book you want to purchase which is not available locally can usually be ordered (if it is still in print) through a bookstore or directly from the publisher. Some mail-order suppliers of Jewish books are listed in the Appendix.

Sometimes you can find the folktales, particularly those drawn from traditional Jewish sources, in collections other than those I have given. So if you have access to different anthologies, by all means check them for the stories listed, along with others that may be appropriate (our heritage contains thousands).

Since the list of books is forever changing and very extensive, it is a good idea to periodically check your local bookstore or talk with a children's librarian. I also highly recommend a booklet published by the Jewish Book Council, "The Selected Children's Judaica Collection," an annotated bibliography arranged by subject area and noted for age level. The Council produces a number of other book lists for adults and children that are useful guides, including "Word Weavers: Collections of Jewish Stories New and Old," a booklet of annotated listings of folktale anthologies. (For information, contact the Council at 15 East 26th Street, New York, NY 10010; 212-532-4949.)

Rather than give full bibliographic information

every time a collection is cited, I have identified anthologies according to the following code:

BA   Aleichem, Sholom. *The Best of Sholom Aleichem*. Ed. by Irving Howe and Ruth Wisse. Washington: New Republic Books, 1979.

FT   Aleichem, Sholom. *Favorite Tales of Sholom Aleichem*. Trans. by Julius and Frances Butwin. New York: Avenel Books, 1983.

BL   Chagall, Bella. *Burning Lights*. New York: Schocken Books, 1988.

CT   Frankel, Ellen. *The Classic Tales—4,000 Years of Jewish Lore*. Northvale, NJ: Jason Aronson Inc., 1989.

HA   *Holiday Anthology* Series. Ed. by Philip Goodman. Philadelphia: The Jewish Publication Society of America, 1949–1992.

TS   Labovitz, Annette, and Eugene Labovitz. *Time for My Soul—A Treasury of Jewish Stories for Our Holy Days*. Northvale, NJ: Jason Aronson Inc., 1987.

HT   Rabinowitz, Shalom. *Holiday Tales of Sholom Aleichem*. New York: Charles Scribner's Sons, 1979.

JF   Sadeh, Pinhas. *Jewish Folktales*. Trans. by Hillel Halkin. New York: Doubleday, 1989.

KT   Weilerstein, Sadie Rose. *The Adventures of K'tonton*. New York: Women's League for Conservative Judaism, 1964.

Of Additional Interest

Works of music have been created around themes related to the holidays, museums have been constructed to house exhibits related to events behind the holidays, and historic sites in Israel connected with those events have been made accessible to the public. Information about them is provided at the end of the chapters where applicable, so that you can listen to the compositions and visit the sites to further support your family's experience of a holiday.

Except in cases where a piece or genre connected with a holiday is particularly unusual or interesting, art is not listed separately. There are so many renditions of holiday themes and observance—by great masters (particularly Rembrandt, who depicted numerous holiday-related Bible scenes), early Jewish artists Moritz Oppenheim, Bernard Picard, Maurice Gottleib, and Alphonse Levy (who beautifully recorded synagogue and home celebrations), and modern Jewish artists such as Marc Chagall, Shalom of Safed, Reuven Rubin, David Sharir, and Jossi Stern. Seeing how artists—Jewish and non-Jewish—have been inspired by the themes of our holidays can be an added source of pride in the Jewish heritage for our young people. A librarian can direct you to books of the collected works of an artist, collections of art of the Old Testament, and other volumes of works that portray the holidays.

APPENDICES

A: Holiday Preparation Calendar

The calendar provides an overview of the Jewish year and highlights interrelationships between various holidays to help you get ready for them.

B: Twenty-five-Year Jewish Calendar

For the next two and a half decades, you'll know exactly when each holiday begins. (That's the first step in being able to prepare!)

C: Additional Resources

The annotated bibliographies throughout the book suggest good materials on specific subjects. Through them you can also get an idea of the range of material available. Be sure to check the Appendix as well. Listed are books within a holiday series or those that cover numerous aspects of a holiday or many holidays together: holiday anthologies, children's sets, cookbooks, songbooks, prayer books, and books of holiday crafts. Also included are a couple of excellent general reference works that are great to have at home and mail-order sources for Judaica items, books, music, and videotapes.

A NOTE ON SOURCES

In quoting from scripture I have largely relied on two editions: *Tanakh—A New Translation of the Holy Scriptures According to the Traditional Hebrew Text*. Philadelphia: The Jewish Publication Society, 1985; and Kaplan, Aryeh. *The Living Torah—The Five Books of Moses and the Haftarot*. New York: Maznaim Publishing Corporation, 1981.

If you need a Jewish Bible, both of the above are excellent choices. The first, in English, has the advantage of including not only the Five Books of Moses but the Prophets and Writings as well. Produced by a committee of scholars representing the three main branches of organized Jewish life, it uses contemporary language that makes the text accessible and alive. Although the volume by the esteemed Rabbi Aryeh Kaplan contains only Torah and the sections of Prophets assigned for Sabbath and festival readings, they appear in both the original Hebrew and contemporary English. Footnotes explain phrases and terms; maps, diagrams, and drawings augment the text; and a table of contents that breaks down each portion into significant subjects makes it easy to locate particular passages.

Throughout the text there are chapter and verse references for information based on scripture. So often when we are taught, we hear "It is written." But where? For example, any of us who went to Hebrew/Sunday school heard the story about how Abraham, our forefather and the first monotheist, smashed his father's idols. Have you ever tried to find it in the Bible? Don't bother; it's not there. That's because it is a rabbinic legend, a *midrash*, used to fill in what Torah does not explicitly say.

I have indicated when a tradition is found in Talmud or *midrash*, and for any from Torah—which is more easily accessible to most readers—exactly where you can locate it—in case you want to explore something more fully. References to "our sages" or "the rabbis" generally indicate the great scholars early in the millennium who codified and commented on our tradition.

A NOTE ON GENDER REFERENCE

I have given a good deal of consideration to how to solve the problem of gender designation in the text.

Although sometimes cumbersome, in the interests of neutrality, I have used "s/he," "wo/man," or "his/her." (I have recently seen texts that, in an attempt to be even-handed, alternate "he" and "she" in successive sentences when speaking about the same generic person. This strikes me as being unnecessarily confusing. It also diverts concentration from the text by calling attention to a political agenda.) There may be instances where I have used a masculine term because it is less awkward, encompasses both genders, or, like it or not, is still the officially recognized collective word in the English language.

Please keep in mind, however, particularly when reading about historic development, that in many instances, the masculine personal pronoun is used simply because it is accurate: traditionally there were things done only by men. This is not a value judgment; it has to do with responsibility as defined by Jewish law and not with the superiority of one sex over the other.

References to God are masculine, because that is the classic and least awkward form and, until some gender-neutral word is adopted into our language, the least confusing. It should also be noted that according to Judaism, God is of no specific gender. In Hebrew, this is obvious. Some of "His" names are actually in the plural, and one, *Shekhinah*, the Divine Presence in the World, is in the feminine. God is neither masculine nor feminine; He is both—just as the original human being was created, in God's image, as a creature with masculine and feminine attributes that were later separated (with some cross-over) so that Adam could have a complementary, equal but different, partner.

CYCLE OF CELEBRATION: THE JEWISH CALENDAR

One of the most distinctive elements of Judaism—and one that has helped preserve our unique way of life—is our calendar. It is a system that recognizes God's involvement in both nature and history, yet encourages us to be masters of our own time.

When God created the celestial illuminations to separate day from night, He also intended that they "serve as signs for the set times" or festivals (*mo'adim*) (Genesis 1:14). Unlike the strictly solar Gregorian calendar (based on the 365 and ¼ days it takes for the Earth to circle the sun), or the strictly lunar Mohammedan calendar (based on the 29 and ½ days it takes for the moon to circle the Earth), the Jewish calendar relies on both the sun and the moon. The sun, which determines the agricultural year, grounds us in nature. The moon, waxing and waning, reflects our history and destiny of renewal after diminishment.

DIVIDING OUR TIME

After the Creation account, the next biblical reference to time comes just before the Exodus, when "this month" is designated as "the first of months of the year for you" (Exodus 12:2). The sages identify the verse as the first commandment, directing us to be responsible for designating divisions of time and avoiding time's oppression by enjoying days of complete rest. Declaring the beginning of any month—necessary in order to determine when to celebrate the "set times" given as "the fifteenth day of the first month" or the "tenth day of the seventh month," and so on—became the basis for establishing the Jewish calendar.

The importance of community in Jewish life dictated that all Jews celebrate holidays at the same time. That meant a standard start of a new month had to be known by everyone so they could count the days before a festival in unison. At the time of the First Temple, the high priest made the determination based on the moon's first appearance in the sky.

During the era of the Second Temple, two eyewitnesses would testify before the Sanhedrin (rabbinical court) that they had seen the crescent sliver. If the witnesses arrived by late afternoon on the thirtieth day after a month began, it was declared to be *Rosh* (literally "head," understood as "new") *Khodesh* (month). If they came later, the following day was proclaimed to be the first of the new month. To let everyone else know, bonfires were set on hilltops in Jerusalem, then in the next ring of settlements, and so on, until the news reached Jewish communities as far away as Babylonia.

When the Romans, who later occupied the Holy Land, prohibited the signal fires, and the Samaritan separatists lit their own fires on different nights to cause confusion, the court resorted to sending messenger relays. With this slower communication system, it could take several days—even weeks—before the official start of the new month was known by communities in remote areas of Palestine or furthest from Jerusalem (which was very far after the destruction of the Second Temple and the dispersal of Jews throughout the world).

To avoid designating the wrong day, those far-flung communities decided to observe Rosh Khodesh on the thirtieth and thirty-first days after the previous one, and since they sometimes did not find out when the month had started until it was half over, they also began to celebrate all festivals (but not fasts) for two days. This practice became the universal custom outside Israel.

Even the relay system had to be abandoned, because under the oppression of Constantine (337–361), all religious observance was prohibited and the Jews of Palestine could no longer proclaim the new moon. A fixed calendar that could specify the days well in advance was needed.

One had actually been in the works, based on mathematics and astronomical study by the rabbis, since shortly after the dispersion. Finally codified by Rabbi Hillel II, it was adopted in 359 (and adjusted for close to five hundred years after that). Although a set calendar eliminated the need for a second day of Rosh Khodesh or holidays, the Jews outside Palestine insisted on keeping it (a demonstration of the power of custom in our tradition). The custom continues today except among Reform Jews and in Israel.

THE CALENDAR STRUCTURE

The Jewish calendar consists of twelve lunar months of either twenty-nine or thirty days. With the short months, the day following the end of the month becomes Rosh Khodesh of the next month and is celebrated for one day. With the long months, the last day of the month and the first of the next month are observed as a two-day Rosh Khodesh.

In biblical parlance, the months are referred to primarily by number (first month, second month, etc.). When the Jews returned to Israel from Babylonia, they introduced the names they had learned there: *Nissan* (corresponding to the "first month" and March–April), *Iyar* (April–May), *Sivan* (May–June), *Tammuz* (June–July), *Av* (July–August), *Elul* (August–September), *Tishrei* (September–October), *Kheshvan* (October–November), *Kislev* (November–December), *Tevet* (December–January), *Shevat* (January–February), and *Adar* (February–March). *Kheshvan* is often called *Markheshvan* (*mar* meaning bitter or mister, because it is a month that contains no special occasions—therefore bitter—and because in compensation the rabbis wanted to give it an air of importance: Mr. *Kheshvan*).

It is often believed that the Jewish year begins in autumn with *Tishrei*. In a way it does: that is when we celebrate what we call the Jewish new year (Rosh Hashanah; more accurately "head" of the year). Even printed Jewish calendars start with *Tishrei* and end with *Adar*, and the count of the year changes then.

While *Tishrei* is the first month for religious matters (such as the beginning of our spiritual year and of Sabbatical and Jubilee years), our festival year begins with *Nissan*, the month in which our redemption from slavery and our life as a holy nation began (see chapter on Pesakh). In the days of the Jewish commonwealths, this was also the date for calculating the length of reign of Jewish kings. (Actually, we have four new years, the other two being *Shevat*, for tithing of trees [see chapter on Tu B'Shevat], and *Elul*, for tithing of cattle.)

The even-numbered months, with the exception of *Kheshvan*, have twenty-nine days each, and the odd-numbered months, with the exception of *Kislev*, have thirty days each. The two were left open to give the rabbis room to manipulate the calendar so that certain festivals would not occur on particular days of the week. For example, if Yom Kippur fell on a Friday or Sunday, complications would arise because of its juxtaposition with Shabbat. Giving extra days in the flexible months, when necessary, avoids those problems.

One other adjustment was necessary. If you add up the days in all the months, you get a total of 354. (The lunar year is technically three hundred fifty-four days, eight hours, forty-eight minutes and thirty-six seconds). The solar year, as we all know, is three hundred sixty-five days (plus six hours and forty-eight seconds). The discrepancy of just under eleven days, if not somehow resolved, would result in each holiday falling that much earlier each succeeding year. That would wreak particular havoc with the festivals that have seasonal significance—putting the spring festival of redemption and rebirth in the dead of winter, the fall harvest festival in the middle of the growing season, and so on.

To compensate, the rabbis inserted an additional (intercalary) thirty-day month seven times in each nineteen-year cycle—creating leap years in the third, sixth, eighth, eleventh, fourteenth, seventeenth, and nineteenth years. Placed between the end of one year and the beginning of the next, the extra month is called *Adar Sheni* (second).

THE HOLIDAYS

The schedule of holidays we observe is a combination of the festivals ordained in Torah, which provide opportunities for us to renew our relationship with God; feasts and fasts added by the rabbis during and just after the Second Temple period, which commemorate significant triumphs and defeats; and the modern commemorative days introduced since 1949, which mark monumental changes in the situation of the Jewish people in the world.

The "set times of the Lord, the sacred occasions which you shall celebrate each at its appointed time" (Leviticus 23:4) include the three pilgrimage festivals (Pesakh, Shavuot, and Sukkot). While superficially marking a stage in the agricultural year, each is a progressive step toward true freedom and spiritual maturity. The other two "set times," Rosh Hashanah and Yom Kippur, encapsulate the purpose of all the festivals: improving ourselves and drawing close to God.

The postbiblical holidays ordained by the sages commemorate our triumph in exile over a threat to our physical existence (Purim), our triumph on the Land over a threat to our spiritual existence (Khanukah), and catastrophes that threatened both (Tisha B'Av and the minor fast days related to it, Shivah Asar B'Tammuz, Tzom Gedaliah, and Asarah B'Tevet). They are paralleled by the days most recently added to the calendar (by law in the State of

Israel and acceptance of the Jewish people): Yom Hashoah (Holocaust Remembrance Day) for the destruction, and Yom Ha'atzmaut (Israel Independence Day) and Yom Yerushalayim (Jerusalem Unification Day) for the resurrection. The two other special occasions are folk festivals that add a bit of levity to the year, Tu B'Shevat and Lag B'Omer.

There is one holiday you will not find as a separate subject in this book: Shabbat (Sabbath), the weekly opportunity for spiritual renewal. It warrants a tome in itself (many have been written). You should be aware, however, that with its release from quotidian routine, the Sabbath is the model for observance of all the major festivals. And like them, it is observed (at least in part) in memory of the Exodus from Egypt, which provided the foundation for the concepts of freedom and mastery of time that pervade Judaism and the Jewish calendar.

BLESSING THE SIGNS OF OUR TIMES

Judaism is adamant against the worship of the sun and moon (and any other objects of nature or otherwise) in themselves, but as orbs created with Divine purpose for human benefit, they are objects to be appropriately appreciated.

As commanded by Torah, the new moon was to be marked with the sounding of trumpets and special sacrifices (Numbers 10:10). It was also an occasion for feasting, as alluded to in I Samuel's account of King Saul's days. The offerings and special blessings for the new moon were later made at the Temple.

In the centuries after the Second Temple was destroyed, the people continued to have a special meal and men in particular did not work on the day(s) of the new month. Women did little housework and children were given time off from school.

At some point, the occasion became a special respite for women. According to *midrash* (rabbinic expansion on scripture), when Aaron told the people to take earrings from their wives and children in order to make the Golden Calf (Exodus 32:2), the women did not willfully comply. In recognition of their refusal to participate in idol worship, they were given Rosh Khodesh as a perpetual holiday, a day on which they did not have to work. In recent years, as Jewish women searched for ways to connect with our heritage, particularly through rituals of their own, they rediscovered Rosh Khodesh. In congrega-

tional settings and outside of them, women have introduced special ceremonies for the occasion.

Aside from them, the observance today primarily consists of additions to the liturgy. (Some particularly pious people also continue the custom begun by the Jewish mystics in the sixteenth century: They treat the day before Rosh Khodesh as a minor day of repentence [Yom Kippur Katan] and use it to fast and pray for forgiveness for transgressions made during the previous month.) At the morning service on the Sabbath prior to Rosh Khodesh, called Shabbat Mevarkhim ("when blessing is made"), the exact time the new month will start is announced and special prayers recited. On the day of the new moon itself, we recite *Hallel* (Psalms of Praise) during the morning service, read a special Torah portion (Numbers 28:9–15, detailing the sacrifices to be made for the new moon), and add special phrases to the other daily services and the grace said after meals.

The Orthodox also have the custom of blessing the new moon (*kiddush levanah*), normally between seventy-two hours after Rosh Khodesh and mid-month, under an open sky so the moon can be clearly seen. It is customary to perform the ceremony in the company of a *minyan* at *motzei* (departure of) Shabbat.

While you might think we bless the sun every day, when it appears anew, the *Birkat* (Blessing) *Hakhamah* ([of] the "Warm") is actually said only when the star is in the same position, on the same day of the week and the same time of day as it was when created. Due to the discrepancy between our assignment of days and weeks in a year and the actual time it takes for the Earth to complete its circuit around the sun (which is slightly longer), the sun's position relative to our viewing perspective on Earth shifts slightly each year. Twenty-eight years of accumulated discrepancies puts it back at its original starting point.

At that time, as Talmud instructs, a special benediction is made. On the Wednesday morning (the sun was created on the fourth day [Genesis 1:14–19]) in *Nissan*,* between the time the sun fully clears the horizon and the third hour of the day, we recite (preferably in a group of people, but alone if necessary) a blessing recognizing God's works of Creation. The next blessing of the sun will take place in the year 2009.

---

*The rabbis disputed whether Creation occurred in *Nissan* or *Tishrei*. We celebrate the birthday of the world in *Tishrei*, but for purposes of the *Birkat Hakhamah*, *Nissan*—one of the other new years—was designated.

COUNTING DAYS AND YEARS

The Jewish accounting of time defines a day from nightfall to nightfall, based on the order of Creation: "and there was evening, and there was morning, a [first, second, etc.] day" (*"vay'hi erev, vay'hi voker, yom—"*) (Genesis 1). This means that like every day, a Jewish holiday begins on the evening (*erev*) prior to the day (rather than at midnight, as it does for most of the world). For example, if *Nissan* 15, the beginning of Passover, coincides with Thursday, April 18, all holiday observances take effect on the evening of Wednesday, April 17. Nightfall is indicated by the appearance of three stars, clearly visible to the un-aided eye. It arrives about fifty minutes after sunset, which marks the transition between one day and the next, between a secular day and a sacred occasion.

Tishrei marks the passing of one year into the next. Most of the world counts years from the birth of Jesus, designating those before that event as B.C. (before Christ) and those after as A.D. (Anno Domini, or year of the lord). We count years from the date of Creation, and use the designations B.C.E., before the common era, instead of B.C., and C.E., common era, instead of A.D. The date of the Jewish year is the common era year plus 3760 (the date B.C.E. traditionally cited as that of Creation). For example, 1994 is 5754 Jewish.

PESAKH

Pesakh (peh'-sakh): the Feast of Freedom. Observed on *Nissan* **15–22** (spring; late March–mid-April).

Known as Passover (and for the unleavened bread—*matzah*—eaten during it), the oldest Jewish festival celebrates the historic delivery of Israel from a life of slavery in Egypt. The first of the three pilgrimages, it is one of the most widely celebrated of all Jewish holidays, a time of family observance, rejoicing for past salvation, and expectation of future redemption.

ORIGINS: WHY WE CELEBRATE PESAKH

WHERE DID IT ALL BEGIN?— HISTORIC FOUNDATION

The Biblical Birth of a Nation

Passover originated with one of the two most significant events of Jewish history: *yetziat* (departure) *mitzrayim* (from Egypt) of the Israelites who had been in bondage. This one occurrence defined the nation of Israel, which was born out of it.

You are probably familiar with at least some portions of the basic story of the Exodus, the name given to this momentous development. The Egyptians were alarmed at the tremendous growth rate among the Israelite population in their kingdom. To eliminate the possibility that the resident foreigners would align with an enemy to attack from within, they enslaved the Israelites. The bondage—applied to building the massive cities of Pithom and Ramses from scratch mud and straw—did nothing to stem the Israelites' prolific increase. So Pharaoh ordered the Egyptian midwives to kill the male newborns of the slaves. When they surreptitiously disobeyed, Pharaoh decreed that every Israelite male infant be drowned in the Nile.

One Hebrew baby was placed in a basket and sent down the Nile in order to save him from the fate of the other newborns. He was later retrieved by the Pharaoh's daughter, who named him Moses (which in Egyptian meant "drawn from [*uses*] the water [*mou*]"). Through the actions of Moses' sister Miriam, his mother was engaged to nurse him. Only after he was old enough to have gained some exposure to his heritage (probably at age three) did Moses' mother turn him over to the princess to raise as her own. From then on, Moses grew up as a prince in Pharaoh's palace.

After killing an Egyptian taskmaster for beating an Israelite slave, the adult and innately just Moses fled to Midian, where he tended flock, married the priest Jethro's daughter Tzipporah, had two sons, and experienced a significant encounter in the desert with God, in the form of the Burning Bush.

At God's insistence, and with the assistance of his older brother Aaron, Moses returned to Egypt to liberate his people. He repeatedly demanded of Pharaoh, "Let my people go!", kept pressure on the vain and hard-hearted tyrant through a series of heaven-sent plagues, and shepherded the finally released slaves to a new physical, psychological, and spiritual reality east of the Reed Sea. (Believed to be one of the lagoons on the shores of the Mediterranean, it was erroneously identified as the Red Sea when Torah [the Five Books of Moses, or in Christian terms, the Old Testament] was translated into Greek in the third century B.C.E.)

The first fifteen chapters of the Torah's book of Exodus chronicle the history from enslavement to emancipation. The account of how the Israelites came to be in Egypt is told earlier, at the end of the Book of Genesis (37–50). Joseph, the son of the patriarch Jacob, was sold by his jealous brothers to a passing caravan leader, who in turn sold him as a slave to an influential aristocrat in Egypt. Imprisoned on false charges because he refused the advances of his boss' amorous wife, Joseph was later recognized for his ability to interpret dreams. When he understood those of Pharaoh to foretell a famine, he was elevated to a position second only to the ruler and devised a plan to ensure the survival of the country.

After being reunited with his brothers (when they were forced to Egypt by famine in Canaan), Joseph arranged for his father's entire family of shepherds—the progenitors of the Twelve Tribes of Israel—to settle in the Egyptian region of Goshen, where they prospered (Genesis 50:24).

How soon the Egyptians forgot the good that Joseph had brought them. After the one-time national hero's death, there was a new Pharaoh "who did not know Joseph" (Exodus 1:8). As a security measure, he imposed the bondage, an oppression that had been predicted by God to Joseph's great-grandfather Abraham: "Know well that your offspring shall be strangers in a land not theirs, and they shall be enslaved and oppressed four hundred years, but I will execute judgment on the nation they shall serve, and in the end they shall go free with great wealth" (Genesis 15:13–14).

Through Moses, God made good on His promise. After the nine plagues that He unleashed on the Egyptians, He instructed the Israelites to "borrow" objects of gold and silver from their Egyptian neighbors. Probably awed, and not a little frightened by the strange goings on in their land and (Torah tells us) holding Moses in esteem (Exodus 11:3), the Egyptians readily parted with their valuables (Exodus 10:2-3).

Then, God provided detailed instructions to the Israelites for a special meal: Each household was to choose an unblemished male yearling lamb, sheep, or goat on the tenth of the designated month, watch over the lamb until the fourteenth, slaughter it at twilight, use hyssop (a marjoram-like herb) to smear its blood on the doorposts and lintels of their homes, and roast the entire animal over fire. Fully dressed, with sandals on their feet and staffs in their hands, they were to eat the lamb hurriedly with unleavened bread and bitter herbs, being careful not to break any of the animal's bones or keep leftovers until morning.

Along with the women and girls, only males who had been circumcised could partake of this paschal offering, and no foreigner—one who had not committed himself to the community through circumcision—could be present. While they were complying, God passed through the land, killing every firstborn Egyptian, human and animal, but kept His promise to "pass over" (*pasakh*) the homes of every Israelite who had marked his dwelling with the blood of the paschal (*pesakh*) sacrifice (Exodus 12:31).

Even before their last meal in Egypt, the Israelites were told—not once but three times (Exodus 12:14, 17, 24)—that in commemoration, this day was to be celebrated in all ages. From the evening of the fourteenth of *Nissan* through the evening of the twenty-first, all leaven was to be removed from their homes and only unleavened bread was to be eaten. They were not to do any work on the sacred first and seventh days.

First Steps to Freedom

During the night, as their firstborn were struck down, the Egyptians urged the Israelites to leave, taking all their flocks and belongings with them. And so, already dressed for a hasty getaway, 600,000 Israelite men, plus women and children (said to have totaled three million), walked out of the house of bondage.

Realizing the valuable human resource he had released, Pharaoh reneged—just as he had following every other plague, once he was out of immediate danger. He sent his chariots and soldiers after the Israelites camped near the Reed Sea, who were immediately ready to turn tail and resubjugate themselves to Pharaoh rather than die in the wilderness. It would be one of their many expressions of loss of faith, indications that getting the people out of the slavery was much easier than getting the slavery out of the people.

Using a strong east wind against the sea all night, God turned the water into dry land, through which the frightened Israelites passed to the other side. When the Egyptians pursued, the waters closed, drowning them, and reinspiring the Israelites with faith in God and their leader Moses. Then they were on their way to Mount Sinai, where they would receive instructions for their mission in life (see chapter on Shavuot).

During their travels, the Israelites received the commandment to observe Pesakh (which later came to mean both the paschal sacrifice and the holiday itself) four more times: It follows several laws of social justice (Exodus 23:14–17), when the *Khag* (feast or festival) *Hamatzot* (of unleavened bread), Torah's designation for the holiday, is included as one of the three (*Shalosh*) seasonal pilgrimage festivals (*Regalim*) to be celebrated annually. It is repeated after Moses' receipt of the second set of tablets containing the Ten Commandments (see "Historic Foundation" in chapter on Yom Kippur) and an admonition against idolatry (Exodus 34:18). In the list of all sacred days and festivals, the Israelites are commanded to commemorate the Exodus with a paschal offering and other sacrifices on each of the seven days, and by eating unleavened bread during the entire period (Leviticus 23:5). Finally, all of the particulars of Pesakh observance and what they represent are summarized (Deuteronomy 16:1–8).

FOR FURTHUR READING/EXPLORATION

From Torah

Exodus, Chapters 1–15, in any Khumash (The Five Books of Moses)

The entire story on which Passover celebration is based, including the commandments of how to observe the holiday, is told.

The Ten Commandments (the movie)

Don't miss the classic film version of the Exodus and journey to Sinai, Cecil B. deMille's epic starring Yul Brenner as Pharaoh, Charlton Heston as Moses, green special effects as the Angel of Death, and Jello as the parting of the Reed Sea. Available on video, it is an exciting and fairly faithful version of the Torah account.

Legends about Moses

"The Birth of Moses," "Moses in the Bulrushes," and "The Coal and the Crown" in CT, pp. 95–101; and "Advice to the Counselors," "The Plight of Newborn Babes," and "The Crown of Pharaoh" in Passover HA, pp. 147–151.

Based on Torah and fanciful *midrash*, these legends about Moses' origins and early years explain why Pharaoh really feared the Jewish population growth, how Moses knew he was a Jew, and why he was "slow of speech."

"The Thornbush" in CT, pp. 107–109, and "Israel in Slavery," "The Test of the Shepherd," and "Moses at the Burning Bush" in Passover HA, pp. 151–153.

More *midrash* explains how Moses demonstrated a key quality of leadership—commitment to social justice—which won him his position as God's servant.

For Adults

Wilson, Dorothy Clarke. *Prince of Egypt*. Philadelphia: Westminster Press, 1949.

Whether or not you accept the author's explanations for the perceived miracles of the Exodus, she does a good job of presenting the emotion and thought behind the Jewish value system as one man, Moses, struggles to find truth. The well-written (if at times flowery) novel closely follows the biblical account and draws on *midrash* and historical and anthropological theory to follow his story from childhood in the Pharaoh's palace through the crossing of the Reed Sea.

For Children

Craig, Diana. *The Young Moses*. Morristown, NJ: Silver Burdett Company, 1984.

The early days of the great Jewish leader are recounted in contemporary language. Ages 10–13.

———. *Moses and the Flight from Egypt*. Morristown, NJ: Silver Burdett, 1984.

A companion book to the above, it takes the reader from Egypt to the crossing of the Reed Sea. Ages 10–13.

Lehmann, Asher. *The Young Moses*. New York: The Judaica Press, 1987.

For young people and based on *midrash*, this novel was originally published in Germany after World War I when Jews faced the kinds of dilemmas in life choices Moses did. The issues still resonate today. Ages 11–14.

Sutton, Rosalind. *Now You Can Read . . . Moses the Leader*. New York: Thomas Nelson Publishers, 1983.

In large type for beginning readers, the book is notable only because it is for children to read themselves. At the end, it asks the reader to tell the story in his or her own words. Ages 6–9.

The Historical Evidence

By Jewish tradition, the Exodus took place on Thursday, the fifteenth of *Nissan* in the year 2448 after Creation (variously identified as 1313, 1308, 1306, and 1280 B.C.E.). Working with stated time spans in the Bible books I Kings and Judges and excavations in Israel, archaeologists and historians generally place it at the latter date.

Although there are no Egyptian records corroborating the Torah's story—not unusual in a culture that erased any evidence of weakness—aspects of Egypt's history provide neat correspondence to the Torah. Historians look back to Amenophis IV, also known as Iknaton (1383–1365 B.C.E.), as a starting point. He abolished multiple idol worship in favor of monotheism of the sun. While he erroneously objectified his deity, he may have gotten the right idea through the influence of the Israelites, one of the foreign groups allowed to sojourn in the rich grazeland of Goshen on the edge of the kingdom. According to one theory, when his short-lived religious revolution was reversed, and polytheistic nature worship reinstated, the Israelites became victims of persecution.

Ramses II (1300–1234 or 1347–1280 B.C.E.), known for his ego, massive building program, and use of foreign slaves, gets the most votes as the Pharaoh who initially pressed the Israelites into forced labor. It ended with the Exodus under his son, Merneptah, who ruled a declining Egypt at the close of the thirteenth century B.C.E. (Torah specifies that two pharaohs were involved in the oppression [Exodus 1:8–10; 2:23].)

This timing coincides with the four hundred thirty years Israel spent in Egyptian exile (Exodus 13:40), counted from the time the patriarch Abraham began his wandering in Egypt-dominated Canaan around the age of seventy. (*Midrash* resolves the discrepancy between these 430 years and the four hundred years told to Abraham: the four centuries began with the birth of Isaac. The covenant God made with Abraham, at the beginning of the Egyptian period, occurred three decades earlier. According to Jewish tradition, Israel sojourned in Egypt only two hundred ten years, beginning when Jacob settled there. That period is said to have been equivalent to four hundred years of suffering.)

The search for artifacts and documents that can verify the Bible's account continues today, and archaeologists and historians still debate its veracity. Scholars (Winston Churchill among them) do not doubt that Israel was in Egypt. Many conclude, using evidence drawn from the political and social situation of the time, and the logic of human psychology, that the Exodus story is based on fact. For one thing, they point out, no other people in the history of the world has ever conceived a national myth that gives itself such a disgraceful past. It could only be a reflection of an actual occurrence.

While not denying that an unusual departure from Egypt took place, some secular scholars—contrary to classic Jewish tradition—claim that the Exodus account is the result of history mixed with fragments of folklore and legend influenced by other nations. They cite, for instance, a common myth of a child hidden at birth, often rescued from a watery death, who grows up to be a great leader and threat to the existing power structure. They also note that the particular rites by which Israel commemorated the event were borrowed from two distinct preexisting seasonal festivals observed by the Israelites themselves, long before the Exodus occurred and combined with new meaning into *Khag Hapesakh/Khag Hamatzot*.

One was celebrated by shepherd families at the time of the spring full moon, when the flocks produced new lambs. It involved rituals similar to the paschal sacrifice designed to elicit good luck and protect the sheep and goats before the tribe left their winter quarters for spring grazing. This festival was supposedly brought with the Israelite shepherds when they settled in the rural areas of Canaan (predominantly the south).

The peasants in the land—the northern farmers—recognized the arrival of spring with a festival related to new grain. Prior to harvesting the barley, the Jews would get rid of all their sour (fermented) dough (used instead of yeast as a leavening agent) and old bread, perhaps to protect against an unproductive year. The first sheaf of the newly cut grain was offered as a sacrifice.

Over time, say these scholars, Israel gave the rites deeper meaning based on their experiences, which included slavery and liberation from it.

Post-Exodus Pesakh

The children of Israel were still wandering in the desert when they celebrated the first anniversary of the Exodus (Numbers 9:1–5). Since they had been commanded that anyone considered ritually impure could not offer a sacrifice (Leviticus 22:3–6), a second Passover, Pesakh *Sheni*, was instituted for those who on *Nissan* 14 had had contact with a corpse. To be held one month later (*Iyar* 14), in the same way as on *Nissan* 14, it was to be observed in the future by anyone who had been prevented from making the sacrifice in *Nissan* because s/he had been either ritually impure or on a journey.

This was the last Pesakh observed by the journeying Israelites until they crossed the Jordan River into Canaan at the Passover season thirty-nine years later. Then, the first religious act ordained was circumcision for every male. With the exception of Caleb ben Yefunah and Joshua ben Nun (of the twelve spies sent to scout Canaan, the only ones who retained their faith in God [Numbers 14:24–30]), the circumcised men who had left Egypt had all died in the wilderness, and those born after the Exodus had not been entered into the covenant because of the rigors of desert existence.

The act of allegiance reaffirmed their part of the covenant made between Abraham, Isaac, and Jacob and God, the deal God offered the Israelites in Egypt and which they accepted at Sinai: He would be their

God and lead them to the Land of milk and honey, and they would be His people, following His laws and acting as His agents for good on Earth. Once each man had become part of the people of Israel, sharing its responsibilities and destiny through this act of identification, the community was able to offer the paschal lamb (Joshua 5:2–10). Every year afterward, the sacrifice would be a reminder of the nation's responsibilities under the covenantal contract.

As long as the elders who guided the people after Joshua's death were still alive, the Israelites remained true to their Redeemer (*Go'al Yisrael*). But in the face of ignorance, lack of leadership, inaccessibility to Torah, and strong pagan influences around them, the next generation, which had not personally experienced the rigors of slavery and the miracles of salvation, wandered away from their parents' traditions. Pesakh, commemoration of one of the greatest things to have ever happened to the Jews, was probably no more than a private family affair for a minority of pious people.

For hundreds of years the Israelites pursued an off-again, on-again relationship with their religion. They revived it under Samuel (the eleventh-century B.C.E. prophet), abandoned it after Solomon's kingdom split into rival idolatrous Israel and Jerusalem-centered Judah (932 B.C.E.), briefly approached it at Judean King Hezekiah's instigation (726 B.C.E.), then largely ignored it until they were within a generation of losing the Temple (619 B.C.E.).

At that time, in a clean-up campaign at the sanctuary, King Josiah's people found some Torah scrolls. Shocked at how much tradition had been lost, the monarch initiated a reformation. All altars outside the capital were eliminated, and Jerusalem was established as the only meeting place for all pilgrimages. A public reading of Deuteronomy, containing the laws, led to immediate repentence by the people, capped by a public celebration of Passover attended by three hundred thousand people. "Since the time of the prophet Samuel, no Passover like that one had ever been kept in Israel . . ." (II Chronicles 35:18).

In and Out of Babylon

The Jews, exiled to Babylon after destruction of the Temple in 586 B.C.E. (see chapter on Tisha B'Av), celebrated the Egyptian redemption as a model for their own hoped-for deliverance. Although in the absence of the sanctuary they could not make the paschal (or any other) sacrifice, they developed new ritual in prayer service.

Those who remained in the Diaspora (Greek for "dispersion," indicating any place Jews live outside Israel and their situation away from the homeland) continued to observe the holiday long after others returned to the Land when the Temple was rebuilt (516 B.C.E.). Jewish life in the Holy Land was revived, largely through the efforts of the scribe and leader Ezra, and though there continued to be periods of neglect and ignorance, such as the one leading up to the Maccabean Revolt, second century B.C.E. (see chapter on Khanukah), Passover from then on continued to be widely celebrated.

While maintaining the Bible's framework for observance, the ritual was expanded and enriched. The penalty for purposely not participating in the Pesakh sacrifice was *karet* (being cut off from the community). So the Jews made tremendous effort to get to Jerusalem. Anyone within a thirty-day journey (about nine hundred miles in those days), including a woman, was obligated to make the pilgrimage. Gradually during the Second Temple period, Pesakh emerged as the greatest Jewish national holiday.

The residents of Jerusalem welcomed the population-doubling pilgrims into their homes, providing free accommodation (the city was considered the common property of all the people); the travelers customarily left the skins of the paschal lambs for their hosts in appreciation. Overflow crowds stayed in surrounding villages or camped in the fields. A carnival atmosphere pervaded, the days and nights filled with festive meals, music, Torah study, and Temple pageantry, which began on the morning of *Erev* Pesakh (*Nissan* 14).

Through a series of signals from the Temple, and the Mount of Olives opposite, the people were informed when to stop eating leavened foods and when to destroy any leavened food left in their possession. Starting at noon on *Nissan* 14, in three groups successively crowding the Temple courtyard, the Israelites brought their paschal offerings, and unlike other sacrifices, slaughtered the animals themselves with the assistance of the priests and to the accompaniment of the Levite orchestra.

As prescribed by Torah, each family unit roasted its own lamb on a portable clay stove set up in the home courtyards. Dressed in white, groups embracing different status and economic strata joined together. With biblical references, they told the story of the night of the Exodus, based on Torah's commandment to pass it on to one's children (Exodus 12:26–27, 13:8, 13:14; Deuteronomy 6:20).

Before the Fall

Two historic developments led to the evolution of Pesakh observance into the form we know today: the dominion of Rome over Palestine and the emergence of rabbinic Judaism.

In the centuries following Ezra's religious revival, controversy over the approach to Torah (and probably not a little over political maneuvering) split Jewish leadership. The Sadducees believed in literally following Torah and only what was explicitly stated in it. The Pharisees, heirs of Ezra and fathers of rabbinic Judaism, believed in extrapolating from Torah according to the Oral Tradition, also called Oral Law (*Torah Sheh B'al Peh*), believed by them to have been given at Mount Sinai along with the Written Law (Torah, or *Torah Sheh Bikhtav*) and passed from generation to generation by word of mouth. It allowed them to interpret the Torah's precepts for changing conditions in the world and the Jewish community.

A major disagreement related to Passover concerned their respective understandings of the Torah's designated timing for the counting of the *omer* (a measure of grain, commonly identified as a sheaf), the agricultural element of Passover and the system for marking off the fifty days between Pesakh and its companion holiday, Shavuot. (At the start of the counting, a handful of meal ground from the grain was burned at the altar, the rest baked and eaten by the priest. A measure was sacrificed every day of the period.) Not a single Jew could eat bread made from grain of the new harvest until the *omer* sacrifice had been made. (The Israelites believed it symbolized protection for the harvest from harmful conditions, particularly winds.)

Although one reference makes the first day relative ("start to count when the sickle is first put to standing grain" [Deuteronomy 16:9]), the original instruction tells the Israelites to offer the first sheaf, which initiates the count of seven weeks, on "the day after the Sabbath" (Leviticus 23:15). The Sadducees insisted that Torah meant the Sabbath that fell during Pesakh and therefore started their count on that Saturday night. The Pharisees took "Sabbath" to mean the day of rest that was the first sacred day of Passover and therefore began their count at the start of the second day of the festival—even if it meant cutting the barley on Saturday, an act normally forbidden that day. (An elaborate barley-cutting ceremony that took place on Shabbat, just to emphasize their point, is described in Talmud.)

It is interesting that the Ethiopian Jews, who did not reject Oral Law as did the Sadducees but were cut off from mainstream Judaism before it was written and explained, understood that "Sabbath" to mean the day after Passover ended, since the entire festival is a period of rest. So they began their count and celebrated Shavuot six days later than the rest of the Jewish world.

The triumph of the Pharisees in the last century prior to the destruction of the Second Temple led to new observances and themes for the holiday. An expanded religious service, which we know as the Passover *seder* (order, for the order of service), began to develop. Looking for symbols of freedom and luxury, the sages found them in the culture to which Israel had been exposed for about two hundred years: Roman banquets and Greek (Hellenistic) symposia: drinking wine throughout the meal (with a blessing of thanks to God), reclining on sofas, eating leisurely, and discussing the topic of the evening.

During the Roman occupation, Passover's theme of redemption fanned the hopes of a messianic deliverance. Having long believed that God would again provide miracles such as those experienced at the Exodus, the Jews anticipated a new Moses who would lead them to freedom on the eve of Passover. With this expectation the Jews continued to celebrate Pesakh as a commemoration of the first redemption and the imminent occurrence of the second. (The last supper of Jesus, which took place during the Roman rule, was the meal of the paschal sacrifice on *Erev Pesakh* 33 C.E.)

Outside Jerusalem, where the sacrifice could not be made (some people symbolically ate roast lamb), Passover was observed with services at the local synagogue and at home with the same family service performed in the capital. It consisted of a *kiddush* (sanctification over wine); eating herbs—or some spring vegetable—dipped in vinegar or red wine; three questions asked by a child about the out-of-the-ordinary rituals being performed at the table; the household head's answers to the questions personalized according to the child's level of comprehension; explanations of the significance of the night of *Nissan* 14; a meal of the paschal lamb, *matzah*, bitter herbs (*maror*), and a pasty mixture of fruit, nuts, and wine called *kharoset*; a cup of wine following the post-meal grace; and for those who had eaten the actual paschal lamb (in Jerusalem only), chanting of *Hallel* (Psalms of Praise, 113–118).

FOR FURTHER READING

Ibn Verga, Solomon. "Passover in Temple Days." In Passover HA, pp. 25–28; and Kitov, Eliyahu. *The Book of Our Heritage*. New York: 'A' Publishers, 1968, pp. 236–239.

Taken from the Talmud, this account of the festival observance based on a report by a Roman eyewitness describes the beauty and aura of the Temple ceremony.

Schauss, Hayyim. *The Jewish Festivals: History and Observance.* New York: Schocken Books, 1974, pp. 48–55, 61–64.

A colorful description of the activities in Jerusalem during the Pesakh pilgrimage, drawn from *midrash*, conjures up the sights, sounds, smells, and sensations of the occasion. Details about the *Erev* Pesakh rites of the Samaritans, who did not accept rabbinic Judaism, illustrate how the holiday was observed two thousand to three thousand years ago.

After the Fall

Like all other aspects of Jewish worship, the paschal sacrifice and everything connected with it had to be reevaluated once the Temple was destroyed (70 C.E.) (see chapter on Tisha B'Av). All that remained possible of the biblical commandments for observance was the prohibition of leavening. Though now truly *Khag Hamatzot*, it retained the name Pesakh (for the passing over), although the *pesakh* (paschal offering) could no longer be made, and became a home ceremony featuring the story of ancient slavery and salvation. That story served as a model for the fight to liberate Jerusalem from Roman occupation in the next century, and for following generations, for the struggle to maintain Jewish life.

As if to bolster their own hopes, the sages elaborated on the number of miracles God performed for the Israelites in Egypt and emphasized the moral significance of the holiday. To commemorate their importance, the paschal sacrifice and its accompaniments appeared on the Passover table in symbolic form, and the typical two cups of wine for festive meals was doubled so one would fall at each of the key points in the ceremony. Detailed, formalized responses to the *seder's* questions began to be set down, and expressions of thanksgiving were added, along with the proclamation that every Jew, in every generation, was to feel that s/he had personally experienced the Exodus.

Rabbi Gamliel, the first-century sage, expanded the story beyond the events of *Nissan* 14 to include all the wonders and miracles of the entire Exodus. He issued the famous dictum included in the written version of the *seder*, that "He who does not stress these three rituals on Passover does not fulfill his obligations: *pesakh*, *matzah*, and *maror*." The three questions became four and were periodically changed in order to reflect altered aspects of the ritual and remain a challenge to children. Specific political de-velopments were reflected in additions, such as interjection of a prayer for a brighter future by Rabbi Akiva. The sage who died a martyr in the second-century Hadrianic persecutions felt that the existing prayer thanking God for the great light of freedom and redemption was incongruous with reality for the Jews living in the shadow of Rome.

Commentary, analysis, and legend were added to embellish the meaning of the Passover story throughout editing of the *Mishnah* (the written version of the Oral Law, second century) and development of the Talmud (commentaries on the *Mishnah*, fifth century) with its tractate devoted to the laws and stories of Pesakh (*Pesakhim*, paschal lambs).

Since Pesakh *Sheni* (called Minor Passover in *Mishnah*) was instituted strictly to allow for sacrifice to be made, absence of the Temple obviated its need. For symbolic commemoration, a prayer of supplication was omitted from daily service. The sages determined that the period of the *Omer*, however, seen as a link between Pesakh and Shavuot, should still be counted, even though the offerings that marked its start and end had been eliminated. It became a period of semi-mourning, when weddings, haircuts, and playing of musical instruments were prohibited (except for on the new moons of *Iyar* and *Sivan*, which fall within it, and its thirty-third day [see chapter on Lag B'Omer]).

During the early Talmud period (second century), one new observance was added: the fast of the first-born. The only fast limited to a segment of the community, it is attributed to Rabbi Judah Hanasi (redactor of the *Mishnah*), who fasted on this day. Ironically, some say that although he was a firstborn son, his action was not in commemoration or appreciation for Israel's firstborn having been spared when the Egyptians were killed in the tenth plague. He simply had a weak constitution and wanted to save his appetite for the anticipated *seder* meal! Thus can customs be born.

Middle Ages to Modernity

Discussions among the sages continued for centuries until the content and format of the *seder* became relatively established and universally accepted. By the eleventh century, the text—a combination of biblical passages, material from *midrash*, and liturgical poems—was virtually the one we use today, and in the next century appeared in a separate publication called the *Haggadah*.

Jews in the medieval European ghettos loved Passover, finding inspiration in the events of the past and eternal hope for the future. Unfortunately, the joyous anticipation generated by the approach of the holiday gave way to abject terror, beginning in the latter part of the Middle Ages with the spread of malicious blood libels at Passover time, which occurs around the date of Easter. In 1144, the first accusation, in Norwich, England, maintained that the Jews had killed a Christian child, repeating the crucifixion of Jesus.

The ridiculous and slanderous lie, enhanced with the claim that the murdered child's blood was needed for the baking of *matzah*, spread all over Europe, inciting massacres against innocent Jews. Christians in Arab lands in the nineteenth century and Nazis in the twentieth century kept the lie alive. The trumped-up cases and murderous rampages even spread as far as America in the 1920s. Recently, the libel has resurfaced in post–Soviet Russia.

The sad reality inspired fictional accounts, the best known being Heinrich Heine's *The Rabbi of Bacherach* and Bernard Malamud's *The Fixer*, based on the 1911 Jacob Beilis case in Russia, which also served as background for Sholom Aleichem's *The Bloody Hoax*. (A book on the court proceedings, *The Beilis Transcripts*, has been published by Jason Aronson.) The legendary Golem, the clay automaton said to have been created by Rabbi Yehudah Lavi of Prague (the Maharal) in the late sixteenth century, existed primarily to guard the community against attacks spurred by the false charges.

Despite the threats, the Jews never ceased observing Pesakh, believing with the indomitable faith for which we are famous (and despised) that the story needed to be told, and deriving renewed strength from it. The only major change was the addition, between the fourteenth and sixteenth centuries, of a number of songs following the service, although these were not universally adopted.

The messages of Passover continued to inspire oppressed Jews throughout the world. Based on the description of Passover in the prophetic books of the Bible to which they had access in the Christian version, the *marranos* (hidden Spanish and Portuguese Jews forced to renunciate Judaism during the fifteenth-century Inquisition and their descendants) continued to observe Passover. Jews in the Warsaw ghetto observed a modified *seder* on *Erev* Pesakh 1943, the night of the start of the ill-fated heroic uprising. Even concentration camp inmates somehow scrounged up the barest essentials and prayed for the deliverance of their people and vanquishing of their oppressors.

In the post–World War II era, the theme of freedom became linked with the fate of displaced, Soviet, Ethiopian, and other endangered communities of Jews whom we prayed would be liberated. It is no coincidence that the most famous of the ships bringing refugees to Palestine after the war was named *Exodus '47*, and that the powerful metaphor was used for the name of the dramatic clandestine airlift that brought close to ten thousand Ethiopian Jews to Israel in 1984–1985 (Operation Moses) and the campaign to fund immigration and settlement of Jews from the former Soviet Union (Operation Exodus).

With its universal messages of freedom from oppression for all people, and its particularistic promises of protection for the people of Israel, Passover remains the most observed holiday among Diaspora Jews.

FOR FURTHER READING

Wiesel, Elie. *The Golem: The Story of a Legend*. Trans. by Anne Borchardt. New York: Summit Books, 1983.

Full of wonder and mysticism, and enhanced by softly surreal pen and ink illustrations, the account weaves the background, accomplishments, and legends about the Golem into the form of a legend itself. The warm and sometimes sad tale beautifully incorporates Jewish history, thought, and religion. (*Note*: There are many versions of "The Golem" published separately—like Isaac Bashevis Singer's [Farrar, Straus & Giroux, 1982]—or as part of collections.)

WHAT DOES IT MEAN?— RELIGIOUS IMPORTANCE

The Foundation of Judaism

Yetziat Mitzrayim, the singular event commemorated by Passover, is nothing less than a defining element of Jewish thought and behavior. It set in motion the pattern for Jewish history, provided the foundation for the Jewish approach to the world, and established the agenda for Jewish national life. Its theme of exile and redemption is the leitmotif of our existence, its message of the absolute right and necessity to be free our core value.

So central are the Exodus and its lessons to Judaism that references to it recur throughout our Bible's accounts of history and its laws, prophecies, and prayers. The life of a traditional Jew is suffused with it not just once a year during an extended festival, but every single day. It is because God brought us out of Egypt that we are commanded to obey Him regarding our two-way relationship, ritual observances, and ethical behavior. Among Torah passages enclosed inside the *tefillin* put on by Jewish men each weekday morning are those pertaining to the Exodus (Exodus 13:1–10, 11–16). Daily services include recitation of the song sung by the Israelites after crossing the Reed Sea (*Shirah* [Exodus 15:1–18]) and a prayer covering the past, and hoped-for future, redemption. And the fact that the Sabbath, the once-a-week respite from the servitude of the work week, memorializes the Exodus (Deuteronomy 5:15) elucidates the meaning of Creation, which the Sabbath also commemorates (Exodus 20:11): Both the world and the liberated Israelite nation were brought forth with specific Divine purpose.

Even the calendar design reminds us of the Exodus. Torah emphasizes that *Nissan*, the month of *nissim* (miracles)—and not *Tishrei*, when the world was created (see chapter on Rosh Hashanah)—is to head the year (Exodus 12:2). The rabbis support its position by breaking down its designation as the month of *aviv* (springtime) into *av* (father) *iv* ([of the] twelve [months], the second part being an abbreviation for twelve, its Hebrew letter *yud* having the numerical value of ten and *bet* of two).

Just as the Earth comes to life again after being constrained by the nature of winter, Israel was renewed. The original naming of months reflected the notion that being reborn with purpose is much more significant than merely coming into existence: As we count the progression of the week with reference to its most important day (Sunday is the First Day [toward Shabbat], Monday is the Second Day [toward Shabbat], etc.), the Bible numbers months beginning with *Nissan*.

The Jewish Notion of Freedom

Had God simply liberated the Israelites from Egyptian oppression, the former slaves would have been a certain ethnic group lucky enough to have had a great-great-grandfather who recognized God's existence, another nation among many. Merely released from the darkness and confinement of bondage into light and lack of restraint, they could have run rampant without direction, expressing pent-up frustration and lashing out at anything in their path.

On the day the Israelites were taken out of Egypt, Moses reminded them to remember it. Later, when they reached Canaan, they were to eat *matzah*, get rid of leaven, and tell their children, "It is because of this that God acted for me when I left Egypt" (Exodus 13:3–8). The sages ask what "this" means. Their having cried out in anguish? Their suffering? The pleasure of eating unleavened bread?

Service to God

Although our God is a merciful God (Exodus 34:6), He did not get the Israelites out from under Egyptian oppression merely to end their suffering and restore control over their lives to individual inclination. From the time God sent Moses back from Midian to confront Pharaoh, He made it clear that He wanted the Israelites to show their appreciation for His benevolence of leading them from the house of bondage to the Land of milk and honey.

The two Torah words generally used for freedom, *khofesh* and *deror*, are not applied to the Exodus. Both imply lack of restraint, complete self-determination, a misconception of freedom prevalent in an undisciplined Western society like America today. This is a kind of liberty that in the end can enslave you to whims and desires that have a way of leading you from what you really want. (While you are free to eat anything you would like, don't you really want to control your weight?)

The Israelites, however, were given *kherut*, freedom to live a certain kind of life, one according to God's system of discipline. It was summarized in the Ten Commandments engraved (*kharut*) on the two tablets of stone that were to be given at the conclusion of the Passover experience at Mount Sinai (see chapter on Shavuot). The sages equate the two —liberty (*kherut*) and the engraving of the law (*kharut*): "Only he is free who occupies himself with Torah" (*Pirkei Avot* 6:2). Rabbi Levi Isaac of Berditchev saw a reflection of the reciprocal relationship between Liberator/Lawgiver and liberated/law abiders in the dual names of the holiday. Israel called it Passover, he said, in recognition of God's mercy in redeeming them. And God called it Feast of Unleavened Bread as a compliment to Israel, who would carefully follow the commandments surrounding it.

The Jewish concept of freedom means the unrestrained ability to have a relationship with God, show obedience to Him, and accept Torah, which sets the Jew on the path in life that will allow him/her to fulfill his/her role in the overall plan for the world. The only way to be free to worship God is to be free of an earthly master. There is a universe of difference between being a servant (*ehved*) of Pharaoh and a servant—like Moses—of God (*ehved l'Elohim*). Under human oppression, those in bondage labor for the aggrandizement of others, or because someone wants to break their spirit. Under God, we can choose obligations that are aimed at benefit for all.

That is why Judaism abhors slavery. No Jew is to be owned, not even by another Jew. If a Hebrew had to enslave him-/herself to someone else—in the case of indebtedness, for instance—it was for a limited period of time (all debts were forgiven at the Sabbatical—every seventh year; all lands reverted to original owners at the Jubilee—every fiftieth year, to keep a socioeconomic balance in the society and prevent development of a serf or landless class). And a servant had to be treated well (so well that the rabbis observed that one who acquired a servant acquired a master for himself!).

A servant who refused liberty at the end of his term had his ear pierced, a symbol of shame that he had not heard God's declaration of independence for all children of Israel. The piercing was done against a doorpost, recalling the site the Israelites smeared with lamb's blood to indicate their readiness to abandon their life of slavery.

Since they are not free to choose their Master (God), slaves may not recite the *Shema*, the Jewish declaration of faith in One God: A person in bondage to another lord is not at liberty to accept God's sovereignty. (The *haggadah* reminds us that the degradation experienced by our ancestors was not just slavery in Egypt but the idol worship—a lack of recognition and negation of God—that preceded it.)

Prior to the Exodus, there was a Jewish nation, a distinct ethnic group that distinguished itself, *midrash* tells us, by maintaining the names, dress, and language of their ancestors. But they were not given Torah until they had forsaken their human masters (by preparing the paschal lambs), had made a commitment to heed God's commandments (by following the instructions for *Nissan* 14), and had been led out of Egypt (the place—physical and psychological—limiting their lives).

Respecting Others

Although we must not be slaves, we are also commanded, repeatedly, not to ever forget we were slaves. The danger of liberty is that once given control, the formerly oppressed can take advantage of their new positions to wield power over others. How often in history have liberation movements, once achieving their immediate aims of toppling the existing structure, succeeded only in establishing a new tyranny (e.g., Church Reformation, French Revolution, Bolshevik Revolution, overthrow of the Iranian Shah . . .)?

The Israelites were to retain the humility of their former lives (the hallmark of the authentic Jewish personality, *khutzpah* notwithstanding) in order to remain sensitive to the plight of others. We treat servants like guests, provide food for widows, orphans, and strangers, are kind to foreigners, use honest weights and measures in our business dealings, help the poor, and do not act with prejudice—particularly toward the disadvantaged—precisely because we were slaves in Egypt. In three dozen of Torah's social laws we are instructed to take certain action based on our early experiences: the hurt we suffered was to teach us to refrain from inflicting pain on others. Our entire religion, which was summarized by Hillel as "do not do to others that which is hateful to you," is drawn directly from our experience as slaves. (You were slaves, you didn't like the humiliation, whippings, and restrictions, so don't degrade, torture, or oppress others.)

Judaism's new concept of freedom and unmatched standard of social ethics was designed to create a just balance in a world that seems to thrive on injustice. If realized, this system would revolutionize the world in ways no liberation movement since the Egyptian Exodus has even approximated. Its unique legislation—which gave the world such concepts as life, liberty, the pursuit of happiness, tolerance, and the six-day work week—governs virtually every aspect of a Jew's personal life and his/her relations to the world: political, legal, ethical, spiritual, environmental, economic. It makes provisions against homelessness and corruption of courts and for monetary retribution, ensuring the dignity of every human being, making everyone feel part of the community, rehabilitation of criminals, and separation of powers in government.

They are laws meant to liberate all people from physical, spiritual, psychological, emotional, and economic oppression. For only when all peoples are released from such restraints will God's grand scheme for the world be fulfilled. And Jews, with our unique heritage, have a particular responsibility to safeguard the freedom of others and to work for the release of those enslaved.

Past as Prologue—and Prototype

Only in dire circumstances would the Jews have followed Moses and God. Having been removed from them served as a reminder that no matter how terrible our situation, we must not lose hope, that there is some ultimate purpose to it: You can live through anything if you know it is not forever. The Exodus demonstrates that our suffering is in fact finite, that in exile we can expect deliverance and renewal.

The message began with the design of the very first *seder*, a model for perpetual hope for the future. It was not a typical celebration of independance, taking place after the fact. It was held while the Israelites were still in bondage, with the expectation that something momentous was about to happen, the belief that the promise of liberation would be fulfilled. The exiled Jews believed that the nation would be revived, that Jerusalem would be rebuilt—because they had an established pattern for the suffering-then-salvation sequence.

"Now we are here, next year may we observe Passover in the Land of Israel, now we are still enslaved, next year may all men be free" (*Haggadah*) has rung true in every age. The belief that the words would eventually become reality has made it possible for Jews to observe Passover without becoming discouraged no matter what the horrendous situation outside their doors. It remains the inspiration for today, when, separated from the ideal we are supposed to be creating in the world, we remain in exile (*galut*). As much as it commemorates the redemption already executed, Passover celebrates the redemption expected (*Geulah*).

Messianic Redemption

Belief that, just as God sent Moses as His servant to redeem us once, a descendant of the House of David will arise as the *moshiakh* (messiah) is a tenet of classical Judaism. It is one of Maimonides' Thirteen Articles of Faith—central beliefs to which every Jew must ascribe—that the redemption will occur: "I believe with a perfect faith in the coming of the messiah and though he may tarry, daily I wait for his coming."

By the second century B.C.E. two concepts of a "messiah" who/which would rescue Israel and return it to former glory had developed. One focused on a human leader—the personal messiah—who would emerge from among the Jews, guide us to independence, and bring the world to accept God. (The word *moshiakh* in Hebrew is derived from *mashakh*, which simply means "to anoint," as to anoint a king, who was supposed to remain faithful to the law of God). The other foresaw a series of cosmic cataclysmic events that would destroy Israel's enemies and world evil and initiate a period of peace—the messianic age—in which the world would be perfected.

Debate over the "true messiah" concept has continued through numerous crises in our history, including the emergence of false messiahs (most notably Shabbatai Zvi in the seventeenth century) and controversy in our own time over the Lubavitcher Rebbe, Menachem Mendel Schneersohn, some of whose followers, believing him to be *Moshiakh*, urged him to reveal himself as such.

Kabbalists of the sixteenth and seventeenth centuries promoted the concept, later enthusiastically embraced by the Reform movement, that we ourselves, through our efforts to perfect the world (*tikkun olam*), would bring messianic redemption. The Lubavitch *Khabad Khasidim*, whose wide-ranging outreach programs are aimed at bringing as many Jews as possible back into the fold of Jewish observance, believe this will happen by following the commandments of Torah. According to the ultra-Orthodox *Neturei Karta* (Defenders of the Faith, who do not recognize the existence of the State of Israel), only an act of God will accomplish it.

By whatever means and in whatever form, belief in a redeeming force and attempts to see it realized are very much a part of our tradition. Its power remains in the fact that the arrival of the messiah has always been seen as a future occurrence providing hope and—as the legendary Eastern European Jew stationed outside his village to greet the messiah found—steady work. Most of all, the undying anticipation fostered the eternal optimism that eventually things can, and will, improve, for the Jewish people and the entire world.

What Does It Mean to Us?—Personal Significance

Self-Liberation

The *haggadah* instructs that each of us ("In every generation . . .") is actually supposed to feel as though we had been slaves and made the transition to a new status. How can we do this—take ancient history and make it into my story and your story?

We who live in an open, democratic society tend to think of ourselves as free. But are we really, just because we are not physically bound to an overlord? What do being enslaved and unencumbered by oppression really mean? And are they mutually exclusive?

In Hebrew, Egypt is called *Mitzrayim*. According to the text on Jewish mysticism, the *Zohar*, the name is derived from *m'tzarim*, meaning "narrow straits" (*mi*, "from," *tzar*, "narrow" or "tight"). When God took us out of *Mitzrayim*, He extricated us from the place of constricted opportunities, tight control, and narrow-mindedness, where movement was severely limited.

Each of us lives in his or her own *mitzrayim*, the external or physical narrow straits of financial or health constraints or, perhaps, personal tragedy; universally the psychological burdens to which we subject ourselves. Like the duality in virtually all of Pesakh's symbols, they work in two ways: They turn us into both slaves and oppressors, of ourselves and others. Passover leads us to question the values and attitudes we hold and which hold us to those roles. (Do we pursue, even worship, things like money and status for their own sake, rather than for how they can make our lives and the lives of those around us better? Do our own insecurities or overconfidence inhibit us from fully participating in life rather than getting the most out of relationships? Do our stereotyping, prejudice, or exploitation oppress other people by robbing them of their dignity rather than affording them the same opportunities we want for ourselves?

As we get rid of leaven and replace it with *matzah*, we are supposed to confront whatever it is that we normally allow to persist in our lives but which should perhaps, like the leaven, be eliminated, and that which we suppress which should, like the back-to-basics unleavened bread, be admitted. (Do you work to live or live to work? Do you play for enjoyment or to avoid having to think? Are you unhappy in a situation but so entrenched in it that you have come to accept it as the norm—as *acceptable*? Does an addiction to food, alcohol, drugs, a pattern of behavior, or another person interfere with leading the life you really want for yourself? Do you allow others to take advantage of your time and resources?)

Pharaoh is seen as the evil enslaver of others. But he was bound by his own ego, which led him to ruin everything he valued, including himself. Even his officials recognized the catastrophe his attitude brought: "Let the men go," they advised. "Don't you realize that Egypt is being destroyed?" (Exodus 10:7). His arrogance simply got in the way.

In order to take the necessary action, we need to believe that things must change for our own good. When we do, we, like Pharaoh, make vows to change. But often, once an immediate need has passed, we, like Pharaoh, who gave and then retracted his permission for the Israelites to leave, revert to old habits. It may be easy, but in the long run, we only hurt ourselves. One lesson of the *Omer* period (see section on "Observance") is how easy it is to slide back into familiar ways. (Witness the former USSR countries who within months of gaining democratic freedoms elected ousted communist leaders to govern them. Remember the ancient Israelites who, not a week out of Egypt, were ready to forego liberty and return to their miserable lives—yearning for the comfort of the familiar evil over fear of the unknown.)

Slavery does offer a certain freedom that can be attractive: the freedom from responsibility for yourself and others, the freedom from having to establish goals, figure out how to reach them, or think beyond the moment. It takes strength and guts to walk out of a known situation, which for all its pain, is predictable. It is human nature to want to stay put, within the stability of the status quo. The danger is that often in those situations you don't even know that you are mired in a negative situation, one you don't realize until too late.

You tell yourself you will look for a better job, sign up for community service, be much nicer to your kids, get out of an abusive relationship, go back to school, pay off your contributions . . . tomorrow. Jacob did not intend to stay in Egypt more than a short time—and look what his sojourning cost. At Passover, we should at least recognize inertia for what it is and not kid ourselves into complacency about our own situation or that of others.

Passover, with its message of hope, tells us that like the Egyptian slaves, we can escape from our straits. Once they had tasted freedom with the paschal lamb, the Israelites gave up the comfort of the familiar, without concern for provisions or how they would get to or exist at their destination. They left Egypt because they believed a better life awaited them elsewhere. As Rabbi Nakhman of Bratslav (eighteenth-century khasidi leader) counseled, when you are about to leave "*mitzrayim*" you should not worry about how you will manage in a new "place." Anyone who does or who stops to get everything in order for the journey will never pick him-/herself up.

As we begin the *seder* with a broken, incomplete piece of *matzah*, we are encouraged to take the first steps toward change even if all the pieces are not in place. We cannot wait until the time is perfect. The European Jews in the prewar years, who were concerned about losing property, did not recognize this. The Ethiopian Jews, at the time of Operations Moses and Solomon, who did not yet have the new clothes they had dreamed of wearing for their entry into Jerusalem, did.

A *midrash* tells that when the Israelites were at the Reed Sea, the Egyptians at their backs, they wailed and moaned and longed for the taskmaster's whip rather than the lash of the sea's raging waves. They hesitated. Moses prayed. And one man, Nakhshon ben Amminadab, recognizing the opportunity before them, plunged into the waters. Only then did the sea subside, allowing the Israelites to continue. Like Nakhshon ben Amminadab, we have to forge ahead, with faith that we will reach the goal and the belief that the attempt to gain freedom is still better than stagnating in slavery.

Passover also reminds us that the process does not stop if we are comfortable with our own progress or situation, with the good fortune of our families. An important aspect of this holiday is recognition of the needs of others. Just as God helped liberate us, people enslaved today need outside assistance to become free. We have been extremely successful in rescuing Soviet and Ethiopian Jews and helping numerous other communities. It is sickening to learn that, according to a United Nations Center of Human Rights report, issued in mid-1993, at least half—*half!*—the world's population lives under social, cultural, economic, and political oppression, including outright slavery, now, on the eve of the twenty-first century.

Rather than allowing ourselves to become inured to suffering, we should use Passover to recharge our sensitivities which, if the message of the holiday has any impact, should lead us to action.

Fostering a Sense of Belonging

"In each generation" echoes a recurring refrain in Judaism: *l'dor vador*, from generation to generation, the slogan of the continuity we consider crucial. It is quite significant that we begin the annual festival cycle by passing the tradition to our children in an important family holiday that takes place at home. While we are personally experiencing the Exodus, our job is also to make our children feel that they are a part of the story, able to identify with the Exodus and with the Jewish people.

This is a difficult task, particularly for those of us who, like the generations born in Canaan, did not experience the rigors of slavery and the miracles of salvation (mirrored in our time by the Holocaust and the establishment of Israel); who turned away from (or were perhaps never exposed to) our parents' tradition and Torah; who have been diverted by overwhelming and omnipresent influences of the prevailing culture.

But it is not an impossible task, because Jewish identity is established within the family, where feelings of freedom, responsibility, and a sense of belonging to something greater than the individual self are fostered. What causes someone to feel part of the community is largely based on what happens in the home—the stories that are told, the songs sung, the symbols used. What could be a better opportunity to begin to shape that Jewish identity than Passover, with its drama, music, and representational food?

Judaism turns those symbols into reality (the bread of affliction transformed into the bread of freedom leads to freedom itself). The process necessitates our being knowledgeable about what the symbols and the national goals are. Educator Avraham Infeld, who dedicates his life to Jewish-Zionist education,

makes the point beautifully. "Being Jewish means allowing Jewish history to make a claim on your life, to turn the collective memory of the people into a personal account. There can be no future without vision. There can be no vision if we are incapable of dreaming, and one who has no memories cannot dream."

If we teach our children so they feel that they are part of our nation, they will be able to participate in the enterprise built on the memories (Exodus) that inspire the dream (redemption), which supports the vision (universal freedom), which fosters the efforts toward making the vision reality (perfected world). We draw on the past in order to build for a better future, like the desert generation who had to give up their former way of life so that the Land of Milk and Honey could be occupied by their children.

TRADITIONS: HOW WE CELEBRATE PESAKH

WHAT DO WE USE?—RITUAL ITEMS

Haggadah

The printed version of the *seder* service, the *haggadah*, is a collection of Bible passages, talmudic narrative, Second Temple supplications, *piyyutim* (liturgical poems) of the Middle Ages, prayers and readings in response to persecutions of the medieval era and modern times, and folk songs. In the words of Heinrich Heine (in *The Rabbi of Bacherach*), it is "a marvelous mixture of age-old legends, miracles of the Exodus, curious discussions, prayers and festive songs."

The word *haggadah* (from the verb *l'haggid*, "to tell") is derived from the Torah verse commanding "and you shall tell [*l'higadeta*] it to your child on that day" (Exodus 13:8). The choice of verb indicates that our responsibility is not merely to recite the story but to use it to inform and instruct. *Haggadah* is also related to the homiletic sayings (the stories, parables, tales) from *midrash*—called *aggadot* (plural of *aggadah*)—used to teach *seder* participants about the history of redemption.

Since the late Middle Ages, when the *haggadah* first appeared as a publication separate from the common prayer book, more than thirty-five hundred versions have been created, some of them magnificently illustrated. Illuminated editions such as the *Birds Head*, *Damstadt*, *Golden* and *Sarajevo haggadot* (plural) provide a record of Jewish social life (costumes, professions) and attitudes (as in the style of representation of the Four Sons [see section on "*Seder*" later in this chapter]) and have contributed greatly to the development of Jewish art. The text has also been illuminated by hundreds of commentaries, which since the fifteenth century have included philosophical, theological, and mystical discussions of the *haggadah*'s contents.

In the last century alone, hundreds of editions have been produced, not only in response to particular artists' creative impulses but to the developing diversity among the Jewish people. Today it is possible to use a facsimile edition of one of the historic illuminated *haggadot* or a *haggadah* representing the philosophy of a particular movement in Judaism (Orthodox, Conservative, Reform, Reconstructionist), social-political philosophy or concern (egalitarian, feminist, secular, Holocaust, contemporary war/oppression), dietary preference (vegetarian, including the wonderfully titled *Haggadah for the Liberated Lamb*), and even national culture.

Haggadot come in Hebrew only, in Hebrew and English or any other vernacular language of Jews, and in Braille, sometimes with transliterations of major segments. Illustrations range from comic book to museum quality featuring the work of modern Jewish artists like Yaakov Agam, Leonard Baskin, Ben Shahn, Shalom of Safed, and Marc Chagall. Contemporary commentators include Elie Wiesel and Rabbi Shlomo Riskin.

Choosing and Using

While the old wine-stained *haggadot* with the antique etchings and archaic language used in some families for generations may hold sentimental value, and the *haggadot* provided free of charge by Maxwell House and other food companies may be appealing for their price, do yourself—and everyone else at your *seder* table—a favor by having at least one *haggadah* that contains commentary. A good commentary not only explains how to perform a ritual and what it means but provides insights as to the deeper significance of parts of the service, including how to apply them to your own situation and time. The purpose of the *seder* is to inspire identification with the experience and its messages. It is supposed to be an enriching, exhilarating experience, which may be difficult to achieve if you have to deal with a leaden unannotated script. The *haggadah* can serve as a starting point for topical discussion; a good one will give you a little push.

Each person at the table ideally has his or her own copy. When they are all the same, it is easier for everyone to keep his or her place (page numbers and English translations vary). With a variety of annotated editions, on the other hand, you have a wealth of resources, and each participant can contribute interesting commentary from the one s/he uses.

A store that sells Jewish books and ritual items will have a wide selection of *haggadot* in the month prior to Passover. (Your library may also have several editions.) Probably the easiest way to find one you feel comfortable with is to review the numerous possibilities for style of translation, illustration, denominational orientation, underlying theme, and so on. (Some people compile their own *haggadot* from a combination of traditional and modern, religious and secular sources.)

FOR FURTHER READING

With all the existing options, and additional *haggadot* being published each year, it is impossible to list even a fraction of popular and recommended choices. The following is just to give you an idea of the possibilities.

For Adults

American Heritage Haggadah. Ed. by David Geffen. Jerusalem: Gefen Publishing House, 1992.

Profusely illustrated with period advertisements, photographs, and drawings reprinted from publications and enhanced by excerpts from sermons and quotes from periodicals, the *haggadah* portrays the American Jewish experience from early in our history through the Persian Gulf War of 1991. It features an original translation of the text.

The Feast of Freedom. Ed. by Rachel Anne Rabinowicz. New York: The Rabbinical Assembly, 1982.

Reflecting Conservative ideology, this vibrantly illustrated *haggadah* includes extensive commentary, readings reflecting the Holocaust and struggle of Soviet Jewry, and an arrangement that helps you use the text to educational advantage.

Gates of Freedom. Ed. by Chaim Stein. Bedford, NY: New Star Press, 1981.

This version of the *haggadah*, representing the liberal viewpoint, incorporates quotes from Talmud, social scientists, writers, and thinkers, Jewish and non-Jewish, on the subjects of slavery and freedom.

Moss, David. *The Moss Haggadah*. Rochester, NY: Bet Alpha Editions, 1990.

A facsimile of the *haggadah* created for a private commission of 1980 and based on years of research and detailed work, this magnificent modern illumination illustrates basic themes of Judaism and Jewish history in novel and emotionally and intellectually stimulating ways. Considered one of the most important and beautiful *haggadot* ever created, it includes a page-by-page commentary by the artist.

The New Haggadah. Ed. by Mordecai Kaplan et al. New York: Behrman House, 1978.

The Reconstructionist *haggadah*, originally published in 1942 to reflect the idealism and aspirations of that age, includes new readings that continue to support its message and developments in world Jewish life.

The Passover Haggadah Legends and Customs. Interpreted by Rabbi Menachem HaCohen. New York: Adama Books, 1987.

Lavishly illustrated with a combination of Persaic-style borders and lettering and highly stylized figures, this version of the standard text is embellished with extensive historic and theologic explanatory material.

Riskin, Rabbi Shlomo. *The Passover Haggadah with a Traditional and Contemporary Commentary*. New York: Ktav Publishing House, 1983.

You may not want to use this *haggadah* for conducting a *seder*; the volume of commentary, while easily readable, overwhelms the service text that is interspersed in it. But, like anything written by Rabbi Riskin, it is well worth reading and will be valuable in preparing for your *seder*. His use of the *haggadah* to initiate discussion of Jewish themes such as freedom, messianism, and particularism versus universalism is insightful and elucidating.

The *Jewish Braille Institute of America* offers several editions of the *haggadah* in Braille, in large print, or on audiocassettes for the visually impaired. All are free. (110 East 30th Street, New York, NY 10016; 212-889-2525)

For Children, Families

ArtScroll Youth Haggadah. Ed. by Rabbi Nosson Scherman and Rabbi Yitzchok Zev. Brooklyn: Mesorah Publications, 1987.

Complete text, simplified translation, and comments in the Orthodox tradition, along with colorful illustrations, make this an appealing choice. Ages 9–14.

Kolatch, Alfred J. *The Family Seder*. Middle Village, NY: Jonathan David Publishers, 1967.

The traditional service is enhanced with explanations and quotations from literature of all ages. Low priced for family use, it comes in an abridged version, *The Concise Family Seder* (Jonathan David, 1987), for those who do not want the entire service but are ready to do more than just have a meal.

Oren, Rony. *The Animated Haggadah*. London: Scopus Films, 1989.

Vibrant claymation figures cleverly illustrate this children's version of the classic text. Large type, transliteration of Hebrew, and the charm and humor of the illustrations are sure to grab children's attention. It includes a couple of pages of suggestions for parents and teachers to use to initiate discussion (added after the original 1985 edition) and is available in a thirty-minute videotape. All ages.

Silverman, Shoshana. *A Family Haggadah*. Rockville, MD: Kar-Ben Copies, 1987.

To be used on its own or with a standard *haggadah*, this one combines tradition and innovation to expand on the text with questions, songs, crafts, and games. Translation and transliteration for blessings and songs—whose melodies are included on a companion cassette, "Songs for a Family Seder"—make it easy to use, particularly for those with little Jewish background. Ages 12–18.

Wark, Mary Ann Barrows. *We Tell It to Our Children: The Story of Passover, A Haggadah for Seders with Young Children*. St. Paul, MN: Mensch Makers Press, 1988.

Using puppetry, amusing and Judaically meaningful lyrics for well-known American folktunes, and many illustrations, this innovative and fun presentation of the Exodus story and world Jewry easily involves everyone—preschool through adult—in the *seder*. It comes in leader (with nine realistic cut-out paper puppets) and guest editions.

See also *Building a Jewish Life/Haggadah* (Grishaver) and *My Very Own Haggadah* (Saypol and Wikler) in Appendix C.

Matzah

Unleavened bread was one of the foods the Jews in Egypt were commanded to eat along with the paschal lamb (Exodus 12:8). In commemoration of that first *seder* meal, and the haste in which the Israelites left Egypt, giving them no time to allow their bread to rise, we eat *matzah* at the *seder* (and instead of bread throughout the holiday).

It is customary to have three pieces stacked on the table. Two are traditional for Sabbath and festivals (when we usually use two *khallot*), as a reminder of the double portion of manna (food from heaven) the Israelites gathered before every day of rest in the desert (Exodus 16:11–22). We need the third to break at the beginning of the service (see below).

The number three is also said to have symbolic significance. Among other things, the number represents: the three measures of fine meal from which Sarah baked cakes for her husband Abraham's three angelic visitors (Genesis 18:6); the three categories of Jews—*Kohein, Levi,* and *Yisraeli*—that make up the Jewish people, or the three patriarchs, Abraham, Isaac, and Jacob, by whose merit we were redeemed from Egypt and whose covenant with God we were redeemed to fulfill.

In recent years, it has become popular to add an additional sheet of *matzah,* representing hope for Jews still enslaved by oppression around the world.

Meaning

Matzah is one of those wonderful transcendent ritual items in Judaism, a symbol embodying a duality to teach a moral lesson. At the beginning of the *seder,* we break one of the cakes of *matzah* and call it the bread (*lekhem*) of affliction (*oni*). It is the meager sustenance of slaves, the meanest fare of the poor, the quickly produced food of those who make a hurried, under-cover-of-dark getaway. Yet later, it represents freedom, the bread we ate when we were liberated from Egyptian bondage.

In both situations, as slaves in Egypt and once we were free, we ate the same flat wafers. What was different was our own attitude when we ate: cowering, accepting our subservience, then claiming our rightful dignity as human beings equal before God. Just as we transform mentally and physically, the symbol of our status is transformed.

Acceptable Forms

For the *seder,* we may use only *matzah* made of the pure and simple ingredients flour and water, prepared and baked in less than eighteen minutes. Any longer and the fermentation that causes leavening occurs. It is so important to avoid allowing the *matzah* to swell that each cake is perforated to let the steam escape (that's why each wafer has rows of little holes). To teach us to remain vigilant in our responsibilities, it must be made from flour that has the potential to become leavened if left unattended.

No *matzah* containing egg, milk, honey, wine, or fruit juice or other enhancements (called *matzah ashirah,* or rich *matzah*) may be eaten, except by the sick or aged who cannot digest the basic recipe. Avoiding the enhanced *matzah* reminds us of the importance of simplicity, of returning to basics, which the plain flour and water *matzah* represents.

(Some rabbinic authorities approve of eating *matzah ashirah* after the *sedarim* [plural of *seder*].)

Until the mid-nineteenth century, when the first *matzah* machine was invented in Austria, the unleavened bread was baked by hand. The innovation sparked controversy over whether it could in fact produce *matzah* acceptable according to *halakhah,* since authorities feared that pieces of dough could get stuck in it and become leavened. Even after it was accepted, *matzah* continued to be baked manually, in the traditional round form, often in communal ovens and bakeries set up just for the holiday. Said to represent the unity of God, the round *matzot* are still preferred by particularly tradition-minded Jews because of Torah's term for the *matzah* baked just before the Israelites left Egypt: *ugot* (round cakes [Exodus 12:39]). Square *matzot,* the kind most of us use right out of the box, are perfectly acceptable.

The pious use the extra special handmade *matzah shmurah* (commonly said reversed, in Yiddish, *shmurah matzah*). Based on the commandment, "And you should keep [watch] the festival of the *matzot*" (Exodus 12:17), the sages believed watching (*shimurim*) required supervising the *matzah*-making process from the time of reaping to ensure that no water, which initiates the leavening process, comes into contact with the wheat, whole or ground, until it is mixed into dough and eighteen minutes are clocked. Made in round cakes, sometimes with unwanted ripples and burned edges, and often tasting even more like cardboard than the prepackaged variety, they are nevertheless coveted because of the attention and care that go into producing them.

Use

Embroidered, painted silk, and other special *matzah* covers containing three pockets, or special boxes to hold square or round *matzot,* can be purchased at Judaica stores or made, but are not necessary. A plate and a napkin for covering the *matzot* during the *seder* are also acceptable.

If you have more than a few people at your *seder,* you will need more than just the three cakes of *matzah* in order for everyone to have their requisite pieces during the service prior to the meal. The additional *matzah* can be placed near the leader, who will distribute it at the appropriate time, or made directly accessible to guests.

K'arah and Its Contents

The centerpiece of the *seder* table is the ceremonial plate, *k'arah,* containing essential ritual foods. It may be a specially designed platter with compartments, indentations, or separate dishes that fit on or into it, each identifying the item it holds. Made of wood, copper, pewter, silver, stoneware, and porcelain, *seder* plates of tremendous stylistic variety are available in Judaica stores (and, sometimes, by manufacturers such as Lenox, in department stores that sell fine china).

Although incorporating aesthetics into holiday observance is encouraged, it is not necessary to purchase a fancy *seder* plate. Children, or an adult so inclined, may make one, or you may arrange the foods on any plate or tray. (Many *Sephardim* traditionally use wicker baskets.) If you host a large *seder*, you may want to have an additional *k'arah* or two so everyone will have access to it (originally, when celebrants reclined on individual sofas at individual tables, each person had his or her own) or place around the table dishes containing extra supplies of the foods that will be consumed.

Whatever *k'arah* you select, it should contain the following:

Karpas

Derived from the Greek word for grass or vegetation, *karpas* is a green vegetable or herb such as parsley, celery, lettuce, endive, watercress, chervil, or scallion. (Potato, though obviously the wrong color, was also used in Europe, probably because of its availability, and is still the choice in many families.) Evidence of the renewal of nature in the spring, the green symbolizes the season of Israel's renewal through redemption, past and future. Near the *karpas*, though usually not on the plate itself, is a bowl of **salt water**.

One often-cited explanation for the use of *karpas* is that the Hebrew word read backwards is *(s)parak*, the term in the book of Exodus used to describe the toil of the Israelites in Egypt, preceded by the letter designation for sixty. The number suggests both sixty types of physical labors the Egyptians forced on our ancestors and the sixty myriad (six hundred thousand) slaves (or "six hundred thousand labored"). As victors of ancient battles were crowned with wreaths of laurel greens, the *seder* greens represent our victory over enslavement.

There is also a simple historical explanation: Formal dinners of the Greco-Roman culture, the basis for our *seder*, began with an *hors d'oeuvre*, customarily a vegetable, usually dipped in vinegar or wine. We replace the vinegar and wine with salt water, which can be seen as a symbol of birth as well as of sweat and tears.

Maror

Bitter herbs (from the Hebrew *marah*, "bitter") represent the nature of our lives under oppression. Grated horseradish, most commonly used among *Ashkenazim*, is just one of the acceptable bitter vegetables—and the *maror* of choice because there is no mistaking its message (your sinuses will be clear for a month after you eat it!). The sages also listed romaine lettuce, endive, chicory, and escarole. They preferred, as do the *Sephardim*, the lettuce, which they likened to Jewish settlement in Egypt: first sweet to the taste, only later is the bitterness realized. They also connected the word for lettuce (*khassa*) to God's having mercy (*khas*) on the Israelites and redeeming them.

Khazeret

Some people use another form of bitter herb, usually whole (pieces of horseradish root, for example), for the second time *maror* is eaten. The term relates to the Hebrew for return, in the sense of repentance (*khazarah*), and also to mercy (*khas*), signifying that when we take the initiative to turn to God (as the Israelites did in pledging their allegiance with the paschal lamb rite), He treats us mercifully.

Many *seder* plates come without a separate section for *khazeret*, because it is common to use only one form of bitter herb.

Kharoset

A mixture of apples, nuts and wine, or other fruits and spices (particularly those mentioned in the Song of Songs—figs, dates, and pomegranates—because they serve as metaphors for Israel), *kharoset* stands for the mortar and clay (*khar'sit*) the Israelites had to use to make bricks and build Pharaoh's projects.

Almonds are a popular ingredient because their name in Hebrew (*shekeidim*) suggests that God was watchful (*shaked*) over Israel. Some add unground spices like cinnamon or ginger to recall the straw the slaves had to collect to mix with the mortar. The color of the wine, added to make the mixture appropriately pasty, recalls the blood of the Israelite infants killed by Pharaoh and of the first plague.

Although it symbolizes something terribly painful, this sweet, tasty concoction is one of the most popular items on the table. In many households, family members sit with spoons poised to dig into whatever *kharoset* remains once it is no longer needed for ritual use. Associated by its dual nature with both physical oppression (clay) and sensual delight (taste, aroma), it suggests the bittersweetness of life and expresses Jewish optimism: Even the most negative condition can contain redeeming features.

Passing down the often unwritten formula for *kharoset*, individual families produce their own distinct flavors. You can find recipes in Passover and other Jewish cookbooks.

Z'roah

The roasted shankbone is one of two symbols on the *seder* plate we do not eat. Representing the paschal sacrifice, it proclaims freedom of religion that the slaves seized when they slaughtered their lambs. It also recalls the "outstretched arm" (*z'roah netuyah*) of God that took us out of Egypt (Deuteronomy 26:8).

You can get the shoulder bone of any kosher animal, containing some meat, from a butcher, or, as many do, use the neck or wing of a chicken. It should be roasted dry, just as the paschal lamb was (but you do not need to do it over an open fire).

Beitzah

The egg, the other symbol we do not eat, reminds us of another part of the paschal offering, the *korban khaggigah* (festival sacrifice) required as an expression of thanksgiving at every festival. On Passover, pilgrims ate the *korban khaggigah* first, to satisfy their appetites, and finished their meals with the paschal lamb. One reason we put both meat and egg on the *seder* plate is to demonstrate our repudiation of the Egyptian custom of not eating any animal product because the Egyptians worshipped the animals as gods. Some connect the egg with its Aramaic word, *beiyah*, meaning want or desire, implying God's desire to deliver His people.

The egg should be hardboiled, then scorched on a stove burner or under a broiler to resemble having been roasted. It remains in the shell.

Arrangement

As with just about every other aspect of the *seder*, there are different opinions as to how the *k'arah* should be organized, based on each authority's concept of not slighting the *matzah*, or any other item, by reaching over it before it has been used. Most people follow a modified version of the pattern established by the Ari (Rabbi Isaac Luria, leading kabbalist of sixteenth-century Safed).

At the center of the plate is *maror*. *Karpas* is below to the left, *khazeret* (if used) below it at the bottom of the plate, *kharoset* below to the right, the bone above

the *maror* to the right, and the egg above to the left. We usually put the three *matzot* the Ari placed at the top of the plate separate from the *k'arah*, or under it, as the Vilna Gaon did: This is practically accomplished with a three-tiered combination *matzah/seder* plate, with holders for the *k'arah* foods on top.

Together, the items on the *k'arah* reflect what has happened to Jews in every dispersion throughout our history. First we experience renewal and birth (*karpas*) and establish ourselves through labor (*kharoset*). Our lives become bitter (*maror*); we sweat and cry (salt water) under oppression (*khazeret*). Through sacrifice we are redeemed (*z'roah*) and we experience rebirth (*beitzah*).

Kittel

The leader of the Passover ritual, who at his table (the substitute for the altar) acts in place of the Temple priest, traditionally wears a white robe (*kittel*) reminiscent of the vestments of the *Kohanim*. It reminds us that the *seder* is not just a family get-together, but a sacred occasion. Lightweight, sometimes edged with gold or silver embroidery and belted over one's slacks and shirt, the *kittel* was also worn by Israelites on festivals as an expression of joy and freedom.

In the Jewish mystical spectrum, white represents God's mercy and loving kindness. (The special garment also recalls that the slaves preserved their Jewishness partly by keeping their traditional clothing, for which God looked kindly on them.) Carrying additional meanings when worn on Rosh Hashanah and Yom Kippur, on those days and this, as well as when donned by a father at his son's *brit milah* (covenant through circumcision) and by a bridegroom on his wedding day, it signifies a transition from one state of life to another.

Previously made by women for their husbands, the cotton wrap can be purchased where religious articles are sold. Today they are used primarily by more traditional Jews.

Four Cups and a Fifth for Elijah

Each person at the table needs a glass (*kos*) for wine (*yayin*) or grape juice, because drinking four cups is required of every participant. Since spills are inevitable (what would Shabbat or a festival be without fresh wine stains on the tablecloth?), it is a good idea to place each wine goblet on a plate or into a shallow bowl, and/or to put an absorbent paper napkin or towel under it.

An additional wine glass, designated as Elijah's cup (*kos Eliyahu*), is placed on the table for use later in the service.

Additional *Seder* Items

To fulfill the *mitzvah* to "recline" during the service as an expression of freedom, **pillows** are usually placed behind the leader, if not every guest. The custom developed from the origins of the *seder* when festive meals were taken Greco-Roman freeman style on comfortable chaises.

Many people have **snack items and candy** on hand to keep children occupied and attentive. **Candles** long enough to burn throughout the *seder* are popular for adding a festive touch to the table. A **pitcher and basin** (or any pouring device and receptacle available) and towel for the hand-washing rituals, and *kippot* (skullcaps, or *yarmulkes*, in Yiddish) for all men present are also needed.

Memorial Candle

On the evening before the *Yizkor* memorial service will be held in synagogue (the last day of pilgrimage festivals and Yom Kippur), anyone who has lost a parent customarily lights a *yahrtzite* candle in memory of the deceased. Since these candles, which come in small cans or glasses, burn for twenty-five hours, they are also popular sources of fire for candlelighting and cooking done after a festival has begun. You can find them in Jewish supply stores and supermarkets that have kosher food sections.

HOW DO WE SHOW WE CELEBRATE?— OBSERVANCE

Set within the home environment and focused on the family, the key to Jewish continuity, Passover is a model for observing a holiday and teaching the tradition. In fact, it is the most important domestic event of all Jewish festivals.

Despite the fact that it is the most labor-intensive, complicated, time-consuming and habit-altering holiday on the calendar, it has always been extremely popular. Its messages have resounded with truth and encouragement, and it speaks even to religious skeptics on a very basic level. Those throughout the ages who had little concern for following the *mitzvot* have often celebrated Passover, in its fullness, at least for the benefit of their children. And despite the minutia of preparation, it was always celebrated with joy, fostering renewed confidence that whatever terrible situations Jews found themselves in would eventually be relieved.

The major observances of Passover are abstention from eating any foods containing leavening and participation in the ritual meal on the first two nights of the holiday (only the first night in Israel and among Reform Jews).

Ushering in Pesakh

As for all biblically ordained holidays, we welcome Passover by lighting festival candles (called to *bentsh* [blessing] *likht* [light] in Yiddish), bringing blessings and light—and symbolically, the illumination of Torah—into the house. As for Shabbat, the woman of the household (or the man if no woman is present) lights at least two candles (corresponding to the two Torah passages commanding us to remember and guard the Sabbath day [Exodus 20:8; Deuteronomy 5:12]). Often a candle is added for each child in the family.

If *yom tov* (holiday) coincides with Shabbat, you must light the candles as you would for the Sabbath, eighteen minutes before sundown. (You can get a calendar that gives the proper time—which depends on your location—from a Jewish bookstore or institution such as *Khabad*, or check your newspaper for the time of sunset). This is done because after sundown, you may not light a fire, and the extra minutes help prevent you from accidentally going over the time limit. If *yom tov* falls during the week, you may light after sunset *from an existing flame*, but it is preferable to light candles at the earlier time, which signals the beginning of a welcome occasion.

By our tradition, a blessing is supposed to precede the *mitzvah* it describes. However, in the case of Shabbat, once you recite the blessing, you have already introduced the Sabbath into your home, which means you can no longer light. So in this situation, we light the candles first, then cover our eyes, so it is as though the candles have not yet been lit. Although technically this is not necessary on *yom tov*, for the sake of avoiding confusion we consistently follow the Shabbat procedure on festivals as well. (It is customary to circle our arms over the flames three times, drawing the spirit of the day of sanctity to ourselves, ending with our hands over our eyes.)

Recite both the blessing for the candles, and the *shehekheyanu*, a blessing made the first time each year that something is experienced: a festival begins, a piece of new clothing is worn, a particular fruit is eaten, and so on.

בָּרוּךְ אַתָּה, יהוה אֱלֹהֵינוּ, מֶלֶךְ הָעוֹלָם, אֲשֶׁר קִדְּשָׁנוּ בְּמִצְוֹתָיו, וְצִוָּנוּ לְהַדְלִיק נֵר שֶׁל [*שַׁבָּת וְשֶׁל] יוֹם טוֹב

Barukh Atah, Adonai Eloheinu, Melekh Haolam, asher kidshanu b'mitzvotav, v'tzivanu l'hadlik ner shel [Shabbat v'shel] yom tov.*

Blessed are You, Lord our God, King of the Universe, Who has sanctified us with His commandments and commanded us to kindle the lights of [Sabbath and of]* the festival.

---

*Said when Sabbath and *yom tov* coincide.

בָּרוּךְ אַתָּה, יהוה אֱלֹהֵינוּ, מֶלֶךְ הָעוֹלָם, שֶׁהֶחֱיָנוּ, וְקִיְּמָנוּ, וְהִגִּיעָנוּ לַזְּמַן הַזֶּה.

Barukh Atah, Adonai Eloheinu, Melekh Haolam, shehekheyanu, v'kiyamanu, v'higgiyanu lazman hazeh.

Blessed are You, Lord our God, King of the Universe, Who has kept us alive, sustained us, and brought us to this season.

Before lighting candles to usher in the second day of *yom tov*, we have to wait for the first day to be fin-

ished, so instead of lighting prior to sunset, we light after nightfall. We use a preexisting flame—twenty-five-hour candle, oven pilot light, stove burner (which had been lit prior to the festival candles on the first evening)—to ignite the wicks .

(On the seventh and eighth days of Passover, which are full festival days, candles are lit as described above. However, since these are not separate holidays in their own right, and we have already said the *shehekheyanu* for this festival, only the blessing for the candles is made. The *yahrtzite* candle in memory of a departed relative should be lit before the festival lights.)

Seder

It has been observed that no Jewish ritual is more followed and thought of more fondly than the Passover *seder*. As Jewish communal surveys and numerous literary works demonstrate, reminiscences of the shimmering holiday table, the aromas of once-a-year foods, the togetherness of family, and especially the familiar tunes stir something in us, bringing more people to the *seder* table than to any other Jewish celebration during the year. As Heinrich Heine observed, "even those Jews who have long forsaken the faith of their fathers and pursued foreign joys and honors are moved to the depths of their hearts when the old familiar sounds of the Passover happen to strike their ears."

Such praise for Pesakh is not to deny that many people today have mixed—if not outright contradictory—feelings about the *sedarim*. Many capitulate to the whines of children and other participants who complain that the wait for the meal is too long, or the process boring or without significance. We all know people who race through the first part of the *haggadah* just to get to the meal and abandon the service after they have eaten, or treat the occasion as a springtime Thanksgiving, a family feast unencumbered by ritual. Sadly, they are missing the point—and the exhilaration that Pesakh offers, robbing themselves and their children of beautiful meaning and memories.

If done right, the *seder* can captivate, excite, and inspire no less than a good stage production or a fascinating seminar. The *haggadah*'s inclusion of prayers and passages from different times and places in our history reflects not just one event but a continuous cycle of exile, oppression, and redemption, through today and into the future. Working from the role of the Exodus in our national life (see "Religious Significance" earlier in this chapter), it emphasizes that the event in Egypt is just a beginning, not only of our journey but of our discussion on *seder* nights.

The Torah commands, and the *haggadah* reiterates, that "in every generation each Jew should regard himself as though he personally went forth from Egypt." By reliving the experience of the Israelites, we too progress from idolatry to slavery and from ignorance to meaningful worship, freedom, and knowledge. Recalling that it was once possible to rise above the debasement and warped values of a surrounding and suppressing society and establish a more equitable order renews our faith that it is possible to do so again. There is tremendous hope in the saga of the Exodus—and Passover can inspire us to seize it.

The key is to keep the *seder* stimulating. Certain elements of the service must, according to *halakhah*, be covered (explanation of the paschal lamb, *matzah* and *maror*, Rabbi Gamliel's dictum, plus telling the story of the Exodus and drinking four glasses of wine). When the tradition says "Whomever expands on the story of the Exodus deserves praise," it does not mean that we should simply read every word of the *haggadah*. Only communicating Pesakh's themes in a way that moves and motivates participants fulfills the *mitzvah*.

Celebrants use all sorts of devices to accomplish the purpose, with variety the rule: different *haggadot* for each of the two nights (or from year to year), stressing a theme (current events, Holocaust, endangered Jewish communities); using dramatic techniques (acting, mime, costumes, puppetry) and songs to present parts of the story (or its modern equivalents), scripted or ad libbed (such as the *Sephardim* have long employed); using props and special effects, updating the service by listing modern-day plagues (diseases, famine, war, homelessness) or using "*Dayeinu*" (see discussion later in this section) to express appreciation for what is right in our world.

Each individual can talk about what freedom or the Passover experience means personally or can share the oppressions from which they fled. Some spend each of the *sedarim* with a different group of people, or in a different setting (how about an "authentic" Greco-Roman style *seder*, on sofas, or reclining on pillows on your living room floor, around a low table?). Maimonides instructed that it is necessary to make changes to draw the children into the proceedings. He suggested such attention-getters as distributing snack foods, moving the table prior to the meal, and snatching pieces of *matzah* from each other.

Many of the rituals are included just to prompt questions, particularly from children, who are the focal point and honored attendees at the *seder*: They are our hope for the future—as Pharaoh knew too well (Exodus 1:22, 10:11).

At the same time, we are all, in some ways, like children. The sages instructed that if no child were present to ask the "Four Questions," the wife must do it, or another man, even a scholar. If no one else is available, the service leader must ask himself. There is always something to learn, especially, for most of us today, about what it means to be children of Israel.

To Participate

If you will not be making a *seder* and cannot attend one made by friends or relatives, contact your Jewish Federation, a local synagogue, Hillel, Family and Children's Service, or other communal organization and ask to be placed with a host family. Since it is a *mitzvah* to invite strangers to the festival table, people are happy to accommodate and generally sign up for the privilege of doing so. As a last resort, you may be able to join a communal *seder*, which many congregations and some organizations hold on one of the nights. (These are not the same as the interfaith/interracial *sedarim* offered during the intermediate days of the holiday as an expression of shared values and concern and/or opportunities to improve mutual understanding.)

Timing

Unlike other festivals, when the candlelighting and *kiddush* which initiate the holiday are done at sundown, the *seder* may not begin until nightfall because that was the time the paschal lamb, *matzah*, and *maror* had to be eaten, and when *kiddush*, over the first of the four cups of wine, must be done. The start should not be delayed longer, however, because you want the children to remain awake, there's no point in unnecessarily delaying the meal, and the last part of the dinner must be eaten prior to midnight.

Basic Structure

Fifteen steps take us through the evening's experience. Each one is designed to prepare us physically or psychologically for the next step we—as our ancestors did—take in progressing from slavery, a life lived only in the moment, to redemption, which we see clearly in the future. They relate to the fifteen psalms that comprise the "Song of Ascents" (120–134), chanted by the Levites as they walked up the fifteen steps to the Temple, and suggest that the *seder* is also an ascent (*aliyah*), from slavery to freedom, the beginning of the forty-nine steps that will take us higher, to Mount Sinai and Torah (see chapter on Shavuot). Through it, we become a holy nation, eventually able to ascend to Jerusalem. (The same word, *aliyah*, is used to denote immigration to Israel.)

To ensure that the components of the *seder* were preserved when not every Jew had a *haggadah*, the rabbis devised a rhymed mneumonic that some families chant at the beginning of the *seder* and then up to the appropriate part as each ritual is reached. Variations on the tune are included in songbooks for Pesakh and on recorded versions of the *haggadah*.

The text of the *haggadah* and numerous commentaries fill entire books by themselves. What follows is an outline of the *seder* ceremony and a few highlights to help you think about what the steps mean.

Kaddesh

The sanctification over wine (usually pronounced *kiddush*, from the word for holy) initiates every Sabbath and festival, customarily over a brimming cup of wine, a symbol of joy. ("Wine gladdens the heart of man" [Psalms 104:15].) It always includes the phrase *Yetziat Mitzrayim*, connecting Pesakh with all festivals of the Jewish year, as all events of Jewish history are connected with the Exodus. Giving a regular meal a spiritual dimension, the *kiddush* on *seder* nights is recited over the first of the four cups of wine.

While it is customary to use red wine because it was thought to be superior (based on Proverbs 23:31), it also recalls the blood connected with Passover (murdered newborns, first plague, doorpost markings, circumcision required to partake of the Passover meal). White wine was often substituted in the Middle Ages because of the blood libels (though that did not always help), and today both red and white are used. Grape juice, for children and those who cannot tolerate wine (especially in Pesakh quantities!), is counted as wine.

After "slaving away" during the previous days and weeks to get ready for the holiday (see section on "Preparation"), the wine helps us make the transition from enslavement to liberty. Each cup helps take us back in time and space, facilitating our ability to relive the experience. The four cups are said to represent the four times Pharaoh's cup is mentioned in the story of Joseph's success at dream interpretation (Genesis 40:11–14) and the four kingdoms that subjugated Israel after the Exodus (Babylon, Persia, Greece, and Rome). They also reflect the four expressions God used when He promised to bring us out of Egypt: "bring you out" (*v'ho'tziti*), "deliver you" (*v'hi'tzalti*), "redeem you" (*v'ga'alti*), and "take you unto Me" (*v'lakakhti*) (Exodus 6:6–7).

We recline when we drink, and eat (except for the *maror* [since the slavery it symbolizes conflicts with the freedom expressed by reclining]), toward the left. It was the position on the ancient sofas, so people could free their right hand (for most, the preferred hand) to feed themselves. (It was believed that leaning toward the right might allow food to enter the windpipe, causing one to choke.)

Urkhatz

We wash our hands (*u*, and, *r'khatz*, washing) by taking a cup of water in the left hand and pouring half its contents in three splashes over the right hand, then switching and pouring the remainder over the left (lefties reverse the order). You can pass a pitcher, basin, and towel from person to person, have one person walk around to each guest's place, or rise from the table to use a sink.

Although we normally say a blessing when washing (because we usually wash in preparation for eating bread), we omit the *brakhah* here because it will be a while until we begin the actual meal. The action may be left over from the ancient practice of washing hands prior to eating anything moist (our next step) because the sages said that unclean hands defiled the liquid.

Today it serves two purposes: to prompt questions from children ("Why is someone walking around the table with a pot of water?" "Why are we washing if we're not ready to eat?" "Why don't we say a blessing?") and to prepare us physically for the Exodus experience: we "wash our hands" of the slave mentality, the first step to independence.

Karpas

The green vegetable or potato is dipped into salt water, the substance both of tears and life genesis. Initially in Egypt the Israelites grew and prospered. But birth of too many led to oppression, salty sweat, and tears of pain. Salt also recalls the Temple, whose loss we mourn, where sacrifices were always salted.

This is another stimulus for questions ("You call that an hors d'oeuvre?" "Where's the rest of dinner?" "Parsley? Why are we eating this stuff that's normally just plate decoration?") and an opportunity for parents to teach children that physical desires are not always immediately met, that a physical act can be invested with spirituality when accompanied by learning and prayer.

Yakhatz

The leader breaks the middle *matzah* in half (*khatzi*), puts the smaller portion (have you ever gotten *matzah* to break evenly?) back on the plate, and wraps the larger portion (suggesting that more is hidden to us than revealed) in a napkin or a special bag for the *afikoman* (as this piece of *matzah* is called). This is another one of the devices promoted by Talmud to keep children awake and prompt them to ask, once again, what is so special about this night. Among *Ashkenazim*, children customarily "steal" the *afikoman* and ransom it at the end of the meal for a reward when the leader cannot find it. (In some families the leader hides it and the child who finds it claims a reward.)

At this point, the *matzah* is *lekhem oni*, the inadequate fare of the poor (slaves to their status), who must suffice with less than a full portion, and often, not knowing where the next meal will come from, saving some for later. The act of breaking the *matzah* puts us in the position of the poor, at least symbolically. Having a partial portion also suggests that life is incomplete for all of us as long as we are in exile.

Shattering it brings to mind the breaking of the bonds that we come, through habit and complacency, to accept, the illusion of security in which we live, financial and especially political, which makes us think that somehow we can exist with the threat of tyranny. (*Kristallnakht* shattered what the Jews of Germany thought was a safe life.) It is taking the first step to liberation.

Signifying the hospitality we are about to extend, breaking the bread also prepares us to break bread with those who need it.

Maggid

The telling of the story of Exodus is the *raison d'être* of the *seder*. It turns the *seder* table into a Jewish environment for learning. One interesting note about it: Except for a truly incidental reference, the name of the hero of the story, affectionately known in our tradition as Moshe Rabbeinu (Moses our Teacher), is not mentioned. The omission was purposeful: to avoid anyone thinking that Moses, rather than God, had effected the redemption and to prevent the possibility of Moses being turned into an object of idol worship—which the Exodus was meant to eliminate. (The sites of Mount Sinai and Moses' burial are unknown for the same reason.)

Opening Our Homes/Hearts

The leader begins by uncovering and lifting the plate holding the "bread of affliction our ancestors ate in Egypt" (*Ha lakhma anya . . .*) and invites all who are hungry to eat with us (fulfilling physical needs), all who are needy to join us in celebrating Passover (ful-

filling spiritual yearnings). We go to the trouble of reexperiencing our servitude in Egypt so that we never forget what it means to be a slave, an outcast. Reaching beyond ourselves to help others is a sign of freedom.

This part of the *seder* originated in Babylonia, where hosts actually went into the streets to extend a welcome. So that everyone would understand the invitation, it was said in Aramaic, the local tongue. For this reason, many people today say it in the vernacular. (Although it is unlikely we would bring someone off the street at this point in the evening, we should think of all those who are hungry, physically, emotionally, and spiritually, all who are strangers, within their own families and to their own heritage, who need our support.) With the persecutions from the Middle Ages on, opening the door became too risky and was eliminated from the beginning of the service. As a sign of hospitality, some people have recently reinstated it.

In contrast, the lines that follow, expressing hope to be in Jerusalem next year and for all to be free, were pronounced in Hebrew. This prevented the Babylonians from understanding the words and thinking that the Jews were planning to revolt.

Matzah *of Hope*

In the past few decades, it has become customary to include special prayers and readings on behalf of Jewish communities still oppressed (most commonly the Soviet and Ethiopian Jews), often over a specially designated piece of *matzah*. (Prayers on behalf of Soviet and Ethiopian Jewry have been altered to reflect the change in their situations since mass immigration to Israel was allowed. Check with an advocacy group or a local synagogue for an updated text.)

The arrival of large numbers of those communities in Israel has not eliminated the need for concern. Not all have reached safety; Jews in certain countries (e.g., Syria) are still endangered, and Jews everywhere live under the afflictions of poverty, sickness, and spiritual malaise. As long as some are oppressed, none of us is truly free, and collectively we are prevented from enjoying universal peace. To emphasize our responsibility in bringing all Jews together, the *Matzah* of Hope is also identified as the *Matzah* of Unity.

Four Questions

The content of the "*Mah Nishtanah*" (why is [this night] different), as the four questions are more popularly known, presents the dual themes of the evening. *Matzah* (the first question) is both the bread of slaves and of free people. Bitter herbs (second question) symbolize servitude as well as an elegant privilege: the hors d'oeuvre dipped into another substance. *Karpas* (third question) represents the suffering of slavery and the rebirth of redemption, as does dipping twice—greens in salt water and later bitter herbs in *kharoset*, which itself commemorates both enslavement (Joseph's brothers, after selling him, dipped his coat in lamb's blood to convince their father he had been attacked by a wild animal [Genesis 37:31]) and liberation (the hyssop dipped in lamb's blood to mark the Jewish households [Exodus 12:22]).

The act of questioning reflects freedom, evidence that we are not restrained in seeking to satisfy our intellectual curiosity through probing and analysis. Questions, not answers, allow us to progress in our learning, to acquire knowledge that lifts us out of ignorance, which can be as brutal an oppressor as a tyrannical taskmaster.

The four questions are not directly answered in the *seder*, a suggestion that formulating the right questions, and searching for the truth in response, is an ongoing process.

Avadim Hayinu *(We were slaves)*

What we really want to know, of course, is why we celebrate Passover, which the *haggadah* explains. The sages debated whether, in following the talmudic principle that we "begin with degradation and end with glory," we start with the debasement of slavery or that of idolatry. Is physical bondage imposed from outside more shameful, or is spiritual bondage, the result of personal choices, a worse humiliation? In including both slavery and idolatry in the *seder* story (the second comes a few pages later in the *haggadah*), we reach back to Abraham, who started the journey to redemption by smashing his father's idols, recognizing One God, and receiving the covenant the Israelites were taken from Egypt to uphold.

Remembering our lowly origins is a means of keeping us from rising so far above afflictions we have escaped that we forget they are very real for too many people. Yet with our eye on glory at the conclusion of the story, we know there is a happy ending, and are encouraged to keep going forward.

Five Sages

A well-known passage of the *haggadah* describes one Passover evening in B'nei B'rak when leading rabbis of the post-Temple era sat up all night, so engrossed in discussing the Exodus that their students had to inform them the sun was about to rise. The report raises numerous questions (among them, especially for children, "how could they have possibly spent so much time at it?"). This is an example of how

the night's themes have held immediacy throughout Jewish history: It is a veiled account of Passover celebrated with political purpose.

The sages of the story lived under Roman occupation—essentially in exile in their own land—when Torah study had been prohibited. On that memorialized Pesakh evening, they were engaged in a crisis session to plan the best course for the community: Were they to merely keep the memories alive secretly, through the darkest periods, finding ways to worship, always hoping for and expecting redemption, or were they to resist openly, fighting for political and religious independence?

One of the participants, Rabbi Akiva, supported the rebellion leader Bar Kokhba ("son of star"), whose rising the eager activist students announced after the all-night debate (see chapter on Lag B'Omer). Later, after the devastating defeat of Bar Kokhba and the end of any kind of dynamic Jewish existence in the Holy Land until the modern era, the *galut* mentality of passivity—out of which grew the image of the meek, defenseless, physically subordinate Jew—dominated until the twentieth century.

Then Zionism reignited the pacifism versus activism debate that was essentially ended by the Holocaust and establishment of the modern Jewish homeland. In recent decades, similar questions were again raised by advocacy groups grappling with determining the most prudent means of obtaining freedom for Soviet and Ethiopian Jews.

The Four Sons

Four times the Torah instructs that a parent teach his/her child the story of Passover (Exodus 12:26; 13:8; 13:14; Deuteronomy 6:20), both in response to questions (three of the passages) and even when a child does not ask. The wording of each suggests a different level of personal involvement with the Exodus story and its commemoration and reflects a different level of commitment to the Jewish people (the intellectually curious "wise" [*khakham*] person, who includes him/herself in the community and is eager for details of all the laws; the rebellious "wicked" [*rasha*] person, who disassociates him/herself from the group and is negative toward its ritual; the "simple" [*tam*] person perhaps immature or naive, who has natural faith; and the unquestioning [*sheh eino yodei'ah lishol*] person, who needs to be treated and taught from beginning to end with sensitivity).

On one level the questions acknowledge that individuals have varying interests and capacity to understand, and that the responses they elicit should be given accordingly. Many commentators contend that the *arba'ah* (four) *banim* (sons, or children) refer not only—or not at all—to minors or aspects of them within all of us. Rather, they stand for ideological groups that threatened rabbinic Judaism in the first and second centuries, when the *haggadah* was written (Hellenes, Judeo-Christians, Sadducees, Essenes), or political attitudes of Jews living under Roman rule (supporters of revolution, those who refused to join the revolt even at its crisis point, those who had been enslaved by Rome, and those who had not been exposed to Judaism and did not know what the revolt was all about).

The most significant interpretation for our age is that ascribed to Rabbi Joseph Isaac Schneersohn (1880–1950), the former Lubavitcher Rebbe, who saw in the *arba'ah banim* the four generations of the American Jewish experience, each one successively removed from European roots of Jewish observance: the religious immigrant; the rejecting second generation; the confused third generation in conflict between the tradition of his/her grandparents' home and the trouncing of *mitzvot* by his/her parents; and the alienated ignorant fourth generation, who never knew his/her great-grandfather and has no basis on which to even form a question. It is the ignorance and indifference that every generation must combat, by making Judaism and Jewish education relevant and appealing so that the next child in line is not so far from our heritage that s/he does not know that Pesakh has arrived or what it signifies.

By now you've probably noticed that there are quite a few "fours" in this ceremony (glasses of wine, questions, ritual foods, sons). The number is used to describe a long list of things with Jewish significance (matriarchs, epochs of the universe, groupings of the tribes in the wilderness, fringes [*tzitzit*] on the corners of ritual garments, species used on the holiday of Sukkot, and on and on). A mystical number in several religions, in Judaism the number four suggests stability and wholeness, as in defining a square that is the base of a house—or the "four corners of the earth" from which the Jews will be collected together at the time of redemption.

The Ten Plagues

Scholars love to give natural explanations for the ten plagues. They may be right and still not negate traditional Jewish belief that the plagues were arranged "by Heaven" (the Jewish definition of miracle is a natural occurrence that comes at the opportune moment), or that they hold relevant symbolic significance. For instance, they are interpreted as measure-for-measure (*midah-k'neged-midah*) retribution for the Egyptians' own actions.

According to this explanation, blood was for the drowned infants; frogs covering everything for the taskmasters being constantly on the Israelites' backs; welt-causing lice getting under the skin for the whip of overseers; beasts to mirror the Egyptians' beastly behavior; cattle disease for stealing the livestock of the Jews when they had been shepherds and herdsmen; boils for making the Jews live in filthy, skin-irritating conditions; hail for the evil words rained down on the Jews; locusts to destroy grains for the straw the Jews had to collect to make bricks; darkness for the general condition slavery imposes on its victims; and death of the firstborn for torture of God's firstborn, Israel.

The plagues have also been understood as means of humiliating the Egyptians for the worthless gods they worshipped, portraying them as bloody (the Nile), obnoxious (a frog-headed creature), diseased (livestock), eclipsed (the sun), and dead (heir to the throne). Affecting the ground itself, the creatures that live on it, and the atmosphere, the plagues demonstrated the Israelite God's sovereignty over earth, nature, life, and death.

The way we incorporate the ten plagues in our ceremony highlights an important Jewish value: We must never sink to the level of our oppressors. We were taken out of Egypt not just to end the brutal subjugation but so that we would not be lost in their unjust, decadent, life-wasting culture. As we recite each of the plagues, we remove a drop of wine from our cups—either with the pinky (symbolizing the "finger of God" Pharaoh's priests recognized as the force behind their troubles [Exodus 8:15]) or with a spoon. Despite all the horrendous actions of our enslavers, they were still human beings. And because our salvation involved their suffering, our joy cannot be complete. For that reason we diminish the wine, symbol of gladness, to express our sorrow. (Since these drops represent plagues, it is inappropriate to lick your finger or spoon after spilling them.)

For the same reason, only the half *Hallel* is recited during the last six days of Passover. *Midrash* relates that when the Egyptians were drowning in the Reed Sea, the angels wanted to sing praises. God rebuked them. "How can you sing Hallelujah when My children are drowning?" Proverbs teaches us "If your enemy falls, do not exult. If he trips, let your heart not rejoice" (24:17). Our tradition teaches us that although we should categorically reject Egyptian practices, we are not to despise the Egyptians, who despite later abuse, did feed and shelter us during the famine. The expression of sensitivity is a reminder that once we win freedom we are to use it appropriately and not apply our new strength to oppress others.

Dayeinu

A *seder* favorite, the lively song with the one-word refrain (much longer in English: "It would have been sufficient for us"), is a progression of expressions of gratitude for each of the fifteen stages in the redemption from Egypt. Although we needed to reach Sinai and then the Temple to achieve our spiritual potential, the song teaches us to appreciate whatever we have, however short of the goal it might be (the glass is half full rather than half empty). Each step provides a promise of something better than the current situation, a reflection of the Jews' eternal optimism. At the same time, the situation at each step is better than the previous one and an accomplishment in itself. Creating a personal *dayeinu*, or a family version as part of the *seder*, can be a powerfully affirming exercise.

Hallel

Following explanation of the symbolic foods (*z'roah, matzah, maror*), and commandment for each of us to feel as though we personally left Egypt, we chant the first part of the "Psalms of Praise." Called Egyptian *Hallel*, it consists of two psalms (113 and 114) dealing with the delivery from Egypt, which were chanted by the Levites in the Temple when the paschal sacrifices were offered. They form one of the oldest portions of the *haggadah*.

Rakhatz

After the second cup of wine, we wash our hands, as in *urkhatz*, this time with the blessing. It is another transition point, as we are about to begin the meal. We refresh our spirits in preparation for the physical celebration of a new physical state.

Motzi/Matzah

Each participant takes a piece of the top *matzah* and the broken middle *matzah* (because there is disagreement as to whether the blessing applies to the bread of affliction or the top festival bread, we take both), salts them and eats, following the *brakhah*, reclining to the left.

Maror

We dip for the second time, immersing the bitter herbs (use a spoon if your choice is horseradish) into the *kharoset*. When the Temple stood, *maror*, representing bondage and exile, was eaten at the end of the *seder*, say our rabbis, because the celebrants knew that they would end up going into exile. Today, when we are in exile, we eat them first, as a prelude to the post-dinner concentration on future redemption.

Korekh

The first-century sage Hillel invented the sandwich (*korekh*) of *matzah* and *maror* because of the Torah injunction to eat the two with the Passover lamb (Exodus 12:8). He understood they were to be eaten together. Each person at the *seder* constructs a sandwich out of two pieces of *matzah* and some *maror*. We do not lean while eating it because the bitter herbs signify slavery, but the sandwich actually combines that state with redemption (the *matzah*).

This duality prompts us to think about how the two factors coexist in our own lives, and how each reminds us of the other: When we are oppressed, the taste of freedom lingers. And when we are free, we recall the pain of oppression. This awareness keeps us mindful of those who still live under slavery and helps us guard our own behavior.

Shulkhan Orekh

Eating a sanctified meal on our set (*orekh*) table (*shulkhan*) is part of the Jewish system of food preparation and consumption (*kashrut*, keeping kosher) designed to elevate every step of the process above animal need to holy service (and likewise, to elevate us above our animal nature to more spiritual consciousness). The model is particularly appropriate for this occasion: The first commandment given to and followed by the Israelites in Egypt concerned preparation of the family meal they would make at home as a sign of their commitment to serve God. It shows how we can use the opportunity of *seder* to strengthen feelings of belonging to our family and the family of Israel while teaching Jewish spiritual values.

Tzafun

The meal is usually not completed without the hidden (*tzafun*) *afikoman*—which means that the child who has successfully hidden or stolen it (in a family that follows one of those customs) is in a good position to be rewarded for relinquishing it. The leader "buys" it back for money, a prepared gift, or the promise to provide the requested ransom. The stand-in for the paschal lamb (or the *matzah* eaten with it), which was the last item eaten in the Pesakh meal, must be consumed prior to midnight, as the *pesakh* was. Nothing is to be eaten afterward (some authorities say water, apple juice, seltzer, coffee, and tea fall outside of "nothing"). If you do not have the actual *afikoman*, take another piece of *matzah* to end the meal.

Usually explained as "dessert," *afikoman* is from the Greek word describing post-banquet revelries. It may have been borrowed by the Jews to identify the desserts that followed a meal. Since no sweets were eaten after the sacrifice, and secular song and dance were prohibited, *afikoman* came to mean the last bit of the paschal lamb, later symbolized by this last piece of *matzah*, which finished the meal, leaving behind its taste of liberty.

Its hiddenness during the part of the *seder* that relived a time of oppression suggests that deliverance can come at any time, when the instigator for it (like Moses, whom some say the *afikoman* represents) suddenly appears.

Bareikh

In the blessing (*birkat*, a form of *bareikh/barukh*) for the food (*hamazon*) just eaten, we thank God for physical, emotional, and spiritual gifts: sustenance, the Land He gave us on which to grow food in security, and our spiritual center there, Jerusalem. It is concluded by drinking the third cup of wine.

Elijah's Cup

We open the door to welcome Elijah the prophet, who will announce the messiah, into our homes. A benchmark in the *seder*—particularly for the children who historically were advised to watch Elijah's cup carefully to see if any wine from it disappeared—it is actually a curious part of the proceedings.

Originally, the custom of opening the door had nothing to do with the prophet. Subjected to the horrifying blood libels of Europe, the Jews had to fearfully open their doors to prove to Christian neighbors that they had nothing heinous to hide.

Another example of duality, the opening of the door also recalls that the time of the Exodus is *leil* (night) *shimurim* (of guarding), when God protects the Jewish people with special watchfulness. (The part of the *Shema* [Hear O Israel] prayer said by traditional Jews before bed each night, asking for God's protection while they sleep, is omitted as superfluous. They recite only the prayer's first paragraph.) Despite that part of our tradition, the sage Maharal counseled that while it was inappropriate for the Jews to bolt their doors on the special night of Passover, in seeking protection for themselves they were not to merely rely on miracles, either.

We express our sense of security under His care with a wide open door—as is the custom in *Sephardi* communities (e.g., among the Djerban Jews in Tunisia)—for the entire duration of the *seder*. The custom may have originated with the opening of the Temple doors immediately after midnight—on completion of the Pesakh meal—and leaving them open until morning.

Until recently, the name of the prophet did not even appear in the *haggadah* except in the *Birkat Hamazon*, and that is standard year-round text. Today, some people greet him with "*barukh habah*" (welcome) and often sing the hope that he will arrive soon ("*Eliyahu Hanavi, Eliyahu Hatishbi . . .*") usually intoned at the close of Shabbat. Traditionally, the opening of the door was followed by an invective against the nations ("Pour out Your wrath . . ."), clearly a reflection of the frustration felt by the Jews of the Middle Ages who, as victims of Crusades, pogroms, and countless indignities, introduced it.

While there is a clear connection between Passover, the holiday of redemption, and Elijah, the advance man of the future redeemer, the custom of including a special cup for the prophet on the *seder* table arose out of disagreement as to whether a fifth expression of deliverance (Exodus 6:8 [see explanation of *Kaddesh* earlier in this section]) called for an additional cup of wine, since it referred to something that would occur later, in messianic days, and not as part of the Exodus. Elijah was identified with the end of days because he was entrusted by God to witness the Jews' continued observance of the *mitzvot* (like *seder* and circumcision, every one of which he is said to attend). With the notion that prior to the messiah's arrival Elijah would solve all doubts and settle differences of opinion, the question of four or five cups was left to his ruling. In case it would be affirmative, the fifth cup was provided but not consumed (except by the Yemenites).

In a rich tradition of folklore, Elijah has often appeared on Earth, usually in the form of a beggar, to help the sick and impoverished. So it was not unusual for people to expect him to show up on their doorstep on the event dedicated to salvation and take a sip.

Like preparation of the paschal lamb, we open the door for Elijah (it's not as if he could not let himself in) because it is we who must act to bring about the desired goal. Based on the practice of the *khasidim*, to show their involvement in trying to facilitate redemption, some families have each person pour wine from his/her cup to fill Elijah's or place their cups around the one for Elijah.

Remembrance for the Six Million

Some *haggadot* include a ritual to commemorate those murdered in one of the most recent oppressions (see chapter on Yom Hashoah). It includes special readings, poems, diary excerpts, prayers, and passages by and about victims of the ghettos and concentration camps, along with the song *"Ani Ma'amin"* (I Believe), the expression of total faith that the messiah will come.

Hallel

The rest of the "Psalms of Praise" (115–118) follow the meal. Pledging service to God, thanking Him for many forms of goodness including freeing us, it concentrates on national redemption. The Great Hallel (*Hallel Hagadol*, Psalm 136), recounting the delivery from Pharaoh and other oppressors, deals with universal redemption. Its refrain *ki* (for) *l'olam* (meaning both "forever" and "for the world") *khasdo* (both "His mercy" and "His loving kindness")—or "For His mercy endures forever" and "For His mercy endures for the world"—stresses that the goal of perfecting the world will be achieved only when all people are freed of all forms of oppression (tyranny, poverty, war, hunger, prejudice, and other obstacles to reaching full potential).

Nirtzah

After we count the *Omer* (see next section) and drink the final cup of wine, we express the desire (*rahtzah*) that our concluded *seder* is acceptable (*nirtzah*), and that we will celebrate in freedom next year. We proclaim "L'shanah haba'ah b'Yerushalayim" ("Next year in Jerusalem"; when in Israel, "next year in Jerusalem rebuilt," *habnuyah*), the dream of Jews since we lost the Temple.

Although we have reclaimed the capital, until conditions in the world are drastically changed, the exile continues. It is not just a geographic boundary. It is a separation in the soul, within a community, among nations. One of the dangers we face as Jews living in a fairly tolerant democratic nation is that we are so comfortable as to not even realize we are in exile. If the preparation for and enactment of the *seder* has been experienced meaningfully, we emerge from it conscious of how the world needs to change drastically, of the exiles in our lives we need to reconcile in order to truly be in Jerusalem, a city whose name suggests peace (*shalom*) and completeness (*shaleim*).

Post-Seder Songs

In the Middle Ages, reluctant to leave the festive table, participants added religious folksongs, number madrigals, nursery rhymes, and hymns that remain a popular part of the celebration. It is fun to sing them when enough people around the table are familiar with the words and music.

FOR FURTHER READING

Seder Melodies. Cedarhurst, NY: Board of Jewish Education of Greater New York and Tara Publications, 1977.

You'll find much of the music for the Passover home service in this compact book and on its companion tape.

Counting the *Omer*

Toward the end of the second *seder* we begin anticipating Shavuot, the next holiday and in essence the conclusion of Pesakh, by counting the days until its arrival. It is customary to stand (based on the "standing sheaves" of the *Omer* sacrifice [Deuteronomy 16:9]), recite the blessing, and say the count for the day:

בָּרוּךְ אַתָּה, יהוה אֱלֹהֵינוּ, מֶלֶךְ הָעוֹלָם, אֲשֶׁר קִדְּשָׁנוּ בְּמִצְוֹתָיו, וְצִוָּנוּ עַל סְפִירַת הָעֹמֶר:

Barukh Atah, Adonai Eloheinu, Melekh Haolam, asher kidshanu b'mitzvotav, vitzivanu al sefirat haomer.

Blessed are You, Lord our God, King of the Universe, Who has sanctified us with His commandments and commanded us concerning counting the *Omer*.

הַיּוֹם יוֹם אֶחָד לָעֹמֶר.

Hayom yom ekhad l'omer.

Today is the first day of the *Omer*.

On each subsequent night of the *sefirah* (counting period), and always at night, when the Jewish day begins, we increase the count and state it in days and weeks. ("Today is the *X* day of the *Omer*, which equals *X* weeks and *X* days of the *Omer*"; "*Hayom X yamim, sheim X shavuah u'X yamim la'omer.*") Some people follow the count by reciting Psalm 67, since it contains seven verses and a total of forty-nine words. Many also say the age-old *Harakhamon* prayer for the final redemption ("May the Compassionate One [*Harakhamon*] restore the Temple speedily in our days"), because its fulfillment would make it possible to reinstate the *Omer* observance to a biblical, not just rabbinic, commandment.

Khol Hamoed

The intermediate (*khol*) festival days (*hamoed*), days three through six or two through six in Israel and for the Reform, have a special designation. Although they are not full festivals, they are still holy relative to ordinary days. Leviticus refers to them as *mikro'ei kodesh*, days of sanctity. Even though there are no biblical prohibitions against work or travel, the rabbis ruled that gainful work is forbidden (you can work if material loss would occur). This was to distinguish the time from normal weekdays and provide greater opportunity for Torah.

We read the Torah in synagogue on each intermediate day, conduct the *Mussaf* (additional) service ordained for Shabbat and festivals, and recite the partial *Hallel* (because only part is said on the seventh day, which is a full festival, we cannot elevate a semi-festival above it).

Synagogue

The liturgy of Pesakh is basically identical to those of the other pilgrimage festivals. The *Amidah* (standing prayer that is the centerpiece of all daily services) refers to the holiday as *Khag Hamatzot* and describes it as *Zeman Kheiruteinu*, time of our freedom.

Prayer for Dew

During *Mussaf* on the first day we recite a prayer for protection against weather conditions that could harm farming efforts: *Tefillat Tal*. *Midrash* says that Isaac gave blessings for dew and sustenance to Jacob on Passover night. In Israel the holiday marks the end of the rainy season and the beginning of a long dry summer when the land, prior to Israel's modern irrigation achievements, was dependent on dew. Seen as a gift from heaven, its absence Divine punishment, the morning moisture is requested as a blessing for life and plenty.

Wearing a *kittel* to reflect a proper solemn and supplicating mood, the cantor recites the prayer, a series of acrostic poems. The *Ashkenazim* say the phrase "Who causes the wind to blow and the dew to descend" on the first day of Pesakh; the *Sephardim* continue to say it until the fall prayer for rain is begun on Shemini Atzeret (see chapter on Sukkot).

Readings from Torah and Prophets

The scriptural selections, drawn from four of the Five Books of Moses, all deal, as you would expect, with the Exodus, laws of the festival, later celebrations of Pesakh, and the sacrifices of the day. Prophetic portions read on the first two days recount Passover celebrations at the time of Joshua and under King Josiah (Joshua 5:2–6:1–27; II Kings 23:1–9; 21–25), and on the last two days we chant a Song of Deliverance by King David—which parallels the Song of the Sea read the same day—and a messianic vision (II Samuel 22:1–51; Isaiah 10:32–12:6).

Intermediate Sabbath

In addition to reviewing the laws of Sabbath and Pesakh (Exodus 33:12–34:26), on the Sabbath that falls within the festival, we read the prophetic account of the revival of dried bones and resurrection of the dead (Ezekiel 37:1–14), a reference to the nation of Israel. Popular tradition says the renewal will occur in *Nissan*.

Shir Hashirim

Each of the Bible's five scrolls (Song of Songs, Ruth, Lamentations, Ecclesiastes, and Esther) is assigned for reading on a festival. For Passover, it is the first, *Shir Hashirim*. Ostensibly a richly imaged sensuous poem of love between a man and woman, it was accepted by the sages as an allegory of the love between God, the people of Israel, and Torah. For this reason, Rabbi Akiva said although "all the books of the Bible are holy . . . this is the holiest." Its themes of spring ("Arise my love, my fair one, and come away. For now the winter is past, the rains are over and gone. The blossoms have appeared in the land . . ." [2:10–12]) and sexuality ("Sweetness drops from your lips, O bride; honey and milk are under your tongue; and the scent of your robe is like the scent of Lebanon" [4:11]) complement the Festival of Spring (*Khag Ha'aviv*) Pesakh is sometimes called. In addition, it contains specific references to Pharaoh and his chariots and symbolic references to the night of watching, the Exodus, the hope and fear of redemption, four different exiles Israel is to endure, and the deliverance from each.

If Pesakh begins on Sabbath or Sunday, the *Ashkenazim* recite *Shir Hashirim* prior to the Torah reading on the first day. The *Sephardim* sing it before the afternoon service on the seventh or eighth day. (In some communities it is customary to also read it at the *seder* after the *Haggadah* has been completed.)

Seventh Day

Tradition holds that the parting and crossing of the Reed Sea occurred on the seventh day following the night of the Exodus. Torah does not mention the specific day or connect the day of crossing with celebration because we do not rejoice when our enemies fall. We do express joy for our deliverance by repeating the exultant "Song of the Sea" originated by Moses and the children of Israel after they had reached safety and included in the morning's Torah reading (Exodus 13:17–15:26). The congregation customarily stands and sings along to a special tune that varies by local tradition.

Since the miracle of the Reed Sea occurred at night, some sects of *khasidim* conduct a special ceremony at midnight, near a sea when possible. (The beach in Tel Aviv is crowded for it.) Many pious Jews stay up most, if not all, night, aiming at improving themselves and their faith by studying excerpts from the Written (Torah) and Oral (as compiled in *Mishnah*) Law and *Zohar* collected in a special book called *Tikkun* (improvement).

Yizkor

On the last day of Pesakh (as well as other pilgrimage festivals and Yom Kippur), a special service for the memory of deceased loved ones and the righteous precedes the additional festival service. Named for the first word of the opening prayer, *Yizkor*, meaning "May God remember," is an ancient practice based on the Jewish belief that one's life does not end when the body dies. Instead, the eternal soul continues to exist in the influence a person has had upon others. We keep the memory of the dead alive by remembering them in these special prayers (and, according to tradition, by resolving to follow in their ways and teachings, presumably according to Torah).

Originally, *Yizkor* was recited on Yom Kippur. Later, after the first Crusades, it became customary to read the names of a community's martyred dead the week before Shavuot. Based on the idea that the living could atone for the dead by reciting the prayers, and by making a pledge to donate money to charity in memory of one's departed loved ones, it became a practice to include *Yizkor* on all festivals when the Torah portion concerns our responsibilities to the poor.

Superstitious Eastern European Jews wanting to avoid the "evil eye" left the sanctuary during *Yizkor* if their parents were still alive. This practice is widely followed to this day (some prayer books even include an instruction to the point). However, it is considered a *mitzvah* for every Jew to say the prayers in remembrance of their loved ones and inspirational people other than one's parents. Anyone who has not completed a year of mourning for a parent does leave, as s/he may be overcome by sorrow and inadvertently disturb others on a day when mourning is prohibited.

Havdalah

Pesakh ends after nightfall, when a shortened version of *havdalah*, the brief and beautiful ceremony to separate (*l'havdil*) sacred and holy time, takes place. Unless the day coincides with Shabbat, when the full *havdalah* (contained in a standard prayer book) done at the close of every Sabbath is made, the *motzi* (departure of) Pesakh version consists only of the blessing over and drinking of wine and the statement of separation. It is done at the close of *Ma'ariv* (evening service) in the synagogue or at home, after three stars have appeared in the sky.

בָּרוּךְ אַתָּה, יהוה אֱלֹהֵינוּ, מֶלֶךְ הָעוֹלָם, בּוֹרֵא פְּרִי הַגָּפֶן.

Barukh Atah, Adonai Eloheinu, Melekh Haolam, borei pri hagaffen.

Blessed are You, Lord our God, King of the Universe, Who creates fruit of the vine.

בָּרוּךְ אַתָּה, יהוה אֱלֹהֵינוּ, מֶלֶךְ הָעוֹלָם, הַמַּבְדִּיל בֵּין קֹדֶשׁ לְחוֹל, בֵּין יִשְׂרָאֵל לָעַמִּים, בֵּין יוֹם הַשְּׁבִיעִי לְשֵׁשֶׁת יְמֵי הַמַּעֲשֶׂה. בָּרוּךְ אַתָּה יהוה, הַמַּבְדִּיל בֵּין קֹדֶשׁ לְחוֹל.

Barukh Atah, Adonai Elokeinu, Melekh Haolam, hamavdil bein kodesh l'khol, bein Yisrael la'amim, bein yom hash'vi'i l'sheshet y'mei ha'ma'aseh. Barukh Atah, Adonai, hamavdil bein kodesh l'khol.

Blessed are You, Lord our God, King of the Universe, Who makes a distinction between sacred and secular, between Israel and the other nations, between the seventh day and the six working days. You are blessed, Lord, Who makes a distinction between the sacred and the secular.

Many people immediately run out to buy bread and consume something they did not have all week—pizza, pasta, ice cream, or beer.

Isru Khag

The day following Pesakh (and the other pilgrimage festivals) is a semi-holiday on which the spirit of the festival is retained so we can sustain it and carry it with us into the work week. Called *Isru* (from *asar*, to tie or bind) *Khag* (festival), today it is marked only by prohibition of fasting and omission of penitential prayers.

Continuation of the *Omer*

In observant circles, marriages do not take place during the counting of the *Omer*, when traditional mourning customs are followed. Haircuts, wearing of new clothes, listening to music, and attending public entertainment are also prohibited out of respect for the thousands of Rabbi Akiva's students who died in the first thirty-two days of *sefirah*—or so the tradition holds (see chapters on Lag B'Omer and Shavuot).

Pesakh *Sheni*

Since the second Passover was instituted only to allow for sacrifice to be made, it has been marked from the time the Temple was destroyed only by the omission of prayers of supplication (*Takhanun*) from the daily services. In commemoration of its former significance, some people eat *matzah* on *Iyar* 14.

WHERE DO WE BEGIN?—PREPARATION

It seems that the laughter of Purim has hardly died down and the effects of its wine have hardly waned when we have to get ready for Pesakh. There is exactly one month between the two, time traditionally devoted to massive housecleaning, food preparation, and study of the holiday laws.

No other holiday in the Jewish calendar requires more advance work than Pesakh—but please do not let that discourage you. (Are you dissuaded from making a lavish wedding, taking an exotic vacation, or moving into a new house because it entails months of planning and activity?) There is something very refreshing about having to examine and alter our physical environment, about having to question and perhaps jolt a complacent frame of mind. When you are scrubbing countertops and scouring crevices, turning your house upside down and inside out, remember that making the transformation between slave and free person—which we are supposed to fully relive—does not happen overnight or without individual effort.

Despite the fact that *halakhah* covers every aspect of the preparation for (and observance of) Passover, probably no other situation or occasion in Jewish life is observed with such a diversity of actual practice. Many Jews today choose not to adhere to the precepts of the holiday. That's another story. The traditional range is not a matter of following particular regulations or not, but the variety of ways in which the laws are interpreted and met. As a Yiddish proverb puts it, "Every Jew has his own code of Jewish law and his own brand of madness." As no two *sedarim* are conducted in exactly the same manner, no two households adhere to Pesakh *kashrut* in exactly the same manner, although the intent and the goal are identical.

Khametz

The reason for the fastidious scouring and scrubbing is that all forms of leavening (*khametz*) must be completely removed from our homes, offices, and cars. There is no stricter law with regard to Jewish dietary habits than this one—which is even more stringent than the prohibition against eating pork. (Although this is not encouraged, you may have pork in your possession, and even feed it to your dog, but you may do neither of those things with *khametz*.)

Khametz literally means sour, or something that has been fermented, an edible food affected by the leavening process, which causes foods to puff up or "rise." It consists of five types of cereal and grain—wheat, barley, spelt, oats, and rye—and includes any pure forms of them, food made from them that is already leavened (bread, cake), or a form that has the potential to become leavened (flour). Grain-based alcoholic beverages (liquor and beer), vinegar (except the pure cider variety or wine vinegar made especially for Passover), processed, canned, and bottled foods containing *khametz* (cornstarch and syrups, too!) are all off limits.

Two additional types of substance are affected by the laws of *khametz*: something inedible that induces fermentation, such as yeast or already fermented dough (*se'or*), and *khametz* that is unfit for human consumption (called *nuksheh*, or *nifsal me'akhilat kelev*: unfit even for a dog to eat). The first is absolutely prohibited. The second is a bit more complicated, with subcategories and differing opinions among rabbinic authorities as to what is permitted.

In general, inedible things like perfumes that contain ethyl alcohol, and the children's modeling clay Play-Doh, both pure *khametz*, must be removed. Then there are items containing the prohibited substances that you do not have to discard or sell as you do *khametz*, and some that you may actually use (for example, those toiletries containing grain alcohol in solid form—such as creams and stick deodorant, some make-up, nail polish, shoe polish, ink, paint, and air freshener). There are authorities who allow year-round medications, vitamins, and toothpaste, and others who say only those specially approved or produced for Passover may be used. It is advisable to check with a local authority regarding specific items.

Ashkenazim also eliminate use of rice, millet, peas, beans, peanuts, corn, and buckwheat, which *Sephardim* allow. The restriction began in the Middle Ages, when these foodstuffs were ground into flour. Although they do not ferment, the products made from them resembled *khametz*, so the rabbis ruled they could not be used. Collectively, they are referred to as *kitniyot* (legumes). While they are forbidden for eating, they may be owned, and some authorities permit the use of their derivatives. (You will find approved-for-Passover brands of corn and peanut oil.)

What It Means

Thinking about *khametz* not just as a food substance but as a psychological and theological metaphor gives us an appreciation for why we become so obsessed with totally eliminating it. The first-century Alexandrian-Jewish philosopher Philo called *khametz*, the stuff that makes baked goods expand and swell up with air, the puff of pride, self-aggrandizement. Allowed to stand around all year, *khametz* gets into nooks and crannies, becoming stale in places we do not even realize it is imbedded—in the way of routine thought patterns and behavior.

When we rout out *khametz*, we are really trying to rout out the negative, stale, deadening, enslaving elements, the egotism and subconscious habits that interfere with fully realizing our potential. Searching every corner of our homes is a physical reflection of a deep soul search, changing our diet an external expression of an internal transformation. Like the Israelites who made a break from accepting slavery and idolatry in Egypt, we can sweep away whatever it is that binds us to meaningless efforts—whether it is outside influences or the internal compulsions that subjugate us to wasteful or harmful actions.

There is only a thin line between virtue and vice, as between polar opposites (love and hate, brilliance and imbecility, pain and pleasure) or between the pride that gives us the impetus to accomplish good things in the world and the pride that makes us so arrogant that, like Pharaoh, we think we are God. The same is true of the difference between *khametz*, which we must completely eliminate during Passover, and *matzah*, which we must eat. The extension of a line of a letter (the ה of מצה, *matzah*, into the ח of חמץ, *khametz* [ץ is the form of *tzaddi*, the letter in the middle of *matzah*, when it becomes the last letter of a word]), and the lapse of a second (flour of one of the five grains mixed with water and baked in 18:01 minutes instead of 17:59 minutes), is not *matzah* but *khametz*. If we stand back and let things develop unchecked, we have the prohibited *khametz*. If we step in to ensure that protective boundaries are not violated, we have the permitted *matzah*. One small stroke, one brief moment, can make all the difference in what we create around us.

Home

For this one week, to be conscious of our change in status, we live differently than we do the rest of the year. Most noticeably, our eating habits change. In addition to food, we cannot use the appliances, utensils, dishes, or work surfaces we normally do, at least without making them kosher (acceptable according to Jewish dietary, and for this week, specifically Pesakh, laws). There is no question that this is an involved process, made less burdensome when shared by family members.

Any area of your home where food has been taken, or could have been taken, must be thoroughly cleaned. This includes bathrooms (remember that some medications, cosmetics, even baby powder, which contains cornstarch, are *khametz*). Do not overlook a playhouse, treehouse, basement, attic, garage, shed, dog house, pet cage, or car.

Shelves and their contents and moldings should be dusted, floors swept and vacuumed, chair and sofa cushions lifted so any morsels that have fallen between can be removed, and even clothing pockets turned inside out. If you ever carry snacks in a handbag or tote, overturn it as well, along with children's schoolbags and lunchboxes. Offices, even if far from home, get the same treatment. Most people begin the process by tackling rooms where food is not usually eaten, or which can be made at least temporarily off-limits for food.

There is just one allowable exception: A non-Jewish boarder, tenant, or guest who has exclusive use of a particular area on your premises does not have to clean his/her quarters (neither do you) and may bring *khametz* into it. It is not considered your property.

You may handle the *khametz* in your possession in one of several ways. You may destroy it, particularly opened packages. You may give it away, for instance to a non-Jewish food pantry. Or you may separate it from everything else in the house—in a room, boxes, or cabinets that are locked or sealed—which will allow you to sell it to a non-Jew for the duration of the holiday (see section "Selling *Khametz*" later in this chapter). A piece of tape is a popular "sealer" and a visual reminder not to open the storage area.

Kitchen

This room obviously requires the most fastidious preparation.

Shelves and Cabinets

All shelves and cabinets need to be cleaned to get rid of crumbs, spills, and opened containers of food containing *khametz*. If you can afford separate sets of dishes, utensils, and cookware for use only during Passover, and have the luxury of sufficient space for dedicated Pesakh cabinets and drawers (which remain off-limits the rest of the year), the cleaned year-round cabinets are simply sealed. If you do not have the space, at least some of your everyday items will have to be packed away.

Once the cabinet surfaces are free of *khametz*, line them with paper (any kind will do). Then you are ready to put your *Pesahdikeh* (the Yiddishized description) dishes and foods on them.

Refrigerator/Freezer

It is possible to *kasher* appliances and utensils on the principle that they expel foodstuffs the same way they absorb them—heat for baked-on residue, boiling for boiled-in morsels, soaking in water for items used only with cold liquids. Since the cold temperatures of a refrigerator and freezer do not cause their surfaces to absorb foodstuffs, washing is the only requirement. After removing *khametz* items, the freezer must be defrosted and all surfaces of both the freezer and refrigerator scoured, including bins and compartments. Line the shelves with paper or foil. Unless you have solid glass shelves, make air slits to ensure circulation.

Oven

An oven, when hot enough, will release the *khametz* that has become embedded in it in the process of baking, roasting, and broiling of foods. Clean it thoroughly, as you normally would (with oven cleaner or on the self-cleaning cycle). The particularly punctilious go after stubborn spots with a blowtorch (small ones are available at hardware stores; make sure you know how to handle one before using it; it could be dangerous). The racks must also be cleaned (soak to loosen caked-on grease, scour with steel wool, or use oven cleaner—or that blowtorch).

After allowing it to go unused for twenty-four hours, with the racks inside, turn the oven to its highest setting for one hour (or use the self-cleaning cycle again). If the interior surface is metal, place a pot of steaming water inside during the process. If it is porcelain (usually painted gray or black), authorities recommend that you use a metal insert, shaped like a box, available in some Jewish bookstores. (Some hardware stores will make them to order.) Instead, you may simply cover the surfaces with aluminum foil.

Stovetop

Clean the entire surface, the burners, and trays thoroughly (the coils on an electric range do not have to be washed), don't use the stove for twenty-four hours, then turn the burners to their highest setting—fifteen minutes for a gas range, five minutes glowing red on an electric. The dishes under the burners may be covered with foil or replaced (hardware and convenience stores and some supermarkets carry them). Some people cover the entire stove surface with foil or metal sheets (purchased through a Jewish bookstore or hardware store).

Microwave

Clean the oven thoroughly, let it stand for the standard twenty-four hours, then put a dish—that has not been used for the past twenty-four hours—of boiling water inside, and turn on the oven until it is filled with steam (about five minutes). Wipe out the inside and it is ready for Pesakh use.

Sink

Scour the entire surface—basin, faucets, spout, drain, garbage disposal. For twenty-four hours, do not run or pour hot water into it. Then reclean it and pour boiling water over all surfaces. Although a metal sink is considered purged of *khametz* it is common practice to put a liner of some sort on the bottom to prevent contact between your Pesakh dishes and the surface used for *khametz* all year. A porcelain or enamel sink, made kosher the same way, cannot be completely rid of *khametz* because it is porous, so a sink liner or stand to keep Pesakh ware from touching the bottom, or dishpan set into the sink, must be used.

Dishwasher

Those with stainless steel interiors—and, according to some authorities, those with porcelain interiors as well—are *kashered* through their own heating process. After running it through a cycle, remove the racks and wash the interior completely. After twenty-four hours of nonuse, run a cycle at full temperature. Some rabbis permit use of the machine and the racks if you run them through the full cleaning cycle at the highest temperature three times following the initial cleaning. Others maintain that plastic or rubber racks need to be replaced, which you can do through a manufacturer's dealer.

Countertops/Tables

Clean surfaces thoroughly, pouring boiling water over them when possible (be careful with this because some materials will warp; lots of towels on the floor will speed clean-up afterward). If you do not or cannot *kasher* your counters this way (for example, if they are tile with grout fillings), clean thoroughly and then cover them with contact paper, foil, or plastic sheeting (heavy plastic available in wide rolls from hardware stores works well). It is customary to use a tablecloth on any dining surface. (A year-round cloth that has been laundered without starch is fine.)

Small Appliances

The motor bases of blenders, food processors, mixers, and so on used year-round can be used for Pesakh as long as the exteriors are thoroughly cleaned and the motor housings are opened so the coils can be brushed free of food particles that have fallen inside. The blades, beaters, and plastic bowls and containers have to be replaced. You can get extra sets at manufacturer service centers (although sometimes it is easier and less expensive to buy a whole new machine).

Dishes, Utensils, Pots

Technically, you can *kasher* for Passover items of glass, metal, stone, wood, and natural rubber used year-round according to the same principle used for major appliances. Items not used directly on the fire, like bowls, utensils and flatware, or pots used to prepare liquid foods, as by boiling, undergo *haggalah* (immersion in boiling water). Anything that has come in direct contact with fire without the addition of liquid is heated until it glows (*libun*). Surfaces on which food is prepared or eaten (like dishes and cutting boards) are purged, like sinks, by pouring boiling water over them (*irui*), and glassware—including Corningware and Pyrex—used only for cold food and beverages and not for pure *khametz* (grain alcohol) is soaked in cold water (*m'ilui v'irui*). In each case, the items to be made kosher must first be carefully cleaned and set aside for twenty-four hours.

However (and this is very important), most people prefer to use separate sets of kitchenware for Pesakh, especially those most concerned with following *halakhah*, and advise others to do the same. It is simply too complex and difficult to *kasher* everything properly. If it is absolutely out of the question to replace your everyday kitchenware (there are many inexpensive options, including disposable foil bakeware and cook and tableware from discount stores and outlets), consult a detailed guide, along with a rabbinic authority who can answer the questions that are sure to arise.

One last note on cleaning: If you decide to stay with a friend or relative or at a hotel that is kosher for Passover, you still need to search for and sell your *khametz*, which still requires cleaning it out of your home and "organizing" what remains in specific storage areas (see section on "*Halakhah*").

FOR FURTHER READING

Greenberg, Blu. *How to Run a Traditional Jewish Household*. New York: Simon and Schuster, 1983, pp. 408–412.

If you plan to ignore the warning about the difficulty of *kashering* your everyday utensils and so on for Passover, and opt to do it, this is a good guide to lead you through the process. Each of the procedures is explained, and options in tools to use in accomplishing them are suggested. (Good luck.)

Bedikat Khametz

Once you have done your best to clean your home and collected the *khametz* items and utensils (except what you need for breakfast on the last day before Pesakh starts), it is time for the *khametz* search-and-destroy mission. For young children it can have the excitement of a treasure hunt; for older ones and adults, it is an opportunity for introspection.

On the evening of *Nissan* 13 (the night before *Erev* Pesakh), we conduct a ceremonial hunt for leaven throughout the house. It starts with recitation of a blessing, and so that it won't be said in vain, as would be the case if you were not to find any *khametz* (a likely outcome after the previous month's intense labor), it is customary to place pieces of bread in easily accessible places. Any number will do, though ten has become traditional (ten plagues; ten commandments; ten mystical characteristics of God; ten sons of Haman who recorded the plot to destroy the Jews on *Nissan* 14, but who themselves were killed [see chapter on Purim]). If you do not use ten, be sure to pick a number you can easily remember so you know when all the pieces have been retrieved.

For the search you will need a candle, something in which to collect the crumbs (a wooden spoon is traditional, but even a piece of cardboard will do), and something to sweep the crumbs into the receptacle (a feather, or a palm leaf from the Sukkot *lulav* is standard). With the family assembled, the head of the house is usually the one to light the candle and say:

בָּרוּךְ אַתָּה, יהוה אֱלֹהֵינוּ, מֶלֶךְ הָעוֹלָם, אֲשֶׁר קִדְּשָׁנוּ בְּמִצְוֹתָיו, וְצִוָּנוּ עַל בִּעוּר חָמֵץ.

Barukh Atah, Adonai Eloheinu, Melekh Haolam, asher kidshanu b'mitzvotav, v'tzivanu al biur khametz.

Blessed are You, Lord our God, King of the Universe, Who has sanctified us with His commandments and commanded us to remove the leaven.

Without speaking, begin the search. (If you speak of matters other than your immediate purpose before completing the search, you must repeat the *brakhah*.) Using the feather or other object to brush the crumbs into the receptacle avoids having direct contact with the leaven. The candle, which allows you to see into every corner, also turns the search back on yourself. "The spirit of man is the lamp of God, searching all the inward parts" (Proverbs 20:27).

To play out the connection, once all the bread has been gathered, in some families each person writes down on a scrap of paper the personal *khametz* s/he would like to eliminate from his/her life. The folded scraps are added to the *khametz* collected in the spoon or cardboard and wrapped (put in a bag, tied up in a cloth or napkin) so that no pieces will be lost.

The expression of nullification that follows (including the bracketed words) should be said in a language you understand, since it is a legal declaration (the original is in Aramaic).

כָּל חֲמִירָא וַחֲמִיעָא, דְּאִכָּא בִרְשׁוּתִי, [דְּלָא חֲמִתֵהּ, וּדְלָא בְעַרְתֵהּ, וּדְלָא יְדַעְנָא לֵהּ] לִבַּטֵל וְלֶהֱוֵי הֶפְקֵר, כְּעַפְרָא דְאַרְעָא.

Kol khamirah vakhami'ah, d'ikah, virshuti [d'lah khamitei ud'lah vi'artei, ud'lah y'danah lei] libateil v'lehevei hefkeir, c'afrah d'ar'ah.

Any leaven that may still be in the house, which I have [not seen or have not removed] shall be as if it does not exist, and as the dust of the earth.

The next morning, we destroy (*biur*) the *khametz* by wind (breaking it into crumbs to be scattered), water (crushing and throwing it into a body of water or a toilet), or the most common means—and the most dramatic for children—fire (burning it outside, often in a bonfire, or if necessary, indoors in a sink). In some city neighborhoods, a community *biur* is arranged through the local fire department.

While your *khametz* is burning, you recite a slightly different nullification, to accommodate the *khametz* left from breakfast and added to that from the *bedikat*. Replace the bracketed section in the preceding *brakhah* with:

דַּחֲזִתֵהּ וּדְלָא חֲזִתֵהּ דַּחֲמִתֵהּ וּדְלָא חֲמִתֵהּ, דְּבִעַרְתֵהּ וּדְלָא . . .

. . . dakhazitei ud'lah khazitei dakhamitei ud'lah khamitei, d'viartei ud'lah . . .

. . . or have not seen, which I have or have not removed . . .

The permanent riddance is a direct response to Torah's commandment to "destroy leaven from your houses" (Exodus 12:15, 19, 13:7). The rabbis understood the purpose as eliminating idolatry from our world, based on a sequence of commandments in Torah: not to make molten gods (Exodus 34:17) and to observe the Feast of Unleavened Bread (Exodus 34:18). Idolatry is limited not to the worship of objects that cannot protect us but to the pursuit of values that do not provide us with real security (money, materialism, celebrity [see "Religious Importance" in chapter on Sukkot]).

Originally, getting rid of leaven had to be completed by the time of the paschal sacrifice, midday, from which time *khametz* could no longer be eaten. To protect anyone from accidentally going over the deadline, the rabbis determined that *khametz* could be eaten only in the first third of the day, or in its first four hours "Jewish holiday time." It is determined by dividing the day—defined as the time between sunrise and sunset—by twelve to determine the number of minutes in each daylight hour (not necessarily, for this purpose, sixty). It works out to approximately 9:30 or 10:00 A.M. as the deadline for eating *khametz* and 10:30 to 11:00 A.M. as the time for destroying it.

If Pesakh begins on Saturday night, the search is done on Thursday night and the burning on Friday morning (see "*Halakhah*" for details).

Selling *Khametz*

Originally, all Jews disposed of whatever *khametz* they owned by selling it in the marketplace, and restocking after Pesakh. This later became a costly proposition for those in businesses like liquor production or baking. The sale of (*mekhirat*) *khametz* was devised to spare them tremendous financial loss. It allowed the Jews to sell the stock with the understanding that it could (and would) be bought back after the holiday. The goods were transferred to the new (temporary) owner.

In the Middle Ages an astute commentator noted that instead of schlepping the merchandise back and forth, the seller could just lease the rooms in which it was stored and provide the key—along with the legally executed contract—to the purchaser. Over time, as Jews had less contact with the outside world, it was suggested that instead of each one having to find a non-Jew with whom to do business, any number of Jews could give power of attorney to a common agent, who would arrange the sale for them.

Although called a "legal fiction," this process, which we follow today, is a totally legitimate transaction. You can arrange for your *khametz* to be sold through a rabbi (if you do not, according to Jewish law you may not derive benefit from it during Pesakh or afterward). If you don't know a rabbi or don't want to call a synagogue, you can go through a local *Khabad* center (check a phone directory under Chabad). Arrangements can be made any time in the weeks before Pesakh up to the deadline for eating *khametz*: The sale must be completed by the time you have to have all leavening out of your possession. This involves filling out a brief form giving the rabbi power of attorney (some will take authorization over the phone) and usually a nominal fee. The rabbi-agent produces a bill of sale. The non-Jewish purchaser makes a small down payment, which is returned with interest at the close of Pesakh, when the would-be purchaser changes his mind. (Since this is a legitimate legal procedure, the non-Jew could decide to go through with the sale, or the agent could decide not to buy it back. There is no record of that ever having happened.) This sale covers only foodstuffs, not utensils, dishes, and so on. Those you may simply keep in storage.

Since one cannot use any of the *khametz* that has been sold until the agent has had ample time to buy it back at the end of Pesakh, most people go out for something fresh for their first *khametz* meal on the night of *Nissan* 22.

Food

Everything we eat during Pesakh must be entirely free of leavening. Since *khametz* is in foods we would not think of as leavened, and in forms we would not readily recognize (e.g., dextrose, sorbitol, decaffeinated tea), we buy foods that are prepared under rabbinic supervision to ensure that they adhere to *halakhah* and that no leaven—or hand, utensil, or equipment touched by leaven—has come into contact with it.

Since food is produced today with sophisticated machinery, with little likelihood of *khametz* getting mixed in (as was the case when everything was made by hand), pure items like coffee, tea, sugar, honey, fresh/dried/frozen fruits and vegetables, kosher meat/poultry/fish, raw nuts (except peanuts and sunflower seeds, which are *kitniyot*), milk, pepper, garlic powders (although some people have a custom of not using garlic—fresh or otherwise—there is no prohibition against it), many dairy products that are kosher all year-round, and paper, plastic, and foil wraps do not require special certification.

Still, many observant Jews use only those labeled as having been manufactured under the direct supervision of rabbinic authority. (There is a wide variety of *kashrut* approvals, local, regional, and national. You will see the names of specific rabbis with the kosher certification on the packaging, along with a variety of symbols—U inside the letter O, Star K, CRC, K inside a triangle. But a package marked "Kosher for Passover"—כשר לפסח—may not necessarily be kosher, and one without a marking may be perfectly acceptable.)

If your baby is on a formula that is not for Passover use and that may contain *khametz* or *kitniyot*, check with your physician about changing it and/or a rabbi about permission to use it. The same is true with medication. Leniency is always the rule when health might be affected, so some items that contain *khametz* may be allowed.

During Pesakh you may not feed your pet *khametz*, which almost all pet foods contain. If you cannot find a variety without wheat or *kitniyot* (Fancy Feast cat food and Alpo and Mighty Dog dog foods are acceptable), you may have to switch your pet to a different diet (check with your veterinarian; some people indulge their animals with table food). Otherwise, arrange to "sell" the animal to a friend or neighbor in an arrangement similar to selling your *khametz* or board it for the eight days (this includes hamsters, birds, etc.).

Once *matzah* is baked, it can no longer become leaven, so it is used in crushed and finely ground form to make the *matzah* farfel and meal we use in cooking and baking for the holiday. You may be surprised to see Pesakh recipes calling for baking soda and baking powder, which are used to make cake rise. Unlike yeasts and sour dough they are not considered leavening (any more than are the eggs used to make fluffy Pesakh cakes). Since baking powder may contain starch (made of flour), you must use the kind made especially for Passover. Baking soda, however, is merely a derivative of salt (sodium bicarbonate) and is therefore approved for Pesakh use. (Be careful with table salt, though, iodine and polysorbates render some brands unfit for Passover.)

There are ways to control the cost of Pesakh provisions: Pay attention to where you do not have to have a *kasher l'Pesakh* label, or where you can buy a *kasher l'Pesakh* product that is available all year for the all-year price. Buy meat, poultry, and fish a couple of weeks before the holiday (prior to price increases); you can store it in your freezer—already cleaned for Passover, with the shelves lined—wrapped and well separated from any *khametz*. You do not have to purchase staples and produce in a kosher grocery; use your regular supermarket. If you shop in advance, keep nonperishable Pesakh purchases wrapped in grocery bags in a closet or room that has been cleared of *khametz*.

FOR FURTHER READING

The Spice and Spirit of Kosher Passover Cooking. Brooklyn: Lubavitch Women's Organization, 1981, pp. 8–10, 20–24.

In addition to a concise and readable explanation of *kashrut*, in general and for Pesakh, the book presents an alphabetized list of food categories and specific items within them and explains which are not approved for Passover and why, and which need special labeling. More strict in some areas than many authorities, it is still extremely useful and informative.

Passover Directory. New York: Orthodox Union.

Published annually, this extensive guide lists items from national brand and private label (local and regional) manufacturers under "OU" supervision which are kosher for Passover. (Available starting two months before the holiday from Orthodox Union, 333 Seventh Avenue, 18th Floor, Attention: Passover Directory Managing Editor, New York, NY 10001; 212-563-4000, extension 146. There is a nominal fee to cover postage.)

Tzedakah

We should not be so obsessed with the preparation of food that we do not consider the many people who go without it. If we fulfill all the precepts of Pesakh preparation and the *seder* but fail to provide for those in need, it is as if we have negated the holiday's significance. We are supposed to think not only of the travails of the past and the glories of the future but of the deficits all around us in our society. We invite "all who are hungry to come and eat" so that even those oppressed by poverty or solitude can at least for one evening feel that they belong to the community and celebrate and feast as equals.

In Rabbi Isaac Meir of Gur's lesson to his *khasidim*, the ninth plague is presented as a message about helping others in need. During the darkness, no one saw his neighbor and no one budged for three days. Someone who ignores his neighbor's suffering deserves the punishment of darkness so that he cannot rise from his place. It is mercy and charity that bring light into the world.

When you are planning your menus and guest lists for the *sedarim*, consider those in need. Many people make arrangements to host Jewish travelers, college students, military personnel stationed in the vicinity, the elderly, or congregation members who are alone (through a synagogue, Hillel chapter, Jewish Federation, or other communal agency).

In addition, we contribute to a special fund (*Ma-ot*) for wheat (*Khitim*), which supplies *matzot* and other Passover provisions for those in need. Even if you have fulfilled all other annual commitments for *tzedakah* (commonly understood as charity, but meaning justice), you are obligated to donate over and above them to *Ma-ot Khitim*. In times past, when community elders showed up on your doorstep, if you did not need to receive, you had to give: everyone, at one end or the other, was involved. To avoid embarrassing anyone, those receiving would not be directly confronted. Many believed they had been visited by Elijah. Today, recipients are told "here is your Pesakh order." In some communities, the boxes are packed and hand-delivered through a massive volunteer effort the week before the holiday.

Some rabbis collect money for *Ma-ot Khitim* when they make the *khametz* sale arrangements. You can also contribute directly to the local fund (check with a rabbi or synagogue office if you cannot find a listing for it). Collection starts at the beginning of *Nissan*.

Getting Set for *Seder*

It is customary to begin reviewing the Pesakh story and preparing for the *seder* at least two weeks prior to the festival starting, at Rosh Khodesh *Nissan*. This is the time to evaluate different *haggadot*, consult varying commentaries, and figure out how you want to convey or have participants explore the significance and personal connections with the *seder's* themes. Come up with songs, games, skits, and questions you can incorporate to keep participants engaged.

Involve your children in the planning. They will be more vested in the celebration and will be great helpers in preparing dramatic approaches, props, and so on and contributing valuable ideas. Especially with young children, it is important to tell the story of Moses and the Exodus several times in advance. As anyone who has had to read a book repeatedly to a child or witnessed a child playing the same videotape over and over again knows, children like to be familiar with their entertainments. Through repetition, you will also be able to teach even two- to three-year-olds the "*Mah Nishtanah*" (don't they learn the songs they repeatedly hear on videos and TV?), allowing them to have a bit of the limelight.

In addition to preparing parts of the *seder* enactment, older children can be engaged in making *matzah* covers, *seder* plates, place cards, and so on, and on the day of Pesakh, parts of the meal and the ritual foods (preparing *kharoset* is a good chore).

Halakhah specifies minimum quantities for ritual foods, which observant Jews follow. If you plan to adhere to them, you will want to premeasure the portions (they can be put into sandwich bags and cupcake liners, one for each participant). Simply rule out a piece of cardboard for the area to be covered for *matzah* and romaine lettuce, and use a measuring cup for horseradish. (Romaine lettuce, though preferred as *maror*, poses a problem for those who

keep kosher because it is very difficult to completely clean the leaves of minute bugs [which we are prohibited from eating] camouflaged in them. A solution is to place the leaves in a bowl of water with some vinegar [make sure it's kosher for Passover], which dislodges the insects. Still examine the leaves very carefully.)

Many synagogues and sometimes other Jewish communal organizations or educational outreach programs run seminars and model *sedarim* to teach novices how to do the service and provide the experienced with new ideas.

Synagogue

Each of the five Sabbaths leading up to Pesakh features a Torah and prophetic reading chosen to remind us of some aspect of or reinforce our spiritual and physical preparation for the upcoming festival: bringing payment for sacrifices to be made after *Nissan* 1 (*Shekalim* [form of currency]; Exodus 30:11–16; II Kings 12:1–17); destroying evil in the world (*Zakhor* [remember]; Deuteronomy 25:17–19; I Samuel 15:2–34); purifying ourselves and our homes, based on the symbolic Red Heifer purification ceremony (*Parah* [heifer]; Numbers 19:1–22; Ezekiel 36:16–38); the month of *Nissan* and regulations for making the paschal sacrifice (*Hakhodesh* [the month]; Exodus 12:1–20; Ezekiel 45:16–46:18); and the future redemption that will come just as the first one did (*Hagadol* [the great]; Malakhai 3:4–24).

The last may have gotten its name (The Great Sabbath) as the others did, for a key word in the *haftarah* (the prophetic portion that completes the Torah reading): "Behold I will send you Elijah the Prophet before the coming of *the great* and terrible day of the Lord." Some say it was named in commemoration of the beginning of the Egyptian redemption, which was on Saturday, *Nissan* 10, when the Israelites started to prepare their lambs, and the miracles begun when the Egyptians did not interfere.

Most think it defines length as much as spiritual height: On this day it became customary for the leading rabbi in a community to deliver a long learned discourse on the themes and laws of Passover. At a time when many people crowded into towns and cities to be with their families, it was a good opportunity to reach large numbers. The rabbis were simply following the example of Moses who, according to *midrash*, spoke to Israel on the laws of Passover prior to the Exodus. (If *Erev* Pesakh falls on Shabbat, the day retains the name but the sermon is moved back to the preceding week so it will have some practical benefit.) In addition to reminding us of the first redemption and announcing the future one, *Malakhai* commands the bringing of tithes, the failure of which, the sages said, causes famine. The connection with Pesakh is through its identity as the time of judgment of the world for famine-preventing crops.

In the afternoon service, the congregation customarily reads the *Haggadah* from "*Avadim hayinu*" through "*Dayeinu*" in commemoration of the miracles that began the Shabbat preceding deliverance, and as a preparatory review.

Fast of the Firstborn

The sunrise to sunset *ta'anit* (fast) *bekhorim* ([of the] firstborn) is the only fast that applies to just a segment of the community: all males who are the firstborn children in their families (if the firstborn child is female, the first son born after her is not obligated). The father of a child too young to fast fasts for him, and if he himself is *bekhor*, the mother fasts for the child on the day of *Erev* Pesakh. Since it is forbidden to abstain from eating on Shabbat (except for Yom Kippur), when *Erev* Pesakh falls on Saturday night, the fast takes place on Thursday.

There is a widely practiced exemption: On the principle that fasting is prohibited on a joyous occasion, Judaism allows for anyone who attends a religious feast to forego fasting. It is customary to hold a celebratory meal on the completion of study of a tractate of Talmud, called a *siyyum* (conclusion). So rabbis initiated the practice of studying a portion of a Talmud tractate after morning services, held especially early on *Erev* Pesakh. All the firstborn are invited to be present for the conclusion and share cake and schnaps afterward, considered a *seudat* (meal) *mitzvah* ([in honor of a] commandment; in this case, studying the Torah).

Erev Pesakh

If you want to be particularly careful in Pesakh observance, after your last *khametz* meal rinse your mouth well and change to a brand new toothbrush. Since you have gotten rid of all the *khametzdikeh* foodstuffs by mid-morning, lunch should be kosher for Pesakh—but by custom you should not have any *matzah* until the *seder*. Pious Jews often refrain from eating *matzah* for two weeks to a month prior to make it particularly special at the *seder*.

All work from the afternoon on (sixth hour of the "Jewish" day) should be directed solely at preparing for the holiday. (It corresponds to the time the paschal lamb was being offered in the Temple, a half-holiday on which ordinary work was prohibited.)

After *Minkhah*, it is traditional to recite the order of the sacrifice, the words substituting for the lambs.

All personal needs—hair cuts, manicures, and so on—should be completed by midday. Some men go to the *mikvah* (ritual bath), and the pious like to bake their own *matzah* (only possible where communal kitchens are set up to accommodate them). The table should be completely set for the *seder*.

Preparing for *Yom Tov*

On Jewish holidays considered sacred occasions—as are the first two and last two days of Pesakh—there are certain activities anyone who follows Jewish law will set aside for the sake of maintaining the proper atmosphere of the occasion, just as s/he does on Shabbat (see section on "*Halakhah*"). Their practical implications need to be taken into account in advance.

Eruv Tavshilin

On *yom tov*, we may bake and cook any food needed for that day itself, because freshly cooked food enhances the joy that is supposed to accompany the occasion. We may not, however, cook for any other day of the week. This is to give the *yom tov* the respect it deserves, but the restriction poses a problem when the day immediately precedes Shabbat (when the second or eighth day of Pesakh is Friday). So a construct called in Aramaic *eruv* (mixture) *tavshilin* ([of] cooked foods) was created to allow us to prepare a special portion for Sabbath on the holiday. It involves making a symbolic meal of two foods—bread (*matzah* in the case of Pesakh) and an egg, fish, or meat—on Wednesday afternoon. Put them on a plate, raise it, and recite a blessing followed by a formula in Aramaic (the vernacular of Babylon and the language of Talmud compiled there).

בָּרוּךְ אַתָּה, יהוה אֱלֹהֵינוּ, מֶלֶךְ הָעוֹלָם, אֲשֶׁר קִדְּשָׁנוּ בְּמִצְוֹתָיו, וְצִוָּנוּ עַל מִצְוַת עֵרוּב.

Barukh Atah, Adonai Eloheinu, Melekh Haolam, asher kidshanu b'mitzvotav, vitzivanu al mitzvat eruv.

Blessed are You, Lord our God, King of the Universe, Who has sanctified us with His commandments and commanded us concerning the *mitzvah* of *eruv*.

בַּהֲדֵין עֵרוּבָא יְהֵא שָׁרֵא לָנָא לְמֵיפָא, וּלְבַשָּׁלָא, וּלְאַצְלָיָא, וּלְאַטְמָנָא, וּלְאַדְלָקָא שְׁרָגָא, וּלְתַקָּנָא, וּלְמֶעְבַּד כָּל צָרְכָנָא, מִיּוֹמָא טָבָא לְשַׁבַּתָּא. לָנוּ וּלְכָל יִשְׂרָאֵל, הַדָּרִים בָּעִיר הַזֹּאת.

41

Bahadein eiruvah y'hei sharei lana l'meifah, ul'vashalah, ul'atzlayah, ul'atmana, ul'adlaka sh'raga, ul'takanah, ul'mebad kol-tzarcana, m'yoma tava l'shabata. Lanu ul'khol yisrael, hadarim ba'ir hazot.

With this *eruv* it shall be permissible for us to bake, cook, and to keep the food warm, to light the candles, and to prepare all necessary things on the festival for the Sabbath. This shall be permitted to us and to all Jews who live in this city.

It is then considered as though we had already cooked for the Sabbath, and any other cooking we do later for it (on the *yom tov*) is incidental. The prepared food must remain in place until after Shabbat. (Many people put it out of the way, on top of a refrigerator, for example, so it is not inadvertently eaten.) A legal fiction, it is a means of reconciling conflicting *mitzvot*. Like all legal fictions (e.g., selling *khametz*), it was created with the intent of sparing people from hardship, the underlying purpose of the whole Jewish way of life.

Use of Fire

Although you may not light a new fire (strike a match, turn on electricity) on the holiday, you may use an existing fire to light another. To light candles on the second night, or to cook, you will need to have a candle, pilot light, or stove burner already lit. Many people use a *yahrtzite* candle or an eight-day festival candle (sold, like the regular memorial candles, in religious supply stores).

WHAT ARE WE SUPPOSED TO DO?— *HALAKHAH*

Recounting the miracles of the *Nissan* 14 and 15, explaining the ritual foods, eating *matzah* and *maror*, removing *khametz* from our possession, and abstaining from eating leavened bread are described in the previous sections on "Observance" and "Preparation" according to *halakhah*. What follows are regulations for festivals in general, as well as more technical aspects of Pesakh preparation and observance that reflect the legal traditions surrounding the holiday.

Days Like Sabbath

Torah commands that the first days of Pesakh, Shavuot, and Sukkot, the seventh day of Pesakh, the eighth day of Sukkot, and Rosh Hashanah are *yom tovim*, when work is prohibited (Exodus 12:16; Leviticus 23:7–36); in the Diaspora, a day is added in each case (see introductory section "The Jewish Calendar").

With the exception of permission to prepare food and transfer fire, there is no difference in *halakhah* between these days and Shabbat. This means that the thirty-nine categories of work prohibited on Shabbat, with those exceptions, are also prohibited on a festival day. These categories, called *melakhot*, are the forms of labor that were involved in building the Tabernacle and its implements in the wilderness (Exodus 25–40) and do not necessarily correspond to what we would normally consider labor.

For instance, you may move furniture in your house but may not even touch a pen. You may sweep the floor with a soft broom but may not carry a handkerchief in your pocket from home to synagogue. While at first glance the system may seem illogical, what is permitted and what is prohibited neatly correspond to the idea of a sacred day of rest, when everything in the world is in harmony.

FOR FURTHER READING

Grunfeld, Dr. Dayan I. *The Sabbath: A Guide to Its Understanding and Observance.* New York: Feldheim Publishers, 1981.

This compact, easy-to-read book is a good introduction to the practical observance of the day of rest. It presents the meaning of Sabbath, concept of *melakhah* (the prohibited work), classification of the thirty-nine categories, and a rundown of what activities fall into each.

Neuwirth, Rabbi Yehoshua Y. *Shemirath Shabbath: A Guide to the Practical Observance of the Sabbath.* New York: Feldheim Publishers, 1984.

The English version of the two-volume guide originally published in Hebrew is much more specific and technical in covering aspects of each category of work. An extremely detailed table of contents is a useful aid in locating the laws on particular concerns, and the format outlining categories and subcategories makes the book easy to use. It is for someone who wants to strictly follow the *halakhah* or understand how the classifications fit.

Festival Laws

Food Preparation

Unlike Shabbat, when each person is supposed to study Torah and feel a personal connection with

God, festivals are occasions for the nation to unite. They were the times of pilgrimage to Jerusalem for communal rejoicing, which encompasses feasting together. Preparing fresh food and carrying needed items from one home to another to allow people to visit back and forth are therefore permitted.

The allowance to use fire for cooking was expanded to provide for other comforts such as illumination and warmth: If you take the flame from an existing one, you may light a fire in a fireplace. You may not extinguish a fire, however.

Honoring the Holiday

Thinking about the holiday, as you do in preparing for it, brings it *kavod* (honor). Therefore, you should personally participate in preparation of needed items (fine foods, for instance) and enter a holiday well groomed and dressed in holiday clothing. It is considered a *mitzvah* to bathe in warm water, wash and, if needed, cut your hair and trim your fingernails on the eve of *yom tov*.

Simkhah

Joy (*simkhah*) traditionally is defined differently for different people. For men, eating sumptuously is considered a fulfillment of joy. According to Maimonides, children should be given roasted grain (popcorn) and nuts and sweets, and women should have new clothes and jewelry.

Pleasure

Eating two meals a day, one at night and one during the day, both of which include bread (or *matzah*), wine (in addition to that used for *kiddush*), and meat, is the means to the *oneg* (pleasure) required on a holiday. Lighting candles, which will provide illumination and an aesthetic enhancement during the night, also brings pleasure. Even if you have limited means, you are supposed to spend whatever is necessary to create pleasure and joy.

Torah Study

Since the words of Torah provide another kind of joy—that of enlightenment and knowledge—there is an obligation to study scripture on *yom tov*.

Dual Joy

Based on King Solomon's dedication of the First Temple, when he preceded the week of Sukkot with a week devoted solely to consecration of the Temple (I Kings 8:65), we do not mix one joy with another. This affords each occasion its rightful honor. Therefore, weddings are not performed during a festival (including its intermediate days).

Feeding Others

Part of experiencing joy comes from providing food and drink for others who need it—a stranger, orphan, widow—which we are obligated to do whenever we enjoy festive meals.

Mourning

So as not to interfere with rejoicing, which must be the prevalent mood of a *yom tov*, the laws of mourning are not observed. For thirty days prior to a festival, eulogies are forbidden. A holiday that arrives while you are sitting *shivah* (seven-day mourning period following the burial of a parent, spouse, or child) suspends the remainder of the week. (If burial takes place during *khol hamoed*, *shivah* does not begin until the festival is concluded, and then it runs its full course. The last day of the festival in the Diaspora, because it is a rabbinic addition, counts as the first day of *shivah*.) Public displays of grief are curtailed so that you do not dampen anyone else's spirits: The mood of the community takes precedence.

Prayers that express acceptance of God's actions in the world, even painful ones, are omitted: *Takhanun*, which usually follows the *Amidah*, *Y'hi rahtzon* (May it be the will) after the Monday and Thursday Torah readings; *Av Harakhamim* (Compassionate Father) normally recited on Sabbath morning; and *Tzedakatekha* (Your Righteousness), usually part of the Sabbath afternoon service. (In addition to the festival days themselves, these omissions apply for the entire month of *Nissan*. Since the majority of *Nissan*'s days are festive, all days in the month are considered to be. The first twelve days commemorate the original tribal gifts to the Tabernacle [Numbers 7:12–83], then come the eight days of Passover, and the day following it.)

Tefillin

The phylacteries put on every weekday morning by men are not worn on festivals (or Sabbath), because as a sign of the relationship between God and man (Exodus 31:13), they would be redundant; festivals and Shabbat are also signs of the connection. There is disagreement regarding the use of *tefillin* during *khol hamoed*. Those in favor advise that they be removed during *Hallel*, Torah reading, and *Mussaf*, which stress the day's festive nature. (Some *Ashkenazim* in the Diaspora wear them; Israelis, *Sephardim*, and *Ashkenazim* who follow the custom of the *Sephardim* do not.)

Additional Prayer

Ya'aleh V'Yavo (May There Rise and Come), requesting that God remember, bless, and redeem Israel, said on all biblically ordained holidays, is inserted into all *Amidah* prayers, plus the *Birkat Hamazon*.

Prohibition of *Khametz*

Those *halakhot* regarding the removal of *khametz* are derived from five passages in Torah (Exodus 12:19,20; 13:3,7; Deuteronomy 16:3,4). The punishment for violating these commandments—being cut off from the community (*karet*)—applies to only one other positive commandment: circumcision. In both cases, the violator separates him-/herself by refusing to demonstrate allegiance and identify with the common destiny. Keeping *khametz* shows refusal to abandon enslavement.

Since any *khametz* owned by a Jew and not sold during Pesakh (*khametz sheh aver alav hapesakh*) may never be used by a Jew, be careful when purchasing *khametz* at the close of the holiday. (Many people will wait until they are certain that merchandise is new before buying it from Jewish-owned shops.)

Khametz *Search*

If you do not search for *khametz* on the evening of *Nissan* 14, you may do it during the day, but still use a candle, not natural light, unless the sun is very strong. If you have not searched by midday, when *khametz* is prohibited, do it later—even on Pesakh, and dispose of it immediately. You remain obligated to perform this symbolic elimination of enslavement even after the holiday, if you fail to do it before, and to burn any leaven that had remained in the house during Passover.

If you leave home within thirty days prior to Passover and will not return until after the holiday, either appoint someone to conduct the search on your behalf or search before you leave, without saying the blessing. You recite the nullification for the *khametz* wherever you are on the fourteenth of *Nissan*. If you leave home more than thirty days in advance of the holiday, check with a rabbi regarding the necessity of conducting the search.

Saturday Night *Seder*

Complications in making the kitchen kosher and conducting *bedikat khametz* arise when Pesakh begins as Shabbat ends. You may not burn the *khametz* or *kasher* the oven on Shabbat because they require fire, and you cannot finish the Pesakh preparation prior to Sabbath because it is customary to have two *khallot* with Friday dinner and the second Sabbath meal, (breakfast) on Saturday. Also, *matzah* should not be used prior to the *seder*.

The procedure is to conduct the search for *khametz* Thursday evening and burn it Friday morning by the time the selling of *khametz* normally takes place. (Since you may still eat *khametz* on Friday, *biur* and *mekhirat* can actually be done anytime until sundown.) Except for the Sabbath *khallot*, all *khametz* should be out of your possession. *Kasher* the kitchen for Pesakh and prepare Shabbat food in Pesakh pots with Pesakh utensils. (You have to cook on Friday for the *seder* meal since it immediately follows the Sabbath.) Be sure to keep the bread separate from the rest of the food, and especially from Pesakh dishes. (Disposable tableware is advisable.)

On the morning of Shabbat, eat *khametz* at the second Sabbath meal. Then dispose of remaining leaven (it may be flushed away, but cannot be burned) or cover it with a vessel until Sunday night, when it should be burned. The formula for nullification should be recited during the fifth hour of the day (late morning).

Seder

All adults are obligated to eat *matzah* and drink four cups of wine. Redemption was achieved largely through the merits of women (the midwives who refused to kill Jewish infants, Miriam, Pharaoh's daughter, Moses' mother). Both men and women were delivered from Egypt.

Wine

Unless necessary for health reasons, you are supposed to drink full-strength wine. Consuming the wine, an act of publicizing the miracle of freedom, is a requirement, even if you have to sell belongings, borrow money, or take on extra work to pay for it.

A cup must contain a minimum of 3.3 fluid ounces. If *seder* falls on Friday night, the first cup of the person making *kiddush* on behalf of everyone else must contain at least 4.42 fluid ounces (the minimum for Shabbat).

Ritual Foods

Each of the items required for the *seder* is supposed to be eaten in minimum quantities, based on equivalents for the bulk of an olive (which must have been huge in talmudic days when the amounts were determined!), referred to as *k'zayit* (like an olive).

The *matzah* for *motzi* is figured to be a piece 7 × 6¼ inches. *Maror* in the form of grated horseradish is 1.1 fluid ounces, .7 fluid ounces for *korekh*. If you use romaine lettuce leaves, each guest should receive enough to cover an area of 8 × 10 inches; if stalks are used, they should cover an area measuring 3 × 5 inches. *Matzah* for *korekh* totals 7 × 4 inches, and for *afikoman* 7 × 6¼ inches.

Khol Hamoed

A number of activities prohibited on Shabbat and *yom tov* are also forbidden on *khol hamoed*. The sages said that anyone who treated the intermediate festival days lightly, by not abstaining from the prohibited labors, was basically worshiping idols. The idea is to maintain the spirit of a festival and give yourself extra time to study traditional text. Determining what is allowed or not is often conditional on specific situations. In general, there is leniency for "work" that enhances one's enjoyment of the holiday. An authority or detailed guide should be consulted for details.

FOR FURTHER READING

Eider, Rabbi Shimon D. *Halachos of Pesach.* Lakewood, NJ: Halacha Publications, 1985.

This is a good two-volume guide for the Torah-observant reader who wants all the details of the holiday's laws. Clear, concise language and organization that chronologically mirrors the activities you do in preparation for and observance of Passover make it particularly useful.

Zucker, Rabbi Dovid, and Rabbi Moshe Francis. *Chol HaMoed: Comprehensive Review of the Laws of the Intermediate Days of the Festivals.* Lakewood, NJ: Halacha Publications, 1981.

Well organized and lucidly written, this book takes the complication out of the intricacies of *khol hamoed* observance. Conditions under which activity is allowed or prohibited are simply and clearly differentiated.

WHAT OTHER THINGS DO PEOPLE DO?— CUSTOMS

Other Times and Places

Unique Observance

Without benefit of talmudic interpretation, the Ethiopian Jews derived their adherence to Torah from their own studied interpretation of its laws. The Ethiopian *seder* was modeled not on the banquets of wealthy free people as in Palestine but on the original Pesakh meal: They ate meat and *matzah* rapidly, as if ready to flee, outdoors in the moonlight. The elders told the story of the Exodus, asked questions of the children, and emphasized the Jews' struggles to reach the Holy Land—which they, with their two-thousand-year history in Ethiopia, and unceasing dreams of Jerusalem, identified with readily. The first day was devoted to synagogue services and the entire week to rest from work. All food prepared was eaten as soon as it was ready, in keeping with the Torah commandment to leave nothing overnight.

Spring Cleaning

Throughout the *Ashkenazi* and *Sephardi* worlds, homemakers moved furniture, examined every corner, cleaned everything in every cabinet, laundered draperies and painted the walls. The Libyan Jews, who made their own whitewash by burning and then crushing the limestone from nearby mountain quarries, slept outside rather than in a room already prepared for Pesakh.

On the morning of *Erev* Pesakh, the beadle went through each Eastern European Jewish town alerting people to burn their *khametz*. The men brought the wrapped spoons and bread morsels to the fire at the study hall near the synagogue. The Jews of China gave their *khametz* to neighborhood beggars.

Food Preparation

In Europe, raisins were turned into wine, hops into mead, root vegetables into pickled condiments, and beets into borscht (a soup) and *eingemakhts* (preserves). Rice, a Pesakh staple for Syrian Jews, had to be carefully sifted to get rid of any wheat chaff that had fallen into it.

The Libyans hollowed out new millstones so they could grind Pesakh wheat for all their needs. Tying scarves around their mouths, they refrained from speaking to avoid having saliva land in the flour and causing it to ferment.

Baking Matzah

At one time, *matzah* was so high that there is a question in Talmud as to whether it could be thicker than four fingers. By the Middle Ages, it had been limited to the width of one finger, but it still had to be baked fresh daily, or it was simply inedible. Gradually it evolved into the thin crisp cracker we know today, which can be made in advance for the entire eight days. (Some, like the Tunisian Jews of Djerba, still make *matzah* by hand that has the look and consistency of pita bread.)

Eastern European communities ran *matzah* bakeries for common use. Each family would provide its own flour and pay the baker to make the *matzah*. Since it was considered commendable for everyone to personally be involved in ensuring that the *matzah* was made with utmost diligence, people often made it themselves in communal facilities. (The medieval synagogue in Carpentras, France, and the Tuscan village of Pitigliano maintained underground *matzah* factories. Sometimes one family invited the community to use its home bakery.) Many poor Jews earned enough to pay for everything they needed to properly observe the holiday by helping out in the *matzah* factories, set up as assembly lines. (One of the arguments against acceptance of the *matzah*-making machine was that it would put people out of work, and they would not have the necessary funds for the holiday.)

Water to be used for the *matzah* dough had to be drawn the previous night and kept cool, since warm water leads to faster fermentation. At the time of water drawing, the Libyans each broke a ceramic vessel used during the year, to signal that *khametz* would no longer be present. As the pious poured the water into a barrel, they recited the Hebrew alphabet to sanctify the water with the holy letters of Torah.

Since Torah identifies *matzah* with the paschal lamb, and the sacrifice was made in the Temple after the sixth hour of the day, it was thought that *matzah* should be baked at that time. Pious Jews often waited until then to bake their *matzot*, at least the ones that would be used for the *sedarim*.

For a time it was popular to fashion *matzah* into figurative shapes or to imprint the cakes with de-

signs. Authorities worried that in the time it took to be creative, the dough would ferment and become *khametz*, so the artistry stopped. The Jews of Cochin made quick hatch marks to identify their *matzot* for the three categories of Jews: two lines for *Kohein*, three for *Levi*, and four for *Yisraeli* ("one" was reserved for God).

In *Sephardi* communities, it was the women who made the *matzah*, since they baked year-round and could work rapidly. As they worked, they sang special songs and recited special poems. Other communities forbade women to speak so their work would not be slowed. Among the *Ashkenazim*, to ensure that the process proceeded with speed, both men and women participated.

Other Preparations

Among some *Sephardim*, women used to observe the fast of the firstborn. The Syrians, who stringently observe it, include their women in the *siyyum* and *seudat mitzvah* following morning services. As an alternative, a community would sometimes arrange for the poor to be married on the day of *Erev* Pesakh. The firstborn were invited, since the wedding meal is a *seudat mitzvah* exempting them from the fast.

It was not unusual for one person to make *kharoset* for an entire town in Eastern Europe, which children would pick up in exchange for a few coins that were then donated for education or the needy. The rabbi might provide *matzah shmurah* for everybody, or the sexton sold it door-to-door.

Gold and silver vessels were often placed on the *seder* tables of *Sephardim* to suggest the jewelry and other riches the Israelites got from the Egyptians prior to their departure (Exodus 11:2). Some placed a bowl containing live fish on the table to represent the crossing of the Reed Sea, recalling the Egyptians' demise.

Seder *Plate*

In North African Jewish communities, as well as India, it was customary to pass the *k'arah* over the heads of everyone at the table in a circular motion. Encompassing all gathered in the historic experience, it was an acknowledgment that "as the world turns," first we were slaves, then we became free.

Afikoman *and Acting Out*

Many communities added dramatizations to their Exodus reenactment, usually of a Jew departing Egypt and wandering in exile expecting redemption.

Prior to the start of *seder* in Djerba, Tunisia, young people come to pay their respects to the rabbi, some carrying sacks and staffs resting on their shoulders, hobo style. It used to be customary that when the middle *matzah* was broken during the service, a member of each household would be sent to neighbors to predict the messiah's arrival.

In some *Sephardi* communities, the cloth-wrapped *afikoman* was tied to the shoulder of a child, who left the company and then reappeared knocking at the door. In the ensuing scripted dialogue, he identified himself as an Israelite on his way to Jerusalem carrying *matzah*. On entering the room, he looked at the specially arranged table and asked "Why is this night different from all other nights?"

Sometimes an adult walked around with the *afikoman* on his shoulder, as though it were bread carried on his back. One of the most elaborate of such ceremonies was dramatized in the Caucasus. The rabbi paced, like our ancestors leaving Egypt, with "their kneading troughs bound up in their clothes on their shoulders" (Exodus 12:34). The young men chose one person to portray a fugitive, dressed in rags, carrying the standard props. When he showed up at the door from Jerusalem to announce the coming redemption, the others did not readily believe him, until he cried, was invited in, and amid joyous celebration, answered questions about life in the Holy Land.

In Morocco, the enactment came at the end of the meal, when the participants quoted "So you shall eat it: your loins girded . . ." (Exodus 12:11). Dramatizations extended to synagogue also, where in some places in Eastern Europe, water was sprinkled on the floor during *Shirah* on the seventh day. The people in the congregation took off their shoes to dip their toes into the water to experience the sea.

From the custom in Kurdistan of binding a *ketubah* (Jewish marriage contract) to the bride's arm, the practice developed of tying the *afikoman* to the arm of a son the parents hoped would marry, wishing that the symbolic act would lead in the coming year to his binding a *ketubah* on his new bride's arm.

Other folk beliefs surround the symbolic piece of cracker. In Asia, Iran, North Africa, and Greece, Jews kept a piece of the *afikoman* in their pockets or houses for good luck during the year, sometimes making a small hole in it so it could be hung like an amulet. Keeping the remains of the *afikoman* in rice, flour, and salt was thought by the Jews of Kurdistan to protect them against the depletion of these staples.

The Moroccans in particular believed this *matzah* had the power to safeguard them during ocean travel, and would throw it into the water to calm it in a storm. (They based the superstition on an appro-

priate verse from Psalms [54:9], whose first letters in Hebrew spell the word *matzah*.) Some believed that if kept for seven years, it could stop floods. Others attributed to it the capacity to stop fire and, when held in hand, to protect a woman and infant during childbirth.

Culinary Customs

Some Moroccan families would not eat black olives for the entire month of *Nissan*: They believed the fruit caused forgetfulness, and *Nissan* was the month in which the Jews were commanded to remember the Exodus. Calling the evening of *seder* Leil (Night) al-Rosh (of the Heads), they customarily ate sheep heads in remembrance of the paschal sacrifice.

Games

With the nuts they received, children devised competitive diversions. These included hitting aligned walnuts and brazil nuts with small steel pellets, guessing whether an opponent had odd or even numbers of nuts in his hands, and tossing nuts into a box from a set distance.

Khol Hamoed

As a time of general joy, when people took time off from work, the intermediate days were used in medieval Europe for election of community leaders, selection of committee members, and completing volunteer projects put off in the day-to-day crush of responsibility. The Moroccans and Libyans made a special *seudah* featuring small dishes and little portions of food for very young children, which the youngsters helped to prepare. Some Moroccans cut a child's hair for the first time during a public celebration during this period. (It was also common to do so during *khol hamoed* Sukkot or, as is still popular in Israel, on Lag B'Omer.)

It used to be the custom to light candles every evening.

Post-Pesakh

At one time it was customary to fast on the Monday, Thursday, and next Monday after Pesakh (and Sukkot) to atone for excesses of indulgence on the holiday. Called *bet* (the second Hebrew letter), *hei* (the fifth Hebrew letter), *bet*, corresponding to the second and fifth days of the week, it had to be postponed to the following month because *Nissan* is devoted to celebration.

On the day after Passover, the Moroccan Jews walked outside of town and recited the blessing over trees, said once a year when new buds appear (see *"Halakhah"* in chapter on Tu B'Shevat).

Maimouna

The Moroccan Jews are known for Maimouna, the exhuberant festival held on the evening and day after Pesakh, and whose origins are unclear. According to one explanation, it is the *yahrtzite* (anniversary of death) of Maimon ben Joseph, the father of the great Jewish philosopher Maimonides (Rabbi Moses ben Maimon, also known by his acronym Rambam), a scholar in his own right who lived in Fez (Morocco) and wrote on Jewish-Islamic relations. He died around 1170.

Others say Maimouna is derived from the Arabic word for wealth and good fortune (literally "protected by God," *ma'amoun*). Since Pesakh is the beginning of the new agricultural year, when the world is judged for produce, it is a time to pray for plentiful crops, symbolic of general prosperity.

Still others connect Maimouna with the word *emunah* ("belief"), claiming it celebrates belief in Israel's redemption. Along the same lines, there is also support (said to be traced to Maimonides' explanation) for the word being an Arabic adaptation of the phrase *Ani ma'amin* (I believe), the classic expression of faith in the coming of the messiah (*ana* for *ani*, placed after the verb *ma'amin*, as is common in Arabic, yielding *ma'amin ana*, which became *maimouna* in the local Judeo dialect). It may have been a greeting exchanged to bolster one another's disappointment that Passover had come and gone without the long-anticipated return to Jerusalem.

Dining tables were decorated with flowers, wheat stalks, and sometimes live fish in bowls (this time symbolizing birth and fertility). Golden rings were hidden in a bowl containing flour, suggesting hoped-for wealth or blessings. A dairy meal of buttermilk, sweets, and special pancakes called *muflita* served with honey was accompanied by singing, dancing, and visiting with friends. The Libyans made a *khallah*-like round loaf with a hard-boiled egg secured in the center with strips of dough. Single men and women received blessings that they would be married in the year ahead. Women wore their fanciest clothes, girls donned white, and children dressed in costumes like the Berbers (native North Africans) and Arabs who shared their celebration and provided flowers, milk, butter, honey, wheat, and other produce for the Jews.

Numerous legends about acts of salvation that occurred on this date arose, and the festival spread through North Africa and to America, where the Maimouna meal provides closure for Passover, and into Israel, where the community gathers in Jerusalem. The holiday traditionally continues the next day with picnics and outings at beaches, fields, and cemeteries.

For the Sabbath after Pesakh, when the approaching start of the month of *Iyar* was announced, *khallah* was sometimes made in the shape of a key. Sprinkled with sesame seeds representing the *mahn* (manna) that began to fall in *Iyar*, the *khallah* stood for the key to our livelihood, which is in God's hands.

Pesakh Sheni

Some *Sephardim* hold a *hillula* (celebration) at the grave of Rabbi Meir Baal Ha-Nes (Meir "master of miracles"). Several Rabbi Meirs were involved with miracles, and although it is not clear which one is buried in the tomb in Tiberias—where the celebrants flock for prayers of intercession and singing, dancing, and feasting—*Iyar* 14 is the anniversary of the rabbi's death. Like that of Shimon bar Yokhai (see chapter on Lag B'Omer) it is an occasion for rejoicing.

Greeting

In the days leading up to Pesakh, we wish each other *"khag"* (holiday) or "Pesakh *kasher* (kosher) *v'samei'akh*" (and joyous), or a *"freilikhen un kushern* Pesakh" (in Yiddish). "*Mo'adim* (festival days) *l'simkhah*" (of joy) is traditional, answered by the *Sephardim* with "*khagim uzmanim l'sassone*" (holidays and special times of rejoicing). Yiddish-speaking Jews and their descendants say "*gut* (good or happy) *yom tov*" (holiday).

Dress

New clothes are customary for Pesakh. (Traditionally, rabbis advised that if one could not afford an entire suit or outfit, at least shoes were to be bought.) If obtaining them is impossible, then clothing should be clean and as good as clothes worn for Sabbath (the attire one would put on to meet and receive an honored visitor, attend a special event, and so on—not the playground and health club attire often seen in synagogues in our informal society). The *seder* leader traditionally wears a *kittel*.

WHAT IS THERE TO EAT?—TRADITIONAL FOODS

Food, always a central aspect of Jewish celebration, is a major obsession on this holiday because of the prohibition of *khametz*. Today we can get practically any foodstuff in a kosher-for-Passover variety, and gourmet and healthful recipes take us far beyond the limits of hardboiled eggs and cream cheese-jelly-and-*matzah* sandwiches.

How you make the *seder* meal festive is largely a matter of local tradition and individual taste. The only restriction—aside from *khametz*, of course—is against eating roasted lamb (to emphasize that we can no longer make the paschal sacrifice since we have lost the Temple). North African Jews generally eat lamb, prepared some way other than roasting, as the main course; *Ashkenazim* avoid it altogether. Some do not eat any kind of meat that has been roasted.

Mirroring the shankbone and egg from the *seder* plate (which may be eaten), Eastern European Jews often made stuffed roasted chicken necks for the meal itself, and it is a widespread, though not universal, custom to start the meal with a whole hardboiled egg in salt water. For some, it is symbolic of the loss of the Temple. The first meal in a house of mourning is traditionally an egg, its roundness representing the wholeness of life and the "wheel of fortune" through which our lives continually change. The connection was also made because the first day of Pesakh always falls on the same day of the week as Tisha B'Av, our national day of mourning for the Temple's destruction.

One other explanation connects the egg to our status in exile. While all other foods soften as they cook, the egg becomes harder, like the character of the Jew in response to oppression.

Khasidim and pious Jews often refrain from eating any *matzah* or *matzah* meal that has been soaked in water, called in Yiddish *gebrokt*. Even though the rabbis have ruled that once baked *matzah* can no longer ferment and become *khametz*, and *matzah* meal and *matzah* farfel are forms of already baked *matzah*, the strict do not take any chances, foregoing such delicacies as *kneidlakh* (*matzah* meal dumplings either delicate as a cloud or as unsubtle as a cannonball depending on your taste, developed through your mother's or grandmother's particular cooking style), *matzah brei* (*matzah* softened by briefly soaking in water, mixed with eggs and scrambled—with additions of cheese and vegetables or cinnamon, sugar, and raisins), and *matzah* farfel kugels. They allow themselves such pleasures on the eighth day when, since it was added for the Diaspora and is not a Torah commandment, they are more lenient.

It is good news to all of us diet/health conscious Americans that Pesakh dishes, normally heavy on the eggs and fat, can just as easily be made with low-cholesterol and low-fat ingredients, as reflected in some of the newer cookbooks. Even *khremslekh*, the classic Pesakh pancakes, can be made with egg whites.

FOR FURTHER READING

In addition to the cookbooks listed in Appendix C (both the Nathan and Zeidler books have selections of *kharoset* recipes from different places around the world), the following are specific to this holiday.

For Adults

AvRutick, Frances R. *The Complete Passover Cookbook*. Middle Village, NY: Jonathan David Publishers, 1981.

With an extensive collection of five hundred recipes arranged by meal course, this sometimes inventive aid for holiday cooking explains the *seder* and *seder* table and provides suggested menus.

Rousso, Nira. *The Passover Gourmet*. New York: Adama Books, 1987.

This very popular book covers both *Ashkenazi* and *Sephardi* dishes. Appealing four-color photographs and an attractive easy-to-follow layout enhance its appeal.

The Spice and Spirit of Kosher Passover Cooking. Brooklyn: Lubavitch Women's Organization, 1981.

In its tenth printing, the book includes helpful, easily followed information on Pesakh *kashrut*, the laws and customs of foods on this holiday and guides to preparation—from a list of everything in the house that must be searched for *khametz* to the *seder* table—as well as instructions for making your own wine and a collection of favorite recipes submitted by Lubavitch women.

Wasserman, Debra, and Charles Stahler. *No Cholesterol Passover Recipes*. Baltimore: The Vegetarian Resource Group, 1986.

The forty-nine-page typewritten booklet contains one hundred low-calorie recipes printed on recycled paper. Eggless versions of such standards as normally egg-heavy *matzah brei* and *matzah* meal pancakes are included, along with meatless stuffed cabbage.

For Children

Tabs, Judy, and Barbara Steinberg. *Matzah Meals—A Passover Cookbook for Kids*. Rockville, MD: Kar-Ben Copies, Inc., 1985.

In addition to more than seventy recipes tested by kids themselves—some of which involve no cooking and can be made by preschoolers—the book includes the Passover story and a *seder* menu for young people. All ages.

DO YOU HEAR MUSIC?—SONGS TO SING

The *shtetl* (small village) of Eastern European Jews produced a number of folksongs about preparing for the holiday, with focus on the *matzah* baker, homemaker, and the children. But the music we identify with is that of the *seder*. In addition to sung passages (some of them to catchy folk tunes adapted for the *seder* by the *khasidim*, who elevated worship music to new levels), there are classic folk songs whose rendition at the close of the *seder* forms a high point in many homes.

The *Seder* Service

As much as it is a story to be told, the *haggadah* is a book to be sung. That is one of the reasons a *seder* can be so much fun and so powerful. So this is one holiday for which you will want to become familiar with at least some of the tunes beforehand. You can easily secure a compact disc or cassette tape for you and your children to listen to and copy. (A number are available—from Israeli schoolkids to Richard Tucker singing the *seder* and Pesakh songs.) Every child should learn the "*Mah Nishtanah*," which is as much a part of one's Jewish cultural heritage as "My Country 'tis of Thee" is of one's American cultural heritage. "*Ha Lakhma Anya*" (This is the bread of affliction), "*Avadim Hayinu*" (We were slaves [in Egypt]), and "*V'hi Shei Amdah*" (God's help has sustained), which are major parts in the Exodus story, all have catchy upbeat tunes, as does "*Dayeinu*," a perennial favorite and whose chorus can be learned on the spot. "*Shir Hama'alot*" (Song of Ascents), Psalm 126, which introduces the post-meal grace; *Birkat Hamazon* itself; "*Eliyahu Hanavi*" (Elijah the Prophet), the refrain wishing for the prophet to quickly bring the messiah; "*Ani Ma'amin*" (I believe), the affirmation included at some *sedarim* in recognition of Holocaust victims; and the rousing "*L'Shanah Haba'ah B'Yerushalayim*" (Next year in Jerusalem) are all Jewish standards sung on other occasions as well.

Your family might also want to learn one of the chants of the order of service; there are several versions.

Folk Songs

Four well-known and popular folk songs appear in a majority of *haggadot*. "*Adir Hu*" (Mighty is He), an alphabetic acrostic sung to a melody popular for hundreds of years, repeats the hope that Zion will soon be restored and the Temple rebuilt. Another alphabetic acrostic, "*Ki Lo Na'eh*" (To Him Praise Belongs), originating probably in France or Germany in the Middle Ages, wraps effusive praise around phrases from various Bible books. The fun in this song is in singing each verse successively faster without tripping over your tongue.

In "*Ekhad Mi Yodei'ah?*" (Who Knows One?), the *seder* host asks the children a series of questions whose answers pertain to Jewish heritage (one God, two tablets of the covenant, three patriarchs . . . eleven stars in Joseph's dream . . . , up to thirteen). Nonreligious number madrigals usually stopped at twelve because of widespread belief that the next number is unlucky. Judaism, which despite persistent folk customs frowns on superstition, holds it in esteem (the age of *bar mitzvah*, number of Maimonides' creeds of the faith, and Attributes of God, and the numerical value of the Hebrew letters in the word *ekhad* [one], which refers to the unity of God, stressed throughout the song).

"*Khad Gadya*" (An Only Kid) is a Jewish "House That Jack Built" or "Old Lady Who Swallowed a Fly," with each development in the story building on the previous one. Written in Aramaic, it differs from similar folktales of the Middle Ages and amusing nursery rhymes in that, aside from being fun to sing, it teaches. Scores of books and articles have been written about its moral significance and historical symbolism.

The song suggests that Divine justice operates in the world promising retribution for all oppressors. No matter how dominant someone is, God rules over all and will eventually even out inequities.

A number of scholars have interpreted "*Khad Gadya*" as an allegory of Israel's fate among nations. Israel (the kid) is redeemed by God from Egypt through Moses and Aaron (two *zuzim*) or, in an alternate reading, by the two tablets of the commandments. Then Israel is subjected to a great empire, which is defeated by a succession of other empires until God redeems His "kid." The cat is said to represent Assyria; the dog, Babylon; the stick, Persia; the fire, Greece; the water, Rome; the ox, Muslims; the butcher, the Crusaders; the Angel of Death, the Ottomans, or according to some, European nations.

Still another analysis reads the song as a record of Israel's relationship to Torah: God "sold" us the Torah for the two words we said at Sinai, "we will do and we will listen" (see chapter on Shavuot). Once in the Holy Land, jealousy (like cats) made us neglect Torah, so hostile nations were sent against us—and so on in a series of neglects and embraces of Torah—through David, Babylonia, return from exile, Hellenism, the Maccabees, and Rome, which caused the current exile, in which we hope for the messiah.

German Jews in the eighteenth century turned the song into a game for children with each scene acted out. You can enhance a simple singing by assigning each of the roles in the song to one of your *seder* guests and having them make the appropriate sound of the animal or object as it is mentioned.

FOR FURTHER EXPLORATION

You can learn how to conduct the *seder*—or participate in its musical parts—from instructional cassettes or by listening to one of the numerous compact discs and audiotapes featuring Passover music. Tara Publications (see Appendix C) produces quite a few songbooks and tapes (including the booklet/cassette set *Seder Melodies*, which contains twenty traditional tunes for the Passover service. There is also a companion tape to Shoshana Silverman's *A Family Haggadah* (see section on *Haggadah* under "Ritual Items" earlier in this chapter).

WHAT TALES ARE TOLD?— STORIES TO READ

Descriptions of Passover celebrations have enlivened numerous literary works, and the themes of the holiday have been used as the backdrop for others, going back to at least the second century, with the play *The Exodus from Egypt*, written by the Jewish dramatist Ezekiel of Alexandria. (*The Passover Anthology*, listed in Appendix C, has an excerpt from it.)

At the beginning of *Peony*, Pearl S. Buck describes a *seder* in Kaifeng, China, in the mid-1800s. Samuel Yosef Agnon's *The Bridal Canopy* weaves Passover through the narration, and Sholom Aleichem effectively uses the commemoration of the ancient libera-

tion movement as the "bookends" for his novel about the stirrings of revolution and Jewish nationalism in early twentieth-century Russia (*Into the Storm*). Both Leon Uris and Elie Wiesel used Pesakh messages and metaphors in their respective novels, *Exodus* and *The Fifth Son*, and several writers have fictionalized the life of Moses.

Among other Jewish philosophers and writers who used the holiday as the subject of essays and poems are Rosenzweig, Heine, Ha-Am, Katzenelson, Herzl, Ibn Ezra, Zangwill, Ibn Gabirol, Halevi, and Bialik.

FOR FURTHER READING/VIEWING

Folktales

"The Bitter Herb." In *Rabbi Nachman's Stories*. Trans. by Rabbi Aryeh Kaplan. Brooklyn: Breslov Research Institute, 1983, pp. 476–477.

The first taste of a *seder* meal might drive someone away, but this lesson shows how much reward awaits one who lasts through it.

"The Man Who Agreed to Be Moses." In JF, pp. 298–299.

Using amusement and wisdom to convince the King that Moses is still alive and among the people, a Jew is able to save his community.

"The Old Man of the Mountains." In JF, pp. 127–128.

A special visitor on the eve of Passover changes a pious woodseller's life of poverty.

"The Prophet Elijah's Magic Box." In JF, pp. 126–127.

Elijah's box provides unlimited funds—as long as its holder uses the money unselfishly.

Schram, Peninnah. *Tales of Elijah the Prophet*. Northvale, NJ: Jason Aronson, 1991.

In the thirty-seven folk stories in this wonderful collection, Elijah appears in a variety of guises to work his miracles and bolster faith. Although the prophet is most closely associated with Passover, this book is a treasure for the entire year. (*Note*: Many volumes of Jewish folktales include stories about Elijah, so you might want to check other collections as well.)

"The Ten Plagues." In CT, pp. 109–113.

The plagues are explained as retribution-in-kind for Egypt's oppression of the Jews.

"The Two Washerwomen on Passover Eve." In JF, pp. 131–132.

Good things come to one who accepts her lot without complaint.

Other Stories

Agnon, Samuel Joseph. "The Passover Celebrants." In Passover HA, pp. 229–236; and *The Bridal Canopy*. Trans. by I. M. Lask. New York: Doubleday, Donan & Company, 1937, pp. 200–206.

A widow and widower, both reluctant to impose on others for Passover, find each other.

Aleichem, Sholom. "Elijah the Prophet." In Passover HA, pp. 219–222.

A young boy faces a difficult dilemma when he falls asleep at the *seder* and meets Elijah. Ages 10–14.

Aleichem, Sholom. "Home for Passover." In BA, pp. 89–102; and FT, pp. 75–92.

Since he was trying to save money, Fishel the teacher had a difficult, though amusing, journey home in order to arrive in time for the start of the holiday. Ages 10–14.

Aleichem, Sholom. "The Passover Expropriation." In BA, pp. 122–128; and FT, pp. 661–668.

When there are more poor people than money in the wheat fund will cover, the poor unemployed young men confront the rich of the town to get their holiday meal. Evocative of a former time in Russia, the story points up an ongoing need. Ages 10–14.

Peretz, Isaac Loeb. "It is Good." In Passover HA, pp. 351–354.

The memory of a rabbi's words helps a young man drafted into the Russian army remember his heritage. Age 10–13.

––––––. "The Magician." In Passover HA, pp. 358–364; and *In This World and the Next, Selected Writings*. Trans. by Moshe Spiegel. New York: Thomas Yoseloff, 1958, pp. 226–230.

A poor couple's Pesakh is made possible by a visit from Elijah the Prophet. Ages 12–15.

Books for Children

Auerback, Julie Jaslow. *Everything's Changing—It's Pesakh!* Rockville, MD: Kar-Ben Copies, 1986.

Cute short poems present preparation for Passover and the activities of the *seder* in an attractive way for a child. Portrayed as welcome activities usually not allowed, it gives a very positive picture of the holiday, complemented by amusing illustrations. Ages 3–6.

Cohen, Barbara. *The Carp in the Bathtub*. New York: Lothrup, Lee & Shepard Company, 1972.

A Passover classic, this is the heartwarming story of how two children try to save the fish they have befriended from being made into their mother's holiday *gefilte* fish. Ages 7–9.

Feder, Harriet K. *Not Yet, Elijah!* Rockville, MD: Kar-Ben Copies, 1989.

The young narrator of the rhymed story keeps Elijah, waiting at the door and impatient to come in, at bay through all parts of the service. This is a cute presentation of the order of *seder*. Ages 6–10.

Goldin, Barbara Diamond. *The Magician's Visit: A Passover Tale*. New York: Viking, 1993.

This is a retold version of the I. L. Peretz story. A one-page explanation of Passover and Elijah is given at the end. Ages 7–9.

Lepon, Shoshana. *The Ten Plagues of Egypt*. New York: The Judaica Press, 1988.

Humorous rhymes and funny, engaging, brightly colored illustrations illuminate the story based on information from *midrash*. Ages 4 and up.

Midoff, Francine. *The Mouse in the Matzah Factory*. Rockville, MD: Kar-Ben Copies, 1983.

A mouse follows the harvested wheat through all the steps of the *matzah*-making process. In large type, simple words are used to show what makes the unleavened bread so special. Ages 4–8.

Miller, Deborah Uchill. *Only Nine Chairs—A Tall Tale for Passover*. Rockville, MD: Kar-Ben Copies, Inc., 1982.

An adorable rhymed story of a family with nineteen guests for Pesakh and only nine chairs presents the *seder* as great fun. Ages 5–9.

Sidi, Smadar Shir. *Passover A–Z*. New York: Adama Books, 1989.

For each letter in the Hebrew alphabet is a word for Passover. A short paragraph explains what each Hebrew word means and the ritual connected with it. Watercolor illustrations enhance the attractive layout. Ages 7–11.

Weilerstein, Sadie Rose. *Ten and a Kid*. Philadelphia: The Jewish Publication Society of America, 1961.

A National Jewish Book Award winner, this extended folktale portrays life in a small Lithuanian town through stories of ten people and the goat that mysteriously arrives on Passover eve. It lovingly expresses the spirit and pattern of Eastern European village life. Ages 8 and up.

Videotapes

Parpar Nechmad/Lovely Butterfly—Passover

Puppets, games, animation, stories, and holiday

songs are used in this award-winning Israeli series to present holidays and their traditions. Although in Hebrew, the tape is geared for those with very little understanding of the language. Ages 2–6.

Shalom Sesame: Jerusalem Jones and the Lost Afikoman
Sarah Jessica Parker stars with the Sesame Street characters in a special Passover program of the Israeli "Sesame Street" set in Israel. The thirty-minute tape is in English and introduces elementary Hebrew words. Ages 2–12.

OF ADDITIONAL INTEREST

Art

Michaelangelo's sculpture *Moses* (at the church of San Pietro in Vincoli in Rome) is famous for the horns growing out of the prophet's head, the result of mistranslation of the word *keren,* meaning ray (or horn) of light shining from the prophet's face following his encounter with God (Exodus 34:29).

Music

In the nineteenth century, Gioachino Rossini created the opera *Mose in Egitto* (Moses in Egypt), and in this century, Arnold Schoenberg wrote (but never finished) *Moses and Aaron,* using solo and choral speaking and singing voices to present his interpretation of the Bible story as a conflict between two great personalities. Darius Milhaud's orchestral ballet suite, *Opus Americanum No. 2—Moses,* takes us through a variety of moods reflecting periods and events in the leader's life. George Frideric Handel and Max Ettinger both composed oratoria, *Israel in Egypt* and *The Song of Moses.* There is also the fanciful Andrew Lloyd Weber rock opera, *Joseph and the Amazing Technicolor Dreamcoat,* which in a variety of music styles tells the prelude to the Exodus.

Moses' experience also inspired the great black spiritual *Let My People Go,* which not only held tremendous significance for the American slaves and civil rights movement but was often heard at rallies on behalf of Soviet Jewry.

YOM HASHOAH

Yom Hashoah (yome' ha show' ah): Holocaust Remembrance Day. Observed on *Nissan* **27** (spring; mid-April–early May).

Yom Hashoah was established to allow us to collectively mourn the thousands of Jewish communities, millions of Jewish men, women, and children, and unquantified unrealized potential liquidated in the greatest atrocity ever perpetrated against our (or any other) people. As a response enveloped by intense emotion and deep questioning, its observance will undoubtedly remain fluid until the perspective of time helps us adequately define its format and place it within the pattern of Jewish commemoration.

ORIGINS: WHY WE CELEBRATE YOM HASHOAH

WHERE DID IT ALL BEGIN?—HISTORIC BACKGROUND

The Catastrophe

On April 12, 1951, the Knesset (Parliament) of Israel declared *Nissan* 27 the day of commemoration for the most devastating oppression we have suffered in our long history: the attempt by the Nazis (National Socialist Party of Germany) and their collaborators to make the world *Judenrein*—to completely annihilate our people from the face of the Earth. Their efforts resulted in the destruction of more than one-third of the world's prewar Jewish population by particularly sadistic means.

Almost five million men and women, and more than one million children, were slaughtered, worked, starved, or tortured to death in what came to be called, in the decade after the fact, the Holocaust. The word is derived from the Greek *holo* (whole) *kaustos* (burnt), a thorough destruction, especially by fire. *Holokaustos* is the translation of the name of the Temple animal sacrifice that ascended (*olah*) in its entirety to heaven as it was burnt whole. Use of the term in connection with the deaths of the six million Jews, the majority of whose bodies were burned in the crematoria of Auschwitz, Treblinka, Majdenek, Birkenau, Bergen-Belsen, Chelmo, and other extermination camps, suggests that they are to be regarded as sacrifices to God. The modern Hebrew word for the Holocaust, *Shoah*, means devastation or ruin.

It began with the Nazis' ascent to power and the naming of Adolf Hitler as chancellor of Germany in 1933. Restrictions on Jews were instituted almost immediately. They were stripped of civil rights (barred from public places and all aspects of public life), property (losing their homes and businesses), and their very status as human beings. (The Nuremberg Racial Purity Laws of 1935 limited German national life to members of the Aryan "master race," effectively classifying Jews as subhuman inferiors and setting the foundation for the heinous treatment of them.)

November 9, 1938, signaled the beginning of the government-sanctioned genocide (a word coined in response to the Nazis' program) of German—and later Eastern European and French—Jewry. On that date, which came to be known as *Kristallnakht* (Crystal Night), mobs rampaged through Germany and Austria, smashing the windows of Jewish-owned businesses and synagogues and torching the buildings. The Jews themselves were fined one billion marks for the damages and forced to their hands and knees—the old and crippled included—to scrub the streets strewn with shattered glass and charred debris.

To make them easy targets, the Germans required the Jews to sew yellow six-pointed stars onto their clothing (a revival of a medieval practice of using clothes to distinguish and sometimes humiliate the Jews). Persecution escalated to forced labor, ghettoization, wanton torture and murder, concentration camp internment, and implementation of "The Final Solution to the Jewish Problem": systematic mass murder—by gunning victims into pits dug to hold tens of thousands, and later, in the gas chambers of the death camps.

The Commemoration

Choosing the date for memorializing unprecedented persecution was somewhat complicated. First of all, unlike other commemorations on our calendar, this one could not be pinned to a specific event or biblical designation. *Hashoah* continued, agonizingly, every day, every season, every year, actively, for twelve years. With countless acts of inhuman brutality against innocents, tremendous numbers slaughtered, thousands of sites of horror, how could one date be chosen to sum up the wrenching memory of it?

There was also the question of whether, despite its magnitude, the Holocaust was "just" one of the many persecutions, expulsions, and slaughters that have punctuated our history (in which case commemoration could be incorporated into existing national mourning days), or whether it had been a unique occurrence that did not fit neatly into the recurring pattern of promise, persecution, and protection in which and by which we had survived two thousand years (which demanded a date dedicated solely to the memory of its victims).

Initially, the Chief Rabbinate of Israel placed the *Shoah* within the context of Jewish history and the set holiday calendar. For *Yom Kaddish Klali* (general day of saying the memorial prayer for the dead), the rabbis chose Asarah B'Tevet (the tenth day of the tenth month), an ancient, and in practice minor, fast day marking the start of the Babylonian siege of Jerusalem that led to the destruction of the first Temple (see chapter on Tisha B'Av).

Since so many people did not know the exact date of death for relatives killed in the Holocaust (*kaddish* is normally said on the anniversary of death), and so many people had died without leaving survivors to say the special prayer for them, the rabbinate declared that the date would serve for Holocaust remembrance in general. There was just one problem: There was no popular support for appending a memorial drawn on fresh, deep, widespread pain to an unfelt, almost forgotten ancient loss.

Many thought that if Holocaust commemoration were to be entwined with a day of mourning already observed, it would be more appropriate if it were tied to Tisha B'Av, a day recalled for a number of the worst calamities to strike us. Even that could not be reconciled. The ancient tragedies already marked by the day were scarred over by the centuries intervening since their occurrence. The Holocaust was an oozing, gaping wound. In addition, for many people, it could not be viewed as part of the pattern of Jewish life—not just in terms of calendar placement but in terms of basic assumptions about our role, relationship with God, and progression through history.

The survivors who had participated in the resistance movement wanted any Holocaust commemoration to highlight the heroic activities of the Jews who had met the Germans with armed strength. For them, only one date had meaning: April 19, 1943, when they actively began to defy the Nazis' efforts to liquidate the Warsaw ghetto. Weakened by hunger and disease, fighting with the disadvantage of few people and fewer weapons, receiving no support from the non-Jewish partisans, their uprising amazingly managed to hold back the enemy for more than three weeks. Recognizing that they could not ultimately win, they were determined not to quietly accept an imposed death but to go down having taken their fates into their own hands.

On the Jewish calendar, April 19, 1943, was *Nissan* 15, the first day of Passover. (The Nazis often chose days significant to the Jews for special suffering, part of the attempt to further demoralize the victims.) While the coincidence of the feast of freedom and a modern struggle for liberation from an evil oppressor was poetically inspirational, choosing *Nissan* 15 for Holocaust remembrance was unacceptable to the Orthodox: they would not allow the grief of Yom Hashoah to overwhelm the joy of our central holiday.

There was one other consideration: a strong desire to place Holocaust remembrance sometime prior and proximate to Yom Ha'atzmaut (Israel Independence Day). Even though the establishment of the State of Israel was in no way viewed as compensation for the Third Reich's crimes, or a result of them, it is a powerful rejoinder. One day we grieve for tremendous soul-crushing losses. Shortly after, we celebrate the triumph of Jewish survival, an important psychological and physical affirmation.

Although displeased, because it still violated the traditional prohibition of mourning during the festive month of *Nissan*, the rabbis accepted *Nissan* 27, four days following Passover and one week before Israel Independence Day, as *Yom Hashoah u'Mered Hageta'ot* (. . . and Ghetto Revolt Remembrance Day).

Very soon after establishing the date, all forms of heroism, not only armed resistance, were recognized and honored by Yom Hashoah. Contrary to a widespread but erroneous attitude, the Jews of Europe did not go meekly to their deaths like lambs to the slaughter. Despite every means imaginable to degrade and dehumanize them, break their bodies and their spirits, rob them of their souls, and turn them into slaves and, worse, into objects (their hair into mattress stuffing, skin into lampshades, tooth fillings into jewelry), they persisted in surviving as human beings and as Jews.

In the face of inhumanity, they asserted their humanity: they sang, they danced, they maintained underground social services; they even retained their sense of humor and made up jokes. Though illegal and punishable by death, in the ghettos they taught their children to read, continued *yeshivah* education, held prayer *minyonim* (groups of ten, the minimum number of men required for public service), consecrated marriages under the *khupah* (wedding canopy), and brought their infant sons into the convenant through circumcision. They recorded what was happening to them, confident someone would one day read the accounts and ultimately discover some meaning in their suffering.

In the camps, too, they managed to retain faith, observe holidays, and express little kindnesses. Even as they walked naked to their deaths, they maintained a spiritual strength and dignity that countered the efforts of their tormentors to reduce them to nothingness.

In recognition of all these acts of defiance, the memorial day became known as *Yom Hashoah v'Hagevurah* (. . . and Heroism), popularly referred to as Yom Hashoah. Increasing awareness of the day among Israelis was mandated by 1953 law to *Yad Vashem* (literally Hand—or monument—and a Name, the Israeli Holocaust memorial museum, archive and educational center whose title comes from Isaiah 56:5: "I will give them, in My house and within My walls, a monument and a name better than sons or daughters. I will give them an everlasting name which shall not perish.").

The day was largely ignored by the Israelis, ambivalent about focusing on the pain, embarrassed by what they often thought had been meek submission to the Nazis, reluctant to promote any contradiction to the image of the new Jew, the strong *sabra* (native Israeli, named for the fruit of a cactus plant that has a tough exterior but is sweet inside). Public commemoration increased after the Knesset passed the 1959 Holocaust and Heroism Remembrance Day Law, which calls for public tribute to the victims of the Nazi war against the Jews. (A 1961 amendment requires that places of entertainment in Israel be closed on the eve of Yom Hashoah.)

Acceptance of the commemoration was substantially helped by the 1960 abduction to Israel of Adolf Eichmann, chief implementer of "The Final Solution," who had been hiding in Argentina. Yet it was not until after the exhilarating victory of the 1967 Six-Day War, which was seen as a balance to the emotional and psychological losses of the Holocaust, and the humbling close call of the 1973 Yom Kippur War, that the country was able to embrace its survivors, seriously study the Holocaust, and openly commemorate those lost in it.

Although established as a secular day (by the government of Israel) rather than a sacred day (which only the rabbinic establishment can do), as a memorial to Jewish dead, it is considered a holy occasion and is widely marked by services and ceremonies in Israel and throughout the Diaspora.

President Carter's Commission on the Holocaust, established in 1979 to recommend an American policy for commemoration, organized the first national ceremony in Washington, DC. Congressional law passed in 1980 mandates an annual national memorial and the encouragement and sponsorship of similar observations throughout the country. Synagogues and Jewish communal organizations and city and state governments sponsor a variety of public commemorative programs, supported by Jewish and non-Jewish organizations, individuals, and government leaders.

FOR FURTHER READING

Blatter, Janet, and Sybil Milton. *Spiritual Resistance—Art from Concentration Camps, 1940–1945*. New York: Rutledge Press, 1981.

Landscapes, portraits, and scenes of life in the camps—as well as depictions of ghettos, transit camps, prisons, and partisans—are evocative of the pain, and the spirit, of the Holocaust's victims. Essays provide background, and biographies of the artists are included.

Dawidowicz, Lucy. *The War Against the Jews 1933–1945*. New York: Holt, Rinehart and Winston, 1975; Bantam Books, 1986.

Considered a definitive work on the subject, in three parts it covers—from a physical and moral viewpoint—how the German National Socialists were able to murder six million Jews, how the Jews responded to the brutality against them, and how the devastation affected Jewish life in Europe.

Encyclopedia of the Holocaust. Ed. by Israel Gutman. Trans. by Mordechai Shalev. New York: Macmillan Publishing Company, 1990.

The well-recognized four-volume set contains nine hundred articles on the Holocaust and related subjects.

Gilbert, Martin. *The Holocaust: A History of the Jews of Europe During the Second World War.* New York: Henry Holt & Company, 1987.

Following a chronological sequence, the massive text draws on first-person accounts, newspapers, diaries, letters, and Nazi records for personalized testimony to the world that existed prior to the Nazis' devastation, and how it was destroyed.

Harrel, Isser. *The House on Garibaldi Street: The First Full Account of the Capture of Adolf Eichmann.* New York: Viking Press, 1975.

Written by the former head of Israel's secret service who was in charge of the operation, this novel-like account details the capture and abduction of Adolf Eichmann.

Lipman, Steve. *Laughter in Hell: The Use of Humor During the Holocaust.* Northvale, NJ: Jason Aronson, 1991.

This collection of jokes and other applications of humor in the ghettos and camps demonstrates how Jews used this special form of resistance, expressing the expectation that good would eventually triumph.

Pictorial History of the Holocaust. Ed. by Yitzhak Arad. New York: Macmillan Publishing Company, 1990.

As much as the Germans documented, in excruciating detail, their crimes against the Jews, according to the introduction, they did not want photographic evidence. Still there is a massive photographic record, provided by Axis soldiers, the Jews, members of the underground, and even occasionally by the Germans themselves. Often disturbingly graphic, this book is drawn from the collection of *Yad Vashem.*

ArtScroll, the respected library of resources produced by Mesorah Publications, has a series of sixteen one-hour cassettes, *History of the Holocaust,* which in their account reflect the survival of the Jewish spirit amid the barbaric actions of the Nazis.

WHAT DOES IT MEAN?— RELIGIOUS IMPORTANCE

Religion attempts to make sense out of the world around us, finding order and meaning in what often seems chaotic and meaningless. Nothing has shaken the foundation of our religion like the chaotic and senseless *Shoah.* Its devastation was so widespread, its perpetration of evil so extensive, it raised searing theological questions about God and His role in the world; about good, evil, and justice; about the value of life and death; and about Jewish destiny. How and why could the Holocaust have happened? Did it fit within the pattern of Jewish history, or was it a unique occurrence that would end it? Could it be read as a fulfillment of an ancient Torah prophecy or did it threaten the integrity of the entire Torah? Could the Jewish people respond to it as we have to previous drastic turning points in our history, or would it totally turn us away from the heritage and its burdens?

Broken Promises

Until the Holocaust, the traditional view of God and His connection with Israel had remained intact: God was our Provider and Protector. Even though bad things would happen to His people—which we saw as the justified result of our failure to honor Him and the way of life He presented to us—periods of oppression would always be followed by salvation, and eventually the persecution-ending, exile-gathering, peace-bringing redemption would occur. As the Passover *haggadah* expresses it, "in every generation enemies rise up seeking to destroy us, but God delivers us from their hands."

This expectation carried the Jews through the failed Bar Kokhba revolt (see chapter on Lag B'Omer), the Crusades, repeated humiliations and expulsions, pogroms and myriad persecutions, even the Spanish Inquisition. But it was shaken (and for some, completely shattered) by the success of the Nazis in decimating European Jewry. The destruction—not only of an astounding number of Jews but of a disproportionate percentage of scholars and rabbis, along with the major centers of Jewish culture and learning—challenged the long-held belief that God intervenes in the world to balance injustice by punishing evil and rewarding good.

Was God dead? Was He just indifferent—or worse, a sadist? If He could not be counted on to live up to His reputation for mercy and intervene, what good was He? And if He did not intervene, by what reasoning did He merit our allegiance? Judaism teaches that maintaining Jewish continuity will bring blessings to one's descendants. But the descendants of identified Jews (anyone with one Jewish grandparent) were the ones who fell into Hitler's trap, the observant along with the secular, the pious along with the *apikores* (apostate). For those left to sort out the implications of the devastation, nothing could possibly justify what was seen as God's brutal and wholesale betrayal of the Jewish people.

This tremendous upset called into question whether the covenant (see chapter on Shavuot)—what was supposed to be an eternal contract between God and Israel—had expired. Without it, there was no sense of order in the universe, no purpose in life, no hope for a better future, no meaning in past or present suffering, no need for Jews or Jewish life. Of course, this was exactly the conclusion desired by the Nazis, who had to eliminate belief in absolute Divine power (which was, according to God's plan, eventually supposed to be universally recognized so that everyone would accept, and benefit by, His standards) and any reference to it in order to wield their own absolute power.

This was also exactly the response of many victims, for whom the covenant had been rendered null and void. They could not believe that God and the Holocaust's degree of evil could coexist. Or they could not recognize a God who would allow such evil to operate. They had no faith that such crimes would never again occur and feeling no hope in life, and expecting no meaning in death, saw no reason to perpetuate Judaism. To spare their descendants the horrors they had endured, they abandoned Judaism, sometimes converting and raising their children as non-Jews.

Fulfilled Prophesies

The ultra-Orthodox asserted that rather than destroying it, the Holocaust actually reaffirmed the covenant. For them the devastation in Europe clearly fit the covenant's projected pattern of Jewish history and was a typical case of God punishing Israel for its sins (see chapter on Tisha B'Av)—in this case, assimilation and Zionism.

Suggesting that more than one million innocent children were brutally sacrificed—either because German Jews wanted to be acceptable to their non-Jewish neighbors, or because European Jews realized that modernity's superficial tolerance of differences between supposedly equal human beings ultimately provided no protection for them—is an abhorrent explanation widely rejected (and another justification for many to deny God a place in their lives).

Despite the discomfort the notion of Divine punishment for sins generates, our tradition does place responsibility for our situations in the world on our shoulders. At the end of his life, when the children of Israel were finally about to cross into the Promised Land, Moses prophetically warned them of what they would bring on themselves if they did not keep the conditions of the covenant: loss of their homeland, degradation, incredible suffering, dispersal to other nations, captivity, disease, idolatry, insecurity, despair, suspense, and terror (Deuteronomy 28:15–68; 32:5). In their distress, they would finally seek God and return to Him, and then they would receive the blessings the covenant promises (Deuteronomy 30:1–5).

As a people, we have experienced other traumatic turning points in our history. They required evaluation and reaffirmation of the Jewish agenda and revolutionary thinking and constructs to allow Judaism and the Jewish people to go forward. After the shocking destruction of the Temple and an entire way of life, the rabbis created new forms of worship, ritual, and structure for the Jewish community. After the Spanish Inquisition, the kabbalists (Jewish mystics) invested existing Jewish practice and new ritual with spiritual and mystical significance and taught that every act could contribute to healing the world.

As Rabbi Irving Greenberg, the popular Orthodox theologian (who has contributed greatly to the examination of Judaism in the shadow of the Holocaust), notes, we were prepared to make and accept such changes because at each stage of our development as a people, we had moved further away from the manifest God—from direct revelation at Sinai to prophetic voice to rabbinic authority—and become more reliant on our own initiation of action. At each stage, God's presence became less obvious, but it was always believed that He was with His people, wherever they were.

The best example of this is the story of Esther, the quintessential account of the Jewish exile in a non-Jewish land. God did not appear and is not mentioned, but it is understood that He acted behind the scenes, able to exert His influence once the Jews themselves had accepted responsibility for their situation and took steps to affect its outcome (see chapter on Purim). As we went out into the world, we were supposed to assume more of the burden of the Israel–God partnership that had been established to improve the world.

Acceptance of our role in countering evil does not necessarily mitigate against the view that the covenant was broken. The fact that He had told us to expect such treatment was no excuse. Whether out of sadism, indifference, shame, sorrow, or the mistaken belief that humans would rise to the potential of our responsibility, God, in letting His people so severely suffer, was seen to have canceled the contract.

Renewing the Contract

In the end, walking away from God and Judaism only leaves a void. What system of belief compares?

(Hermann Broder, the central character of Isaac Bashevis Singer's postwar novel, *Enemies: A Love Story*, finds all sociopolitical alternatives bankrupt.) No model of social justice or rationale for longstanding hope has been devised to supplant the Jewish view of the world and Jewish destiny.

In reply to the Holocaust, the overwhelming response has been to reconnect with Jewish tradition in some way, to rebel against Hitler's attempt to destroy Jewish lives and values by asserting them, to counter his plan to eliminate witness to evil by more forcefully refusing to give up as the world's conscience. Confronted with the power of evil in the world, we have chosen to renew our job to fight against it. The Holocaust proved that our mission is far from finished, and if we do not fulfill it, it is unlikely the world will adopt it. Against unrelenting efforts to destroy us, we Jews have responded by embracing life, giving birth, rebuilding, and providing support for fellow Jews and Jewish causes in unprecedented volume.

At the beginning of Creation, the vessels meant to hold Divine light proved too weak and shattered. So another means of sending spirituality into the world was devised. The first set of tablets of the Ten Commandments, the tangible contract between God and His people, were smashed and had to be replaced.

The post-Holocaust world—a world in which we know the possibilities of evil—demands no less an opportunity for repair. The covenant, along with the Jewish people, tradition, and memory—even if torn up or torn from us—like the dream it represents, was not fully destroyed. Without satisfactorally being able to answer the questions thrust on us by the Holocaust, we have, as Rabbi Greenberg explains, volunteered to pick up the crumpled, sullied agreement, proclaiming our intention to move ahead under its terms, waving it in God's face, challenging Him to meet our commitment by fulfilling His promises. As Rabbi Shlomo Riskin, another popular Orthodox theologian, says, we have suffered the curses, we will continue trying to mend the world, and we expect to enjoy the blessings. In the end, the response of the Jewish people to the Holocaust has been to reaffirm our expectation of fulfillment of the Exodus message, that delivery follows devastation, and to decide to heed the biblical command (Deuteronomy 30:15–19) to "choose life and good" so that the Jews and our descendants will live.

FOR FURTHER READING

Deuteronomy in any *Khumash*, Chapters 28–30; 32:1–43.

The blessings and curses predicted for Israel, because of the nation's choices in following or forsaking God, are given in discourse and in a song taught to the people by Moses as an eternal reminder of the warnings and promises.

Eliach, Yaffa. *Hassidic Tales of the Holocaust*. New York: Oxford University Press, 1982.

The stories, written during and after the Holocaust by *khasidim*, and often recording actual occurrences, demonstrate tremendous faith and the spiritual strength that guarantees ultimate Jewish survival.

Fackenheim, Emil. *To Mend the World: Foundations of Post-Holocaust Jewish Thought*. New York: Schocken Books, 1989.

The religious implications of the Holocaust are considered in a series of essays.

———. *God's Presence in History—Jewish Affirmations and Philosophical Reflections*. New York: New York University Press, 1970.

The third section, "The Commanding Voice of Auschwitz," examines Jewish faith and the role of the Jew after the European devastation.

Greenberg, Rabbi Irving. *The Jewish Way: Living the Holidays*. New York: Summit Books, 1988, pp. 305–372.

The chapter on Yom Hashoah is a rich and rewarding exploration of Judaism's—and more so, the Jewish people's—response to the Holocaust.

Holocaust: Religious and Philosophical Implications. New York: Paragon House, 1989.

An anthology, this book was compiled to make a variety of written works often used by Holocaust scholars more widely accessible. In one place are essays by such leading Holocaust thinkers and writers as Primo Levi, Raul Hilberg, Yehuda Bauer, Elie Wiesel, Emil Fackenheim, Eliezer Berkovits, and Irving Greenberg.

Job, in the Writings (*Ketuvim*) section of the Jewish Bible.

The classic account of suffering, Job deals with the question of why evil exists in the world. The book has been a source of solace for many Holocaust survivors and others who have experienced personal tragedy.

WHAT DOES IT MEAN TO US?— PERSONAL SIGNIFICANCE

Emil Fackenheim, a leading postwar Jewish philosopher, has put forth a six hundred and fourteenth commandment regarding our lives after the Holocaust: It is forbidden to grant Hitler posthumous victories. We are not to give up on God, we are not to relinquish the idea that the world will become the place we historically dreamed it would, we are not to turn our backs on Judaism, Jewish history, or the Jewish people, and we are not to forget the martyrs of the *Shoah*.

His commandment has its critics. But it echoes the essence of the 613 commandments in Torah, which regulate every aspect of our existence: live ("choose life"). Traditionally we have done so by remembering—who we are, where we came from, what we have to contribute, who came before us—and rebuilding our confidence, our culture, our connections to past and future.

We always talk about remembering in conjunction with the Holocaust. Remember the six million. The world must remember so that a holocaust can never again happen. Remember those who perished in order to honor them and give their deaths meaning.

It is memory that has allowed us to last through thousands of years of history. Our religion and our people are founded on the collective memory of revelation at Sinai (see chapter on Shavuot). Scripture throughout commands us to remember: Remember the Sabbath day (Exodus 20:8), observe the Sabbath as a reminder of the Creation (Exodus 20:11) and of the Exodus (Deuteronomy 5:15); remember, continually, the Exodus (see chapter on Pesakh); remember what the evil Amalek did (see chapter on Purim).

All those memories define us and help us keep focused on the goal of our national mission. As the Baal Shem Tov (the founder of the *khasidi* movement) taught, "Forgetfulness leads to exile while remembrance is the secret of redemption," words that appropriately guard your exit from the history museum at *Yad Vashem* in Jerusalem. The wall above the eternal flame in the Hall of Remembrance of the United States Holocaust Memorial Museum in Washington, DC, also invokes memory. "Only guard yourself and guard your soul carefully, lest you forget the things your eyes saw and lest these things depart your heart all the days of your life. And you shall make them known to your children and to your children's children" (Deuteronomy 4:9).

The biblical citation etched into that wall, while an apt admonition in the face of Auschwitz, is out of context. What the original usage enjoins us never to forget is the experience at Mount Sinai and the laws given to us there, the positive context for purposeful living.

What we have to keep in mind in recalling the Holocaust is that memory must function, as it does in the Bible, as a positive force. It should not be used to inflict guilt and exact vengeance and certainly should not be (as unfortunately occurs) the defining element of Jewish life. We cannot raise our children to be healthy, constructive Jews by cowering them with expectations that the anti-Semitic world will force Jewish identification on them. Being Jewish mainly because the Holocaust happened or because anti-Semitism continues is not sufficient reason to hang on to a culture.

The Jews who maintained their heritage for thousands of years did so not because they were surrounded by rabid anti-Semitism. (Until Hitler's demonic program, they always had the option to abandon Judaism for another belief system.) They did so because their way of life had value.

While you are teaching your children about this painful period, remember to teach them that: Don't talk only about the destruction but about what was destroyed: the rich culture, the intellectual accomplishments, the colorful tradition that was Eastern European Jewish life. Our heritage, our unique value system, our contributions to the world are what we must remember along with our troubled history. These are the memories that will prompt us to effectively engage in the revitalization of Jewish life.

The question each of us must ask is "How will I participate in Jewish renewal?" It may be through your children: raising them to be informed, identified Jews. (One suggested response to the tremendous loss of Jewish life is that each family have one more child than it had planned, to replenish the population, and its potential progeny, cut down by Hitler.) Strengthening the community by supporting—with money and volunteer efforts—the institutions devoted to promoting Jewish life (physical, spiritual, emotional, and intellectual) is a widespread response. Helping ensure that Israel continues to grow and progress so there will always be a safe haven for Jews is of utmost importance.

If you are creative, produce art, literature, music, dance, or film on Jewish themes. Whether or not you are creative, read Jewish books, visit Jewish museums, attend Jewish programs, subscribe to Jewish periodicals. And, most of all, learn.

Learning has always been a cornerstone of Jewish continuity and renewal. In biblical days, the Israelites emerged from periods of idolatry, devastation, and exile by returning to Torah—reading it, trying to understand and live by it. From the ashes of the respected European *yeshivot* destroyed in the 1940s have arisen new Jewish academies and other educational programs in Israel and in America (many of them supported by funds from Jews who are not themselves particularly tradition minded or Jewishly well educated!). Day school, supplemental, family, and adult educational programs are continually being expanded. Make sure your children have access to formal Jewish education (don't overlook a good Jewish youth group or summer camp), and take advantage of learning opportunities yourself (don't overlook the possibility of organizing or attending a study group in someone's home).

All of these acts, while honoring the memory of the generations that preceded us, will create positive new memories and strong new Jewish realities for the generations that follow.

FOR FURTHER READING

The memoirs by Bella Chagall, autobiographical stories of Sholom Aleichem and accounts of Israel Zangwill paint vivid word pictures of Eastern European Jewish life. They can be useful for family learning and discussion, especially when supported by photographic essays (see below).

Dobroszycki, Lucjan, and Barbara Kershenblatt-Gimblett. *Image Before My Eyes: A Photographic History of Jewish Life in Poland, 1864–1939*. New York: Schocken Books, 1977.

The three hundred photos that provide a pictorial account of all aspects of Jewish life in Poland, one of the largest communities prior to World War II, are supplemented by explanatory commentary.

Salamander, Rachel. *The Jewish World of Yesterday*. New York: Rizzoli, 1991.

Chapters on religious practice, political activism, and family life and archival photographs cover life in the Jewish ghettos and major cities in Central and Eastern Europe between 1860 and World War II. The text of this coffee-table glimpse of what was lost is enhanced by selections by Einstein, Freud, Kafka, and Singer.

Vishniac, Roman. *A Vanished World*. Farrar, Straus & Giroux, 1983.

This incredible collection of photographs, a small sampling of the sixteen thousand taken by the photographer with a hidden camera between 1934 and 1939, records the life of Eastern European Jewry as it was being decimated.

TRADITIONS: HOW WE CELEBRATE YOM HASHOAH

WHAT DO WE USE?—RITUAL ITEMS

Due to the nature of this commemoration and the fact that observance is still in formation, there are no needed ritual items per se; however, two practices gaining adherence make use of easily accessible symbols.

Memorial Candles

Usually lit on the anniversary of death for parents (and by some people for grandparents), and on the evening prior to the *Yizkor* memorial service held on the last day of pilgrimage festivals and on Yom Kippur, these candles last a full day. The regular white ones are readily available in Jewish supply stores and supermarkets that have kosher sections. Yellow ones, produced especially for Yom Hashoah, can be ordered (see below). If you are going to light the candles, you will need six of them.

FOR FURTHER EXPLORATION

Yellow memorial candles are distributed by the Federation of Jewish Men's Clubs every year in time for Yom Hashoah. They must be purchased by the case (forty-eight candles), but small boxes and bags are available so you can divide and distribute the forty-eight candles among extended family members, friends, or members of congregations or organizations. To receive an order form, contact the Federation between December and January, in time to be added to their mailing list (475 Riverside Drive, Suite 244, New York, NY 10115, 212-749-8100).

Yellow Tulips

Flowers symbolize the rebirth that comes in spring, and for Yom Hashoah represent the renewal of the Jewish people. The color of choice comes from the yellow six-pointed ("Jewish") stars the Nazis forced the Jews to wear on their clothing. The tulip is specified because in addition to being a spring bloom likely to mature in time for Yom Hashoah, it is the national flower of Holland, one of the few countries (along with Denmark, Sweden, and Bulgaria) that refused to turn its Jews over to the Nazis and actively tried to ensure their safety.

You can purchase the flowers from a florist or plant bulbs in the fall so they will blossom in time for the occasion. Six are sometimes displayed (as are the candles), one for each million Jews murdered by the Nazis.

HOW DO WE SHOW WE CELEBRATE?— OBSERVANCE

Until the Holocaust, the "newest" important commemoration on the Jewish calendar was Tisha B'Av, and that is almost two thousand years old. Even the minor holiday Tu B'Shevat, as a festive day, has half a millennium of observance behind it. Many of the rituals and customs we follow in celebrating our holidays evolved over time, developing and taking hold not just because they may have been commanded but because they represented something meaningful. It may be generations before the commemoration of Yom Hashoah takes its "final" shape. In the meantime, certain formats are emerging for public and private ceremonies, and practices drawn from Judaism's existing trove of mourning, remembrance, and affirmation rituals are being tentatively applied for the day.

In the United States, Yom Hashoah is often observed on the Sunday closest to *Nissan* 27, though commemorations may be scheduled on the weekday evening of the day, or close to April 19. While they generally take place in a communal setting, there is growing encouragement of home recognition of the day as well.

In the Synagogue

Many congregations create their own services, built around Psalms (traditionally recited in memory of the dead); selections from Lamentations, the sacred book read on Tisha B'Av; and literature written by victims of the Holocaust. (*Gates of Prayer*, the Reform movement's daily and festival prayer book, includes selections to be read on the occasion). The Mourn-

ers' *Kaddish* and *Eil Molei Rakhamim* (Exalted, Compassionate God), part of the traditional service for mourning the dead and the prayer recited at graveside, are frequently used. These services often add remembrances of the Righteous Gentiles (*khasidei umot ha'olam*), those non-Jews who risked their own lives to protect Jews during the Nazis' reign of terror.

It is also common to incorporate periods of silence (which has been repeatedly suggested as the most appropriate response, an opportunity to meditate on the troubling questions raised by the Holocaust). Some congregations sit in darkness. Lighting candles is becoming more and more prevalent to recall the dead and introduce light and all it signifies: obscuring the kind of ignorance that makes genocide possible, life, Torah learning, God's spirit. Typically, six memorial candles are lit to represent the six million martyrs. In some places, a seventh candle honors the non-Jewish victims or the Righteous Gentiles.

Other services consist of the liturgical drama *Night Words: A Midrash on the Holocaust* by David Roskies. Created in 1971, it works as a *seder* for Yom Hashoah evening. It is a powerful script that congregants themselves read, in parts assigned to them as they arrive, remove their shoes, and situate themselves on the floor in the posture of mourners. Elie Wiesel and Albert Friedlander have created a scroll modeled after the five biblical *megillot* (Song of Songs, Ruth, Lamentations, Ecclesiastes, and Esther), each of which is assigned for reading on a specific holiday.

FOR FURTHER READING

A Holocaust Commemoration for Days of Remembrance—for Communities, Synagogues, Centers and for Home Use. Ed. by Rabbi Irving Greenberg and David Roskies. Washington, DC: Holocaust Remembrance Foundation, 1982.

Two alternate orders of service are based on personal accounts of the Holocaust, each fifteen to twenty minutes long, and are meant to be used in conjunction with a speaker, film, or other presentation.

Roskies, David. *Night Words: A Midrash on the Holocaust.* Washington, DC: B'nai B'rith Hillel Foundation, 1971.

Weaving modern Yiddish, Hebrew, and English poetry with biblical excerpts, philosophical passages, Holocaust accounts, traditional prayer, and raw facts, the service's thirty-six roles represent the three dozen righteous individuals said to exist at any moment and on whose merit the world continues.

Wiesel, Elie, and Albert H. Friedlander. *The Six Days of Destruction—Meditations Toward Hope.* New York: Paulist Press, 1988.

This new "scroll" uses the Genesis story of Creation, with an account focused on an individual for each day, to give a history of the Holocaust. A service for Jewish communities and one for interreligious groups follow.

Public Events

A ceremony attended by the President of the United States, members of Congress, and other government officials is held in Washington, DC, annually. Remarks by dignitaries, lighting of memorial candles, prayers for the dead, U.S. Army Band renditions of *"Ani Ma'amin,"* the "Partisans' Hymn," and other relevant songs are usually included. Since 1986, the Eisenhower Liberation Medal has been awarded to a member of the United States Armed Forces (or his/her survivor) who was involved in the liberation of the camps.

In communities throughout the country, programs take a variety of forms: Survivors speaking about their harrowing experiences; discussions with the children of survivors; accounts of the war; readings of diaries, memoirs, memorial books, and literature of the Holocaust; performances incorporating first-hand accounts, history, and music. Singing the "Partisans' Hymn" (during which survivors traditionally stand) and *"Ani Ma'amin"* is often included at these public assemblies. The programs are usually well publicized in local Jewish and secular newspapers in the weeks before Yom Hashoah.

In some locations, especially college campuses, night or twenty-four-hour vigils are held. They may start with a film or lecture on the richness of the world that was destroyed. Presentations on life in the ghettos and camps, examples of the culture of those environments, discussions with survivors, and often a memorial prayer or service may follow. Vigils may feature the continual reading aloud of names of victims, sometimes over the background recitation of psalms.

In New York, the annual Warsaw Ghetto Uprising Memorial takes place on April 19 or the nearest Sunday. It features speeches by survivors and public figures and ceremonies similar to those for Yom Hashoah.

For Further Reading

A Memorial of Names. College Park, MD: B'nai B'rith Hillel Foundation Jewish Student Center, 1979.

The list of names in this book, used for Hillel's vigil, is so long that two people reading simulta-neously for twenty-four hours complete only a fraction of them. (Available from Hillel, P.O. Box 187, College Park, MD 20740, 301-422-6200, for the cost of printing [$10 in 1993].)

In Israel

Yom Hashoah in the Jewish homeland is a national memorial day. On the eve of the commemoration, when a special ceremony takes place at *Yad Vashem*, all theaters and places of amusement are closed. During the day, banks, schools, and most businesses are not open. At 11:00 A.M., a siren blast brings the entire country to a halt. Media broadcasts are interrupted, cars come to a standstill, and drivers get out of them to stand at attention for two minutes of silence. Throughout the day and all around the country, numerous memorial observances take place.

In the Home

There is no "official" private ritual—any more than there is an "official" synagogue or community ritual—for Yom Hashoah. However, as Jews throughout the world continue to grapple with the meaning and implications of the Holocaust, and try to find the most appropriate means of remembering it and properly honoring its victims, some are introducing family commemorations. There is a particular need for them because most public ceremonies are for adults only, and as with all Jewish holidays, it is imperative that we teach our children the significance of this one. This means that as for other holidays, we need to introduce particular activities, rituals, and music.

In time, there may be a *haggadah* for Yom Hashoah. At present, the two most prevalent means of observing the occasion in the home are lighting six *yahrtzite* (memorial) candles (yellow, if possible) and displaying yellow tulips.

An attempt was made early on to create a special *menorah* for Yom Hashoah, which may yet be realized (in ceremonies at which a seventh candle is lit, a *menorah* is sometimes used). Until then, a line, circle, or star of individual memorial candles can be arranged on a table or windowsill. Some people place six tulips on the table with the candles or in their windows to be seen by those outside. Others plant them, so they will bloom in front of their homes in time for *Nissan* 27. (It has been suggested that yellow tulips should adorn the outside of every synagogue and Jewish institution.)

Having your children help with the planting and tending of the flowers is one way to involve them with a commemoration that is inherently difficult to present to young people. A ceremony of arranging the flowers and lighting the candles is followed in many homes by the singing of "Ani Ma'amin," an affirmation of faith in the future.

Considering the suffering endured by millions of people, it has been suggested that any meals eaten on Yom Hashoah be sparse and simple, with no sweets or embellishments. Many advocate a fast. In conjunction with abstention from normal entertainments (music, television), dinnertime and the rest of the evening could be devoted to discussions (stimulated by a book the family has read or a movie the family has watched), reading selections of Holocaust literature, or looking at books of poems and drawings by children who died in the camps. Talking about family members who suffered and/or died in the Holocaust and applying conditions and lessons of the Holocaust to current situations in the world are also appropriate.

Children should be encouraged to share what they have learned in school (the Holocaust is taught in Jewish schools and, at least in states in which Holocaust education is mandatory, public schools), including any songs of the Holocaust. Their questions should be welcomed.

Tzedakah

The significance of *tzedakah* in Judaism comes home in a story told about the Italian Jewish community. Even in the closing days of World War II, when the Nazis were losing and knew it, they would not divert attention or resources from killing as many Jews as possible. The only exception was when they could ransom their victims in order to build the private coffers they would need to protect themselves from the Allies.

The Nazis bargained that they would not deport the Jews remaining in Rome if they handed over fifty bullion of gold. After years of war and deprivation, the community could only come up with twenty-five bullion. They appealed to the Vatican, not to give them the difference, but to only lend it to them. The Vatican refused. For lack of money to buy their lives, the Jews were marched to their deaths.

Twenty-eight years later, the Roman Jews who had rebuilt the community were praying in synagogue when they learned that the Yom Kippur War had begun. They stopped their service, closed the doors, and voted to immediately send the equivalent of fifty bullion of gold to Israel.

Saving Jewish lives, and Jewish life, is what *tzedakah* is all about. As a contribution to bringing justice to the world by righting imbalances, each gift is an expression of belief that life on Earth can be better, that the world *can* be perfected. The Jews made this assertion after the war, raising an unprecedented amount of money to help the displaced and to support efforts for the establishment of a Jewish homeland. (The best-known Jewish American umbrella fundraising effort, United Jewish Appeal, resulted from the American Jewish community's response to the outbreak of hostility against the German and Austrian Jews on *Kristallnakht*.)

Traditionally, Jews also make contributions to charitable causes in memory of the deceased. On this occasion of remembering the vast number of people who were murdered, it is entirely appropriate to donate money either to those institutions dedicated to honoring Holocaust victims (such as *Yad Vashem* in Jerusalem, the U.S. Holocaust Memorial Museum in Washington, DC, the Simon Wiesenthal Center in Los Angeles, or a Holocaust museum, memorial, or center in your vicinity) or to those Jewish schools, synagogues, institutions, and organizations devoted to Jewish survival and continuity. A gift in a multiple of *khai* (Hebrew for life, with a value of eighteen: ח, *khet*, eight; י, *yud*, ten), always significant in Judaism, has particular symbolic strength.

WHERE DO WE BEGIN?—PREPARATION

If you want to have tulips bloom in front of your home in time for Yom Hashoah, you will need to plant them in the fall.

Otherwise, you may want to order the flowers from a florist. Yellow memorial candles must be ordered several months in advance. You may want to arrange for your synagogue or organization to buy them.

To be ready to have a more extensive commemoration at home, during the week or two prior to Holocaust Remembrance Day, you will want to choose books or a movie to review with your family, or jot down questions to initiate discussion on the subject of the Holocaust, anti-Semitism, hatred, heroism, humanity, the richness of European Jewish life before the war, and so on. If you have photographs, letters, and memorabilia of family members who were victims of or affected by the Holocaust, don't forget to locate and organize them for display or use.

WHAT ARE WE SUPPOSED TO DO?— *HALAKHAH*

Neither a biblically nor rabbinically ordained holiday, Yom Hashoah has no religious sanction, and therefore there is no *halakhah* connected with it. However, most authorities would agree that, consistent with our history and religious tradition, it is a *mitzvah* to remember. Just as every Jew in every generation recalls the slavery of Egypt and the salvation of Exodus, every Jew—survivor, child of survivor, generations that come many years after those who experienced the devastation—must remember what we, and the rest of the world, experienced.

The purpose of the memory should not be to exact revenge on the children of the perpetrators or, as is usually claimed, so that it will not happen again. (Genocide has happened again and is happening again. It is questionable whether our memory, our chastisements of the world can change what seems to be inevitable human nature.) We remember in order to honor the dead and give some meaning to their lives. And we remember, too, as a warning to ourselves, of the limits of assimilation, the dangers of complacency, the conquering will to live, and our ongoing role in the world.

In time, as our commemorations become more established, certain practices (like fasts from food or speaking—*tzom shtikah*, a medieval kabbalistic practice) and rituals may take on the force of *halakhah* when they are adapted by the majority of the community and practiced as custom over a long period of time. (It is said that a practice accepted and adopted by a majority of the community can be just as important, and binding, as a commandment of God: "*minhag Yisrael Torah hi.*")

WHAT OTHER THINGS DO PEOPLE DO?— CUSTOMS

Dress

This is another area in which there are no set guidelines, although over time, some of the practices initiated by select families or groups could become accepted practice. In some congregations, it is customary for people to adopt the mourning custom of not wearing leather shoes, either donning cloth or rubber foot covering or removing their shoes outside the sanctuary. Although it may seem offensive to some people, participants at some commemorations, or throughout the day of Yom Hashoah, wear yellow armbands or yellow stars that have been sewn onto their coats or jackets. Shoddy clothing, clothing torn as a symbol of mourning, or a black ribbon that has been torn, for the same reason, have all been suggested as appropriate.

WHAT IS THERE TO EAT?— TRADITIONAL FOODS

Home observance of Yom Hashoah is not widespread enough for there to be customary practices regarding meals on this day. The majority of people probably do nothing out of the ordinary at all. However, those who want to create a meaningful impact in their families often model dinner on a typical camp meal—stale, almost rotten bread, potato peels, extremely diluted soup. The contrast of such a meal with what one normally eats could actually be more significant than a fast.

DO YOU HEAR MUSIC?—SONGS TO SING

Music, which we so often use to express joy and exultation, is an effective reflection of the whole range of human emotion. In the ghettos and concentration and death camps, it mirrored the situation around the condemned Jews—sadness and grief—but also their inner strengths: defiance and hope. As Shoshana Kalisch, a survivor of Auschwitz and compiler of a sampling of the songs of her environment, points out, singing in the face of Nazi atrocities was a unique form of resistance, a means of helping the victims retain their belief that life did have meaning, and encouraging others whose spirits flagged.

Two songs emerged as anthems of the victims of the *Shoah*. "*Ani Ma'amin*" (I Believe) portrays the Jews' unshakable allegiance to their tradition. Even as they were marched into the gas chambers, they sang the affirmation based on the Thirteen Articles of Faith by Maimonides (the twelfth-century Jewish philosopher and scholar): "I believe with a perfect faith in the coming of the messiah. I believe, and although he may tarry, in spite of it all I believe." Though their own salvation was lost, they had no doubts as to the outcome for their people.

"*Zog Nit Keyn Mol*" (Never Say [you're going your last way]; also known as Partisans' Hymn) had immediate impact. When twenty-year-old Hirsch Glick, a poet and partisan living in the Vilna ghetto, heard the news of the Warsaw ghetto uprising, he immediately wrote words to a well-known Russian melody by Soviet composer Dimitri Porkass. The song spread throughout the ghetto, to others, and to the camps. A testament to the Jews' defiance and their undying faith, it became the hymn of the Jewish resistance fighters and internationally recognized as a song of courage.

FOR FURTHER READING

Kalisch, Shoshana, with Barbara Meister. *Yes, We Sang! Songs of the Ghettos and Concentration Camps.* New York: Harper & Row Publishers, 1985.

Compiled by a survivor of Auschwitz who lost most of her family, the collection of twenty-five songs (with piano accompaniment, transliterated Yiddish and English translation) expresses the strength and grief of the Jews' lives. Each song is enhanced by introductory narrative about the circumstances of its origins and the lives of its composers or performers, often entwined with the author's experiences.

WHAT TALES ARE TOLD?— STORIES TO READ

Thousands and thousands of volumes of nonfiction and fiction have been written on the Holocaust. There are vast amounts of material available for every age group, and more is produced each year. Poets, novelists, historians, theologians, philosophers, and ordinary people who lived through extraordinary circumstances have examined and/or reported on the Holocaust from a myriad of angles.

Names like Anne Frank, Elie Wiesel, and Primo Levi are immediately recognized, and their books are well worth reading. But there are scores of others. A number of good resources can guide you to the memoirs (of children and adults), community memorial books, diaries, biographies, novels, histories, photo essays, collections of artwork, and analyses most appropriate for the ages of your children and most interesting for you.

FOR FURTHER READING

Bibliographies

Cargas, Harry James. *The Holocaust: An Annotated Bibliography.* Chicago: American Library Association, 1985.

Roughly five hundred titles recommended for institutional collections (and therefore those most beneficial for the public) are arranged by category, with separate sections for fiction, drama, poetry, art, literary criticism, and collections. The annotations go a long way to giving a real feel for each entry.

Szonyi, David M. *The Holocaust: An Annotated Bibliography and Resource Guide.* New York: Ktav Publishing House, for the National Jewish Resource Center, 1985.

Scholarship, memoirs, and other nonfiction by category, selected literature for young people, audiovisual material, music resources, traveling exhibits and resource kits, education and commemorative centers and research institutes and archives in the United States and Canada, an introduction to high school Holocaust curricula, survivor and children of survivor groups, and Yom Hashoah services are all listed. While the annotations are quite sparse, this is a useful guide, particularly for the subject areas not covered in other bibliographies.

The Selected Children's Judaica Collection. (see "Stories to Read" in "Dear Reader").

The listing of selectively chosen and age-evaluated books for children 7–14 and up is introduced by guidelines on telling our children about the Holocaust. (The Jewish Book Council, which publishes this booklet, also produces a newsletter-size Holocaust annotated bibliography, primarily for adult readers, covering ten different subject areas.)

For Adults: Fiction

Hersey, John. *The Wall.* New York: Alfred A. Knopf, 1950.

This classic fictionalized account of the events leading up to the destruction of the Warsaw ghetto is based on the experiences of Emmanuel Ringelblum, one of the most noted historians of the Holocaust period and a resident of the ghetto. (Ringelblum's day-by-day record of his life during this period was published as *Notes from the Warsaw Ghetto* [New York: Schocken, 1974].)

Yevtushenko, Yevgeny. *Selected Poems.* Trans. by Robin Milner-Gillard and Peter Levi. Baltimore: Penguin Books, 1974.

The collection contains the most famous poem written about the most famous *Einsatzgruppen* (shooting squad) massacre of 33,000 Jews during Rosh Hashanah 1941, named for the city of the slaughter, "Babi Yar."

For Adults: Nonfiction

Anthology of Holocaust Literature. Ed. by Jacob Glatstein et al. New York: Atheneum, 1977.

The sixty-five selections were all written by victims and eyewitnesses.

Frank, Anne. *The Diary of Anne Frank: The Critical Edition.* Ed. by David Barnouw and Gerrold van der Stroom. New York: Doubleday & Company, 1989.

In addition to the original diary that Anne Frank herself edited and rewrote is this version edited by her father. This volume also includes a comparison of the father's version with the first published Dutch edition, with notes about omitted details. The diary is supplemented with information about the Frank family's life before and during the war, their betrayal, Mr. Frank's life after the war, and a report on the diary's authenticity. (In 1987, Miep Gies, who helped hide the family, published her memoirs about the war years in *Anne Frank Remembered* [New York: Simon and Schuster, 1987].)

Spiegelman, Art. *Maus: A Survivor's Tale.* New York: Pantheon Books, 1991.

In this highly acclaimed two-volume work, the cartoonist son of a survivor tells of his father's Holocaust experiences and his own coming to terms with his father and his father's life, in the form of a comic strip, with the Jews portrayed as mice and the Germans as cats. It is incredibly honest and moving.

Wiesel, Elie. *Night.* New York: Hill & Wang, 1960; Avon, 1969.

A memoir—one of the first written by a survivor about his life during the Holocaust and one of the best ever written—the book is based on Wiesel's experiences at Auschwitz and is appropriate reading for anyone over the age of thirteen. (Wiesel's novels and reminiscences *Accident, Dawn, Gates of the Forest, Legends of Our Time, One Generation After,* and *The Town Beyond the Wall,* and his play *Zalman, or the Madness of God,* all deal with Holocaust themes.)

For Young Adults

Frank, Anne. *The Diary of a Young Girl.* New York: Pocket Books, 1965.

The classic account was written by a teenage Dutch girl who hid in a secret attic in Amsterdam with her parents, sister, and four other people until they were betrayed to the Nazis. Ages 14 and up.

————. *Tales from the Secret Annex.* New York: Doubleday, 1984.

Written separately from her famous diary, these short fictions, essays, fables, and vignettes about her life are well done and sensitive. Ages 12–14.

Friedlander, Albert H. *Out of the Whirlwind: A Reader of Holocaust Literature.* New York: Schocken Books, 1976.

This valuable volume combines excerpts from diverse literary works, novels, memoirs, and diaries, including some of the best known; scholarly works

by well-known thinkers of the post-Holocaust era; and a section devoted to questions raised in the aftermath of the devastation. Ages 14 and up.

Roseman, Kenneth. *Escape from the Holocaust.* New York: UAHC Press, 1985.

Presenting several options for each of various situations set during the Holocaust, the interactive book allows readers to determine what they would do and see the ramifications of their decisions. It is surprisingly and perhaps too benign, presenting myriad opportunities for escape, which were not available to the majority of Holocaust victims. While giving teens the chance to take action, and valuable in helping them confront history and Jewish values, the book's approach to the Holocaust is superficial and simplistic and needs to be supplemented. Ages 12–15.

Schur, Maxine. *Hannah Szenes—A Song of Light.* Philadelphia: The Jewish Publication Society of America, 1985.

A victim of the Nazis in Hungary, Hannah, a Zionist and poet, fled to Palestine but returned to her native land in 1943 as part of a resistance operation to try to save other Jews—and sacrificed her life, at age twenty-three, as a result. This acclaimed biography, interspersed with her poems, is one of the many inspiring stories about heroes of the Holocaust. Ages 8–12.

For Children

Adler, David A. *The Number on My Grandfather's Arm.* New York: UAHC Press, 1987.

A young girl learns about the Holocaust when she notices her grandfather's odd tattoo. This is a sensitive introduction of the subject for young readers. Ages 6–8.

Ginsburg, Marvell. *The Tattooed Torah.* New York: UAHC Press, 1983.

Based on the true story of the discovery and restoration of the Brno (Slovakia) Torah, the book describes the dark days of World War II and the rebirth of Judaism in the children of the congregation that became the Torah's new home. Ages 6–10.

I Never Saw Another Butterfly: Children's Drawings and Poems from Terezin Concentration Camp 1942–1944. Ed. by Hana Volakova. New York: Schocken Books, 1978.

The way station to Auschwitz, Terezin (or Theresienstadt) was the model camp shown to foreigners—but of 15,000 children encamped there, only one hundred survived the war. Named for one of the poems, this famous anthology's contents express the misery, courage, and optimism experienced by the young victims in the last years of their lives. Ages 10 and up.

Klein, Gerda Weissman. *Promise of a New Spring.* Chappaqua, NY: Rossel Books, 1981.

Starting with a simple and brief history of the rise of the Nazis and the concentration camps, this picture book uses the metaphor of a forest that must put down new roots and regenerate itself after its natural order has been destroyed by fire to explain the Holocaust and the response of survivors. Ages 6–10.

Wild, Margaret, and Julie Vivas. *Let the Celebrations Begin!* New York: Orchard Books, 1991.

When they know their camp is about to be liberated, the women scurry to create toys out of scraps of cloth for a party they plan to give the children. Based on a recollection, it is an upbeat story for young people but may bring tears to the eyes of adults reading it to them. Ages 5–8.

OF ADDITIONAL INTEREST

Films

As with written works, there is no dearth of movies dealing with the Holocaust as a broad subject, and as it affected families and individuals, in documentaries, fiction, and dramatized versions of true stories. Many of the commercial films are available for rental from video shops. Public and Jewish libraries, Jewish resource centers, and Holocaust centers often have some of the titles in their collections.

In the context of entertainment, the 1972 blockbuster *Cabaret* chillingly portrays life in Berlin in the early years of the Nazi regime, which is traced in the 1961 documentary *The Life of Adolf Hitler. Night and Fog* (1955), the brilliant but graphic film still among the best of its kind, by the noted French director Alain Resnais, depicts concentration camp life. *Shoah*, Claude Lanzmann's two-part, nine-and-a-half-hour epic based on years of research, tracking survivors and interviewing people who lived within sight and smell of camps, was greeted as a landmark achievement when released in 1985. (A transcript of the French film's English subtitles is available as *Shoah: An Oral History of the Holocaust* [New York: Pantheon Books, 1985].)

There are a number of wonderful theatrical run movies about the fate of individuals and families, some fictional (many adapted from novels), some

based on true stories: *Shop on Main Street* (1965), *Garden of the Finzi-Contini* (1971), *The Sorrow and the Pity* (1972), *Lacombe, Lucien* (1973), *Les Violins du Bal* (1974), *Voyage of the Damned* (1976), *Julia* (1977), *Au Revoir Les Enfants* (1987), *Triumph of the Spirit* (1989; possibly one of the best evocations of personal life in a concentration camp), *Europa, Europa* (1992), and the brilliant *Schindler's List* (1993), as well as the filmed version of *The Diary of Anne Frank* (1959).

Both *Judgment at Nuremberg* (1961) and *Man in the Glass Booth* (1975) are effective Hollywood versions of Nazi war crimes trials (the first is based on the actual proceedings against eleven Nazi officials, the second a fictional account of the Eichmann trial). *The House on Garibaldi Street* (1979) dramatically portrays the capture of Eichmann in Argentina.

Enemies: A Love Story (1989) is from Isaac Bashevis Singer's novel about difficult love among survivors. *The Nasty Girl* (1990), based on a recent occurrence, shows the lengths people are still willing to go to keep their wartime collaboration hidden, while *Le Chambon: Weapons of the Spirit* (1988), tells the inspiring story of the small Protestant village in south-central France that protected five thousand Jews.

Music

A number of books to have come out of the Holocaust, as well as traditional text dealing with the subject of faith, have been used as the basis for musical creations. Several cantatas and a one-act opera are based on *The Diary of Anne Frank*. Samuel Adler composed a musico-drama (with libretto by Albert Friedlander) borrowing the theme of the near-sacrifice by Abraham of his son Isaac (see chapter on Rosh Hashanah): *The Binding: Modern Akeida*. In Elie Wiesel's cantata *Ani Ma'amin*, with music by Darius Milhaud, the patriarchs are asked to intervene to save the children of the Holocaust. A number of adaptations, including a choreography, have been made of *I Never Saw Another Butterfly*. Dmitri Shostakovitch set Yevgeny Yevtushenko's "Babi Yar" to music in his *13th Symphony* for orchestra, voice, and choir, and Arnold Schoenberg incorporated the *Shema* into his *Survivor from Warsaw* for male speaker, chorus, and orchestra.

Museums and Resource Centers

There are more than one hundred Holocaust museums, memorials, and resource centers throughout the United States. The most well known are the *Beit Hashoah*/Museum of Tolerance of the Simon Wiesenthal Center in Los Angeles and the much heralded

United States Holocaust Memorial Museum in Washington, DC, which opened on the Mall in the heart of the capital in April 1993. Many others have useful resources, including exhibits and educational materials, to help us remember what happened and to teach our children. A listing is included in Szonyi's Holocaust bibliography and one can be obtained from the United States Holocaust Memorial Museum.

In Israel, in addition to *Yad Vashem*, a must on the itinerary of every visitor to the state and mandatory for official state visits, there is another museum devoted to Holocaust memory: *Beit Lohamei Hagettaot* (The Ghetto Fighters' Museum), at the *kibbutz* of the same name founded by the surviving partisans (north of the city of Acre).

The sites of several of the concentration camps—where there are memorials, museums, and in some cases actual camp structures—can be visited: in Poland, Auschwitz, Chelmo, Majdenek, and Treblinka; in Germany, Bergen-Belsen, Buchenwald, and Dachau; in Austria, Maulthausen; in the Czechoslovak Republic, Theresienstadt; and in the Netherlands, Westerbork.

Educational Materials

Each year the U.S. Holocaust Memorial Museum produces a number of pieces useful in teaching about the Holocaust. While the majority are designed for classroom use, and preference in filling requests for them is given to teachers, they are available to anyone as long as supplies last. There may be a charge for certain items. (Write to the museum's Education Department, 100 Rauol Wallenberg Place SW, Washington, DC 20024-2150, or call 212-488-0400.)

Among the resources available are a list of Holocaust resource centers in the United States, a selective annotated bibliography, a selected annotated videography, guidelines for teaching the subject in a sensitive and productive manner, primarily directed for use with groups, and the *Days of Remembrance* planning guide, published each year and containing primary source material, suggested formats and checklists for Yom Hashoah events, the program from the previous year's national commemoration, bibliographies, and resource directories. Coordinated lesson plans for high school students and adults may also be requested.

YOM HA'ATZMAUT

Yom Ha'atzmaut (yome hahtz'mah oot'): Israel Independence Day. Observed on *Iyar* 5 (spring; late April–early May).

The first holiday added to our calendar in close to two thousand years, Yom Ha'atzmaut marks the return to our homeland promised by scripture. A day of thanksgiving and joy, it is celebrated with a festival religious service and secular frivolity.

ORIGINS: WHY WE CELEBRATE YOM HA'ATZMAUT

WHERE DID IT ALL BEGIN?— HISTORIC FOUNDATION

At 4 P.M. on the fifth of *Iyar* 5708 (1948), the fiery Zionist leader David Ben-Gurion, surrounded by members of the Provisional Council of State on the bunkerlike ground floor of the Tel Aviv Art Museum, issued a proclamation to the world: "We, members of the people's council, representatives of the Jewish community of *Eretz Yisrael* and of the Zionist movement . . . by virtue of our natural and historic right and on the strength of the resolution of the United Nations General Assembly hereby declare the establishment of a Jewish state in *Eretz Yisrael*, to be known as the State of Israel" (Declaration of Independence of the State of Israel).

With that announcement, the two thousand years of waiting to be restored to our homeland—two thousand years of longing, wandering, and suffering—ended.

The Zionist Dream

From the moment God instructed Abraham to leave his father's home and go to the Land He would show him (Genesis 12:1), *Eretz Yisrael* became the focal point in Jewish life. It was part of an inseparable triumvirate with the Jewish people and Jewish God, its character a reflection of our people's soul, its condi-

tion a reflection of our behavior. Torah, Prophets, and Writings continually talk about the Land and our relationship to it—either the destination, the home, the place from which we were exiled, or the place to which we would return.

The sages considered the commandment to inhabit the Land of Israel equal in importance to all the precepts of Torah combined. Since the Land was given to us by God, our connection to it is sacred. Maimonides instructed that we are supposed to live there even if it means leaving a more comfortable abode elsewhere, and the thirteenth-century sage Nakhmanides said that we are to fight to get it out of foreign dominion and not allow it to become desolate. Having this involvement with the Land was seen as being such an essential part of a complete Jewish life that a spouse whose partner refused to accompany him or her to *Eretz Yisrael* was granted a divorce.

The yearning for it expressed after the first (Babylonian) expulsion became the theme psalm after the seemingly "permanent" second (Roman) one: "If I forget thee, O Jerusalem, Let my right hand forget her cunning. Let my tongue cleave to the roof of my mouth, if I remember thee not; If I set not Jerusalem above my chiefest joy" (Psalms 137:5–6).

No celebration was completely happy (a glass broken at a wedding was a reminder of the Temple's destruction), no persecution completely hopeless ("Next year in Jerusalem" proclaimed at Pesakh and Yom Kippur was a wish and expectation). Facing Jerusalem during prayer and conjuring return in the three daily services by asking God to rebuild Jerusalem speedily in our days kept the pain of the loss fresh, the desire for restoration strong. Many Jews obtained vials of Palestine soil, which was sprinkled into their coffins when they died so that they could, in a sense, return to the Holy Land.

Pious Jews did travel to Palestine, particularly toward the end of their lives, and money collected in the Diaspora helped support the small impoverished remnant that lived there throughout the exile. Yet despite the intense emotion and faith surrounding the reestablishment of Jewish government and life in Zion (a traditional synonym for Israel and Jerusalem), the Jewish people did not act to make it happen. The lesson they had derived from the disastrous Bar Kokhba revolt (see chapter on Lag B'Omer) was that they should not take matters into their own hands but wait for Divine deliverance. That attitude lasted until the late nineteenth century.

The anti-Jewish laws of 1881 and resulting pogroms in Russia, and the Dreyfus Affair of 1894 in France (in which a French Army captain was unjustly accused of treason just because he was Jewish), finally convinced many Jews that the end to anti-Semitic persecution, and acceptance into their respective national societies that they had hoped would result from the Enlightenment (with its "Rights of Man," religious tolerance, and opportunities for secular education), would never come to be.

One of those Jews was Theodor Herzl, a Viennese playwright, novelist, and journalist who had previously advocated that the Jews convert *en masse* in order to avert anti-Semitism. Hearing the mobs cry for the death of his people at Dreyfus' degradation ceremony (which he covered along with the treason trial for Vienna's *Neue Freie Presse*) convinced him otherwise. Herzl realized that as long as a wrong was committed by, or merely attributed to, any Jew, all Jews were suspect. The only solution was not assimilation but nationalism: the Jews had to have a land of their own.

The essay he penned in response to what he witnessed in France, *Der Judenstaadt* (The Jewish State), promoted the idea of establishing a Jewish homeland in what had been the Jews' historic Middle Eastern home. Though others (Moses Hess in *Rome and Jerusalem* and Leo Pinsker in *Auto-Emancipation*) had suggested the notion before him, Herzl was the first to establish a political movement based on it and a course of action to accomplish it.

When his meetings with wealthy influential Jews and heads of state (first of Turkey, which ruled Palestine at the time, then of Germany and England in the hope they could influence the sultan) failed to bring results, he gathered Jewish leaders from throughout the world at the First Zionist Congress in Basel, Switzerland, in 1897. Coalescing support with the rallying call "If you will it, it is not legend," Herzl called subsequent congresses that attracted increasing numbers of delegates. From them came the World Zionist Organization (an umbrella structure focused on the establishment of a Jewish home) and the Jewish National Fund (which raised money to purchase land in Palestine so Jews could settle there).

Resettlement of the Land

Although not free of Turkish harassment, the Jews were permitted by the Sultan to live in Palestine and found their villages, farms, and institutions. Between 1882 and 1903, twenty-five thousand pioneers (*khalutzim*) from Russia, Poland, and Romania were part of *Aliyah Aleph*, the first mass immigration of Jews to the Holy Land since their return from Babylonian exile.

After Herzl's untimely death in 1904 at age 44 (due to heart disease, perhaps brought on by his relentless missions in pursuit of his goal) and throughout World War I, his successors continued the negotiations for a Jewish home. As postwar rule of Palestine was about to pass from Constantinople to London, England's Foreign Minister, Lord Arthur Balfour, influenced by his longtime association with Zionist leader Khaim Weizmann, sent to the Jewish philanthropist Lord Rothschild a letter that became famous as the Balfour Declaration. The critical sentence stated: "His Majesty's Government view with favor the establishment in Palestine of a national home for the Jewish people."

The Jews rejoiced. The Arabs protested, but their worldwide efforts were not sufficient to prevent the League of Nations from awarding the Mandate for Establishment of a Jewish Homeland in the Territory to Britain in 1922. The *yishuv* (Jewish community in Palestine, literally "settlement") prepared by developing a labor movement, self-defense force, and structure for future self-governance. The Arabs prepared by stepping up hostilities against them. Under pressure from the Arabs, the British began to waffle on the Balfour Declaration. They claimed (despite what had been the Foreign Minister's sincere support) that its intent was ambiguous.

Jewish immigration to Palestine was curtailed—most severely by issuance in 1939 of the infamous White Paper (referred to by the Jews as the Black Paper). It presented a gutless and hollow interpretation of Lord Balfour's letter and caused countless tragedies by refusing entry to Europe's unwanted Jews.

The *yishuv* fought against the British (while at the same time fighting *with* them against the Nazis) with *Aliyah Bet*, an illegal immigration that smuggled 125,000 Jews into the country. In addition, acts of sabotage and aggression were carried out by the country's underground self-defense forces: *Haganah* (Defense), which became the core of the new state's army, and the more militant *Irgun Tzvai Leumi* (National Military Organization) and *Lekhi* (Freedom Fighters for Israel), known by its detractors as the Stern Gang after its founder, poet Abraham Stern.

Establishment of the State

After the First Zionist Congress, Theodor Herzl had written in his diary that there would be a Jewish state, "in five years, perhaps, and certainly in 50." Fifty years later, on November 29, 1947, members of the United Nations, no doubt chastened by the world events of the previous decade, voted to partition Palestine into two tiny states, one for the Jews and one for the Arabs. The plan created a checkerboard of the mandate territory that left the Jews vulnerable. Still they immediately accepted. The Arabs would not.

The British, doing little to discourage or avoid Arab hostility against the Jews, as quietly as possible waited out their last months in the Middle East. On the morning of May 14, 1948, they lowered their flags, took their belongings, and as the joke about British departures goes, left without saying good-bye. (The other part of the joke is that Jews say good-bye without leaving.)

The Declaration of Independence of the state proclaimed that day—which granted freedom, justice, and peace to everyone, guaranteed freedom of religion, and safeguarded the holy places of all faiths—also extended a hand "to all neighboring states and their peoples in an offer of peace and good neighborliness." It appealed to them "to establish bonds of cooperation and mutual help with the sovereign Jewish people settled in its own land." The State of Israel was prepared, the Declaration continued, "to do its share in common effort for the advancement of the entire Middle East."

The response took less than twenty-four hours: Egypt, Lebanon, Syria, Jordan, and Iraq, plus troops from Saudi Arabia, simultaneously invaded the tiny nascent refuge for the people no other nation in the world wanted. They outnumbered and outgunned the Israelis. An international arms blockade on the region further handicapped the fledgling nation.

Anyone available—recently arrived refugees, schoolchildren, women—was enlisted. Jews in other countries clandestinely collected and smuggled armaments, raised money, and lobbied decision makers. Many others volunteered their services directly to the new state, World War II veterans often joining in combat. Lack of training and poor organization hampered the Israelis and caused unnecessary casualties. Yet just three years after the Holocaust, with another enemy screaming for their extermination, the Israelis had one advantage. While the Arabs' objective was to kill them, the Israelis' objective was the most basic drive: survival.

The War of Independence lasted until early 1949. When fighting stopped, the Israelis had been able to push the Arabs out of the new sections of Jerusalem they had invaded, but lost the beloved Old City with its historic religious monuments to Jordanian control. Elsewhere, Israel had been more successful, extending her borders from the precarious partition plan to embrace the Negev in the south and the Galilee in the north. The gains came at a heavy price: six thousand people, almost one percent of the population (comparable to a loss for the United States of two million), had died in the hostilities.

First Egypt, then the other countries contiguous with Israel, agreed to a cease fire. Iraq refused to negotiate an armistice altogether, and except for Egypt, which signed a peace treaty in 1979 after three more major armed confrontations, the original aggressors remained in a state of war with Israel. But Israel, an independent homeland for the Jews, had come into existence.

Celebrating Independence

Clearly this development in Jewish history called for commemoration, and in 1949, Israeli law established *Iyar* 5 as a national holiday, Yom Ha'atzmaut (Independence Day). Less clear was just how the day would best be observed. Was the proper mood joy for the victory, or sorrow for the fallen? Was the achievement to be credited to the efforts and sacrifices of those who struggled and died to create the state, from the early pioneers to the war heroes? Or was the establishment of the modern state of Israel part of a biblical fulfillment and therefore loaded with messianic implications?

The underlying conflict between the secular and religious philosophies necessitated compromise even in the wording of the Declaration of Independence. For the secularists, mention of God would have attributed the establishment of the state to Divine deliverance—which they were not prepared to do. For the religious, leaving out mention of God would have credited only human efforts. Everyone was comfortable with the concluding phrase, "With trust in the Rock of Israel, we sign our own hands as witnesses. . . ." Since Hebrew has no capital letters, Rock (or rock) would be read either as meant by the psalmist ("Rock and Redeemer") or as the strength of Israel.

The chief rabbinate was reluctant to assume the authority necessary to declare a holy day after a lapse of two thousand years. Yet the rabbis unequivocally saw the achievement of independence and victory over destruction as a miracle: the beginning of our long-awaited redemption, which we were obligated to commemorate with a feast day. Like a traditional Jewish festival of thanksgiving, it was to be celebrated in synagogue, with special additions to the liturgy and festive attire, and at home with a festive meal and singing. Daily and business pursuits were to be suspended.

Secular authorities stressed aspects of family celebration, suggesting a home observance similar to a Passover *seder*. For that purpose, the Israel Defense Forces issued an Independence Night *Haggadah* containing a service that includes drinking three cups of wine (for the state, armed forces, and Jewish people) and provides a selection of readings and prayers.

Memorials to those who had died trying to bring the state into being were a large part of Yom Ha'atzmaut—such a large part they threatened to obliterate the joy. So the two aspects of independence observance were separated, with *Iyar* 4 designated as Yom Hazikkaron, Israel's Memorial Day (see section on "Preparation"). Then the mood of Yom Ha'atzmaut became exuberant, and the most popular celebrations moved from the synagogue and home out into the streets.

Until after the country's twentieth anniversary, a major feature of the day was the massive military parade, meant as much to intimidate hostile neighbors as to bolster pride and self-confidence at home. Displays of nationalistic decorations, parades, parties, fireworks, folk dancing, torchlight processions, and long-distance relay runs became standard. Over the years, other events, like the International Bible Contest for Jewish youth, special sports competitions, art exhibits, cultural performances, and the Hebrew Song Festival have been added to the day's festivities.

The number of Yom Ha'atzmaut observances outside Israel continues to grow. Some congregations in the Diaspora have adopted new liturgies for the day, and cities with substantial Jewish communities annually organize programs to demonstrate solidarity with the Jewish homeland.

FOR FURTHER READING

For both adults and children, there are a number of biographies and autobiographies or memoirs of people who were instrumental in Israel's independence and early leadership—among them Weizmann, Ben-Gurion, Dayan, Meir, and of course Herzl (including the two-volume biography by Jacob deHaas, ardent supporter and Zionist Congress secretary who lived through the growth of the Zionist movement with Herzl; Amos Elon's masterful and detailed *Herzl*; and for young adults, Miriam Gurko's *Theodor Herzl, The Road to Israel*). Any of them will add to your understanding of Israel's birth and development.

For Adults

Collins, Larry, and Dominique Lapierre. *O Jerusalem!* New York: Simon and Schuster, 1972.

Detailed, exciting, and poetic, this epic account of Israel's struggle for independence starts from the events leading up to it and continues through the ceasefire. It is a classic.

Eban, Abba. *My Country—The Story of Modern Israel.* New York: Random House, 1972.

Rather than presenting all the facts and historic detail, Eban conveys a sense of what modern Israel's early decades—from the years leading to independence through 1972—felt like.

Elon, Amos. *The Israelis: Founders and Sons.* New York: Penguin Books, 1981.

The discussion of the history, politics, and philosophies by which Israel was established, and how attitudes changed in the next generation, provides an insight into the country as well as a context for looking at the problems Israel faces in the Middle East. This is an enlightening look into the Israeli mind.

————, and Fifty-five Photographers. *The Israelis: Photographs of a Day in May.* New York: Harry Abrams, 1985.

All aspects of life in Israel are portrayed in the 318 photos chosen from among the 40,000 taken by a corps of Israeli photographers who traversed the country on May 10, 1984.

Herzl, Theodor. *The Jewish State.* Trans. by Harry Zohn. New York: Herzl Press, 1970.

Starting with an analysis of the problem of anti-Semitism, Herzl's essay provides a detailed practical plan—from liquidating assets in the Diaspora to town planning in Palestine—for turning the idea into the State of Israel.

The Israel-Arab Reader: A Documentary History of the Middle East Conflict. Ed. by Walter Laquer and Barry Rubin. New York: Penguin Books, 1984.

Here is an overview of developments in the Jewish homeland from the first settlers in 1882 through PLO statements of 1983, provided in letters, agreements, proclamations, government policy statements, UN resolutions, speeches, and other official documents. It is a good source book.

Kurzman, Dan. *Genesis 1948.* New York: The World Publishing Company, 1970.

The author, a *Jerusalem Post* reporter, writes like a biographer and novelist to bring the history of Israeli independence alive.

The Zionist Idea: A Historical Analysis and Reader. Ed. by Arthur Hertzberg. New York: Atheneum, 1981.

Through the writings of great Jewish thinkers and poets, the development of the ideology that resulted in the State of Israel is traced. The selections show the internal intellectual and moral forces operating in Jewish life from the mid-1800s until the mid-1900s, which were as responsible as the external forces (like anti-Semitism) in the establishment of Israel.

For Children

Adler, David. *A Picture Book of Israel.* New York: Holiday House, 1984.

A much more straightforward introduction to Israel than Burstein's lively book (below), this one is written for older children and contains a somewhat broader range of information. The black and white photographs are nothing special; you might want to use the text while looking at one of the coffee-table books on Israel whose photos really show off the country. Ages 6–10.

Burstein, Chaya M. *What's An Israel?* Rockville, MD: Kar-Ben Copies, 1983.

This is a wonderful introduction for the young child to Israel's cities, countryside, and major attractions. As Benjy has fun-filled and meaningful experiences in Israel, he (and the child) learns. A few simple Hebrew words are introduced and there are short lists of basic facts, games, puzzles, mazes, and pictures to color. Ages 2–4.

Elon, Amos. *Understanding Israel.* New York: Behrman House, 1976.

In seven units and eight photo essays, the book covers issues, Jewish values, and themes related to various stages in Israel's development from the first *aliyah* to contemporary life. A valuable element is the posing of questions to make readers think about the relationship between being an American and being a Jew. Ages 13–15.

Sidon, Ephraim. *The Animated Israel—A Homecoming.* London: Scopus Films, 1987.

With two children, a tree, and a bird who vow to remain faithful forever, this moving fable tells the story of the Jewish people from independence in ancient Israel to renewed independence in modern Israel. Produced in honor of Israel's fortieth anniversary, the book is written in simple, effective rhyme. Ages 6–10.

WHAT DOES IT MEAN?— RELIGIOUS IMPORTANCE

Gateway to Redemption

For two thousand years, Jews had dreamed about, yearned for, imagined, and idealized Israel. "Next year in Jerusalem" was not the rote phrase so many of us absently say, but a living hope. The planned return to Israel was not a macho nationalistic drive to regain territory stolen from its rightful owners. It was a prerequisite for being able to accomplish our mission, an essential piece of a whole Jewish life, a sacred obligation.

The establishment of the State of Israel looked like the day of redemption we had been waiting for. It seemed to fit the pattern of deliverance the ancient Jews experienced and the prophets promised to their children. The chief rabbinate was encouraged but cautious (hence, "the beginning" of the flowering of our redemption). Never before had a people been dispersed, remained distinct, and returned thousands of years later to reclaim and rule a piece of property from which they had been forcibly expelled. Never before had such near total devastation been followed almost immediately by the community's resurrection. There were signs of Ezekiel's dry bones (37:1–14) all over it.

Still, some questioned whether it could just be an anomalous moment in history. After all, the Maccabees (see chapter on Khanukah), seen as saviors in their day, had been successful—but only briefly. Bar Kokhba (see chapter on Lag B'Omer), considered the Messiah, had recaptured Jerusalem for an even briefer period of time. Would the new Israelis eventually follow in their footsteps?

The circumstances surrounding the establishment of Israel suggested something different. It occurred during an opportune moment before the Iron Curtain firmly descended (and U.S.–USSR cooperation, needed for establishment of the state, dissipated), anti-Semitism rose, post-Holocaust sympathy waned, or the British changed their departure timetable. (And was it just coincidence that the Talmud instructed that anyone who saw a crowd of 600,000 Jews—a number the rabbis considered critical for a Jewish population base—in Israel was to make a special blessing, and that at the time of Israel's independence, there were just over 600,000 Jews in the Land?) Within months, days, even hours, the windows of opportunity could have closed. Recognizing that fact, although he risked Arab attack, Ben-Gurion made the now-or-never decision.

According to a story current in Israel prior to the Six-Day War, when a rabbi was asked about that impending crisis, he replied it would be resolved either the natural way or by miracle. The natural way, he explained, would be to settle it by miracle. And it would be a miracle to settle it in a natural way (recorded in Emanuel Feldman's *The 28th of Iyar*).

Nakhmanides believed that the redemption would come in a natural course of events, with the consent of nations, and would begin with just a partial ingathering of the exiles. As it did. Considering what had happened in prior decades, and what was going on in the world, wouldn't we say what he defined as a course of events was a miracle? Earlier sages had observed that those who benefit from Divine delivery do not recognize what they have experienced as such. (The Tourism Ministry did not encounter difficulty when, in the 1980s, it referred to Israel as "The Miracle on the Mediterranean.")

Even if secularists would not call it that, achieving statehood was still a phenomenal change in the status of the Jewish people and every bit the chance for a cultural and spiritual, as well as political, resurgence the prophesies promised, an opportunity to build the foundation for the just society Torah envisions and prescribes. We were back in control in our homeland, the only place on Earth where all *mitzvot* apply and where all can be performed (Deuteronomy 11:31–32), and, therefore, where our full potential, in every aspect of life, can be achieved.

For Further Reading

Deuteronomy 28–30, in any *Khumash*

The stirring talk by Moses to the Israelites just before they crossed the Jordan into the Promised Land outlines Israel's history of exile and return.

What Does It Mean to Us?—Personal Significance

Since the Jewish homeland is no longer the abstract dream it was to our grandparents and their grandparents, but a real place of tremendous possibilities, we are theoretically closer to fulfilling the biblical prophesies regarding ingathering and perfection of the world. This raises a logical question for a Jew: Should I live in the Jewish state?

Dreaming that the Jews would come home, Ben-Gurion found it incongruent, because of Israel's historic significance and the Jews' suffering-filled history, that they did not readily accept the invitation. (The 1950 Law of Return, the first piece of legislation passed by the Knesset, grants any Jew the right to immigrate to Israel and become a citizen immediately. An American may retain dual citizenship as long as s/he does not volunteer to serve in Israel's army; draftees do not lose American citizenship.)

The displaced Jewish refugees of World War II, Jews endangered by overt persecution, and religiously inclined Jews readily responded. But despite the pressures individual Israelis have been known to place on their cousins in the Diaspora, despite the acrimonious barbs on the subject tossed in the Israel–Diaspora relations debates, most Jews living comfortably in Western societies remain unlikely to pack up and move east. (An old joke defines a Zionist as a person who thinks it is great for a child to make *aliyah* to Israel—someone else's child.)

It may even seem odd that, being patriotic citizens of one country, we should feel so attached to another that we celebrate its independence as though it were our own. But in numerous ways, it is. For millennia, for the vast majority of our people, *Eretz Yisrael* was the center of the Jewish universe. Through history, prayers, songs, customs, stories, and celebrations, it remained a part of every Jew. Today, official tour guides advise visitors, "Enjoy everything you see here. It's yours."

The heroic birth of modern Israel restored to Jews throughout the world a sense of pride in our heritage, and its continued existence gives us a feeling of security. No matter how safe we think we are, it provides a psychological crutch: If something disastrous were to occur, we know there is one place on Earth that would welcome us. (The argument is often made for continued residence in the Diaspora based on the observation that never before in history have Jews reached the status we have in a democratic country that guarantees our rights. We have to remember that two hundred years is a short experiment in terms of world history. The Jews of Spain during the two-hundred-year run of their Golden Age and the Jews of cultured civilized Germany, in which they could so readily assimilate, failed to foresee the horrors that later befell them.)

Many of the Jews who died in the Holocaust were rejected at the border of country after country. Ships carrying refugees (like the *St. Louis*, which was returned from U.S. shores) were sunk rather than allowed to discharge their condemned cargo in any of numerous nations. They and countless others could have been saved had an Israel, with open arms for all Jews, regardless of age, health, profession, or skin color, existed then. Look what its existence has meant to Soviet and Ethiopian Jews.

If our history in the world has reinforced anything (aside from anti-Semitism's senseless persistence), it is that we Jews, like it or not, are inextricably bound to each other. We may not want to live in Israel, but we may have to some day. We ourselves may not have to live in Israel, but other Jews who dwell in societies not as free as ours, and whose welfare we, as our brothers' and sisters' keepers, are responsible for, may need to find safe haven there. Therefore, it is up to every one of us to make sure that Israel remains viable, so that when and if we, or our children, or our cousins, need it, it is there.

But we should not look at Israel as just a safety net. No other place has the history or spiritual significance for us that Israel does. Soon it will be the largest Jewish community in the world, with some of the best minds and most advanced technologies. With tremendous potential in all fields of endeavor, it will continue to develop as the dynamic center of Jewish culture and achievement.

The question for each of us is how can we best maintain a connection with Israel and contribute to its strength and survival. You can find as many ways as you have interests and opportunities to pursue them. Use Yom Ha'atzmaut to explore possibilities, to review materials you have collected about programs, organizations, and so on, or to gather information.

Become knowledgeable about Israel by attending lectures or taking classes, subscribing to Israeli periodicals, reading books about Israel and/or by Israeli authors. Familiarize yourself with Israeli culture: attend performances given by Israeli artists—musicians, dancers, actors. Listen to tapes of Israeli music in your home or car, participate in Israeli folk dance classes, view exhibitions of Israeli art. Support Israel's economic independence by investing in Israeli business or industry, contributing to organi-

zations here or in Israel that support human services and economic development, or by buying Israeli products.

Develop relationships with the people of Israel. Start by learning Hebrew, not only so you can communicate with them but to be better able to understand how they think. Be a Volunteer for Israel (spending a month providing needed human resources to free the overtaxed Israelis to work at their regular jobs). Buy a second home there.

Get your children involved in Zionist youth groups and camps (such as Young Judea, the youth movement of Hadassah). Make sure they learn Hebrew, too. Encourage them to have Israeli penpals with whom to practice the language, learn about the country, and arrange exchange visits. Send them on an Israel summer program (or take a family mission). Arrange for your child to have his/her *bar/bat mitzvah* in Israel, or to "twin" with an Ethiopian Israeli child of *bar mitzvah* age (arranged through the North American Conference on Ethiopian Jewry, headquartered in New York and Jerusalem).

Get involved with a Zionist organization yourself (find one through the umbrella World Zionist Organization) or support organizations for Israeli institutions (American/Canadian friends of an Israeli college, museum, sports organization, cultural institution).

From the beginning of our history, Jews outside the Land of Israel have had a lot to do with what happened or could happen within it—from Abraham to Joseph to Moses to the prophets to the sages of the Talmud in Babylon to the leaders in the Diaspora who kept the Zionist idea alive. Like them, each of us has an incredible opportunity to contribute to the realization of an ancient dream and a modern necessity.

For Further Reading/Watching

For Adults

Devir, Ori. *Off the Beaten Track in Israel: A Guide to Beautiful Places*. New York: Adama Books, 1989.

Maps, magnificent color photos, and detailed directions lead you to archaeologic, historic, and scenic sites in the countryside of Israel. You can learn a lot just by reading this book—even if you never visit the places described.

Sofer, Barbara. *Kids Love Israel/Israel Loves Kids: A Travel Guide for Families*. Rockville, MD: Kar-Ben Copies, 1988.

Valuable for both the visitor or resident in Israel, the well-organized guidebook presents more than two hundred sites in major cities and lesser known locations. With an emphasis on young travelers, it suggests lots of activity-oriented places, including hands-on exhibits at museums, outdoor adventures, interactions with diverse kinds of people, and visits to historic sites that come alive—including active archaeological digs and recreated villages.

For Children

Burstein, Chaya M. *Kids Catalog of Israel*. Philadelphia: The Jewish Publication Society of America, 1988.

With this terrific comprehensive guide, your kids will learn what Israeli children say, how they celebrate holidays, what they eat, dance and play, what American and Israeli youth have in common, and how they are different. Aspects of Israel's history, stories, places to see in Israel, and so on, are all included. Ages 8 and up.

Videotapes

Parpar Nechmad—Lovely Butterfly: Independence Day

From the Israeli-produced award-winning series, the tape features the country's most popular TV stars and puppets and animation to present games, stories, and songs about the holiday. Although in Hebrew, it is geared for those with little understanding of the language. Ages 2–6.

Shalom Sesame: The Land of Israel; Tel Aviv; Kibbutz; The People of Israel.

The well-known Muppets and group of celebrity friends (led by Itzhak Perlman) star in these programs, covering their visit to Israel. Each mixes animation, song, comedy, and learning in thirty minutes to introduce the cities, countryside, and mix of population. Each show is available individually or as a set along with one on Jerusalem. In English, with some elementary Hebrew. Ages 2–12.

FOR FURTHER EXPLORATION

American-Israel Friendship League

The nonprofit, nonsectarian, nonpartisan organization is committed to developing and expanding a mutually supportive relationship between both countries through cultural, artistic, and scientific exchange. Headquartered in New York, it maintains regional offices in San Francisco, Tucson, and Glendale (CO).

Israel Aliyah Center

People who are considering living in Israel can get printed material and personalized guidance through an aliyah center or Israel program desks (at Jewish Federations, Community Centers, or Israel consulates). In addition to immigration, the center helps with arrangements for two-month *kibbutz*, five-month *kibbutz-ulpan* (Hebrew instruction), and a broad range of temporary Israel living experiences. An extensive listing of possibilities is available.

Israel Investment and Trade Center

If you are interested in investing or doing business in Israel, you can receive personalized guidance from this center in Boston, Los Angeles, or Chicago. (Representatives at Israel consulates in other cities [see below] are also available to assist you.)

United Jewish Appeal

The umbrella fundraising organization (known in your community as the Jewish Federation or Jewish United Fund) runs national, regional, and local missions programs to Israel throughout the year for various age groups, singles, families, leaders, and so on. (Other Jewish organizations—including American Jewish Congress and Hadassah—also offer numerous travel programs to Israel.)

Volunteers for Israel

For the cost of a subsidized airline ticket good for a six-month stay in Israel, people of any age can spend three weeks working on an Israeli army base (or occasionally in a hospital) to help the Israeli national effort. Thousands of people participate each year. Headquartered in New York, the international organization has offices throughout the United States and in Canada.

For additional information on Israel, contact the Consulate General in Atlanta, Boston, Chicago,

Houston, Los Angeles, Miami, New York, Philadelphia, or San Francisco, or the Embassy of Israel in Washington, DC.

TRADITIONS: HOW WE CELEBRATE YOM HA'ATZMAUT

HOW DO WE SHOW WE CELEBRATE?— OBSERVANCE

The number of Israel Independence Day celebrations held on (or, outside Israel, near) *Iyar* 5 (which falls in April or May) has continued to increase since the start of the Third Jewish Commonwealth. For Jews throughout the world, it is a time of great festivity and gratitude, with commemorations religious and secular, in synagogues and on the streets.

Synagogue

While not widely adopted in the Diaspora, special liturgies are fairly common in Israel, where government leaders regularly attend the festive prayer services. The one for evening designed by Israel's Chief Rabbinate in 1949 begins with psalms of thanksgiving (107, 97, 98) and ends with a single blast of a *shofar* and a prayer that as we have witnessed the beginning of redemption, we will also merit hearing the *shofar* announcing the messiah.

Their morning service includes the introductory psalms customarily recited on Shabbat and festivals, *Hallel*, also recited on festivals but here without the introductory blessings, and, again without the preceding blessings, the prophetic portion Isaiah 10:32–11:12. A preview of the messianic era, it contains the familiar line, "The wolf shall dwell with the lamb, the lion lie down with the kid" (11:6).

The choice of this particular reading suggests the Rabbinate's belief that Israel independence is in fact a redemption on par with the Exodus, since the same *haftarah* is read in the Diaspora on the last day of Passover. Still, many rabbis were and are reluctant to put the two in the same category. That is why they omit the blessings: It is fine, and appropriate, to express gratitude to God for this incredible shift in our national fortune—so we say *Hallel*. But if this is not *the* historic redemption we have been waiting for, the introductory blessing—which states that our recitation is a commandment of God—along with God's name, would be said in vain. The same reasoning holds for the *haftarah*.

Not everyone has agreed with the rabbis' reticence. Some feel that the official service comes up short in reflecting the magnitude of the unique occurrence it celebrates, one which fits the pattern of exile and redemption recurrent throughout Jewish history. So organizations and congregations on their own say the blessings prior to *Hallel* and the *haftarah*. They include the *shehekheyanu*, in thanks for being brought to this point, which is fully accepted as appropriate for anyone who regards Israel independence as an occasion of real joy. During the *Amidah*, they recite *Al Hanissim* (For the Miracles), just as we do on Khanukah and Purim.

Some also read the Torah (Deuteronomy 7:1–8:18, describing what would happen after the Israelites entered the Land, or Deuteronomy 30:1–10, about being returned to the Land after exile and misfortune). A prayer for the welfare of the State of Israel, one in memory of those fallen, prayers for Jerusalem, and a Zion Lover's Prayer have also been added to services, along with the song expressing belief in the coming of the Messiah, "*Ani Ma'amin.*" Many of these changes were incorporated into the *makhzor* (festival prayer book) developed by *Hakibbutz Hadati* (the religious *kibbutz* movement).

Communities around the world have added their own touches. An announcement of the number of years since the establishment of the state prior to sounding the *shofar* at the *Ma'ariv* service is modeled on the Yemenite Tisha B'Av custom of proclaiming the number of years since the destruction of the Temple. *Ma'ariv* in some communities is chanted to the *yom tov nusah* (holiday melody). A *Tikkun L'Yom Ha'atzmaut*, an anthology of readings and prayers (parts of *Kabbalat Shabbat, Shema, Leshanah Haba B'Yerushalayim, Shir Hama'alot*—perhaps sung to the tune of Israel's national anthem—and *Ani Ma'amin*), is used by some Moroccan and other congregations for *Ma'ariv* and *Shakharit*. Some add Psalm 27 ("The Lord is my light and my help").

The Conservative movement prayer book includes a customized version of *Al Hanissim* along with suggested readings related to Israel. The Reform movement prayer book includes a service written especially for Independence Day.

FOR FURTHER READING

Bokser, Ben Zion. *Prayers and Readings for Israel Independence Day*. New York: Hebrew Publishing Company, 1967.

Along with a selection of psalms, songs, prayers, and scriptural selections appropriate for Yom Ha'atzmaut, the book provides instruction for how they can be incorporated into a service for the occasion.

Neriah, Rabbi Moshe Zvi. *Order of Prayer for Yom Ha'atzmaut*. New York: Department for Torah Education and Culture in the Diaspora of the World Zionist Organization, 1978.

The book is worth having for the selection of source materials at the end regarding the Land, love of it, obligations to it, and its restoration. Much of the rest of the text consists of the regular evening service, all in Hebrew, and special additional prayers for Yom Ha'atzmaut, in Hebrew and English. (Available for a nominal fee from the publisher as listed above, 110 East 59th Street, New York, NY 10022; 212-339-6080.)

Home Observance

For many families, Yom Ha'atzmaut is an occasion for a special meal together. Even without doing a *seder* people often want to add something, like singing at the table—as they would on the Sabbath or festivals. (Candlelighting and *kiddush* are not as yet accepted practices for this occasion.)

Listening to tapes of Israeli music, reading stories about Israel, and watching one of the increasing number of videos that have something to do with Israel are good family activities. It would not be unusual to use Israeli flags, pictures of Israel, souvenirs of trips to the country, or products made there as decorations in honor of the holiday.

Tzedakah

In the years when Herzl's goal was still a dream, metal "blue (collection) boxes" were common in Jewish homes. Distributed by the Jewish National Fund (*Keren Kayemet L'Yisrael*), they instructed the holders to contribute regularly to "Redeem the Land of Israel." The money collected from these *pushkehs* did indeed buy tracts of land so the Jews would legally own them.

Today the Jewish National Fund (JNF) remains dedicated to the physical land and its resources in order to maintain quality of life for the people inhabiting it. With the priorities of afforestation and land reclamation, its projects include water and soil conservation, care of natural woodlands, maintenance of parks and recreation sites, and road building. It has been an important source of jobs for immigrants who were part of the great influx in the late 1980s and early 1990s. You can still have a "blue box" in your home (so that family members can add their contributions just before Shabbat or holiday candle-lighting). Many people give directly to JNF or buy trees in honor of special occasions (see chapter on Tu B'Shevat).

Any organization that contributes to the security or development of Israel, or works toward improving Israel–Diaspora relations, is an appropriate object for Yom Ha'atzmaut donations. You might consider, for example, Israel Bonds (which supports the economic infrastructure of the country), Friends of the Israel Defense Forces (which provides special services for Israeli soldiers), Melitz Centers for Jewish-Zionist Education (which brings Israeli and American Jews together), and Hadassah, the Zionist Women's Organization (which maintains Hadassah Hospital and scores of programs in Israel).

Public Festivities

Israel

Streets and buildings are brightly decorated with flags and lights. At nightfall a siren blast signals the start of Yom Ha'atzmaut, when the speaker of the Knesset, surrounded by dignitaries, lights a torch at the grave of the father of modern Zionism, Theodor Herzl. Twelve others—one for each of Israel's tribes—are lit by individuals chosen as representatives of areas of achievement in the nation's history, culture, and struggle for survival. Salvos numbering the years of independence make up the concluding gun salute. With giddy abandon, public and private parties, outdoor bands and orchestras, fireworks, and dancing in the streets last well into the night.

Parades (without the military component since 1968) march through cities the next day. The President of Israel hosts a reception for the diplomatic corps and soldiers who have had distinguished careers, and an open house for everyone else. At a special ceremony at Hebrew University in Jerusalem, the Minister of Education and Culture awards the prestigious Israel Prizes for outstanding accomplishment in literature, art, and science. The International Bible Competition for Youth and the Hebrew Song Festival finals also take place. Picnicking and hiking short distances in places not previously explored are popular activities.

Diaspora

Cities that have active Jewish communities have devoted the day (or one close to it) to public demonstration of solidarity with and support for Israel. Synagogues, Hebrew schools, Jewish community centers, and Zionist organizations produce a variety of programs.

For many years, a performance troupe from Israel toured the United States in the weeks around Yom Ha'atzmaut for special salute to Israel programs. For decades, New York has held an Israel Day Parade. Other cities have also organized parades, when funding has been available, or presented Israel-oriented fairs, songfests, concerts, and Walks with Israel (in which participants are sponsored with pledges of money for Israel). It is common to display the Israeli flag and wear its colors, blue and white (from the traditional prayer shawl: white for mercy, blue—the color originally derived from a specific marine creature—representing the sea reflecting the color of the sky, suggesting the Heavens and God's throne, representing His presence).

Events are usually publicized in local Jewish periodicals in the weeks prior to Independence Day. You should also be able to get information about them from your local Jewish Federation or Jewish Community Center.

For Further Reading

Program Guide for Yom Ha'atzmaut and Yom Yerushalayim

Published every year by the American Zionist Federation, this guide provides background information and ideas for home, school, and community celebrations (available from the organization's offices in New York, Chicago, and Los Angeles).

Where Do We Begin?—Preparation

A day of intense mourning precedes the exhilaration of Yom Ha'atzmaut in Israel. Set aside to honor all those who died defending the country, Yom Hazikkaron (Martyr and Heroes' Memorial Day) is like no Memorial Day most Americans have ever witnessed or experienced. Flags are lowered to half-mast, and memorial candles are lit in homes, schools, and synagogues. At mid-morning, the wail of a siren focuses all attention on those whose lives had made everything surrounding the mourners possible. For two minutes, the entire country stops: Cars halt. People come to their feet. Even young children know how and why to stand serenely, sorrowfully.

Religious services include Psalm 9 (about God striking down Israel's enemies), *Yizkor* (the memorial service also conducted on the last day of each pilgrimage festival and Yom Kippur), the army's version of *El Molei Rakhamim* (the prayer said at graveside), and Psalm 144 ("Blessed is the Lord, my Rock, Who trains my hands for battle . . . save me from the hands of foreigners").

Most impressive, though, is the crowd solemnly winding to Mount Herzl and other military cemeteries. Throughout the day people from all parts of society come together—the old and young, *sabras* and immigrants. There is no one in Israel who has remained untouched; everyone has lost someone dear in the decades of fighting. They place the flowers universally brought and linger over the graves, too many testifying to the youth of war victims. Outside the burial grounds, you cannot go anywhere without encountering wreath-adorned roadside monuments, where former servicemen and soldiers stand guard and more ceremonies and services take place.

As the first stars appear, the siren calls everyone to attention again, initiating the most incredible transformation. It is as though a switch were suddenly thrown: The entire nation in the merest instant brushes away its tears, casts off its somber air, and literally begins dancing in the streets. A carnival atmosphere erupts. Having paid respects to those who sacrificed themselves for independence, it is time to celebrate what they helped create. In traditional Jewish manner, the survivors move forward exuberantly to embrace life.

Outside of Israel, some congregations hold memorial services for Yom Hazikkaron. It has been suggested they become more widespread, and that other prayers and readings be recited, such as Israel's Declaration of Independence, poems by fallen *Tzahal* (Israeli Army) soldiers, and David's lament over the battle deaths of Saul and Jonathan, "How mighty are the fallen!" (II Samuel 1:19–27).

Any other advance activity depends on how you and your community observe Yom Ha'atzmaut. You may need to purchase tickets for a performance event, register and secure sponsors for a Walk with Israel, decorate with pictures and items purchased in Israel, or prepare food for a special Independence Day picnic or more formal meal.

What Are We Supposed to Do?— *Halakhah*

Mourning

The mourning customs followed for festival days (see chapter on Pesakh) are in effect. However, there is no interruption of the restrictions of the *Omer* period in which Yom Ha'atzmaut falls.

Coincidence with Shabbat

If *Iyar* 5 falls on Friday or Saturday, Yom Ha'atzmaut celebrations are held on the previous Thursday. This ensures that the Sabbath will not be desecrated by celebratory activities and that celebration will not be cut short by the preparation for and arrival of Shabbat.

WHAT OTHER THINGS DO PEOPLE DO?—CUSTOMS

Greeting

People wish each other *"khag samei'akh"* (happy festival). The formal greeting among very religious people is *"moadim l'simkhah"* (have a happy festival), to which the response is *"le geulah shleimah"* (toward a complete redemption).

WHAT IS THERE TO EAT?—TRADITIONAL FOODS

People often try to eat "Israeli foods" on this national holiday (although the dishes identified with the country—*falafel, tahina, hummus, baba gannouj, pita,*—are actually all part of the regional cuisine adopted by the Jews who settled there). Items associated with milk and honey or the seven species for which Israel is blessed (wheat, barley, grapes, pomegranate, olive, fig, and date) (Deuteronomy 8:7) are also popular.

DO YOU HEAR MUSIC?—SONGS TO SING

The most significant song associated with Israel Independence Day is, of course, the country's national anthem, *"Hatikvah"* (The Hope), the theme song of the Zionist movement and the settlers in Palestine. Naphtali Herz Imber, who wrote the words in 1878, read his poem to the farmers in the early settlement Rishon Lezion (which means First to Zion) when visiting the village in 1882. His audience loved it. One member, Samuel Cohen, composed the melody based on a folktune from his native Moldavia (apparently the same folktune used by Bedrich Smetana for "The Moldave").

The song captures our undying hope of return to Zion: "As long as a Jew's heart beats within his breast, and he faces forward to the east with his eye on Zion, our ancient hope continues, the hope of two thousand years, to be a free people in our own land, in Eretz Zion and Jerusalem."

The lively *"Im tirtzu, ein zo aggadah,"* Herzl's urging to the Jews to make Israel a reality ("If you will it, it is no legend"), is appropriate, as are songs that joyfully express Israel's survival, such as *"Am Yisrael Khai"* (The People of Israel Live) and *"David Melekh Yisrael"* (David King of Israel Lives). *"Haveinu Shalom Aleikhem"* (We Bring You Greetings of Peace), reflecting our hopes of final redemption, is also the message we tried to introduce in the region. There are scores of folksongs, many from the pioneering days of the *yishuv*, which extol the Land and describe living and working on it, as well as songs of the army and fighting, including the touching *"B'Arvot Hanegev"* (In the Wilderness of The Negev [a soldier has fallen]).

WHAT TALES ARE TOLD?—STORIES TO READ

The Bible is a good initial source for background to the saga that led to the establishment of Israel. Deuteronomy, in addition to providing a preview of exile and return, outlines how the Jews are to live on the Land. Amos and Micah (in Prophets) also stress proper behavior. Prophets Jeremiah and Ezekiel foresee the return of Israel to the Land. Yehudah Halevi, Hayyim Nahman Bialik, and Rachel were among poets who expressed great love for the Land.

A number of books, particularly for young people, demonstrate the ingathering with stories of children from different parts of the world who have made *aliyah* and established new lives in Israel.

FOR FURTHER READING

For Adults

Michener, James. *The Source.* New York: Random House, 1965.

It's worth struggling past the first chapters of this novel about the development of the Land and people of Israel through history, told in parallel stories about members of a modern archaeological team working at the dig site of an ancient settlement, and of the people whose world the dig uncovers.

Uris, Leon. *Exodus.* Garden City, NY: Doubleday & Company, 1958.

Beginning with the journey of the actual ship *Exodus,* which unsuccessfully tried to reach Palestine with its Jewish war refugees, Uris gives a fictionalized account of the establishment of the State of Israel. A bestseller, the book generated tremendous pro-Israel support in America and reawakened Jewish sentiment among the Soviet Jews who circulated underground copies after 1967. The movie made from the novel is worth seeing, but the book provides much more background to Israel's independence, including the Holocaust.

―――. *The Haj.* Garden City, NY: Doubleday & Company, 1984.

Experts on Arab culture say that this novel accurately portrays the mentality and history of the Arabs with whom Israel must establish peace—and insights into why so many attempts to do so since the beginning of the state have failed. Through the relationship of two families, one Jewish, the other Arab, Uris presents Israel's establishment and growth from the point of view of the Arabs who lived in Palestine before mandate days.

Vilnay, Zev. *Legends of Judea and Samaria* (vol. 2); *Legends of Galilee, Jordan and Sinai* (vol. 3). Philadelphia: The Jewish Publication Society of America, 1978.

Folktales, folklore, history, mystical occurrences, and other interesting tidbits about scores of places throughout the Land of Israel, since Bible days and through the ages, capture the unique character and allure of the Land. (See also *Legends of Jerusalem*, volume 1 of the set.)

For Children

Carmi, Giora. *And Shira Imagined.* Philadelphia: The Jewish Publication Society of America, 1988.

At each site that Shira and her parents visit in Israel, they see what is there now. When her parents explain what it was like before, Shira "imagines" a brightly colorful scene that incorporates objects familiar to her. The picture book is meant to be a first look at Israel for young children. Ages 4–8.

Levitin, Sonia. *The Return.* New York: Fawcett Books, 1988.

The National Jewish Book Award winner tells the exciting story of a girl who flees Ethiopia to make a new life in Israel, as her people had dreamed about for two thousand years. Age 12 and up. (*Falasha No More* by Arlene Kushner tells a similar story, for readers ages 5–11, about a little boy. *My Name is Rachamim* by Jonathan P. Kendall, for ages 7–11, portrays an Ethiopian family's perilous journey to the Promised Land. Ruth Gruber's exciting and poignant *Rescue*, for young and not-so-young adults, tells the story of Ethiopian Jewry.)

Meir, Mina. *Alina: A Russian Girl Comes to Israel.* Philadelphia: The Jewish Publication Society of America, 1982.

Photographs and text express the difficulties of learning an entirely new culture and show how Alina finally feels that she is at home. Ages 6–10.

Shamir, Moshe. *The Fifth Wheel.* Berkeley: Benmir Books, 1986.

Kolbo goes from adventure to adventure through the countryside of northern Israel, meeting typical and colorful characters from all walks of life. His journey from Kibbutz Hermonim to Haifa and back covers a lot of geography and is a popular story in Israel. Ages 10 and up.

Shteiner, Puah. *Forever My Jerusalem: A Personal Account of the Siege and Surrender of Jerusalem's Old City in 1948.* Jerusalem/New York: Feldheim Publishers, 1987.

This vivid and eloquent memoir of the 1948 siege of Jerusalem is told by a woman who experienced it as a young girl. With lots of dialogue, it reads like a novel. Ages 12 and up.

Zim, Jacob, ed. *My Shalom, My Peace—Paintings and Poems by Jewish and Arab Children.* Tel Aviv: Sabra Books, 1975.

The beautifully moving and perceptive words and pictures in this collection were created by children between the ages of six and fifteen. This book gives a lovely view of hopes and dreams for the region and is for readers of any age.

Of Additional Interest

Videotapes

Each Consulate General of Israel has an extensive library of videotapes covering the diversity of life in Israel: art and culture, science and technology, the land and people, politics and security, relations with other countries and the world, archaeology and travel, Jerusalem, Holocaust, immigration, nature, and holidays. Anyone, even those who do not live near a consulate, may borrow the tapes for two weeks at a time. Call or write to the consulate in your region for a videography.

Sites in Israel

It is possible to trace the birth of the State of Israel through visits to a number of museums in the country. **Herzl Museum** (Jerusalem) documents his life with a significant collection of personal memorabilia and reconstruction of his Vienna study using its original furnishings. Several re-creations or restorations provide a sense of what life was like for the early pioneers in Palestine. These include the **Old Yishuv Court Museum** (Jerusalem, Jewish Quarter), where the atmosphere of a nineteenth-century Jewish home in the capital has been re-created by a young member of the family who lived there prior to evacuation in the War for Independence. **Tel Hai Museum** (Kibbutz Tel Hai, in the Galilee) is a reconstruction of the settlement begun in 1907 and evacuated under Arab attack in 1920. **Museum for the History of Gedera and the Biluim** (Gedera, east of Ashdod off the southern Mediterranean coast), **Museum of the History of Tel Aviv-Yafo** (Tel Aviv), and **Rishon Lezion History Museum** (Rishon Lezion) record the early days of these communities.

The history of various defense organizations and clandestine activities is well documented at **Beit Haganah** (Tel Aviv); **Golani Brigade Museum** (Golani Junction in the Galilee); **Museum of Clandestine Immigration** (Port of Haifa), which includes one of the illegal ships, the "*Af-al-pi-khen*" or "In Spite Of"; **Beit Hashomer** (Kibbutz Giladi, in the Galilee), dedicated to "The Watchman" protective force, which played a large role in development of modern Jewish settlements in the area; and **Museum of Heroism** (Acre), housed in the prison where members of the Jewish underground were held and executed in the last years of the British mandate.

Memorials to those fallen in Israel's wars are housed at **Beit Gidi** (Tel Aviv), documenting the battle for Jaffa in 1948; **Yad Lebanim** (Petakh Tikvah), to those who fell in that settlement in 1948; and **Ein Dor Museum of Archaeology** (Kibbutz Ein Dor, in the Galilee), where there is a special room that honors members of the *kibbutz* lost in all of Israel's wars.

You can visit the restored **Independence Hall** (Tel Aviv), where Ben-Gurion proclaimed the State of Israel. Exhibits trace the development of the state's two symbols, the *menorah* and Star of David, and the period between the UN Partition and Israel Declaration of Independence. The **Weizmann Museum and Weizmann House** (Rehovot) document the life of Israel's first president, Khaim Weizmann. **Ben-Gurion's House** (Tel Aviv) and the **Ben-Gurion House and Gravesite** (Kibbutz Sde Boker, in the Negev) are also open to the public.

For additional information, contact the Israel Government Tourist Office in Atlanta, Chicago, Dallas, Los Angeles, New York, or Toronto.

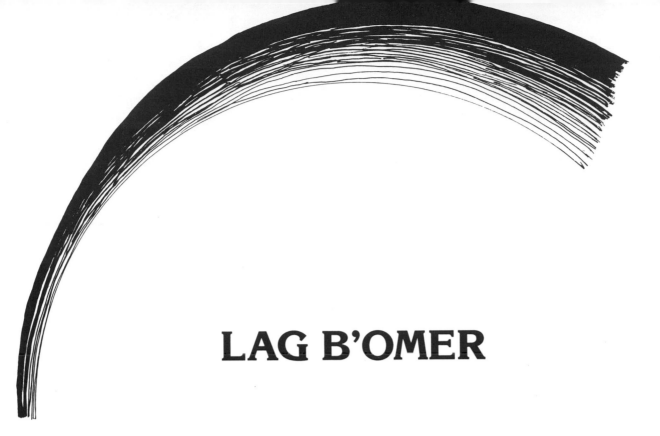

LAG B'OMER

Lag B'Omer (lahg' buh oh'mair): Folk celebration in memory of scholars. Observed on *Iyar* 28 (spring; early–late May).

A minor holiday, Lag B'Omer developed a following among ordinary people and was added to the calendar as a noted but nonsacred day. Supported by a series of legends around second-century sages, it is observed as a spring outing and is especially popular among school children and the *Sephardim*.

ORIGINS: WHY WE CELEBRATE LAG B'OMER

WHERE DID IT ALL BEGIN?— HISTORIC FOUNDATION

Lag B'Omer is one holiday whose origins we may never know for certain. Like many Jewish festivals, it might have roots in the cycle of planting and harvest, but the two most popular explanations concern great men in our history, both of whom lived under the oppressive Roman occupation that followed the destruction of the Second Temple (see chapter on Tisha B'Av).

Akiva and the "Star's" Light

Rabbi Akiva was a great second-century Jewish scholar and leader. Although the Romans had prohibited the practice of Judaism and the teaching of Torah, he continued to transmit the tradition to students who were attracted to his *yeshivah* (academy of Jewish learning). They were extremely talented; however, because they failed to treat each other with respect, they were afflicted by a terrible plague that claimed 24,000 of their lives.

According to our tradition, we mourn during the *Omer* period (see chapter on Pesakh) because of the deaths of the *yeshivah* students, but interrupt our grief to mark the end of the plague. Lag B'Omer (which means the thirty-third day of the *Omer*; the Hebrew letter *lamed* [ל] has the numerical equivalent of thirty and *gimmel* [ג] of three) may have been the day the dying actually ended, a day marking a suspension in the deaths (most communities resume the mourning practices of the *Omer* on the thirty-fourth day), or a day chosen to represent the day on which no additional students lost their lives.

It is commonly believed that "plague" was a euphemism. The burdens of spiritual oppression, land confiscation, and heavy monetary tributes to which the Jews were subjected under Rome were capped when the conquering rulers decided to erect a temple to their god Jupiter in Jerusalem (which they had renamed Aelia Capitolina). Unwilling to stand for that outrage, the Jews rebelled.

Shimon Bar Kosiva distinguished himself in leading a small army against the occupying troops. Said to have been strong enough to uproot a tree with his bare hands while riding a horse, he emerged as a new Judah Maccabee, whose guerrilla attacks had been so successful against the Greeks three centuries earlier (see chapter on Khanukah).

Thoroughly impressed with him, Rabbi Akiva changed Bar Kosiva's name (which meant "son of deceiver") to *Bar* (son of) *Kokhba* (star), a shining light who would guide the Jews to renewed independence, based on Numbers 24:17: "A star shall go forth from Jacob, and a staff shall rise from Israel, crushing all of Moab's princes, and dominating all of Seth's descendants." Believing him to be the messiah, Akiva encouraged his students to join Bar Kokhba's efforts against the Romans. When they prepared to join the revolt, they dressed as hunters so they could carry bows and arrows to the woods without arousing suspicion.

Bar Kokhba was successful—for a while. He recaptured and for three years held Jerusalem, until Emperor Hadrian heard about the rebel victories and reinforced his troops in Palestine. In the ensuing putdown of the revolt, the Romans killed tens of thousands of Jews, including, in 132 C.E., the supposed messiah and his men. According to the records of the third-century Roman historian Dio Cassius, in addition to approximately 600,000 Jews slaughtered, countless others died of sickness and fire, and fifty fortresses and almost one thousand of the most important Jewish settlements were destroyed. In 135, after the devastating defeat of the last Jewish stronghold, Betar (southwest of Jerusalem), Jews were prohibited from being within sight of Jerusalem (except on the day of mourning for its destruction, Tisha B'Av), and Jewish life in Palestine was effectively ended until the modern era.

Although parts of the Talmud were written as the events were unfolding, the commentary barely discusses the Bar Kokhba revolt, an omission that suggests the rabbis' attitude toward the entire episode. Believing that it would ultimately be a futile cause of tremendous bloodshed (which it was), many of the rabbis opposed the rebellion. Thinking Bar Kokhba arrogant, they feared it would turn him and Akiva's followers into martyrs and inspire similar useless efforts in the future. That is why the cause of the students' deaths was veiled as disease rather than reported as the result of war.

During the Gaonic period (the time of the great Torah scholars between the sixth and eleventh centuries) the rabbis could more objectively assess the historic occurrences. They recognized the end of the "plague" as the date Bar Kokhba and company had recaptured Jerusalem and made it an official semiholiday. (This corresponds with the idea that Lag B'Omer marked a "suspension" of dying, because the war continued after this temporary victory.)

Recognition was not afforded Bar Kokhba himself until Jewish nationalism developed at the end of the nineteenth century. However, that did not stop him from being turned into a folk hero by the Jews who, enduring generations of persecution and dreaming of a return to their homeland, used the legend to prop up their hopes. In Eastern Europe and later in America, it became customary for Jewish school students to go to parks or woods on Lag B'Omer, picnicking, recounting stories about the heroes of the holiday, and playing with bows and arrows in commemoration of the fighting against the Romans.

For Further Reading

For Adults

Finkelstein, Louis. *Akiba—Scholar, Saint and Martyr.* Northvale, NJ: Jason Aronson Inc., 1990.

This is a readable, comprehensive look at the life, political leadership, ethical thinking, religious contributions, and martyrdom of one of our greatest sages.

Yadin, Yigal. *Bar Kokhba: The Rediscovery of the Legendary Hero of the Last Jewish Revolt Against Imperial Rome.* New York: Random House, 1971.

Written by the professor of archaeology who led the excavations, this fascinating account follows the discoveries—including fifteen dispatches written or dictated by the military commander himself—which brought Bar Kokhba from the realm of legend to real life and reconstructs life and developments during his time.

For Children and Young Adults

"How Rabbi Akiva Became a Scholar," "Everything G-d Does Is for the Best," "Charity Saves from Death," "The Debt Paid by the Sea," "The Doctor and the Farmer," and "The Death of Rabbi Akiva." In CT, pp. 312–318.

These short tales about the life and teachings of Akiva portray his great intelligence and tremendous faith.

Whitman, Amram. *Bar Kokhba.* New York: Bloch Publishing Company, 1985.

In this novel for young adults, the excitement, dangers, and hopes experienced by the Jews during their doomed fight for freedom come alive in action and dialogue. Ages 12–15.

Yokhai and the Light of Torah

One of Akiva's greatest students was Rabbi Shimon Bar Yokhai. Like his teacher, Yokhai openly defied the decree against the study and teaching of Torah. Sentenced to die after Bar Kokhba's death in battle and the fatal torture of Akiva (which we recall in memorials to the Ten Martyrs on Tisha B'Av and Yom Kippur), he went into hiding with his son Eleazar. For thirteen years, accompanied only by Torah and other sacred writings, they lived in a cave, sustained by a carob tree that grew at its entrance and a spring just outside it. According to one story, students visited them one day each year—said to have been Lag B'Omer—for the purpose of learning and bringing them food. Like the students in the Bar Kokhba account, they also carried bows and arrows and disguised themselves as hunters. Father and son emerged only after Hadrian's death and were recognized as great sages.

Before he died—on the thirty-third day of the *Omer*—Yokhai revealed to his disciples the sacred wisdom he had discovered through his years of intense Torah study. Tradition says that the day was filled with endless joy and with great light, and that the sun did not set until he had completed telling his students all he wanted to relate. His words were recorded in what was to become the basic text of *kabbalah* (Jewish mysticism), the *Zohar* (splendid, brilliant light). (The book first appeared in the thirteenth century, brought to light by Moses ben Shemtov de Leon. Although generally believed to be a product of the Middle Ages, it was attributed to the insights and teachings of Yokhai.)

Yokhai's last request was that his death and its anniversary be observed with celebration, rather than with the mourning and fasting that normally accompany the loss of a great scholar. He was happy that his life's work had been finished. Anticipating a mystical marriage of his soul with God, he rejoiced as a bridegroom does on his wedding day and wanted everyone to share his joy.

Upon his death, the story goes, a rainbow appeared in the sky for the first time since his birth. The symbol that God would not destroy the earth as He had with the flood of Noah's time (Genesis 6:13–9:17), the rainbow, during Yokhai's lifetime, had been replaced by the righteous sage himself as God's commitment to sustain the world.

It was not until the Middle Ages that the connection between the joyous *yahrtzite* (death anniversary) of the father of Jewish mysticism and the thirty-third day of the *Omer* was made. Rabbi Khayim Vital and the sixteenth-century kabbalists of Safed (a town in Israel's northern Galilee region, near Lake Kinneret and Tiberias) started the custom of gathering the night before Lag B'Omer in nearby Meron, the mountaintop site of the supposed tombs of Yokhai and his son, and singing and dancing around bonfires until dawn.

The celebration spread throughout the *Sephardi* world and was termed *hillula* (Aramaic for "festival" or "celebration"). Used especially to denote a wedding celebration, the word was later applied to the *yahrtzite* of famous rabbis and scholars (whose souls wed with God), occasions often accompanied by pilgrimage and rejoicing. In addition to celebrations in

Yokhai's memory, children often played with bows and arrows. Here they were said to symbolize the rainbow (in Hebrew the archer's bow and the multicolored arc are both *keshet*) that appeared when the rabbi died.

FOR FURTHER READING

"Shimon bar Yohai and the Cave." In CT, pp. 326–327.

The folktale relates how Yokhai came to hide from the Romans and what he learned in his years in the cave.

"The Most Precious Thing in the World." In CT, pp. 327–328.

This example of the Rabbi's approach to a problem shows how his wise suggestion saved a marriage.

The Agricultural Connection

Late spring, the time of year in which Lag B'Omer falls, is nerve-wracking for farmers. Between the barley and wheat crops, they worry about how weather, insects, or plant disease might affect their food supplies and livelihoods. The fear that the earth might not resume producing sustenance was universal in primitive societies. Late spring was certainly not a time when farmers could be merry and frivolous.

The farmers' concern mirrors the concerns experienced by the post-Exodus Israelites in the desert just after their liberation, which occurred at this time of year. Having exhausted their provisions from Egypt, they complained about their situation and expressed the wish to return to the house of bondage, where at least they had their fill of bread (Exodus 16:3). The next day, God told Moses that they would receive manna (bread from heaven) in another day, on *Iyar* 18, which is Lag B'Omer. According to some authorities, this is the reason we celebrate the date.

Once the Temple was destroyed, and the Jews could no longer bring the barley offerings that marked each day of the *Omer* period, which began during Pesakh, or the wheat bread that ended it on Shavuot, the people became especially sad. They may have felt the particular loss of the sacrifice through which they sensed they could ensure a good outcome for the produce. They were also in mourning for the Temple itself. The restrictions of the period may have been institutionalized reflections of these feelings, with the thirty-third day a brief built-in relief.

Secular scholars and historians have pointed out that the Romans believed that souls came back to Earth at this time of year to haunt the living and would be appeased only by funerals. Late spring, a nonproductive period between growing seasons, was viewed as an inauspicious time for human production, too. Therefore, for thirty-two days (basically coincident with the month of May) no weddings took place (Roman folk sayings about unlucky May marriages were later echoed in England, France, and Germany), and on the thirty-third day, a festival was held. The time frame served the Jews for their own commemorations. The pagan prohibitions, like other non-Jewish customs that have crept into Judaism throughout our history, could have been adapted because they fit our own needs.

Others have drawn parallels with the medieval European May Day celebrations, when children customarily shot bows and arrows in the woods (originally to chase demons who could spoil vegetation), and bonfires were lit to frighten the demons and witches so they could not harm livestock. Evil spirits were thought to be particularly prevalent on May 1, which was preceded by Walpurgis Night (Witches' Sabbath). The German peasants went into the woods to shoot at the spirits, and in England archery contests were held (perhaps the origin of the Robin Hood legend). The Jews may have adopted the custom because it suggested shooting at our own "demons," the oppressors who occupied our Land and threatened our way of life.

WHAT DOES IT MEAN?— RELIGIOUS IMPORTANCE

Although Lag B'Omer, by any definition, is not a sacred occasion, both the Akiva and Yokhai versions of its origin underline a main principle of Jewish life. The importance of Torah—of maintaining it, studying it, and ensuring Jewish continuity through teaching it—was the motivating factor in the lives of both men.

Though they endangered themselves in the process, these rabbis resisted the Romans to uphold the values of Judaism, spreading their learning and love of Torah, promoting it as the only worthwhile way of life. A *midrash* relates that when Pappus ben Judah came upon Akiva holding a public lesson, in clear defiance of the Roman decree, he wondered if the sage were not afraid of the government. Akiva responded with a parable.

A fox walking by a river asked the fish in the water, swimming rapidly in every direction, why they were fleeing. To get away from the nets and traps set by men, they replied. So the fox invited them to come up on dry land to escape. But the fish retorted, "If we are afraid in a place where we can stay alive, how much more fearful we would be where we are certain to die!"

As afraid as the Jews were to study Torah in defiance of Rome, they believed they had much more to lose by trying to live without it. They recognized that Torah, which provided an unparalleled moral structure and guided them to personal and communal fulfillment, was their "sole means of survival and long life" (Deuteronomy 30:20).

The deaths of Akiva's students, the failure of the Bar Kokhba revolt, the destruction of Betar, and the execution of Akiva severely darkened the Jewish world. As a result of the Roman oppression, however, Shimon bar Yokhai shined the brilliant light (*Zohar*) on our understanding of the universe. The process of learning, illuminating the world, and inspiring others is what Torah and Judaism are all about.

WHAT DOES IT MEAN TO US?— PERSONAL SIGNIFICANCE

Until he was forty years old, the poor shepherd Akiva ben Joseph could not even read and had no interest in education. He fell in love with Rachel, the daughter of his rich boss, who also loved him, but said she would marry him only if he became a Torah scholar. At his age, he thought it an impossible task. But one day, while watching the sheep, he noticed that the continual passage of water on a stone had created a groove in it. He realized that if rock could be worn down by steady drops of water, certainly he could learn by continually applying himself. He married Rachel and became one of the greatest Torah scholars to have ever lived. Once he himself was learned, he taught others.

By his example, we learn that it is never too late to begin to learn about our heritage. Little by little you can make accomplishments. It is unlikely they would be of the magnitude of Akiva's (unless, like him, you dedicate yourself solely to learning—which he did for twenty-four years) but would certainly be worthwhile. Akiva's life also demonstrates that it is not enough to have knowledge; you must share it with others, as he did, despite the hardships involved.

We learn about the necessity of balancing learning with other aspects of life from Shimon Bar Yokhai. After Yokhai spent twelve years in his cave, the legend goes, the prophet Elijah appeared to tell him that the Roman Emperor Hadrian, who had sentenced Yokhai to death, had died. The first thing Yokhai and his son saw upon emerging were farmers busy plowing and seeding their fields. It seemed to them a waste of time that should have been devoted to Torah. The anger reflected in Yokhai's eyes burned the fields and trees. A heavenly voice challenged him, "Would you destroy My world?!" and ordered the two back to the cave for an additional year.

They learned, through more Torah study, that the greatest holiness is in the physical world, that we are supposed to use the material to become spiritual and serve God. When Yokhai finally came out of hiding, he applied himself to healing the world.

Together, Akiva and Yokhai demonstrate the important messages of our heritage: learn, teach, and do. Even if you have spent little or no time in your life reading about or attending a program or class about some aspect of Judaism, there is no reason you cannot do so now. Once you have increased your knowledge, share it with your spouse, child, sibling, parents, friend, or neighbor. You will also be able to apply what you have learned to help make the world a better place.

One of the keys to doing so, as we learned at Passover, is to treat all people with respect. It is a courtesy we often disregard within our own community. Even though each one of Rabbi Akiva's students was reputed to be special in a unique way, each one recognized only his own style of serving God, discounting his fellow students. With all their learning they ignored a fundamental principle of Judaism, love of a fellow Jew (*Ahavat Yisrael*).

Attributing their deaths to this transgression is supposed to teach us the importance of embracing all members of the community and accepting diversity within the whole. Yokhai's forced return to the cave to refine his perspective teaches that not everyone has to be involved in the same pursuits: It is enough if the intentions and goals match.

Consider what you are doing, or failing to do, to promote *Klal Yisrael*, the unity of the Jewish people. Do you belittle Jews who have chosen to be either more or less observant or traditional than you? Do you say disparaging things about a particular group of Jews based on their dress, behavior, or lifestyle? Do you let opportunities to challenge the negative comments of others pass? The judgments that accompany perceived differences are often a result of ignorance, theirs and yours. The entire community can be richer and stronger if we drop our prejudices (it is said that the worst anti-Semites are Jews) and speak with and try to learn from each other—the scholar from the farmer, the farmer from the scholar, the *streimel*-wearer from the *kippah*-shunner, and vice versa. The more you know, the better prepared you will be to determine what form your service to God could take.

TRADITIONS: HOW WE CELEBRATE LAG B'OMER

How Do We Show We Celebrate?— Observance

Though both call it Scholars or Students Day, *Ashkenazim* and *Sephardim* seem to have developed two different styles of celebrating the folk festival, for two different reasons.

Ashkenazim and Akiva

In America (as Eastern Europe before) Lag B'Omer is primarily an occasion for Jewish school students. In remembrance of the life of Akiva and the Bar Kokhba revolt, students have traditionally been taken on outings—to forests, woods, and parks—for archery (reminiscent of the scholar-soldiers and their bows and arrows), hikes, picnics, and sporting events.

In Israel, children go on *tiyulim* (outings) to play

with bows and arrows. On hilltops and empty lots throughout the country, they make bonfires, sing and dance around them, and roast potatoes.

Sephardim and Rashbi

Hillula

Hundreds of thousands of *khasidim* and others attuned to *kabbalah*, *Sephardim* throughout Israel and nearby countries, and anyone else who likes a good party, stream to Mount Meron in northern Israel for the *hillula* of Rabbi Shimon Bar Yokhai (referred to by his acronym Rashbi—*Ra*bbi *Sh*imon *B*ar Yokhai). Since 1833, an ancient Torah scroll has been carried in procession (accompanied by flowers and rose water thrown from overhead balconies) from synagogue Beit Abu in nearby Safed (known for its connections to mysticism) to the outskirts of the city. From there, the celebrants (who used to walk the entire distance) are transported by vehicle to the tomb at the top of the mountain, where a huge bonfire is lit at midnight.

The entire route up the mountain is lined with the cars, campers, and tents of pilgrims. Their fires dot the entire site. Oriental music and the smoky scent of lambs roasting on spits pervade the air.

In recent years, the *hillula* has taken on more of a carnival atmosphere, with hawkers selling all sorts of flea market merchandise, and representatives of every *yeshivah* and Jewish institution offering *brakhot* for a price. The closer to the graves, the more dense the crowds jostling to get to the burial places to plea for cures for illness, pain, and infertility. Those praying for miracles light candles in the indentations in the stone walls. Many people leave candy or personal items at the tomb.

Since ancient days it has been customary to throw silk scarves and other clothing into the main fire (called *hadlakot*, or ignitings) despite rabbis' protestations that it was wasteful. (There is a rabbinic prohibition against needless destruction.) Over the years the organizers of the *hillula* have attempted to persuade people to sell the garments and distribute the proceeds to the poor in honor of Yokhai.

Some say the bonfires reflect the ancient communications system between settlements (at their recapture of Jerusalem, Bar Kokhba and his men lit signal fires that were relayed by successive groups of villages throughout the country). There is also a strong connection between fire and Shimon Bar Yohkai himself.

Proverbs likens the soul to a candle (20:27). In the *Zohar*, attributed to Yokhai, the comparison is explained. If you watch a flame, you will see that it moves back and forth and stretches itself, continually reaching higher, like the soul striving for spiritual fulfillment. (This is one of the explanations of why a religious Jew "shuckles" back and forth when he prays: He is imitating the movement of fire, helping his soul become elevated.) It is said that the soul of a *tzaddik* (a righteous person), like a huge flame, rises to the highest level after s/he dies.

The next day, the celebrations continue on Meron. In the parks of nearby Safed, families gather for picnics featuring lively music, dancing, and a profusion of food.

The Haircut

Since ancient days it has been customary to wait until a Jewish boy turns three before giving him his first haircut. That age marks the time that he is ready to begin learning and taking on responsibility as a Jew. Along with getting his hair cut in such a way that leaves the *peiyot* (the hair on the sides of the head forbidden to be completely removed) (Leviticus 19:27), he receives his first *kippah* (skullcap) and *tzitzit* (ritual fringes worn under clothing), and is introduced to Torah study. With his first lesson he receives candy and honey so that he will associate learning and Torah with sweetness.

The tradition of giving boys the first haircut (called *khalakah* in Hebrew, *upsherenish* in Yiddish) at Meron was begun by the Ari (Rabbi Isaac Ben Solomon Luria), most revered of the sixteenth-century Jewish mystics. The ceremony may have become associated with Lag B'Omer simply because haircuts are not allowed during the *Omer* period and relaxation of that restriction on this one day provided the opportunity to celebrate the "coming of age" of little boys who had turned three since the beginning of Passover.

Believing that they will secure health, happiness, and long life for the child, *khasidim* and *Sephardim* in particular bring their three-year-old sons to Yokhai's place of burial on that day. Parents especially try to have a rabbi or dignitary participate as friends and family members each take a snip of the long locks, often throwing them into the bonfire. It is common for a joyous party to be held afterward.

WHAT ARE WE SUPPOSED TO DO?— *HALAKHAH*

Relief from Restrictions

In the forty-nine-day period between Pesakh and Shavuot, there are only thirty-two days on which the prohibitions of mourning ordained for *sefirah* are permitted. On the seven days of Pesakh, two days of Rosh Khodesh *Iyar*, one day of Rosh Khodesh *Sivan*, plus seven Shabbatim, which are all festival days, mourning ceases. The Gemara (commentary on the written version of the Oral Law) states that Akiva's students died only on the thirty-two nonfestival days. That is why the mourning practices are imposed on them and the thirty-third day represents a day of relief.

There are differences of opinion, however, as to whether the prohibitions are supposed to last for thirty-two days (the entire *Omer* period of non-exempted days) until the thirty-third day (symbolic of the period of dying) or after the thirty-third day. The most common observance is to suspend the *Omer* restrictions on the thirty-third day and then resume them on the thirty-fourth, until Shavuot. If you are unsure about the custom followed in your city, consult a local rabbinic authority.

Marriage

A wedding, permitted on Lag B'Omer, is to be held during the day. While it should not begin the night before (mourning is supposed to continue into at least part of the thirty-third day), the marriage feast may extend into the evening and night of the thirty-fourth day.

Haircuts

If Lag B'Omer falls on Sunday, it is permissible (and customary) to have a haircut—not allowed since before Pesakh—on Friday, in honor of Shabbat.

WHAT OTHER THINGS DO PEOPLE DO?— CUSTOMS

Other Times and Places

Candles and Contributions

In *Sephardi* communities, it was customary on Lag B'Omer to light candles and raise communal funds. Sale of tapers in memory of Rabbi Shimon Bar Yokhai, Rabbi Meir Ba'al Ha-Nes—presumably a different one than the man whose tomb is in Tiberias (see "Customs" in chapter on Pesakh)—and other *tzaddikim* buried in Morocco was accompanied among the Jews of that country by study of *Zohar* and singing. The occasion was called *Leilui* (Night) *Nishmat* (of the Souls) *Hatzaddikim* (of the Righteous).

The Judeo-Spanish attended synagogue on Lag B'Omer, where each person made a contribution to have a candle lit in Yokhai's memory. In Syria also, evening ceremonies included auctioning the honor of lighting candles to raise money for local *yeshivot*.

Tunisian Hillula

Nowhere were such proceedings more elaborate than Tunisia, where the Jews of Djerba have long hosted a two-day *hillula*. Before the majority of North African Jewry (particularly the sizable community in Tripoli, Libya) left their native countries for Europe and Israel in the decades after the 1967 Six-Day War, tens of thousands traveled to the small traditional Jewish village of Hara Seghira on the island off the southern coast of Tunisia. (The celebration still draws a large gathering, mostly from Tunisia, but also from France, Israel, and Morocco.)

Pilgrims bring to life the usually quiet hostel built opposite the historic synagogue just for the occasion. Many of the women, wearing white dresses and robes and the traditional jeweled wedding head-pieces, bracelets, and anklets, gather on the balcony that overlooks the entire courtyard, which is filled with men, women, and children. Amid music, singing, and drinking, honors are auctioned for the privilege of placing layers of colored veils on a huge traveling *menorah*. The tremendous wedding-cake-shaped candelabra has holders for hundreds of candles around its multiple brass tiers. When it has been richly decorated—after a sufficient number of donations—a joyous procession of the pilgrims, local people, and musicians leads the *menorah* through the residential areas of the community.

Later, in the synagogue, pilgrims buy candles to place in the *menorah*, on available spots in the sanctuary, or particularly for women seeking special blessings, in the small crawl-space grotto under the Ark—said to be the remains of the first synagogue built on the spot, when the Jews arrived after the destruction of the first Temple in 586 B.C.E. It is believed that if a woman who wants to find a marriage partner or conceive a child places a raw egg in the space, lets it cook overnight in the heat of all the candles around it, and eats it the next day, her prayers will be answered.

WHAT IS THERE TO EAT?— TRADITIONAL FOODS

The only food regularly associated with Lag B'Omer is the hardboiled egg, which may be connected with the mourning of the previous days (eggs, symbolizing the wholeness of life, are the customary first food in a house of mourning) but was probably chosen because hardboiled eggs were easy for children to take on their Lag B'Omer picnics. Among the *Sephardim*, typical North African dishes, such as couscous, are often served.

WHAT TALES ARE TOLD?— STORIES TO READ

Aside from the folktales, legends, and biographical works listed earlier, there is little available specifically for Lag B'Omer.

FOR FURTHER READING

Weilerstein, Sadie Rose. "What Happened to K'tonton on His *Lag'B'Omer* Picnic." In KT, pp. 55–64.

The thumb-sized Jewish boy is rewarded for the way he treats the creatures of the forest. Ages 3–8.

OF ADDITIONAL INTEREST

In Israel

It is possible to see artifacts and visit sites connected with the days of Akiva and Bar Kokhba. The military dispatches from Bar Kokhba discovered among the Dead Sea documents are displayed at the **Shrine of the Book**, part of the Israel Museum in Jerusalem and home of the Dead Sea scrolls. Some of the thousands of Bar Kokhba coins (inscribed "Year One of the Redemption of Israel," "Year Two of the Freedom of Israel," and "Freedom of Jerusalem") are also on display at the **Israel Museum**.

To protect themselves and their rich olive oil business from the Romans, the Jews in Palestine during the second century moved underground into an incredible labyrinth of caves in the limestone area south of Jerusalem. Discovered and excavated in the 1970s and 1980s, the caves, administered by the neighboring *Moshav* (communal farm) **Amatzia**, are open to the public. The ingenuity of the builders, who created secret entries through cisterns, false alleys and small windows to trick and trap intruders, and floors to preserve leaks of valuable olive oil make it a fascinating place to visit.

YOM YERUSHALAYIM

Yom Yerushalayim (yome' yeh roo' shah lie' yim): Reunification of Jerusalem. Observed on *Iyar* **28** (spring; early–late May).

The last holiday added to the Jewish calendar, Yom Yerushalayim, celebrates the reestablishment of Israeli control over our entire eternal capital and spiritual center through the reuniting of the Old City of Jerusalem with the new. Observance is continually expanding outside of Israel because of the significance of the sacred city in Jewish history and continuity.

ORIGINS: WHY WE CELEBRATE YOM YERUSHALAYIM

WHERE DID IT ALL BEGIN?—
HISTORIC FOUNDATION

Jerusalem Lost and Found

According to the United Nations Partition Plan for Palestine, Jerusalem, the city considered holy by the world's three major monotheistic religions and the scene of battle for control since David led the Israelites to it two hundred years after the initial conquest of the Land, was to have been internationalized. During the War of Independence (see chapter on Yom Ha'atzmaut), the Arabs surrounded it, leaving those within the ancient capital without electricity or sufficient food, water, and ammunition—an eerie reenactment of the sieges in 586 B.C.E. and in 70 C.E.

When the war ended, the cease-fire line ran through Jerusalem, with the Jews on the wrong side. The Old City, the section with historic and emotional significance for us, ended up under Jordanian control. Despite the terms of the armistice, which guaranteed access to the historic district, not a single Jew was allowed to go to Judaism's holiest remaining site, the Western Wall (*Kotel Ha Ma'aravi*).

According to Jewish tradition, the Wall—which was not part of the Temple itself but the last standing section of the great retaining and defense structure for the Temple Mount built by Herod—was where God's presence on Earth, the *Shekhinah*, moved when Her ("God's Spirit" is feminine) previous abode in the Temple's Holy of Holies was destroyed. For that reason it was the holy spot in Israel Jews most wanted to visit, for there, they believed, they stood in God's presence.

So from the time of the destruction of Jerusalem in the year 70, pious Jews undertook often treacherous journeys to find their way to the Wall, where their heartfelt supplications were accompanied by such expressions of emotion that non-Jews named the location the Wailing Wall. Being blocked from it after the War of Independence, when we were so close, was frustrating and painful.

Having never signed a peace treaty with Israel following their defeat in 1949, the neighboring Arab nations remained in a state of war. Terrorist and sniper attacks across the borders were common. Agricultural settlements in northern Israel were often shelled by artillery. All Israeli homes had to be equipped with bomb shelters, in which many children of the post-independence generation spent their nights.

Two days after Yom Ha'atzmaut in 1967, Gamal Abdul Nasser, President of Egypt, began massing troops in the Sinai Peninsula and insisted that the United Nations remove its peacekeeping forces from the region. The next week, he closed the Straits of Tiran, strangling Israel's Red Sea supply route. Israel called up just about every able-bodied man between the ages of eighteen and fifty-five, secular and religious, student and employee, professional and laborer.

The pressure on Israel was becoming unbearable.

101

Arab rhetoric, the inaction of world powers, the overwhelming weight of nations supporting her foes, the extent of the enemies' forces training their weapons on every border created a feeling of isolation within Israel. Jews in Israel and around the world feared that the nation, just a quarter-century after Auschwitz, was on the brink of annihilation.

On June 5, Israel did what was necessary for survival: The country made a preemptive attack, beginning what would be the Six-Day War. In its first strikes, it destroyed the grounded Egyptian air force and hundreds of tanks, along with the majority of Syria's planes. Two days later, on June 7, 1967—*Iyar 28, 5727*—stunned, ecstatic, and awed Israeli soldiers stood before the *Kotel*, praying, singing, weeping. The chief chaplain entoned the memorial prayer for those lost in the battle. The *shofar* cried out again and again, obliterating gunshots from the nearby streets as the area was secured. The blue-and-white flag was hoisted, *Hallel* chanted. Those back at command headquarters heard the incredible announcement: "All of Jerusalem is in our hands!"

The war continued for only four more days. A month earlier, Israel had desperately wanted to avoid it, had feared for its very existence, was suffering economically with the call-up of virtually all of its men of working age. Now, in addition to Jerusalem, Israel held territory captured on all three fronts, from all three aggressors: the Sinai Peninsula and Gaza (Egypt), the Golan Heights (Syria), and Judea and Samaria (Jordan's "West Bank").

To an even greater degree than after independence was won, Israel and being Jewish were seen in a different light. American Jews who previously had had no particular interest in Israel felt vicarious pleasure in its fortunes. Israel's triumph, won by strong, directed, brave men and women clearly in control of their own fates, led to a surge of Jewish identity, a feeling of pride in being Jewish, and an awakening of Jewish nationalistic feelings. In the Soviet Union, news of Israel's spectacular and unexpected victory spurred the refusenik movement (Jews who applied for permission to emigrate from their country to Israel but were "refused" by their government, fired from jobs, and often harassed and/or imprisoned).

Cementing and Celebrating Unification

Despite claims on Jerusalem by other religious groups, for whom it also has significance, only for us Jews was it ever a national capital or the focus of a people's literary, religious, spiritual, and historic experience. Both the secularists and the religious were anxious to establish immutable sovereignty over the entire city, the rightful seat of government, and the religious center for world Jewry. Within a few years, both groups lent widespread support for making *Iyar* 28 Yom Yerushalayim. Their two approaches led to a mixture of secular and religious celebrations that take place predominantly in Israel but are increasing in number in the Diaspora as well.

In 1992, in honor of the twenty-fifth anniversary of reunification, the office of the Israeli Prime Minister initiated a program to foster commitment to Jerusalem as the eternal capital of the Jewish people and the political center of the Jewish state. Copies of the "Jerusalem Covenant" (printed in Hebrew, English, French, Spanish, German, and Russian) were distributed to Jewish communities throughout the world. Each was to organize a signing ceremony involving local leaders, organization members, dignitaries, and other supporters, and then display the Covenant as testimony to local identification with the Holy City. Guest books were placed near the signed Covenant to allow other supporters to add their names through 1996, the trimillennium of King David's conquest of the city, when a year of activities is planned in honor of that anniversary.

FOR FURTHER READING

Narkiss, General Uzi. *The Liberation of Jerusalem—The Battle of 1967*. London: Vallentine, Mitchell, 1983.

Commander of the central front and one of the first officers to break into the Old City, the author gives a day-by-day, moment-by-moment account of the turning point in Jewish history, replete with the emotions and concerns prior to battle.

Rabinovich, Abraham. *The Battle for Jerusalem, June 5–7, 1967*. Philadelphia: The Jewish Publication Society of America, 1972.

Based on three hundred interviews, the author, a reporter in Jerusalem before and during the battle, and in the Old City in the first hours after the Israeli troops entered, gives a personalized and suspenseful account.

WHAT DOES IT MEAN?— RELIGIOUS IMPORTANCE

A highly unusual spiritual atmosphere pervaded Israel in the weeks leading up to the war and the months following it, even among those who normally scoffed at anything vaguely religious. Perhaps it was the need in the face of seemingly insurmountable odds to have faith in something beyond themselves, or the tremendous desire to believe the promises for a better future, that they would be delivered by a merciful God, which had continuously sustained the Jews in previous precarious situations. For the first time in generations, there was widespread feeling—documented in newspaper articles, diaries, and books about the war—that God was playing an active role in the events around them.

People increased their *tzedakah* contributions, spent more time in Jewish learning, were more careful to perform *mitzvot*, and treated others with more courtesy than usual. They prayed more fervently, confident that with their efforts, God would not allow another two-and-a-half million Jews to be murdered. Even Jews who normally ignored religion easily mentioned God in conversation. Many people saw whatever was happening—the anxiety, the economic burden, the war no Israeli wanted—as part of His master plan. Spiritual leaders adeptly recognized the contemporary signs of ancient prophesies and reassuringly related current events to traditional text.

Reports of battle experiences considered supernatural filtered back from the fronts. There were even instances of tough military veterans sensing that something extraordinary was underway. After the capture of Jerusalem, and certainly by the seventh day, there was widespread feeling—even among those usually loathe to acknowledge, never mind credit, God—that a miracle had indeed occurred. After so many years, and so much devastation, perhaps God *was* again looking toward His people. Even those hardened to spiritual expression were swept up in the talk and thought that perhaps the messianic days long-ago promised were at last on their way.

With the overwhelmingly secular nature of Israel's population, however, the Israelis credited themselves—their strength, their intelligence, their superior army—for the triumph and any movement toward redemption. That attitude created a feeling of invincibility. Unfortunately, it caused people, even within the government and military, to misread and ignore signs of trouble leading up to the disastrous Yom Kippur War.

If the circumstances surrounding the War of Independence had created a window of opportunity through which Israel was renewed, the Six-Day War threw open a window of opportunity through which the world could be redeemed. With Jerusalem in our possession, all the concrete prerequisites for accomplishing our mission were in place. It remained for the Israelis and the Jews of the world to take advantage of the situation to achieve Judaism's long-standing goals and bring the world closer to perfection by establishing a just society. The advent of Yom Yerushalayim had the potential to be a far-reaching turning point in Jewish and world history.

FOR FURTHER READING

Feldman, Emanuel. *The 28th of Iyar*. New York: Bloch Publishing Company, 1968.

An American rabbi on sabbatical in Israel decided to stay as tensions mounted. He kept a journal, recording his own feelings and observations, as well as a record of developments and the reactions of the people around him. With humor and pathos, his account captures the mood of the country and relays the increased spirituality at a time that the hand of God was clearly felt.

WHAT DOES IT MEAN TO US?— PERSONAL SIGNIFICANCE

Jerusalem has always existed on two levels: the physical and the ideal. The physical was the political and religious center of the country, the seat of government, and the focus for pilgrimage and prayer. The ideal was the spiritual symbol of the nation, the vision of prophets and dream of exiles, the image in the minds and feeling in the hearts of generations of Jews who never saw the city but knew it by the essence of its name: peace (*Yerushalayim—shalayim, shalom*).

The Six-Day War gave us back the physical Jerusalem. Israel is committed to retaining it—undivided—as the state's capital, despite the fact that practically the entire world refuses to recognize it as such (only Costa Rica has established its embassy there), and the Arabs insist its status be negotiated as part of the peace process.

Take every opportunity to express support for the city to remain the capital of Israel and the Jewish nation, in letters to government leaders or special ceremonies (like those for the Jerusalem Covenant). You can also contribute to the stability, growth, and beauty of the city through organizations devoted to improving the quality of life there (such as Teddy Kollek's Jerusalem Foundation and various support organizations for the city's cultural and social service institutions).

Those who want to abolish Tisha B'Av claim that the State of Israel is the Third Temple, and therefore we no longer need to mourn over the destruction of Jerusalem and exile. But the Jerusalem we longed for was never just a geographic destination under our administration. It was to be a place of harmony within the nation and between nations.

Though the mood of Yom Yerushalayim is decidedly different from that of Tisha B'Av, our thoughts on both days are similar. Mourning for the loss of Jerusalem and the battle to reclaim it will not be finished until we have achieved peace—not just the political variety but the overriding harmony the prophets described. That is the more difficult task. How do we create the Jerusalem of ancient visions? Since it is a reflection on the civic level of the situation between individuals, we can start in our own hearts, in our own lives, in our own interactions with other people. Brotherhood requires mutual respect and tolerance, the acceptance of others who have different opinions and philosophies. We must be able to stand together with other Jews, accepting diversity within unity, before we can expect to stand shoulder to shoulder with the other nations. And that is something we can each strive for on a daily basis.

FOR FURTHER READING

The Jerusalem Covenant. Jerusalem: Ministry for Jerusalem Affairs, 1992.

If you can get a copy of this specially produced booklet (it is uncertain how long supplies will last), it is worth having. Beautifully produced, it provides annotation, in the format of the Talmud, with text in the center and commentary surrounding it. The Covenant itself relays history, emotion, and hope in the Jewish connection with the city. (Available from World Zionist Organization Torah Education and Culture Department, 110 East 59th Street, New York, NY 10022; 212-339-6080.)

TRADITIONS: HOW WE CELEBRATE YOM YERUSHALAYIM

HOW DO WE SHOW WE CELEBRATE?— OBSERVANCE

As you would expect, most recognition is given to Jerusalem Unification Day in Israel, although it is just as appropriate to celebrate it in the Diaspora, for the same reasons we celebrate Israel Independence Day. Special ceremonies and other programs outside of Israel—including some citywide commemorations such as services and musical presentations—are growing in number.

In Israel and in Diaspora congregations that choose to observe the occasion, daily services include *Hallel* and Psalm 107 (praising God for His steadfast love). Outside of synagogue, films about Jerusalem, concerts of songs devoted to the city, and prayers for its continued unity are all parts of observance. Israelis often take day-long hikes around the Old City walls, and there have been mass rallies in Jerusalem, attended by representatives of Jewish communities throughout the world.

DO YOU HEAR MUSIC?—SONGS TO SING

The Six-Day War—and particularly the capture of Jerusalem—is so closely identified with one song it is as though it had been written specifically for it. At the Hebrew Song Festival on Yom Ha'atzmaut just before the fighting began, Naomi Shemer presented her "*Yerushalayim Shel Zahav*" (Jerusalem of Gold), which she had written the previous month. Its haunting melody and sad words mourned the desolation of Jerusalem bereft of Jews.

Shemer was in the desert entertaining the troops when she learned that the Old City was in Israel's hands. Immediately she changed the images of abandonment and decay in the last stanza to reflect the new situation of people and sounds once again enlivening the city. The song caught on like wildfire and remains a favorite in the Israeli music repertoire.

WHAT TALES ARE TOLD?— STORIES TO READ

Histories of the city of Jerusalem (starting with II Samuel 5, about David's conquest of the city) and personal accounts abound. Some of the most interesting reading may be found in legends and in novels that use Jerusalem as a setting.

FOR FURTHER READING

For Adults and Children

Children of the World Paint Jerusalem. Jerusalem: Keter Publishing, 1978; New York: Bantam Books, 1978.

As part of the tenth anniversary celebration of the reunification of Jerusalem, the city's mayor, Teddy Kollek, invited the children of the world to express their impressions of and feelings for the Holy City through paintings. Of the unexpected 150,000 entries from forty-three countries, four hundred were selected for an exhibit at the Israel Museum. One hundred ten of these (including thirteen from foreign winners) were chosen for this fascinating and moving book that reflects the cultures in which the young artists live and the hopes and dreams universal among children.

For Adults

Millgram, Abraham E. *Jerusalem Curiosities.* Philadelphia: The Jewish Publication Society, 1990.

These stories of oddities and peculiarities of Jerusalem and life in that city help convey its unique role in world history. This enlightening book is great preparatory reading for anyone planning a trip to Israel.

Sonnenfeld, Rabbi Shlomo Zalman. *Jerusalem Gems: Great Tales About Everyday People in Old Jerusalem.* Brooklyn: Mesorah Publications, 1987.

Written by a fourth-generation Jerusalemite and member of an old *yishuv* family, this collection records incidents in the lives of famous and unknown men and women trying to live righteously in the Eternal City a few generations ago.

Vilnay, Zev. *Legends of Jerusalem.* Philadelphia: The Jewish Publication Society of America, 1973.

Stories, folklore, and accounts of historic and spiritual occurrences said to have happened in Jerusalem, or to people and things associated with it and the Temple, are collected in this compendium of material about the Holy City. It provides a view of its history and the mystique surrounding it.

Wiesel, Elie. *A Beggar in Jerusalem.* New York: Random House, 1970.

The dreamlike account conveys the sense of imminent destruction the Israelis felt prior to the War of 1967 (especially with reflections of the Holocaust) and their exhilaration upon reaching the Wall.

Videotape

Shalom Sesame: Jerusalem

The Sesame Street characters and celebrity friends visit major sites in the capital. The program contains songs, comedy, and animation. Available as a single cassette or with four other thirty-minute programs on Israel. Ages 2–12.

OF ADDITIONAL INTEREST

In Israel

It has long been a tradition to insert written petitions (*kvitlakh*, in Yiddish) in the spaces between the stones of the *Kotel.* If you could not go to the Wall yourself, you could send a supplication with someone else or pay a company to do so. Now it is also possible to fax your prayer to the *Kotel,* thanks to a service established by Bezek, Israel's telephone company (972-2-612-229).

Two museums in Jerusalem help tell the story of the battles for the city. *The Tourjeman Post* distributes a brochure giving the background from 1917, while the building and its exhibits concentrate on the period of the great divide, 1948 to 1967. At **Ammunition Hill**, which had to be conquered before the Israelis could enter the Old City, a reconstruction of the battle condition memorializes those who died there. Changing exhibitions sometimes feature the moving letters and pictures of the soldiers who participated in the crucial battle.

Despite the practical problem of having two Moslem mosques on its site, there are those who believe the erection of the Third Temple is imminent—and they want to be ready to reinstate biblical Temple service as soon as it occurs. Rabbis, goldsmiths, silversmiths, weavers, and other artisans working under the auspices of The Temple Institute have been engaged since 1987 in creating authentic Temple utensils based on information provided by the Bible, Talmud, and archaeological research. The magnificent finished items—priestly vestments, Levite musical instruments, gold and silver vessels—are displayed and explained at the **Treasures of the Temple** exhibit in the Old City's Jewish Quarter.

The **Tower of David Museum of the History of Jerusalem** presents four thousand years of the city's history in intricate models and dioramas of exacting and historically accurate detail. The Citadel, where the museum is located, is at the Old City's Jaffa Gate. Nearby is an entry point for the less than three mile **Ramparts Walk** along the top of the city walls, which features observation points. (If you want to explore areas outside the segment between Jaffa and Zion Gates, along the Armenian and Jewish Quarters, check with local authorities. Although one can also walk in the opposite direction, along the Moslem Quarter and into East Jerusalem, Middle Eastern politics and tensions being what they are, it is not always safe to do so.)

The conquests of the Six-Day War provided access for archaeologists to key sites for excavation, and incredible finds have been unearthed, including parts of David's City and passageways to the Temple Mount, which are open to the public. (Check with local tourist offices regarding access and advisability of visiting sites located in Arab sectors.)

More information on these sites and related tours is available through the Israel Government Tourist Office in Atlanta, Chicago, Dallas, Los Angeles, New York, or Toronto.

SHAVUOT

Shavuot (sha-voo'oat; Yiddish: shuh-voo'-us): Giving of the Torah to Israel. Observed on *Sivan 6–7* (spring; late May–early June).

Shavuot, the second pilgrimage holiday, began as an agricultural festival marking the transition between the barley harvest and the start of the wheat-ripening season. Later it was identified as the anniversary of the Revelation at Sinai of the Law that transformed Israel from a liberated people to a truly free people. Its message and the event it commemorates make it one of the most significant religious occasions of the year.

ORIGINS: WHY WE CELEBRATE SHAVUOT

WHERE DID IT ALL BEGIN?—HISTORIC FOUNDATION

A Direct Message from God

In the third month after the Israelites left Egypt, they reached a place in the wilderness called Mount Sinai. There, after being announced by thunder and lightning, and the blast of a *shofar* (ram's horn), enshrouded by a cloud enveloping the mountain, God told the nation what He wanted from them. For the only time in human history, God did not limit revealing Himself to only one visionary who would report to others what He had said. Every Israelite at the foot of the peak experienced the phenomenal Revelation.

"I am the Lord your God, Who brought you out of the land of Egypt, out of the house of bondage," He began in the first of the *Asarei* (Ten) *Hadiberot* (Sayings, commonly called Commandments), which established the foundation for proper behavior between humans and God and between one person and another. "You shall have no other gods. . . . You shall not take the Name of the Lord in vain. . . . Remember the Sabbath day to keep it holy. Honor your father and your mother. . . . You shall not murder. You shall not commit adultery. You shall not steal. You shall not bear false witness. . . . You shall not covet. . . ." (Exodus 20:2–14; Deuteronomy 5:6–18).

Even though they had been prepared for three days (during which time they pledged to do whatever God asked of them [Exodus 19:8]), the actual occurrence was so overwhelming that the people were afraid they would not come out of it alive. (A *midrash* depicts God holding Sinai over Israel's head, threatening to turn the mountain into their grave if they refused to obey, an image used to convey the coercion they felt. After all, what choice did they have while standing in the presence of their Judge, Jury, King and Redeemer? The rabbis explain it was not until Purim, when God was completely hidden from them, that the Jews could accept the covenant in faith, rather than out of fear.) Insisting that Moses assume his usual role as intermediary, the Israelites were given the remainder of God's instructions, the complete Torah, through the prophet.

Despite their trepidations, this unparalleled event made every one of the Israelites direct witnesses to God's existence and the extent of His involvement in the world. From that moment, every single Jew—not just the priest, the prophet, or even those physically present at the historic moment—was empowered to serve God. Every Jew who would ever live is said to have been at Sinai (including converts), and each had a role to play in making God's plan for a perfect world a reality. The authority of Torah in Jewish life—as a God-given set of laws and regulations—and the authority of the learned of each generation to interpret it—not to change it by addition or deletion (Deuteronomy 4:2, 13:1) but to appropriately apply it to changing situations on Earth—were established.

Following the Revelation, Moses ascended Mount

Sinai, where he was given the two stone Tablets (*Lukhot*) of the Covenant (*Habrit*) on which God had engraved the Ten Commandments. Everything else God told him he recorded on a scroll—the Torah—which he gave to the priests and elders before his death (Deuteronomy 31:9).

Chapters 19 and 20 of the Bible book Exodus describe the incredible encounter. If the Exodus created a unique physical nation, by giving people who had individually endured the same miserable fate as slaves a common, and community-forging, redemption, the Revelation at Sinai created the unique spiritual nation by giving the people a common, and unique, mission that held great consequences not only for Israel but for the world they were charged to influence.

As significant as this formative event was, you would assume that, like for the Exodus, Torah would go to lengths to mark the date and describe an appropriate commemorative ritual. But it does neither. In fact, until the first century of the Common Era, *Matan* (the giving [of]) *Torah* was not celebrated as a holiday at all, and Shavuot, with which it became associated, was strictly an agricultural festival.

A Harvest Holiday

Among the laws given to the Israelites at Sinai were those pertaining to the holidays they were to observe once they reached and successfully cultivated the Land that had been promised to them.

One of those special occasions was Shavuot, the second pilgrimage initially identified as *Khag Hakatsir* (Feast of Reaping) (Exodus 23:16) and later as *Khag Hashavuot* (Feast of Weeks) (Exodus 34:22, Numbers 28:26, Deuteronomy 16:10, II Chronicles 8:13). When the firstfruits (*bikkurim*) of the field (referring to wheat) were ready to be harvested, the Israelites were to bring an offering of new grain, in the form of two loaves of leavened bread made from choice flour (Leviticus 23:17–22). On this sacred occasion, a law for all times and places, they were also to cease their normal work.

There was one minor technical problem in keeping the holiday. Unlike every other Jewish festival, for *Khag Hakatsir/Shavuot*, or *Yom Habikkurim* as it was also known (Numbers 28:26), Torah specifies no fixed date. It simply says to count seven complete weeks from the day the first sheaf of barley is waved (the beginning of the *Omer*) and celebrate this new festival on the fiftieth day (Leviticus 23:15).

The first sheaf was to be offered "after the Sabbath" connected with Passover (Leviticus 23:11). (Identification of what "after the Sabbath" meant was a point of contention between two philosophical branches within Judaism, the Sadduccean and the Pharissean.) Later, start of the seven-week count is even less precise: "when the sickle is first put to the standing grain" (Deuteronomy 16:9). Since the start of the harvest depends on when the barley ripens, the indefinite timing makes sense. However, it was not left at that.

The Pharisees' conviction that counting the *omer* began the day after the paschal sacrifice (see chapter on Pesakh) set Shavuot, occurring fifty days later, on *Sivan* 6. That celebration at the end of the period of barley harvesting was festive because it also coincided with the start of the wheat and fruit harvests. With the combined harvest of the two grains and the produce of the trees and vines, the farmers could determine how well fed and prosperous they would be for the year.

All seven kinds of food plants for which Torah praises the Land—barley, wheat, grapes, figs, pomegranates, olives, and dates (Deuteronomy 8:8)—were covered in the commandment to take "some of every firstfruit of the soil which you harvest from the Land that the Lord your God is giving you" and offer it to Him (Exodus 23:19, 34:26; Deuteronomy 26:2-11). This produce, which did not ripen all at once, or at the same time as the first wheat, could be offered anytime beginning at Shavuot and through the fall festival Sukkot.

In Temple Times

All of the festivals ordained in Torah required burnt offerings (in this case one bull, two rams, and seven sheep [Leviticus 23:18–20]). But unlike on other holy days, when offerings were made in addition to specific rituals that defined the occasions, sacrifice was Shavuot's exclusive observance.

The wheat was the gift of the entire community. The two loaves (*shtei halekhem*) brought in thanksgiving for the wheat harvest were used in the ritual of waving—as were the barley sheaves on Pesakh for the first grain harvest and the four plant species on Sukkot for the completion of the agricultural year—before being eaten by the priests. Firstfruits of trees, on the other hand, were required of every Jewish household. Each farming family brought what it felt compelled to offer for this "freewill contribution," based on how blessed with good crops it had been (Deuteronomy 16:10).

Initially, the Israelites made their sacrifices at local sanctuaries. But a religious reformation instituted around 619 B.C.E. to unite the nation and spiritually reinvigorate the Jews abolished the provincial altars and designated Solomon's Temple as the only site for all pilgrimages and sacrifices. From then on, the people had to journey to Jerusalem to express their recognition that God was part owner of the Land, and that whatever grew there was a result of the partnership between Him (providing the land, sufficient rain, favorable conditions) and humans (plowing, planting, tending, reaping).

The peasants prepared by going to their fields, orchards and vineyards to discover the first ripe stalk or cluster of grapes, or date, pomegranate, or olive. Tying each *bikkur* with a piece of grass or thread, they declared it a firstfruit. At the time for the journey to Jerusalem, they added the designated pieces to their choicest produce piled in baskets—gold and silver ones among the wealthy, wicker ones from the peasants—adorned with greens and flowers. (The people traveling long distances brought dried figs and raisins so their offerings would not spoil.) The pilgrims gathered in the nearest town, then proceeded to a district center, and from there to the capital, adding people to the procession at every stage.

An ox whose horns had been gilded, wearing a wreath of olive leaves, led the way as a flute player accompanied happy, singing Israelites to the Temple Mount. Every individual—including the King of Israel himself—carried a gift basket on his shoulders, entered the Temple courtyard, and recited the declaration drawn from Torah (Deuteronomy 26:5–10) connecting him to the past, all the way back to Abraham ("the wandering Aramean"), and to the future (the expected outcome of the harvest, which the *bikkurim* suggested). In fulfillment of the accompanying commandment to rejoice with the Levite and stranger (Deuteronomy 26:11) the city was the site of great celebration after the ceremony (*Bikkurim* 3:1–8).

Due to its occurrence in the midst of the summer harvest, its short duration, and the staggering of formal *bikkurim* presentations among different regions that allowed for various ripening dates, the Shavuot pilgrimage did not attract the attendance enjoyed by the other *Shalosh Regalim*, Pesakh and Sukkot. The fact that it was for farmers only and limited to those who made the trip to the Temple further limited attention to it.

Through the first century, unlike the other holy days that were by then recognized for their historic significance, Shavuot seems to have remained strictly an agricultural festival. Both Philo, the Alexandrian Jewish philosopher, and Flavius Josephus, the Roman Jewish historian who recorded details of contemporary Jewish life, failed to mention any other aspect of the holiday.

FOR FURTHER READING

Shihor, Samuel. "King Agrippa and the Firstfruits." In Shavuot HA, pp. 288–291; and *The New World Over Story Book*. Ed. by Ezekiel Schloss and Morris Epstein. New York: Bloch Publishing Company, 1968, pp. 189–193.

Based on the Talmud's sense-arousing description of the Shavuot pilgrimage, the story follows a young boy to Jerusalem, where he is assisted by the king in following the last promise he made to his recently deceased father. This is a great story to read aloud to young children. Ages 5–13.

Zeitlin, Solomon. "The Bringing of the First Fruits During the Second Commonwealth." In Shavuot HA, pp. 145–147.

The description of the pilgrimage for *bikkurim* includes the phrases chanted or recited by the priests and pilgrims.

Post-Temple Transformation

Without rationale or ritual outside of *bikkurim*, Shavuot would have disappeared completely after the destruction of the Temple if a spiritual dimension had not been added. Particularly in the wake of the Bar Kokhba debacle (see chapter on Lag B'Omer), when the Jews' faith that they would be redeemed flagged, the rabbis recognized that they had to renew the people's hope. That meant forging connections between current and future situations with formative events in Israel's history.

As they did for every other observance, the rabbis gave Shavuot a place along the Jewish continuum by attaching it to the people, rather than to their homeland. The notion of the human–Divine cooperation needed for a successful harvest was broadened to encompass the God–Israel partnership necessary for all earthly endeavors. The logical choice for a related occurrence in Israel's history was the Divine Revelation at Mount Sinai, when God presented Himself and His plan for life on Earth to Israel.

The groundwork for linking Revelation with Shavuot had been established during the last centuries of the Temple's existence, when the Pharisees were engaged in a philosophical-theological struggle with the Sadducees over the essence and direction of the religion. For the Sadducees, who were aristocrats connected with the Temple priests, it rested in the system of sacrificial rites and was based on literal reading of Torah's word. The Pharisees, who tended to be common folk, believed that there was more to God's teaching than what met the eye, that prayer and study were no lesser means to do God's will than was sacrifice, and that Torah was meant to be interpreted on different levels.

Getting close to God, the Pharisees felt, was a matter of not just bringing Him gifts but trying to understand Him the way one would try to understand any partner: by learning what and how He thought and felt—which is all presented in Torah. That text defined the terms of His ongoing relationship with Israel and the world, a relationship that began with the courtship of the Exodus and led to marriage at Mount Sinai. It was the marriage contract by which God and Israel agreed to serve each other. By this reasoning, the date of the wedding of God and Israel was a most important one.

However, nowhere did scripture specify when that momentous occasion occurred. Torah merely says that the Israelites arrived at Sinai "*bayom hazeh*," on this day (Exodus 19:1). That was purposeful, said the rabbis, to teach us that Israel's getting the Torah is a perpetual, ongoing process that transcends time, place, and ritual. It is given to every generation in every locale. Each time it is understood a little deeper through study, each time a commandment is followed, the Torah is transmitted and received.

Still, in order to recast Shavuot as *Zeman Matan Torateinu* (the season of the giving of our Torah), the rabbis had to find compelling evidence of the coincidence of dates in the text itself. The legacy of the Pharisees, who identified the first day of the *Omer* as *Nissan* 16, served them well. Through a process of interpretation of the time markers in Exodus 19, and comparison of certain phrases in that text with similar ones in other parts of the Bible, the rabbis determined that the Revelation had taken place on *Sivan* 6—fifty days after Passover, fifty days after the first count of the *Omer*, the same day as Shavuot.

There was further evidence in the root of the word *Shavuot*. *Shavuah*, meaning "week," comes from the word *sheva*, which means "seven." Seven is a holy number, a number signifying perfection, the highest level of attainment in the material sphere after which we are beyond the limits of earthly time. Seven days rounded out Creation and form a week, seven years make a sabbatical cycle (Leviticus 25:2–4; Deuteronomy 15:1), seven times seven years comprise the jubilee cycle (Leviticus 25:8), which begins in the seventh month, the month of our highest spiritual attainment (the month of Rosh Hashanah, Yom Kippur, and Sukkot). And Shavuot arrives at the end of a period of seven times seven weeks. Derived from the same root as *shavuah*, the word *shevuah* means taking a vow. (The Talmud tractate named Shevuot is not about this holiday, but about oaths.) At Sinai, God and Israel exchanged their vows.

Although there were some dissenting opinions, the majority of rabbis accepted the date. Now the period of counting the *omer* took on new meaning as the spiritual link between Exodus and Revelation, with Shavuot providing a finale to Pesakh. Consequently, the rabbis referred to it in Talmud as the day of *Atzeret* for Passover, the same term used to describe the last day of Sukkot. For that holiday it indicated the conclusion of the ingathering, the pulling together of all achievements. Here it is the conclusion of the process of liberation, the attainment of true freedom.

As Torah study grew in importance in Jewish life, celebrating the text also became more important. Two sages in the third century (Elazar and Joseph) stressed the requirement of feasting and rejoicing on the anniversary of the giving of the Torah.

Middle Ages and the Modern Age

In the weeks before Shavuot in 1096 the Crusades began, claiming hundreds of Jewish lives in the Rhine valley. To honor the dead without interfering with the joy associated with the holiday, a communal prayer for those martyred in that barbaric outbreak of anti-Semitism was introduced for the Sabbath prior to Shavuot. The timing was considered doubly significant, because the day fell during the *Omer* period, which commemorates the massacre of an earlier persecution, that of Akiva's students by the Romans (see chapter on Lag B'Omer). Along with *Av Harakhamim* (Father of Compassion), the first form of the memorial prayer, the list of the rampage's victims was read.

Since more people attended synagogue on Shavuot than on the Shabbat prior to it, the memorial service was moved to the holiday itself and expanded to encompass the one done on Yom Kippur since talmudic days, which honored all dead, not only martyrs but also pious Jews and deceased loved ones. (In time, it was added to the liturgies of the last days of the other pilgrim festivals as well.)

When Simkhat Torah developed several centuries later (see chapter on Sukkot), the intense expression of joy for Torah was shifted to that occasion. It was not that the people of the time felt that the beginning of our covenantal life had lost any significance, but they recognized that, as in a good marriage, depth of understanding and appreciation for one's partner grows over time. The love and attachment at a twenty-fifth or fiftieth wedding anniversary is more substantial, and more substantiated, than at the wedding. So, too, there is more reason for joyous celebration after the Torah has been examined, studied, and lived with than when it has merely been presented.

For the kabbalists, in particular, though, Shavuot remained an opportunity to express intense devotion to Torah. A *midrash* says that even though the Israelites knew that God was going to give them an incredible gift on the afternoon of *Sivan* 6, at noon they were still asleep. Moses had to go to their shelters (according to one version), or thunder and lightning had to be used (according to another) to rouse them. So in the sixteenth century, the Jewish mystics—who believed that every action of every individual affects the state of the world—developed an all-night vigil to compensate for the sleeping Israelites' affront to God. A compilation of selections from Torah, Talmud, and *Zohar*, called *Tikkun* (improvement, or remedy) *Leil* ([for the] night [of]) *Shavuot*, was published for use on the holiday (although the learned often chose their own texts). Dark-to-dawn study on the first night of the holiday became customary.

Early in the nineteenth century, the German reform movement, which had eliminated *bar mitzvah* as the "coming of age" ceremony for its thirteen-year-old boys, instituted a new initiation into Jewish responsibility for its boys and girls: confirmation. Designed as the culmination of a course of study for teens, it was originally held on the Sabbath during Pesakh, Sukkot, or Khanukah. Within a few years, it was moved to the holiday appropriate for expressing commitment to Jewish ideals and Jewish life, when the voluntary acceptance of God's law is commemorated. Adopted by the Conservative movement and even some Orthodox congregations after being introduced in America in 1846, confirmation grew in popularity, becoming a widespread feature on the first night or first morning of Shavuot.

In Israel the pioneers of the early twentieth century who reclaimed the Land refocused on the agricultural aspects of the holiday. In modern *bikkurim* festivals, children dressed in white, wearing floral wreaths, and carrying baskets of produce from their local villages and *kibbutzim* (communal farms) joined parades and processions to ceremoniously present their firstfruits amid great pageantry. Reading poems, singing, dancing, displaying artwork, and presenting dramatic performances accompanied the donations, which were sold to benefit the Jewish National Fund.

Shavuot continues to be observed this way in Israel and, throughout the Jewish world, with synagogue service.

WHAT DOES IT MEAN?— RELIGIOUS IMPORTANCE

Jewish belief and behavior rest on the historic occurrence of the Divine Revelation, the cornerstone of Judaism, and on the body of knowledge that was revealed.

Hearing the Voice of God

As religions go, Judaism is not very dogmatic—except on two points: belief in one God, and belief that Torah, Judaism's sourcebook, is the word of God spoken directly by Him to the entire nation of Israel. While there had been differences of opinion as to what form God's communication took, and how the Israelites perceived His contact with them (they heard everything, they heard only the first two commandments and the rest through Moses, they heard only an unintelligible sound interpreted for them by Moses, Moses heard every word spoken by God in a language he could comprehend, Moses intuited the entire code), the fact that He revealed Himself, a fact critical to Jewish thought, remained unchallenged until the late 1700s.

Then the Enlightenment, with its emphasis on the rights of each individual to follow his or her conscience, and the sublimation of faith to scientific evidence, led to differences in approach to the account of Revelation. There were those who maintained that Torah was absolutely true, a record of the word of God. There were those who insisted it was absolutely not the word of God, but the work of humans. And there were those less rigid on either view, seeing it as a divinely inspired human product representing a joint effort of God and His children.

Some of those who continued to believe that God had spoken to the Israelites distinguished between the ethical and ritual laws He had given them. Recognizing the purpose of the former, they retained them but deemed the latter obsolete and expendable. Jews who rejected the notion of Divine Revelation still saw great value in Torah (whose Sinai story, they said, expressed the Israelites' understanding of something extraordinary that had happened to them in the desert): It reflects what we recognize to be true of human nature and psychology and provides a common moral system that guides our actions in the world. For these people, it is holy not because it was given by a supernatural being but because human beings invest it with religious meaning and purpose.

The faithful whose worldview was not shaken by the Enlightenment continued to accept Torah as a complete, integrated system whose *mitzvot*, whether ethical or ritual, all have purpose within the whole, even if humans cannot discern their meaning. According to traditional Jewish thought, Jewish law, being God-given, is eternal and universal, its authority absolute. We can explain the *mitzvot* (as we can Revelation) according to any system of philosophy we like, but they remain true and binding. We do *mitzvot* not because we understand why, but simply because they are commanded.

If you reject this notion, and believe that the Torah was not given by God, Judaism is reduced to a cult whose laws, while they might reflect some Divine thought, are manmade and therefore subjective, subject to shifting standards as societal mores change. If they are alterable over time, the laws can be transformed beyond recognition or altogether abolished—along with the system, the people, and the promise they define.

That is why the law was revealed publicly to everyone—not, as is usually the case with religious illumination, to one individual in a secluded setting. As God told Moses, He wanted the people to hear for themselves so that they would ever after trust that Moses was accurately conveying His concerns (Exodus 19:9). Hearing with their own ears and seeing with their own eyes, they would have no reason to doubt, and they would be able to give an eyewitness account to their children, who would pass the national history to their children (just as we pass on the experience and lessons of the American Revolution, the signing of the Declaration of Independence, the Civil War, the Holocaust and those experiences and lessons become part of the consciousness of those who were not physically present at those world-changing occurrences but are no less affected by them).

Whichever explanation you accept, the revealed word of Torah stands as our national myth, which is not in any way to suggest that it is not true. A myth is a story based on a community's actual experiences (real historic events) designed to make sense of the world, create identity, and generate loyalty to the community. Subjective, as is all reality, myth answers existential questions and defines the community's outlook. To the extent that ongoing experience supports it, the myth remains the explanation of how and why a nation came to be and what its role is, and continues to be transmitted to successive generations.

Our shared tradition and common reference point in the search for meaning in life has withstood the rise and fall of philosophies, cultures, and governments for more than three thousand years. And it continues to work on some level whether you take the national myth literally or not.

This was demonstrated beautifully during a nasty debate in Israel's Knesset, as related to and by the educator Avraham Infeld. Shulamit Aloni, the education minister controversial for her liberal religious stance, was being characteristically chastised by the Orthodox wing. "How dare you say such things to me!" she admonished them. "How can you use such terms? After all, aren't we all brothers and sisters? Didn't we all stand together at Sinai—even if it never happened?"

The message that we are supposed to embrace on some level, at least as an element of our national culture, is the one the Israelites were reminded of in Deuteronomy's recapitulation of their history and laws: "Has any nation ever heard God speaking out of fire, as you have and still survived? Has God ever done miracles, bringing one nation out of another nation with such tremendous miracles, signs, wonders, war, a mighty hand and outstretched arm and terrifying phenomena, as God did for you in Egypt before your very eyes? You are the ones who have been shown so that you will know that God is the Supreme Being and there is none besides Him" (Deuteronomy 4:33–35).

Based on this shared history, we are supposed to attest to other nations about His involvement and standards in the world—and more. In addition to making Israel a passive witness, through the covenant we became a full-fledged partner with God, the messenger through which God's plan would become known and the activist through which it would be implemented.

The Chosen People

When the Israelites arrived at Sinai, God promised "if you will obey me faithfully and keep My covenant, you shall be My treasured possession among all the peoples. . . . you shall be to Me a kingdom of priests and a holy nation" (Exodus 19:5–6).

Perhaps no other label has caused as much problem for Jews, or been as misunderstood, as "chosen people" (a term, by the way, that does not appear anywhere in scripture; it is based on a talmudic interpretation of "treasured"). We were not singled out by God because of any inherent virtue (our stiff-necked nature and continual backsliding into idolatry and other abominations are painstakingly recorded) or for privileged treatment (as our history painfully demonstrates). All we possess over and above our non-Jewish neighbors is the obligation to fulfill Torah, simply because we made the commitment to do so.

Any nation could have taken the responsibility. As *midrash* relates, God asked the children of Esau "Will you accept My Torah?" They asked what was written in it. "You shall not murder." Esau's descendants would not give up their heritage of living by the sword. So God offered Torah to the children of Amnon and Moab, who also wanted a preview. They were told the Torah says you shall not commit adultery. But adultery was a national pastime they refused to abandon, so they would not accept it. The children of Ishmael also had their chance, but could not limit their economic status by abiding the commandment "You shall not steal." When God finally gave Israel the option, they all said, as one, "*na'aseh v'nishma,*" we will do and we will hear."

The Israelites leaped before they looked, promising to obey before they fully heard what would be required of them. God had demonstrated His caring, through all He had done for the patriarchs and matriarchs, and all He had done for the former slaves; He had "proven Himself" through all the history that preceded Sinai, so He deserved their allegiance. They opted to accept the Torah, the covenant for an eternal partnership through which they would help God complete Creation by perfecting the world. Had they not, tradition says, the earth would have returned to chaos, metaphorically if not physically, for what would the world be without moral law?

Chosenness refers only to this relationship with God, not to Israel compared with other nations. What Israel was chosen, and chose, to be is an example of how human beings should act toward each other. What they chose to take on was the responsibility, as teachers and priests, of being held to a stricter standard of judgment as they demonstrated universal truths that are available to anyone—regardless of race, nationality, or birthright.

Torah was given in the desert, a no-man's-land, at Mount Sinai, whose location is not known, so that no nation, even the "chosen people," could ever claim it as its alone. Although the Torah obligates no one but the Jews to its laws, according to talmudic tradition, it was proclaimed simultaneously in seventy different languages, so that every nation on Earth would understand that it could also accept its precepts. Israel is merely Torah's caretaker.

Torah

In their directness and simplicity, the Ten Commandments proclaimed by God from Mount Sinai touch minds and hearts with such truth that no concepts have had more influence on religious thought or had more moral impact on humanity. The ancient world had never heard anything like them; the world since has not devised a better code of behavior.

Within the Decalogue are actually two sets of laws, one reflecting the human–God relationship, the other the relationship among people; one pertaining to the human being as an individual, the other as a member of society. Read as pairs across the tablets (One and Six, Two and Seven, etc.), they mirror and illuminate each other.

Since murder takes the life of a human being created, with the help of God, to be like God, it diminishes God's image. Adultery, allowing lust to become a driving force, is tantamount to worshipping another god. In stealing (which in particular applies to kidnapping), you deal falsely with another person, equivalent to using God's name inappropriately. Desecrating the Sabbath, which is supposed to be kept as testimony to God's power over nature (Creation) and history (Exodus), gives false witness to God's role in the world. And coveting, particularly the main object of the commandment, another's wife (Exodus 20:14, Deuteronomy 5:18), leads to the break-up of family, the sabotaging of a child's respect and honor due his or her parents.

Revelation at Sinai continued beyond the tenth commandment, encompassing an additional 603 ethical and ritual laws, a total of 613 *mitzvot* (commandments, and not, as the word is sometimes understood, "good deeds"). The 248 positive *mitzvot* were said to correspond to what the rabbis believed were the number of bones in the body, and the 365 negative *mitzvot* were said to correspond to the days of the year. Together they suggest that we devote every part of our bodies, every day of our lives, to following God's word.

These comprise the Torah, the essence of our unique faith and lifestyle, the historical gene, as Rabbi Shlomo Riskin so beautifully says, which unites all generations, our national treasure, "the precious vessel of God with which the world was created" (*Pirkei Avot*).

The word *Torah* is derived from the word *horah,* meaning "to teach" (teacher is *moreh,* or *morah* in the feminine, and teaching, *hora-ah*). It is said that everything in the world can be found in the Torah by delving into its layers of meaning. It teaches us all we need to know in order to live in this world: public, private, material, spiritual, business, pleasure, personal, interpersonal. In its Five Books of Moses (Genesis, Exodus, Leviticus, Numbers, and Deuteronomy) or, in Hebrew (named for the significant word in the first phrase of each book), *Bereshit* (in the beginning), *Shemot* (the names), *Vayikra* (and [God] called), *Bemidbar* (in the desert), and *Devarim* (the words), are history, ethics, prophesy, and psychology. The printed form (as opposed to the carefully hand-written parchment scroll) is called *Khumash*, from the Hebrew word for five (*khameish*).

(The Hebrew Bible also contains *Nevi'im* [Prophets], the accounts of the visionaries, spiritual leaders, and kings of Israel, and *Ketuvim* [Writings], additional texts attributed to prophets, kings David and Solomon, and select sages. Together, all three sections are known by the acronym *Tanakh*—<u>T</u>orah, <u>N</u>evi'im, <u>K</u>etuvim.)

Our tradition maintains that at the same time Moses received the written document (Torah *Sheh Biktav*), he was given a corollary elucidation of it, the Oral Law (Torah *Sheh B'al Peh*). Without it, it would be impossible to comprehend what many of the Torah's laws mean. Our understanding of how Sabbath is to be kept and remembered, what exactly *tefillin* are, and how *kashrut* is to be observed, for example, comes from these explanations of how to derive deeper and varied meanings from the text. (If you look at a Torah scroll, you will see that unlike the *Khumash*, it does not include the dots and dashes used in other printed texts to indicate vowel sounds. [All letters in the Hebrew alphabet are consonants.] While tradition maintains that Moses was taught the correct pronunciation for the superficial meaning, the absence of vowels is one way of allowing for various readings and interpretations.)

Moses did not record these instructions but taught them to Joshua, who passed them to the Judges, who transmitted them to the Elders, who continued the chain of memorizing the instructions and passing them on orally to each succeeding generation—the Prophets, the Men of the Great Assembly, the great sages—until the traditions were officially recorded as the *Mishnah* (around 200 C.E.). The rabbis feared that because of mounting persecution against the Jews, the laws would be lost to future generations if not preserved in written form.

Sages later added their commentaries on the *Mishnah*, which became the Gemara. Together, *Mishnah* and Gemara form the Talmud (from the Hebrew word for study, *lamad*; student is *talmid*), the combined heritage of rabbinic thought reflecting the way the unchanging law was interpreted with relevance to meet the needs of the Jews at any time in history.

For Further Reading

For Adults

Aseres Hadibros/The Ten Commandments. Ed. by Rabbi Nosson Scherman and Rabbi Meir Zlotowitz. Brooklyn: Mesorah Publications, 1986.

Part of the acclaimed ArtScroll series, this slim volume provides detailed explanations of the most famous laws in the world.

Chill, Abraham. *The Mitzvot—The Commandments and Their Rationale.* New York: Bloch Publishing Company, 1974.

Organized in the order in which Torah presents them (so they can be studied with the weekly portions), each of the 613 *mitzvot* is explained in several clear and concise points and then elucidated with select commentaries from a range of historic sources.

"Commandments, 613." In *Encyclopedia Judaica*. Vol. 5. Jerusalem: Keter Publishing House, 1971, pp. 759–783.

The sages disagreed as to exactly which laws constitute the 613 said to be contained in Torah. This list, the accepted enumeration of Maimonides, includes their biblical sources based on rabbinic interpretation and is arranged under subheads by category.

Kaplan, Rabbi Aryeh. "The Commandments." In *Handbook of Jewish Thought.* New York: Mazmaim Publishing Corporation, 1979, pp. 59–81.

The chapter is a great introduction not of specific commandments, but commandments in general: how they were given, their nature, why we observe them and other basic facts. All are given in brief, simple numbered points. (This book is one of the best available introductions to classic Judaism.)

Kitov, Eliyahu. *The Book of Our Heritage: The Jewish Year and Its Days of Significance.* Trans. by Nathan Bulman. Jerusalem/New York: 'A' Publishers, 1968, pp. 89–104.

The explanation of the Ten Commandments, based on talmudic interpretation and *midrash*, presents the broader implications of each, how they relate to each other, and how their significance in Jewish law is derived from scripture.

For Children

Cone, Molly. *Who Knows Ten? Children's Tales of the Ten Commandments.* New York: UAHC Press, 1965.

An introduction to each commandment and a version of how the Israelites heard and reacted to it is followed by a story, in ancient or modern setting, demonstrating how it applies to everyday life. Ages 8–11.

Cowan, Paul. *A Torah is Written.* Philadelphia: The Jewish Publication Society of America, 1986.

Explaining Torah, its use and importance, the photo-illustrated text describes the work of one particular scribe in Brooklyn who created a Torah scroll.

The book follows every step of the process beginning with the making of the parchment. Ages 7–11.

Topek, Susan Remick. *Ten Good Rules*. Rockville, MD: Kar-Ben Copies, 1991.

Appealing illustrations accompany presentation of the Ten Commandments in language geared for young children. (For that reason, some of the commandments have been rewritten from a negative to a positive format.) Ages 3–6.

WHAT DOES IT MEAN TO US?— PERSONAL SIGNIFICANCE

Connecting with Torah

Unlike the other festivals, Shavuot is not a day of recollection on which we merely pretend to experience the event it commemorates. We do not reenact Revelation, we *enact* it, and we continue to do so the day after Shavuot and the next day and throughout the year. There is no specific date, no identified place, no unique ritual associated with *Matan Torah* because the Law is given to each of us in our time, wherever we are, with our own means of finding its relevance for us as individuals.

Unless we receive Torah, by using it in our daily lives, the gift is meaningless. Our sages tell us that the world rests on three things: Torah (study), *avodah* (Divine worship), and *gemilut khasadim* (acts of lovingkindness). The second and the third emanate from the first. It is not enough to simply learn what is in the sacred text, Torah study being one of the 613

mitzvot (Deuteronomy 6:7). We must serve its author by applying it to our actions in the world. It was not enough for the king of Israel to write one *Sefer* (book [of]) Torah to be deposited in the royal treasury, a symbol of its worth (Torah, not precious stones and metals, is Israel's wealth). He was enjoined to write a second one, to accompany him wherever he went and whatever he did, so that he would live by it. "Great is the study of Torah," say our sages, "for it leads to proper action" (*Kiddushin* 40b).

Tradition claims that an angel comes to every one of us when we are in the womb and teaches us the entire Torah. Then, just before birth, the angel touches us between the nose and mouth (creating the philtrum, that distinct impression) to make us forget it all. But that first instruction (like the mother's voice that is immediately recognized by the newborn who has heard it for nine months, or music that resonates with familiarity for a child who heard it in utero) makes us receptive to it later. This is sweet *bubbe-meiser* (grandmother's story), but it makes a point: Studying Torah is like a return, a rediscovery of something we already know, a way of saying that it is inherent knowledge, ringing true because it is such a basic part of each one of us.

The key is to find a way you can relate to it. There are said to be seventy facets to Torah, different ways (like the seventy languages in which the Ten Commandments were proclaimed) in which it can be understood, based on one's particular needs and abilities. They fall into four distinct levels commonly associated with Torah learning: *pshat*, the literal meaning; *remez*, the suggested interpretation; *derush*, the moral lesson; and *sod*, the mystical significance. Just as the manna given to the Israelites in the desert was said to taste like whatever food they desired, our spiritual sustenance can satisfy individual yearnings for truth and meaning.

The idea of taking on hundreds of *mitzvot* may seem overwhelming—although you might be amazed at how many you follow in the course of just being a decent human being. (Actually, only 369 are in practical force today, and just 270 apply to everyone, since many deal with Temple sacrifice and others are in effect only in Israel.) While it would be ideal to accept the whole package, and Judaism strives toward perfection, it does not expect it. (Our greatest leaders and heroes are shown to us with all their flaws. Read carefully about Moses [Exodus], who dealt directly with God. He did not behave properly enough to merit being allowed to reach the Promised Land. Read the stories about King David [I Samuel 16–31; II Samuel; I Kings 1–2]. For all his greatness and accomplishments, he was hardly a paragon of virtue.)

Instead, Judaism is concerned with your intent and the direction in which you are moving. Every single *mitzvah* you do is judged as meritorious and not discounted by any *mitzvah* you fail to fulfill. Just as one step in the wrong direction makes it that much easier for you to make another mistake, doing one *mitzvah* can lead you to do another. Each has tremendous value in and of itself.

You can start with the Ten Commandments. Generally, most of us would say that we do a pretty good job of adhering to them. However, like everything else in Torah, they have deeper and more subtle meanings than what a surface reading reveals.

It is unlikely that you have taken a knife, gun, or other lethal instrument to a fellow human being. But do you do anything that could hurt someone's reputation or publicly embarrass him/her? Both are forms of murder, for they diminish a person. Idolatry is not restricted to genuflecting before useless figures of stone or metal but includes counting on material possessions or transient power for protection.

Perhaps you would never have an extramarital affair. But are there other ways you disrespect a spouse or threaten the foundations of your marriage? Are you satisfied with what you have, or content to work to gain what you want—or are you so obsessed with having someone else's wealth, power, position, or possessions that your life is affected? Do you give your parents the honor and respect they deserve just because they brought you into the world and nurtured you? Part of the commandment to study Torah is to give it to the next generation. What kind of example are you providing for your children (whom you want to "honor *their* mother and father" and be able to teach their children to "honor their grandmother and grandfather")?

How do you relate to God? Have you made any attempt to discover the meaning and purpose of His laws, to evaluate their value or uncover their relevancy for your life—or do you reject them in ignorance or because you think they are inconvenient?

The Israelites were gently chastised in advance for any excuses they might find for not developing a relationship with Torah. "Surely this instruction which I enjoin upon you this day is not too baffling for you. Nor is it beyond reach. . . . No, the thing is very close to you, in your mouth and in your heart, to observe it" (Deuteronomy 30:11–14).

Remember that part of the responsibility is to teach Torah to your children. There are several versions of the Ten Commandments that present the concepts on their level. You can ask your children to think of situations in their lives that illustrate each command-ment. Expose them to Bible characters and stories (which have been adapted for children as young as two years), and encourage them to retell the stories in their own words. It can inspire a lifelong process, like all learning. Shavuot was the beginning of a great adventure for the Israelites. It can be equally as great for you and your family.

Unity

The rabbis explain that one of the prerequisites for the giving of Torah was that the nation of Israel be united. Rashi noted that when Israel "encamped" in the wilderness (Exodus 19:2), the verb used is in the plural. Later in the same verse, when they "encamped" before Mount Sinai, the verb is in the singular, indicating that they had come to be of one mind, one purpose, one heart. And when they responded to Moses' initial communication from God, and subsequent instructions, "all the people answered as one, saying "All that the Lord has spoken we will do!" (Exodus 19:8, 24:3).

Unity means that we value and respect each other as individuals with something to contribute. It is a major principle of our religion, the foundation for strength and continuity. At the Revelation the entire community heard and together accepted one set of laws. Since the community is made up of individuals, each of us is obligated to share the message given at Sinai, and with the world. So it is the responsibility of each individual Jew to fulfill its precepts, and not to expect that someone else is doing the job for him or her.

A pair of wonderful folktales deliver the same message. A couple so poor they did not have enough money to properly celebrate Passover agreed that every week each of them would put a coin from his and her meager earnings through the slot of a special box, and leave it there. Not one week passes before the husband thinks "There is no need for me to put my hard-earned money into savings as long as my wife is adding hers," and so he spends whatever he has in hand. And the wife thinks, "Why should I contribute the few pennies I have left over from running the household as long as my husband is filling the kitty?" Come next Passover, there is no money for provisions.

With similar thoughts the residents of Khelm, known for their "cleverness" but not their intelligence, try to ensure a stock of wine for their next Purim fest. They decide that every week each man will bring a small part of his Shabbat wine to the synagogue and pour it into a communal barrel. One Khelmite thinks, "With everyone else contributing their wine, if I put in water instead, no one will notice." Unfortunately, he is not an original thinker. When the barrel is opened for Purim, the Khelmites have only what they had deposited all year: pure water.

When each person thinks someone else is doing the job, we can collectively end up with nothing. As the saying goes, a chain is only as strong as its weakest link. Torah is the connection that has kept the chain of Jewish continuity alive. The secret of our survival is continually listening to God's voice and being alert to opportunities to carry out His strategies, to safeguard the national treasure, and to pass it along to the next generation. You would not lose sight of the family jewels; neither should you misplace the national treasure.

For Further Reading

Berman, Melanie, and Joel Lurie Grishaver. *My Weekly Sidra*. Los Angeles: Torah Aura Productions, 1986.

The basic message of each of the fifty-four weekly portions is presented in simple language and activities to help children understand the concepts. The name of each portion is given in English and Hebrew, a key quotation from each section of Torah is highlighted, a question around which parents and teachers can initiate discussion is presented, and an opportunity for each child to comment on how s/he would fulfill the message of the portion is included. There are many pictures to color and learning activities as well. This is a great addition to a home library. Ages 6–8.

Cassway, Esta. *The Five Books of Moses for Young People*. Northvale, NJ: Jason Aronson, 1992.

Suitable to be read aloud, the key stories of the Bible are told with humor, emotion, and engaging language. The book provides a beautiful way to introduce children to the people, events, and values of Torah. Ages 4–10.

Eisenberg, Ann. *Bible Heroes I Can Be*. Rockville, MD: Kar-Ben Copies, 1990.

This charming picture book takes one character trait or activity of each of the major Bible characters and, with a few simple words and beautiful illustrations, shows how the child is naturally like them. A good way to begin to build identification. Ages 2–5.

Nissan, Mindel. "A Gift for All." In *The Complete Festival Series*. Vol. 2. Brooklyn: Merkos L'Inyonei Chinuch, 1967, pp. 176–189.

A *midrashi*-style story relates how Moses convinced all the people—scholars, merchants, workers, women, and children—that each had a stake in Torah. Ages 11–14.

Samuels, Ruth. *Bible Stories for Jewish Children*. New York: Ktav Publishing House, 1954 and 1973.

In two volumes—*From Creation to Joshua* and *From Joshua to Queen Esther*—the key stories of Jewish scripture are covered concisely. They can be read aloud to young children, or older children can read the stories themselves. Ages 6–10.

See also resources to help you discuss God with children, listed in the chapter on Rosh Hashanah.

For Further Exploration

Discovery Seminars

Aish HaTorah College of Jewish Studies runs a program designed to increase pride in being Jewish and interest in Torah study and Jewish life. The centerpiece is an elaborate series of sessions, using a modern national survival model, proving the Revelation at Sinai with scientific and mathematical evidence that appeals to modern, skeptical minds. It is a fascinating and thought-provoking presentation done periodically at sites around the country, either as a weekend retreat or a one-day experience. (For information, call a local Aish center—Cleveland, Columbus, Detroit, Lakewood [NJ], Los Angeles, Miami, New York, St. Louis, Washington [DC], Toronto, London, Jerusalem—or the Discovery USA office in New York, 718-377-8819.)

TRADITIONS: HOW WE CELEBRATE SHAVUOT

What Do We Use?—Ritual Items

Since there are no unique rituals associated with Shavuot, there is almost nothing special needed in order to observe it. In addition to the first item below, you might encounter the others, which are used for two widely practiced customs.

Memorial Candle

On the evening prior to the *Yizkor* service, held on the second day of Shavuot, it is customary for anyone who has lost a parent to light a *yahrtzite* candle at home. (Some people also light for grandparents.) You can purchase the candles at a Jewish supply store or a supermarket that has a kosher food section. Contained in a small can or juice glass, it burns for twenty-five hours. Many people use the candle as a source of fire with which to light candles or the stove on the second day of *yom tov*.

Tikkun Leil Shavuot

To support the one major activity connected with Shavuot—Torah study—special anthologies originally drawn from traditional text by the kabbalists have been compiled. They contain brief sections of every Torah *sidra* (weekly portion) and the first and last sentences of each tractate (major division) of the *Mishnah*, and may include excerpts of *Zohar* (the central work of Jewish mysticism), a few sentences from each book of Prophets, accounts of the most significant sections of *Tanakh*, and Maimonides' list of the 613 *mitzvot*. The *Tikkun Leil Shavuot*, as it is called, is often in Hebrew but does come in English/Hebrew versions. Available in some Jewish bookstores, copies may be provided by your synagogue. (While the *Tikkun Leil Shavuot* is used in traditional circles, synagogues and communal organizations often design their own programs of study for the night of Shavuot that do not rely on the *Tikkun*.)

Decorative Greens

Synagogues and homes are traditionally adorned with fresh greens and flowers in honor of the holiday that occurs in the spring. Small trees, leafy or flowering plants, boughs, and floral arrangements are placed around the sanctuary and near the ark, as well as around the house and on the dining table.

Favorite flowers for the occasion are lilies—standing in for the lily of the valley to which Israel is compared in the Song of Songs (2:1–2)—and roses, chosen because of a playful reinterpretation of a verse from the Book of Esther (8:14): "the decree (*dat*) was proclaimed in Shushan" becomes "the law (*dat*) was given with a rose (*shoshan*)." Lilies and roses often have been placed directly on the *Sifrei* (plural of *sefer*) *Torah*, individually, in wreaths, or in garlands.

As an agricultural holiday, Shavuot has always been linked to plant life. In particular, the baskets used to transport firstfruits to the Temple were adorned with flowers and leaves. According to another explanation for the decorative scheme, the greens recall Sinai itself. The fact that the Israelites were warned not to allow their livestock to graze near the mountain (Exodus 19:12–13) indicates there

was a grassy oasis at its base. The greens serve as vibrant reminders that Torah is "a tree of life to those who hold fast to it" (Proverbs 3:18). Some rabbis claimed—even though they are in contradicton to the foundation for the holiday of Tu B'Shevat—that we use branches because Shavuot is the day of judgment for fruit trees.

Rabbi Elijah, Gaon (meaning "excellency" or "genius") of Vilna, Lithuania, the leading sage of his era (1720–1797), tried to have the custom of decorating with flowers and leaves discontinued when similar practices became widespread among Christian churches for Whitsun, the day Jesus' disciples are said to have been divinely inspired (the Christian version of Pentecost, Greek for fiftieth and the archaic term for Shavuot). Most communities ignored him (although in some, the development of special papercuts, particularly those featuring floral motifs, may have been a direct response to his ruling).

How Do We Show We Celebrate?—Observance

A Jewish folk saying identifies Shavuot as the best of all Jewish holidays, because we can eat whatever we want (unlike Pesakh with its restrictions against leaven), wherever we want (unlike Sukkot, when we must have our meals in the *sukkah*), and whenever we want (unlike Rosh Hashanah, when we have to wait through long services, or Yom Kippur, when we are not to eat at all). In addition, it provides us with an opportunity to reaffirm our connection with the very foundations of our faith: It is the anniversary of our eternal commitment to God. Just as a spouse does not blithely skip over a wedding anniversary, Jews cannot ignore this day.

When We Observe

Orthodox and Conservative Jews celebrate Shavuot for two days, while the Reform and Israeli Jews celebrate one. Technically, this is one time that the second day for the Diaspora is totally unnecessary. Since the festival arrives fifty days after the beginning of Passover, there was never any doubt as to its date. But so as not to set one biblically ordained holy day apart from another, the Diaspora communities added the second day of Shavuot for the sake of consistency.

Ushering in the Holiday

As for all festivals, we begin Shavuot by blessing the festival candles at home (see "Observance: Ushering in Pesakh" in chapter on that holiday for full explanation). The one difference here is in timing: While on Shabbat we light prior to sunset, and on a festival that does not coincide with Shabbat we may light at sunset or later (as long as we use a preexisting flame, such as a candle or pilot light), on Shavuot we *must* wait until nightfall (unless, of course, the holiday coincides with Shabbat). This is because we are commanded to count forty-nine full days for the *Omer*, and the count is made only after a day is complete. So we wait until three stars appear (the traditional indication of nightfall, and the start of a new day).

In addition to the *brakhah* for kindling, we recite *shehekheyanu* for the arrival of the holiday.

בָּרוּךְ אַתָּה, יהוה אֱלֹהֵינוּ, מֶלֶךְ הָעוֹלָם, אֲשֶׁר קִדְּשָׁנוּ בְּמִצְוֹתָיו, וְצִוָּנוּ לְהַדְלִיק נֵר שֶׁל [*שַׁבָּת וְשֶׁל] יוֹם טוֹב.

Barukh Atah, Adonai Eloheinu, Melekh Haolam, asher kidshanu b'mitzvotav, v'tzivanu lehadlik neir shel [Shabbat v'shel] yom tov.*

Blessed are You, Lord our God, King of the Universe, Who has sanctified us with His commandments and commanded us to kindle the [Sabbath and]* festival lights.

---

*Said when Sabbath and the holiday coincide.

בָּרוּךְ אַתָּה, יהוה אֱלֹהֵינוּ, מֶלֶךְ הָעוֹלָם, שֶׁהֶחֱיָנוּ, וְקִיְּמָנוּ וְהִגִּיעָנוּ לַזְּמַן הַזֶּה.

Barukh Atah, Adonai Eloheinu, Melekh Haolam, shehekheyanu, v'kiyamanu, v'higgiyanu lazman hazeh.

Blessed are You, Lord our God, King of the Universe, Who has kept us alive, sustained us, and brought us to this season.

Since the second day is regarded as a duplicate of the first, both blessings are repeated at the start of the festival's second day, again after nightfall. (If you are lighting a memorial candle, do so before you light the festival candles.)

The festival meal, as usual, begins with the *kiddush* (full text of the festival *kiddush* can be found in a comprehensive prayer book), which must also be done after nightfall. *Shehekheyanu* follows it, again on both nights, as long as the person who makes *kiddush* is someone other than the one who lit the candles (only one *shehekheyanu* per person).

בָּרוּךְ אַתָּה, יהוה אֱלֹהֵינוּ, מֶלֶךְ הָעוֹלָם, בּוֹרֵא פְּרִי הַגָּפֶן.

Barukh Atah, Adonai Eloheinu, Melekh Haolam, borei pri hageffen.

Blessed are You, Lord our God, King of the Universe, Who creates the fruit of the vine.

The *motzi* for bread is said over two loaves, which are standard for every Shabbat and festival and have added meaning and sometimes distinctive shapes for Shavuot (see "Traditional Foods" later in this chapter). Traditional Jews precede it with the blessing for handwashing (always done prior to a meal that begins with bread):

בָּרוּךְ אַתָּה, יהוה אֱלֹהֵינוּ, מֶלֶךְ הָעוֹלָם, אֲשֶׁר קִדְּשָׁנוּ בְּמִצְוֹתָיו, וְצִוָּנוּ עַל נְטִילַת יָדָיִם.

Barukh Atah, Adonai Eloheinu, Melekh Haolam, asher kidshanu b'mitzvotav, v'tzivanu al netilat yadayim.

Blessed are You, Lord our God, King of the Universe, Who has sanctified us with His commandments and commanded us regarding washing the hands.

בָּרוּךְ אַתָּה, יהוה אֱלֹהֵינוּ, מֶלֶךְ הָעוֹלָם, הַמּוֹצִיא לֶחֶם מִן הָאָרֶץ.

Barukh Atah, Adonai Eloheinu, Melekh Haolam, hamotzi lekhem min ha'aretz.

Blessed are You, Lord our God, King of the Universe, Who brings forth bread from the earth.

Study

Following the holiday meal, many people proceed to synagogue for *Ma'ariv*, followed by an all-night (or into-the-night—many last only until 12 A.M.) Torah study session based on the kabbalists' practice. We remain awake to show that, unlike the situation of our heavy-lidded ancestors at Sinai, there is no need to bring us to our senses; we are ready to receive Torah. The *tikkun* (which refers both to the study session and to the text used for it) was the only observance developed specifically for Shavuot. (Although *tikkunim* were later introduced for Pesakh and Hoshanah Rabbah, this is the one most widely observed.)

In addition to wanting to compensate for the Israelites, the mystics had the idea that at midnight, the heavens open and favorably receive the thoughts, study, and prayers of those who remain awake on the anniversary of the Revelation. (Some promoted the legend that, as on Hoshanah Rabbah [see chapter on Sukkot], wishes are fulfilled at that moment. The Moroccan Jews believed staying up all night guaranteed you life for the next year.) It was likened to the hours of preparation prior to a wedding. The chapter headings in the anthology used for study were said to represent the jewels used to adorn a bride prior to her marriage, and the *tikkun* process was the *bedecken* ceremony (when the groom verifies the identity of his bride and places the veil over her face), which precedes the wedding.

Through the ages scholars have followed the *Tikkun*, but among the learned who knew how to study traditional text, it was also common to devote the time to Talmud. Today, the *tikkun* might consist of a series of seminars on a variety of topics based on ancient or modern texts, Jewish history, or current events. In Israel, the Western Wall is a popular site for the study session. In the United States, in addition to communal settings, a *tikkun* especially for children may take place at home, in which age-appropriate books and Bible stories can be the basis for activities and discussion. (There is no reason a group of adults cannot get together to study in someone's home—and while you may not want to do it late at night, there is also no reason it cannot become an ongoing activity.) Refreshments such as cheesecake and coffee are usually served. Breakfast might follow a sunrise *Shakharit* service for those who participated in a communal study group.

Liturgy

With a few additions, the prayer services for Shavuot coincide with those for the other festivals. (The regular daily and Sabbath *siddur* is used in many synagogues, since it contains the basic changes in prayers. A special festival prayer book, a *makhzor* specifically for Shavuot, contains more of the *piyyutim* associated with the occasion, which embellish the story of Revelation.) The *Amidah* refers to the occasion as *Zeman Matan Torateinu*, the Season of the Giving of our Torah. Full *Hallel* (Psalms 113–118) is recited following the *Shakharit Amidah*, and the priestly blessing, if any *Kohanim* are present in the congregation, is done during *Mussaf*.

Akdamut

On the first day of Shavuot, a special hymn is recited responsively by the reader and congregation, each taking two verses, after the Torah scroll has been opened and the first person has been called to it. An introduction (*akdamut*) in Aramaic to the Ten Commandments, it is an exaltation of God, His wonders in the world, Torah, and the reward waiting at the end of days for those who devote themselves to it.

The first forty-four verses are a double acrostic of the Hebrew/Aramaic alphabet (first two verses start with *aleph*, next two with *bet*, etc.). The initial letters of the last forty-six verses spell the author's name and a blessing: "Meir, the son of Rabbi Yitzkhak, may he grow in Torah and good deeds, Amen. Be strong and of good courage." The syllable *ta* at the end of each line, representing the last and first letters of the Hebrew alphabet, signifies the endless cycle of Torah study.

Tradition holds that Rabbi Meir, the eleventh-century cantor of Worms, Germany, wrote the hymn of praise to God, Israel, and Torah in response to being forced to publicly debate the precepts of Judaism as opposed to those of Christianity. While celebrating the Jewish people's resolve to retain Torah despite oppression, he chose to write his hymn in Aramaic so only Jews would have access to its meaning. Meir's purpose especially was to strengthen the people's faith during the Crusades, the first of which claimed his wife and son.

Instead of *Akdamut*, the *Sephardim* and Yemenite Jews read one of several versions of a *ketubah* (marriage contract) between Israel and God modeled on the traditional format for a Jewish bride and groom. It generally includes prophetic verses alluding to the covenant between God and Israel (Jeremiah 31:31; Hosea 2:21–22), substitutes the gifts between God and Israel (Torah, *tefillin*, *tallis*, Sabbath, and festivals and their observance) for what a bride and groom normally promise each other, and lists God and Moses or Heaven and Earth as witnesses. It is invariably dated 6 *Sivan* 2448 (the year Revelation occurred, counting from Creation at year 0).

Yatsiv Pitgam

In traditional *Ashkenazi* congregations, the *haftarah* (prophetic reading) on the second day is uncharacteristically interrupted after the first verse for the beautiful chant of another *piyyut*. Literally "Irrefutable Decree," the poem known as "The Myriad Angels' Songs" is also an acrostic that reveals the author's name (Jacob ben Meir Levi, Rabbenu Tam [Our Perfect Master] of Troyes, the illustrious grandson of the great Torah commentator Rashi). In beautiful pastoral imagery it expresses awe at Revelation and the power of God, and seeks protection and blessings for His people. In addition to mentioning the giving of the Law, the poem may have been included in Shavuot's liturgy because Rabbenu Tam was almost killed by Crusaders on the second day of the festival.

Azharot

A special group of *piyyutim* summarize the 613 commandments in rhymed form. Called *azharot* (warnings) because the numerical value of that word is 613, they were composed by Shlomo ibn Gabirol, the celebrated poet of the Jewish Golden Age of Spain (900–1100). *Sephardi* and Oriental congregations that include the poem in their *Mussaf* or *Minkhah* services concentrate on the 248 positive commandments on the first day and the 365 negative commandments on the second.

Scriptural Readings

The selections from Torah and Prophets encompass both the agricultural and historical aspects of Shavuot. On the first day, we read Exodus 19–20, recounting the three-day preparation immediately prior to the revelation at Sinai and the giving of the Ten Commandments to the entire nation.

The Decalogue is read on two other occasions during the year: on the Sabbath whose reading is *Yitro* (Exodus 18:1–20:23), in which they are first enumerated, and on the Sabbath when we read the portion *Va-Etkhanan* (Deuteronomy 3:23–7:11), when they are reiterated. It is customary to stand for all three readings (except in some *Sephardi* communities), as though we are again *ma'amad* (standing [at]) *Har* (Mount) *Sinai*, ready to accept the laws. For this holiday, a different cantillation makes the reading more dramatic.

There were controversies surrounding both the special reading of the Ten Commandments and the custom of standing. In Temple days, the priests recited the Decalogue daily. When first-century sects and Christianity began to challenge Judaism and assert that since the ten represented the whole of the religion the other 603 could be abandoned, the rabbis eliminated highlighting the few so the people would not think they could ignore the total.

Maimonides was among those who later prohibited standing while they were read, claiming the attention made those ten select aspects of the law seem superior to the others, which gave the wrong impression. He was overruled by those who understood the gesture as one of welcome to God's presence—and His present to Israel.

The concluding verses of the Torah reading on both days cover the special sacrifices required for Shavuot (Numbers 28:26–31).

Like each person at Sinai, the prophet Ezekiel had his own vision of God, which is relayed in the *haftarah* (1:1–28, 3:12), meant to parallel the experience of the Revelation. The fantastic image of the radiant and mobile God appeared to him at the beginning of the Babylonian exile eleven years before the destruction of Solomon's Temple. It suggests that God had left the Temple and was present with His people outside the Land.

The Torah reading on the second day, Deuteronomy 15:19–16:17 (beginning with 14:22 if it coincides with Sabbath), describes the requirements of the pilgrimage festivals and their connections with the harvest and animal sacrifices. Habakkuk 2:20–3:19, the second day's *haftarah*, is a prayer uttered by the prophet during the Assyrian exile (after 722 B.C.E.), expressing the expectation that God will again deliver His people.

The Book of Ruth

Of the five scrolls in the Writings section of the Hebrew Bible, the one assigned to Shavuot is Ruth. It tells the story of a Moabite princess who, after the death of her Jewish husband, brother-in-law, and father-in-law, pledges her allegiance to her Jewish mother-in-law, adopts Judaism, and because of her virtue, merits becoming the matriarch of the Davidic-messianic line. Its few short pages contain one of the most moving and well-known verses of scripture: "For wherever you go, I will go; wherever you lodge, I will lodge; your people will be my people and your God my God" (1:16).

The sages explain that Ruth was written to teach us that those who act kindly to others will be rewarded. The main figures in the story—Ruth, who did not want her widowed, childless mother-in-law to have to return to Bethlehem stripped of all honor with which she had left; Naomi, the loving mother-in-law who embraced her Moabite daughter-in-law and guided her into a suitable redeeming marriage; and Boaz, the judge and kinsman who provided the poor stranger Ruth with all the sustenance she and Naomi needed, and accepted his responsibility to marry her—are exemplars of *gemillut khasadim*, one of the pillars of the world. Learning from Torah so we can act in similarly righteous ways is one of the messages of Shavuot.

It is also generally believed that the Book of Ruth was chosen for Shavuot because her story takes place against the backdrop of the barley and wheat harvests in Judah (2:23), tying in with the agricultural nature of the festival. Especially significant is its illustration of the laws of *pe'ah* (leaving the corners of a field unharvested) and *leket* (leaving behind individual stalks that fall from the bundles that have been reaped), which allow the needy to also reap and which are commanded immediately following the instructions to observe the festival of Shavuot (Leviticus 23:22).

As we learn in the last paragraph of the story, its title character is the great-grandmother of King David, the king who dedicated his life to serving God and Torah, and who, by tradition, was born and died on the anniversary of the day the Torah was revealed. His descendant, the Messiah, will bring about redemption, the goal of Revelation.

Most appealingly, this is a story about the voluntary embrace of Torah and Judaism, a model of what being Jewish means: accepting the destiny of the Jewish people, living among Jews, being part of the community, and serving One God.

Maimonides pointed out that prior to the giving of the Torah, all human beings on Earth were bound to the seven Noahide Laws (dating from the righteous gentile Noah, whose family was the only one of his generation to survive the great flood [Genesis 6:13–8:14], and delineated in Talmud). Adherence to them constitutes morality in non-Jewish society (do not deny God, do not blaspheme God, do not murder, do not engage in adultery and other sexual abominations, do not steal, do not eat the limb torn from a living animal, and establish courts to enforce the other laws). From the moment of the Revelation on Mount Sinai, the Jews committed to accept the additional 606 that make up our body of commandments. That count is the numerical value (according to *gematria*) of the name of the Moabitess Ruth (*reish*, ר, two hundred; *vov*, ו, six; *taf*, ת, four hundred), who adopted the laws as her own.

In traditional congregations, the Book of Ruth is read, either from a scroll or a printed *Khumash*, on the second day prior to the other scriptural readings. Reform congregations often read it at confirmation services. *Khasidim* read it as part of the *tikkun* rather than at services, or each member of the congregation reads it individually (on *Sivan* 6 in Israel; on the second day in the Diaspora) prior to the Torah reading. Some *Sephardim* read it before *Minkhah*, often completing chapters one and two on the first day, and three and four on the second.

Yizkor

Following the *Shakharit* Torah reading on the second day of Shavuot, the service in memory of deceased martyrs, *tzaddikim*, and loved ones takes place, as it does on the last days of all the major holidays. (The Reform generally do not include this service on Shavuot, and in Israel it is held on the morning of the previous day.) Some have the custom of leaving the sanctuary during *Yizkor* if their parents are still liv-

ing, based on an old superstition, but it is considered more appropriate to remain with the congregation and pray on behalf of the people Israel has lost, including your relatives (see "Observance" in chapter on Pesakh and "Historic Foundation" earlier in this one for further explanation).

Confirmation

While its future is in question, the "graduation" ceremony for Jewish teens between fifteen and seventeen years of age who have completed some kind of education program established by their synagogues remains a feature in many congregations on the first evening or first morning of Shavuot. Recognition of the confirmands is worked into the holiday service.

Conclusion

As for all festivals, the end of sacred time is marked by the brief ceremony *Havdalah*, performed in the synagogue after *Ma'ariv*, or at home after nightfall. If the end of the festival coincides with the close of Shabbat, we recite the full complement of blessings (contained in a prayer book). On a weeknight, only blessings over wine and separation are said (see "Observance" in chapter on Yom Kippur for explanation of differences, and in chapter on Pesakh for *brakhot*).

Isru Khag

Like the days following the other pilgrimage festivals, the one after Shavuot is a semi-holiday designated to help us hold onto the spirit of the holy day just a bit longer. According to Talmud, whoever observes an *issur* (continuation) for the festival by eating and drinking (which substitutes in post-Temple life for the sacrifices) is considered to have "built the altar and offered up a sacrifice on it," based on Psalms 118:27: "Bind the festival [offering] with cords onto the horns of the altar."

In the case of Shavuot, *Isru Khag* served a practical purpose during Temple days (see section on "*Halakhah*"). In our time, while the mourning laws of festival days hold (see "*Halakhah*" in chapter on Pesakh), for all intents and purposes, *Isru Khag* goes virtually unnoticed.

WHERE DO WE BEGIN?—PREPARATION

Spiritual

For the Israelites, Shavuot was the culmination of the process of transcending innate, animal nature to liberate the human being. As we learn at Pesakh, the release from physical bondage alone is not freedom. True freedom is knowing what you want to do—what you truly want being what is good for both the body and soul—and having the discipline to achieve it, which means being able to control the natural desire for immediate gratification that can distract you.

The period that connects the two levels of freedom, *Sefirat Haomer* (see chapter on Pesakh), began with the cutting of the first sheaf of barley that ripened. Barley is animal fodder. An animal is a being whose consciousness consists of the immediate situation. Having no vision of what is beyond the self is the least Jewish of attitudes. As we count the days representing the duration of the barley harvest, we rise toward the start of what was the wheat harvest. Wheat is human food, a symbol of *khokhmah*, intelligence (based on the rabbis' dictum that a child does not utter its first word until it has tasted bread).

The offering brought to the Temple at the start of the *Omer* was meal ground from the barley grain, a raw material representing the first step in the production of leavened bread, which was the offering at the end of the *Omer*, on Shavuot. The message is that without Torah, which gives us the insights to recognize what we want, and the moral standards and social ethics to guide us to accomplish it, we are like animals who respond to instinct. Raw barley needs to give way to the refined wheat, the grain to meal and bread. Raw natural intelligence needs to be refined to become the wisdom through which potential can be reached. Once our animal selves, which are always present, are under control, we are ready to learn how to get the most out of life.

That is why counting the *Omer* continued even after the development of a standard calendar eliminated its initial necessity: to let the majority of people—farmers occupied with field work—know exactly when to make pilgrimage to Jerusalem. It remained an opportunity to help us move out of enslaving patterns of thought and behavior.

For the ancient Israelites, each day was a step away from the defilement of Egypt and a step toward spiritual purity. Like the Israelites who began to get ready for their encounter at Mount Sinai as soon as they crossed the Reed Sea, we use the seven weeks beginning on Passover to similarly prepare ourselves for the arrival of Shavuot. During this time, we are supposed to evaluate our behavior and work to improve ourselves, particularly by being more faithful to God and dedicated to His ways, more humble, and unified with all other Jews (Exodus 19:2).

The sages devised a construct to help us follow in the Israelites' footsteps. It is based on seven Divine qualities in the kabbalistic design of the universe, which were represented by the illustrious leaders of Israel (in one variation): love (Abraham), respect (Isaac), compassion (Jacob), efficiency (Moses), beauty (Aaron), loyalty (Joseph), and leadership (David). These virtues, in their extreme, become vices (lust, fear, indulgence, obsessiveness, vanity, submissiveness, and stubbornness) that we have to strive to avoid. So the sages dedicated each week of the *Omer* to one of the characteristics and each day of the week to one of them. The unique combination on each of the forty-nine days (love-love, love-respect, love-compassion . . . respect-love, respect-leadership, and so on) helps us gain insight into our own behavior in relation to them, and focus our efforts on self-improvement, to make each day of *Omer* important.

Torah study in general is customary and appropriate. Some people read portions from every book of the Bible, and review of the Ten Commandments is common. Many read *Pirkei Avot* (Ethics of the Fathers), a particularly accessible section of Talmud. Study culminates in the *Tikkun Leil Shavuot*, meant to make up for omissions or deficiencies in our devotion to Torah during the preceding year. It helps us to be particularly receptive to the body of law we will be given the next morning.

FOR FURTHER READING

Pirkei Avos—Ethics of the Fathers. Ed. by Rabbi Nosson Scherman and Rabbi Meir Zlotowitz. Brooklyn: Mesorah Publications, 1989.

This new translation of the Talmud tractate (literally Chapters of the Fathers), full of pithy sayings and concise lessons, is supplemented by commentary drawn from classic rabbinic sources. Each of its six chapters is traditionally read on the Sabbaths between Pesakh and Shavuot. (There are a number of editions of *Pirkei Avot*, including the respected three-volume edition *Ethics from Sinai* with commentary by Irving Bunim [Feldheim Publishers]. Some *makhzorim* for Shavuot also contain *Pirkei Avot*, and ArtScroll has a version for young people as part of its Youth Series [Mesorah Publications]).

FOR FURTHER EXPLORATION

48 Ways to Wisdom. This set of forty-eight individual audiotapes was produced from lectures given at Aish Hatorah, a *yeshivah* in Jerusalem for Jews with little religious background. Each tape deals, from a Jewish perspective, with some aspect of everyday emotions and concerns about personal matters and interpersonal relationships, and almost all provide concrete suggestions of simple things to do to help improve your thinking and behavior. There is a lot of illuminating and helpful information here. (Available through Aish Hatorah educational centers in Cleveland, Columbus, Detroit, Lakewood [NJ], Los Angeles, Miami, New York, St. Louis, Washington [DC], Toronto, London, and Jerusalem.)

Personal

All of the semi-mourning restrictions imposed for the *Omer* period are suspended as of Rosh Khodesh *Sivan*. The day of the new moon iself is a semi-holiday when mourning is not permitted. The three (*shalosh*) days (*yomei*) of setting bounds (*hagbalah*) immediately preceding Shavuot—when the Israelites had to refrain from climbing Mount Sinai and be particularly pure in their physical actions—are also considered festival days since they anticipate the Revelation. The day in between, *Sivan* 2, called *Yom Hameyahut* (Privileged or Choice day), borrows the status of the surrounding occasions. (Talmud gives it further distinction by identifying it as the day God told the Israelites they would be a kingdom of priests and a holy nation [Exodus 19:6].)

During these three days, it is customary to get a haircut and buy new clothes, which were prohibited earlier in *Sefirah*. In traditional circles, men go to the *mikvah* prior to the start of the holiday. Some also go on the morning of Shavuot in remembrance of Israel's purification prior to receiving the Torah.

Tzedakah

One of the ways of improving our spiritual standing is by helping others. As with all occasions in Jewish life, it is appropriate to make donations to Jewish causes. Those that perpetuate Jewish learning (Jewish schools, *yeshivot*, scholarship funds, and Jewish camp programs) are particularly suitable at this time. Some people set aside amounts on every night of the *Omer* corresponding to the count of the day (in pennies, dimes, dollars, etc.).

Home

To adorn your home in the traditional manner, you will want to buy, or cut from your garden, flowers and greens and arrange them in vases or strew them on tables. Some people also display leafy or flowering houseplants.

You and your children may want to make papercuts, a folk art decoration that was customary in Eastern Europe in the 1800s. These are made by folding a square or circular piece of paper in quarters, sixths, or eighths, cutting shapes along the folds, then opening up the paper to reveal a symmetric design. For Shavuot, floral patterns are most common, and the finished papercuts are hung in windows so that the sunlight will cast their shapes in shadow.

If you want to cook and light candles on the holiday in accordance with Jewish law, you will need to use a preexisting flame, from a long-lasting candle or pilot light, for example (see chapter on Pesakh, regarding these preparations, as well as for arrangements when the holiday falls immediately prior to Shabbat).

WHAT ARE WE SUPPOSED TO DO?— *HALAKHAH*

With the exception of specific sacrifices and the order of the prayer service, no attention is given to Shavuot in the literature of *halakhah*. As a festival and a pilgrimage holiday, it shares the *halakhot* of the other such holy days (see chapter on Pesakh).

Counting the *Omer*

If you forget to count in the evening (see section on "Observance" in chapter on Pesakh), make the count the next day, but without the blessing. If you skip one count, you may start again whenever you remember to do so, but you may no longer say the blessing for the remainder of *Sefirah*. This is because the *brakhah* is based on the command to count every single day. (*Omer* scrolls are often used in synagogues, where the count is made at the conclusion of the evening service. You can use calendars that allow you to flip one page for each date, which can easily be made from a notebook, or create a chart with boxes to check off.)

Tikkun

If you stay up all night for study, the rituals and prayers you would normally do and say in the morning are omitted since they were performed the previous day, and are not said anew if sleep has not intervened.

Joy

Torah commands us one time to rejoice on Shavuot (Deuteronomy 16:11), since part of the harvest is complete. However, because we have not yet seen all the fruits of our labors, our full expression of joy is reserved (see chapter on Sukkot). We rejoice by eating festival meals accompanied by wine and sharing our good fortune with those in need.

Isru Khag

While it is customary not to fast or deliver a eulogy on the day after any festival, for Shavuot those prohibitions are law. This is because this day had to serve as a practical addition to the holiday itself. Sacrifices could not be made on behalf of individuals (as opposed to those for the nation) on *yom tov* itself because there was simply not enough time in one day, and when Shavuot coincided with Shabbat, the labor involved was prohibited. On the other pilgrimage festivals, these problems were solved by having *khol hamoed*, the intermediate days, when the sacrifices

could be made. Without that time, Shavuot had to extend into *Isru Khag* for the same purpose.

WHAT OTHER THINGS DO PEOPLE DO?— CUSTOMS

Other Times and Places

Omer *Period*

Some people had the custom of studying the Talmud tractate *Shevuot*. With forty-nine pages and sharing the name of the holiday the counting period prepares us to observe, it was considered appropriate.

Women traditionally did not work after sunset during *Sefirah*. Although their laborious preparation for the last festival, Pesakh, would have been enough to excuse them, the custom is said to be in recognition of the women who buried Akiva's students at night (see chapter on Lag B'Omer). Since there were so many deaths, the entire community's life would have been disrupted by daytime funerals.

Greens

Despite the admonition of the Vilna Gaon, using plants and flowers to decorate homes and synagogues for Shavuot was fairly widespread, particularly in Europe. Fresh grass was sometimes scattered on the floor of a house, and spices and roses on the synagogue floor, a reference to the *midrash* claiming that the Israelites had to be revived after fainting out of fear when they heard God's voice. Another *midrash* says that the fragrance of spices filled the world as each commandment was issued. Because flowers were used to decorate the *Sifrei Torah*, in Italy the holiday was called the Feast of Roses, and in Persia the Feast of Flowers.

Papercuts

The prohibition by the Vilna Gaon of using decorative greens may have led to the adaptation of the folk art of paper cutting specifically for Shavuot. While the craft in general was widespread, its application for this holiday was limited geographically to Galicia, Bukovina, and adjoining areas of Poland and Russia, especially Lithuania and the Ukraine. In the nineteenth and early twentieth centuries, *kheder* and *yeshivah* students and older men with time on their hands created the intricate lacy patterns. The papercuts—called *Shavuoslekh* (little Shavuot) or *roiselekh* (little roses) for their characteristic shape and design—were the only Jewish papercuts seen from the street. (The works of the Jewish artists Maurice Gottlieb and Mordecai Antokolski are said to have attracted the attention of non-Jewish patrons who later helped the artists enter art academies.) Floral motifs were prevalent, inspired by words of the *Akdamut* hymn, the legend that Mount Sinai burst into flower at the giving of the Torah, the classic image of Torah as the Tree of Life, and the Song of Songs' image of Israel as a rose. Some papercuts had text—*Khag Hashavuot Hazeh* (This Shavuot Festival)—and some depicted classic Jewish symbols: the crowned Torah scroll, tablets of the commandments, star of David, animals real and mythological, and zodiac signs.

Enactments of Weddings and Battles

On the morning of the first day of Shavuot, the devout went to the *mikvah*, so they would be prepared to greet the Torah, like a bridegroom getting ready to meet his bride at the marriage ceremony. North African communities dressed their *Sifrei Torah* in white, like brides, and held symbolic wedding processions after morning services. These were sometimes followed by mock battles representing the war against evil of messianic times (suggested in the hymn *Akdamut*, which precedes the Torah reading on the first day).

Pilgrimage

After the agricultural processions of Shavuot had been eliminated, another kind of visit became popular among *khasidim* and Oriental Jews. As the anniversary of King David's death, Shavuot became the time to visit the traditional site of his tomb on Mount Zion in Jerusalem. Some congregations lit *yahrtzite* candles on the second day of the holiday in his honor.

Hundreds of candles lit on behalf of deceased relatives illuminated the synagogues of Kurdistan, where each individual brought fruit to be blessed in their memory. In Kurdistan, people also made pilgrimage to the shrines of holy men buried in their country. Singing, dancing, and special refreshments accompanied the processions. The biggest procession was for the prophet Nakhum, buried near a hill called Mount Sinai, which the men climbed in order to recite the Ten Commandments at its summit. On *Isru Khag*, crowds walked past the tomb, gave charity, and received from the *gabbai* (sexton) fruit and sweets that had rested on the grave throughout the night.

Sometimes a person who had read the Ten Commandments hosted a banquet, or members of a congregation, after eating their meals at home, visited the honoree for merriment and refreshment.

In Babylon, Shavuot was called the Feast of Visitation. It was traditional to visit the gravesites of noted ancestors.

The Moroccans joyfully danced to their cemeteries on *Isru Khag Shavuot* as they buried damaged and unused text and scripture in the *genizah* (the storage place for such materials, which may not be discarded or destroyed). Coinciding with the date of burial of the Jews slaughtered at Betar (see chapter on Lag B'Omer), the occasion was marked by singing and musical accompaniment to properly commemorate those whose bravery brought honor to the Torah.

In Eastern Europe, the *khasidim* made a different kind of pilgrimage, traveling great distances to be able to spend the festival with their learned and esteemed rebbes.

Start of School

During the Middle Ages, it became customary to introduce boys around the age of five to Hebrew and Torah study on the morning of Shavuot. Letters of the alphabet and verses of scripture would be written on a tablet enhanced with dabs of honey or bits of candy, which the children were invited to lick. They would then associate Torah and learning with sweetness (based on Psalms 119:103: "How pleasing is your word to my palate, sweeter than honey"). After the initial lesson, honey cakes or eggs on which verses had been written might then be given to the children to eat.

Dousing

The comparison of Torah with water ("Your springs [teachings] will gush forth in streams in the public squares" [Proverbs 5:16]) led to customs among the North African Jews which seem uncharacteristically rambunctious for the mood of the day. Men battled each other with goatskins of water, each trying to pour more on the next. Sometimes the person who had recited the last verse of *Azharot* was treated to a cold shower. Women more delicately sprinkled each other.

These activities are also said to reflect appreciation for the role of water in two incidents in Israel's life. After his birth on *Adar* 7, according to rabbinic tradition, Moses' mother hid him for three months, until Shavuot, *Sivan* 6, then placed the infant in a basket in the Nile River, which protected him from the Pharaoh's decree. When so overwhelmed by Revelation that the souls of the Israelites departed, God sent a heavy dew to revive His people. Throwing water imitates and expresses gratitude for the resuscitation.

In Babylon and Persia, instead of water, the Jews threw apples from the synagogue roofs, because the Israelites' response to Torah ("we will do and we will hear") was compared to the apple tree, whose fruit develops before its leaves. Among some Judeo-Spanish, it was customary to conduct *hakafot* (circuits) in the sanctuary with the Torah and to throw candies at those called to read it when the scrolls were lifted (as on Simkhat Torah). (See chapter on Sukkot.)

Greeting

The standard greeting, "*khag samei'akh*" (Hebrew) or "*gut yom tov*" (Yiddish), "happy holiday," is exchanged on Shavuot.

Dress

Clean Shabbat clothes are appropriate for the festival.

WHAT IS THERE TO EAT?— TRADITIONAL FOODS

Cheese

Although everyone agrees that the food of choice for Shavuot is cheese (most typically blintzes, crepelike pancakes filled with farmer cheese, or a *Sephardi* equivalent such as *burekas*, cheese-filled dough pockets), there are differences of opinion (some quite charming) as to why it is a custom.

Some derive the practice directly from scripture, saying we eat dairy to symbolize the "Land flowing with milk and honey" (Exodus 3:8) promised to the Israelites, or that "milk and honey are under your tongue" (Song of Songs 4:11). These passages along with "The precepts of the Lord are . . . sweeter than honey" (Psalm 19:9–11) also indicate we should eat honey, which is customary in some communities.

A sage discovered that the initials of the four Hebrew words in Numbers 28:26, which describe the sacrificial meal offering on Shavuot, spell *mei khalav* (from milk), suggesting that dairy food is the acceptable dinner for the festival. At Sinai, the Israelites were considered to be as innocent as newborns, whose food is milk.

Those of kabbalistic bent equate the numerical value of the word *khalav*, forty (ח, eight; ל, thirty; ב, two), with the number of days Moses spent on Mount Sinai receiving the Ten Commandments and other teachings (Exodus 24:18). Others look to the mountain itself, which is termed in Psalms mount of *gavnunim* (68:15), meaning many peaks. They connect that description with the Hebrew word *g'vinah*, meaning cheese.

Scholars who trace all Jewish customs and rituals to practices common among various ethnic groups claim that spring harvest festivals characteristically featured dairy dishes, perhaps because cheese was produced during that season.

There is also support for the custom based on the spiritual development among the Israelites in the wake of Sinai. After the Torah was given, they were obligated to follow its laws, including those governing dietary practice. As they returned to the camp from Revelation, they could not eat the previously prepared meat, which had not been done according to the laws of *kashrut*. Since butchering and cooking fresh meat would take too long for the tired, hungry Israelites, they took the dairy food that was readily available. Symbolizing modesty, the dairy was also seen as appropriate for the occasion of receiving the Torah, which should always be approached with humility.

In some Jewish communities it is customary to follow the traditional dairy meal with a meat dish (after waiting the requisite thirty minutes per the laws of *kashrut*, except in places where the rabbis waived the normal separation). The two foods represent the two loaves brought on the festival. We are also supposed to eat meat as a contribution to our joy on a festival day. This can cause practical problems, however, not only in terms of the time lapse but because you cannot mix milk and meat dishes and utensils. Therefore, it is more common to have a dairy meal on the first evening of Shavuot and then serve meat the next day.

Along with blintzes and *burekas*, cheesecake is a widely popular Shavuot item. Some eat *kreplakh*, three-cornered dumplings which are often filled with meat but can be cheese filled or even vegetable filled. They are supposed to remind us of the Torah, which is comprised of three sections (Torah, *Nevi'im*, and *Ketuvim*) given to Israel, comprised of three categories (*Kohanim*, *Leviim*, and *Yisraelim*), through Moses, the third child of Amran (after Aaron and Miriam), following three days of preparation (Exodus 19:11) in the third month of the year (Exodus 19:1).

Khallah

As for most holidays, special designs were devised for the traditional braided bread. A ladder with seven rungs represents the seven spheres God traversed to descend to Mount Sinai. Long loaves of bread stand for the length and breadth of the Law (Job 11:9), and square loaves, with their four corners, represent the four layers of meaning inherent in Torah.

Round loaves in tiers were called *Siete Cielos* (seven heavens) in oriental countries; in others they represented the mountain and were known as Sinai Cake. Large loaves or cakes with raisins and/or almonds were also called Sinai (or, in local terms, *pashtudan* or *fladen*).

The traditional two loaves, common for Shabbat and all festivals, have added meaning for the two loaves of the wave offering brought to the Temple. They are sometimes baked with their sides touching to resemble the tablets or the zodiac sign for the month of *Sivan*, Gemini (twins).

Among North African Jews, it is customary to eat *matzah* left from Passover in bowls of milk and honey, as a reminder that Shavuot is the finale of Pesakh.

Do You Hear Music?—Songs to Sing

Like virtually every other aspect of Shavuot, the songs connected with it are largely part of the synagogue liturgy. A number of folk songs and *khasidic* melodies, built around short phrases, extol Torah and God, Who gave it to us. Among them are "*Torah Tzivah Lanu*" (The Torah is our Inheritance), "*Barukh Eloheinu*" (Blessed is our God [Who Gave Us the Torah of Truth]), "*Yisrael V'Oraita*" (The People of Israel and the Light of Torah), "*Yamakh Moshe*" (Moshe Joyfully [Welcomes the Gift of Torah]), "*Yismekhu Adirim*" (Rejoice in the Great Gift), and "*Ki Mitzion*" (For Out of Zion).

Two popular folk songs learned by every Hebrew school student, youth group member, and Jewish camper exuberantly proclaim Israel's and God's existence and our belief in redemption. Each consists of only one sentence: "*Am Yisrael khai, od Avinu khai*" (The people of Israel lives, Our Father still lives), and "*David Melekh Yisrael, khai v'kayam*" (David, King of Israel lives and endures [suggesting the Messiah]). The Hebrew folksong "*Eretz Zavat Khalav (khalav u'd'vash)*" (Land of Milk and Honey) and the Yiddish standard "*Oif'n Pripetchik*" (By the hearth [the rabbi teaches little children the *aleph bet*]) are also appropriate for the occasion.

What Tales Are Told?— Stories to Read

Surprisingly, for a holiday of Shavuot's significance, there is little written specifically about its history and themes. Neither Sholom Aleichem (except his use of gathering greens as a backdrop) nor Bella Chagall, who both lovingly recorded Eastern European holiday observance, treated this one. Aside from books on the Ten Commandments (see "Religious Significance" earlier in this chapter), there is little available for children. However, since the subject of Shavuot is Torah, any material drawn from our rich tradition based on scripture is appropriate. Treasuries of folktales, such as those listed in the introduction, provide a wealth of choices, as do Bible stories adapted for children. You may also want to check with a librarian, Jewish bookstore, or the Jewish Book Council directory for suggestions of titles that deal with various aspects of Jewish life.

For Further Reading

Folktales

"We Will Obey and We Will Hear," "The Contest of the Mountains," "Divine Blackmail at Sinai," "The Revelation at Sinai," and "Moses and the Angels Wrestle Over the *Torah*." In CT, pp. 122–132.

Based on Talmud and *midrash*, these legends surrounding the giving of the Torah explain why and how Israel received it and why it was given on Mount Sinai. ("The Contest of the Mountains" is the subject of a play, *Dialog dos Montes*, by Rabbi Rehuel Jessurun, written in Portuguese and performed in the *Sephardi* synagogue of Amsterdam on Shavuot 1624. A brief excerpt appears in Shavuot HA, p. 235.)

Other Stories

Asch, Sholom. "We Will Do and We Will Obey." Trans. by Rufus Learsi. In Shavuot HA, pp. 202–215.

The Jews of Zlochov, Ukraine, driven from their homes by an approaching pogrom, have the opportunity to rediscover the faith expressed by their ancestors at Sinai.

Pessin, Deborah. "At Sinai." In Shavuot HA, pp. 272–276.

A young boy is rewarded when he eagerly awaits Moses' return from Mount Sinai. The story captures the emotion of the event. Ages 7–10.

Weilerstein, Sadie Rose. "How K'tonton Wished a Wish on Shevuoth Night." In KT, pp. 65–70.

The Jewish Tom Thumb, in the course of enjoying all the traditions of Shavuot, earns his wish to be a scholar, but in a way he hadn't expected. Ages 3–8.

TISHA B'AV

Tisha B'Av (teesh'-ah buh-ahv'; Yiddish: tish'-uh buhv'): National day of mourning. Observed on *Av* **9** (summer; late July–mid-August).

Tisha B'Av, the commemoration of the destruction of the first and second Temples, is also the anniversary of a number of other catastrophes in our history. As the embodiment of national disaster, it is a time for grief and remorse, yet also for renewed hope for redemption. We observe it by refraining from any pleasure-producing activities.

ORIGINS: WHY WE CELEBRATE TISHA B'AV

WHERE DID IT ALL BEGIN?— HISTORIC FOUNDATION

Loss of First Temple

For all the blessings bestowed on the Land of Israel (Deuteronomy 7:12–14, 8:7–9), its location between continents has always been a dubious advantage: wonderful for commerce, but an open invitation to conquest. Just after 600 B.C.E., the Babylonians won control over Assyria (which had previously conquered the northern Kingdom of Israel and expelled its Ten Tribes). Influential Judeans (residents of the southern Kingdom of Judah, part of the territory captured) were exiled to Babylon. Under Judah's last king, Zedekiah, whom the Babylonians had installed to be a puppet, those allowed to remain retaliated with a revolt for independence.

On the tenth of *Tevet*, 587 B.C.E., King Nebukhadnezzar moved his army against the capital. On the ninth of *Tammuz*, six months later, the Babylonians breached the walls of the city weakened by famine and disease. One month later (given in different sources as *Av* 7 [II Kings 25:8] and *Av* 10 [Jeremiah 52:15], and designated in Talmud as *Av* 9), the chief of Nebukhadnezzar's guards, Nebuzaradan, set the Temple and every significant building in Jerusalem on fire.

The loss was devastating. (Imagine the city in which you live depleted of food and water, ablaze in every direction, littered with the rubble of fortifications and houses and the victims of starvation, disease, armed combat, smoke inhalation, and flame.) The Temple treasures and vessels were carried off to Babylon, and thousands of Jews were forced to march there in chains.

The Bible books II Kings (24–25) and Jeremiah recount this period of history from the admonitions that preceded destruction through the end of the Jewish community on the Land. The Judeans who had abandoned God for idols and idle pursuits were repeatedly warned that if they did not act justly, as they had been commanded, an enemy from the north would turn their home to desolation and ruin.

Events occurred as predicted. For the next seventy years, Jeremiah instructed, the exiles were to build a new community in Babylon, where they would prosper. Those who had not been marched to the conquering kingdom were supposed to stay on the Land and live quietly under Babylonian rule (Jeremiah 40:9).

To govern the remnant—the poorest of the Jews—Nebukhadnezzar appointed Gedaliah, a noble who had served as a minister under Zedekiah. Although warned that his life was in danger, Gedaliah refused to take protective or preemptive measures. When a member of Judah's own royal house murdered him and his Babylonian advisors on Rosh Hashanah, the Jewish leaders were afraid Babylon would see the attack as open rebellion and respond with bloody retribution.

They refused to heed Jeremiah's assurances that they would be safe and blessed in the Land, but doomed if they returned to Egypt, as they planned: It would mock everything God had tried to do for them since bringing them out of slavery (Jeremiah 42). Under the direction of Yokhanan ben Kareah, they did flee to Egypt (a doubly bad move, since it was later invaded by Nebukhadnezzar). That was the end of Jewish presence in Israel and of any hope of securing the foundation for restoration of the Jewish commonwealth.

No matter how comfortable their lives in Babylon might have become, the exiled Jews were distraught, refusing to sing ("How can we sing a song of the Lord on alien soil?" [Psalms 137:4]), determined to constantly recall Jerusalem ("If I forget you, O Jerusalem, let my right hand wither . . ." [Psalms 137:5], and adopting the ancient expression of grief and remorse, fasting (Zekhariah 8:19).

The three days that marked successive stages in the loss of Jerusalem—the tenth of *Tevet* for the beginning of the siege; the ninth of *Tammuz* for the break in the walls; and the third of *Tishrei* (postponed since fasting is prohibited on Rosh Hashanah, *Tishrei* 1 and 2) for the true beginning of exile following Gedaliah's murder—were marked by sunrise to sunset fasts. *Av* 9, commemorating the actual *khurban* (destruction) of the Temple, became a full-day fast. (The date may have been a compromise to accommodate the discrepancy between the II Kings and Jeremiah accounts of when the Temple was demolished. Historians note that *Av* 9 was a preexisting fast day in Babylonia, where the commemoration began, and may have been conveniently adopted by the exiles for their own purposes.)

A Second Chance, A Second *Khurban*

As Jeremiah promised, after seven decades the Jews were allowed to return to Jerusalem, where the Temple was rebuilt—not as lavishly as Solomon's version, but a national sanctuary nonetheless. The prophetic book Zekhariah records that in the fourth year of Persian King Darius' reign (518 B.C.E.), while the Temple was under reconstruction, a delegation from the Diaspora went to ask the priests and prophets in Jerusalem whether they were supposed to continue observing the four fast days.

After pointing out that denying themselves sustenance was not a ritual done for God's sake, but a reminder to act justly and with compassion for others, Zekhariah predicted that "the fast of the fourth month [*Tammuz* 9], the fast of the fifth month [*Av* 9], the fast of the seventh month [*Tzom Gedaliah, Tishrei*

3] and the fast of the tenth month [*Tevet* 10] shall become occasions for joy and gladness, happy festivals for the House of Judah" (Zekhariah 8:19). That seemed to indicate that they could be suspended (as some scholars say they were). But the prophet added a key proviso: "you must love honesty and integrity," suggesting that the end of exile was more than a physical matter. Redemptive rejoicing required a certain moral precondition.

Rav Papa, the fourth-century sage, claims that the fasts were converted to holidays and celebrated that way throughout the second Temple era, 516 B.C.E.–70 C.E. The Jerusalem Talmud notes that they remained optional days of mourning observed as fasts by the pious: Although the Jews had returned to the Land, they did not necessarily enjoy self-rule, and although they once again had a Temple, it was a poor replacement for the one they had lost.

After approximately six hundred years of residence on the Land there was a reprisal of the events of 586, almost to the day. This time it was orchestrated by the Romans, who had been in Israel for 180 years since being invited to intercede in a battle within the House of Hasmoneans (see chapter on Khanukah). After four years of armed combat in Israel, they were able to break through Jerusalem's walls on *Tammuz* 17, 70. Once again the inhabitants were trapped, reduced to a starving, disease-ridden community imperiled by their own factions of zealous terrorists warring with each other over the best approach to take against the enemy. None worked. On the ninth of *Av*, the Romans set the Temple and much of the city ablaze. The fires burned through the night and well into the next day.

Titus, the conquering general, carted home the vessels, golden *menorah*, and ark (depicted on the Arch of Titus, which celebrates his triumph. It still stands in the archaeological garden of the Roman Forum near the Colosseum; Jews traditionally do not walk under it). Again those captured were taken away in chains, and those left behind continued to resist.

Years before the siege of Jerusalem began, a small group had found refuge on an anvil-shaped plateau near the Dead Sea, which one hundred years earlier had been fortified by the paranoid Herod, King of Judea, as the kingdom of Judah was called beginning in the Hellenistic period, fourth and third centuries B.C.E. Fighters who had escaped the destruction of the capital joined them there. For two years, the community of 960 men, women, and children held out against the Romans, who were intent on eradicating every last Jewish stronghold. When the defenders realized they would not prevail once their attackers completed an assault ramp and wheeled their battering ram to the top, the Jews decided to kill themselves rather than be taken. They left their stores of food and water so the Romans would know they had chosen to die in freedom rather than become enslaved, the antithesis of Jewish life. (Masada, the site of this dramatic episode, became a symbol of the Jewish and Israeli fighting spirit, the site of inductions for select units of the Israeli army, and the basis of the slogan for independence, "Masada shall not fall again!")

Outside and within Israel, the Jews continued their armed struggle against Rome, first in Alexandria (117), then in Betar (135) (see chapter on Lag B'Omer), where they were decisively defeated—both times on the ninth of *Av*. To emphasize their complete victory, the Romans plowed over Jerusalem, changed its name to Aelia Capitolina, and rebuilt it with pagan temples and heathen gods. They renamed *Eretz Yisrael* Palestina.

Dealing with Desolation

As devastating as the first destruction was, this one was a much more decisive blow. Many of the surviving Jews were carted off as slaves. The remnant was severely crushed in a bloody slaughter, and anyone left was forbidden to come within viewing distance of what had been Jerusalem (except on *Av* 9, when they could mourn at the ruins). No prophet wandered in their midst promising a speedy restoration. The ascetic practices adopted by a large number of Jews reflected the dimensions of their sense of loss.

Rabbi Joshua tried to convince them of the futility of such actions. According to their reasoning for forfeiting meat and wine, which had been offered on the altar that no longer existed, they would also have had to give up bread, in remembrance of the meal offering, and fruit, since firstfruits could no longer be sacrificed, and water, because of the elimination of the water ceremony on Sukkot. And, as another sage pointed out, since studying Torah and following its precepts, including circumcision and redemption of firstborn sons, were prohibited by Roman law, they might also think it proper to forego marriage and having children.

Instead, the rabbis had to incorporate appropriate expressions of loss while affirming traditional Jewish faith that out of tragedy comes possibility, out of exile comes redemption. So they established a pattern of mourning balanced between two attitudes: Anyone who did not grieve over the destruction of Jerusalem would not live to rejoice over her renewal, and while not grieving at all was impossible because the devastation had already occurred, to mourn too much was beyond human endurance.

Almost immediately, they restored Tisha B'Av as a national day of mourning, marked by a twenty-five-hour fast and the personal abstentions associated with the expression of grief for loss of a loved one. Again there was a discrepancy over the actual date of the defeat, with the historian Josephus claiming the tenth, the Talmud citing the ninth. Rabbi Yokhanan ben Zakkai, a leading sage of the time, said if it had been up to him, he would have chosen the tenth because the greater part of the destruction occurred then. The rabbis, however, chose to mark the beginning of the end, which coincided with the ancient observance of destruction and with the fall of Betar and the leveling of Jerusalem. By the end of the first century observance was mandatory.

After Betar and the barbaric persecutions by Emperor Hadrian, which included the martyrdom of ten of our greatest sages, the other fast days observed after the first destruction were reinstated (with the fast of *Tammuz* 9 moved to *Tammuz* 17, the date related to the greater loss). They conveniently provided needed outlets for a people anxious to express its grief. (This welcome embrace of self-denial may be difficult for us, in our age of self-indulgence, to understand, but when Judah Hanasi [third-century compiler of the *Mishnah*], in a conciliatory mood toward Rome, wanted to abolish the fast of Tisha B'Av, the people wouldn't accept it.)

The rabbis ordained that every year on Tisha B'Av the Jews were to read *Eikhah* (Lamentations). The scroll attributed to Jeremiah gives a graphic and heart-rending eyewitness account of the destruction of the First Temple, but is no less relevant in commemorating the detruction of the second. (Using the ancient text, like reviving the ancient date, was also politically expedient. With its description of events that had occurred six hundred years earlier, it avoided offending the new Roman rulers.)

The whole tenor of Judaism, until then a religion marked by joyful celebration and aesthetic worship, became more doleful. The rabbis decreed that reminders of the incompleteness of existence outside of *Eretz Yisrael*, and the diminishment of joy in the absence of the Temple, be incorporated into everyday life. For weekday meals with guests, one place at the table was to be left unset, and one or two dishes were to be omitted from the menu for any banquet. Women were not to wear all their jewelry at once, and an area approximately twenty-inches square in a new home was to be left unpainted or unplastered and designated in memory of the Temple. At a marriage, the groom was to put ashes on his forehead where the *tefillin* normally sits, and would break a glass at the conclusion of the ceremony. Instrumental accompaniment and music, aside from hymns and songs of praise to God, which had contributed to the beauty of Temple service, were removed from worship.

Instead of eliminating consumption of meat and wine from all meals as a constant reminder that the animal sacrifices and wine libations were no longer possible (a restriction the community would be unable to keep in the long run), the rabbis included a recounting of the Temple sacrifices in the daily liturgy.

Those who saw the Temple site from the vantage of the desert would rend their clothes and then tear them further when they saw Jerusalem—or any other destroyed Judean city. Special prayers were also to be said. These practices continued even after the cities had been rebuilt, because they remained under foreign rule.

Anyone viewing the Western Wall was to recite "Her gates have sunk into the ground. He has smashed her bars to bits" (Lamentations 2:9). Prayers beseeching God to rebuild Jerusalem were added to the daily liturgy, and exclamations of desire to return to that city were added to the prayers of holidays most closely associated with redemption: Yom Kippur (personal), Pesakh (national), and Sukkot (universal). Wherever a Jew went, whatever a Jew did, s/he was reminded of Israel's ultimate goal.

The idea behind all these institutions was to allow the people to vent their grief and yet be able to maintain some sort of normal life. To that end, the ruling that emerged from the Gemara discussion between Rabbis Meir, Judah, and Simeon ben Gamaliel regarding whether mourning for the Temple should last the entire month of *Av*, only the first nine days, or just the week of the ninth was for the most lenient choice.

A Day for All Misfortune

The magnitude of the destruction that had occurred not once, but twice on the same date, and the fact that some of the worst disasters to befall the Jews afterward also occurred on *Av* 9, made that day a symbol of national catastrophe. The rabbis claimed that when the Israelites were wandering in the desert *Av* 9 had already been designated to embody all Jewish misfortune.

As a prelude to having the Israelites possess the Land He had promised them, God told Moses to send representatives of the Twelve Tribes to scout Canaan and report back to the people. After forty days of spying, on the ninth of *Av*, the twelve gave the impression that they could not prevail against the inhabitants, robbing the people of belief in their own capabilities. Rather than heeding the assurances of Joshua and Caleb, who encouraged self-confidence, or having faith in God, Who promised to protect them in their conquests, the people began to weep and complain about having been taken out of Egypt.

Disgusted with their causeless crying, Talmud explains, God essentially said, "You want to cry? I'll give you something to cry about. This will be a day of mourning for you forever." The generation of slaves was condemned to wander one year for each day the spies had spent in Canaan and to die without entering the Land. (According to legend, each year on the eve of Tisha B'Av, a certain number of Israelites dug their own graves and were told to sleep in them, a sleep from which they never awoke.)

This incident set the pattern of rejection of God and the Land of Israel, which repeatedly brought ruin upon the Israelites. The pattern repeated in the two ensuing exiles: Because they turned to idolatry—a blatant rejection of God and His values—and engaged in adultery and murder (reasons given for loss of the First Temple), the Jews were sent away to Babylon. Then, when they rejected God through the senseless hatred (*sinas khinam*) to which the second destruction is attributed, they again were told, in essence, that they did not deserve to live on a land that was supposed to be peaceful.

Tammuz 17 was likewise given ancient historic significance as the day the first Tablets of the Covenant were broken by Moses because the Israelites, impatient and uncertain about his return from Mount Sinai, couldn't refrain from making the Golden Calf (Exodus 32:1–5). Just forty days after Revelation, the people acted as though God were not among them. Centuries later, it was the stones of the walls protecting Jerusalem that were smashed as the enemy approached. By acting against each other, not respecting their fellow Jews as equal human beings, the people again behaved as though they were not living with God. Also on that day, the daily sacrifice (through which the people drew close to God) ended because the animals were no longer available; a Torah scroll was burned in the Temple (a reminder of the destroyed Ten Commandments, which represented all of Torah); and someone named Apostumus placed an idol in the Temple sanctuary (an act tantamount to erection of the Golden Calf).

Day of Repeated Infamy

Contrary to what we would expect, the further away in time the Jews got from the initial cause of their grief, the more stringent their mourning practices grew. During the Gaonic period (sixth to eleventh centuries), it became customary to read other grief-inducing texts in addition to Lamentations, such as Job and the passages describing destruction in Jeremiah. Meat and wine were banned during the nine days before Tisha B'Av (eleventh century), then abstention was made optional for the entire three weeks beginning *Tammuz* 17 (thirteenth century), a restriction some pious Jews had already taken on themselves, particularly in Palestine. Eating new fruits during the three weeks was banned, and by the sixteenth century, marriages were prohibited during this period. It had already become customary to not put on *tefillin* (considered ornaments and therefore signs of joy inappropriate on a day of mourning) until the afternoon of Tisha B'Av.

The need for more expressions of grief resulted, no doubt, from the series of massacres and expulsions that occurred on the ninth of *Av*. The Jews of York, England, were slaughtered in 1190, and in 1290 King Edward decreed that all Jews be expelled from the country. The Jews of France were imprisoned on *Av* 9, 1305, and informed they had to leave that country within a month. In 1492, they were expelled from Spain and in 1555 forced into a Roman ghetto. In 1571, the Jews were ghettoized in Florence, in 1630 expelled from Mantua, and in 1670 forced out of Vienna. A two-week pogrom erupted against the Jews of Padua in 1684 because they observed Tisha B'Av rather than a Christian festival.

Medieval Jewish liturgical poets created numerous elegies (*kinot*) about the tragedies that befell our people, and these were added to the liturgy for the day of Tisha B'Av. Observance was not restricted to the pious. Even those who may not have accepted the idea, promoted earlier by the prophets and then by the rabbis, that Jewish suffering was the result of Jewish sinning, regarded the three weeks leading to the major fast as an opportunity to repent, ever hopeful that their actions would hasten redemption.

Devastation on Tisha B'Av continued into the modern age, beginning with Russia's *Av* 9 mobilization for World War I, which a year later led to the expulsion of all Jews from the border provinces. Arab attacks against Jews over access to the Western Wall erupted on Tisha B'Av 1929, and deportations from the Warsaw Ghetto to Treblinka began on this day in 1942.

Because of its character, Tisha B'Av was seriously considered as the day of commemoration for the Holocaust. The idea was finally rejected because it was necessary to give this unique catastrophe in our history its own memorial (see chapter on Yom Hashoah).

Most modern Jews find it difficult to relate to the ancient tragedies associated with Tisha B'Av, partly because we have a more immediate and far more gruesome destruction to contend with, the Holocaust, with its own day of mourning. We also have our sovereignty back. The Reform movement, having seen the dispersal of Jews throughout the world as a new opportunity to fulfill our mission to humanity, long ago ceased to regard the Temple's destruction as a tragedy (although in recent years the movement has given Tisha B'Av modern significance), and few Jews retain the desire to return to the rituals of Temple life.

At the same time, Jewish camps take advantage of Tisha B'Av, the only summer holiday, for special programs. Also, observance of Tisha B'Av has increased in recent years, probably a result of the *ba'al teshuvah* (masters of return) movement, the tens of thousands of Jews who are rediscovering their heritage. They and other observant Jews recognize that as long as the quality of life promised in the vision for restoration has not been achieved, there is reason to grieve.

FOR FURTHER READING

Bloch, Abraham P. *The Biblical and Historical Background of the Jewish Holy Days*. New York: Ktav Publishing House, 1978, pp. 231–251.

An account of the course of the war that led to the destruction of the Second Temple and explanation of how the dates for the fasts connected with it were determined are discussed.

Culi, Rabbi Yaakov, and Rabbi Yitzchak Bakhov Agruiti. *The Story of Tisha B'Av*. Trans. by Aryeh Kaplan. New York/Jerusalem: Maznaim Publishing Corporation, 1981.

First published in 1773, this collection of stories primarily from Talmud was compiled, and much more recently translated into English, to provide appropriate reading materials about the calamities surrounding the fall of Jerusalem and the reshaping of Judaism that followed it to those without access to the original sources. It includes traditional accounts of the course of the wars and legends surrounding them (some of which strain credulity).

Josephus, Flavius. *The Jewish War*. New York: Penguin Books, 1969.

This is the classic account of the war between Rome and the Jews, written by the historian who had been a leader of the Jewish revolt, was captured by the Romans, and became a Roman citizen and friend to

Vespasian and Titus. Though some of his details are suspect, much of our information about this period in history is based on his writings.

Roseman, Kenneth. *The Tenth of Av.* New York: UAHC Press, 1988.

This engaging book puts the reader in first-century Jerusalem, in the midst of the burning city. At the end of each of its vivid pages, it presents the choices the Jews made at the time. In the course of opting to fight or flee, follow Judaism or Christianity, become a teacher or merchant, live in Palestine or the Diaspora, the reader—who chooses his/her own path throughout the book—learns about history, Jewish values, historic figures, and what Jewish survival entails. While this Do-It-Yourself Jewish Adventure is directed to young teens, even adults will find it appealing and extremely informative. (Another book in this series, *The Cardinal's Snuffbox*, similarly treats another ninth of *Av* catastrophe, the Spanish Inquisition.)

Yadin, Yigal. *Masada: Herod's Fortress and the Zealot's Last Stand.* London: Weidenfeld and Nicolson, 1966.

The site of one of the most dramatic events in our history was proven to be more than legend when the excavations undertaken by volunteers from throughout the world, under the direction of Yadin between 1963 and 1965, uncovered exciting and significant evidence confirming Josephus' description of what had occurred there (based on the testimony of two Masada residents who hid instead of committing suicide with their compatriots). This is the story of the dramatic archaeological dig, its findings, and the history they brought to life.

WHAT DOES IT MEAN?— RELIGIOUS IMPORTANCE

In the context of Jewish destiny, Tisha B'Av marked more than the destruction of a city, the scourging of a countryside, a political development. The entire Jewish way of life, which since the Exodus had been focused on the Land, and the entire Jewish way of worship, which since the desert Tabernacle had been focused on God's earthly abode, were no longer possible. Along with the base of the Temple, the foundations of a belief system and a relationship had been shaken. In addition to everything material and spiritual, the possibility and opportunities for great achievement inherent in their living on the Land had vanished.

The ancient Jews, whose world was completely brought down around them, faced the same kinds of agonizing questions of faith and continuity that Holocaust survivors in our own time have had to ponder. What did the destruction say about the covenant and the God–Israel connection? Was Judaism supposed to continue? Could it? If so, what would it look like in the absence of the Temple, in exile from the Land, in the face of such complete devastation?

Exile as Punishment

Throughout our history, whatever happened to us was seen as a reflection of our nation's relationship with God. When He was pleased with us, we prospered and won in battle; when He was not, we experienced hard times and lost. Everything we had been taught and had witnessed during the desert wanderings—the extended length of which itself was a result of Divine displeasure—reinforced the connection. We were promised blessings for living in a way that would accomplish our mission and warned of curses that would befall us if we did not follow the commandments issued for our and the world's good.

So when they were led off in captivity to Babylon, the Jews only had to read Torah—which clearly stated that the Land would cast them out for immoral behavior—to realize that they were being punished for sinning against God. The prophets (Isaiah, Hosea, Habakkuk, Zephaniah, Jeremiah) for generations had warned them of the coming punishment. When it finally arrived, it was so severe it made the people question whether their violations of the terms of the covenant had caused God to revoke it.

Like the earlier prophets, those who experienced the loss of Jerusalem reassured the survivors that even though God had punished them out of the anger they provoked, His undying love would allow Him to forgive them. Jeremiah explained that God's presence was universal, that He would not abandon them, but had gone into exile, too, and would restore them to their homeland.

The second destruction created an even greater crisis of faith. Particularly with no prophetic guidance (not that the people had always listened to it anyway), there was confusion over the proper response, both during the war and after it. Were they to stay and fight, flee to another stronghold and try to outlast the enemy, escape from the besieged city and secretly teach their culture and religion, or adopt different religious practices altogether—either within the context of Judaism or outside it?

Many of the Jews who returned to Israel after the Babylonian exile, facing harsh conditions and lasting foreign subjugation, could no longer believe that loyalty to God would make any difference in their lives (Malakhai 3:13–14). Likewise, many of those quashed by Rome also despaired. Some came to believe that Christianity, which had developed as a sect within Judaism in the last decades of the Temple's existence, was not, after all, a renewal of the connection between God and Israel. They began to see it as a new covenant to replace the one obliterated by the destruction of the Temple. Christian Jews broke away and began evolving into an entirely separate religious community, taking with them Jews whose faith had been shattered along with Jerusalem's walls.

Others, led by the great sages, continued to see Israel's fortunes and misfortunes within the established pattern of Exodus (redemption) and exile, of rewarding compliance and punishing sin, of Israel having the free will to act, and God having the power to intervene to steer the nation back on the course of its moral mission. A critical part of the pattern is its intrinsic hope. The prophets who made the most gruesomely dire predictions always had visions of ultimate salvation. The worst sinner could repent. Between the cracks, one could again sow seeds, from the rubble, rebuild. If Judaism were to continue, however, it needed a new structure, one that was not reliant on particular places or physical structures.

From Sacrifice to Study

Trapped in the besieged Jerusalem, Rabbi Yokhanan ben Zakkai realized that people reduced to sustaining themselves on tea made from straw, as were the defenders of Jerusalem, would not be able to withstand Rome's onslaught. And he knew that the "independence or nothing" attitude adopted by the Jewish zealots in control, who refused to allow any living person to leave, was a policy of suicide that would put an end to Israel's true mission.

So Zakkai and his disciples staged his death so he could be carried out in a coffin in order to meet with Vespasian. All he asked of the Roman commander was permission to establish an academy of Jewish learning at Yavneh (a town in the Galilee). His request was granted. Zakkai realized that making the Jews as knowledgeable as possible about their culture and religion would preserve in another form the rituals no longer possible to perform. It would allow every one, not just the priests, to participate in Jewish life.

Following the lead of their predecessors, the Pharisees, the rabbis promoted the idea that getting close to God did not require burning an animal carcass but could be accomplished by expressing Jewish values in every aspect of one's life. Holiness was no longer housed just in an external place, but was an internalized characteristic of each person. Words (recounting Temple service, praising God, said in honesty to other people) and actions (routine behavior performed in spiritual awareness, interpersonal dealings carried out according to Jewish law, deeds of lovingkindness) could define Jewish life. Jeremiah had spoken of this "new covenant": "I will put my Teaching into their innermost being and inscribe it upon their hearts" (31:33). Torah study, through which anyone could learn how to live by Jewish values, was elevated to such a high priority in Jewish observance, the sages said it equaled all other commandments.

The means may have changed, but the message was unaltered: the goal of Jewish existence was still a redemption of universal peace. To underscore it, the rabbis said that the day of the destruction of the Temple is the day of birth of the messiah.

The Talmud relates that Rabbis Gamaliel, Eleazar ben Azariah, Joshua, and Akiva went to Jerusalem together. When they reached the Temple Mount, a jackal emerged from the remains of the Holy of Holies. Recalling that any common person who went near the spot would be put to death (Numbers 1:51), and seeing it turned into the haunt of fearless animals, three of the sages began to weep. Akiva laughed. He remembered the prophecy "and I call reliable witnesses, Uriah the Priest and Zekhariah the son of Berekhiah" (Isaiah 8:2). In the First Temple days of Uriah, Micah wrote "because of you, Zion shall be plowed as a field, Jerusalem shall become heaps of ruins and the Temple Mount a shrine in the woods" (3:12). Zekhariah, who lived at the time of the Second Temple, wrote "There shall yet be old men and women in the squares of Jerusalem" (8:4). Seeing that Uriah's prophesy had come to pass, Akiva explained, made him certain Zekhariah's would also come to be.

The sustaining lesson we learned through catastrophe was that in the aftermath of tragedy, an unavoidable part of an imperfect life, we move forward, perhaps in a different manner, but guided by the same values toward an unchanging goal. In the new revised system, anyone and everyone—each a component of the holy nation—could contribute to bringing it about.

FOR FURTHER READING

Ezekiel, in any Jewish Bible
   After the prophesy of Jerusalem's destruction, the prophet foresaw the return of the exiles and reconstructed Temple in his vision of the valley of dry bones.

Isaiah, chapters 40–66, in any Jewish Bible

Attributed to a prophet who lived much later than the author of the first thirty-nine chapters, the latter part of the book expresses consolation to the exiles in Babylon and later addresses those who returned to Israel after the Temple was rebuilt.

Jeremiah, in any Jewish Bible

With historic detail and vivid poetry, the prophetic book beautifully tells the story of the fall of Jerusalem and the exile to Babylonia.

WHAT DOES IT MEAN TO US?— PERSONAL SIGNIFICANCE

Have you ever been in a relationship that ended? Or watched a great chance come and go? Or made a choice you later wished you could reverse? How many times in your life have you said "I should have" or "if only. . . ." It is difficult enough to let go of something you have in hand. But often a large part of the pain comes from the sense of loss over what you *could* have had.

You would not engage in "what ifs" if you were happy with a current situation. Displeasure with it and sadness for squandered potential or lost opportunity can be incapacitating: It's extremely difficult to stride ahead when you are continually looking behind you. The rabbis of the postdestruction decades recognized this. So they concentrated the period and practices of mourning to free the people, so they would be able to move forward with their lives. If in your mourning you focus on identifying what is wrong and figuring out how to make it right, the experience can be cathartic and constructive.

That is exactly the purpose of a fast day: to give you a chance to momentarily retreat from your imperfect present, the imperfect world, to step back and indulge in your dissatisfaction with it, and then step forward and take action that will lead to positive change. Tisha B'Av allows you to experience loss for what was and what might have been, individually and collectively. If used well, it can help you create what can be, personally and communally.

There may be any kind of past loss or regret in your life whose hold you need to relinquish. But what is it Jewishly that you miss? If it's the smell of chicken soup on Friday night, the sales techniques of Maxwell Street, the colors and characters of the Lower East Side, or Bubbe and Zaide's Yiddish-accented speech, you've got a case of nostalgia, the source of melancholy reminiscence, perhaps, but not a reason to cry. As the once-popular poster of an oversized bagel suggested, there's more to two thousand years of Jewish civilization than this.

A concern for Tisha B'Av—which came about because the possibility of living a full Jewish way of life ended—should be the kinds of *meaningful* connections to the Jewish past, and future, you are missing. Lacking the knowledge to make time-honored traditions relevant and to infuse your everyday life with Jewish value, being illiterate about Judaism (can you explain Sukkot, identify Abraham, and name the Twelve Tribes of Israel with the same ease you explain Thanksgiving, identify George Washington, and name the original thirteen American colonies?)— these are things to mourn. Having not had a Jewish summer camp experience, first-hand exposure to Israel, or an exceptional Hebrew school teacher are legitimate disadvantages to regret and worthwhile aspects of Jewish life to consider on Tisha B'Av.

But once the day of mourning for what might have been ends, we stop "crying over spilled milk" and go out to fill the bottle. There's still time for you to increase your knowledge and for your children to take advantage of the opportunities you missed.

In the collective arena, most of us find it difficult to identify with the moaning and weeping the Jews of past centuries went through on this holiday. Unlike them, we have Israel and position through our status as citizens of other countries. But if we step back from our seemingly secure position, we realize that we still lack much of what they mourned. We have not eliminated anti-Semitic persecution from the world or established the universal peace that guarantees a life of dignity, self-sufficiency, and mutual respect for all; we have not effected a spiritual reconciliation to accompany our renewed sovereignty over the Land, nor have we been able to achieve unity—regardless of UJA (United Jewish Appeal) slogans ("One People")—which the Temple, as a national symbol and gathering place, promoted.

These deficits provide national goals to ponder during our day of withdrawal and introspection, and they have local communal implications. For instance: The senseless hatred that brought down the Temple is said to have been caused by "the root of all evil." Even the position of spiritual leadership, *Kohein Gadol*, went to the highest bidder. In our communities and institutions today, is the situation much different than it was at the end of the Second Temple? Who gets the greatest honors in the synagogue? The top positions on organization boards? Should you be trying to influence organizations in your community to add requirements for scholarship and character so that along with the necessary financial leadership you have the intellectual, spiritual, and moral leadership models and direction critical for long-term success?

Another example: The rabbis also blamed the destruction on *lashon harah* (evil talk): gossip, rumor, innuendo, even saying nice things that could prompt someone to respond with a negative comment. Trying to eliminate it is undoubtedly even a much more difficult task than trying to change our communal culture. Let's be realistic. How many of us can resist listening to or passing along a juicy tidbit?

The problem, which the rabbis considered one of the most serious offenses because of the destructive power of words, goes deeper. Even if a comment is not made initially with malicious intent, it can wind up causing serious irreparable damage. The remarks of individuals can have national repercussions. For instance, consider how you or the people around you express discontent with Israel. Is it done in constructive ways and without providing ammunition to our enemies? Does the criticism come out of sincere concern for the future of the country and its people, or because as a Jew you feel embarrassed by Israel's actions?

Words—whose power we should think about on Tisha B'Av—can be tools as well as weapons, can build up as well as tear down. Think of ways you can be constructive. Soothe ruffled feathers. Take advantage of opportunities to counsel cooperation and mutual respect in communal settings, stressing common ground and common goals rather than differences. (And on the personal level, encourage your children so that they develop confidence in themselves, the ability to "conquer the land"—their own challenges—which the Israelites facing Canaan for the first time lacked.)

Rabbi Levi Yitzhkak of Berditchev, the *khasidi* master, said that we cannot expect to achieve the "rebuilt Jerusalem" of our collective dream until we eliminate from among ourselves the destructive forces that devastated Jerusalem. All of them (idolatry, adultery, murder, hatred) represented turnings away from the Jewish way of life, as does ignorance, one of the most destructive forces we face in today's Jewish communal crisis.

The Chinese character for crisis consists of two symbols: one for danger, the other for opportunity. That combination sums up the history and meaning of Tisha B'Av. In past generations, emphasis was on the former, because the Jews continued to live in the wake of loss and the threat of persecution. So on Tisha B'Av they grieved over the destruction and passively hoped for the redemption. Never before in history, because of the political and cultural environments in which they lived, could the Jews act on the

opportunity; in response to the different threat we face, we can. While we still grieve for the loss of wasted possibilities and recognize the danger of not taking bold, positive steps, we do have the chance to bring redemption closer. It's an opportunity you don't want to miss.

FOR FURTHER READING

See *Jewish Literacy* (Telushkin) in Appendix C.

TRADITIONS: HOW WE CELEBRATE TISHA B'AV

WHAT DO WE USE?—RITUAL ITEMS

Kinot

Instead of the regular *siddur*, we use a special prayer book for the holiday, *Kinot* (Elegies), which contains the prayer services (*Ma'ariv*, *Shakharit*, and *Minkhah*), the text of Lamentations, a selection of additional elegies, and the scriptural readings for the day. Copies are usually provided by the synagogue or service organizers.

How Do We Show We Celebrate?— Observance

In the antithesis of the slogan for *Adar* (see chapter on Purim), the rabbis observed "When *Av* comes in, all merriment must go out." The restrictions established for Tisha B'Av and the weeks preceding it are intended to eliminate anything that would detract from mourning or lead to levity. We limit everyday comforts. We read elegies lamenting the tremendous loss and suffering of our people. Everything is meant to help us relive the devastation of Jerusalem, experience the grief of exile. (As an incentive, the rabbis cautioned that only those who mourn the destruction of the Temple would merit the privilege of seeing it rebuilt, based on Isaiah 66:10: "Rejoice with Jerusalem and be glad for her all you who love her! Join in her jubilation all you who mourned over her.")

Ushering in the Holiday

In reenacting the response to the destruction of Jerusalem and other tragedies of Jewish history, every Jew becomes a mourner. That is why many of the things we do on Tisha B'Av are borrowed from the customs and rituals we follow to express grief when we lose members of our immediate families. We restrict our physical comfort and express humility by not wearing leather shoes. Likewise, the clothes we put on should be simple and already worn, not fresh from the laundry or dry cleaner. For the same reasons, we sit on low stools or on the floor. We do not eat or drink. When we go to sleep this night, we change our habits in a way that will lessen comfort— for example, using fewer pillows than normal (the pious used to replace theirs with stones), taking the mattress off the boxspring, or using a sleeping bag on the floor. We refrain from sexual relations.

From before sundown, when all restrictions of the holiday take effect, idle chitchat and frivolous behavior are shunned. We forego the usual ways of welcoming a holiday both because of its nature and when it starts. Our last meal prior to the fast must be completed before sundown, and since at least the beginning of *Av*, we have not consumed wine. So there is no *kiddush*. We do not light candles, which are elements of joy. In fact, it is customary to reduce

illumination as much as possible, to acknowledge the dark days of our suffering.

The Fast

The rabbis said that anyone who eats or drinks on Tisha B'Av, except those exempt for health reasons, would not see the joy of Jerusalem. In addition to being an ancient means of expressing remorse and sorrow, fasting on Tisha B'Av is also a reflection of the famine, repeatedly referred to in Lamentations, which wracked the defenders of Jerusalem. (Among the most horrendous details of the siege are those pertaining to the mothers who, in the throes of starvation, cooked and ate their own children [Lamentations 2:20, 4:10].)

The *seudah* (meal) *mafseket* (interrupting), or the meal that comes between normal eating and the abstention from food, is supposed to be a sparse, lonely affair. Limited to one dish and foods traditional in a house of mourning, it is customarily eaten while you sit on the floor or on a low stool. Since, according to Jewish law, when three people eat in each other's company they recite the *Birkat Hamazon* together (known as *zumin*, invitation, as the leader invites the others to say grace with him), it is customary for several observant people eating in the same room to position themselves as though each is eating alone.

Synagogue

According to tradition, communal discord brought down the Jewish sanctuary and the Jewish commonwealth. The sins cited in the fall of the First Temple were acts between individuals that caused rifts in the whole society: adultery, murder, and idolatry, which meant that people were choosing their own gods, relinquishing their common goals and values to follow different masters. The senseless hatred blamed for the second destruction made enemies among people who should have viewed each other as brothers and sisters, fracturing what might have been a united front against a common enemy. Joining with other members of the community in prayer, a major part of observance for the ninth of *Av*, could be seen as compensation for this fatal fragmentation.

Evening

It is customary to go to the synagogue for *Ma'ariv* services at nightfall. You will notice that the sanctuary is only faintly lit, and the *parokhet* (ark curtain) has either been removed or replaced with a black cloth. The Torah scrolls and *bimah* (reading desk) may also be draped in black. Without greeting each other (another custom of mourning), members of the congregation quietly find places on the floor or on chairs or benches that have been turned on their sides. Often they remove their shoes.

Following *Ma'ariv*, read in a slow, mournful voice, *Eikhah* (Oh how [lonely sits the city]), known in English as Lamentations and sometimes in rabbinic literature as *Kinot*, is chanted in its own sad melody. (The tradition that senseless hatred caused the destruction of the Second Temple is derived from the initial letters of this first phrase of the book—*Eikhah yashav badah ha'ir*—which spell *eybah*, hatred.) Traditionally ascribed to the prophet Jeremiah (but more recently said to have been composed by various poets), it is the eyewitness account of a survivor (or survivors) of the destruction of the First Temple, a suite of five elegies whose suggestive imagery was thought by the sages to be as descriptive of the Roman destruction as it had been of the Babylonian.

Since the rabbis looked forward to the time that the days of mourning for the Temple's destruction would be converted to days of rejoicing for its renewal, they did not want *Eikhah* to take permanent form. For that reason, we do not read it from a parchment scroll (as, for example, we do for Esther on Purim) but from a printed book.

If you do not understand Hebrew, read the English translation. Its evocative language has the power to transport you to ancient Jerusalem, to make you sense what it was like to see your entire universe collapsing around you, to make you feel the pain of a parent unable to feed a child, the disgrace of a once self-sufficient citizen reduced to groveling in the streets. (The description of Jerusalem of 586 B.C.E., which reads like a description of Jerusalem of 70 C.E., in large part also reads like an account of Warsaw in 1943.)

The motif in Judaism of life over death, renewal after devastation, hope after destruction appears strongly in the midsection of Lamentations ("The kindness of the Lord has not ended. . . . The Lord does not reject forever, but first afflicts, then pardons. . . . Let us search and examine our ways and turn back to the Lord. . . ." [3:22, 31, 40]). In keeping with this philosophy, it is customary not to end the reading of any book of the Bible, or any portion of a book, on a negative note. For that reason, after the book finishes in distress ("For truly, You have rejected us, bitterly raged against us"), the next to the last verse of *Eikhah*, "*Hashiveinu*" ("Take us back, O Lord . . . renew our days as of old!"), is repeated by the entire congregation.

Most of the *kinot* chanted after *Eikhah* were composed during the difficult times of the Crusades and the Spanish Inquisition. Describing the transgressions of the Jews and their love for Israel, the most popular ones were written by Elazar Hakallir (the eighth-century liturgical poet), Judah Halevi (1085–1145, the Spanish philospher also considered to be the greatest postbiblical poet), and Solomon ibn Gabirol (another product of the Golden Age of Spain, 1021–1058). Embodying a timeless quality that has given them lasting impact in the liturgy, they express the prayers and dreams of a persecuted people who look to God for hope. Often in acrostic or altered acrostic form, they frequently draw on imagery from Talmud and Midrash.

Most liturgies begin with a *kinah* of Hakallir, and end with a series known as Zionides, which extol the glory of Zion. In a favored elegy, written by Halevi, the poet expands on Jeremiah's vision of the weeping woman identified as the matriarch Rachel (Jeremiah 31:15). He imagines himself walking on Jerusalem's holy ground and encountering Mother Zion, who asks about the welfare of her children throughout the world. Other *kinot* recited were written in response to tragedies in Jewish history. One commemorates the public burning of the Torah in Paris, another the massacres of German Jews during the first Crusade, another the slaughter of the Jews of York, and a recent one the annihilation of European Jewry in the Holocaust.

In the full *kaddish* (the prayer said in honor of the dead, but which praises God for the living) at the end of the service we delete the line *titkabeil* ("May the prayers and supplications of the entire Family of Israel be accepted"). It would contradict what we have just said in *Eikhah*, "You have screened yourself off with a cloud that no prayer may pass through" (3:44).

Congregations sometimes design special programs to give the Tisha B'Av experience current relevance, adding readings, stories, or discussions to the evening service and Lamentations.

Morning

Like mourners prior to a funeral, men generally do not put on their *tallesim* or *teffilin*, which are regarded as signs of joy. (Religious men who normally wear a *tallit katan*, also called *arba kanfote*, the fringed undergarment, do so even on Tisha B'Av. Some, like the Syrian Jews, put on their prayer shawls and phylacteries at home but remove them before going to synagogue; those who do wear them for the *Shakharit* service remove them before the reading of

Eikhah and/or *Kinot*.) Lights are not used in the sanctuary.

On fast days, the central *Amidah* prayer usually contains an addition, *Nakhem* (comfort), which requests consolation for the mourners of Jerusalem and the experience of exile. Since during the early part of the day, which corresponds to the time prior to a funeral, mourners are not open to being consoled, this prayer is omitted until the afternoon service. By then, grief is considered to have somewhat abated.

We do say the fast-day prayer *Aneinu* (answer us), which looks for response to our fast of distress. Prayers normally part of daily service that express sentiments or thoughts that contrast with the subdued and dejected feeling of the day are omitted. These include the Psalm of the Day, Hymns of Unity, Hymn of Glory, and the Priestly Blessing, usually said by the *khazzan* at the end of the *Amidah*. (It requests the granting of peace, like the traditional Jewish greeting, and greetings are not exchanged on Tisha B'Av.)

Normally mourners do not attend synagogue services during the week immediately following a burial (*shivah*), but since everyone is a mourner on the ninth of *Av*, anyone grieving for the loss of a family member may attend and may even be called to the Torah.

In keeping with the hushed aura of mourning, the *Sephardim* do not announce the *aliyot* but quietly tell the men to be called for the three Torah reading sections in advance, and they just go up in turn. (The *Sephardim* also omit their normal custom of joyously raising the Torah prior to reading.) In some congregations, it is the practice to say *Barukh dayan emet* (Blessed is the true Judge), the phrase said on hearing of a death, when called for an *aliyah*. The *yad* (literally "hand," the pointer used to note the place for reading the Torah) may be replaced with a simple instrument, such as a reed.

The Torah reading is Deuteronomy 4:25–40, the warning that the Israelites would be banished from the Land if they followed other gods, and the reminder that they would be blessed and live well on the Land if they followed the commandments. We are supposed to learn that any transgression, regardless of its severity, will be forgiven if we sincerely repent. Between *aliyot*, we make a *mishabeirakh* ("Who blesses") only for someone who is sick. (Normally, this special petition is made during this part of the service for various kinds of personal requests.)

The prophetic portion, Jeremiah 8:13–9:23, describes God's grief at the transgressions of His people and His plan to make Jerusalem and Judah desolate,

and to exile the Jews in punishment. Except for the last two verses, which refer to God's kindness (suggesting again that repentance will result in renewal), the *haftarah* is chanted to the same melody as Lamentations.

After the Torah has been returned to the Ark, we again sit on the floor for *kinot*. (Some congregations begin by repeating *Eikhah*.) We are not supposed to talk or leave the synagogue at this time. The central elegy of the morning is *Artzei Halebanon* (Cedars of Lebanon), a painful record of the martyrdom of the ten rabbinic teachers who were brutally murdered during the Hadrianic persecutions for thwarting Roman law prohibiting Torah education. Akiva, Gamaliel, Yishmael ben Elisha, and the other seven martyred sages are the subjects of another well-known *piyyut*, which we recite during the *Mussaf* service on Yom Kippur. In *Sephardi* congregations, members take turns reading the Bible book of Job, the classic tale of human suffering.

Afternoon

The *Minkhah* service includes the parts deleted from *Shakharit*. Interestingly, we do not recite the prayers normally omitted on festivals because they would hamper the feeling of joy (see "Halakhah" in chapter on Pesakh). This is consistent with the optimism built into Tisha B'Av—"the birthday of the messiah." From midday on, the mood lightens somewhat. While we continue to recall misfortune, our focus shifts to the hope of redemption embodied in every episode of suffering. (That is why restrictions on work and household activity are also lifted at this time.) The men may now put on their *talleisim* and the congregation resumes sitting on regular seats.

The scriptural readings underscore the positive message: Exodus 32:11–14 (Moses' success in convincing God not to destroy Israel after the Golden Calf abomination, but to uphold His promise to the patriarchs to bring them to the Land) and Exodus 34:1–10 (about the second set of Tablets, the attributes of God, and the covenant with His people) are standard readings for all fast days, known as *Vayekhal*, the first word of the Torah portion ("And [Moses] began" [to plead]). Isaiah 55:6–56:8, also read on public fast days, is a consolation to the anguished exiles in Babylon, reminding them of God's mercy and promising the restoration of the Land and the people to it.

Now the *Amidah* can include *Nakhem*. In Israel, two revised versions—one issued by the chief rabbinate and one by the religious kibbutz movement—reflect the reunification of Jerusalem. In the *kaddish*, *titkabeil* is reinstated.

Study

On the festivals, we engage in Torah study because it is one of the forms of joy that heightens our experience of the holiday. In keeping with avoidance of pleasurable activities, on Tisha B'Av we abstain from "the precepts of the Lord [which] gladden the heart" (Psalms 19:9). Only those parts of *Tanakh* and Talmud that deal with destruction, catastrophe, and mourning are permitted. A standard text, of course, is the book of Job. Also allowed are the warnings and descriptions about the impending punishment of the world in Jeremiah, *Midrash Eikhah* (rabbinical stories and commentaries on Lamentations and the second destruction), the scroll of *Eikhah* with commentaries, tractate *Mo'ed Katan* on the laws of mourning and excommunication, the account of the destruction in tractate *Gittin*, and the last chapter of *Taanit* in the Jerusalem Talmud, which details the destruction of the Temple.

We are forbidden to engage in analysis of text because it stimulates the mind, also a pleasurable activity. We may not even answer a question of Jewish law, unless it involves a sick person or an immediate need. When teaching children about the holiday, subjects appropriate for adult study may be used.

Conclusion of Tisha B'Av

While the blessing for the new moon (*kiddush levanah*) (see "The Jewish Calendar" at the beginning of this book) may be recited prior to Tisha B'Av, since it should be done in a joyous mood, it is common to wait until after *Ma'ariv* at the conclusion of the mourning period.

The preferable procedure is to wash your hands, break the fast with some food other than meat and with a beverage other than wine, change into your regular shoes, and go outside in the company of ten men. If doing all the preparatory steps would mean a *minyan* would not be available, they can be omitted. It is a lovely way to end the day and the three weeks, because the blessing that praises God for creating the heavens likens the moon to the Jewish people, who will be renewed as the moon is renewed.

Although the fast ends at nightfall, we do not drink wine, eat meat, or hold a celebration until noon on *Av* 10, since the Temple burned all through the night of *Av* 9 and into most of the next day. (The pious used to maintain the fast until midday on *Av* 10.) The other restrictions of the mourning period should also be continued until midday on the tenth.

Shabbat and Tisha B'Av

When the ninth of *Av* falls on the Sabbath, observance of the day of mourning is postponed until the tenth. (We are prohibited from expressing grief, or from fasting, on the Sabbath, a day of peace and joy. The fast of Yom Kippur, whose nature is entirely different, is the only exception.) *Havdalah*, the ceremony that separates sacred and profane time, is postponed until the close of the fast day. The blessings over light (created at the end of the first day of rest) and spices (used to strengthen us at the departure of a soul-filling day of rest) are omitted because they relate only to the Sabbath. The *Havdalah* blessing over wine is recited along with *hamavdil* (the passage dealing with separation).

Continued Consolation

Prophetic Voice

The upswing of hope begun on the afternoon of Tisha B'Av continues on the following Sabbath. Called *Shabbat Nakhamu* (Console) after the first line of the day's prophetic reading ("*Nakhamu, nakhamu ami*, Console, console my people . . .") (Isaiah 40:1–26), it is also the first of seven *haftarot* of consolation, all drawn from the Book of Isaiah, that deliver a message of comfort in the seven weeks following Tisha B'Av and lead us to the period of repentance and Rosh Hashanah (49:14–51:3; 54:11–55:5; 51:12–52:12; 54:1–10; 60:1–22; 61:10–63:9).

Tu B'Av

Six days after Tisha B'Av, on the fifteenth (*tu*; with the Hebrew letter *tet* [ט], nine, and *vov* [ו], six) of the month, there used to be a minor festival. Talmud remarks that there were no days as festive in Israel as those of Yom Kippur and *Av* 15, when the girls dressed in white and danced in the vineyards to attract husbands.

Several legends and several theories try to explain the fifteenth of *Av*'s origins. *Midrash* relates it to how the ninth of *Av* became designated as a day of disaster. It says that in the last year the Israelites spent in the desert, the elders who dug their graves and slept in them on the ninth of *Av* did not die. Thinking they had miscalculated the date, they returned to the graves the next night, and the next, until, by the fifteenth, they realized they were being spared and would be allowed to enter the Land: The sin of the spies had been forgiven.

Another explanation is more closely tied to the way the day was observed. It identifies the date as the end of the prohibition against an Israelite woman marrying a man from another tribe if she had inherited land from her father (Numbers 27:4–8). The prohibition had been in effect until the conquest of Canaan was completed and Israel became secure enough to not worry about transfer of property between tribes. It may also have been the end of the ban against intermarrying with the tribe of Benjamin, punished because of their depravity which led to the rape and murder of the wife of a Levite (Judges 19–20). (The next chapter of Judges describes how the Benjaminites, once accepted back into the community of Israel, selected wives from among the girls dancing in the vineyards during a festival at Shiloh.) Both explanations, like the wedding motif of Yom Kippur, suggest the reunion of Israel and God, which marked the end of a period of estrangement.

After the fall of Betar, the Romans inflicted additional punishment for the Jews' revolt by prohibiting them from burying their dead. Three years later, a new emperor overturned the cruel decree. Permission to bury the remains—given on 15 *Av*—was so significant, a special blessing of thanks (*hatov v'hameitiv*, Who is good and does good) was added as the fourth *brakhah* of the *Birkat Hamazon*.

In Temple days, *Av* 15 was the last time firewood could be brought to the sanctuary for the sacrifices (after that the waning sun was not strong enough to dry the wood) and was observed with festive dancing and the lighting of torches and bonfires.

While some *kibbutzim* tried to revive the celebration with music, poetry, dancing, and love songs, most vestiges of it are seen in traditional Jewish circles where penitential prayers are omitted during daily services. The bride and groom married on *Av* 15 do not fast, as is customary prior to a wedding; *yeshivah* classes are suspended after morning services, and teachers provide refreshments for the students.

For Further Reading

Tisha B'Av Compendium. Trans. and annotated by Rev. Abraham Rosenfeld. New York: The Judaica Press, 1989.

Providing the full text used for synagogue services on Tisha B'Av, this widely popular version of *Kinot* has an extensive selection of elegies, including one by the translator in honor of Holocaust martyrs.

Where Do We Begin?—Preparation

A three-week period of grieving precedes Tisha B'Av. Known as *bein hametzarim* (between the straits, or between the fences), from *Eikhah*—"All her pursuers overtook her in the narrow places" (1:3)—the sages identify it as a general period of affliction for Israel. (They relate *metzarim* to the word *tzarah*, meaning "affliction," which you might recognize in its Yiddish form, *tzuris*.) It corresponds to the twenty-one days from the breaching of the outer wall of Jerusalem to the day the city fell.

We relive the mounting despair of the besieged Jerusalemites, and the suffering of Jews throughout history who experienced catastrophe after massacre after slaughter at this time of year, by adopting progressively more intense mourning practices. Some begin on *Tammuz* 17 and last for the full "Three Weeks," while others are adopted from Rosh Khodesh *Av* for the "Nine Days." The most restrictive apply during the week in which Tisha B'Av occurs.

Three Weeks

Our period of mourning begins with one of the three minor fasts related to the loss of Jerusalem, *Shivah Asar* (17) *B'Tammuz*. It lasts from dawn until nightfall. (The two other minor fasts of destruction, *Tzom* [fast {of}] *Gedaliah* on *Tishrei* 3, when the last Jews fled Judah, and *Asarah* [tenth {of}] *B'Tevet*, when Nebukhadnezzar first attacked Jerusalem, are observed the same way.)

As of *Tammuz* 17, no weddings are held, there is no attendance of musical performances or playing instruments, dancing, pleasure trips, haircuts, or purchasing or using new items—clothing, luxuries, fruits—which would require the *shehekheyanu* blessing. Since the blessing thanks God for "bringing us to this season" and "this season" is one of catastrophe, it is obviously inappropriate.

With the amalgamation of misfortune accrued to these days throughout our history, the three weeks became known as a time when the Jews seemed to court trouble. (Even in Yokhanan ben Zakkai's time it was thought of this way. The sage urged teachers to avoid corporeal punishment for fear of serious consequences.) As a result, the rabbis advised that all situations of danger be avoided. We are not supposed to swim in deep water, ride in an unstable boat (like a canoe), undergo minor or cosmetic surgery, or go to court in a lawsuit with a non-Jew.

The pious set aside time each day to reflect on the loss of the Temples.

Nine Days

In the last few centuries, activity has become more restricted than in prior times. During this period, we are not supposed to bathe, even in cold water. That means no baths, showers, swimming, wading, floating, or soaking. This is the area that most offends modern sensibilities, especially since the nine days fall during the hottest time of the year. There are exceptions, in honor of Sabbath, for the sick and for laborers who get dirty on the job; otherwise, we are limited to cold sponge baths without soap and shampoo. (The *Sephardim* follow these restrictions only during the week of Tisha B'Av.)

Although historically some people have taken on restrictions regarding meat and wine consumption from *Tammuz* 17, the general custom is to give them up at the beginning of the month of *Av*. Ritual slaughterers since the eleventh century, in the days of Maimonides, have put away their knives on Rosh Khodesh, retrieving them only to prepare meat for the sick, the Sabbath, or a *seudat mitzvah* (meal connected with a commandment, such as a *brit*, *bar mitzvah*, *pidyon haben*, or *siyyum* following a course of study). It is a widespread custom not to eat food that has been cooked with meat, even if the meat itself is not consumed.

Since restrictions on washing and laundering clothes begin on Rosh Khodesh *Av*, any clothes that you or your family need to wear must be readied in advance. Many people put on new or freshly laundered clothes briefly before Rosh Khodesh, which allows them to wear those items during the nine days.

Shabbat Khazon

The Sabbath immediately preceding *Av* 9 is known as the Sabbath of Vision (*khazon*) for the prophetic reading Isaiah 1:1–27. After recounting heinous transgressions, it offers the hope of reconciliation, which will come when the people "cease to do evil, learn to do good." The Sabbath of Vision and *Shabbat Nakhamu*, which provides words of consolation a week later, embrace Tisha B'Av from opposite sides, cushioning the blow of the day of destruction, allowing the mourners to go into it knowing there is salvation and emerge from it reassured that redemption will come. The entire portion may be chanted to the melody of *Eikhah*; more appropriately, only the verses of admonition are rendered in that subdued chant.

Tisha B'Av on Shabbat

When the ninth of *Av* falls on Saturday or Sunday, which means that the fast and its restrictions are observed on Sunday, and you attend the evening service, you need to have a pair of nonleather shoes available at the synagogue to change into at the transition between Sabbath and the day of mourning. In an Orthodox congregation, the shoes are brought prior to sunset on Friday, since carrying anything outdoors on the Sabbath is prohibited by Jewish law.

WHAT ARE WE SUPPOSED TO DO?— *HALAKHAH*

All the laws connected with Tisha B'Av and the weeks preceding it are designed, like the customs of the period, to decrease joy and avoid frivolity, and like the preparations for the holiday, they increase in intensity.

Fast of *Tammuz* 17

The abstention from food lasts only from seventy-two minutes before dawn (*amud hashakhar*, literally, the rise of morning) until fifty minutes after sunset (nightfall), and does not apply to pregnant women or nursing mothers (unless they feel they will not be hurt by it), a woman who has given birth within thirty days, or someone who is sick but not necessarily in mortal danger. People who do need to eat during the day should take only what is necessary for well-being and avoid eating luxurious items or excessively. The same ruling applies to minors who understand the meaning of the fast. Males of thirteen years and over and females of twelve years and older are required to fast.

While other personal comforts and pleasures are permitted, abstaining from taking a hot bath or shower, unless the fast coincides with *Erev* Shabbat, is advised. Having a haircut or shaving is prohibited. (They are permitted on the fast days of *Tevet* 10 and *Gedaliah*, which otherwise share the same *halakhot* as *Tammuz* 17.) One who is not fasting should not be called to the Torah (read if at least six people in the *minyan* are fasting) or lead the prayer service.

Celebration

If no other date is feasible, a wedding may be held on the eve of *Tammuz* 17 but not after that during the three weeks. If *Sheva Brakhot* (seven blessings, the meals marked by recitation of the benedictions traditionally held on the seven evenings following a wedding) fall during the three weeks, it is permissible to dance and sing as long as musical instruments are not played.

At other meals during this period, singing without instrumental accompaniment is allowed as long as it does not lead to a joyous or raucous mood. Since grief should not be observed on Shabbat, normal Sabbath singing takes place.

Once Rosh Khodesh *Av* begins, all rejoicing is forbidden. If an occasion for celebration occurs on or after Rosh Khodesh *Av* (such as a *brit milah*), the expression of joy (for example, in the amount and style of refreshments served) should be reduced from what it would normally be. Giving gifts is inappropriate. (Consult an authority about procedures to follow when the *brit* coincides with Tisha B'Av itself.)

Music

During the three weeks, you may not attend concerts, opera, musical theater, and so on. Programs such as sporting events at which music is incidental to the main activity are permitted until Rosh Khodesh *Av*. If you are a music teacher, professional musician, or music student, you may play your instrument.

Pleasure and Comfort

Aspects of house building, repairing, decorating, and landscaping that are considered sources of pleasure are restricted during the nine days. If you are concerned about these matters, consult a detailed guide or local rabbinic authority.

New and Laundered Clothing and Needlework

Except for undergarments and children's clothing and preparation for Shabbat or a *brit*, you are not supposed to wash or clean linens or clothing, or use new or clean linen or clothes during the nine days. (You may purchase shoes needed for the ninth of *Av*.) If you must prepare garments for a trip or wedding, consult a rabbinic authority about how arrangements may be made.

Shehekhiyanu

Except for on Shabbat, or an opportunity for a *mitzvah*, such as *brit* or *pidyon haben*, all situations that call for saying *shehekhiyanu* are to be avoided during the three weeks. (If Tisha B'Av falls on the Sabbath, even though the restrictions of the holiday will not be observed until Sunday, the blessing may not be recited.) If a new fruit will not be available after the ninth of *Av* but will last until Shabbat, it should be

eaten on the Sabbath, when the blessing may be made. It is permissible to purchase and wear new *tefillin* (but not a new *tallit*, since it is a garment) during the three weeks; a new *tallit katan* may be bought and used until Rosh Khodesh *Av*. Other clothing and luxury items may not be purchased or used.

Meat and Wine

During the nine days, meat (which includes chicken), wine, and brandy (which contains wine), all sources of joy, are prohibited—except on Rosh Khodesh and Shabbat, or a *seudat mitzvah*. The restrictions include any food made from meat (such as soup), even if it does not contain meat, and foods and beverages that contain wine or grapes. Children over the age of six are also bound by the restrictions.

To avoid drinking the cup of wine normally taken at the end of the post-meal grace, or post-Sabbath *Havdalah*, give it to a child. If no children are present, after *Havdalah* drink the wine yourself, but do the *birkat* without it.

Haircuts

Beginning *Tammuz* 17, you should not get a haircut, except on Thursday in order to honor the Sabbath. If you have been in mourning for thirty days that end after *Tammuz* 17, you may get your haircut then. If being ungroomed would result in loss of a job or ridicule, you may get a haircut and shave, and a woman is permitted to shave her legs. A child's hair may not be cut during the week in which Tisha B'Av occurs.

Washing

During the nine days, you are limited to washing one part of your body at a time. Soap or shampoo may be used only if you cannot remove dirt otherwise. A laborer or other worker who normally gets dirty in the course of doing a job may use soap or shampoo as necessary. During a heat wave, you are permitted to take a cold shower, and for medical reasons, you may bathe or shower in hot water. A woman preparing for ritual immersion may wash with hot water.

If you customarily immerse in a *mikvah* on Friday in honor of Shabbat you may continue to do so during the nine days. When Rosh Khodesh *Av* falls on *Erev* Shabbat, you may bathe or shower as you normally would for the Sabbath. Otherwise, on *Erev* Shabbat during the nine days, it is permissible to wash your hands, feet, face, and hair with hot water. If you bathe or shower every *Erev* Shabbat, you may do so before midday, but use soap or shampoo only if it is impossible to get clean without it.

Swimming is prohibited for boys thirteen years of age and older and girls twelve years of age and older. Younger children may take cold showers or swim, and those under six may wash as usual. You may wash an infant and rub baby oil on its body.

On Tisha B'Av itself, except for hygienic reasons, it is forbidden to even place a finger in water—hot or cold—except to remove dirt from your hands. When rinsing your hands after using the bathroom, you should wash only up to the finger joints. (If you normally have to wash your eyes to cleanse them, particularly on rising in the morning, you may do so by passing your dampened fingers over them.) If you perspire heavily, you are allowed to use deodorant but no other cosmetics, beauty aids, lotions, or fragrances.

If you have to wash food in order to prepare it for the post-fast meal, it is permissible—since it is unavoidable—to get your hands wet.

Fast of 9 *Av*

Everyone of religious majority (age thirteen for a male, twelve for a female) is required to observe the fast that begins, along with the other restrictions of the day, at sunset. This includes pregnant women and nursing mothers. You may not even rinse your mouth in the morning and until the fast ends. Someone who is ill, even if life is not threatened, may eat, but only as much as is necessary. The food should be as bland as possible. You may not prepare the meal to be eaten after the fast before midday.

Leather Shoes

If the only leather on your shoes consists of decorative strips, you may wear them, but if the shoes are covered with leather or if they have leather soles, you may not.

Work

While the work prohibitions of *yom tov* and Shabbat (see "*Halakhah*" in chapter on Pesakh) are not in effect, it is traditional to refrain from a normal work schedule unless doing so would result in loss. (Rabbi Akiva said that anyone who worked on Tisha B'Av would not see any benefit from it.) Writing, business pursuits, and housework are not to take place before midday. A non-Jew may work for you earlier in the day but should do so in a secluded area.

FOR FURTHER READING

Felder, Rabbi Aaron. *Moadei Yeshurun, A Compilation of Jewish Laws and Traditions Dealing with Chanukah, Purim, Sfirah, Fast Days and the Three Weeks.* Vol. 1. New York, 1979, pp. 126–150.

Presented in clear concise language, logical order, and easy-to-follow outline format, this guide to the laws of Tisha B'Av and weeks leading up to it is particularly useful in its presentation of specific situations, including those arising from modern life.

WHAT OTHER THINGS DO PEOPLE DO?— CUSTOMS

Other Times and Places

Precautions

The Libyan Jews so strongly believed that the three weeks augured danger that they would not allow children born at that time to be seen outside during daylight hours.

A Month by Another Name

It is widespread practice to call the month in which the day of mourning for the Temples occurs *Av* through the ninth, and afterwards to call it *Menakhem* (consolation) *Av*, to indicate hope for comfort and renewal.

Expressing Grief

From biblical times, the pious put ashes on their heads—in the place where the *tefillin* are worn—as a sign of mourning. Some congregations would put the Torah on the floor and sprinkle it with ashes while reciting verses like "The crown has fallen from our head. Woe to us that we have sinned" (Lamentations 5:16).

In Yemenite synagogues, just before the chanting of *Eikhah*, a community leader proclaimed the number of years since the destruction of the Second Temple and announced that redemption had not yet arrived. Grief was encouraged by the observation that anyone who did not witness the building of the Temple was regarded as having experienced its destruction in his own lifetime. In Algeria, the *shofar* was blown, as it was in ancient fast-day ceremonies at the time of the Temple, when the priests sounded horns and declared the fast in times of distress, and a procession of wailing mourners in sackcloth would prostrate themselves in front of the altar.

After the morning service, it was common practice to visit a cemetery to pray at the graves of close relatives, martyrs, and the righteous for speedy restoration of Zion. It was preferable to go alone to avoid frivolous conversation and actions.

Expressing Joy

The tradition that the messiah will be born on Tisha B'Av led to special preparations as the day's mood changed. In Libya, while the congregation was engaged in chanting *kinot*, the young boys would ride around the fields on donkeys, hopeful of meeting up with the messiah, who, according to folklore, would arrive as a poor man also riding on a donkey. The women of Jerusalem whitewashed their walls and scrubbed their floors in anticipation of his impending arrival, and in other communities it was customary to sweep out the house on the afternoon of *Av* 9. For the same reason, many women put on jewelry or perfume in the afternoon of the fast day.

Shabbat Nakhamu was a joyous occasion in small Jewish communities throughout Eastern Europe. After the hiatus for celebrations, a succession of weddings took place, often beginning on Friday night and continuing, as was typical in past generations, for several days.

Israel

On *Erev* Tisha B'Av restaurants and places of entertainment are closed, and broadcast music programs are replaced with the chanting of *Eikhah* and suitable talks. The Western Wall is a popular place for Tisha B'Av prayers. During the day, people also walk along the Old City walls, visit archaeological dig sites that have uncovered approaches to the Temple Mount, or visit *Yad Vashem*, the memorial to victims of the Holocaust.

FOR FURTHER READING

Chagall, Bella. "Tisha B'Av." In BL, pp. 244–247.

In this reminiscence from the eyes of a child who had been enjoying glorious summer weather, the author describes the heartfelt misery the adults around her expressed for being in exile.

Greeting

The custom of not exchanging greetings on Tisha B'Av is taken directly from the *shivah* period following a burial, when mourners and those who come to comfort them do not greet each other. (In fact, it is common practice for a visitor not to say anything to a mourner, but to wait for the mourner to speak first.) This is particularly understandable since the traditional Jewish greeting was "*shalom aleikhem*" (peace to you), rejoined with "*aleikhem shalom*" (to you peace)—structured so it began and ended with the word of utmost goodwill and blessing. One is hardly at peace at a time of mourning, especially mourning over the devastation of war.

If someone greets you, you should not ignore it, but respond in a subdued way so as not to cause embarrassment. After midday, when other restrictions imposed to foster grief are lifted, it is appropriate to exchange good wishes.

Dress

The restriction against wearing leather shoes begins at twilight. In former times, people often went barefoot; now when people go without shoes, it is usually in synagogue only.

A common sign of mourning used to be the donning of sackcloth and ashes. While that does not seem to have ever been the custom for Tisha B'Av, we do indicate a time of distress, disarray, and struggle by avoiding freshly cleaned and pressed clothes and anything particularly fine, even if it is old. Jewelry is inappropriate.

WHAT IS THERE TO EAT?— TRADITIONAL FOODS

Cutting back on gustatory enjoyment customarily begins with the meal prior to the one that brings in the fast. Although you do not want to deplete your strength, the rule is to eat bland, basic food and as few tasty dishes as possible (traditionally these included salads, pickles, condiments, etc.)

The *seudah mafseket* is supposed to be limited to one dish (this includes two or more foods cooked together, such as a casserole). An egg or lentils are preferred. Both are served for the initial repast in a house of mourning because, as items that are completely enclosed within their outer coverings, without any openings, they are like mourners who in their grief hold to themselves. Being round, they also suggest the complete cycle of life. In some communities, it was customary to sprinkle ashes on the egg or to eat with it a piece of bread dipped in ashes, a practice based on Lamentations 3:16, "He has broken my teeth on gravel, has ground me into the dust." (The pious often limited themselves to bread, salt, and water.)

It is permissible to bring in the fast with a meal of a few kinds of fruit or raw vegetables (although many refrain from a salad per se). Coffee and tea are fine, but it is customary to drink less of any beverage accompanying the meal than you normally would. Meat and chicken are forbidden for this meal, and eating fish is discouraged.

WHAT TALES ARE TOLD?— STORIES TO READ

Most of what is available for Tisha B'Av is folktale based on talmudic sources about various aspects of the ninth of *Av* and the ancient catastrophes of the day. For all of us, and particularly children, it is important, as it is for commemoration of modern devastation (Yom Hashoah), to convey the greatness of what was, why Jerusalem and Judaism were and are worth fighting for, rather than simply focusing on destruction itself. There are numerous histories of Jerusalem and the First and Second Temple periods, as well as a myriad of stories about Temple days and the sages, which are available in numerous collections.

FOR FURTHER READING

"The Birthday of the Messiah," "Shame Destroys Jerusalem," "The Spies," and "Titus and the Gnat." In CT, pp. 338–340, 286–287, 139–143, and 302–303.

Based on often-quoted *midrashim*, these stories tell of hope inherent in the day of mourning, the origins of the ninth of *Av*'s character, the disrespect between fellow Jews that led to Jerusalem's loss, and the retribution exacted on the arrogant Titus for sacking the holy city.

Roskies, David G. *The Literature of Destruction: Jewish Responses to Catastrophe.* Philadelphia: The Jewish Publication Society, 1988.

The one hundred powerful selections spanning two thousand years of history show how Jews have placed violence against them in the continuum of Jewish experience defined by the God–Israel relationship and the sin-punishment-renewal cycle. Margin notes explain terms and provide sources and historic references.

Vilnay, Zev. *Legends of Jerusalem.* Philadelphia: The Jewish Publication Society of America, 1973.

Stories, folklore, accounts of historic and spiritual occurrences said to have happened in Jerusalem, or to people and things associated with it and the Temple, are collected in this compendium of material about the holy city. It provides a view of its history and the mystique surrounding it.

OF ADDITIONAL INTEREST

Music

While making or enjoying music is one of the prohibitions of the Tisha B'Av season, at some other time you might want to listen to Leonard Bernstein's symphony *Jeremiah*. It includes a vocal rendition in Hebrew of Lamentations.

In Israel

The excavations around the Temple Mount and in and around the Old City of Jerusalem, made possible by the reunification of the city in 1967, have uncovered remains from the periods of both Temples. They are generally open to the public, but since some are located in Arab sectors of the city, be sure to check with local authorities before venturing out to see them. You will want to check with the tourist office to find out about walking tours of First Temple and Second Temple Jerusalem, which are offered periodically.

Safely within the Jewish Quarter of the Old City (13 Teferet Yisrael Street) is **The Burnt House**, which provides tragic evidence of the last days of Jerusalem in 70 C.E. As fascinating as the restoration of the home of the priestly Kathros family mentioned in the Talmud, and the artifacts that give us a glimpse of their lives, the most exciting part is the unrestored room of charred beams, broken pottery, and ashes which, with other finds, confirms Josephus' accounts of the conquest by Rome.

Other views of aristocratic life in old Jerusalem can be seen at the **Siebenberg House**, the result of an extraordinary private excavation commissioned by Theo Siebenberg under his own house, when he became convinced that the site had to have been prime real estate during Second Temple days; and the **Wohl Archaeological Museum/Herodian Quarter**, the remains of six mansions from 37 B.C.E. to 70 C.E., including luxurious household items.

The **Museum of the History of the City of Jerusalem, Ramparts Walk**, and **Treasures of the Temple** (see descriptions at end of chapter on Yom Yerushalayim) should also be investigated.

In southern Israel, near the Dead Sea, it is possible

to visit **Masada**. The most spectacular and exhilarating (not to mention exhausting) approach is up the "snake path" on the east side, which you must begin before sunup, after which it gets too hot on the strenuous forty-five-minute climb. When you reach the top you will be rewarded with a magnificent sunrise over rosy Jordanian hills. You may choose the somewhat easier and less heart-pounding Roman ramp on the west, or easier still, the base-to-summit cable car. Herod's palace, with frescoed walls and mosaic baths, and the nearby synagogue, *mikvah*, cisterns, and storehouses can be seen.

ROSH HASHANAH

Rosh Hashanah (Roesh Hah-shah-nah'; Yiddish: rush' uh-shun'-uh): Jewish New Year. Observed on *Tishrei* **1 and 2** (late summer–early fall; September).

The Jewish year reaches its spiritual heights during the intense ten-day period that begins with Rosh Hashanah, the day on which the entire world and every person is judged for the way life is being lived. It is a serious yet joyous opportunity for assessing one's existence and for reordering priorities. Taking note of our place as Jews within all of humanity, and including prayers for the welfare of every nation, it is also the most universal of Jewish holidays.

ORIGINS: WHY WE CELEBRATE ROSH HASHANAH

WHERE DID IT ALL BEGIN?—HISTORIC FOUNDATION

The Biblical Basis

It is a credit to the genius of our sages that Rosh Hashanah occupies such an important place in the Jewish year. The holiday we know is far different from the new year originally celebrated. It wasn't even called by the same name. (When the words "Rosh Hashanah" appear in *Tanakh* [Ezekiel 40:1] they refer to Yom Kippur.) Torah calls the first day of the seventh month *Yom Zikhron Teruah* (a memorial of sounding [the ram's horn]) and *Yom Teruah* (a day of sounding). A day of complete rest, it is to be a sacred occasion when the *shofar* is blown and sacrifices are made to God (Leviticus 23:25, Numbers 29:1–6).

Prior to the Babylonian exile (sixth century B.C.E.), most Jews probably didn't even recognize the first of *Tishrei*. Ignorance of the Bible was common, idolatry was rampant, and the opportunity to witness the sacrificial rites and hear the *shofar* blasts mandated for the festival was limited to those who gathered at the Temple in Jerusalem. The blowing of the *shofar*, the one act that clearly distinguished *Tishrei* 1 from other festivals, wouldn't even have been enough to impress the Israelites, who heard the horn sounded at every new month and on a variety of other occa-

sions as well. Their attention was likely focused on the pilgrimage festival Sukkot, two weeks later.

The Postexilic "New Year"

After King Cyrus began permitting the Jews to return to Judah in the century or so after the destruction of the Temple, he dispatched Ezra to govern Jewish affairs in the Land. On *Tishrei* 1, 450 B.C.E. (give or take a few decades), the scribe and Torah scholar assembled his people in Jerusalem. Confronting him was a community unaware of the significance of the day, ignorant of the precious heritage that had been passed down for one thousand years before them, and weakened by extensive assimilation (as evidenced by the large number of intermarriages Ezra had just dissolved).

With the Levites (the Israelite tribe that comprised the priesthood) serving as translators and interpreters, from dawn until noon Ezra read to the people from the Books of Moses. The congregation wept when they realized how much they had lost by ignoring Torah. Instructing them not to mourn, Ezra and the Levites reassured them: "Go, eat choice foods and drink sweet drinks and send portions to whomever has nothing prepared, for the day is holy to our Lord. Do not be sad for your rejoicing in the Lord is the source of your strength" (Nehemiah 8:1–13).

In essence, Ezra effected a rapprochement between the people of Israel and the God they had abandoned, and defined Rosh Hashanah for them. It was a time to acknowledge God as their true ruler and to begin the return to Torah. This was not a day to lament over what they had forgotten or what they had done wrong in the past, but to rejoice that they could begin to recapture their collective memory and work toward being better in the future.

In Times of Temple II and Talmud

During the Second Temple period, when synagogues were built outside of Israel's capital, people who did not go to Jerusalem could hear the *shofar* sounded. Then, following the destruction of the Temple (70 C.E.), worship had to be reformatted. Over a period of centuries, the sages designed a system to replace the sacrificial rite. To prayers formerly uttered by the high priest in the Temple, they added new ones, and Jewish history amplified the day's themes.

It was natural for a people subjected to a succession of mortal rulers, and the inconsistencies such sovereignty entails, to deal with the issue of kingship and the question of who truly reigned over them. The answer, of course, was God. By the time the *Mishnah* recorded common Jewish practices (200 C.E.), the rabbis had asserted that *Tishrei* 1 was the day the Jews reaffirmed their loyalty to God as the Supreme King, not only over them but over the entire world.

As the King of the World, God was also seen as its Chief Judge, and *Tishrei* 1 was considered the day of passing judgment. Perhaps influenced by Babylonian and Hellenistic myths and symbols, the sages developed a rich imagery using the metaphor of a trial, during which each living being on Earth is evaluated.

In this construct, the Jews, because of their particular responsibilities, go to court, where every petitioner prays for a year of blessings. One's good deeds and repentance serve as Advocates, while the Adversary, personified in Jewish lore as Satan, takes the role of Prosecuting Attorney or Accusing Angel, arguing against the merit of the individual and of the Jewish people. (The Jewish Satan [in Hebrew sah'-tahn] is something altogether different from the Christian concept of the red-cloaked, short-horned Devil incarnate. It represents the evil inclination [*yetzer harah* in traditional Jewish thought] latent in every human being, counterbalanced by the good inclination [*yetzer hatov*].)

The scales of the zodiac sign corresponding to *Tishrei* symbolize the scales that weigh how much one's *yetzer hatov* has been able to subdue the *yetzer hara*. The side to which they tip determines whether s/he is to be written in the Book of Life, Book of Death, or Book of Limbo—the three volumes opened in heaven at the start of Rosh Hashanah for recording the names of the righteous, the wicked, and those who fall in between and must wait until the Day of Atonement ten days later for their final sentences.

Commemorating World Events

People became uncomfortable with the fact that unlike other holidays, Rosh Hashanah, because it focused on the individual and his/her relationship with self, others, and God, had no connection with any historic occurrence or with the cycle of nature and the seasons. So the rabbis determined that the day does in fact mark noteworthy anniversaries, each of them a kind of new beginning. On this day (as recorded in Talmud), the patriarchs Abraham, Isaac, and Jacob were born and died, Abraham prepared to sacrifice his son Isaac, the matriarchs Sarah and Rachel and the prophetess Hannah were remembered by God and subsequently able to conceive, and Moses declared the emancipation of the Israelites from Egyptian bondage.

Above all other historic events cited for Rosh Hashanah was the beginning of beginnings: the Creation of the world. The timing of Rosh Hashanah on the first day of the seventh month echoes the original seventh day, and the seventh day of every week, a break from encounter with the physical world, a time of rest and renewal. (Seven—a number "beloved above" according to the sages—signifies completion in earthly terms and is recurrent in Jewish law, observance, and history.)

In talmudic calculations, it was actually on *Elul* 25 that God began His magnificent endeavor, and what occurred on *Tishrei* 1 was the endpoint of His effort: the creation of humankind. This tradition clearly tells us that the real beginning of the world is humanity, in its physical and qualitative senses.

From Then to Now

By the time the Talmud was completed around the year 500, the holiday's observance as we know it was well established. While it refers to the new year throughout, Talmud devotes a special tractate, *Rosh Hashanah*, to the festival's laws. It was in these commentaries that *Tishrei* 1 took on the name Rosh Hashanah (literally Head of the Year). Other designations highlighted various aspects of its nature: *Yom Hadin* (Day of Judgment), *Yom Harat Olam* (Birthday of the World), and *Yom Hakeseh* (Day of Concealment, alluding to the position of the new moon on the first of *Tishrei*, the Torah's limited indication of the nature of Rosh Hashanah, and the unknown aspect of our sentences).

Aside from laws pertaining to *shofar* and service, the rabbis ordained, and accordingly set the calendar, that Rosh Hashanah would never fall on a Sunday, Wednesday, or Friday. This brilliant provision precluded the companion holiday Yom Kippur from ever falling immediately before or after a Sabbath (which would mean two consecutive days when, according to *halakhah*, it would be forbidden to cook or to bury the dead).

During the Middle Ages, liturgical poets added their literary interpretations of the motifs of the holiday, and common folk instituted a ceremony symbolizing the discarding of one's sins. Otherwise, the observances, mood, intention, and prayer themes of Rosh Hashanah have basically remained constant.

WHAT DOES IT MEAN?— RELIGIOUS IMPORTANCE

In addition to the fact that Rosh Hashanah is essentially a religious occasion, its meaning and observance embrace defining principles of Judaism.

The Nature of God

Four times a day and, if possible, at their deaths, pious Jews declare the creed of Judaism: "Hear O Israel, the Lord our God, the Lord is One" (*Shema Yisrael, Adonai Eloheinu, Adonai Ekhad*), referred to as the *Shema* (Deuteronomy 6:4). It asserts the Jew's acknowledgment that there is only one God in the universe, that all life stems from Him on an ongoing basis, that His rule is supreme. From the beginning of Creation, His role included judging His world, seeing it as "good," "very good," or "not good" (Genesis 1,2).

On their first day of existence, the first human beings did the one thing God had specifically instructed them not to do: eat from the Tree of Knowledge of Good and Evil (Genesis 2:15–16, 3:1–7). For their violation, God judged Adam and Eve, and instead of immediately implementing the death penalty He had promised as punishment for disobeying Him, God tempered his harsh sentence with mercy and gave them another chance.

This was to be a model for all future generations: As the Talmud explains, on the anniversary of the first "trial" in the world, Adam's descendants would also stand trial, they would repent, and God would remove Himself from the Throne of Judgment and sit on the Throne of Mercy in order to pardon them.

When Ezra comforted the wayward, decimated Jewish community of Jerusalem, telling the people to rejoice, he conveyed the message that God would accept their return to Him, that He listened to their prayers and would meet their change of attitude, heart, and behavior with forgiveness. God was no enforcer of predetermined fate, but as a lawgiver and embodiment of goodness (acting justly and mercifully) and sustainer of life (creating the world initially and continually), He was a loving parent and the model of what human beings could hope to achieve in character and conduct. Holding close to us this one God who allows us to learn from our mistakes makes Judaism a religion of tremendous optimism and hope.

The Nature of Man

Mankind was a unique culmination of God's creative activities, a combination of the purely spiritual (God Himself) and the purely physical (the world He made): clay from the earth, breath from God, form and content, substance and sum, body and soul. And as such, s/he was a bridge between the two worlds, the conduit for bringing heaven to Earth.

When God created humans in "His image," it was not to have a physical likeness of Himself. (In fact, Judaism ascribes anthropomorphic features to God only to make His actions comprehensible to us. In Judaism, God has no such form or characteristics.) "The image" refers to God's moral essence, as reflected in the way He instructs human beings to behave toward one another and in relation to Him.

That man can repent and be forgiven means that each of us, although independent to choose which options to pursue, is morally responsible for the choices we make and held accountable for them. Given free will by a God, Who as much as He wanted obedient servants did not want unthinking slaves, we have the capacity to mold our own lives. What we make of them depends on how we manage the constant struggle between the two conflicting aspects in our make-up: the *yetzer hatov*, the tendency toward saintliness, and the *yetzer hara*, the pull toward savagery. Our duty is to subdue the latter and stengthen the former in order to act morally for personal and common good.

The laws provided to us in Torah guide us to act properly. When we don't follow them and do wrong, we must take the consequences. Yet even if we are judged on Rosh Hashanah as undeserving of life (which means we're on the wrong course for our own good), we have the chance during the intervening seven days—in which time a whole world was created!—to recreate, or if you prefer redirect, our own lives.

Communal Responsibility

In addition to being held accountable for our actions, each individual is also responsible for the situation of the community and of the entire world. According to Maimonides, we are supposed to imagine that the scales determining our futures are even, that each one of us and the world as a whole is half meritorious, half guilty. One wrong act could tilt the balance toward the negative side, threatening our destruction. Conversely, one good act will be for the collective merit and bring us closer to salvation.

You don't have to believe in the notion of heavenly weights and measures to understand the underlying concept: Each one of us contributes to the state of the world, in however large or small a way. Our words and actions have ramifications that go beyond us as individuals. They affect our families, our neighborhoods, our communities, our country, our globe. The famous Talmud example instructs that when several people are sailing in a boat, no one has a right to bore a hole under his or her own seat. Human purpose in the world involves everyone in trying to keep the vessel buoyant and sailing smoothly.

Repentance

Judaism didn't need modern psychology to affirm that the discomfort we experience when we do something wrong—embarrassment, guilt, depression, anxiety—are destructive forces and therefore counter to life. (Wrongdoing is a form of death. How often do these feelings eat away at us inside? Don't we say, "I could have died!" or "I felt like dying!"?)

Judaism is all about life, that we should live, that we should live in a way that allows us to experience the greatest peace with ourselves, others, the world around us, and with God, the giver and sustainer of life. So there has to be a way to make up for our transgressions and eliminate their destructive results, which separate us from life. In fact, Talmud asserts that a mechanism for making up for wrongs preceded creation of the universe itself, because without it, the world could not possibly last.

This system, which tells us not to dwell on the wrongs and hurts, not to wallow in eternal guilt, and helps us move ahead in a positive way, is called *teshuvah*. It means turning away from (wrongdoing) and returning (to good, to God, to the commandments). It means that our errors need not be permanent blots on our records, that all is not lost just because we strayed, even great distances. Until the last moment of life, we have the opportunity to admit failure and improve.

This is a tremendously reassuring attitude. It means we get a second chance, provided our repentance is sincere and purposeful. As Talmud emphasizes: "Just as when a garment becomes soiled it can be made white again, so can Israel return to God after they have sinned, by doing penance" (*Exodus Rabbah* 23:10). "The Holy One, blessed be He, said to Israel, '. . . present to Me an opening of repentance no bigger than the eye of a needle, and I will widen it into openings through which wagons and carriages can pass'" (*Song of Songs Rabbah* 5:2). Once we initiate the process, with the faintest thought, we are on the way to relief.

Teshuvah allows us to express the negative thoughts and feelings about inappropriate actions we often repress, to purge ourselves of them, and wipe the slate clean, reestablishing our fundamental relationships, not the least of which is the internal balance within the self. Much more than a single act of asking forgiveness and forgetting, it is a process that, because it takes time, leads to self-transformation by helping us deal with the past, make the most of the present, and prepare for the future.

During the ten days between Rosh Hashanah and Yom Kippur, we use the word *khet* to connote wrongdoing. Although generally translated as "sin," implying some mortal flaw or heinous crime, it comes from an archery term that means "missing the mark," implying failure to meet potential, or a lost opportunity to act properly. Maimonides taught that *teshuvah* is not just for violations of *mitzvot*, transgressions of Jewish law and major offenses. Wrong thoughts, attitudes, and dispositions also require *teshuvah* for they, too, affect our level of morality, which continually needs review and improvement.

The first step is to recognize what we did wrong, realize that it is a waste of life and potential, and express *regret* about it. This helps us overcome the tendency to sublimate, rationalize, or deny it. We admit it to ourselves and to God, and if the offense involved others, we confess to any wronged party.

The second step entails *rejecting* the offensive behavior; we stop doing the wrong thing. Of course it's easier said than done. (It might be helpful to try listing what we think is gained by doing this thing, what is lost by doing it, what we fear we might lose by abandoning the behavior, and what we stand to gain through change.) Then we *resolve* never to fall back into it, in effect changing a habit, a pattern, perhaps a way of life. The measure of effectiveness of our progress toward transformation doesn't come about until we are faced with an opportunity to engage in the same behavior for which we have repented, and we successfully *restrain* ourselves.

Tanakh contains numerous references to *teshuvah*, including the commandment to do it, both as it involves other people (Numbers 5:5–7) and God (Deuteronomy 30:1–6). A rich heritage of *aggadah* on the theme indicates its importance in the Jewish way of life. Despite all the Jewish mother jokes and tales of woe, guilt is not one of our values, for with it you convince yourself you cannot change. That means you stagnate. On the contrary, through repentance, a uniquely Jewish concept, you can continually grow.

Our sages actually placed those who do *teshuvah* on a higher plane than those who have never erred. "And let not the man who is doing *teshuvah* imagine that he is kept far from the rung of the righteous, because of the iniquities and sins he has sinned. It is not so; rather he is as beloved and desirable to the Creator, as though he had never sinned. Yes—even more—his reward is great, for having tasted sin, he has forsaken it and conquered his impulse" (*Berakhot* 34b).

It is considered an act of merit to help someone repent, and it is forbidden to remind one who has done *teshuvah* of his/her sins. S/he is, after all, a new person.

What Does It Mean to Us?— Personal Significance

Since this holiday is all about the moral and spiritual quality of each individual life, the significance the holiday can have for you lies entirely in what you, as an individual, make of it. In just about every aspect of Rosh Hashanah's observance you can find something to relate to your situation. So in addition to the specific points below, you'll find insights throughout this chapter.

The first human being, whose creation we celebrate on Rosh Hashanah, was the pinnacle of a process, each step of which built on the previous and which was all part of Divine purpose. Inherent in Creation was the fact that the world, as good as it was (and "God . . . found it very good" [Genesis 1:31]), was unfinished, and that humans would work in partnership with God to perfect it: Creation continues throughout time.

Just as the world evolves, developing from what was before, so does each life. Despite the sages' designations, rather than being a holiday of Jewish history, Rosh Hashanah is a holiday of personal history: It presents us with the opportunity to review where we have been and to renew ourselves in positive ways. Because the world and all its possibilities is reborn in each person, each person can be reborn to grow closer toward his or her potential. Such is progress.

As part of the process, we confront our own morality every day. On Rosh Hashanah, we also confront our own mortality. Standing before God to take credit or censure for our actions brings us face-to-face with death (we are, after all, on trial, the outcome of which will determine whether we are written into the Book of Life or its opposite). The Creation epic has taught us that the universe is not random but was created with Divine purpose giving significance and dignity to every life. So as we confront death, Rosh Hashanah makes us focus on the meaning of our individual lives.

At annual review time on your job, before giving you his or her analysis and determining whether you qualify for a raise, a good superior will ask you to evaluate yourself against your job description and any stated goals established for the year. At the new year, you are up for a raise, too, a raise in your spiritual status. The evaluation used to measure worthiness is called *kheshbone hanefesh*, an accounting of the soul.

You ask yourself: What am I doing with my life? Is it worthwhile? Where is it taking me? Is this where I want to go? What have I accomplished in the past year? What did I set out to do that I failed to accomplish? What are the ramifications of my successes and failures, for me and for others, in my overall plans? What do I need to change to reach my goals, my potential? What am I doing to contribute to the balance of scales in my life, in my family's life, in my community, in the world? How do I interact with the people around me—family members, friends, coworkers, strangers? What negative aspects of my personality do I need to deal with? How can I change them? What am I doing wrong? What can I do better? How can I be closer to the Divine ideals of how I should behave in relation to God and others?

The way you answer these questions and the ways you resolve to improve yourself can have tremendous impact. Humankind was initially created as a single being to teach us that one individual has the capacity to fulfill Creation. This means that every single person has the potential for the same, and is therefore of infinite value. (How do you measure a wasted life?) This places on every one of us the responsibility to work toward the highest level of fulfillment.

By making choices leading in that direction, choices that will keep us healthy mentally, physically, and spiritually, we write ourselves into the Book of Life. "Life" and its negation are not merely biological terms. The Torah defines life as the path it has outlined, through a series of psychologically sound, logical, humane, and common-sensical laws that guide how we are to take care of ourselves, treat others, and appreciate God. Death is deviation from the commandments, because there are consequences when the laws are transgressed. (If we are to learn from Adam's mistake, when we don't obey, we make life more difficult for ourselves.)

Study after study has shown that people suffer when they feel their lives have no overriding direction or purpose. As Maimonides admonished (in words as applicable today as they were in the twelfth century): "Awake you sleepers from your sleep, and you slumberers, arise from your slumber—examine your deeds, repent and remember your Creator. Those of you who forget the truth in the vanities of the times and dwell all year in vanity and emptiness, look into your souls, improve your ways and actions, let each of you forsake his evil path and his thoughts which are not good" (*Hilkhot Teshuvah*, 3).

Such soul-searching can be a difficult and painful process, particularly for anyone who determines that major changes are warranted. Everything doesn't have to happen at once, however. What matters is the direction in which you are going. To keep things manageable, you might want to determine a priority or choose the most doable items on your accounting.

As a practical approach, as you go through *kheshbone hanefesh* and *teshuvah*, choose something in each of three areas to concentrate on during this holiday, and resolve to improve them in the coming year: in yourself, in your relationships with others, and in relation to God (or, if you prefer, the community). You can use the process and goals to help your children do the same. The idea is not to do things better for a short period of time, but to raise yourself to a new level of performance and spirituality and work toward maintaining the higher standards throughout the year.

FOR FURTHER READING

Moments of Transcendence: Inspirational Readings for Rosh Hashanah. Ed. by Rabbi Dov Peretz Elkins. Northvale, NJ: Jason Aronson, 1992.

The observations of philosophers, psychologists, poets, religious leaders, popular pundits—and a comedian—ancient, modern, Jewish, and gentile, have been gathered in this useful book. The thought-provoking and sometimes moving entries are organized in sections on themes of the day and major parts of the service. This is an excellent resource to consult as you prepare for the holiday and is a good companion to have in synagogue.

TRADITIONS: HOW WE CELEBRATE ROSH HASHANAH

WHAT DO WE USE?—RITUAL ITEMS

Shofar

The only Rosh Hashanah ceremony from biblical time still practiced involves the *shofar*, an ancient musical instrument. It is usually made from a ram's horn, to recall the animal that was sacrificed in place of Isaac (see discussion of the *Akeidah* in section on "Observance").

The talmudic law dictating each step in the detailed process of converting a horn into a ritual instrument allowed for differences between communities. *Ashkenazi shofarim* tend to be straighter (though still curved, symbolizing that we must bend our will before God) than the often long, ornately curled ones of the *Sephardim*, so they could be easily concealed from anti-Semitic neighbors. Since one person in the synagogue blows the *shofar* for all to hear, it is not necessary to have your own, although many families do. The *shofar* can be blown at home or in another setting (such as a hospital) for those who are unable to attend communal services.

Makhzor

Instead of the *siddur*, which contains the order of services for weekdays and Sabbaths, on Rosh Hashanah (and other festivals) we use a special prayer book called a *makhzor* ("cycle," for the pattern of holidays that brings us back to the beginning). Most synagogues provide *makhzorim* for worshippers; depending on the version yours uses, you might want to have your own that contains commentary, allows you to read Hebrew and English line for line, or otherwise facilitates your following and understanding the service.

FOR FURTHER READING

For Adults

The Complete ArtScroll Machzor—Rosh Hashanah. Trans. and Commentary by Rabbi Nosson Scherman. Brooklyn: Mesorah Publications, 1988.

This is a wonderful version of the traditional prayer book, with clear instructions, extensive commentary on origins and meanings of the prayers, and sections on the laws and customs of the holiday. The layout aligning Hebrew and corresponding English paragraphs facilitates following the text in both languages. A highly regarded *makhzor*, it is published for both the *Ashkenazi* and *Sephardi* rites.

The Metsudah Machzor—Rosh Hashanah. Trans. and Anthology of Classic Commentaries by Rabbi Avrohom Davis. Far Rockaway, NY: Metsudah Publications, 1983.

This is the *makhzor* for someone who does not understand Hebrew but wants to read it with comprehension. The book provides linear translation, with short phrases of English and Hebrew on the same page, so that you can read both languages simultaneously. There are few instructions, and the commentary is limited.

For Children

Abrams, Judith Z. *Rosh Hashanah, A Family Service.* Rockville, MD: Kar-Ben Copies, 1990.

Designed for use with young children, the simple service helps explain the concepts of Rosh Hashanah—*tefillah* (prayer), *teshuvah* (repentance), and *tzedakah* (what the author calls sharing)—with a section on each. For the Torah reading, the book age-appropriately uses the Creation story (rather than stories of Isaac's birth and the *Akeidah*). A couple of simple songs and suggested activities for home and school are included. A companion cassette tape is available. Ages 4–8.

Orkand, Robert, Joyce Orkand, and Howard I. Bogot. *Gates of Awe, Holy Day Prayers for Young Children.* New York: Central Conference of American Rabbis, 1991.

Though produced by the Reform movement, this introduction to prayer for the Days of Awe may be useful for anyone. Explaining that prayer helps us think about God, it contains simple blessings that introduce God and identifies key items and personalities with brief stories about their importance. The text is enhanced with beautiful watercolor illustrations. Ages 2–6.

Kittel

A lightweight belted white robe, the *kittel* is worn over street clothes by religious men. (On Rosh Hashanah the *khazzan* and prayer leader generally wear them, while on Yom Kippur many of the men attending a traditional synagogue will.) It symbolizes the attire of the angels, to whose spiritual level we aspire, and brings to mind the simple white shroud in which Jews are buried, prompting thoughts of mortality and feelings of humility. A *kittel* can be purchased at a store that sells Jewish supplies.

HOW DO WE SHOW WE CELEBRATE?— OBSERVANCE

Ten Days of Repentance

Rosh Hashanah begins a solemn, but decidedly not sad, period, ending with Yom Kippur, during which we focus on our behavior and how we can improve. The rabbis connected the two holidays that in Torah's terms seemed to have no direct relationship. By creating the thematic unity of the trial (Rosh Hashanah) and sentencing (Yom Kippur) linked by a period of appeal, they embued the two holidays and intervening week with a single and sustained meaning and mood.

Popularly called the High Holy Days, which sounds like a Christian designation, the period is better described by its activity, *Aseret Yamei Teshuvah* (Ten Days of Repentance), or its aura, *Yamim Nora'im* (Days of Awe), both of which capture the seriousness, spirituality, soul-searching, and supplication that are part of this season. They begin with our attempts to elevate ourselves toward heaven and judge ourselves against its standards.

Remembering that when Adam disobeyed God he faced the death penalty, we ask ourselves what we face, what we deserve—good or bad. Those are *awesome* thoughts that engender feelings powerful enough to affect Jews who have little or nothing to do with Judaism the rest of the year. These days and their agenda speak to real human needs, to intensely personal pains and fears (the discomfort of error, the burden of guilt for wrongdoing, the anguish of unknown consequences), and to cherished hopes and dreams (the warmth of improvement, the joy of achievement, the anticipation of reward).

Proper Mood

Just as God's harsh judgment is tempered with mercy, the seriousness in our task should be tempered with joy. We are confident that God will forgive us for our shortcomings and give us the chance to do better. This approach expresses our belief in the process of *teshuvah*, our implicit trust in God's goodness, and our understanding of the nature of God. This is a spiritual joy, not the frivolity and abandon of a secular new year. It is the true joy of peace of mind, of a soul at rest.

Ushering in Rosh Hashanah

Like Shabbat and other festivals, Rosh Hashanah begins with candlelighting (preferably done by the women of the household, but by men if no woman is present) and the appropriate blessings:

בָּרוּךְ אַתָּה, יהוה אֱלֹהֵינוּ, מֶלֶךְ הָעוֹלָם, אֲשֶׁר קִדְּשָׁנוּ בְּמִצְוֹתָיו, וְצִוָּנוּ לְהַדְלִיק נֵר שֶׁל [*שַׁבָּת וְשֶׁל] יוֹם טוֹב.

Barukh Atah, Adonai Eloheinu, Melekh Haolam, asher kidshanu b'mitzvotav, v'tzivanu lehadlik ner shel [Shabbat v'shel] yom tov.*

Blessed are You, Lord our God, King of the Universe, Who has sanctified us with His commandments and commanded us to kindle the light of [the Sabbath and of*] the festival.

---

*For when Sabbath and the holiday fall on the same day.

בָּרוּךְ אַתָּה, יהוה אֱלֹהֵינוּ, מֶלֶךְ הָעוֹלָם, שֶׁהֶחֱיָנוּ, וְקִיְּמָנוּ, וְהִגִּיעָנוּ לַזְּמַן הַזֶּה.

Barukh Atah, Adonai Eloheinu, Melekh Haolam, shehekheyanu, v'kiyamanu, v'higgiyanu lazman hazeh.

Blessed are You, Lord our God, King of the Universe, Who has sustained us, kept us alive, and allowed us to reach this season.

Some people bless their children, as they do on *Erev* Shabbat, using the standard form (below) and/or a personalized version:

(For a son):

יְשִׂמְךָ אֱלֹהִים כְּאֶפְרַיִם וְכִמְנַשֶּׁה.

Y'simkhah Elohim k'Efraim v'k'Menasheh.

May God make you like Ephraim and Menasseh.

(For a daughter):

יְשִׂמֵךְ אֱלֹהִים כְּשָׂרָה, רִבְקָה, רָחֵל וְלֵאָה.

Y'simeikh Elohim k'Sarah, Rivkah, Rakhel v'Layah.

May God make you like Sarah, Rebecca, Rachel, and Leah.

(Continue for both):

יְבָרֶכְךָ יהוה וְיִשְׁמְרֶךָ. יָאֵר יהוה פָּנָיו אֵלֶיךָ וִיחֻנֶּךָּ. יִשָּׂא יהוה פָּנָיו אֵלֶיךָ, וְיָשֵׂם לְךָ שָׁלוֹם.

Y'varekhekha Adonai v'yismarekhah. Ya'eir Adonai panav eilekha v'khunekhah. Yisah Adonai panav eilekhah v'yahseim l'khah shalom.

May the Lord bless you and watch over you. May the Lord shine His face toward you and show you favor. May the Lord be favorably disposed toward you and may He grant you peace.

Following evening services in the synagogue (similar to those of a regular evening, with the exception of the type of melodies used), we enjoy a festive meal at home. Like any festival meal, it is preceded by *kiddush, shehekheyanu* (if someone other than the person who lights the candles makes *kiddush*), the blessing over handwashing and *motzi* over bread. (You'll find the full festival *kiddush* in a *makhzor*.)

בָּרוּךְ אַתָּה, יהוה אֱלֹהֵינוּ, מֶלֶךְ הָעוֹלָם, בּוֹרֵא פְּרִי הַגָּפֶן.

Barukh Atah, Adonai Eloheinu, Melekh Haolam, borei pri hagaffen.

Blessed are You, Lord our God, King of the Universe, Who creates the fruit of the vine.

בָּרוּךְ אַתָּה, יהוה אֱלֹהֵינוּ, מֶלֶךְ הָעוֹלָם, שֶׁהֶחֱיָנוּ, וְקִיְּמָנוּ, וְהִגִּיעָנוּ לַזְּמַן הַזֶּה.

Barukh Atah, Adonai Eloheinu, Melekh Haolam, shehekheyanu, v'kiyamanu, v'higgiyanu lazman hazeh.

Blessed are You, Lord our God, King of the Universe, Who has sustained us, kept us alive, and allowed us to reach this season.

בָּרוּךְ אַתָּה, יהוה אֱלֹהֵינוּ, מֶלֶךְ הָעוֹלָם, אֲשֶׁר קִדְּשָׁנוּ בְּמִצְוֹתָיו, וְצִוָּנוּ עַל נְטִילַת יָדָיִם.

Barukh Atah, Adonai Eloheinu, Melekh Haolam, asher kidshanu b'mitzvotav, vitzivanu al netilat yadayim.

Blessed are You, Lord our God, King of the Universe, who has sanctified us with His commandments and commanded us regarding washing the hands.

בָּרוּךְ אַתָּה, יהוה אֱלֹהֵינוּ, מֶלֶךְ הָעוֹלָם, הַמּוֹצִיא לֶחֶם מִן הָאָרֶץ.

Barukh Atah, Adonai Eloheinu, Melekh Haolam, hamotzi lekhem min ha'aretz.

Blessed are You, Lord our God, Who brings forth bread from the earth.

Instead of dipping the bread into salt (as we normally do since it represents the sacrifices made on the Temple altar that were sprinkled with salt—which also suggests the tears shed by Jews throughout history), we dip it into honey.

This is followed by a piece of apple dipped in honey, symbolizing a sweet year, which we eat after we recite:

בָּרוּךְ אַתָּה, יהוה אֱלֹהֵינוּ, מֶלֶךְ הָעוֹלָם, בּוֹרֵא פְּרִי הָעֵץ.

Barukh Atah, Adonai Eloheinu, Melekh Haolam, borei pri ha'eitz.

Blessed are You, Lord our God, King of the Universe, Who creates the fruit of the tree.

The focal point for the celebration of this holy day remains the house of worship.

Synagogue Sights and Service

Out of the Ordinary

As soon as you walk into the sanctuary you will notice that things are different from the rest of the year. To reflect joy and purity, white ark curtains, Torah scroll sheaths, and *bimah* (reading desk) cloth replace the usual ones that are blue or maroon. In an Orthodox *shul*, during the repetition of the *Amidah*, you might see the *khazzan*, sometimes accompanied by members of the congregation, not only "bend the knee and bow" but completely prostrate himself in remembrance and reenactment of the Temple service. (We don't normally bow down because this act was part of Temple service that we refrain from doing out of respect for our destroyed spiritual center.)

Sometimes traditional Jews gesture wildly and shout their prayers as if they will reach heaven faster and somehow better convey the worthiness of the petitioner. (The Baal Shem Tov, founder of the *khasidim*, likened such actions to those of drowning men thrashing about, trying to pull themselves out of overwhelming waters, and instructed that we therefore should not make fun of these people.) Often the worshippers stand with their heads slightly bent in contrition.

In a *Sephardi* synagogue, three *khazzanim* (or a *khazzan* and two *seganim*, or associates) stand at the *bimah*. This triumvirate is reminiscent of Moses being supported by Aaron and Hur as he presided over the battle of the Israelites against Amalek, the extreme manifestation of the *yetzer hara* (Exodus 17:12). The *khazzan* and his assistants pray to God that the congregation will triumph over its adversaries and adversity. Sometimes silent partners, the *seganim* often trade off leading the service with the *khazzan* and each other.

In the Judeo-Spanish rite, prayers are recited in Hebrew and Ladino. Some Conservative and Reform congregations have choirs and instrumental accompaniment.

A Logistical Note

Unfortunately, in America, large numbers of people who normally do not attend a synagogue want to be present for some portion of services on Rosh Hashanah and Yom Kippur. Synagogues are built to accommodate their members, with a little room for growth, but generally cannot handle the crowds that appear two or three days a year. Whether the services are given in their normal setting, or shift to a nearby school, theater, or other larger facility, it has become necessary for tickets to be sold for them. If you are not a member of a synagogue who receives tickets for the cost of annual dues, call in advance to order them. Special arrangements are usually made for students or those who are in unfortunate circumstances, so that no one is turned away for lack of funds. In fact, no synagogue will turn you away if you do not have a ticket, although you might have to stand in the back, at least during the most popular parts of the services. (For a list of synagogues, call your local Jewish Federation or rabbinical council, check the Yellow Pages, or look in a local Jewish newspaper for listings. Many congregations advertise during the weeks prior to the holidays.)

Deciphering the Prayer Book

Most of us are not adept at following a sport, playing a musical instrument, or speaking a foreign language the first time we try. Each activity has its own structure and terminology whose particularities you need to learn before you are fully able to participate. You shouldn't expect a prayer service to be different. While one of Rosh Hashanah's powerful images is of three heavenly books (to record the righteous, the wicked, and those in between) being opened, you're far from alone if for you the guidebook that takes us through the festival remains closed.

Even with modernizations, alterations, and use of more English than Hebrew in many versions, large numbers of Jews unfamiliar with the *makhzor* often feel uncomfortable with the services and unmoved by the experience of what they think is fulfillment of a religious obligation. The Baal Shem Tov said that someone who prayed, even if he did not know the meaning of his prayers, would still be blessed, because his worship would reach heaven. Others say that it is not the form of worship (incomprehensible prayers) but the sincerity that matters, as movingly illustrated in the stories of the poor, uneducated or mute men who could express their prayers only by reciting the *alef-bet* (Hebrew alphabet), speaking in the vernacular, or blowing through a flute.

These are acceptable options but not totally satisfying if you want to be comfortable and able to participate with the community (we pray together in synagogue rather than at home alone) and be affected by the services on a personal level.

The *makhzor* for Rosh Hashanah is admittedly ancient. A type of anthology, it summarizes Jewish thought on God and man through selections from Bible and Talmud, prayers from Temple and talmudic days, and liturgical poems of the Middle Ages. But it is not archaic. Its central elements have remained constant for the past fifteen hundred years and across more than fifty different rites, because they resonate with truth and relevance that transcend individuals and the times and places in which we live.

Some *makhzorim* contain detailed commentaries that help us better understand what the services

mean. In addition, there are books that follow the order of the services, providing information about the development of various elements, why they have been included, and how they are significant. These are invaluable aids, especially when taken to synagogue and used as companions to the *makhzor* (see suggested titles under "For Further Reading").

Understanding Prayer

We cannot avoid the fact that the way we observe this festival is by praying, a major obstacle for many of us; even those who are "religious" often express difficulty with it. But it doesn't have to be.

First of all, what is prayer? We think of it as petitioning God—"remember us, bless us, grant us, give us"—for whatever we desire. This is not the Jewish concept. The Hebrew "to pray," the reflexive verb *hitpaleil*, implies reflection and self-examination. When we pray, the idea is not to influence God to give us what we want, but to concentrate on what we need to do to achieve what we want, to get from where we are to what we can, and should, be. Through our prayers, we speak to God privately, believing that He welcomes our communication, hears and acts on our pleas. Yet the process is not other-, outer-directed. Our offer of praise and supplication is not for God's benefit; it is self-, inner-directed, for ours.

The words of prayers were set down because most people at all times in our history have been incapable of articulating the thoughts and feelings so eloquently communicated in the predetermined formats. They also express the ideal situation, the goal toward which we strive. They serve as the established standards without which we could not meaningfully judge ourselves.

Stripped of accolades and what sometimes come across in translation as stilted phrases, they tell us about the nature of the universe and our place within it. If we focus on what we are really praying/saying, we'll think about how we fit in. While we are expressing universal hopes, we'll be evaluating personal situations. If we comprehend this, the day is not just a recitation of praises or repetitions of requests for peace and the well-being of all mankind, for forgiveness and salvation for Jews and the Jewish people. It becomes a reflection on what our lives are and can be about.

Following the Services

Rosh Hashanah, like every other day, has three basic services: *Ma'ariv* (evening, after sundown, when the

Jewish day begins), *Shakharit* (morning), and *Minkhah* (afternoon). There is also, as for Shabbat and all festivals, the *Mussaf* (additional service) following *Shakharit*, corresponding to the special Temple sacrifice commanded in the Torah for those days (Numbers 29:1–6).

The motif of life—of God as Creator of life; of our striving to live better lives as individuals, a people, and part of the human race; of our hopes of being granted long and positive life—runs through the entire liturgy. The major themes of the day, which are fundamental tenets of Judaism, are most prominently presented during the *Amidah*, particularly of *Mussaf*. At first glance the themes might seem remote. But they can be cast in contemporary personal terms.

In *Malkhuyot* (from the Hebrew *melekh*, "king"), we acknowledge that God is the King of all Kings, that His rule extends over all nations. While thinking about what having an absolute authority in the universe means, and what our loyalty to Him entails, we should consider what forces in actuality rule our lives (pursuits, objects, emotional crutches, other people?) and whether they deserve the kind of influence we give them.

Zikhronot (from the Hebrew *zikhron*, "memory") reminds us that God remembers all our deeds, not only the bad, for which we repent, but the good, by which we merit forgiveness. The *zikhronot* section is acknowledgment that God plays a role in the world, punishing the wicked and rewarding the good. The history in which He participates is also the history that irrevocably connects us to Him and to the Jewish people. We might consider during these prayers what in our memories hinders us from moving forward—old hurts, grudges, guilt over mistakes—and what can work to our advantage—gratitude for past material and emotional support, relationships, accomplishments of which to be proud. It is also the place to renew our connection with the Jewish community, whose history and destiny we share.

Shofarot (from the Hebrew *shofar*, "ram's horn") recalls the Revelation of God at Mount Sinai, when the ritual instrument was sounded, and evokes the future revelation of God at the time of redemption, which will also be announced by *shofar* blasts. Both times the *shofar* is the clarion call to establish justice on Earth. This is a place to evaluate our own behavior by comparing it with the moral standards and to recognize any obstacles we present in creating the ideal.

The ten proof texts that each section contains (three from Torah, three from *Nevi'im* [Prophets], three from postbiblical writings, and a summary pas-sage from Torah) ascertain the absolute veracity of the themes, emphasized, lest there be any doubt, by the sounding of the *shofar* at each section's conclusion. Highlighting God's universal role as well as His special relationship with the people of Israel, these passages give significance to our finite lives, occurring for a brief moment in the eternity stretching from before the creation of the world millennia in the past to beyond its redemption sometime in the future: We are part of the tradition of the progression of people helping to move the world forward.

Liturgical Poems

Much of the services' lyricism comes from the *piyyutim*, a distinct feature of festival liturgies. Composed throughout the Jewish world over a period of one thousand years, the liturgical poems use the illusions of talmudic and midrashic sources to assert passionate commitment to Torah, Israel, and God and express desperate longing for redemption. The *piyyutim* may have originated during periods of persecution, when Jews were prohibited from studying Torah, teaching the commentaries on the law, or reciting certain prayers. These poems would have been temporary replacements, combinations of instruction and worship, to allow unbroken transmission of Judaism, whose widespread use led to later sanction. (Then again, they may simply have been the products of creative individuals eager to express themselves liturgically.)

The best-known and most stirring *piyyut* is said during the *khazzan*'s repetition of the *Mussaf Amidah*. Although some dispute the authenticity of the story behind its composition, no one denies the power of the words or melody of *Unetanneh Tokef* (Let Us Now Relate the Power [of this day's holiness]).

According to the legend behind the poem (included in full in some *makhzorim*), in the tenth century, Rabbi Amnon of Mainz faced pressure from the Bishop to convert to Christianity. In distress after giving the impression that he would consider it, the rabbi failed to reappear before the church leader. The cleric retaliated by having the rabbi's hands and feet amputated.

The poem is Amnon's unswerving affirmation of God's greatness and justice, which he uttered in front of the *Aron Hakodesh* just before his death on Rosh Hashanah. The powerful evocation of God's judgment of the world, containing the poignant image of sheep passing before Him, was inserted into the liturgies of all Jewish communities for the first day of Rosh Hashanah and for Yom Kippur. (Overtaken by the graphic picture of the fearful and solemn judgment day, worshippers in Eastern Europe would cover their heads with their *talleisim* and cry out the words of the poem amidst tears and sobs.)

Other Prayers

Just before *Mussaf* the *khazzan* intones a special prayer, *Hineni* (Here I Am [impoverished]). With deep feeling, he beseeches God's acceptance of his prayers on behalf of the congregation, although he himself is unworthy. Chanted slowly and soulfully, it is moving in its humility.

Some congregations include a prayer for the State of Israel during their services.

Selections from Torah and Prophets

The Portions

On the first day we read about the birth of the patriarch Isaac (which, according to tradition, occurred on Rosh Hashanah) and his growth to manhood; the banishment of Hagar (the concubine of Abraham, the first patriarch and monotheist) and Ishmael (the son of Abraham and Hagar, born when Abraham's pious wife Sarah was unable to conceive); and Abraham's treaty with Abimelekh (the king of the region of Gerar who acknowledged God's relationship with Abraham) (Genesis 21).

The *maftir* (last Torah verses read), from a second scroll, recounts the prescribed sacrificial offering for Rosh Hashanah (Numbers 29:1–6). In the *haftarah* (I Samuel 1–2:10), Hannah pleas for a son, whom she promises would be dedicated to the service of God. (Her whispered prayers are the basis for the nine blessings of the *Amidah*, and the fact that we recite them quietly to ourselves during the "silent" version. The son she eventually bore became the prophet Samuel, the religious voice during the reign of the first King of Israel, Saul.)

On the second day, we read one of the most affecting Bible stories, the near sacrifice of Isaac (referred to as the *Akeidah*, from the Hebrew "to bind") by Abraham, his father, based on the commandment of God (Genesis 22). After the same *maftir* as day one, the *haftarah* we read gives Jeremiah's account (31:2–20) of Israel's future redemption. It includes a passage about the refusal of Rachel to be consoled for the exile of her children. (Rachel was the beloved wife of the patriarch Jacob, son of Isaac, who gave birth after years of barrenness to Jacob's favorite two sons; they and the ten sons Jacob fathered with other women were the progenitors of the Twelve Tribes of Israel.)

The Meaning

Although we do not read the Creation account, as might be expected on the birthday of the world, themes of birth and motherhood are well represented in these readings. Sarah, Rachel, and Hannah had repeatedly beseeched God to end their barrenness. By tradition, on Rosh Hashanah God "remembered" these pious women and allowed them to bear children. This illustrates a major motif of Rosh Hashanah, that God remembers humankind and notices and acts on our prayers.

The incident of Hagar and Ishmael in the wilderness—on one level also about motherhood—tells us something about how judgment takes place. A *midrash* relates that the angels demanded to know why Ishmael (banished at the insistence of Sarah for his bad influence on her son Isaac), whose descendants, the Moslem nation, would cause so much harm to Israel, should not have been left to die. God justified the salvation of Ishmael because of "where he is" (Genesis 21:17); based on his actions at that moment, he did not deserve to die. Similarly, on Rosh Hashanah, we are judged by our state on that day. Even if we sinned all year, if we sincerely regret our actions, we are judged by the reform, not the former transgressions.

The *Akeidah*, often seen as proof of Judaism's abhorrence of the heathen practice of child sacrifice to deities, is generally understood as the supreme test of religious conviction, the classic example of Jewish faithfulness to God. With his request, God basically asked Abraham what he was willing to give up in order to follow His word. Though distressed at the prospect of sacrificing his son—the one for whom he had waited many years, and through whom God had promised to fulfill His pledge of making Abraham the father of a great nation—Abraham believed in his values and trusted that God would only command him to do something that was ultimately for his and the collective good.

The powerful story begs us to ask ourselves what we are willing to give up for the preservation of our values, our tradition—in essence, our futures. How do the values we hold dear conflict with other demands on our lives? What do we hold onto, what do we sacrifice, and what do our choices say about who and what we are and what remains for us? Just as Abraham answered "Here I am" (*hineni*) when God called him to the test, we need to be prepared to step forward and act to preserve what really matters.

The rabbis teach us that the willingness of Abraham and Isaac (said to be thirty-seven years old at the time of his near demise and just as ready as his father to trust in God's plan) also serves as vicarious atonement, a credit to be used by successive generations. And more, it has served as a message of hope to those throughout the centuries who gave up much to remain Jewish, believing that in the end they, like the patriarchs, would be blessed because they remained true to something that was greater than themselves. (For this reason, the story is recited during every morning service throughout the year.) Similarly, their test is supposed to provide comfort to all Jews on Rosh Hashanah as we face our own trials.

FOR FURTHER READING

For Children

"The Akeidah." In CT, pp. 68–75.

Details from *midrash* amplify the Torah story we read on the second day of Rosh Hashanah.

Cohen, Barbara. *The Binding of Isaac.* New York: Lothrop, Lee & Shepard Company, 1978.

Isaac tells his grandchildren the story of how he was nearly sacrificed, handling their questions (and ours) in a warm and reassuring way. The beautiful paintings illustrating the text evoke the mood and mystery of the story. Ages 7–12.

Ife, Elaine. *Now You Can Read . . . Samuel.* New York: Thomas Nelson Publishers, 1983.

Printed in large type for beginning readers, the book fills in what happened before and after what the *haftorah* for Rosh Hashanah tells us about Hannah and her son. It gives a good sense of what living in the Temple was like. Readers are asked at the end to tell the story in their own words. Ages 5–8.

Shofar

Following the Torah reading, we finally hear the greatly anticipated initial blasts of the *shofar*. The congregation stands as the *makrei* (reader) calls out the notes (except in *Sephardi* synagogues), and the *ba'al tekiah* (master of the blast, or trained *shofar* blower) produces the specified sounds, alternately wailing and willful, supplicating and demanding. In accordance with talmudic rules, the blasts consist of a combination of *tekiah* (a long, straight blast, nine beats long, typically used to herald good news), *teruah* (an alarm sound, nine staccato blasts, like a sobbing or bleating), and *shevarim* (an alternate form of the Torah's *teruah*, three broken blasts, each three beats long, reminiscent of wailing).

Customarily, one hundred blasts are sounded on each day of Rosh Hashanah: thirty blasts during the *shofar* service between *Shakharit* and *Mussaf*, ten at the conclusion of each of the major sections of the *Mussaf Amidah* during the *khazzan*'s repetition, and forty following the full *kaddish* at the end of the *Mussaf* service. The last blast is a *tekiah gedolah* (big *tekiah*), a single, extended blast that, held for what seems to be much longer than human lung capacity, often draws murmers of approval from an appreciative congregation, as though the longer the blast the more readily accepted their prayers will be.

The count of one hundred is based on *midrash*. It says that the mother of the brutal Canaanite conquerer Sisera whimpered 101 times in anguish over the son she presumed had been killed in battle against Deborah the Prophetess (Judges 4). Despite her anxiety and grief, she took solace from friends' assurances that he was detained merely in collecting spoils (Judges 5:28–30). Each blast of the *shofar* nullifies each cry of the cruel woman for her barbaric son. But in recognition of a mother's pain, we leave one of her anguished moans uncountered.

The *Sephardim* add a *tekiah* at the end of the service, just before *Aleinu*, so that they sound 101 blasts. That is the numerical value of the name of Michael, the angelic protector of Israel (Daniel 12:1). The extra blast is to summon him to do battle on our behalf.

If Rosh Hashanah falls on Shabbat, the *shofar* is not blown (see "Halakhah").

The Shofar *in History*

The ceremonial horn holds numerous associations for Israel. Whether in celebration or warning, the *shofar* called the community together. It signaled Temple sacrifice and proclaimed the time of the new moon, fast and feast days, the start and end of the Sabbatical (every seven years) and Jubilee (every fiftieth year). *Shofar* blasts announced the coronation of kings (which we allude to in *malkhuyot*), preceded the giving of the Torah (Exodus 19:19), when we chose God at Sinai (and which we recall on Rosh Hashanah with *zikhronot*), and will broadcast the coming of the messiah (Zekhariah 9:14) and the ingathering of the exiles to Israel (Isaiah 23:13) for final judgment and redemption (which we pray, during *shofarot*, will arrive speedily).

In war, the *shofar* also called advance and retreat (as when blasts helped bring down the walls of Jericho [Joshua 6:20]). In fact, the *shofar* is not sounded until after the Torah reading because of its role in battle. During Roman rule of Palestine, the conquering army took a *shofar* blast emanating from a synagogue as a call to arms and rushed in to massacre the innocent worshippers. By moving the *shofar* service to midday, the Jews proved to the Romans that they were assembled to pray, not plan insurrection. Also, by noon, the spies planted in synagogues when *shofar* blowing was prohibited had left, allowing the Jews to fulfill the *mitzvah*. The timing continued, for the sake of custom, even after the prohibition was rescinded.

What Shofar *Signals for Us*

In the soul-wrenching emotion-laden sounds summoning primal hopes and fears, we hear the echo of those turning points in our collective history, along with the encouragement to turn our personal lives around. Derived from the same root as the word *improve* (*shipeir*) and related to the word for beauty or goodliness, *sheper*, the *shofar* summons us to make ourselves better. As Maimonides expressed it, the sound of the *shofar* is a great wake-up alarm.

When Moses went up Mount Sinai to receive the second set of tablets of the Ten Commandments, *shofar* blasts reminded the people not to return to the idolatrous practices that had resulted in the first tablets being broken (see next chapter). The blasts remind us how easy it is to forget commitments made in the intensity of a spiritual or near-death experience and fall back into the bad habits we promised to abandon. As we pray to God to end disharmony between the forces of nature and the factions of nations, to make peace and restore the Temple, the sound of the *shofar* reminds us to retreat in our battles with others and with nature and advance in our war against the negative aspects of ourselves. At the same time, as it did in ancient days, the *shofar* calls us to unite as a community to work with mutual respect and purpose.

Tashlikh

On the first day of Rosh Hashanah, before sunset (between the *Minkhah* and *Ma'ariv* services), Jews traditionally proceed to a body of running water, preferably one containing fish, and symbolically cast off (*tasklikh*) their sins. The ceremony includes reading the source passage for the practice, the last verses from the prophet Micah (7:19): "He will take us back in love; He will cover up our iniquities. You will cast all their sins into the depths of the sea." Selections from Psalms, particularly 118 and 130, along with supplications and a kabbalistic prayer hoping God will treat Israel with mercy, are parts of *tashlikh* in various communities.

The custom developed around the thirteenth century and became widespread despite objections of rabbis who feared superstitious people would believe that *tashlikh*, rather than the concerted effort of *teshuvah*, had the power to change their lives. Religious leaders were particularly opposed to the practice of tossing bread crumbs, representing sins, into the water, and even shaking one's garments to loosen any evil clinging to them was discouraged.

Superstitious rites most likely did influence the ceremony. Primitive people believed that the best way to win favor from evil spirits living in waterways was to give them gifts. Some peoples, including the Babylonian Jews, sent "sin-filled" containers out into the water. (The Talmud describes the practice of growing beans or peas for two or three weeks prior to the new year in a woven basket for each child in a family. In an early variation of the Yom Kippur *kapparot* ritual, the basket, representing the child, was swung around the head seven times and then flung into the water.) Kurdistani Jews threw themselves into the water and swam around to be cleansed of their sins.

To make the practice symbolic rather than superstitious, the rabbis gave it ethical meaning. Through *midrash*, they connected the water with the *Akeidah*. When Abraham was on his way to sacrifice Isaac, they said, Satan (which could be understood as the voice inside Abraham telling him not to kill his beloved son) tried to stop him. When Abraham refused to heed his voice, Satan became a raging river blocking Abraham's way. Abraham proceeded nevertheless. When the water reached his neck and he called out for God's help, the waters immediately subsided.

Water was also seen as symbolic of the creation of the world—and of all life. Kings of Israel were crowned near springs, suggesting continuity, like the King of Kings' unending sovereignty. Since the prophets Ezekiel and Daniel each received revelation near a body of water, it was seen as a place to find God's presence. As the element of purification, water also represents the opportunity to cleanse the body and soul and take a new course in our lives. (Later rabbis continued to protest against the ritual, on grounds that it encouraged new sins by creating a social situation where people could gossip and men and women mingle, as Isaac Bashevis Singer's story "Tashlikh" illustrates.)

Although the rabbis preferred that *tasklikh* be done at a body of water containing fish (man cannot escape God's judgment any more than fish can escape being caught in a net; we are just as likely to be ensnared and trapped at any moment as is a fish), since this is, after all, a symbolic ceremony, any body of water will do—even water running out of a hose or a faucet.

If the first day of Rosh Hashanah falls on Shabbat, the *Ashkenazim* do *tashlikh* the second day (so as not to carry prayer books to the water, which would violate Sabbath laws). *Sephardim* perform the ritual even on the Sabbath. The ceremony can take place anytime during the holiday season through Hoshanah Rabbah at the end of Sukkot.

Second Day

Rosh Hashanah is the only holiday whose second day is celebrated in Israel as well as in the Diaspora. Technically, the need for the second day was eliminated, as it was for all other holidays, when the calendar was established. Prior to that time, Rosh Hashanah had posed a particular problem because, unlike every other holiday, it falls on the first day of the month. If the witnesses to sighting of the new moon (which determined the beginning of the month) failed to testify or did not show up until late in the afternoon of the thirtieth day of *Elul*, it would have been too late for the people to observe what should have been a sacred day.

So our sages created "one long day" composed of the last day of the sixth month (*Elul*) and the first day of the seventh month (*Tishrei*) and called it *yom arikhata* (lengthy day). Although we go through all the ceremonies of two distinct days, the purpose of the construct was to impress upon the people that the entire time period is sacred. For that reason, observance for both days was retained as the worldwide standard (except much later in some Reform congregations, which observe only one day of Rosh Hashanah).

On the evening of the second day, candles are lit at home. So that the *shehekheyanu* can again be recited, it is customary for the person doing the *brakhot* to have on a new piece of clothing or to place on the table a fruit not yet eaten that year to become the object of the blessing. Since you are not supposed to make a new fire (see "Halakhah" in chapter on Pesakh), observant Jews take their flame from a candle already burning or from a pilot light.

Except for different *piyyutim*, a smaller number of hymns, and different Torah readings, services on the second day are essentially like those of the first.

Conclusion

We mark the end of the sacred day and passage into regular time with the brief ceremony used on all festivals, *Havdalah*. [Unlike Shabbat, for Rosh Hashanah only the blessings over wine and separation are made.]

For Further Reading

Agnon, Samuel Joseph. *Days of Awe: A Treasury of Traditions, Legends and Commentary on Rosh Hashanah, Yom Kippur and the Days Between.* New York: Schocken Books, 1965.

The 1966 Nobel Prize winner for literature studied thousands of texts and excerpted from three hundred sources of Hebrew literature, ancient and modern, sacred and secular, to compile this condensation of our tradition on this period of the year. Laws, customs, folktales, parables, and tidbits from throughout history follow the order of observances from preparations for the holidays through the end of the Ten Days.

Apisdorf, Shimon. *Rosh Hashanah–Yom Kippur Survival Kit.* Columbus, OH: Leviathan Press, Columbus, 1992.

Get this book. If all you do is read the introduction you will benefit. But do yourself a favor and don't stop there. This easy-to-read *makhzor* companion focuses on one or two themes of key prayers, suggests how to give the service more relevance, presents six different ways of relating to prayer, poses questions to ask yourself, and includes other ways of making the most important days of the Jewish year meaningful. Wonderful metaphors and modern parables drawn from the author's own experience bring concepts to life. (Available from 66 Merkle Road, P.O. Box 43209, Columbus, OH 43209; 1-800-860-0774.)

Arzt, Max. *Justice and Mercy: Commentary on the Liturgy of the New Year and the Day of Atonement.* New York: Holt, Rinehart and Winston, 1963.

Progressing prayer by prayer through each of the services for the Days of Awe, the book provides biblical and talmudic sources, origins, significance, and explanations. Traditional and spiritually oriented, it is a good volume to consult in preparation for attending services or to take along to the synagogue to use as a companion to the *makhzor*. (An alternative is Jeffrey Cohen's *Understanding the High Holyday Services: A Popular Commentary to the Machzor.* London/Boston: Routledge & Kegan Paul, 1983.)

WHERE DO WE BEGIN?—PREPARATION

Spiritual Readiness

When there is a major event in our lives—a wedding or *bar mitzvah*, a business presentation or sports competition—we don't just wake up the morning of the anticipated action and do whatever is required. We spend weeks, maybe months or longer, making sure all the details are arranged, that we are physically and psychologically primed. Our sages realized that preparing for the most important occasions in our spiritual year demanded no less.

Originally, the annual focus on repentance was limited to the one-day observance we know as Yom Kippur. But those sages knew that if atonement were going to have any lasting impact on getting us to redirect our lives, it had to be more than a one-day symbolic ceremony. So they extended the period of self-examination and self-correction to a full thirty days prior to Rosh Hashanah, the entire month of *Elul*—like the grace period the court granted a debtor in which to pay off creditors.

Although *teshuvah* is acceptable any time, it was believed that God is particularly favorable to mankind during *Elul* and the first ten days of *Tishrei*. This forty-day period corresponds to the one Moses spent on Mount Sinai receiving the second set of tablets of the Ten Commandments. While he was gone, the Israelites camped at the base of the mountain and repented for having turned away from God to worship the Golden Calf (Exodus 32), which had resulted in the destruction of the original tablets. We use the time ending with Yom Kippur to give up our own false gods (greed, jealousy, gluttony, money, fame—whatever our particular harmful indulgences) and reaffirm our commitment to the one God. (Not coincidentally, forty is the number symbolic of life transition, appearing repeatedly in Jewish scripture and tradition to illustrate turning points, for example, the length of the flood, the length of Moses' sojourns on the mountain, the years of Israelite wandering in the desert, the age at which a man is considered well-educated enough to delve into Jewish mysticism.)

Since repentance, prayer, and charity are considered merits that counterbalance our "missed marks," which have the potential to reverse what would have been a negative outcome for us, the month of *Elul* is the time to intensify efforts in all three areas. We go through the process of *teshuvah*, rise early for special penitential prayers, and give donations.

Prayer

Selikhot

Special services, *selikhot* (forgiveness), begin at midnight on the Saturday prior to Rosh Hashanah (if the holiday falls earlier than Wednesday, *selikhot* begin the Saturday night of the preceding week). This pro-vides at least four days in which to recite the penitential prayer service, based on the desire among pious Jews to fast during the entire Ten Days of Repentance. Since the time span includes four days during which fasting is prohibited (the two of Rosh Hashanah, the Sabbath between Rosh Hashanah and Yom Kippur, and the day before Yom Kippur), the four days prior to Rosh Hashanah compensate.

Four days also defined the period in which animals to be sacrificed were examined for blemishes. As we are preparing for self-sacrifice, in a sense, we should have at least four days to examine ourselves for, and try to correct, spiritual imperfections.

The beginning of the week was chosen as the start of *selikhot* because the Jews, by and large Sabbath observant, were filled with the spirit of the just-ended day of rest and therefore in the proper frame of mind to begin praying for forgiveness. According to tradition, midnight is the hour of Divine goodwill, when the heavens are most open to prayer. On every other day of the week before Rosh Hashanah, *selikhot* take place before dawn. The Talmud also calls this a time of favor and compassion when the spirit of God hovers over the Earth.

Today, most Jews who attend *selikhot* go to the midnight service, generally preceded by a coffee and cake reception. Some liberal congregations use the occasion to have people come together and through prayer, song, and apology work out any differences they have had during the year.

While the special *selikhot* prayer books vary from community to community (the *Sephardim*, who recite *selikhot* during the entire month of *Elul*, use the same contents every day; the *Ashkenazim* change daily), they share the themes of professing human guilt and acknowledging God's grace, asking for God's mercy and blessing, and reminding God of the hardships of exile and His positive responses to the Jewish people's cries for help in the past. (Books are usually provided by the synagogue. A version for children, *Selichot: A Family Service* by Judith Z. Abrams, is published by Kar-Ben Copies.)

In addition to a number of psalms and *piyyutim* on the same subjects, a key portion of the services is recitation of the Thirteen Divine Attributes of Mercy. They were revealed to Moses when he asked to know God in order to be assured of His favor (Exodus 33:12–34:7). The Talmud says that when Moses implored God to forgive Israel for its lapse into idolatry, God replied that whenever in the future the Jewish people would be threatened with calamity or discipline, they would be able to arouse God's mercy by reciting these attributes with sincere devotion.

Personal

Cemetery Visits

Even nonobservant Jews often show their respect to the deceased by visiting the graves of parents, grandparents, and other loved ones during the week before Rosh Hashanah. It has been customary among the *Ashkenazim* since the Middle Ages, when *Erev* Rosh Hashanah trips to the tombs of the pious and scholarly began. Many still believe that the departed, especially the righteous, even if not relations of yours, can be beseeched to pray on your behalf.

In Israel, particularly under the cultural influence of *Sephardim* who hold great stock in the power of such prayer, this custom has turned into a tour business, with several companies busing believers from a wide range of backgrounds to the gravesites of matriarchs, patriarchs, and other particularly pious Jews. Visitors touch the tombs, throw candy or leave other foods, and pray, often tearfully, to find a life partner, conceive, have a loved one healed, enjoy health and prosperity. Making a *tzedakah* donation, if not giving money directly to needy people at a grave site, is also customary, as is giving *tzedakah* anytime a cemetery is visited. The traditional Prayer for the Departed (*El Molei Rakhamim*, God Full of Mercy), recited at the gravesite, is found in a standard *siddur* and is provided by funeral homes.

It is common practice to place a few pebbles or small stones on the headstone, based on an old folk custom indicating that someone has been to visit the burial site as an expression of respect for the deceased. The gesture may date back as far as biblical days, when graves were typically designated with piles of rocks. Vandals often dispersed them, so mourners added stones to make sure the graves remained marked.

Annulment of Vows

Following *selikhot* on the morning before Rosh Hashanah, religious Jews gather in the synagogue in groups of three for the *hatarat nedarim* ceremony. Taking turns, each declares, according to a talmudic formula (included in traditional *makhzorim*), before the symbolic court of the other three that he be absolved from vows, made consciously or unintentionally, which he failed to complete. The absolution covers only vows of a personal or religious nature, not any involving promises to another person. (Throughout most of Jewish history, making vows based on planned piety or in thanks for the expected granting of a request to God were common. Since they were generally couched in Divine terms, they could not just be ignored when unfulfilled.)

The fact that any unfulfilled oaths or vows have to be excused emphasizes the sanctity of one's word, not only in the form of vows (which, once made, are considered to carry the force of a positive Torah commandment) but in anything we say. It makes us more aware of the words we use and how we use them.

Tickets

If you do not belong to a synagogue and plan to attend services, be sure to arrange for tickets in advance.

The Body

It is traditional on *Erev* Rosh Hashanah, prior to donning Sabbath clothes, to bathe and get a haircut. These acts are symbols not only of purity and cleanliness but of belief in God's mercy. In previous centuries, this was in striking contrast to the prevailing secular custom, when defendants arrived for their court trials unshorn and dressed in black, signifying their anxiety over the anticipated outcome. Religious men still go to the *mikvah* (ritual bath) in preparation for the holiday.

Home

Parchments

Those concerned about the *kashrut* of their *mezzuzah* scrolls and *tefillin* should check to make sure that the writing has not faded and that the letters on the parchment's surface have not chipped. If so, the scrolls need to be replaced.

Tzedakah

Before candles are lit, many families deposit money in a special box (provided by the Jewish National Fund or another Jewish organization, purchased at a Judaica store, or made from a can or jar). The money is set aside on the holidays (and Friday night, when it is also customary to add to the *tzedakah* box before lighting candles) and later donated to a Jewish cause.

Children

Without any of the external attractions other holidays offer, it can be difficult for children to relate to this inner-focused one, and they need help in understanding what it means. The kinds of questions you pose for yourself can be presented on their level.

Ask them what they remember from the previous year and talk about how the family will celebrate the holiday. Ask them what they think they did well last year and what they were unhappy about in their behavior or performance. Perhaps they can think of ways they helped or hurt you, or a sibling, or a friend. Guide them in talking through their feelings about what they did—good and bad—and how they can get rid of any bad feelings and have more good ones. Help them set goals for the year.

This may be a time their questions about God arise—or a time for you to introduce the subject. Prayer books for children and the sources listed below may be helpful.

For very young children, you might want to focus on the theme of the birthday of the world, and on that wonderful musical instrument, the *shofar*—what it is, the role it has played in our history, how it is made. If you do not have a *shofar* at home, borrow one from a friend or a synagogue or observe or buy one at a store that carries Jewish books and supplies, so they can handle it, hear it, maybe even blow it. You can also talk about the special foods we eat (see "Traditional Foods").

Food and Fire

If you want to use fire—for cooking, to light candles, etc.—on the second day in accordance with *halakhah*, you need to leave a source, such as a stove pilot light or a twenty-four hour candle, burning from before the start of the first day, and take any flame needed from that. If Rosh Hashanah falls immediately before the Sabbath and you are concerned about following Jewish law, on Wednesday you need to make an *eruv tavshilin* so that you will be able to cook in preparation for Shabbat (see "*Halakhah*" in chapter on Pesakh).

FOR FURTHER READING

Sasso, Sandy Eisenberg. *God's Paintbrush.* Woodstock, VT: Jewish Lights Books, 1992.

This warm, embracing book helps children understand God through vignettes of everyday activities, feelings, and thoughts. Throughout, it asks readers (or listeners) how they would react or feel in God's place. Ages 5–9.

Wolpe, David J. "Letting God In." In *Hadassah Magazine.* August/September, 1992, pp. 42–43.

Written by the author of *The Quest for God* and *The Healer of Shattered Hearts: A Jewish View of God*, the article provides practical suggestions of how to incorporate God into family life, make Him real, and deal with your children's natural curiosity about God without feeling uncomfortable.

See also *Building a Jewish Life—Rosh Hashanah/Yom Kippur* (Grishaver) and *My Very Own/Rosh Hashanah, Yom Kippur* (Saypol and Wikler) in Appendix C.

WHAT ARE WE SUPPOSED TO DO?— *HALAKHAH*

Festival Laws

The Sabbath-like restrictions that apply to all *yom tovim*, the laws covering the preparation of food, eating a formal meal and feeding the stranger and the needy, the wearing of clean clothes, and rejoicing in the occasion, apply equally to Rosh Hashanah (see "*Halakhah*" in chapter on Pesakh).

Teshuvah

Doing *teshuvah* is one of the 613 *mitzvot* commanded in the Torah (Deuteronomy 30:2,10). Fulfilling it requires Moses Maimonides' three steps: regretting the sinful past behavior, restraining yourself from repeating the behavior, and resolving never to do it in the future.

Prayer

The laws covering changes in wording and inclusion or exclusion of particular parts of the regular liturgy all relate to the special nature of the Ten Days and the Divine judgment that takes place.

Word Changes

"The holy God" (*haEl hakadosh*) and "King Who loves righteousness and justice" (*Melekh oheiv tzedakah u'mishpaht*) become "The Holy King" (*Melekh Hakadosh*) and "The King of Judgment" (*Hamelekh Hamishpaht*). The *kaddish* following *selikhot* contains the sentence usually said only after the *Amidah*, "May the prayers and petitions . . . be accepted" (*titkabail tzlotehone u'vautehone*). *Le eilah* (to the heavens) is added to every *kaddish* to emphasize that God rules from His heavenly throne. (Using the normal wording instead of "Holy King" necessitates repetition of the prayer; forgetting to say "King of Judgment" does not because the usual wording also conveys the notion of sovereignty.)

When Rosh Hashanah falls on Shabbat, the words of certain *piyyutim* not moved to the second day are changed from "a day of *shofar* blowing (*yom teruah*) to "a day of remembering the blowing of the *shofar*" (*yom zikhron teruah*).

Avinu Malkeinu

We recite Our Father, our King after the *khazzan's* repetition of the *Shakharit* and *Minkhah Amidah*, except on Shabbat. This is because it was first intoned at a public fast, and no fast can be ordered to fall on a Sabbath. (Yom Kippur, ordained by Torah, falls outside this law.) Some say we omit *Avinu Malkeinu* on Shabbat because on that day we don't ask for our needs to be met.

The Talmud relates that Rabbi Eliezer recited twenty-four benedictions so God would bring rain, all to no avail. So Rabbi Akiva stepped forward and called out "Our Father, our King! You are our Father. Our Father, our King! We have no King but You. Our Father, our King! We have sinned before You. Our Father, our King! Have mercy upon us. Our Father, our King! Deal kindly with us for the sake of Your name." His prayers were answered immediately. Because of their relevance in theme, and the outcome they produced, we repeat the series of requests for material and spiritual blessings throughout the Ten Days of Repentance.

Hallel

Although Rosh Hashanah qualifies as a festival, the hymns of praise normally included on such days are not said. Complete joy must accompany their recitation, and although we are not to be sad on Rosh Hashanah, the fear of judgment modifies our mood enough that we cannot say *Hallel* in the proper frame of mind: "How can Israel sing hymns of praise when the King is seated on His throne in judgment and human lives hang in the balance?" (*Rosh Hashanah* 32).

During prayer, some authorities permit the pious to shed tears to awaken God's mercy.

Zekhirus: Ritual Purity

Special care is to be taken during this period of judgment not to violate prohibitions in your relationships with other people and with God. In actions and spiritual piety (such as eating kosher foods), vigilance is required, and you are supposed to study Torah and Talmud.

Shofar

The Talmud covers all aspects of the *shofar* ritual, the central part of the Rosh Hashanah service, from the proper fashioning of one, to who must sound and hear it, to how the *shofar* blowing takes place.

Obligation

The commandment specifies that one is to hear rather than blow the *shofar*. It applies to every man and woman, with the exception of those who are mentally incompetent or hearing impaired. Although minor children are also exempt, parents should introduce their children to the sounding of the *shofar* from the age of three. Since the *mitzvah* falls on each individual, a congregational setting is not required, but it enhances the proclamation of God's kingship and rule. Arrangements should be made to blow the *shofar* for anyone who cannot attend synagogue for the communal sounding.

Blasts

The ritual requires nine blasts of the *shofar* consisting of three the Torah calls *teruah* (which may or may not be what we call *teruah*), each preceded and followed by an extended blast called *tekiah*. *Halakhah* resolves the Gemara's disagreement as to whether all nine are scriptural (from Torah) or scribal (from the sages) in origin, based on Leviticus 25:9, 23:24, and Numbers 29:1. There are to be one straight blast, a broken blast, and again one straight blast, in sets of three, with the two broken blasts the same length as one single straight blast.

To unify the varying forms of the broken blast developed in different communities, and avoid dissention among the Jews following the destruction of the Temple, Rabbi Abbahu of Caesaria ruled that both versions would be incorporated into the service. The order was established as three groups of *tekiah*, *shevarim* (three broken)-*teruah* (nine staccato), *tekiah*; three groups of *tekiah*, *shevarim*, *tekiah*; and three groups of *tekiah*, *teruah*, *tekiah*, thirty blasts in each set.

Since blowing the *shofar* is an exercise of skill rather than performance of work prohibited on Sabbath, it is not a violation of the day of rest. However, except for a short period when the sages convened in Yavneh after the destruction of the Second Temple, blowing the *shofar* on the Sabbath outside of the Temple has been prohibited. This prevents someone from carrying a *shofar* in an area of public domain—such as from home to *shul*, to a hospital (to sound it for a sick person), or to an expert to ascertain whether it is kosher or not. (Carrying in the public domain is prohibited on Shabbat.)

Acceptable Horns and Procedure

Defined as a hollow horn into which a bony projection intrudes, a *shofar* can be fashioned from the horn of any kosher animal except that of an ox or steer. Gemara stipulates that since the horns of the ox and steer are composed of many layers, they appear to be several *shofarot* inside each other, while a *shofar* must be singular. Horns of the steer and ox are also to be avoided because they recall the sin of the Golden Calf.

Detailed instructions tell how a *shofar* is to be made. It should have no holes or cracks (although what kind of crack renders a horn unfit is a matter for an expert to determine), a curve to represent our humility before God, and no augmentation that would create a separation between the *ba'al tekiah*'s mouth and the *shofar*. Since the purpose of the *shofar* blasts is to summon God's mercy on those before Him, the *ba'al tekiah* is expected to be pious as well as capable of sounding strong, clear blasts of proper length.

Prior to sounding the *shofar*, Psalm 47 is recited seven times, in accordance with the kabbalists of Safed. God's name appears in the psalm seven times, representing the seven *sefirot* or levels of heaven He created. Keeping the *shofar* covered until it is used, the *ba'al tekiah* recites the blessing for *shofar* blowing and the *shehekheyanu*.

Joy

We should leave the synagogue following Rosh Hashanah services in an upbeat, confident mood. Without being gluttonous, we are to eat as well as our means allow, study Torah at the table, and unless a nap is absolutely required to counter a headache that would interfere with attending *Minkhah* services, return to synagogue to recite psalms with the congregation.

Shehekheyanu

The concept of Rosh Hashanah as one long day raised questions about the propriety of reciting the *shehekheyanu* with *kiddush* and candlelighting on the second night, and sounding the *shofar* on the second day. Since both days have the same sanctity and the blessing has already been recited on the first day, there is no need to repeat it on the second. But it is a *mitzvah* to say blessings. Therefore, when *kiddush* is recited the second night, and the candles lit, a new fruit (one not yet eaten this year) placed on the table, or a new garment worn by the person making the *brakhah* serves as the object of the blessing. However, if you do not have a new fruit or new garment, you are not precluded from saying the blessing. (An individual may say *shehekheyanu* only once, so if the same person does candlelighting and *kiddush*, the blessing is not repeated.) The *shofar* blower also tries to wear a new garment for the second day (except when the first day falls on Shabbat, in which case the *shehekheyanu* has not yet been said since the *shofar* has not yet been sounded).

For Further Reading

Rosh Hashanah—Its Significance, Laws and Prayers. Ed. by Rabbi Nosson Scherman and Rabbi Meir Zlotowitz. Brooklyn: Mesorah Publications, 1983, pp. 79–89.

This guide clearly summarizes the laws covering requirements for the individual (as opposed to those who perform public activities, such as *shofar* blowing) from preparation through both days of Rosh Hashanah.

WHAT OTHER THINGS DO PEOPLE DO?— CUSTOMS

Other Times and Places

Study

Throughout much of our history, the forty-day period between *Elul* 1 and *Tishrei* 10 has been a time to pray more fervently, study more diligently, recite psalms more regularly, and follow the *mitzvot* more carefully. Since the days of the Babylonian captivity, Jews would take time off from work to participate in Bible study groups and examine their lives. (Later, the Moroccan Jews chose a night during *Elul* or the Ten Days to entirely devote to learning principles from the *Mishnah*, laws from Maimonides' writings, and Psalms. Forsaking sleep and talk, they allowed themselves only tea and coffee while they studied.) Many made it a habit to conduct no secular conversations during the forty days as a way of purifying the soul.

From mid-*Elul* until after Sukkot, Eastern European children had only half-days of school, but didn't really get to enjoy the time between the summer and fall semesters as vacation. They, too, used the time for study and self-examination.

Prayer

The ancient Jews introduced two customs for the month of *Elul*, which are followed to this day: sounding the *shofar* every morning after *Shakharit* (except on Shabbat, when it was considered a disturbance of the universe, and on the last day of the month, so that there would be a break to separate the *shofar* blowing done throughout *Elul*—which was only a custom—and that done on Rosh Hashanah, which was a commandment), and reading Psalm 27 at every service until the last day of Sukkot. A plea to God to help us when we are surrounded by enemies (including the internal ones that lead us astray), it also expresses longing to dwell in the House of the Lord. (*Ashkenazim* say it after *Shakharit* and *Ma'ariv*, *Sephardim* after *Shakharit* and *Minkhah*.) Per *midrash*, verses of this psalm refer to the holidays of the season: "The Lord is my light [Rosh Hashanah] and my help [Yom Kippur], whom should I fear? . . . . He will shelter me in His pavilion [Sukkot]."

To rouse the Jews in Eastern European and Middle Eastern villages for the early *selikhot* services, the *shammash* (beadle) would knock on windows or doors, sometimes with a special hammer, occasionally one carved in the shape of a *shofar*. The children in Yemen were so eager to join the adults that each one tied one end of a string to his or her toe and hung the other end out the window so the beadle could pull on it as he passed.

Symbols and Superstitions

When medieval women visited the cemetery during *Elul*, they would stride around the perimeter, unrolling a spool of cotton string onto the ground. They gave the rewound twine to a candlemaker to use as wicks for candles, preferably out of white wax, that would be long enough to burn twenty-four hours. These were then donated to the synagogue for use on Yom Kippur. (In Germany, the women made the candles themselves on *Tishrei* 8, the day before *Erev* Yom Kippur and the anniversary of the dedication of the First Temple. Prayers and supplications recited over every wick asked dead relatives, particularly pious women, to intercede for those still alive.)

A variety of customs, further indicating how superstitious our predecessors were, developed from the belief in Satan as our adversary. The new moon of *Tishrei* was not blessed, so the "evil" one would not realize Rosh Hashanah had arrived. (It is customary not to bless the new moon until after the close of Yom Kippur.) The *shofar* was sounded in part to confuse his being able to keep track of the day. (If he did not realize it was Rosh Hashanah, the reasoning went, he could not present his accusations before God.) After Psalm 47, six verses were added to form an acrostic spelling *kra* (destroy) *Satan*.

In recognition of the different type of joy expressed during the Ten Days of Repentance, weddings do not take place. Those who thought that one who is happy on the night of Rosh Hashanah is assured of happiness all year (such as the Afghanis) created the proper atmosphere at home after synagogue. There is a similar belief, expressed in the Jerusalem Talmud, "if one sleeps at the year's beginning, his good fortune likewise sleeps." Therefore, it is customary not to sleep during the day on Rosh Hashanah, or be idle, which is tantamount to dozing. Study of scripture commonly filled the time between synagogue services. A number of *Sephardi* Jewish communities try to read through the Book of *Tehillim* twice during Rosh Hashanah since the total number of its psalms (150×2) equals the numerical value of the Hebrew word *kaper*, meaning "pardon."

Despite the general practice of avoiding sour or

bitter foods, in France and Jerusalem pickled olives were distributed as people left synagogue on Rosh Hashanah. They suggested what the worshippers' priorities should be, as the Talmud explains: "Let my sustenance be as bitter as the olive in Thy Divine charge rather than sweet as honey in the charge of flesh and blood."

Charity

Jews have long gathered at the Western Wall in Jerusalem the day before Rosh Hashanah to pray and distribute *tzedakah* among the poor. The Afghanis made their donations in the form of meat, from the sheep they slaughtered after they annulled their vows.

Fasting

It was commonplace for pious Eastern European and Judeo-Spanish Jews to fast part of the day on *Erev* Rosh Hashanah. They refrained from eating between their pre-dawn, pre-synagogue tea and crackers and noon. The fast indicated their willingness to place service to God above physical aspects of life and made them "advance men" in gaining God's favor, based on a parable from *midrash*: A king journeyed to a province to collect the overdue payment of tribute. At some distance from his destination, a delegation (the most pious and scholarly who fast before Rosh Hashanah) met him, admitted they were remiss in their debt, and begged for pardon. The gracious king forgave them one-third of their debt. As he approached closer, more people arrived to plead for mercy (those who fast during the intervening days); he forgave another third. When he reached the gates of the town, crowds (everyone fasting on Yom Kippur) gathered to honor him, so he granted total forgiveness.

Often the fast was not broken until the men had purified themselves in a *mikvah*, as was customary before festivals and specifically ordained for before Rosh Hashanah and Yom Kippur. In some places, the Jews bathed in a cold stream, immersing three times in the presence of witnesses to complete the ritual process.

Greeting Friends and Relatives

Following services on Rosh Hashanah morning, the men and children in Turkish Jewish communities went visiting while the women stayed home to receive guests. They served white or light-colored sweets on traditional silver trays to symbolize happiness in the coming year. When the guests could eat no more, but did not want to insult their hostesses, the men would wrap the extra goodies in their white handkerchiefs, carried especially for the purpose of transporting the sweets home.

From the very beginning of *Elul*, sidewalk vendors set up their tables throughout cities in Israel to offer a wide array of new year cards. A national holiday in Israel, Rosh Hashanah is a time of exchanging gifts, particularly baskets of fruit and candy, among friends and business associates (much as American companies do during the end of the secular year holidays). Bonuses and gift certificates send Israelis flooding to the stores.

Greeting

We traditionally wish each other "*leshanah tovah tikateivu v'tikhateimu*" (may you be inscribed and sealed [in the Book of Life] for a good year), often shortened to "*leshanah tovah*" (a good year). Variations include "*lehshanah tovah u'metukah*" (a good and sweet year) and "*tikatev lekhayim tovim u'leshalom*" (may you be written for a good life and peace).

Since the Talmud states that the righteous are inscribed for good within the first three hours of the new year (unlike the rest of us, who must wait for our final decrees until the end of Yom Kippur), after *Erev* Rosh Hashanah you should not greet a friend with the wish that s/he be "written" because it implies you don't consider that person to be among the most righteous. The proper form between the two holidays is therefore "*leshanah tovah tikhateimu*" (may you be sealed for a good year).

You are also likely to hear "*gut yom tov*" (happy holiday) or "*gut yohr*" (good year) among those of Yiddish-speaking Eastern European backgrounds. Among *Sephardim*, "*tizkeh leshanim*" (may you merit long life) invites the response "*tizkeh vetikhyeh veta'arikh yomim*" (may you merit, may you live, and may you have length of days).

The custom of sending new year's cards containing one of these or related greetings developed from the instruction of the Maharil (Rabbi Jacob Molin). In the late fourteenth or early fifteenth century, he wrote that from the beginning of *Elul*, any personal letter should mention that the writer is praying on behalf of his friends, that they may be inscribed and sealed for a good year. It became common in the Diaspora to send such messages, and by the late nineteenth century in Eastern Europe, the new year greeting card industry had begun.

Dress

Clean Sabbath clothes are appropriate for synagogue. Since talmudic times, it has been popular to wear white on Rosh Hashanah, the color of both joy and purity, based on a verse from the prophet Isaiah: "Though your sins be scarlet, they shall become white as the snow" (1:18). Any pious man, today usually at least the rabbi and *khazzan* of the synagogue, wears a *kittel*.

It is a widespread custom to wear new clothes so that, as they say in Bulgaria, the whole year will be new. (The Moroccans do not wear new clothes since they could make one haughty.) When putting on new clothing for the first time, it is appropriate to say a blessing (unless the new item is leather, such as shoes, because its fashioning resulted in the loss of life for an animal). It is followed by the *shehekheyanu*, recited for any new item or event each year.

בָּרוּךְ אַתָּה, יהוה אֱלֹהֵינוּ, מֶלֶךְ הָעוֹלָם, מַלְבִּישׁ עֲרֻמִּים.

Barukh Atah, Adonai Eloheinu, Melekh Haolam, malbish arumim.

Blessed are You, Lord our God, King of the Universe, Who clothes the naked.

בָּרוּךְ אַתָּה, יהוה אֱלֹהֵינוּ, מֶלֶךְ הָעוֹלָם, שֶׁהֶחֱיָנוּ, וְקִיְּמָנוּ, וְהִגִּיעָנוּ לַזְּמַן הַזֶּה.

Barukh Atah, Adonai Eloheinu, Melekh Haolam, shehekheyanu, v'kiyamanu, v'higgiyanu lazman hazeh.

Blessed are You, Lord our God, King of the Universe, who has kept us alive, sustained us, and brought us to this season.

What Is There to Eat?— Traditional Foods

At no other time in the year is the idea that symbolic acts produce positive outcomes so effusively expressed than at Rosh Hashanah. Throughout the Jewish world, customs regarding the eating of certain foods for their sympathetic qualities developed.

No Rosh Hashanah meal would be complete without apples and honey. In addition to representing a year of positive blessings (sweetness), the apple, according to mysticism, represents the *Shekhinah* (the feminine spirit of God), which is now judging each person. The honey symbolizes the sweetness with which we hope the judgment will be made. Many people keep honey on their dining tables through the end of Sukkot and serve apples for dipping into it throughout the festival season.

We also eat foods that are round (indicating the continuation of life and the endless nature of God's sovereignty) and that grow in abundance (representing prosperity and fertility). The Talmud suggests pumpkin, fenugreek, leek, beet, and dates. All varieties of sweet cakes, particularly honey cake and *teiglakh* (a mound of small balls of fried dough mixed with dried fruits and honey), were developed.

Khallot are altered from the normal long, braided loaves used on Shabbat and other festivals. Round ones, often studded with raisins for extra sweetness, are customary. Some bake the breads decorated with, or in the form of, ladders (according to a *midrash* describing the ladders God makes in heaven on Rosh Hashanah, on which some people will be raised and some lowered), crowns (representing God's reign as King of the Universe), or birds (showing God's mercy, based on Isaiah 31:5: "Even as the birds that fly, so will the Lord of Hosts protect Jerusalem").

European Jews typically eat carrot *tzimmes*, a mix of carrots and honey that may also include some combination of white and sweet potatoes, dried fruit, meat, and wine. The Yiddish word for carrot is *meren*, which means to increase, as we hope our merits will. Carrots are also sliced into rounds, resembling coins in color and shape and therefore suggesting prosperity.

We avoid sour and bitter foods, along with nuts. Nuts are irritating to the throat, a potential interference with prayer, and according to *gematria* the numerical value of the Hebrew word for nut, *egoz* (אֱגוֹז), equals that of the word for sin, *khet* (חֵטְא). (Egoz = seventeen, khet = eighteen – 1; the value of the word itself—one—is often subtracted or added in the *gematria* formula.)

According to Ezra's admonition (Nehemiah 8:10) we are supposed to enjoy a substantial meal after Rosh Hashanah services. In most families, it takes place both evenings of *Erev* Rosh Hashanah, as well as midday after the synagogue break between *Mussaf* and *Minkhah* on both days. On the second night, we eat a new fruit of the season so we can justly say the *shehekheyanu*.

Always good at throwing a party, the *Sephardim* developed a special *seder* done on the first, sometimes also the second, evening of Rosh Hashanah. In addition to the above traditional *brakhot* and foods, they eat a series of items that are symbolic of or that have names containing allusions to some desired protection or blessing. Prior to partaking of each, they recite a *yehi rahtzon* (may it be [God's] will), which often makes a play on words between the Aramaic name given in Talmud for a food and the Hebrew word that resembles it in sound.

Typical items include the head of a sheep (symbolizing the planned sacrifice of Isaac), or the head of a fish, to ask that we be like the head and not the tail; beet greens or swiss chard (*selek*), that all our enemies may go away (*yistalku*); carrot (*gezer*), that the harsh sentence (*gezar din*) to be imposed on us will be torn up; pomegranates, that we may be as full of good deeds as the pomegranate is of seeds, or that we may have as much prosperity; leek (*karti*), that our enemies may be cut off (*sheyikaretu*); chick peas (*kara*), cold (*kar*) on the inside, symbolizing the "cooling down" of God's stern judgment.

Some *Ashkenazi makhzorim* contain a number of *yehi rahtzon*s, as do some *Sephardi* cookbooks. You can even make up your own in English (beet is obvious; carrot, garrote, perhaps; pepper and lettuce suggest several possibilities).

Since along with being instructed to feast we are taught to "send portions unto him for whom nothing is prepared" (Nehemiah 8:10), it is customary to invite the needy for Rosh Hashanah, symbolically by providing money through appropriate organizations. It can also be accomplished by inviting someone who does not have any place to go for the holiday meals to join you.

FOR FURTHER READING

See Gilda Angel's book for the *yehi rahtzon seder* and recipes for the items used in it in the listing of cookbooks in Appendix C.

DO YOU HEAR MUSIC?—SONGS TO SING

Like almost everything else connected with this holiday, the music centers on what goes on in the synagogue: There are no folk songs or traditional melodies except those attached to the liturgy. Some date back to the Spanish Inquisition, when many Jews publicly renounced Judaism, but privately and secretly retained their traditions. Certain melodies served as signals and passwords so that secret worshippers could avoid detection.

This music, as much of the rest of the *nusakh* (musical rendition) for the Rosh Hashanah services, is different from that normally used during the year.

Even the *trop* (cantillation) for the Torah readings changes. There are recordings of them, and you may feel more comfortable in synagogue if you familiarize yourself with the sound of the liturgy beforehand. You can even learn some key tunes so that, even if you cannot sing the words, you could at least hum along during the service.

Some musical highlights of the service that you might want to learn in advance are The Thirteen Attributes, "*Avinu Malkeinu*" (both discussed earlier in this chapter), "*B'Rosh Hashanah*" (On Rosh Hashanah, acknowledgment that we are judged), "*V'Kol Ma'aminim*" (And all Believe, an expression of our faith in God's character and His role in the world), and "*B'Sefer Hakhayim*" (In the Book of Life, a request that we be written in it).

FOR FURTHER READING

High Holidays and Sukkot Melodies. Cedarhurst, NY: Board of Jewish Education of Greater New York and Tara Publications.
The major tunes of the services of the fall season, with words transliterated into English, are included in the booklet, which has a companion tape.

WHAT TALES ARE TOLD?— STORIES TO READ

Folktales for the holiday convey a sense of the role spirituality played in the lives of Jews of previous centuries, and the sense of wonder with which they approached this season. From the stories and reminiscences of writers like Issac Bashevis Singer, Isaac Loeb Peretz, and Bella Chagall, we can get a feeling for how our grandparents or great-grandparents in Eastern Europe celebrated. And among newer books are several that effectively present the past or provide meaningful contexts for today's observance.

FOR FURTHER READING

Folktales

"Adam and Eve's Repentance." In CT, pp. 32–34.
As a follow-up to the Genesis story, which conveys no sense of remorse on their part, this story tells how Adam and Eve felt after they disobeyed God and what they did to try to regain His favor.

"The Creation of Adam." In CT, pp. 18–21.

A charming tale about how God created humankind over the objections of angels, it also explains why God chose the nose as the entry point of the soul. It concisely and beautifully says a lot about the natures of man and woman.

"If Only I Could Pray." In TS, pp. 105–106.

Even a man who never learned his Jewish heritage found it is never too late to have a relationship with God and Judaism.

Nissan, Mindel. "The Fireman." In *The Complete Story of Tishrei*. Brooklyn: Merkos L'Inyonei Chinuch, 1957, pp. 50–52.

The parable about a boy who thought it was the sounding of a bugle that put out all the fires in a town teaches what the *shofar* can and cannot accomplish.

Peretz, Isaac Loeb. "If Not Higher." In *The I. L. Peretz Reader*. Ed. by Ruth R. Wisse. New York: Schocken Books, 1990, pp. 178–181; and Rosh Hashanah HA, pp. 241–244.

Depicting Eastern European Jewish life, this story about how a pious rabbi ascends to heaven during his penitential prayers illustrates what serving God really means.

Another Story

Singer, Isaac Bashevis. "Tashlikh." In Rosh Hashanah HA, pp. 267–273.

A love-struck young *khasid* is able to meet the girl of his desires at the *tashlikh* ceremony. Ages 12–15.

Books

Aronow, Sara. *Seven Days of Creation*. Sepher-Hermon Press, 1985.

In this sweet book, rhymes tell what each part of Creation meant. The one for the seventh day gives information on how we prepare for and celebrate Shabbat. All ages.

Baude, Pierre-Marie, *The Book of Creation*. Saxonville, MA: Picture Book Studio, 1991.

A shepherd father agrees to tell how the world and its components came into being only after his son has been sensitive to everything around him. The poetic quality of the lengthy text conjures the image of the elder storyteller passing cultural secrets to the next generation. It incorporates the joy of Creation, appreciation for everything on Earth, and a message about living in peace. The award-winning illustration recalls Japanese painting and Southwest Indian prints. Ages 12 and up.

Cohen, Barbara. *Even Higher*. New York: Lothrop, Lee & Shepard, 1987.

A retelling of Peretz's *If Not Higher*, the book is about a visitor to the village of Nemirov who attempts to find out where the rabbi goes during prayer when the villagers claim he goes to heaven to speak with God. Ages 5–9.

Fass, David E. *The Shofar That Lost Its Voice*. New York: Union of American Hebrew Congregations, 1982.

Avi practices the *shofar* for the children's service. When he can't make a sound anymore, he travels inside and learns the beautiful meanings of the notes. Ages 9–12.

Goldin, Barbara Diamond. *The World's Birthday, A Rosh Hashanah Story*. San Diego: Harcourt Brace Jovanovich, 1990.

Daniel wants to have a birthday party for the entire world. In thinking about Creation, he finally figures out how to do it. Charming vibrant illustrations and a one-page explanation of the holiday add to the appeal of the book. Ages 3–8.

Kimmel, Eric A. *Days of Awe: Stories for Rosh Hashanah and Yom Kippur*. New York: Viking, 1991.

The three incredibly moving stories in this book show us the key concepts of the holidays in simple everyday life. Adapted from traditional sources and conveying the awe and beauty of the season, the stories deal with charity, prayer, and repentance. Ages 8–12.

Levin, Carol. *A Rosh Hashanah Walk*. Rockville, MD: Kar-Ben Copies, 1987.

This lovely book follows a group of children on Rosh Hashanah as they learn the meaning and how-to's of *tashlikh*. The section on the walk itself is told in pleasing verse, and the illustrations, a combination of photography and drawing in browns and blues, is very effective. Ages 3–8.

Levitin, Sonia. *A Sound to Remember*. San Diego: Harcourt Brace Jovanovich, 1979.

Often teased by other boys in the village because of his clumsiness and awkward speech, Yacov is chosen to blow the *shofar* and helped by the rabbi to succeed. This is a lovely story with a message about communicating with God. Ages 4–8.

Sidi, Smadar Shir. *Little Daniel and the Jewish Delicacies*. New York: Adama Books, 1988.

Sad at being the shortest boy in synagogue, Daniel vows to grow taller by next year. After eating his way through the holidays with no regard for why he consumes special foods, he realizes what growing really means. Ages 5–7.

Waskow, Arthur, David Waskow, and Shoshana Waskow. *Before There Was a Before*. New York: Adama Books, 1984.

By a father and his two grown children, this beautifully written book tells the Creation story with love, gentleness, and humor. Evoking the Earth's smells, sounds, colors, and sensations, it expresses the interrelatedness of all life. The refreshing look at an old story is great for parents and children to read together. All ages.

YOM KIPPUR

Yom Kippur (yome' key-poor'; Yiddish: yome kip'-per): Day of Atonement. Observed on *Tishrei* **10** (fall; late September–mid-October).

On Yom Kippur, the holiest day of the entire year, physical needs are sublimated to spiritual pursuits so that the entire nation of Israel can reconcile itself with one another, with God, and to its role in the world. The endpoint of the process of self-examination and repentance begun forty days earlier, it marks the resolution of the judgment period begun on Rosh Hashanah. It is designed to leave us purified, ready to face life with renewed vigor and purpose.

ORIGINS: WHY WE CELEBRATE YOM KIPPUR

WHERE DID IT ALL BEGIN?— HISTORIC FOUNDATION

A Biblical Commandment

Yom Kippur began shortly after completion of the portable Tabernacle (house of worship) in the Sinai (Exodus 35–40). As recorded in Torah, God gave Moses explicit instructions for this "Sabbath of Sabbaths" (*Shabbat Shabbaton*). Named *Yom Hakippurim* (later shortened in the vernacular to the singular, Yom Kippur), Day of Atonements, it calls for complete rest, prohibition of work, self-denial (or "affliction of your souls"), and specified sacrifices (Leviticus 16, 23:26–32; Numbers 29:7–11).

The purpose of the holiday and its activity was "to make atonement for the Israelites for all their sins once a year" (Leviticus 16:34) so that they would be "clean before the Lord" (Leviticus 16:30). In order to accomplish it, Aaron (and each descendant who would succeed him as *Kohein Gadol*, or high priest) performed an intricate ritual.

Through immersion, vestment changes, and the blood of the sacrificed bull, ram, and a goat chosen "for God," the *Kohein Gadol* purged himself, his household, the Israelite community, the Shrine (curtained-off part of the Tabernacle that contained the Tablets of the Ten Commandments and over which God's spirit hovered in a cloud), the Tent of Meeting (the wandering Jews' sanctuary), and the sacrificial altar of all transgressions committed by the entire nation.

He then put his hand on a second goat and confessed the sins of the Israelites, essentially laying their wrongdoings on the head of the innocent animal. By sending this goat (whose purpose had been designated at the same time the other was chosen for dedication to God) out into the wilderness "for *Azazel*," the priest symbolically rid the community of its mistakes.

Those who rationalize biblical narrative based on the beliefs and practices of primitive peoples define the unexplained *Azazel* as a demonic force dwelling in the desert. The rabbis themselves suggest it was a kind of bribe to the Adversary (see chapter on Rosh Hashanah) so he wouldn't make new accusations against Israel. Breaking the name into *az* (strong or rough) and *ayil* (ledge or buttress) could indicate the inaccessible rocks or cliffs where the animal would die. The *Septuagint*'s translation yields *ez*, goat, and *azal*, Aramaic for "go" or "went," which is related to the Hebrew *lazel*, meaning "to remove."

Whatever the specific definition, the original scapegoat was understood as something other than what the word has come to mean. It was not unjustly blamed for causing the problems of the community and subsequently punished. It was merely a vehicle for transporting them as far away as possible. The society could benefit by the banishment of the animal only after its members had owned up to the wrongful behavior for which they themselves were guilty.

183

The First Yom Kippur

According to tradition, the conceptual model for the annual observance occurred earlier, when Moses returned from his third trip up Mount Sinai with the second set of tablets bearing the Ten Commandments. He had broken the originals when he discovered that the people had created an idol, the Golden Calf (Exodus 32:1–6). Moses tried to convince God not to completely destroy the ungrateful wayward lot of Israelites who, within a few months after they had been redeemed from slavery, after the unique experience of receiving direct communication from Him at Sinai, betrayed their saving God for a lump of precious metal.

Having secured another chance for the Israelites, Moses returned to the camp. Then, on the first of *Elul*, he again ascended, this time for the replacement text (Deuteronomy 10:10). While he was gone, the community fasted daily from sunrise to sunset, until the day of their leader's anticipated return—the tenth of *Tishrei*. Then they fasted from sunset to sunset. Moses found them remorseful and announced that God accepted their repentance and commanded that the date remain the Day of Atonement throughout all generations.

After the Commandment

Despite the fact that observing the tenth of *Tishrei* in the prescribed manner is "a law for all time" (Leviticus 16:29), like Rosh Hashanah it may have been widely ignored during the First Commonwealth, a period of religious ignorance and laxity. The Talmud indicates it was totally suspended during the dedication of Solomon's Temple (I Kings 8), which began two days before the holiday and seems to have continued with food, drink, and festivities nonstop through Sukkot.

Post-Babylonia

In the Talmud, Rabbi Simeon ben Gamaliel makes a curious statement for what was supposed to be a solemn day on which the nation reconciled itself with God: "There were no happier days in Israel than the fifteenth of *Av* and Yom Kippur." That's because for a time, the Day of Atonement had a split personality with dual purposes.

In the afternoon following the prescribed ritual, young girls dressed in white danced in the vineyards to catch the attention of eligible men. The poor wore borrowed clothes to eliminate apparent differences between the modestly situated and the aristocrat, and each maiden would encourage potential husbands to choose for her particular assets (the beautiful chiding them not to consider family position, the homely reminding them that inner beauty was paramount). Rabbi Gamaliel's comment referred to the many good marriages that resulted from the festival.

The overriding need to focus all attention on internal, spiritual concerns later determined a uniform character for the day. In the few hundred years following the Jews' return from their first exile, the holiday evolved into the holiest occasion of the year. Except for symbolic substitutions for previously performed ritual, it has changed little since.

Jewish writings tell us a great deal about the day's observance during the Second Temple period. Seven of the eight Talmud tractate *Yoma*'s chapters detail the high priest's Temple service. Apocryphal books Ecclesiasticus and Jubilees (written in the second century B.C.E.) document fragments from the Qumram Caves near the Dead Sea (the end of the Second Commonwealth) and the works of Philo of Alexandria, the Jewish philosopher who lived in the early years of the Common Era, support and supplement what our sages recorded.

In addition to providing specifics about the preparation and performance of the high priest's duties based on Leviticus 16, the records tell us that the tenth of *Tishrei*—often referred to as "The Fast," "The Great Fast" (*Tzoma Rabba*), or "Great Day" (*Yoma Rabbah*) in Talmud, and also as "Holy Day" (*Yom Hakodesh*)—was scrupulously observed not only by the pious or religious fanatics but also by those who never acted religiously in other aspects of their lives or other days of the year (as is the case today). Those who did not go to Jerusalem spent the entire day in their local synagogues abstaining from food and drink. Without the high priest as intermediary, they actively confessed and prayed on their own behalf.

For the thousands who did celebrate in Jerusalem, entering the Temple in the extended procession behind the high priest, participating in the prayers and witnessing the rituals, the atmosphere vibrated with the intensity of the drama and mystery of being close to God. Warned by Torah that he would not leave the Shrine alive unless he performed the Yom Kippur service properly (Leviticus 16:2–28), the high priest spent the week prior to the holiday living on the Temple grounds in concentrated preparation, attended by the sages who helped him cleanse himself; review the law, procedure, and scripture; and guard against any last-minute impurities that would render him unfit for service.

Unlike other days of the year, on this one the *Kohein Gadol* was required to officiate. And only on this, the holiest day of the year, could the holiest representative of the holiest nation enter the holiest place on Earth. The high priest, and only he, stepped into the Holy of Holies (the permanent version of the Tabernacle's Shrine), the innermost chamber of the Temple, considered God's earthly dwelling place. It was a privilege frought with anxiety, for one impure thought by the priest in such close proximity to the Ruler of the Universe would have resulted in his death. A personal tragedy, it also would affect the Israelites he represented in atoning for sin.

To be shielded from the full glory of God, the priest created a screen of smoke, as he had in the Shrine. Three times during the day he entered and emerged. And ten times he said the word not uttered at any other time or place: the ineffable name of God (*Shem Hameforash*), giving full body to the Tetragrammaton we recognize as the Hebrew letters *yud, hei, vov, hei* (YHVH) and say as *Adonai* (or religious Jews as *Hashem*, The Name). This was the name by which God identified Himself to Moses at the Burning Bush (Exodus 3:14), a composite version of the verb "to be" (*l'hiyot*), defying tense and thereby suggesting timelessness and ongoing creation. The pronunciation was so guarded only a high priest could learn it from his predecessor; we no longer know what it is. Overcome with feelings of humility and awe, at hearing the first syllable, everyone in the Temple congregation prostrated themselves on the ground.

The goat chosen by lot for *Azazel*, his horns tied with a piece of wool dyed red, was led into the wilderness by a designee. Ten way stations intervened between the Temple and the cliff twelve miles distant, from which the goat was pushed to its death.

As the trip progressed, the high priest chanted the portions of Torah dealing with Yom Kippur. Using a system of signal flags the animal's escort relayed the message back to the Temple that the sins of Israel had been successfully disposed and, as the red wool had turned white (Isaiah 1:18), the people had been absolved of their transgressions. With this news, and the emergence of the *Kohein Gadol* unharmed from God's chamber, the community rejoiced in the feast prepared by the priest.

Post-Temple

While gazing at the ruins of the Temple following the Roman siege (70 C.E.), Rabbi Joshua remarked, "Woe to us that the place where Jews were forgiven for their sins is destroyed." His teacher, the scholar and leader Rabbi Yokhanan ben Zakkai, replied, "We have another medium just as good for the forgiveness of sin. It is: Do good to mankind. For it is writ-

ten, 'I desire mercy, not sacrifice' (Hosea 6:6)" (*Avot de Rabbi Natan* 4).

The fact that we don't always "do good" to each other dictated the need for a day of atoning in the first place. With the destruction of the Temple the means of achieving its purpose simply shifted from an external physical ritual—sacrifice, expulsion of the *Azazel* goat—to an internal psychological process—*teshuvah* and prayer.

In fact, the rabbis had worked hard to get the people to recognize that the rites and prayers of Yom Kippur were not magical formulas that in and of themselves would absolve the nation and its individuals of sin. This message was easier to convey once the collective purge represented by the priest's confessions and the scapegoat was replaced by personal examination and catharsis.

From this more mature view, it is easier to understand that the goats had functioned as an external representation of an internal dilemma. The goat chosen for *Azazel* was one of two identical animals, same size, same sex, same color, same level of ritual purity. By lot one was picked to die after serving God, the other to be relegated to death in the wilderness. Each person has the same choices that determine the path of his/her life: to cast his/her lot with God, directing him-/herself to achieving a high moral and spiritual level, or turning away from society to wander in a moral wasteland, which will lead to certain ruin. The word *Azazel* then suggests one who is lost or disappears (*azel*) to the force (or strength, *az*) of sin.

Through the Ages

Because of its deep psychological import, the Temple rite, in the form of being recalled, remained essential on Yom Kippur. Services changed only with poetic embellishment of descriptions drawn from Talmud, *piyyutim* of the Middle Ages, and the addition of a controversial introductory service, *Kol Nidrei*, on *Erev* Yom Kippur.

As in ancient times, Yom Kippur continued to draw people, if only temporarily, back to their religion. Even those who do not have other connections with Judaism or the Jewish community during the rest of the year have always been drawn to the synagogue for at least part of the day, and take upon themselves the time-honored major form of affliction, fasting.

Throughout history, Jews risked their lives to participate in the communal cleansing, even in the most dire circumstances. They gathered secretly in secluded cellars during the Spanish Inquisition. In makeshift corners in the Warsaw ghetto, in a worksite forest or field or behind a barracks in a concentration camp, the Jews could not let the day pass without being honored with their prayer and, even though already starving, forsaking food that could have saved their lives. (Yom Kippur was one of the days the Nazis would provide better food than normal to the Jews as an additional torment.) The Jews in Mandate Palestine risked punishment by the British when they insisted on blowing the *shofar* at the Western Wall, and in the Soviet Union, long before the refuseniks had international support, Jews who had ostensibly forsaken their religion would often chance going to synagogue.

The tremendous power of the day is wonderfully illustrated by the story of Franz Rosenzweig (1886–1929), philosopher and founder of the Frankfurt Lehrhaus, a Jewish Free University for adult education. Raised in an assimilated Jewish home where he had received little exposure to the meaning, significance, and joy of his own religion, he had planned to convert to Christianity. He decided to prepare himself to do so as a Jew, rather than a pagan, by attending Yom Kippur services. In a small Orthodox *shul* in Berlin, he was surprised to find a vitality and modern relevance to Judaism, and felt the closeness of God. Realizing that Judaism provided what he thought he could find only in the church, and more, he changed his plans and became a tremendous influence on Jewish life, even after his death.

With its potential for emotional and psychological impact, deeply experienced by our forebears and not at all lessened by the absence of the Holy of Holies or *Azazel*, it is no wonder Yom Kippur retains such a hold on Jews generally disengaged from their religious heritage. Even secular *kibbutzim*, which for years ignored the holiday, have begun to observe it in some fashion. Perhaps it is fear that motivates them. Or reluctance to discard a last vestige of their tradition. Or recognition that there just could be something in it for them.

It is because of the almost universal observance of Yom Kippur that the Arabs made a serious tactical error when they decided to attack Israel on the holiday in 1973. Since virtually every Jewish Israeli was in synagogue or at home, mobilization of the Israel Defense Forces was much faster and easier than it would have been on a workday, when logistical chaos could have engulfed the country.

FOR FURTHER READING

Exodus 32–34, in any *Khumash*.

The incidents that led to the first Yom Kippur are recorded. (Additional details appear in Deuteronomy 9:8–10:11).

Leviticus 16, in any *Khumash*.

This chapter, on which observance of Yom Kippur is based, details the requirements of the individual and the rituals to be performed by the high priest.

Makhzor for Yom Kippur.

The *Avodah* section of *Mussaf* follows the *Kohein Gadol's* Temple service.

Schauss, Hayyim. *Guide to the Festivals, History and Observance.* New York: Schocken Books, 1974, pp. 133–141.

The detailed description of the Temple Service and changes in the holiday since it was observed in ancient days includes information on similar rites in other religions. There's also a description of Eastern European celebration of Yom Kippur.

WHAT DOES IT MEAN?— RELIGIOUS IMPORTANCE

You cannot fully understand the last of the Ten Days of Repentance without knowing something about the first, so you will find it helpful to refer to the previous chapter. The Jewish New Year it explains begins the intense process leading to a key pursuit of Judaism: atonement.

Read that as the quest for at-one-ment. It is striving to balance our souls and our selves (our true needs and potential versus our diverting desires and actuality). It is the attempt to counter our personal inclinations with concern for common good. And it is the reconciliation of humans as wasters of opportunity with God as Creator of an infinite number of chances to do the right thing. Stemming from a concept of the world in which humankind and the rest of the universe are in harmony, Yom Kippur provides the opportunity for us to correct any disparities that result in disunity.

The Human–God Relationship

Partners in Progress

God created human beings to work *with Him* in likeminded, shared-value partnership to perpetuate and perfect the world. Unfortunately, partnerships do not always run smoothly. A spouse has an extramarital affair. A business colleague neglects to fulfill a job's responsibilities. A party to a contract does not deliver promised goods. These failures get in the way of successfully meeting the objectives of the partnership agreement. They also create barriers between the people involved, impeding what could be mutually supportive and satisfying relationships.

We, the Jewish people connected throughout all time and place, accepted the contract for the endeavor called Judaism when we agreed to abide by the Torah offered to us at Mount Sinai (see chapter on Shavuot). Referring to the image in our tradition of Israel as the bride of God, some view it as a marriage contract. (This view gives new meaning to the custom of maidens dancing in the vineyards to attract husbands. Instead of being seen as taking advantage of an opportune holy occasion for betrothal, or a remnant of a primitive preharvest fertility rite, it becomes a reenactment in human terms of the first Yom Kippur, when Israel renewed her vows to God, fully embracing Him and His commandments.)

That contract, which we call a covenant, specifies that God will be our God, bringing blessings, protecting us, being accessible to us, and we will be His people, carrying His standards of morality to the world by exemplifying how people are supposed to treat each other. A condition of our acting as God's representatives on Earth is that we be holy, dedicated to aspiring toward the best that we and the world can be.

When we idle after idols—money, recognition, immediate gratification—when we fail to act properly toward our fellow human beings, when we forsake quality by going for the easy path, we create negative ramifications on several levels. The direct results of our behavior cause objects, relationships, even people, to be broken. They prevent the world from moving forward toward completion. This means we can no longer live up to our side of the covenant. And this creates distance between us and our fundamental partner in the endeavor of life.

Just as the Torah teaches us how to right the wrongs we do to other people, it teaches us how to "make up" with God. Atonement, and the self-examination and confession that precede it, are the means of removing the obstacles to continuing our partnership and to enjoying a mutually fulfilling relationship. Through the annual repurification we once again become holy, which means we meet the precondition of our ongoing covenant and are in the position to carry out our function according to it.

The Wholeness of Holiness

Being a holy nation—not set apart by God, but by our behavior—means being able to control our physical desires. The laws particular to Judaism, those which go beyond the ethical standards that apply to all humans equally, are designed to elevate us above our animal drives: *kashrut* (eating), *brit milah* (sex), *tefillin* and *mezzuzah* (thoughtless instinct). They exist to help us master the desires that, when indulged, lead us away from health and healthy relationships and distract us from concentrating our energies on meaningful pursuits.

Our tradition asserts that every single Jew, even one who ignores the laws, or is ignorant of them, has the potential for holiness. According to a kabbalistic version of the Creation, before the light God made to dispel the darkness, He created an illumination so powerful it would have allowed mankind to see from one end of the earth to the other. But the vessel into which the light was directed proved too weak to contain it and exploded into myriad glimmering shards. One of these bits of Divine light entered every Jewish soul, and therefore rests inside every Jew.

Referred to in Yiddish as *pinteleh yid*, this little spark can be understood as the inextinguishable Jewish essence, the potential for holiness each Jew possesses (and perhaps that inexplicable something that draws even the Jew most separated from the community to the synagogue on Yom Kippur). All the attention of introspection during this holiday season can fan the spark into a flame, making the God within us recognizable. It happens as we clear away the impurities of wrongdoing.

The term usually used for this process of atonement, *kapparah*, and *kippur* share a root meaning "to cleanse thoroughly, to scour, to erase." It conveys the idea that wrongdoing is a stain to be thoroughly removed. It is according to basic Jewish precept that wrongdoing *can* be totally eliminated, that human beings, regardless of what evil we do, can regain our initial purity. Of the world's major religions, only Judaism sets aside a specific day for the completion of the process. At its close, we can stand again as the first human beings did immediately after Creation, unobstructed by prior transgressions or guilt, with the entire world of possibilities available to us.

This doesn't happen because God reaches into our depths with a scouring pad to rub out the blotches on our souls. It happens because we redirect our inner drives to meet our true, purposeful goals. While God grants us atonement by mercifully accepting our repentance and believing our sincere resolutions to do better, the purification we experience comes from our own efforts.

No matter how great our efforts, we will not attain God's level of holiness; we're not expected to because we are only human. Even Moses, who was closer to God than any other prophet, standing before Him and speaking directly with Him, was never allowed to see His face (Exodus 33:20). (He also didn't arrive at his destination but could only gaze at the Promised Land from a distance [Deuteronomy 32:48–52].)

And the high priests, from Aaron on, the only men allowed to enter the chamber in which God's presence rested, could not face God, but separated themselves from Him by creating a veil of smoke by burning incense.

There will always be something, like the smoke, or the curtain at the entrance to the Holy of Holies, between us and the ideal level of holiness. But the value is not in the endpoint (ultimately death) but in the way we transform ourselves along the way. Life is a process, sometimes viewed in Judaism as a ladder on which we go up and down. We are supposed to push ourselves to climb up the ladder. What we learn on the journey, about ourselves, life, and God, leads us to contribute to creating the conditions for the arrival of the Messiah, an eternal process of improvement.

WHAT DOES IT MEAN TO US?—
PERSONAL SIGNIFICANCE

A well-known Talmud passage records the visit of a non-Jew to Hillel. He promises to convert if the great sage can teach him the Torah while he stands on one foot. Hillel replies, "Do not do to others that which is hateful to you" (which we know, reworded, as the Golden Rule). "The rest is commentary. Now go and study." The ethical guideline is the essence of Judaism. Reflecting on how well we follow it is the essence of Yom Kippur.

Like Rosh Hashanah, Yom Kippur is very much about you. As you read through this chapter, you will see how every aspect of its observance relates to you as a unique individual who has a particular role in life, and you as a singular component of the Jewish people that has a particular mission in the world.

Ten days ago, you assessed your life, where it is going and whether its purpose is worthwhile. Today you concentrate on how well you measure up to standards of behavior for human beings, on who you are as a person, for the individual qualities that define you—honest or dishonest, sweet or bitter, scornful or supportive, debased or holy—ultimately determine the path you take and its endpoint.

One of our sages instructed his students to repent for all their wrong choices the day before death. When they pointed out that they wouldn't know when that would occur, he replied, "Then surely you must repent today in case you die tomorrow." If we heeded Rabbi Eleazar's teaching, we would continually be aware of what we are doing with our lives, continually making adjustments to be sure we stay on track, regularly avoid putting off things likely to go unfinished if we do not do them today. Since we fail to follow Eleazar, we need at least one day a year to express remorse for our mistakes and our intentions to do better.

The confession we make on this holiday is identical to the one we are supposed to recite just before we die. But Yom Kippur provides us with more than a trial run. Facing imminent death, we can admit our wrongdoings and express regret for them, but we don't have the chance to actually change our behavior. On the Day of Atonement, that possibility still exists. On your deathbed, if you do not like the answers to the questions "Has my life been worthwhile? Did I accomplish what I wanted to achieve? Did I achieve something meaningful? Was I a good person?" there's nothing you can do to change them. But if you don't like your answers on the tenth of *Tishrei*, you can take action on the eleventh.

On Rosh Hashanah you identified things in yourself and in your relationships with others that you want to improve in the coming year. That gave you goals. Now you need specific tasks that will allow you to meet them. The sixty-seven categories of behavior for which we ask forgiveness during the confession provide a convenient list from which you can pick items appropriate to your situation and agenda.

Focus on the ones you fail to do to help yourself and others, or the things you are guilty of doing that create hindrances. Recognize how they limit or enhance the way you conduct your everyday life. They define your character.

For each of the improvements you want to make, concentrate on two or three concrete actions you can take, beginning immediately, which will contribute to the overall goal. For instance, if you have a negative outlook, you might decide that at the beginning and/or end of each day, you will list three things for which you can be thankful. If you are prone to gossip, you might limit phone conversations. If you are impolite to service personnel, you might make efforts to smile at or greet them, and remember to say "thank you." If you abhor beggars in the street, you might distribute blankets on cold nights, prepare or distribute food in a soup kitchen, or graciously give one a bag of groceries.

Behaving more morally, more humanely—what in Yiddish might be called in *menchlikeit* manner—is what will make you feel closer to God (on Rosh Hashanah you also chose something to improve in relation to Him). That is the key to achieving the "spirituality" of this day, which is supposed to be the climax of the year, a religious phenomenon par excellence. Although we spend it in prayer, pouring our hearts out to God, believing that He cares enough to listen and that He will act on our pleas, we are supposed to recognize that it is merely a means to better ourselves and the world.

Our tradition includes moving tales of rabbis who leave *selikhot*, or fail to appear for *Kol Nidrei*, because they are busy rocking a crying baby whose mother is not home or returning a stray cow to a non-Jewish neighbor. Although they are late in getting to the house of worship, with these and other *mitzvot* to aid the aged and poor, the rabbis of these stories are engaged in truly spiritual endeavors.

The challenge is to continue to be directed by concern for others once the holiday ends, to avoid relapsing into habitual patterns of thought and action. Next Yom Kippur you will confess again, in all sixty-seven categories, with the rest of the nation. But if you have made the day meaningful for yourself this year, you will be able to choose different areas in which to live more spiritually.

FOR FURTHER READING

Moments of Transcendence: Inspirational Readings for Yom Kippur. Ed. by Rabbi Dov Peretz Elkins. Northvale, NJ: Jason Aronson, 1992.

Drawn from ancient and modern, traditional and nontraditional sources (ranging from Talmud to a pop psych poster!) the insights presented in this book provide relevant contemporary perspective on the holiday's themes—and can also give a lift throughout the year. Like the volume for Rosh Hashanah, it makes a nice *shul*-time companion to the *makhzor*.

TRADITIONS: HOW WE CELEBRATE YOM KIPPUR

WHAT DO WE USE?—RITUAL ITEMS

With one addition (see below), the objects needed to fulfill the religious requirements of the holiday are those used for Rosh Hashanah: *shofar*, *makhzor*, and *kittel*.

FOR FURTHER READING

For Adults

See previous chapter for books that supplement the prayer book.

The Complete ArtScroll Machzor—Yom Kippur. Trans. and Commentary by Rabbi Nosson Scherman. Brooklyn: Mesorah Publications, 1988.

This highly regarded Day of Atonement prayer book shares qualities of its companion, the Rosh Hashanah *makhzor*.

The Metsudah Machzor—Yom Kippur. Trans. and Anthology of Classic Commentary by Rabbi Avrohom Davis. Far Rockaway, NY: Metsudah Publications, 1983.

This is the companion to the Rosh Hashanah Metsudah, valuable for anyone who wants to follow the English and Hebrew simultaneously.

For Children

Abrams, Judith Z. *Yom Kippur, A Family Service.* Rockville, MD: Kar-Ben Copies, 1990.

Designed for use with young children, the simple service explains the same concepts as the Rosh Hashanah edition: prayer, repentance, and charity. It beautifully presents how to have a relationship with God. A couple of simple songs and suggested activities for home and school are included. A companion cassette tape is available. Ages 4–8.

Memorial Candle

Anyone who has lost a parent (or grandparent) customarily lights a candle in memory of the deceased just before sundown on the eve of Yom Kippur (since *Yizkor* will be recited the next day). Available at grocery stores that have kosher food sections, or at Jewish supply stores, the candles contained in small glasses or cans burn for twenty-five hours.

HOW DO WE SHOW WE CELEBRATE?— OBSERVANCE

Since the holiday is dedicated to spiritual pursuits, you may anticipate Yom Kippur as unnatural and uncomfortable, particularly if it is the only spiritual thing you do all year. But like every other aspect of Judaism, the acts we perform on this holiday have rich psychological underpinnings. Once you understand them, you will find them relevant and recognize that they are merely tools for our own growth.

All activity is centered in the synagogue, where services last virtually all day, usually with a short break between forty-five minutes and an hour and a half long, depending on the speed and style of the *khazzan*. But no one takes attendance, so if this is beyond your endurance, stay only part of the day. Partial participation is better than none, and you can acclimate yourself gradually to spending hours in synagogue.

If you prepare yourself by knowing what to expect and learning what the service means, you'll find that the day can have the kind of emotional and spiritual impact it did for our grandparents and great-grandparents and continues to have for committed Jews throughout the world. The kinds of companion books mentioned in the chapter on Rosh Hashanah and in this chapter are highly recommended. In addition, the information following is intended to provide a foundation and useful perspective for some of the day's highlights.

Priming the Soul

In its instructions for observing the tenth of *Tishrei* (Leviticus 16:29,31; 23:26,29,32; Numbers 29:7), Torah specifies that we are to "afflict our souls." After searching Scripture and *Mishnah* in order to determine what affliction means, the rabbis identified five activities from which we abstain on the most solemn, but not mournful (despite the posture of many Jews, particularly of Eastern European background) day of the year. The purpose is not to punish ourselves but to gain control over our bodies and their potentially harmful appetites, which can become ends in themselves: Rambam describes the prohibitions of

Yom Kippur as "resting," as if not doing them were relief from ordeals. While not engaging in our normal daily concerns and pleasures, we become more conscious of how our physical urges so often lead us into trouble.

In Talmud's terms, for a brief time we elevate ourselves to the status of angels, who have no corporeal needs and whose sole role in the universe is to serve God. (The rabbis also explain that the things we abstain from are all those that make the soul comfortable in the body. By engaging in activities that make it uncomfortable, the soul is more likely to rise up from the body, taking us to a higher spiritual plane.)

Fasting

Derived directly from the Torah, abstaining from eating and drinking from before sundown until after the following sunset is probably the greatest test of self control during this holiday. How are we supposed to accept the promulgated notion that fasting frees us to worship when hunger pangs and distaste in a parched mouth create strong distractions to concentration on lofty spiritual thoughts?

The abstention in and of itself cannot create a sense of spirituality. The idea is to be able to refrain from giving in to our impulses. We prove to ourselves that we can control our bodies in the extreme; under normal circumstances we should cerainly be able to prevent our desires from leading into damaging excesses. Allowing the body to rid itself of the toxins eating produces mirrors our efforts on this day to purge ourselves of the impurities of unhealthy thoughts and deeds.

Of course, in the extreme, the restriction of food and water results in death. On Yom Kippur, this concept is significant in two ways. First, as on Rosh Hashanah, the act of standing to be judged in a sense entails facing death, for we are waiting to see what the verdict in our trial will be, whether or not we will be written in the "Book of Life." By denying ourselves material sustenance, we symbolically engage in self-sacrifice, a recognition that we deserve to be punished. (The weight-conscious will take heart in the fact that fasting reduces the body's fat content.) That innocent animals lost their lives for human wrongdoing (their fat was burned at the altar) should have made people aware of their actions. Today it's not animals, but what, we should ask ourselves, is being sacrificed when we err?

Experiencing hunger that we know is temporary should also encourage us to do something for those who suffer from lack of food. This is the real purpose of the fast, as Isaiah explains in the day's prophetic reading. A problem since biblical times, it has not abated yet, with recurring wars, famines, and other natural disasters leaving millions to die of starvation. When we resume feeding our bodies, we are revived and, as people who have experienced near death attest, feel like we are starting over. When we do so, it should be with our priorities in order.

Since Torah stipulates that the fast begins on the ninth day, but we are to deny ourselves only on the tenth, it is understood that the fast begins before sundown and concludes the next day at nightfall.

To revive themselves during the long hours without food, worshippers sometimes sniff smelling salts (in former times, tobacco or snuff), spices, sprays of mint, flowers, or a clove-filled *etrog* (citron) prepared after the previous Sukkot. Among the religious, spices are used this way just to give them the opportunity to say a *brakhah*. (The rabbis instructed that one hundred benedictions be said daily, which is more difficult on Yom Kippur because of its restrictions.) If you smell spices, the blessing to be said is:

בָּרוּךְ אַתָּה, יהוה אֱלֹהֵינוּ, מֶלֶךְ הָעוֹלָם, בּוֹרֵא מִינֵי בְשָׂמִים.

Barukh Atah, Adonai Eloheinu, Melekh Haolam, borei minei v'samim.

Blessed are You, Lord our God, King of the Universe, Who creates species of fragrance.

Sexual Relations

The normal and healthy drive, encouraged on Shabbat because it is an act seen to involve God and assist Him in ongoing creation, is prohibited on Yom Kippur. Again, it is an appetite whose satisfaction can lead one into sin.

Washing

Cleansing oneself for pleasure or comfort is prohibited. Observant Jews do not shower, bathe, or wash their hands or faces, unless they are soiled with mud. The focus of this day is on internal, rather than external, cleanliness. You should not think you are rid of soil just because you have applied soap and water to your skin.

Anointing

The application of oil to the body was once done regularly, particularly after bathing, and was part of the cleansing process. Today, anointing generally refers to the use of face and hand creams, which on Yom Kippur are not to be applied except for medicinal purposes. As for the prohibition against washing, thoughts should be directed to what needs to be cleaned out from the inside.

Wearing Shoes

You may notice a lot of people wearing sneakers, particularly the basic canvas and rubber models, to synagogue. It is not for comfort, although they certainly function that way with all the standing we do during the services. Wearing shoes (sandals in biblical days) of leather was forbidden in holy places, as we learned from Moses' experience before the Burning Bush (Exodus 3:5), where he removed his sandals. The *Kohanim* removed their shoes when giving the Priestly Benediction in the Temple (as the *Kohanim* do today when they stand before the Ark in front of the congregation for the *dukhan* service, during which they make the blessing). Since the day of Yom Kippur entails a reliving of the Temple experience, we forego our leather shoes as well.

(As usual, the rabbis offer another reason: After Adam and Eve's sin, the earth, which was supposed to have been holy ground, became contaminated. We normally wear shoes to keep from having direct contact with the defiled ground. But on Yom Kippur, when we make atonement with God and focus on attaining the purity of Creation, the earth is holy, and so we don't have to separate ourselves from it.)

On the physical level, leather shoes protect the feet, providing comfort, while footwear of other materials or going barefoot does not. On the Day of Atonement, we forego bodily pleasure. Because of their comfort, and also their expense, even in biblical times leather shoes were considered a luxury (Song of Songs 7:2) and thought to contribute to a feeling of pride and haughtiness in the wearer. Since Yom Kippur, and the entire Ten Days of Repentance, are designed to produce feelings of humility, wearing leather shoes would interfere with one's proper frame of mind. (Despite the admonitions of overzealous rabbis, the prohibition is specifically for leather shoes—whether the top or sole is of leather—and not other items made from the skins of animals. Coats, hats, watchbands, and so on are all permissible.)

Ushering in Yom Kippur

Although certain rituals completed prior to sundown on *Erev* Yom Kippur are not parts of the holiday itself, they are considered essential elements in its observance.

Prefast Meal

Timed to end well before sundown, both so that the fast begins on *Tishrei* 9, as ordained, and so that you can arrive in synagogue in time for the initial services, eating the *seudah hamafseket* is considered as much a *mitzvah* as fasting the next day (see "Traditional Foods"). Since the holiday has not yet begun, you do not recite the *kiddush* over wine, but it is appropriate to do a *motzi* (as religious Jews do at any meal) after the ritual handwashing:

בָּרוּךְ אַתָּה, יהוה אֱלֹהֵינוּ, מֶלֶךְ הָעוֹלָם, אֲשֶׁר קִדְּשָׁנוּ בְּמִצְוֹתָיו, וְצִוָּנוּ עַל נְטִילַת יָדָיִם.

Barukh Atah, Adonai Eloheinu, Melekh Haolam, asher kidshanu b'mitzvotav, v'tzivanu al netilat yadayim.

Blessed are You, Lord our God, King of the Universe, Who has sanctified us with His commandments and commanded us regarding washing the hands.

בָּרוּךְ אַתָּה, יהוה אֱלֹהֵינוּ, מֶלֶךְ הָעוֹלָם, הַמּוֹצִיא לֶחֶם מִן הָאָרֶץ.

Barukh Atah, Adonai Eloheinu, Melekh Haolam, hamotzi lekhem min ha'aretz.

Blessed are You, Lord our God, King of the Universe, Who brings forth bread from the earth.

As for Rosh Hashanah, you dip the bread into honey. *Shir Hama'alot* (Psalm 126), which expresses the desire to return to Zion, precedes the *Birkat Hamazon* as it does on Shabbat and festivals. Following the meal, it is traditional to put a clean white cloth on the table in honor of the festival. Books of Jewish significance are often placed on it to represent that prayer and Torah will suffice as sustenance on this day.

Candles

Based on Proverbs and Prophets, candles are often used to illuminate the house: "For the commandment is a lamp [candle], and the teaching is light" (Proverbs 6:23) recalls the Ten Commandments, the synopsis of the Torah that Moses brought to Israel on Yom Kippur. A *midrash* compares man's soul to a lighted candle, and Isaiah's admonition to "honor the Lord with light" (58:13) refers to this holiday when, since we cannot honor the day with feast, we do so by kindling many lights and wearing festive clothing. There should be at least one candle that will burn a full day, to provide a source for *Havdalah* at the close of the holiday.

It is also customary to light a memorial candle for deceased parents, prior to kindling the *yom tov* candles with a blessing unique in that the name of the holiday replaces the standard "*yom tov*." *Shehekheyanu* follows it.

בָּרוּךְ אַתָּה, יהוה אֱלֹהֵינוּ, מֶלֶךְ הָעוֹלָם, אֲשֶׁר קִדְּשָׁנוּ בְּמִצְוֹתָיו, וְצִוָּנוּ לְהַדְלִיק נֵר שֶׁל [*שַׁבָּת וְשֶׁל] יוֹם הַכִּפּוּרִים.

Barukh Atah, Adonai Eloheinu, Melekh Haolam, asher kidshanu b'mitzvotav, vitzivanu l'hadlik ner shel [Shabbat v'shel] Yom Hakippurim.*

Blessed are You, Lord our God, King of the Universe, Who has sanctified us with His commandments and commanded us to kindle the light of [the Sabbath and of]* Yom Kippur.

---

*When *Erev* Yom Kippur and *Erev* Shabbat coincide.

בָּרוּךְ אַתָּה, יהוה אֱלֹהֵינוּ, מֶלֶךְ הָעוֹלָם, שֶׁהֶחֱיָנוּ, וְקִיְּמָנוּ, וְהִגִּיעָנוּ לַזְּמַן הַזֶּה.

Barukh Atah, Adonai Eloheinu, Melekh Haolam, shehekheyanu, v'kiyamanu, v'higgiyanu lazman hazeh.

Blessed are You, Lord our God, King of the Universe, Who has kept us alive, sustained us, and brought us to this season.

Blessing Children

Many parents bless their children before going to synagogue. Just prior to their deaths, at the peak of their holiness, the patriarchs blessed theirs, and Moses blessed the children of Israel. On *Erev* Yom Kippur, we are, in a symbolic way, about to purify ourselves and experience death, so we offer similar blessings, expressing the hope that our children not sin, study Torah, love God, and be granted fulfilling lives. Longer than the normal Shabbat *brakhot*, they form a beautiful expression of anything a parent could wish for a child. (The Hebrew can be found at the front of a standard *makhzor*).

May God make you like [for a boy] Ephraim and Menasseh/[for a girl] like Sarah, Rebecca, Rachel, and Leah. May God bless you and safeguard you. May God illuminate His countenance for you and be gracious to you. May God turn his countenance to you and establish peace for you. May it be the will of our Father in Heaven that He instill in your heart His love and reverence. May the fear of God be upon your face all your days, in order that you not sin. May your craving be for the Torah and the commandments. May your eyes gaze toward truth; may your mouth speak wisdom; may your heart meditate with awe; may your hands engage in the commandments; may your feet run to do the will of your Father in heaven. May He grant you righteous sons and daughters who engage in the Torah and the commandments all their days. May the source of your posterity be blessed. May He arrange your livelihood for you in a permissible way, with contentment and with relief, from beneath His generous hand, and not through the fits of flesh and blood; a livelihood that will free you to serve God. And may you be inscribed and sealed for a good, long life, among all the righteous of Israel.

Synagogue

We observe Yom Kippur, unlike any other holiday on the calendar, exclusively in the synagogue. The day has the largest number of prayer services of any day of the year: five—*Ma'ariv* (evening, on *Erev* Yom Kippur, preceded by *Kol Nidrei*), *Shakharit* (morning), *Mussaf* (additional), *Minkhah* (afternoon), and *Neilah* (closing) on the day of the tenth. (If you attend services in a traditional synagogue, you may see people standing not only for the parts of the service that re-quire the congregation to rise but for the entire proceedings. This is a custom originally based on a *midrash*, claiming that when the Adversary will behold all of Israel upright before God, he will be forced to liken the Jews to angels who stand before God free of sin.)

With its unbroken devotion to prayer, Yom Kippur may seem, for those unused to attending services, even more daunting than Rosh Hashanah. To get something out of the experience, read or reread the section on prayer in the previous chapter and obtain a book that will guide you through the *makhzor*. It will make an incredible difference in your appreciation and observance of the holiday.

Liturgy

Expanding on the themes of the Rosh Hashanah services, the notions of sin as alienation from God, reconciliation as a human need, atonement as a possibility through inner change, and individual accountability for the status of the world pervade the prayers. A phrase from Ecclesiastes expresses the universal need to go through the process: "There is not a righteous man upon earth who does good and does not sin" (7:20).

In his Yom Kippur confession, the high priest used three different words for sin, which the Talmud explains express progressive stages in our gradual movement away from God: *khet*, an unwitting offense (and the word graciously used in our confessions), *avon*, an act of insolence, and *pesha*, an overt act of rebellion. On Yom Kippur, we take the steps that will lead us back in the other direction.

Confession

The central aspect of the liturgy is the confession of sin, *Viddui* (literally "declaration"). The same as the prayer said prior to death (and by a groom, who is forgiven for his sins and considered a new man when he weds), it deals with moral transgressions between one person and another.

It consists of two parts, the *Viddui Ze'ira*, minor declaration, beginning *Ashamnu* (We have become guilty), and made up of a one-word transgression for each letter of the alphabet, a total of twenty-three, and *Viddui Rabbah* (major declaration), beginning *Al khet* (For the sin . . .), consisting of two more specific expressions of wrongdoing for every letter of the alphabet, a total of forty-four. (The *Sephardim* reduce the catalogue to a few lines.)

Together they cover a range of human behavior of an ethical nature (entrapping a neighbor, running to do evil, haughty eyes, hard-heartedness, immoral-

193

ity, scorning, being obstinate, giving evil counsel, and so on). Ten times during the course of Yom Kippur we recite *Viddui*. (This coincides with the ten times the high priest pronounced the name of God and recalls the Ten Commandments Israel accepted on Yom Kippur, the tenth day of the seventh month and the last of the ten days of repentance.)

The *Ashamnu* is said both to ourselves and aloud as a congregation, the *al khets* to ourselves, with the exception of the refrain. It divides the list into four sections and is sung together three times: "For all these, O God of forgiveness, forgive us, pardon us, atone for us" (*V'al kulam, Elohei selikhot, s'lakh lanu, m'khal lanyu, kaper lanu*). It is customary to stand with your head bowed and to hit your breast (lightly thump your right fist over your heart) as each *khet* is mentioned, since the heart is viewed as the seat and source of sin (Ecclesiastes 7:2). It is natural to feel a pang as you come to a *khet* that applies to your own behavior (the rabbis said you should experience such feeling). If you committed a wrong somehow omitted from the list, you are supposed to add it to your private declaration.

The fourth- or fifth-century originators of the recitation chose the alphabet acrostic format to emphasize that each sin, represented by a letter, destroys the world, which according to *midrash* God created using the letters of the Torah. (The Hebrew alphabet is believed to be a complex and mystical system whose letter forms and names contain intricacies that hint at the secrets of the world and give the words they comprise levels of meaning.) By essentially going through God's building blocks as we admit our shortcomings and ask for His forgiveness, we remind Him how He felt when He gave us the Torah at Mount Sinai—like a groom for a bride on their wedding day. It is a way to encourage His mercy.

Aside from the general experience of prayer, a lot of us have difficulty with this formula for communal confession. Most of us are good, decent people, trying hard to live our lives properly, with concern for others. We may resent having to admit to something we may have successfully resisted, never contemplated, or maybe never even knew existed. We may believe that with all our upright living and social awareness, we have nothing to confess, or at least nothing on a scale of sixty-seven categories.

One of the first things you notice in this long list of transgressions is that they are confessed to in first-person plural: *we* have betrayed, *we* have robbed, for the sin that *we* sinned before you. . . . Everyone confesses to every sin. This is to emphasize that each of us is part of and responsible for the entire community of Israel.

It makes us recognize that as individuals, we are inseparable parts of the Jewish people. Our status as a nation, the extent to which we are together living up to our mission, affects all of us and vice versa. If a fellow Jew sins, it is as if you yourself sinned. Like it or not, we *are* our brothers' and sisters' keepers. By confessing together, we share the burden of our shortcomings and express our responsibility for each other.

Part of the strength in Judaism comes from the concept that every Jew, deceased and living, from Mount Sinai until the present moment, appears before God as one entity. Each of us is as much an integral part of the collective Israel as our hands or legs or eyes are to our individual bodies. The interrelatedness is so deep, our tradition holds that every Jewish soul that would ever be on Earth, whether embodied at the time or not, was actually present at Sinai. We *were* the desert-bound ex-slaves who accepted responsibility for fulfillment of the covenant onto ourselves—all Jews, forever. And it is because we are intimately connected through time and space that Judaism places such emphasis on the collective.

Through this relationship, one Jew can, and is obligated to, act on behalf of others. As personal as *teshuvah* (repentance) and atonement are, Yom Kippur worship is not something to be done in solitude any more than you pray only for your own needs. A successful final outcome for the Jewish people depends on our common efforts as individuals.

The Talmud says "If an individual repents, God forgives him and the entire world" (*Yoma* 86b). We have the models of Moses and the *Kohein Gadol* to show us that one person can bring atonement for the nation. For this reason, we recall the matriarchs, patriarchs, and other righteous members of our community throughout history, so we will be judged based on their merits. At the same time, each of us is to be the one person becoming more holy for everyone's benefit and not count on someone else to carry us along with his or her efforts.

As a community, we have surely run the gamut of offenses during the previous year. Within the litany of communal wrongs, each of us can apply the appropriate ones to ourselves. But the *makhzor*'s convenient itemization serves us well in another way. It reminds us of errors in judgment, missed chances to do good, and certain infractions that we might have forgotten, or indicates wrongdoings that we might not think of as *khets*. (Do you know that gossip is against Jewish law—even spreading positive information about another person? What about showing contempt for parents or teachers? Or foolish speech?) As broad headings, each item mentioned can start us thinking about subcategories that ring bells for us.

Divine Attributes of Mercy

When Moses asked God to reveal Himself so that the prophet would be better able to represent Him to the Israelites, God arranged for Moses to stand in a mountain cleft and see Him from behind. As God passed by, He indicated His nature: "Lord [merciful before one has sinned], Lord [merciful to the repentant sinner], All Powerful, Compassionate, Gracious, Slow to Anger, Abundant in Kindness and Truth, Preserver of Kindness for thousands of generations, Forgiver of Iniquity, willful sin and error, and Who Cleanses" (Exodus 34:4–9; *Rosh Hashanah* 17b). A total of twelve times during Yom Kippur we chant after the cantor "*Adonai, Adonai, El rakhum v'khanun, erekh appayim, verav khesed v'emet, notzer khesed la'alafim, noseh avon vapeshah v'khata'ah v'nakkeh.*"

According to *midrash*, Moses was instructed to tell the Israelites that whenever they needed God's mercy, they could appeal for it by reciting these Thirteen Attributes of Mercy. On the one day a year devoted to winning God's favor, we intone the description that, as much as it summons God's forgiveness, reassures us that it will be given. It is no wonder we repeat it, with increasing fervor, seven times alone during the last service of the day.

Recurring Refrains

A number of other prayers embodying key themes of the Yom Kippur process recur throughout the liturgy. They express recognition of our place relative to the King of the Universe and our deepest hopes to be granted a favorable life. They all have catchy, easily learned tunes that invite participation.

Kol Nidrei

With its beautiful haunting melody; the crescendo increasing through each of its three consecutive renditions, taking it through sadness, warmth, beseeching, and ultimately confidence; the two Torah scrolls previously paraded around the sanctuary held by synagogue leaders flanking the *khazzan*; and the full attention of the congregation (often a larger crowd than at any other point in the Yom Kippur service, with the possible exception of *Yizkor* or *Neilah*)—the chant that ushers in Yom Kippur seems the essence of spirituality. For many people, it is a defining point of the holiday.

Actually just an introduction to Yom Kippur's first service, *Ma'ariv*, expressed before the sunset signalling the start of *yom tov*, Kol Nidrei is not even a prayer. Meaning "all vows," it is a legal formulation which relinquishes one from the responsibility of fulfilling certain promises.

Its origins are uncertain and its history rocky. It may have begun during a time when Jews were forced to convert to Islam or Christianity, and did so only outwardly, to save themselves. (Romantic legend has it that the plaintive tune we find so soul-wrenching, as if a musical rendition of our bitter history, was composed in secret by Jews during the Spanish Inquisition.)

Recited since before the ninth century, it probably had less dramatic origins than the remorse of cryto-Jews. Torah considers a vow sacred. One is not to be made casually, and once expressed, it must be fulfilled (Numbers 30:3; Deuteronomy 23:22–24). The Talmud provides a loophole by stating that anyone who won't be fulfilling an oath—and this is only an oath of a personal, usually religious nature that does not involve another individual—should declare so at the beginning of the year. (Although *hatarat nedarim* still takes place before Rosh Hashanah, as it did in talmudic times, during the Middle Ages Yom Kippur was chosen as the occasion for the communal declaration since more people attended synagogue then.)

Centuries-long controversy arose between proponents of the annulment and opponents who objected to granting a blanket release from promises that by their nature had the force of law. They argued, with justification, that it undermined the value of one's word. Many rabbis still forbade it after a descendant of Rashi, the great eleventh-century Torah commentator, changed the language so that the declaration is in advance for vows that will be made in the coming year, rather than after the fact for vows that had been made since the last Yom Kippur. Nevertheless, since people continued to make unfulfillable vows, the custom remained.

Anti-Semites, neglecting the fact that *Kol Nidrei* does nothing to free one of responsibilities to others, seized on it as proof of a Jew's untrustworthiness. After repeated complaints to Russian authorities in Kurland in the mid-1800s, a special Hebrew introduction had to be written into the prayer books stating that the declaration applied only to vows exclusively involving the person who made them and only applied to that person's relationship with God. At the same time, *Kol Nidrei*'s melody so enticed Christians that it was once routine for them to visit synagogues on *Erev* Yom Kippur so they could hear it. (The composers Beethoven and Bruch both used it in their works.)

Between 1844 and 1961, when it reinstated the declaration, the Reform movement abolished *Kol*

Nidrei (often using Psalm 130, as the Jews of Palestine had before the existence of *Kol Nidrei*, to open their service). The Reconstructionists tried to but ended up introducing a new form written by the movement's founder, Mordecai Kaplan.

Except for the Italian rite, which uses a Hebrew version, *Kol Nidrei* is in Aramaic, the vernacular at the time it was written. The Italian Jews and *Sephardim* retain the original language of retroactive release, while the *Ashkenazim* take the proactive approach.

Since it is prohibited, in accordance with Talmud, to ask for release from vows on Sabbath or a festival, unless the vows directly concern those days, *Kol Nidrei* must be recited prior to the start of Yom Kippur. Because of this timing, the men wear their *talleisim*, which are usually not put on for evening services. (The *mitzvah* concerning the wearing of ritual fringes specifies that they be seen [Numbers 15:39], interpreted to mean during daylight. If one arrives late and puts on the *tallit* after sunset, the usual *brakhah* is omitted.) The sight of the men in their prayer shawls, a sea of white gently swaying to the bittersweet chant, adds to the aura of the occasion.

The men standing next to the *khazzan* make up the symbolic court needed for annulment of vows and represent Aaron and Hur, who stood on either side of Moses, supporting his arms in the battle against Amalek (Exodus 17:12). Each repetition of the declaration, said three times like any court's proclamation, expresses greater comfort in standing before the Judge. The first is almost suppressed, a whisper of awe at being in the King's palace, especially to make a request. The last shows confidence and relief at recognizing that the Ruler is a merciful father figure.

While it is as easy to dismiss the meaning of *Kol Nidrei* as it is to excuse any ill-conceived vows we might make in the next twelve months, we should look beyond its dull legalese. We all know how difficult it is to live up to promises, especially the ones we make to ourselves. (How many new year's resolutions have you broken? How many times have you relapsed into smoking, overeating, etc.?) Once we are away from the intensity of the situation that fostered the promise, it is easy to give in to the habitual behavior we vowed we would break. It takes a tremendous amount of willpower and self-discipline to follow through on our good intentions. When we succeed, we are living up to our word. During this declaration, we should think about what our word really means, not only to ourselves but to anyone who trusts us based on what we say.

Fasting with Sinners

Just before the cantor begins *Kol Nidrei*, he recites (three times, as it is another legal statement) a declaration permitting the congregation to pray with transgressors. Instituted to allow those who had been banned from the community (and those who had removed themselves from it by pretending to convert to another religion) to take part in the rites of repentance, it was based on the Talmud's assertion that a public fast is not a fast unless all Jews, including sinners, participate. (It points out that just as the Torah includes the malodorous spice *khelbanah* among the essential ingredients of the incense offering [Exodus 30:34], transgressors are accepted as part of the Jewish people.) However, if we remember the passage from Ecclesiastes, that there is not a person on earth, no matter how righteous, who has not sinned, we realize that all of us gathered in the synagogue have transgressed and should feel compassion and closeness in our shared experience of the day. Just as we wish others will forgive us, we should be moved to forgive others. Even those who show up only once a year, or those who have been away from Judaism a long time, are still considered part of the community. And while the community welcomes them back with open arms, they have the perfect opportunity to express the desire to be included.

Uninterrupted Service

According to a traditional belief that the Yom Kippur evening service that follows *Kol Nidrei* should not end, some worshippers spend the night in the synagogue. They might sleep there, and to continue their devotion beforehand they usually study Talmud tractates *Yoma* and *Keritot* or read Psalms. The Kabbalists believe that since "the gates of understanding" are open, it is a good night to study the secrets of the Torah (Jewish mysticism).

To be sure that people would not weaken themselves to the point that they would be unable to participate in the next day's services, rabbis often suggested to congregants that they would do better to rest during the night. Some Reconstructionist congregations close their evening services with personal meditation that allows worshippers to leave gradually, whenever they are satisfied with their thoughts on forgiveness, so that the service never officially ends.

Shakharit

The morning Torah reading, Leviticus 16, details the unique service performed by the high priest on Yom

Kippur. It begins with a reference to the tragic death of Aaron's sons when they were consumed by the "strange fire" (Leviticus 10:1–2) they produced in defiance of God's specific directions. (The *Sephardim* introduce the reading with a special *piyyut*, a dirge in memory of the sons, designed to produce tears. The response is based on the rabbinic teaching that one who cries on Yom Kippur for the passing of Aaron's sons will not during his or her life lose a child.)

The passage serves to warn us not to take any transgression, however seemingly minor, lightly, and that not even the highly placed are immune to the dangers of sin or punishment for it. Judaism teaches that the standard by which one is judged becomes more stringent as one's status or knowledge increases. Aaron himself, brother of Moses, leader in Moses' absence, the high priest who made peace in the community and brought many people close to Torah, could not save his sons.

In fact, he was responsible for their deaths: "The sin of the father is visited upon his sons" when a parent sets a bad example that is followed by his children. Though not punished immediately for it, Aaron sinned by allowing the Israelites to make the Golden Calf; he was the one who wrongfully used fire to mold the idol. The death of his sons by flame, for their illicit fire, was his punishment as much as theirs.

The detailed description of the sacrifices of the day is capped by the *maftir* reading, commanding us to fast and reviewing the order of sacrifices (Numbers 29:7–11).

The *haftarah* (Isaiah 57:14–58:14) tells us what this day is supposed to be about. The prophet criticizes those who think that going through the motions of self-affliction as purely physical acts will lead to atonement. The ultimate purpose of a fast day, he admonishes, is not to show God or others how pious we are by standing all day, fasting, beating our chests and calling out His name. External acts are good only to the extent that they lead us to more moral behavior: freeing the oppressed, feeding the hungry, taking other justice-oriented action.

Yizkor

The memorial service for souls of the departed follows *Shakharit* (see chapter on Pesakh for full explanation). A custom since talmudic times, it may have been introduced at the Yom Kippur service in recognition of Aaron's sons, and was later given added meaning because of historic developments (see chapter on Shavuot) and added to the services on the other festivals. Reflecting on human mortality is especially appropriate on this day, as it generates feelings of humility. Although some whose parents are still alive leave the sanctuary out of superstition, it is considered a *mitzvah* for everyone to participate in the service. However, anyone who has not completed a year of mourning for a parent should leave, because s/he could be overcome with sorrow and inadvertently disturb others on a day when mourning is prohibited.

Since giving charity is an integral part of the remembrance, most synagogues conduct their annual appeals for funds just before the service begins. (Sometimes it is done privately, with congregants folding down flaps on a prepared pledge card to indicate the amount of their donation to the synagogue. In some places, gifts are announced in the belief that it encourages others to be more generous.)

Sephardim conduct their version of *Yizkor* before *Ma'ariv* the previous evening, the time when some congregations hold their appeals. Conservative congregations add introductory readings and verses from Psalms, and the Reform, who shorten the traditional text and add Psalm 23 and poems from the Middle Ages, hold *Yizkor* just before *Neilah*.

The service begins between 11 A.M. and noon in most synagogues. Those who exited the sanctuary return for the closing prayer, *Av Harakhamim* (Father of compassion) for all the Jews martyred for their faithfulness. This is often followed with special prayers for Holocaust victims and soldiers who died defending the State of Israel.

Mussaf

The focal point of the early afternoon service is a review, in all its detail, of the *Avodah* (service) performed by the *Kohein Gadol*, the ceremony of sacrifice, scapegoat, and seclusion in the Holy of Holies. The rendition we read is a version of the text from the Talmud poetically enhanced.

You may get an idea of the emotional pitch this service generated in past generations if you visit a traditional synagogue. There, at the part of the ceremony in which the high priest mentioned the *Shem Hameforash*, the entire congregation, not just the *khazzan*, will often kneel on the floor, then prostrate themselves, their heads nearly touching the ground (or, in crowded synagogue rows, they will touch their knees and foreheads to the ground) as those who attended the Temple service did, calling out "Blessed be His glorious sovereign Name for ever and ever" (*Barukh Shem kavod malkhuto l'olam voed*).

This phrase, part of daily prayer, is normally said in an undertone. Since it was forbidden at one time by rulers who considered it subversive, the Jews acquiesced—except on Yom Kippur, when they insisted on shouting it, as had their forebears at the Temple. Except for the Reform, who say it aloud year-round to demonstrate their freedom in our society, the practice is continued by tradition, based on two *midrashim*.

When Jacob was about to die, says one *midrash*, he called his sons to his bedside so he could reveal to them all that would happen until the end of time. When the Divine spirit departed from him, thwarting his plan, the dying patriarch wondered if perhaps some taint in his family had caused the situation. His sons replied, "Hear O Israel [Jacob, their father], the Lord your God, the Lord is one [the text of the *Shema* (Deuteronomy 6:4)]. Our faith in God is complete, In our hearts, just as in yours, there is only one God." To which Jacob replied "*Barukh Shem. . . .*" The rabbis who could not agree as to whether these words should be incorporated into the *Shema*, since they are not directly quoted in the Torah, compromised by adding them in undertone.

The other tale relates that Moses heard the angels reciting the verse when he went up Mount Sinai, and that he taught it to the Israelites. But since he felt humans did not have a right to the property of higher beings, he instructed that it be said quietly. On Yom Kippur, when we elevate ourselves to the level of angels, it is permissible for us to say it openly.

The prostration occurs four times, at each retelling of the high priest's confession, when he pronounced God's name, and at *Mussaf Aleinu*, which also recalls the Yom Kippur *Avodah*. Outside of very traditional *shuls*, only the *khazzan* prostrates himself, or the congregation simply bows, as do the *Sephardim*.

The Reform movement eliminates the description of the sacrifices, limiting its *Avodah* to the confession, without the prostration. Prayers stressing Israel's moral responsibility are added. The Conservative keep most of the traditional *Avodah*, which they recite in the vernacular rather than in Hebrew, and include new prayers relevant to contemporary life.

Although it is easy in our ecologically minded, animal rightist environment to understand the Reform movement's rejection of symbolic sacrifice, if we know some Hebrew, we can at least gain an appreciation for how the ancient Jews derived spiritual benefit from a practice we generally find primitive and abhorrent.

The word for sacrifice, *korban*, comes from the verb *hekriv*, meaning "to sacrifice," or "to draw close." "Near," or "close by" (or "relative") is *karov*, and "relationship" is *kirvah*. Sacrifice then was a way to get closer to God. It was not a value because it was a gift to Him but because it changed the feelings of the giver. When we "make a sacrifice," don't we do so in order to be nearer reaching a goal, or in order to help another person, which makes us feel closer to that person? That's the feeling the ancient Israelites had toward God, and the feeling we, through our form of service—prayer—can hope to achieve.

Ten Martyrs

Shortly after the *Avodah*, we read an incredibly moving poem depicting the gruesome deaths of famous talmudic sages brutally killed by the Romans during Hadrian's reign. Historically inaccurate (all ten men did not die at the same time), it was written after the Crusades to put the martyrdom of Jews into the perspective of our people's history of being sacrificed for our beliefs. Evoked on Yom Kippur so that the sacrifices of the martyrs may bring forgiveness for their descendants (that connection-through-time-and-space notion), it is often followed by prayers for and readings about victims of the Holocaust, who will sometimes give the readings. (A different version of the martyrdom of the sages is recited on Tisha B'Av.)

Minkhah

Unlike other festivals, the afternoon service includes a Torah reading (like the afternoon service on Shabbat). There is also a *haftarah*.

Illicit Liaisons

The Torah portion, Leviticus 18, details forbidden sexual relations. A "hint" to God, according to *midrash*, that just as He commanded us not to uncover our bodies for immoral purposes, He should not expose our sins, it may have been chosen as a further reminder of the base behavior that results from the weaknesses we try to overcome on the Day of Atonement. Since this was once a time for young men to choose brides, the laws on liaisons were an appropriate way to instruct young people. Later it was considered a warning against temptation, as the women customarily attended synagogue in elegant attire. (Some congregations follow the minority choice in the Talmud and instead read the next chapter of Leviticus, which deals with holy behavior and social justice.)

Jonah

For the prophetic portion, we read the children's favorite, the book of Jonah. It tells the story of the reluctant prophet who spent time in the belly of a "great fish." Rather than warn a Gentile city that it would be destroyed if its inhabitants did not repent, as God sent him to do, Jonah tried to sail to a faraway destination. He couldn't bear the thought that the non-Jews would better heed God's word than would his own intractable people.

He did not recognize that as a Jew, his role entailed being a universal voice, spreading God's word to all nations. In the end, Jonah learned what we learn from his story: God cares about all living things. While Jonah believes in strict justice—he would just like God to destroy the place and be done with it—God judges with compassion and, rather than wanting to destroy them, prefers that the Ninevites repent. And when the Ninevites' repentance is accepted, it is not because they have performed rituals but because they changed their behavior. We're supposed to recognize that if these people could repent, anyone can.

The other message is that it is impossible to evade God's presence or a destiny of service to Him. Although Jonah tried to sail away, God never lost track of his whereabouts. Like it or not, Jonah could not escape from his destiny any more than the Jewish people can escape from ours: obligation to the people of all nations, to the world, to serving God.

For Further Reading

For Children

Patterson, Geoffrey. *Jonah and the Whale*. New York: Lothrop, Lee & Shepard Books, 1991.

One of the more appealing of the many versions of the Bible story, this one is well written and vibrantly and expressively illustrated. Ages 5–8.

Neilah

As the sun's rays begin to retreat to the tree tops, we begin the last service of the day, *Neilah*, or *Neilat haShearim* (closing of the gates). Originally referring to the shutting of the Temple gates at sunset, the image of the heavenly gates, which had stood open all this time to receive our supplications, slowly coming together to block accessibility to forgiveness, adds great poignancy to these last moments of appeal. The Ark is representationally kept open throughout the service, and all who are physically able stand for its entirety.

Suddenly, it might seem as though the day has ended all too fast, and we might be overtaken by a sense of urgency in getting in all our pleas for God's favor. However, since we believe, because of God's nature, that our outcome will be good, the service is chanted in a confident, happy melody. We make our last confessions, but the focus of our prayers shifts to acknowledgment of God's grace. All previous requests to write us in the Book of Life are replaced by requests that we be sealed in it.

As *Neilah* ends, the congregation joins the *khazzan* in the final declaration of faith: The *Shema* is chanted just once (repetition might be misconstrued as implying there is more than one God). We repeat the rejoinder phrase, "*Barukh Shem kavod . . .*" three times, emphasizing God's rule in the past, present, and future. And seven times we recite "*Adoshem, Hu HaElohim*" (The Lord, only He is God [I Kings 18:39]), escorting the Holy Presence back through the seven heavens (which God revealed to Israel at Mount Sinai to prove that there was no other God but Himself). In loud voice, the congregation is proclaiming its loyalty to God and affirming that He and He alone is the force behind nature and history.

One blast of the *shofar* concludes the service. It recalls the proclamation of the Jubilee (*Yovel*), which was announced by *shofar* on Yom Kippur every fiftieth year (Leviticus 8–10). When we lost track of the start of the cycle, it became customary to blow the *shofar* annually in commemoration. But the symbol of the Jubilee holds for every year, for it emphasizes freedom from past burdens and the opportunity for everyone to start over again (Leviticus 25:10–17).

It is greeted with a rousing round of *L'shanah haba'ah b'Yerushalayim*, next year in Jerusalem, the goal of Jews throughout our historical and spiritual wanderings.

At this point, everyone is anxious to rush home from synagogue, or to the homes of friends or relatives, to break the fast. But there are still the regular evening service (*Ma'ariv*), *Havdalah*, and the blessing of the new moon, which had been put off until now. Altogether, they add about fifteen minutes to your time in synagogue. As great rabbis have pointed out, the way you take leave of someone is as important as the way you greet that person. Think about the awe and anticipation you felt just twenty-five hours ago. Think about everything you have meditated on during the day, all you tried to accomplish. Think about in Whose presence you stood all these hours, what you requested, and what you promised. And think about others in the congregation who want to finish the worship. In this context, you will probably be reluctant to disrespectfully race out of the sanctuary.

199

Conclusions

Havdalah

The ceremony of separation between holy and ordinary time that takes place after every Shabbat is slightly different on Yom Kippur. We omit the benediction over spices. (According to tradition, on the Sabbath each Jew receives an extra soul—*neshamah yeterah*—which leaves at the end of the day. The spices are to revive us from this loss. Since Yom Kippur is a day of afflicting our souls, unless the Day of Atonement coincides with the Sabbath, we don't receive extra souls and therefore do not need the spices.) And since the flame we use to kindle the *Havdalah* candle has been burning all day, we do not use the Sabbath's benediction over new light (recalling the fire Adam made for the first time at the conclusion of the first Shabbat). Instead, we say a blessing about the permissibility of using fire again.

New Moon

In a happy mood impossible until this point in *Tishrei*, because of the impending judgment that had been ahead of us, we may now properly bless the moon (*kiddush lavanah*). Some congregations go outside to do so.

Mitzvot

In the tradition that completion of one *mitzvah* leads to performing another ("They go from strength to strength" [Psalms 84:8]), and since Yom Kippur is supposed to awaken us to more devoted living, pious Jews often precede or interrupt the breaking of the fast by erecting at least the first posts of their *sukkot*. It expresses readiness for the next holiday, to emerge from the internal focus and take positive action in the outside world (see next chapter).

WHERE DO WE BEGIN?—PREPARATION

As one of our scholars of a previous century pointed out, if you knew that you faced sentencing from the king of your country, all your attention, energies, and efforts would be directed toward defending yourself. Consumed with worry about the outcome, and knowing that you had to do everything possible to influence it, you would take a leave of absence from your job and refuse to be distracted by other matters.

Obviously, he was making a point about being in anticipation of facing your life-or-death verdict from God. It behooved everyone, he suggested, to cut back on normal activities in order to spend time alone, devoted to self-examination, focusing psychological and emotional energy and physical activity on the purpose of the holidays.

Spiritual Readiness

The day of sentencing is the last of the forty-day period that begins on the first of *Elul*. Since all the preparation for Rosh Hashanah, and the new year itself, is preparation for Yom Kippur, it will be helpful for you to review the section on preparation in the previous chapter. The mood, special prayers, extreme care in carrying out *mitzvot*, and caution in not transgressing them continue during the intervening days of repentance as we focus more keenly on the specific improvements we can make. And of course, you cannot be ready to engage in the significance of Yom Kippur if you have not done *teshuvah* (see chapter on Rosh Hashanah).

A time of mending existing relationships, it is considered unsuitable for starting new ones, positive or negative, so weddings and lawsuits are avoided during the ten days.

Tzedakah

Since charity is one of the three ways (with prayer and repentance) of "averting the evil decree," or influencing the balance in your favor, the period prior to the Day of Atonement is particularly auspicious for donating to worthy causes. Synagogues usually have *tzedakah* boxes to accept contributions, but today you are likely to be solicited by mail or phone by any number of deserving and needy social service organizations in the Jewish community. This is a good time to pay any outstanding pledges made in the past year.

Fast of *Gedaliah*

The third of *Tishrei* (or the fourth, if the third is a Sabbath) marks the murder of the last Jewish governor of Israel on the New Year after the destruction of the First Temple. (The sun-up to sun-down fast is postponed since Rosh Hashanah is a festival, when fasting is prohibited.) One of the four days of mourning connected with loss of Jewish sovereignty in the Land of Israel, it falls at this point coincidentally but conveniently shares in its liturgy and readings from *Tanakh* the messages of this holiday season: sin, repentance, and forgiveness (for full explanation, see chapter on Tisha B'Av).

Shabbat *Shuvah*

The Sabbath between Rosh Hashanah and Yom Kippur is named Sabbath of Penitence after the prophetic reading for the day (Hosea 14). Its first words, "*Shuvah Yisrael*," exhort Israel to "Return . . . unto the Lord your God." Before it was standard for rabbis in Eastern Europe to deliver a *drash* (sermon) at every Sabbath morning service, it was customary to do so on this day. Lengthy and impassioned talks on the related topic of *teshuvah* were supposed to be given in a spirit of encouragement, without attacking or disparaging the congregation. While there's no guarantee of the tone of a sermon today, you can be sure the topic will be the same.

Reconciliation

Since admitting wrongdoing and asking forgiveness before God cannot atone for any transgressions you have made in relation to another person, it is essential to ask forgiveness of anyone you may have hurt during the previous year. As with our confessions in synagogue, we don't always realize that we have done something wrong and may not recognize that a word or an act has in fact hurt another person. Often this is the case with people who are closest to us—spouses, children, parents, siblings, friends. Therefore, in addition to making amends with anyone who was harmed in a specific way, it is customary to apologize to those nearest and dearest by saying "please forgive me for anything I might have done in the past year to cause you any pain." It can be uncomfortable at first, especially if you don't normally express such sentiments, but it can make you feel incredibly close to those whose pardon you seek. (This is a model of how you can feel when you ask God to pardon you.)

When someone asks you for forgiveness, you are supposed to grant it.

Kapparot

Though largely abandoned today, this atonement ritual can still be witnessed in religious enclaves like Williamsburg in Brooklyn and Mea Shearim, Israel, and in many *Sephardi* neighborhoods. It is one of the strangest ceremonies you will see in Judaism, one that smacks so much of superstition and pagan rite that it has generated much opposition and has been eliminated among most Orthodox as well as Conservative and Reform communities.

For the authentic ritual, a male takes a rooster and a female a hen. After tying its legs together, the person (who does the ritual for him-/herself or on behalf of others) swings the chicken over his/her head while reciting "this is my (our) exchange, this is my (our) substitute. This rooster (chicken) will go to its death while I (we) will enter and proceed to a good long life and to peace." The fowl is then killed and given to charity or eaten in the pre-fast meal and its value donated to charity. Leaving its innards for other birds to feed on is considered a *mitzvah*.

Palestinian Arabs sold so many white fowl for the ritual to the Jews that they called the day the Festival of Chickens. That bird may have been chosen simply because it was the most readily available domestic animal. (Since the ceremony entails sacrifice, in the absence of the Temple, any creature that had been suitable for the altar is forbidden.) Fish were sometimes used, but in some cultures, chickens carried additional significance: The Persians believed the rooster had magical powers to eliminate evil spirits (it drove them away with its daybreak crowing). The word for the bird in Hebrew, *gever*, also means man, giving the substitution added meaning. (In modern Hebrew, *gever* is Mr., *giveret*, Mrs.)

Often today money is used in place of the chicken and then donated. The ceremony, which a parent can do for a child, or one member of the family for others, can take place anytime from two days before Yom Kippur until the morning of Yom Kippur Eve, but the preferred time is just after dawn that day.

Remission of Vows

Those who did not annul their vows the day before Rosh Hashanah often do so on the afternoon prior to Yom Kippur, even though the communal annulment will take place with *Kol Nidrei*. The remission covers only vows of a personal nature that affect the person him-/herself.

Personal

Cemetery

Though it is customary to visit the graves of one's deceased relatives during *Elul*, some people go to the graves of pious individuals just before Yom Kippur starts.

Stimulant Withdrawal

It is a good idea to begin to cut down on consumption of chocolate and caffeinated drinks like coffee, tea, and cola at least a week prior to *Tishrei* 10. The headaches some people experience on Yom Kippur result from caffeine withdrawal and can be avoided if you wean yourself from the stimulant gradually.

Mitzvot

Prior to the holiday, it is appropriate to pay all outstanding debts. In accordance with performing extra *mitzvot* to appear more meritorious on Yom Kippur, in the week before the holiday, many people purchase the *etrog* and *lulav* they will need for Sukkot, the next holiday.

Body

Before *Minkhah*, which is held early on Yom Kippur to give people ample time for the prefast meal, religious men immerse in the *mikvah* for the sake of purity.

Tickets

If you are not a member of a synagogue and plan to attend services, be sure to arrange for tickets in advance.

WHAT ARE WE SUPPOSED TO DO?— *HALAKHAH*

Rest on the Sabbath of Sabbaths

All thirty-nine categories of labor prohibited on Shabbat are also forbidden on the Day of Atonement. That means the restrictions on carrying objects outside and food preparation that are lifted for other *yom tovim* are still in effect on Yom Kippur. The laws that apply to other festivals—rejoicing, caring for the stranger and needy, wearing clean clothing—all apply (see "*Halakhah*" in chapter on Pesakh). Ac-

cording to the principle that we are supposed to add from the profane to the sacred, all forbidden acts are to be stopped shortly before twilight and are prohibited until after nightfall.

The day is additionally sanctified through the five "afflictions" or self-denials we follow.

Fasting

We abstain from satisfying our hunger and thirst based on two Torah commandments: "You shall afflict your souls" (Leviticus 16:29) and "For any soul which is not afflicted on that day will be cut off" (Leviticus 23:29). The rabbis ascertained the connection between affliction and fasting from additional verses in the Bible (Leviticus 23:30; Deuteronomy 8:3).

Females over the age of twelve and males over the age of thirteen are to abstain from food or beverage for the duration of the holiday. Children under the age of nine are not allowed to fast and from nine until the age of religiously recognized maturity should gradually learn to forego eating or drinking (usually by postponing breakfast for longer and longer periods of time).

If a doctor asserts that fasting could endanger your health, you need not fast. There is a famous story about a rabbi who insisted that his entire congregation eat on Yom Kippur during a cholera epidemic so that the worshippers would not lose strength and succomb to the disease. If any number of doctors state that fasting would not be harmful, and one doctor disagrees, or you yourself feel you must eat, you are supposed to eat.

A pregnant woman likewise determines if she must have food. During childbirth or within three days of giving birth, a woman does not fast. If she feels it is necessary, she can eat in the period within three to seven days after giving birth.

If you need to break the fast, you should try to do so by taking very small quantities, smaller than the size of a date, pausing between each piece, so that within nine minutes you will not have eaten more than the volume equivalent of three eggs. When life and health are at risk, whatever is needed for one's welfare is to be given, as necessary.

Other Self-Denial

The four additional forms of "affliction" (*inui*) practiced on Yom Kippur, although not specifically mandated in the Bible, were derived from its idea of a day of complete rest by the sages.

Washing

Prohibited for pleasure, cleansing yourself for hygienic purposes is permitted. If your hands or feet are mud-soiled, if you have to wipe a film out of your eyes upon rising in the morning, or if you are sick, you are allowed to wash. A bride within thirty days of marriage may wash her face. (In former times, the king was also permitted to wash his face.)

Anointing

The application of oil or cream is permissible only for medicinal purposes.

Marital Relations

A husband and wife must refrain from intimacy during the Day of Atonement.

Wearing Leather Shoes

After childbirth, a woman may put on leather shoes. Otherwise, shoes must be of some other material, such as canvas, rubber, plastic, or wood.

Ritual Purity

The laws that apply for Rosh Hashanah continue through the end of the period of atonement.

Prayers

Early-morning *selikhot* services begun in the week prior to Rosh Hashanah continue through Yom Kippur, as do the alterations in wording of prayers made for Rosh Hashanah. When Yom Kippur falls on Shabbat, the *Ashkenazim* recite *Avinu Malkeinu* only at the *Neilah* service. Otherwise, it is recited after each Day of Atonement service except *Minkhah*.

Viddui, the declaration of sins, is said three times a day between Rosh Hashanah and Yom Kippur, during *selikhot* recited before the morning service, *Minkhah*, and *Ma'ariv*. (The *Khabbad khasidim* say it once in *selikhot*, once during *Shakharit*, and once during *Minkhah*.) The number of repetitions corresponds to the Torah verse "forgiving iniquity, and transgression and sin" (Exodus 34:7). It also represents the three people who must serve as witnesses to the annulment of vows. (On the day of *Erev* Yom Kippur, it is said only once, at *Minkhah*.)

The *mitzvah* of confessing on *Erev* Yom Kippur is at nightfall. However, to ensure that you will enter the holiday in a state of repentance, you should confess before the prefast meal, in case the food and drink confuse you; you should confess after the meal in case you transgressed in any way during it; and you should also confess at the evening service, in case any wrongs were committed in the intervening time.

Conciliation

Since Yom Kippur cannot atone for transgressions between one person and another, everybody should make amends directly with the people involved by *Erev* Yom Kippur. If an injured party refuses to forgive, according to Jewish practice, the offender must apologize in front of three witnesses. If forgiveness is still refused, the offender is considered absolved (except if the injured is a teacher, in which case forgiveness cannot be requested too many times), and the person who refuses to grant the pardon after being asked three times is considered to be in the wrong.

Even if an injured party has died before you could seek a pardon, you must seek his/her absolution by confessing at his/her grave in front of ten witnesses.

Teshuvah

As Yom Kippur is the climax of the period of repentance and forgiveness for individuals and the community of Israel, everyone is obligated to do *teshuvah* and confess on the Day of Atonement.

WHAT OTHER THINGS DO PEOPLE DO?—CUSTOMS

Other Times and Places

Spiritual Preparation

Particularly conscientious prayer leaders used to go into seclusion for seven days after Rosh Hashanah, in order to improve their behavior and study the order of the service. In solitude, concentrating on holiness, they were like the high priest in Temple days. Extremely pious Bulgarian Jewish merchants sometimes gave their shop keys to non-Jews so that on Yom Kippur, they would be totally free of any everyday material concerns.

Paying Debts

In Libya, after morning services on *Erev* Yom Kippur, a community meal was served to the rich and poor. This was the time for people to pay all pledges made in synagogue during the previous year. Trustees sat in the courtyard at foliage-decorated tables as people passed by and made their donations to welfare institutions, for the *khazzan* and *shammash* of the synagogue. The afternoon before the start of the holiday was the time for the Eastern European Jews to make similar collections. Various fund-raising organizations would set out plates or *pushkehs* (collection boxes) at synagogue entrances, marked "clothing the naked," "feeding the hungry," "Talmud Torah" (Jewish education), and "Return to the Land of Israel." (Some also included plates for "call to the Torah" and a precursor to our "High Holy Day" tickets, "seat in the synagogue.")

Self-Punishment

Rarely seen today, from the time of Rashi (eleventh century) until earlier this century, older and pious Jews used to submit themselves to symbolic lashings (*malkot*). A common form of punishment at one time (even prescribed in the Torah for various offenses), on *Erev* Yom Kippur it was purely representational. The flogger, in Eastern Europe a poor man in the town, spread hay on the floor. The penitents, wearing their overcoats, would stretch out face down and say their *Ashamnu* confessions while the flogger delivered light, token blows using a leather strap and three times recited Psalms 78:38, beginning "For He is merciful and forgives iniquity." Each repetition of the verse consists of thirteen words, for a total of thirty-nine, the number of lashes formerly given to sentenced criminals. (In one of the Torah's instructions regarding flogging, it specifies that forty may be given [Deuteronomy 25:3]. But it was felt that if one received the full count prior to Yom Kippur, he might think he had eliminated all his wrongdoing, so the sages took away one lash to remind him he still had to improve.)

Light

During the Middle Ages, synagogues were ablaze with candles, set in lamps, boxes that had been filled with sand, and candelabras. Singing Psalms 97:11, "Light is sown for the righteous and gladness for the upright in heart," accompanied the kindling.

The candles were often prepared on *Tishrei* 8, the anniversary of the beginning of the dedication of Solomon's Temple, using wicks from cotton thread paced out in the cemetery. Each family had two candles that burned all day, one for the living, which usually was left at home, and one for the dead. Some-

times both were taken to synagogue, one for themselves, one for the deceased relatives, or one for body, one for the soul.

Dress

In Spanish-Portuguese synagogues in the United States, known for their upper-class decorum, the men carry Torah scrolls during *Kol Nidrei* dressed in formal evening clothes, including high silk hats (the attire also worn in British synagogues). They followed the opening service with special prayers for the government, the congregation, the two Torah carriers, the congregations that established America's first synagogues, Jerusalem, those held in captivity, those traveling, the sick, and uniquely, women, for the work they had done in preparing the white clothes for the *Sifrei Torah*, *Aron Hakodesh*, and *bimah*.

In another example of the similarity between Yom Kippur and a wedding day, the Libyans had their young boys dress in their best clothes and sing wedding songs in the synagogue courtyard.

Synagogue

During the *Mussaf* prostrations, paper or cloth, such as a *tallit*, kept the worshipper's body from coming into direct contact with the floor. (In Frankfurt until the fourteenth century, grass was strewn on the floor.) The custom developed when synagogue pavements were often stone, and outside the Temple, Jews had to take precautions not to appear to be following an idol, since other peoples worshipped stone (Leviticus 26:1).

When Libyans perform the priestly blessing, each head of a family extends his *tallit* over the heads of his children, including married sons, who place their hands on the heads of their sons as the blessing is said.

The Syrians allow anyone who wants to to come forward between *Minkhah* and the closing service to kiss the *Sifrei Torah* and ask forgiveness for any negligence he might have engaged in in relation to the sacred scrolls.

Break Fast

Sephardim sometimes break their fast with a light dairy meal, then put in the first nail of the *sukkah*, and follow by eating a heavy meat and vegetable soup. Afterward, it is customary to visit one's grandfather to receive a blessing for the new year.

In several *Sephardi* communities (Libya, Morocco, Bombay Bene Israel), the day following Yom Kippur was a holiday, *Yom Simkhat Kohein*, a day of rejoicing for the high priest. Like the high priest of Temple days, the *Kohanim* would celebrate with feasting, visits to friends and family, giving donations to the poor, and foregoing all work.

Eager to avoid slipping back into lax ways, people sometimes try to arise earlier than usual for morning prayers the day after Yom Kippur. Their synagogues might oblige by starting the services fifteen minutes prior to the normal time.

For Further Reading

Chagall, Bella. "Day of Atonement in Vitebsk, Russia." In BL, pp. 82–95, and *Yom Kippur* HA, pp. 179–186.

The evocative detailed account of preparation at home and synagogue on the holiday shares the emotion expressed by worshippers. Ages 10 and up.

Greeting

Prior to the start of Yom Kippur, we wish each other "*gemar khatimah tovah*" (may the final decree be good) and "*tzom kal*" (an easy fast). At the end of the day it is appropriate to say "*gut yom tov*" or "*khag samei'akh*" (happy holiday). *Sephardim* wish each other "*tizkeh leshanim*" (may you merit long life), to which the response is "*tizkeh vetikhyeh veta'arikh yomim*" (may you merit, live, and have length of days).

Dress

Sabbath clothes are appropriate for attending synagogue. Even more so than on Rosh Hashanah, it is customary to wear new clothes, especially white ones. Particularly in a traditional *shul*, you are likely to see many women in white dresses and a number of men other than the prayer leaders each wearing a *kittel*.

Although silver ornamentation on a *kittel* is acceptable since it is likened to white, gold is not, because it recalls the Golden Calf. (In eighteenth-century Eastern Europe, men replaced the rope ties of their robes with belts on silver buckles carrying a prayer, based on Leviticus 16:30, about being cleansed of sin.) For this reason (and humility), women are supposed to refrain from wearing gold and flashy jewelry in general.

Since leather shoes are forbidden people generally wear canvas beach shoes, sneakers (be careful in your choice, as most running and sports shoes are leather), even house slippers. People attending Conservative and Reform synagogues are generally less strict in observance of this restriction than those in more traditional synagogues.

What Is There to Eat?— Traditional Foods

Although we do not eat on Yom Kippur itself, several traditions apply for the pre- and post-fast meals.

Prefast

Even though there is no commandment to eat on the day prior to Yom Kippur (it is implied in conjunction with the one to fast, Leviticus 23:32), the sages asserted that anyone who does is considered by Torah to have fasted on both that day and the holiday itself. Eating before the fast not only gives us the energy to make it through the next day's fast but shows us that we serve God both by abstinence and by enjoyment of physical pleasures done in the proper spirit.

Our dining before Yom Kippur shows that we rejoice in our anticipated reunion with God. The self-denial we will shortly experience is merely a means to an end, not an end in itself and not a Jewish value. A Jewish life is not about other-worldly spirituality but about spiritual existence very much grounded in the physical world.

For this meal, *khallot* are often baked in the shape of wings, for the angels the Jews resemble on Yom Kippur (Isaiah 6:2), or ladders, on which we climb to higher spiritual levels. After the *motzi*, it is dipped in honey.

You want to guard against eating anything that will cause thirst, and most people like to eat lightly to ready their bodies to experience food deprivation. A customary meal begins with chicken soup (formerly made from the rooster or hen used for the *kapparot* ceremony), often served with *kreplakh*. These meat-filled dough pouches, also traditional for Purim and Hoshanah Rabbah, symbolize stern judgment (the meat) enveloped in mercy (the soft, flexible dough). Poultry, traditionally boiled, is the typical entree (although beef is all right as a substitute). It is customary to keep the food bland, because salt, pepper, and other spices will create the desire for water. Intoxicating drinks are to be avoided so that one's prayer is not affected, and we do not consume food and beverages containing caffeine, so that we will not later suffer the ill effects of deprivation.

Light, sweet vegetables and desserts, such as those typical for Rosh Hashanah, are also served.

Break Fast

A *midrash* relates that after the fast, a heavenly voice calls out "Go and eat your bread joyfully, drink your wine in good spirit, for the Lord has accepted your efforts" (Ecclesiastes 9:7). Based on this, and the custom of the high priest to make a feast upon his successful completion of the Yom Kippur service, the night following the Day of Atonement is considered a minor festival when it is appropriate to eat and drink. The synagogue usually provides a sip and a bite—juice and cookies or some plain cake—and then friends and families often join together for a breakfast meal. Although in some places it has been the custom to have a full dinner, it is more common today to eat a brunch-like dairy repast.

Do You Hear Music?—Songs to Sing

As is true for Rosh Hashanah, the music for this holiday is concentrated in the liturgy, some of it quite moving. Aside from the *Viddui*, a number of *piyyutim* and the entire *Avodah* (reenactment of Temple service) distinguish the Yom Kippur service from that of the new year. You will be able to pick up some of the melodies just by hearing them repeatedly in the synagogue, but as with Rosh Hashanah, you may feel more comfortable and be better able to participate if you become familiar with them in advance.

In addition to the prayers listed for Rosh Hashanah, requests that we be remembered, written and sealed in the Book of Life punctuate the service in the refrains "*Zakhreinu l'khayim*" (Remember us for Life) and "*Ukh'tov l'khayim tovim*" (And inscribe for a good life). Also significant is the proclamation "*U'teshuvah, u'tefillah, u'tzedakah ma'avirin et roah hag'zeirah*" (But repentance, prayer, and charity remove the evil of the decree), recognition that by our own actions we can put ourselves in a favorable position.

Other tunes to learn are those for "*Ashamnu*" (We have become guilty . . . , the short confession; "*Anu Amekha*" (We are Your people), a summation of the entire Yom Kippur process, based on verses from the Bible, phrases of endearment expressing the intimate connection between Israel and God, and recognition of our failings; "*Shema Koleinu*" (Hear our voice), a prayer that we have the will to return to God; "*V'al Kulam*" (and for all), the *Viddui* refrain asking God to forgive us for all our transgressions; "*Ya'aleh Takhanumeinu*" (May our entreaty rise), a prayer that our prayers go to heaven at nightfall and arrive before God's throne at dawn so that our salvation and reconciliation will come at dusk; "*Salakhti*" (For-

given), the verdict we hope to get from God; "*Ki Ninneh KaHomer*" (Like clay in the hand of the potter), showing our submission to God; and "*L'shanah haba'ah b'Yerushalayim*" (Next year in Jerusalem), the age-old wish of Jews in exile.

Among the *Sephardim*, "*El Nora Eilah*" (God that does wonderously), chanted just before *Neilah*, is a popular tune whose liveliness indicates the confidence of worshippers at that point in the day.

For Further Listening

There are some wonderful recordings of the Yom Kippur liturgy, including "*Kol Nidrei*," performed by Max Bruch, Jan Pierce, or Richard Tucker, and other noted cantors singing selections from the Days of Awe services. A librarian or Jewish bookstore manager can direct you to what is available (or check mail order sources in Appendix C).

High Holidays and Sukkot Melodies. Cedarhurst, NY: Board of Jewish Education of Greater New York and Tara Publications.

The tunes for the major parts of the services are included in the booklet (with words transliterated into English) and on the companion tape.

What Tales Are Told?—Stories to Read

Major Jewish writers from the Middle Ages to modern times have created wonderfully inspirational and philosophic writings about Yom Kippur.

Poet Judah Halevi's *The Kuzari* (A Book of Argument in Defense of a Despised Religion), philosopher Moses Maimonides' *Moreh Nevukim* (Guide for the Perplexed), talmudist Jonah ben Abraham Gerondi's *Shaare Teshuvah* (Gates of Repentance), and scholar Abraham ben Hiyya's *Hegon Hanefesh* (Meditation of the Soul) treat aspects of the Day of Atonement and have influenced philosophical and ethical literature since the medieval period.

Tremendous insight into the significance of the Days of Awe is provided in the many tales told of and by the *khasidi* rabbis. Like the movement's founder, Rabbi Israel Baal Shem Tov (1700–1760), who saw only good in people, and the compassionate Rabbi Levi Isaac of Berditchev (1740–1809), they not only submissively prayed to God but *demanded* that He remit their sins. Their teachings demonstrate a dynamic interaction with God, rather than a once-a-year formal or detached relationship, we can aspire to on Yom Kippur.

Solomon Ibn Gabirol and, in more recent years, Israel Zangwill composed poems. Sholom Aleichem, Martin Buber, Isaac Loeb Peretz, Elie Weisel, and Samuel J. Agnon are among the writers who reflect some aspect of the holiday in their stories.

FOR FURTHER READING

Folktales

"The Golden Calf." In CT, pp. 133–137.

Fantastic elements from *midrash* enhance this expanded version of Israel's sin at Mount Sinai.

"I Am A Jew." In TS, pp. 125–129.

When a tenth man is needed for a *minyan*, the rabbi brings in someone who long ago had abandoned Judaism but learns it is never too late to rejoin the community and repent.

Ish-Kishor, Sulamith. "At the Beginning of the World." In *Heaven on the Sea and Other Stories*. New York: Bloch Publishing Company, 1924, pp. 57–61.

As the Hebrew letters present their cases to God for being the first letter of Creation, their natures are discovered. Ages 7–11.

Kranzler, Gershon. "Maftir Jonah." In *Jewish Youth Companion*. Brooklyn: Merkos L'Inyonei Chinuch, 1957, pp. 73–78.

On Shabbat *Shuvah* in a small town in Poland, a congregation gets the message that salvation doesn't come to those best able to pay for Torah honors but to people who honor those less fortunate.

Levin, Meyer. "The Boy's Song." In Yom Kippur HA, pp. 247–249.

An entire congregation's supplications are accepted only because of the sincerity of the musical prayers of a shepherd boy who can express himself only with a flute. (There are variations of this tale, including "The Shepherd's Pipe" in JF, p. 396, and "The Yom Kippur Flute" in CT, pp. 475–477.)

Nissan, Mindel. "The Open Makhzor." In *The Complete Story of Tishrei*. Brooklyn: Merkos L'Inyonei Chinuch, 1957, pp. 121–125.

The Baal Shem Tov story about a boy uneducated in things Jewish finding his way back to his heritage teaches what prayer is all about and how anyone who has trouble with it can get help. (There are numerous variations of this story, including "If Only I Could Pray" in TS, pp. 105–106; "The Prayerbook" by Martin Buber in Yom Kippur HA, pp. 243–247; "The Boy Who Gave God The Whole Prayerbook" in JF, p. 395; and "A Mother's Prayerbook" in CT, p. 560.)

"Repentance." In TS, pp. 115–117.

After he observes Yom Kippur on the wrong day because he was isolated, a poor Jew learns the importance of living in a Jewish community and asking for help from others.

"The Tailor's Reckoning with God." In JF, p. 393.

A simple tailor confesses all his transgressions before God, but he also reminds God of all the ills He brought to him and his family. As the tailor forgives and forgets, the story demonstrates the wonderful dynamic involvement Judaism believes is possible to have with God.

Zeligs, Dorothy. "The Tear of Repentance." In Yom Kippur HA, pp. 350–351.

An angel searching Earth for the most precious thing in the world finds it as a man decides not to go through with an evil act.

Other Stories

Aleichem, Sholom. "The Day Before Yom Kippur: Sketches of Disappearing Types." In FT, pp. 319–328.

Three of the "cruelest" men in the village change their gruff disrespectful ways and humble themselves to ask forgiveness from everyone on *Erev* Yom Kippur. Ages 10–14.

Frishman, David. "Three Who Ate." In Yom Kippur HA, pp. 256–262.

With great trepidation but strong conviction, the rabbis insist their congregation eat on the holiest day of the year to avoid falling victim to the cholera epidemic that was claiming thousands of lives.

Weilerstein, Sadie Rose. "How K'tonton Was Forgiven on Yom Kippur." In KT, pp. 76–80.

K'tonton feels so badly about a situation he has created that causes problems for another being that he learns he has to admit his mistake. Ages 3–8.

Books

Cohen, Barbara. *First Fast*. New York: UAHC Press, 1987.

A wager between a younger and older boy before Yom Kippur teaches them about honor, honesty, and integrity as a difficult choice must be made. Ages 5–9.

———. *Yussel's Prayer: A Yom Kippur Story*. New York: Lothrop, Lee and Shepard Books, 1981.

This is a retelling of the classic story of the uneducated boy who, with his simple and novel way of praying to God, wins acceptance of the prayers of the insincere congregation. Ages 5–9.

Kimmel, Eric A. *Days of Awe: Stories for Rosh Hashanah and Yom Kippur*. New York: Viking, 1991.

The three incredibly moving stories in this book show us the key concept of the holiday season in simple everyday life. Adapted from traditional sources and conveying the awe and beauty of the times, the stories deal with charity, prayer, and repentance. Ages 8–12.

SUKKOT

Sukkot (soo-kote'; Yiddish: sook'-us): Feast of Booths. Observed *Tishrei* **15**–*Tishrei* **22** (fall; late September–mid-October).

    Hoshanah Rabbah (hoe-shah-nah' rah-bah'; Yiddish: hoe-shah'-nuh rah'-buh): Day of the Willows. Observed on *Tishrei* **21**.

    Shemini Atzeret (shmin'-ee aht-tzehr'-rette; Yiddish: shmin'-ee aht-ser'ress): Eighth Day of Assembly. Observed on *Tishrei* **22**.

    Simkhat Torah (sim-khat' toe-rah'; Yiddish: sim-khus' toe'-ruh): Rejoicing of the Torah. Observed on *Tishrei* **23**.

Sukkot, the longest, last, and for a long time, the greatest of the festivals specified by Torah, and the third of the pilgrimages (after Pesakh and Shavuot), has both seasonal and historic significance. It begins and ends with the fulfillment of God's promises to bring us to a bountiful Land after years of wandering and to return us to it after years of exile. As a celebration of the rewards of individual and national efforts for material and spiritual achievement, it is considered the most joyous time of the year.

ORIGINS: WHY WE CELEBRATE SUKKOT

WHERE DID IT ALL BEGIN?— HISTORIC FOUNDATION

A Torah Law

When the Israelites were still wandering in the Sinai, they were given holidays for the future. Among them was a fall festival, one of the three pilgrimages (*shalosh regalim*; see also chapters on Pesakh and Shavuot) to be celebrated after the Israelites had settled and successfully cultivated the Land. Entries in four successive books of Torah gradually reveal its nature and significance.

Khag HaAsif (Festival of Ingathering) was to take place once the produce of the vineyards and product of the threshing rooms was collected (Exodus 23:14–17; 34:22). Beginning on the fifteenth of the seventh month, this *Khag Adonai* (Festival of God) would last seven days, the first a sacred occasion when no work was to be done. The Israelites were to take the "product of hadar trees, branches of palm trees, boughs of leafy trees and willows of the brook" (later called the four species) and rejoice with them before God.

Then another dimension was added as a "law for all time": For the duration of the festival the Israelites were to live in booths (*sukkot*) "so that future generations will know that I made the Israelite people live in *sukkot* when I brought them out of the land of Egypt, I the Lord your God" (Leviticus 23:39–43).

Rabbi Akiva explained *sukkot* literally as physical structures that protected the Israelites from the sun. (Many dispute his opinion, saying if anything, the wandering Jews used tents, not open-roofed sheds, the materials for which would not have been available in the desert. Secular historians claim that the booths originated later, adapted for ritual either from autumn pagan ceremonies or from the shelters constructed in the fields by farmers who were harvesting their crops. Rabbi Eleazar provided the widely accepted interpretation: The booths were the Clouds of Glory that surrounded the Israelites on their journey, providing protection and guidance. In other words, they formed a spiritual construct.

Another sacred occasion was to follow the week, a day called Shemini (eighth) Atzeret (solemn assembly) (Leviticus 23:36). Not completely understood, *atzeret* (also used to designate the last day of Passover [Deuteronomy 16:8]) comes from the root *atzar* for "restrain" and literally means to tarry or hold back. A *midrash* explains that as the children of Israel are about to take leave of God after having rejoiced with Him for a week, God, like the parent of a child about to end a cherished visit, says "It is difficult to have you leave me. Stay another day." As one greater in number than the perfect seven, the next day of the holiday (the eighth, beyond the period needed to create the world) represents a day after time—eternity—suggesting the longed-for messianic age.

Each of the eight days had its own complement of sacrifices, beginning with thirteen and decreasing by one each day through seven (a total of seventy). One sacrifice was made on the eighth day (Numbers 29:12–28).

In Deuteronomy's reiteration of festivals, this one is called Sukkot to stress its connection with our history. We are enjoined not just to celebrate the "Festival for God" for His agricultural and other blessings but to rejoice along with our entire families, our servants, the Levite (priest), the stranger, the fatherless, and the widowed in the community (16:13–15). The passage that follows this instruction, commanding the appointment of judges and delivery of justice, emphasizes the relationship between Israel's ethical behavior and prosperity in the Land: "Justice, justice you shall pursue, that you may thrive and occupy the Land that the Lord your God is giving you" (Deuteronomy 16:20).

The connection with judgment also rests in the placement of Sukkot, not only at the end of the annual festival cycle that starts with Pesakh but at the resolution of the assessment defined by the Days of Awe. According to *midrash*, the protective clouds provided shortly after the Exodus disappeared when the Golden Calf emerged. Following the repentance and forgiveness of the first Yom Kippur, when the people began constructing the Tabernacle that was to be God's temporary dwelling place in the desert—indicating that they wanted Him to live with them—the clouds returned to provide temporary shelter for the Israelites in the desert, indicating God's renewed embrace of them.

In the Land and Off It

The specifics of the Jewish harvest festival were designed to protect the Israelites from the pagan influences they would encounter once they entered Canaan. While heathens worshipped nature itself, the Jews were to worship the Creator and Renewer of nature. While the pagans celebrated with excess and debauchery, the Israelite pilgrims were to focus on the moral significance of the festivities.

The purpose of rejoicing was not sensual abandon but to honor and thank God for His blessings, spread good fortune, and act with sensitivity. (The oddly placed admonition following the commandments of Sukkot to "not seethe a kid in its mother's milk" [Exodus 23:19; 34:26]—fundamental in our practice of *kashrut*—was included here, as Maimonides pointed out, to eliminate the "revolting custom" of serving such dishes at pagan harvest festivals—revolting because they mixed death, the slaughter of an animal, with new life, the sustaining milk.)

On the other hand, properly directed joy was not to be hampered at this culmination of the spiritual (repentance and renewal), agricultural (harvest), and historic (successful settlement of Israel) growth. Three times the Torah commands us to experience elation in connection with the holiday: "You shall rejoice before the Lord your God seven days" (Leviticus 23:40); "You shall rejoice in your festival" (Deuteronomy 16:14); and "You shall have nothing but joy" (Deuteronomy 16:15).

Although Torah gave it the same status as the other pilgrimages, Sukkot became the predominant agricultural celebration. Reference to *HeKhag*—The Festival—only meant Sukkot, and the biblical books covering the period of Israel's independent kingdom mention this holiday more than any others. Having finished their work for the year, the peasant pilgrims did not have to rush home to tend crops and with peace of mind *could* tarry in Jerusalem. Consequently, the festival became known as *Zeman Simkhateinu*, the Season of Our Rejoicing.

Even before there was a Temple in Jerusalem (the designated site of festivals before God), the Israelites made pilgrimages to sanctuaries in other locales, such as Shiloh (Judges 21:19–21; I Samuel 1:3). When Solomon completed his Temple (955 B.C.E.) the very first observance held there was celebration of Sukkot, with which the dedication coincided. The focal point for pilgrimage shifted to the capital, and within a few centuries, provincial altars were abolished.

Getting everyone away from local pagan harvest rites to a common Israelite celebration gave the religious leaders at least a fighting chance to appropriately direct the level of joy, although being in the holiest place in the kingdom was still no guarantee. Two hundred years after Solomon's reign, the prophets Isaiah, Amos, and Hosea observed that the overzealous pilgrims marching in sacred procession, singing hymns, and playing musical instruments in praise of God often overindulged, creating the atmosphere of a bacchanalia. The prophets' protests about the drunkenness and disorderly behavior did not stop the Jews. Exile did.

During their sojourn in Babylon (beginning in the sixth century B.C.E.), Sukkot was suspended. It was, after all, a holiday tied to the Israelites' territorial sovereignty and the Land's agricultural abundance. Without them, there was not much reason to celebrate.

When the displaced returned to Palestine in the next century, they enthusiastically embraced the Torah commandments about Sukkot that were read to them on Rosh Hashanah by Ezra. The newly motivated Israelites ran out to get olive, pine, myrtle, palm, and other leafy branches for construction of their temporary shelters, which they set in every available space, public and private. Nehemiah observed that "the whole community that returned from captivity made and dwelled in booths" (8:17), which they had not done since the generation of Joshua, the first to inhabit the Land. (He may have been referring to the extent of celebration or use of certain materials rather than the ritual of booths itself.)

Even though the Jews were back on their own ground, the rabbis recognized the need to refocus this land-oriented festival. As with other annual events, Sukkot was separated from its physical aspects of agriculture, nature, and the seasons. Instead, its religious, moral, and nationalistic content was stressed.

Torah had provided a means for spiritual rejuvenation of the landed Jewish nation, at least once every seven years (Deuteronomy 31:10–13). On the second day of Sukkot at the end of each sabbatical year, all the people were to gather for a public reading of Deuteronomy, the Torah book that reviews the laws of Israel. The priests blew trumpets throughout Jerusalem to summon all, including women and particularly children, who would be influenced by what they heard for the rest of their lives. Surrounded by the populace, the king sat on a large wooden platform erected in the Temple's Women's Court and read aloud. In reviewing their responsibilities and duties, this ceremony, called *Hockheil* (gathering), was a source of inspiration for the assembled.

Second Temple

After the connection to the Land had been minimized and Pesakh overtook Sukkot as the greatest Jewish holiday, Sukkot retained its joyousness and appeal. As described in Flavius Josephus' *Jewish Antiquities* (which includes reports of Sukkot celebrations in particular years) and Talmud (which in addition to references scattered throughout has a tractate, *Sukkah*, devoted to the holiday), pilgrims came from throughout the Land of Israel and every Jewish community in the world. Gathering in regional centers for the arduous trip, in colorful caravans they set out by chariot, donkey, camel, boat (as far as the Mediterranean shore), and most often on foot (as the great Rabbi Hillel is said to have done from Babylon, a journey of two weeks). Although the commandment obligates only men, entire peasant households traveled.

Once in Jerusalem, which was festive in garlands of olive, palm, and willow branches, fragrant with fruits and flowers, they participated in prayers, hymns, and singing and watched religious processions in the Temple. The four species (definitively identified through Oral Tradition as palm, willow, and myrtle bound together into a *lulav*, and an *etrog* [citron]) were now part of the ritual: Each day of Sukkot, the priests, holding the *lulav* and *etrog* in hand, marched around the altar, which had been adorned with freshly cut willow branches. As they circled, they recited a psalm asking God to "please save us" (*Hoshiah na*).

Simkhat Beit Hashoavah

At this most joyous season of the year, with all the electric anticipation along the caravan trails, the stirring ceremonies, and the lively singing and feasting, the epitome of celebration took place surrounding a water ritual: the Rejoicing (*Simkhat*) at the Place of (*Beit*) the Water Drawing (*Hashoavah*).

Every day of the year, after the sacrifice was burned, an offering of wine was poured on the altar. During Sukkot, there was also a water libation (*nisukh hamayim*). Some have suggested that it was a folk rite, an inducement for rain made by pouring out water at the season's onset, transformed by the rabbis into a symbolic Temple ritual.

Each morning of Sukkot, the priests went to the pool of Siloah (Silwan) near Jerusalem to fill a golden flask. *Shofar* blasts greeted their arrival at the Temple's Water Gate. They then ascended and poured the water so that it flowed over the altar simultaneously with wine from another bowl. When the priest was about to pour the water, the people shouted "Raise your hand!" because of an incident that occurred in a previous year: The high priest Alexander Jannaeus (103–76 B.C.E.) showed contempt for the rite by spilling the water at his feet, a transgression for which worshippers threw their citrons at him.

The pelted priest had demonstrated his alliance with the Sadducees, who literally followed Torah and only what was specifically in Torah. (Explained as an oral instruction given to Moses at Sinai, this water rite was not mentioned in The Five Books.) The deliriously happy celebration connected with the water drawing developed when the Pharisees (who believed in the Oral Tradition and interpretation of Torah and gave us the rabbinic Judaism we know today) triumphed over them in the first century.

Based on Isaiah's promise "With joy shall you draw water out of the wells of salvation" (12:3), rejoicing began at the end of the first day and took place every night except Shabbat. Talmud recorded that "one who had never witnessed the Rejoicing at the Place of the Water Drawing had never seen true joy in his life." (Although the celebration was for the *libation* that would be made the next morning, it was named for the preparation for the ritual—the water drawing—which the rabbis said showed that getting ready was sometimes of greater merit than the *mitzvah* itself because of its positive effect on the person doing it.)

Talmud describes the festivities in detail, from the lighting of immense candelabrum set in the Temple courtyard (each holding gallons of oil and fit with wicks made from priests' worn-out vestments), which generated such intense light that they illuminated every courtyard in the city. A Levite orchestra of flutes, trumpets, harps, and cymbals accompanied torchlight processions, and men who had earned the capacity for real spiritual joy through their purity, character, and scholarship danced ecstatically to the hand-clapping, foot-stomping, and hymn-singing crowds.

We do not imagine our distinguished sages as acrobats and tumblers, but they were often agile physically as well as mentally: Rabbi Simon ben Gamaliel juggled eight lighted torches and raised himself into a handstand on two fingers, a gymnastic feat no one else could master. Others juggled eight knives, eight glasses of wine, or eight eggs before leaders and dignitaries.

At dawn, as the rejoicing subsided, the priests enacted what some have identified as the transformation of another folk rite, one to rekindle a diminishing sun approaching the autumnal equinox. With trumpet blasts, the *Kohanim* descended the steps to the Women's Court, marched to the Eastern Gate, turned their faces west to the Temple, and proclaimed, "Our fathers who were in this place stood with their backs to the Temple and their faces eastward and worshipped the sun, but our eyes are unto the Lord" (based on Ezekiel 8:16).

Seventh Day

During the Temple service at the end of Sukkot week, the priests' procession circled the willow-adorned altar seven times instead of once. Each time they recited a refrain of *Hoshiah na*. At the conclusion of the seventh circle, they struck the willows—the branches of trees associated with life-giving water since they thrive near rivers and brooks—on the ground around the altar, an unexplained custom that was possibly another rain rite.

The sacrifices made throughout the week—a total of seventy—were understood to represent the seventy nations that then existed in the world. Their well-being, like Israel's, depended on whether or not they would receive the rain needed for food supplies. Blessings like rain were understood as rewards for proper behavior (Deuteronomy 11:13–15). (In his vision of messianic times, Zekhariah presents lack of rain as punishment for the nations that fail to make pilgrimage to Jerusalem on Sukkot to worship God, which would show that they accept His sovereignty [14:16]. This prophecy, and those of Isaiah and Micah calling on all nations to show their acceptance of God's sovereignty by going to His Temple—combined with the connection between Sukkot and fulfillment, the ultimate being messianic redemption—encouraged many proselytes to join the pilgrims in Jerusalem.)

Therefore, the final day of the festival, when the last sacrifices were offered on behalf of the other nations, was identified as the occasion when the earth is judged regarding replenishment of water, and consequently, when mankind's fate, collectively and individually, is sealed. (Rabbinic literature identifies this *Yom Darvata*, Day of the Willow, as *Yom Hakhitum*, Day of Sealing, an extension of Yom Kippur.) Striking the willows then had the added connotation of casting away of sin or symbolizing the thrashings one would receive in punishment for sin.

Shemini Atzeret

The one set of sacrifices made on the closing day of the festival season was for Israel, which all week had placed concern for others above self-interest.

A prayer for rain was included in the day's supplications, and at the evening services, the direction in which the smoke from the sacrificial fire wafted was taken as an omen. If it blew north, the poor would gratefully anticipate a good year, because it indicated a wet season, when crops would be plentiful. Blowing south, indicating a dry year, was heralded by the rich, who would earn higher prices for limited supplies. West portended famine, and east was read as good for all.

Post-Temple

Sukkot changed little after the destruction of the Second Temple and, despite our extended exile, remained the most joyous of Torah festivals. People continued to build booths. In remembrance of the Temple, during the first century Rabbi Yokhanan ben Zakkai instructed that ceremonies using the four species be performed every day of the week except on Shabbat, even though it was a biblical commandment only for the first. (Leviticus 23:40 says to take the four on the first day, and rejoice with them before God—which meant only in the Temple—on all seven.)

Though it sounds extreme, *midrash* includes the *lulav* and *etrog* along with circumcision, study of Torah, and eating *matzah* as a religious obligation for which we are to be prepared to struggle and die. An Aramaic letter on papyrus, sent before Sukkot 134 C.E. by the Jewish military commander (and found among the Dead Sea documents) attests to the great effort of Bar Kokhba and his soldiers to obtain sets of the four species during the Hadrianic persecutions of Jews remaining in Palestine. (Providing for soldiers to fulfill their religious duty even in the midst of military campaigns has also been done for the Israel Defense Forces throughout modern Israel's history.)

As symbols of a revived Jewish state, the *lulav* and *etrog* were depicted on coins of the Bar Kokhba period (as they had been on the first coins minted by a Jewish nation, under Simon the Hasmonean [see chapter on Khanukah]). For centuries they were popular decorations, engraved on ritual items and patterned into floor mosaics in ancient synagogues, among them the fifth-century Mount Carmel and sixth-century Beit Alfa. (The *lulav* even became important for the Christians, who adopted it for their Palm Sunday rite.)

The willow ceremonies were temporarily discontinued, then established for one day, in post-talmudic terms called Hoshanah Rabbah (the many *hoshanah*s —a contraction of *hoshiah na*—or "The Great Salvation"). With prayer the accepted replacement for sacrifice, and the scripture-reading table (*bimah*), like the dining table at home (both sanctified by words of Torah), recognized as the stand-in for the Temple altar, the processions and beating of the willows eventually resumed. During the Middle Ages, customs of Yom Kippur such as dressing the Torah scrolls in white vestments and the cantor's wearing of a *kittel* were adopted for Hoshanah Rabbah, this final day of judgment.

For the second day of Shemini Atzeret observed in the Diaspora, something new developed. Until sometime between the ninth and twelfth centuries (depending on whose history you accept), different parts of the Jewish world followed different cycles of reading the Torah. Then the triennial system ending before Pesakh used in Palestine was dropped in favor of Babylon's annual cycle, with the last portion of Deuteronomy assigned as the portion for the second day of Shemini Atzeret.

In connection with the reading, it became customary to remove the *Sifrei Torah* from the Ark and circle around the *bimah*, a ceremony for which hundreds of prayers were composed (also called *hoshanah*s, for the last word of each prayer). Named Simkhat Torah,

Rejoicing of the Torah, the occasion was soon accompanied by vivacious dancing and hymn singing in synagogue and lavish festival meals at home.

The impetus for the exuberant support of and adherence to Torah was provided by persecutions of the fourteenth century, when expulsions, blood libels, and Crusades were directed against Jews who refused to forsake the text. With symbols and activities of marriage, such as a service suggesting the wedding of Israel to the law, the celebrations demonstrated that the Jews' devotion was unflagging and their feeling insuppressible. (The British diarist Samuel Pepys noted, in rather disdainful terms, the carryings on in a London synagogue in 1663, in disbelief that he was watching a "decent" religious community. The congregation later regulated itself to display greater decorum.)

Soon it became customary to immediately turn to the beginning of the Torah and start the reading cycle again, expressing the desire to continually study the sacred guidebook. Due to its nature, the new holiday superseded the biblically ordained and much more subdued Shemini Atzeret.

Despite loss of the original agricultural significance of Sukkot, the erection of booths brought a bit of nature to the gray ghetto and urban conditions of the Jews in past centuries. In deteriorating Diaspora situations, Sukkot increasingly was associated with exile and wandering: The Jews were again like the homeless former slaves in the wilderness, dreaming of entering the Promised Land. (Willow in particular became entwined with the despair of exile that resulted from sin, based on our first experience of it (see chapter on Tisha B'Av) and as immortalized in Psalms (137:1–4): "By the rivers of Babylon, there we sat, sat and wept, as we thought of Zion. There on the willows we hung up our harps."

The erection of booths sometimes caused problems for the Jews, as exemplified by the incident in a Galician town in the last century. An official ordered the *sukkot*—which he presumed had been built without government approval—torn down. The mayor, a friend of the Jews and knowledgeable about their customs, gave them ten days to do so. (The incident was turned into a folktale.)

Modern Times

The revival of Jewish life through Zionism is the latest stage of our long journey that began with the Exodus. The custom of building *sukkot* in Jerusalem for pilgrims from surrounding countries, which had ended centuries before Jewish nationalist stirrings, was reestablished in the early 1900s. Pilgrims from within Palestine began making the trek to pray on the Mount of Olives opposite the Temple site, around which they walked seven times on Hoshanah Rabbah.

The settlers emphasized the renewal of Jewish life through restoration of the Land. *Etrogim* became one of the earliest crops, the beginnings of Israel's once dominant citrus industry. When Jerusalem was divided during the War for Independence (1948), the devout moved their prayer to Mount Zion.

American Reform Jews reintroduced the holiday's harvest nature in the 1930s, with a reenactment of the pilgrimage that is still seen today. Groups of children carrying various fruits and vegetables sing hymns as they march around a model *sukkah* erected in the synagogue, which has been liberally decorated with fruits and flowers.

In the Warsaw ghetto, Holocaust labor camps, and Stalinist Soviet Union, Jews continued to celebrate Sukkot. It gave them hope for a positive endpoint to their own journeys in exile.

Outside of Orthodox circles, Simkhat Torah somehow became categorized in the American community as a holiday for children. Conversely, in the 1950s, seemingly out of nowhere, Jews—not just the old, but young adults—defying official religious repression began to gather at synagogues in Moscow and Leningrad on Simkhat Torah. They sang Hebrew songs and danced traditional folk steps. Of all the holidays to pick for a reconnection with Judaism and the Jewish people, they wisely chose the joyous communal embrace of the heart of our heritage. Their courageous stance encouraged more to join them in following years and spurred Simkhat Torah rallies in America, protesting Soviet treatment of Jews, which contributed to the eventual easing of emigration.

Largely based on the return of Jews from what was the Soviet Union to Israel, Evangelical Christians believe the messiah is on his way. Expecting the arrival during Sukkot, thousands of them gather in the Holy Land each year for the Feast of Tabernacles Conference, organized by the International Christian Assembly. Since 1980, these supporters of the State of Israel have joined tens of thousands of Israelis in their annual Sukkot processions through Jerusalem.

FOR FURTHER READING

Schauss, Hayyim. *Guide to the Jewish Festivals: History and Observance.* New York: Schocken Books, 1974, pp. 175–186.

Based on information from Talmud, a very colorful description of the pilgrims en route to Jerusalem, and at the Temple, includes preparation and the sounds, sights, and feeling of the festival.

Wiesel, Elie. *Jews of Silence.* New York: Holt, Rhinehart & Winston, 1966, pp. 44–66.

The author vividly recalls his Simkhat Torah celebration in Moscow with crowds of Jews whose nationalistic sentiments had been awakened.

Yechezkieli, Y. "In the Valley of Death." Adapted by Moshe Barkany. In *Seasons of the Soul.* Ed. by Rabbi Nisson Wolpin. Brooklyn: Mesorah Publications, 1981, pp. 78–84; and in Sukkot and Simhat Torah HA, pp. 198–200.

The inspiring record describes how inmates in a Nazi labor camp managed to celebrate all the Jewish holidays of the fall season.

WHAT DOES IT MEAN?— RELIGIOUS IMPORTANCE

In not commemorating a specific event in our past, but representing particular conditions that were more than one-time occurrences, Sukkot established models for periods that would recur throughout our history. Like the *matzah* of Pesakh, which symbolizes the situation both before and after the Exodus (the bread of slavery and of salvation), this holiday's central image, the *sukkah*, also embodies duality, standing for both homelessness and settlement, wealth within poverty and the reverse.

The Real Source of Security

While the Israelites were wandering the desert with nothing—not even the ability to provide for their own basic needs—they had to recognize and rely on God as the means of their survival. He provided manna for food (Exodus 16:4–16), clouds for shelter (Exodus 33:14–17; Numbers 9:15–23), water to drink (Exodus 15:22–25; 17:5–7; Numbers 20:7–12), and conditions to prevent their clothing from deteriorating (Deuteronomy 29:4). His *sukkot*—protection—inspired in them the faith that they would reach the designated Land, as promised.

Once they arrived, they planted and harvested foodstuffs, built houses, dug wells, and wove and sewed garments. But they were not to then feel that they were self-sufficient. All they created and enjoyed, while developed through their own efforts, was no less provided by God than the desert sustenance had been. Though much more obvious in times of want, the booths they lived in for a week each year were reminders of how they began, and that regardless of their state, whatever they had came from the Supreme Provider and Protector. As Torah warned when this was readily recognized, "When you later have prosperity, be careful that you not say to yourself, 'It was my own strength and personal power that brought me all this.' You must remember that it is God your Lord Who gives you the power to become prosperous" (Deuteronomy 8:17–18).

It was an important lesson: Generations after the Israelites settled the Land, their "permanent" homes were destroyed because they failed to keep the conditions of the covenant (see chapters on Shavuot and Tisha B'Av), and they again became homeless wanderers. The shelter they "owned," wherever in the world they went, was the *feeling* of protection, a belief in God's guardianship that provided a sense of security much stronger and much more durable than any tangible structure. This security sustained their belief, through generations of uprootings and millennia of wandering, that they would eventually be brought home again.

Likewise, living in a *sukkah* today teaches us that the firmest foundation is not cinder block or stone but faith in God. Did a wall ever stop a Crusader or Cossack? Is real security sitting shut up in a house, insulated from problems around you—like the Jews of South Africa today, behind barbed wire and walls guarded by killer dogs? In one instant, fire, flood, earthquake, or hurricane can destroy what we think of as shelter. Despite barred windows, deadbolted doors, and alarm systems, intruders can enter our homes and walk out with all our valuables—including our lives. At best, the roofs over our heads and walls around us are temporary physical safeguards.

When we realize how transient material possessions are, how fragile life situations can be, we gain a profound appreciation for whatever we have received and how much we owe for those blessings. Being thankful actually defines Jewishness, as reflected in our name: We are known as Yehudim (Jews), after the fourth son of Jacob and Leah, whom she named Yehudah (Judah), in thanks to God (*hodiyah*) (Genesis 29:35).

A Jew, with blessings for every aspect of life, is someone constantly aware of God's role and grateful for what He provides and, whether viewing it as good or bad, believing it is ultimately for the best. In the *sukkah*, sitting under its airy branches of *s'khakh* (its covering), we look (*sahkah*) up and out, "seeing" God's provision for us, a model for our own responsibilities in the world.

Sharing the Bounty

The purpose of our receiving gifts from God is to make it possible for us to follow His example and provide help for others. When we move out of our secluded homes into the thin-walled, open-doored *sukkah*, there is less of a barrier between ourselves and those around us. This tenuous box open to the elements causes us to become somewhat like the poor who endure physical hardships throughout the year.

Philo, the first-century Alexandrian Jewish philosopher (and Maimonides after him), noted its moral imperative. For him, the timing of the holiday at the autumnal equinox (the point where the sun crosses the equator from the northern to southern hemispheres and day and night are of equal length) suggests balance and the opposites that maintain it. When we enjoy good fortune, status, comraderie, achievement, or peace, we should remember the unfortunate, common, lonely, struggling, and wartorn.

That is why providing for the needy is an essential component of celebrating this festival, why at every step of our journey through the Jewish year we are reminded that we began in bondage. For the poor invited into the *sukkah*—who, like the ex-slaves, can become prosperous and esteemed—the experience fosters hope. For those of means—who, like so many people of wealth and influence, can fall from power and possession—it is meant to humble. Sitting in the *sukkah* stresses that all of us are equal before God, Who in the end produces the justice we fail to enact on Earth.

Our Role through Our History

The fulfillment of Sukkot marks not just our first-time arrival in the Promised Land and is not just the annual harvest of what has been sown in the fields. It is also the absolute culmination of the progression that began with the Exodus.

The same word we use to describe the agricultural aspects of the festival is the one we use when we talk about the messianic age: ingathering—of crops, of the Jewish exiles from all parts of the earth. In other words, when we have accomplished our mission, we will not only reap grapes and grains, fruits and vegetables from the seeds sown and cultivated but the freedom, mutual respect, well-being, and peace that proliferate when moral standards are upheld.

It is no coincidence that the commandments of Sukkot follow the Torah's enumeration of laws of social justice (Exodus 23:6) and are followed by a reminder to provide justice (Deuteronomy 16:13–18). We were led to the Land so that we could implement these values, welcoming strangers in our midst, leaving gleanings of the field for the hungry, caring for the widow and orphan, rehabilitating criminals, and educating indentured servants. Our Torah-based society would be a paragon for the human community on Earth. When it has been accomplished, as Zekhariah tells us, all the nations of the world will gather in Jerusalem together to praise the just God of this just nation.

According to legend, at that time God will construct a *sukkah* out of the skin of the Leviathan, a mythical sea animal of immense proportions said by the Talmud to have been created on the fifth day of the world for just this purpose. Representing a protective mantle of peace and harmony to shelter all, it is the image and hope with which we leave the *sukkah* each year (see "Observance"), a reminder of the goal to be kept in view as we go back to our everyday lives in the world.

Approaching Life with Joy

The building blocks to redemption, acts of kindness such as bringing happiness to others by sharing what God gives us, materially and spiritually, is what Torah means by "rejoicing." These are acts that bring us close to God, the standard of our potential. That is why Sukkot, during which we give others the benefit of our wealth (our crops, our money, the teachings of our Torah) and approach reaching the goal of Godliness, is the holiday most defined by "joy" (*simkhah*).

We learn from this festival that joy, connected with working toward our highest capabilities, is a fundamental attitude in Jewish life. We celebrate with *simkhah* at occasions throughout the year and each year prior to the final ingathering. Regardless of the amount we harvest, we rejoice: The poor pilgrim who could not afford livestock to sacrifice brought a jar of flour or a bottle of wine for the altar. We are joyful not only in times of accomplishment or well-being. As Elie Wiesel observed, the Jews of Auschwitz managed to dance on Simkhat Torah, study pages of Talmud from memory while lugging heavy rocks, and sing Sabbath songs while they were being worked to death.

That is appropriate behavior for a Jew. For joy reflects a feeling of optimism about the future, and no matter what the immediate situation, a Jew believes in the promise of redemption: "I believe with perfect faith in the coming of the Messiah, and though he may tarry, daily I will wait for his coming" (Maimonides' Thirteen Principles of Faith).

It is an attitude that, along with the teachings of Torah, sustained the Jewish people. The rabbis said that in the world to come, we will be rewarded for the joy we felt in performing *mitzvot*, rather than for the actual observance of the commandments. In other words, indication of motivation is seen as more important than going through the motions. Literature of the *khasidim* contains many references to joy in service to God. In fact, the movement arose to reestablish that spirit in Jewish worship, which its founders saw as having become too oppressive.

The cheerful, positive attitude with which we approach God should be applied to our interpersonal relations as well. Common sense and experience teach us that people respond better to a happy face than a sad one ("When you're smiling, the whole world smiles with you. . ."; "Receive all men with a cheerful countenance," the sage Shammai instructed.) Expressing resentment or impatience when we hand someone *tzedakah* or provide a helping hand detracts from the fact that we are extending ourselves. Smiling at someone can make his/her day—and ours.

We have also observed that approaching life this way can alleviate the pain of difficulties. Believing that things are for the best and will work out in the end eliminates a great deal of anxiety and contributes to peace of mind. The optimistic outlook, so beautifully expressed by the Jews in Auschwitz who went singing to their deaths, is the mark of a faithful Jew who trusts in the protection of God, who finds comfort in the shade of His *sukkah*, reassurance in the shadow of His presence, hope in the glory of His sheltering cloud.

FOR FURTHER READING

Goldberger, Moshe. *A Practical Guide to the Mitzvah of Bitochon.* Staten Island: Kolel Yeshiva of Staten Island, 1982.

Not for religious skeptics, this booklet explains the principle of absolute trust in God, how it leads to complete peace of mind, how it operates in relation to major concerns in our lives such as choice of occupation, finances, social needs, and insurance coverage, and why we should work on developing it. (Available from P.O. Box 82, Staten Island, NY 10309.)

WHAT DOES IT MEAN TO US?—
PERSONAL SIGNIFICANCE

Just five days ago, on the most solemn day of the year, you learned in the face of death that what really matters is living purposefully in a way that will bring you closest to God—to the realization of the highest moral standards. From the closed setting of the synagogue, you now move outside to do something constructive in the world. First you build a leaf-topped booth that provides you with a physical and psychological environment that is different from your regular home.

Instead of shutting you off from the difficulties and unpleasantness beyond your walls, the *sukkah* wraps you in sensitivity to the blessings you enjoy and the plight of others. While all holidays and Sabbath create Jewish *time*, with this uniquely Jewish structure you literally construct Jewish *space* around you and your family. It is a transitional environment between the religious intensity of Yom Kippur and the material preoccupation of normal daily life, where you can begin applying the lessons of the Day of Atonement.

The mystics regarded the *sukkah* as the perfect synthesis of physical and spiritual: In order to fulfill the *mitzvah* of dwelling in it, you must enter the *sukkah* with your entire being, body and soul. Inside, you carry on mundane day-to-day functions enveloped in its inherent spirituality. While you sit in the *sukkah*, with its references to a time of universal peace, you are reminded of how much better the world can be.

At the end of the week, when you find yourself still sitting in a "temporary" home (since from Judaism's point of view, until we perfect the world, we remain in exile), you are prompted to question how you can help hasten redemption, our universal and eternal goal.

It is impossible to live in our world without being reminded every day that people are starving and lack shelter. The problem is that we can easily become insensitive. We are bombarded with unceasing news about those who are famine stricken, wartorn, ethnically persecuted, and hit by disaster. We literally come face-to-face with the unemployed, unhoused, unwashed, and unfed on our streets. When we are working so hard to provide decent lives for our own families, it is understandable that many of us just want to shut out all that need and deprivation, often rationalizing that the suffering people cause their own misfortune.

In previous generations, in Jewish communities all over the world, there were always poor people who depended on the generosity of others for survival. The rule was that if you did not need to request communal assistance, you were required to contribute to providing it. Sukkot is a great time to discuss what your family can do to guard yourselves against becoming hardened to less fortunate people and their legitimate needs, and to decide on ways you can help them so that the sensitivity you feel during the holiday lasts beyond it.

Contributing to a relief organization or urging your legislators to take what you feel is appropriate action in the world are routes taken by many people. If you are uncomfortable dispensing money directly to the homeless, you can donate to a legitimate organization, distribute bags of food, contribute to or work in a food kitchen, help establish/promote/gain offerings for a job bank, or venture out on especially cold nights to distribute blankets or warm unused clothing from the recesses of your closets. For inspiration, you might look to the seven illustrious men of Israel you invite to join you in the *sukkah* (see "Observance"). Each one embodies a particular quality, mirroring a facet of the character of God that needs to pervade the world.

While you are in the position of being able to assist others, you might also consider whether or not you pause often enough to be grateful for all that you have. When you recite *brakhot* are they just foreign words said by rote? Are they formulas you include only on holidays? To maintain conscious appreciation for whatever you enjoy, you might introduce a daily or weekly prayer into your family life. Many people thank God for all the good things of the previous week on Shabbat, when they light candles or bless their children. Encouraging children to enumerate, at candlelighting or before bed, the people and things they are glad to have in their lives is a good way to foster the awareness in them. (Observant Jews accomplish the lasting recognition by saying blessings for virtually every aspect of their existence and activity.)

If we exit the festival with this increased sensitivity, we will be doing our part to bring redemption. Many communities announce the end of Simkhat Torah with the proclamation, "And Jacob went on his way" (leaving the household of his deceitful father-in-law Laban) (Genesis 32:2). It is a reminder that as we depart from our festivities and return to regular existence, we do so as Jews, like Jacob, with our own ways, ways based on awareness of God and a mission much greater than our individual selves, which should influence everything we do, say, and think.

The Jewish way is of course presented in the Torah, a book unfortunately, like Jewish education and Simkhat Torah celebration, too often relegated to children. Certainly it is for children—and for adolescents, young adults, and older adults. The sages say there are seventy different levels to it, so that it not only has ageless application but can be understood from a broad range of perspectives, intellectual capacities, and interests. Each person can understand it in his or her own way. That is why we read it again and again, as we would see a well-crafted drama, or listen to a magnificent symphony, or look at an intricate painting repeatedly, discovering new elements, nuances, and meaning with each encounter.

For young children, Bible stories are colorful tales about relevant people with whom they can identify, as readily as with cartoon, television, and other popular culture characters. (The four-year-old grandson of an acquaintance of mine thinks Moses is a contemporary and questions his grandfather about the leader as though the two are fast friends.) For teens, biblical personages and situations are no less real, expressing a full range of human emotion and quality and offering the moral values young people need but are too often denied in today's system of formal education.

For adults, Torah—full of pathos, psychology, drama, love, comedy, conflict, and philosophy—contains all the elements considered essential for blockbuster novels today, and in the context of a good read provides universally applicable guidance for how to get the most out of life. "Study the Torah again and again for everything is contained in it," counsel our rabbis (*Pirkei Avot*). "Constantly examine it, grow old and gray over it; and swerve not from it, for there is nothing more excellent than it."

In blessings traditionally given to children, particularly at the *brit* and baby naming, we pray that they will perform good deeds, come to the *khupah* (wedding canopy), and grow in study of Torah. This is a very telling wish for a child. Unlike the Romans who wanted muscular, rugged soldiers, and the Greeks who wanted athletes—or American Jews who may wish for doctors and lawyers—historically Jews above all wanted children who would maintain their bond to Judaism through Torah, to understand its messages and exemplify its ethics. For this would mean that they could, through their own behavior, go out, as we do from the *sukkah*, live meaningful worthwhile lives, and change the world.

As in the case of the children commanded to attend the *Hockheil* reading of Deuteronomy, what your children learn of Torah in their youngest years will affect them the rest of their lives—in terms of knowledge, values, and feelings of connectedness to Judaism and the Jewish people. The example they see in your own involvement with Torah learning can easily convey the message that this is a book to carry through, and to carry you through, life. You have a built-in opportunity to begin learning together now, at the start of the Torah-reading cycle.

FOR FURTHER READING

Refer to the materials listed in the chapter on Shavuot.

TRADITIONS: HOW WE CELEBRATE SUKKOT

WHAT DO WE USE?—RITUAL ITEMS

Sukkah

The *sukkah* is the temporary dwelling, referred to as "booth" or archaically as tabernacle (from *taberna*, hut, which is why you may hear the holiday referred to as the Feast of Tabernacles), in which we are supposed to eat our meals and sleep during the week of the harvest festival.

Although there are regulations regarding the minimum size, maximum height, and acceptable dimensions for its walls, the element that makes a *sukkah* more than an agricultural shed is its "roof": a canopy made from stalks or branches arranged to provide more shade than sunlight and allow you to see the stars through it. In other words, it is something that originally grew from the earth through which we can look up and see heaven. In fact, the word *sukkah* is derived from the word for the roof—*s'khakh*, meaning "covering"—indicating the most important element of the structure. It is a reminder that during the Israelites' forty years of wandering, God "covered" all their needs.

Since we are supposed to live in the *sukkah* according to our normal standards (as "dwell" in the commandment "and you shall dwell in booths" [Leviticus 23:42] indicates), we should surround ourselves with the finest accoutrements of our permanent homes—furnishings, linens, tableware. However, most people today do not transfer their favorite couches or their dining room sets into the *sukkah*. Folding tables and chairs are common.

It is a *mitzvah* for every Jew to participate in building and decorating a *sukkah*. (A *sukkah* decorating party, for the immediate family or an extended group including friends, is a great way to get into the spirit of the holiday.) If you have absolutely no space in which to contruct one (don't overlook a balcony, rooftop, area of common ground in front of an apartment building; there's a famous story of Rabbi Akiva building one on a ship's deck despite the warnings of a colleague that it would blow away), try to assist in building a synagogue or community *sukkah*, or help a friend. (Some families, unable to do any of these, at least build a model that becomes part of their table decorations.)

Construction

You can use just about any materials to make the walls: cinder blocks, scrap lumber, old doors, bamboo shades, canvas or nylon sheeting attached to a frame of wood or metal piping with nails or grommets and rope.

Beams can be placed across the top to support the *s'khakh*. In Israel, authorities trim the palm trees in time for the holiday and leave the branches in piles on the streets for people to take home. In this country, parks departments often oblige with the by-product of fall pruning. If you cannot obtain leafy branches, bamboo, straw, reeds, and thin boards may be used.

Our enjoyment of the *mitzvah* is enhanced when we consider its aesthetics, so it is appropriate to make the *sukkah* as beautiful as possible. Gourds, fruits, birds made from hollowed eggshells, cranberry garlands, popcorn strands and paper chains, pictures and wall tapestries, along with representations of the seven species that grow in Israel (wheat, barley, grape, fig, date, pomegranate, olive), are all traditional. Some people use cards they have received for the new year and previous years' *etrogim*, either dried or clove-studded. Spotlights, strings of small bulbs, hanging lanterns, and other fixtures or candles are used to provide illumination.

Pre-fab *sukkot* are available through Jewish bookstores and sometimes synagogues (and are often advertised in Jewish publications around the holiday season).

Despite the regulations regarding erecting a "kosher *sukkah*" a *khasidic* tale teaches us about the importance of following the intent of the law over the letter of it, and encourages even the novice to erect a *sukkah*. A humble man, who had spent more than he could afford to get the choicest materials for his *sukkah*, invited Rabbi Nakhman of Bratslav to visit. The rabbi accepted and went with a disciple. As soon as they entered, the student whispered to the Rabbi that the structure did not conform to all the laws. After they had left, the rabbi chastised the disciple. "This Jew went to such trouble to make the booth, and you raise questions about its validity because of legal technicalities?!"

Four Species

We take up the *lulav* and *etrog* to fulfill the commandment regarding the *arba'ah* (four) *minim* (species). The long elegant *lulav* consists of one palm branch (*lulav*, the largest element of the bundle and therefore the name of the whole assembly) embraced by a holder with a pocket on the left containing two willow branches (*aravot*) and one on the right containing three myrtle branches (*hadasim*).

There is usually at least one ring holding the leaves

together, and traditionally three of them up the length of the *lulav* above the holder, said to represent the partriarchs Abraham, Isaac, and Jacob (or, continuing a theme of the Days of Awe, the wicked, the righteous, and those in between). The holder, often woven, can be made only of palm leaves because the three plant types may not be separated by any foreign material, which would also disrupt the proper number of species.

Some rabbinic interpretation was necessary to identify two of the four flora not specified in Torah (Leviticus 23:40). The "product of hadar trees" they said had to be the *etrog* (citron), because no other tree has bark, leaves, and fruit that are equally fragrant and flavorful, exemplifying beauty (*hadar*). Since Torah uses the singular for "fruit" we use one *etrog*. "Boughs of leafy trees" were recognized as myrtle. Since Torah uses three words to describe this species (*anaf* [branch], *eitz* [tree], and *avot* [thicket]), we use three *hadasim*. The plural designation for "willows of the brook" suggested two *aravot*.

Meaning

Exactly why these particular plants were chosen and how they are to be arranged and used may remain one of Torah's mysteries. That has not stopped rabbis from offering numerous explanations. On the superficial level, the *etrog* and components of the *lulav* together represent the entire plant kingdom and emphasize Sukkot's agricultural nature as well as, by their shapes, masculine and feminine forces. Life on Earth could not be sustained without them and the four basic elements they also suggest: air (the palm standing upright), fire (the yellow citron), earth (the low-growing myrtle), and water (the willow that lives next to rivers and brooks).

Maimonides (*Guide for the Perplexed*) saw them as symbols of the change from the Israelites' existence in the wilderness, "a place . . . there was not even water to drink" (Numbers 20:5), to their rejoicing in a country full of fruit trees and rivers reflecting God's fulfillment of His promise of "a good land, a land of brooks of water [willow], and fountains issuing from valleys [where *etrogim* grow] and hills [where myrtles thrive], a land of . . . honey [date palms]" (Deuteronomy 8:7–8).

The qualities of the four species are likened to those of four categories of Jews. The *etrog*, possessing both taste and aroma, stands for Jews who have knowledge of Torah and do good deeds. The palm's fruit (date), with taste but no aroma, represents people with Torah knowledge. The myrtle, with no taste but aroma, represents the opposite, and willow, with

neither aroma or taste, stands for those self-concerned and ignorant of Torah.

We serve God with all four elements held together, the spiritually lofty with the mundane, the scholar, aristocrat, merchant, and laborer. In society, all elements must likewise hold together, so that the wise and righteous can influence those less so, and because each contributes its part to society's functioning and progress when they unite for common welfare. As our sages put it, "As one does not fulfill his duty on Sukkot unless all four species are bound together, so some will not be redeemed unless all Jews hold together," a strong message about the need for unity among our diverse segments.

Similarly, those that bear fruit (citron and palm), the wise, must be bound closely with those that do not (willow and myrtle), for the prayers of the sages produce mercy for everyone else, and the non-scholars provide physical comfort for the sages and their disciples.

From the body of Israel the rabbis moved to the body of the individual, seeing through their shapes the palm as backbone, the citron as heart, the myrtle as eye, and the willow as mouth. Together they express our desire to use all our vital components to worship God, and to atone for transgressions resulting from an envious eye, malicious mouth, or lustful heart. In mysticism, each species represents one letter in God's name. The *lulav* is the *vav* ("and") uniting them as a conduit for Divine energy into the world.

Myrtle represents beauty and mercy, like the heroine of the Purim story who had the same Hebrew name (*hadas* [*sah*]). Since myrtle stays fresh for days after it is cut, it became an ancient symbol for success and immortality. In contrast, willow leaves droop as soon as the branches are cut. On the one hand representing our exit from the desert to the Land full of water, it also symbolized our exile from the Land and the sadness and longing we have felt at the separation. However, just as the leaves fall and grow again, God continually provides new life and hope for the Jews.

Considered perfect and full and therefore a symbol of purpose in life, the *etrog* is not bound to the other species, each imperfect due to the lack of one quality or another. Because of what it represents, an *etrog* used in the Sukkot ritual must be flawless. The critical element is the *pittam*, the protuberance at the top of the citron. The remaining part of the blossom through which the developing fruit had been nourished, it must be intact in order for the *etrog* to be kosher (ritually valid).

It is considered desirable to have your own *lulav* and *etrog*, for they are used every morning of the holiday, at home and in synagogue. However, the synagogue usually has one set for anyone who needs to use it.

Obtaining

The concept of *hidur mitzvah*, beautifying the commandment, that all *mitzvot* should be performed with regard to aesthetics, has traditionally been carried to extremes for Sukkot. While we should buy the choicest example of each species, people throughout our history have in particular sought the perfect *etrog*, often paying excessive prices for the privilege of owning one. The sages advised that we spend up to one-third more than what we would normally expect to pay. To prevent exploitation by the once-a-year opportunity for citron sellers to clean up in the concentrated market, each year a few religious leaders agree on a maximum price.

It is considered an enhancement of the *mitzvah* to choose your own *lulav* and *etrog*. If you are in Israel or a religious Jewish enclave, you can go to one of the stores selling them, or to an open Sukkot market, such as those in front of Mashbir Department Store in Jerusalem or Kings of Israel Square in Tel Aviv, where you will see religious Jews choosing each of the four species separately, going from shop to shop or booth to booth with a magnifying glass—literally—to ensure the quality of their selections.

Most of us do not have the opportunity for such choices but have to order our four species from a Jewish supply store or through a synagogue. Many congregations take orders from members during the Days of Awe and deliver the items in time for Sukkot. The *lulav* and *etrog* are purchased as a set.

To protect the *etrog*—though it is hardy, you do not want to damage or lose its *pittam*—it is kept wrapped in flax in the box in which it is delivered, or transferred to a special *etrog* box. This could be something as makeshift as a plain wooden or metal receptacle, or as elegant as a carved olive wood or engraved silver container especially designed for the purpose. They are available at stores that sell Judaica items and can be modern or antique.

You can keep the *lulav* fresh by placing it in the refrigerator wrapped in a damp towel or aluminum foil, enclosed in a plastic bag with a few drops of water, or in a vase with just enough water to keep the bottom moist.

Aravot

For Hoshanah Rabbah, branches of willows are needed for the "beating" ceremony, symbolic of summoning rain. Some people use the *aravot* from their *lulavim*; additional switches are often made available through synagogues, and some Jewish bookstores sell them. It is traditional to use five twigs bound together with a palm leaf. In addition to inducing rain and obliterating sin, the willow beating is said to represent elimination of a danger to the community: The Jew it symbolizes, ignorant of Torah and negligent in helping others, although acceptable in the mix of all Jews, threatens communal welfare and continuity when acting alone. Thrashing it is also said to express our sadness at still being in exile.

Simkhat Torah Flags

Reminiscent of the standards carried by the Twelve Tribes of Israel as they progressed through the desert (Numbers 2:2–31; 10:14–28), paper flags are carried by children as they follow the processions on Simkhat Torah. Sometimes provided by the synagogue, the flags can be purchased in Jewish bookstores or made by the children themselves.

Memorial Candle

As for all other holy days on which the memorial service *Yizkor* is recited, it is customary for anyone who has lost a parent (or grandparent) to light a *yahrtzite* candle the evening before the service is held. The candles can be purchased at a Jewish supply store or in supermarkets that carry kosher items. The candles come in small cans or glasses and burn for twenty-five hours, long enough to last from candle-lighting time through the end of *yom tov*.

HOW DO WE SHOW WE CELEBRATE?— OBSERVANCE

Think about the anticipation most people experience as Thanksgiving approaches. We look forward to the warm embrace of family and friends and allowing ourselves to splurge on lavish meals. That's the kind of feeling Sukkot, the original thanksgiving, is meant to generate. This is a holiday suffused with happiness. The Torah commands three observances to foster it: living in the *sukkah*, gathering together the four species, and rejoicing during the holiday. (In the liturgy, the festival is referred to as *Zeman Simkhateinu*, the Season of Our Rejoicing.)

There is the excitement of a new and different living arrangement for a week, out in the cool, crisp autumn air; the anticipation through the party-like atmosphere of erecting and decorating the structure;

the novelty of eating and possibly sleeping in a harvest booth scented with palm or pine and fall fruits. Having gotten through the deprivations of Yom Kippur, we relax in the relief of reaching a milestone of accomplishment and can let ourselves go in the singing and dancing that cannot help but raise our spirits.

Orthodox and Conservative Jews in the Diaspora celebrate for nine days: the first two as full holidays, days three through seven as *khol* (intermediate) *hamoed* (festival days), and the last two as full holidays, Shemini Atzeret (day eight) and Simkhat Torah (day nine). In Israel and for the Reform, the festival lasts eight days, with the first and last as full holidays and the last as a combination of the solemn Shemini Atzeret and the spirited Simkhat Torah.

The intermediate days are alike in character to *khol hamoed* Pesakh, the other extended festival in our year. Comparable to eating *matzah* for the former, the commandment for the latter is dwelling in the *sukkah*. While there are no biblical prohibitions against work and travel on these days, in traditional circles people sometimes refrain from doing any nonessential work and do not write.

Dwelling in the *Sukkah*

For the entire period of Sukkot, we eat our meals and, where weather permits, sleep in the *sukkah*. If you do not have your own *sukkah*, ask a friend who has one to invite you for at least one meal, or make *kiddush* in a synagogue *sukkah* (this is easy because it is generally organized to take place after services).

Candlelighting

As for all Jewish holidays, we usher in Sukkot by blessing and lighting candles and reciting *shehekheyanu*. If at all possible, it is done in the *sukkah*.

בָּרוּךְ אַתָּה, יהוה אֱלֹהֵינוּ, מֶלֶךְ הָעוֹלָם, אֲשֶׁר קִדְּשָׁנוּ בְּמִצְוֹתָיו, וְצִוָּנוּ לְהַדְלִיק נֵר שֶׁל [*שַׁבָּת וְשֶׁל] יוֹם טוֹב.

Barukh Atah, Adonai Eloheinu, Melekh Haolam, asher kidshanu b'mitzvotav, v'tzivanu lehadlik ner shel [Shabbat v'shel] yom tov.*

Blessed are You, Lord our God, King of the Universe, Who has sanctified us with His commandments and commanded us to kindle the [Sabbath and*] festival lights.

---

*When sabbath and a full festival day coincide.

בָּרוּךְ אַתָּה, יהוה אֱלֹהֵינוּ, מֶלֶךְ הָעוֹלָם, שֶׁהֶחֱיָנוּ, וְקִיְּמָנוּ, וְהִגִּיעָנוּ לַזְּמַן הַזֶּה.

Barukh Atah, Adonai Eloheinu, Melekh Haolam, shehekheyanu, v'kiyamanu, v'higgiyanu lazman hazeh.

Blessed are You, Lord our God, King of the Universe, Who has kept us alive, sustained us, and allowed us to reach this season.

If the candles are in danger of being blown out, they should be moved into the house.

Ushpizin

Maimonides admonished that anyone who sits comfortably with his family within his own walls and does not share with the poor is performing a *mitzvah* not for joy but for the stomach. In addition to extending personal invitations to the needy (in former times it was customary to have at least one poor person at a Sukkot meal; today donation of funds often is a substitute), we open our homes symbolically. With a formula established by the kabbalists in the sixteenth century, based on the earlier *Zohar*, on each night of Sukkot we invite one of seven exalted men of Israel to take up residence in the *sukkah* with us. "When a man sits in the shadow of faith [*sukkah*] the *Shekhinah* [Divine Presence] spreads Her wings on him from above and Abraham and five other righteous ones of God (and David with them) make their abode with him. . . . A man should rejoice each day of the festival with these guests."

The inspiration for *hakhnasat orekhim* (hospitality to guests) goes back to our first partriarch, and the first guest honored, Abraham. He would sit outside waiting for the opportunity to invite dusty wayfarers into the shade of his tent, and then run to prepare a meal of the choicest ingredients. (A *midrash* based on the apocryphal Book of Jubilees claims that the first booth, on which the holiday Sukkot is based, was built by Abraham when he greeted the three Angels who came to tell him his wife Sarah would at last bear a child [Genesis 18:1–10]. Jubilees [16:21] traces other observances of Sukkot to Abraham's tents in Beersheva, where he erected an altar and circled it while praying.)

We perform a short ceremony to welcome the *ushpizin* (Aramaic for "guests"). The full text for the invitation that they join us, including prayers that our fulfillment of the *mitzvah* of *sukkah* will be worthy of Divine favor, is printed in a full daily/festival *siddur*. Then, on the first day we say "I invite to my meal the exalted guests, Abraham, Isaac, Jacob, Joseph, Moses, Aaron, and David. May it please you, Abraham, my exalted guest, that all the other exalted guests dwell here with me and with you—Isaac, Jacob, Joseph, Moses, Aaron, and David." On each day, a different one of the seven is singled out, in order.

The *Sephardim*, who often set aside a special chair laden with holy books for the *ushpiz*, invite the patriarchs, then the leaders/prophets (Moses and Aaron), then royalty (Joseph and David). They often send provisions to the poor along with a note saying "This is the share of the *ushpizin*." Recently, it has become popular in some circles to invite matriarchs and other important women of Israel—Sarah, Rachel, Rebecca, Leah, Miriam, Abigail, and Esther—either paired with the men or on their own.

In addition to serving as a reminder of our duty to the poor (it is said that the *ushpizin* would refuse to enter a *sukkah* where the poor are not welcome), each of these exalted personages represents uprootedness. (Abraham left his father's home for the land God promised to show him [Genesis 12:1], Isaac went to Gerar during a famine [Genesis 26:1], Jacob fled from his brother Esau to the habitat of Laban [Genesis 28:2], Joseph was sold to merchants and taken to Egypt [Genesis 37:23–36], Moses fled to Midian after inadvertently killing an Egyptian [Exodus 2:11–15] and he and Aaron wandered the Sinai for forty years [beginning with Exodus 13], and David hid from Saul in the wilderness [I Samuel 20, 21].)

Each in his wanderings contributed to the world through a respective personal characteristic (a version of those cited in reference to self-improvement on Shavuot): lovingkindness, strength, splendor, glory, holiness, eternity, sovereignty. Reflecting the periods of homelessness and wandering in their lives, our temporary dwellings can inspire us to emulate the benefits they brought to the world. Many people put up plaques or pictures of the *ushpizin*, containing the blessing and scenes from their lives. (Laminated ones are available in Jewish supply stores.)

Kiddush *and Other* Brakhot

Once our guests—worldly and otherwise—are comfortably established beneath our shelter, we recite a special festival *kiddush* (full text found in a *siddur*), followed by the blessing used every time we take a meal in the *sukkah*:

בָּרוּךְ אַתָּה, יהוה אֱלֹהֵינוּ, מֶלֶךְ הָעוֹלָם, בּוֹרֵא פְּרִי הַגָּפֶן.

Barukh Atah, Adonai Eloheinu, Melekh Haolam, borei pri hagaffen.

Blessed are You, Lord our God, King of the Universe, Who creates the fruit of the vine.

בָּרוּךְ אַתָּה, יהוה אֱלֹהֵינוּ, מֶלֶךְ הָעוֹלָם, אֲשֶׁר קִדְּשָׁנוּ בְּמִצְוֹתָיו, וְצִוָּנוּ לֵישֵׁב בַּסֻּכָּה.

Barukh Atah, Adonai Eloheinu, Melekh Haolam, asher kidshanu b'mitzvotav, v'tzivanu leisheiv basukkah.

Blessed are You, Lord our God, King of the Universe, Who has sanctified us with His commandments and commanded us to dwell in the *sukkah*.

If a person other than the one who did candlelighting makes *kiddush*, *shehekheyanu* is then said and refers to both the first day of the festival and the first use of the *sukkah*. On the second day, candles are again lit with the *brakhah* and *shehekheyanu*. This time, *shehekheyanu* immediately follows *kiddush* (so it refers only to the new holy day) and then *leisheiv basukkah* is recited.

Traditional Jews then do the ritual hand washing and blessing over bread:

בָּרוּךְ אַתָּה, יהוה אֱלֹהֵינוּ, מֶלֶךְ הָעוֹלָם, אֲשֶׁר קִדְּשָׁנוּ בְּמִצְוֹתָיו, וְצִוָּנוּ עַל נְטִילַת יָדָיִם.

Barukh Atah, Adonai Eloheinu, Melekh Haolam, asher kidshanu b'mitzvotav, v'tzivanu al netilat yadayim.

Blessed are You, Lord our God, King of the Universe, Who has sanctified us with His commandments and commanded us regarding washing the hands.

בָּרוּךְ אַתָּה, יהוה אֱלֹהֵינוּ, מֶלֶךְ הָעוֹלָם, הַמּוֹצִיא לֶחֶם מִן הָאָרֶץ.

Barukh Atah, Adonai Eloheinu, Melekh Haolam, hamotzi lekhem min ha'aretz.

Blessed are You, Lord our God, King of the Universe, Who brings forth bread from the earth.

On intermediate days, we continue to say the blessing for dwelling in the *sukkah*. Since the end of the festival in the Diaspora coincides with Shemini Atzeret, an independent holiday, there is disagreement over whether or not we are still supposed to live in the *sukkah* on that day. Common practice is to eat meals but not say the blessings. (In Israel, the *sukkah* is not used at all after the seventh day of the festival.)

When we leave the *sukkah* for the last time, we express our hope that we will deserve to sit in the *sukkah* that will be built at the time of the Messiah, which we pray will be during our lifetime:

יְהִי רָצוֹן מִלְּפָנֶיךָ, יהוה אֱלֹהֵינוּ, וַאלֹהֵי אֲבוֹתֵינוּ, כְּשֵׁם שֶׁקִּיַּמְתִּי וְיָשַׁבְתִּי בַּסֻּכָּה זוּ, כֵּן אֶזְכֶּה לְשָׁנָה הַבָּאָה לֵישֵׁב בְּסֻכַּת עוֹרוֹ שֶׁל לִוְיָתָן. לְשָׁנָה הַבָּאָה בִּירוּשָׁלָיִם.

Y'hi rahtzon milfanekhah, Adonai Eloheinu, veilohei avoteinu, k'sheim shekiyamti v'yashavti basukkah zu, kein ezkeh l'shanah haba'ah leisheiv b'sukkat oro shel livyatan. L'shanah haba'ah b'Yerushalayim.

May it be Your will, Lord our God and God of our fathers, just as I merited and sat in this *sukkah*, so may I merit the coming year to sit in the *sukkah* of the skin of Leviathan. Next year in Jerusalem.

Comfort and Joy

Since the *sukkah* is a memorial to God's protection, it is meant to enhance the joy of the festival. If you do not feel joy, you cannot appropriately fulfill the *mitzvah* of dwelling in the *sukkah*. This understanding led to an unusual approach by the rabbis. While they generally encourage us to perform *mitzvot* beyond the requirements stated, in this case they encourage us *not* to stay in the *sukkah* when conditions make it uncomfortable.

Exceptions to the stringent talmudic laws about sleeping in the *sukkah* developed in Europe, where inclement weather made it unreasonable. It was because the structures were often uncomfortable that women and children were generally excused from even having meals there. (Women were not obligated anyway, under the general principle that they are not bound to *mitzvot* that must be performed at certain times of the day. However, they voluntarily took the *mitzvah* of dwelling in the *sukkah* on themselves, and therefore it is customary for them to fulfill it.) If it rains enough to "spoil the soup," as the rabbis say, you are supposed to leave. (The laws for the first night are somewhat different, as explained in the section on *Halakhah*.) Anyone exempted who remains in the *sukkah* despite discomfort is classified by the rabbis as an ignoramus!

Those anxious to perform the *mitzvah* of eating in the *sukkah* despite terrible conditions fulfill the obligation by reciting *kiddush* and eating just a small piece of bread or cake. The idea is that it is preferable to be comfortable in your house enjoying the holiday than to be miserable in the *sukkah*, cursing the discomfort and, worse, the cause of it.

However, do not overlook what a backyard adventure sleeping in the *sukkah* can be for children, especially if it is equipped with toasty sleeping bags. Sometimes an entire family "sleeps out" at least one night during the week.

To enhance the celebration it is customary to sing in the *sukkah*. Some people prepare special readings for each night, such as a relevant eight-part story, text on the *ushpiz* of the day, appropriate sections of Ecclesiastes (the scroll assigned to this festival), or psalms that deal with God's shelter (27, 31, 34, 36, 57, 63, 91).

Taking Up the *Lulav* and *Etrog*

In a traditional Jewish home, every member of the family fortunate enough to have its own *lulav* and *etrog* recites the benediction over them first thing in the morning, before breakfast, every day throughout the festival. (You can actually bless the four species anytime during the day.) When possible, the *brakhah* is made in the *sukkah*.

Procedure

The way we hold the four species prior to and following recitation of the blessing is determined by technicalities of saying benedictions. For all *mitzvot*, we are supposed to first say a blessing, then immediately perform the *mitzvah*. So that there will not be a lapse of time in the case of the *lulav* and *etrog*, we should have them in hand when we say the blessing. However, since we cannot fulfill the *mitzvah* until after the *brakhah*, they have to be in hand differently beforehand and afterward.

The generally followed custom is to stand, pick up the *lulav* in your right hand (since the *lulav* is composed of three of the four species it is considered dominant and therefore is held in the usually dominant right hand) with the spine (the long green shaft running its length) toward you, and the *etrog*, with its *pittam* down (opposite the way it grows), in your left (closer to the heart, whose shape it resembles). On the first day only, *shehekheyanu* follows the *brakhah*, which covers all four species.

בָּרוּךְ אַתָּה, יהוה אֱלֹהֵינוּ, מֶלֶךְ הָעוֹלָם, אֲשֶׁר קִדְּשָׁנוּ בְּמִצְוֹתָיו, וְצִוָּנוּ עַל נְטִילַת לוּלָב.

Barukh Atah, Adonai Eloheinu, Melekh Haolam, asher kidshanu b'mitzvotav, v'tzivanu al netilat lulav.

Blessed are You, Lord our God, King of the Universe, Who has sanctified us with His commandments and commanded us concerning the taking of a palm branch.*

---

*Only one of the species is mentioned since the date palm from which it is taken is taller than the others and covers all.

Then turn the *etrog* so the *pittam* faces up and, keeping your hands close enough together that so the *lulav* and *etrog* touch, with enough force to slightly rustle the leaves, wave the *lulav* in six directions: east, south, west, north, above, and below. Since we face east, this means in front of us, right, over the right shoulder, left, up, and down. (The *Sephardim* wave right, left, front, back, up, and down. The Syrian Jews actually turn to the direction and wave three times in front of themselves and up and down in each position.)

The customary procedure is to hold the *lulav* and *etrog* with your hands together, extend your arms out, shake the four species, draw your arms back toward you, and repeat twice more. Then go to the next direction. It is a moderately rapid movement; don't labor over it.

Those who do not bless the four species at home do so at synagogue following the *Shakharit Amidah* just before *Hallel*. On the Sabbath, we do not use the four species in order to avoid their being carried from home to synagogue or from one home to another.

Meaning

Like the four plant types themselves, the wavings (*na'anu'im*) have symbolic significance. They represent Israel's acceptance of God's sovereignty over all of nature (the four directions), heaven (up) and earth (down). Talmud likened the motion to the offering of *omer* brought on the second day of Passover and waved in four directions to contain ill winds and to a sacrificial offering on the altar. Lifting the *lulav* expresses joy (as when you lift a child or a trophy into the air) and victory, publicly proclaiming Israel's successful emergence from the Divine Judgment of Rosh Hashanah and Yom Kippur. (When people used to appear before a judge, the one who exited holding palm branches was recognized as the victor.) According to *midrash*, the outcome of the Yom Kippur judgment of all nations of the world is not revealed until the first day of Sukkot. The procession of Israelites around the altar (or *bimah*), their *lulavim* held aloft, proclaims Israel's victory and hints at messianic fulfillment as promised in Isaiah (55:12): "You shall leave in joy and be led home secure. Before you mountains and hills shall shout aloud, and all the trees of the field shall clap their hands. . . ." When we shake the *lulav*, the palm leaves hit against each other as if hands clapping, bringing to mind God's promise to Israel.

Hallel

We recite the Psalms of Praise (113–118) every day because, with a unique complement of sacrifices, each is considered a holiday in its own right. The wavings are done twice during the verse of *hodu l'Adonai*, give thanks to God (Psalms 118:1), twice in *ana hoshiah*, we implore you, save us (Psalms 118:25), and twice in the last *hodu l'Adoshem* (Psalms 118:29). *Hodu* contains six words (excluding the name of God); we wave in one direction as each word is slowly enunciated. (Just follow the service leader.) The pattern is followed for the six syllables of the phrase beginning *ana*, and then for the six words in the verse of *hodu* in the concluding paragraph of *Hallel*.

Hoshanot

Immediately after the *khazzan's* repetition of the *Mussaf Amidah*, we recite special prayers, the *hoshanot* (multiple of *hoshanah*). Medieval poems and prayers predominantly composed by the eighth-century Rabbi Elazar Hakallir, they ask God to deliver us. Each consists of twenty-two verses or stanzas in alphabetical order.

For the service, Torah scrolls are taken from the Ark, which remains open, and held at the *bimah* by members of the congregation. Everyone who has the four species holds them throughout the service. After introductory verses, the *khazzan* leads everyone (only men in Orthodox congregations) carrying the *lulav* and *etrog* around the *bimah* as they read the *hoshanah* of the day. (Since the contents are connected with the days of the week, the order changes depending on when the festival begins.) The congregation repeats each line. On the Sabbath, the Ark is opened and verses said, but the *Sifrei Torah* are not removed and no procession takes place (remember, we do not pick up the four species on the Sabbath).

Because they already have the *lulavim* and *etrogim* out, for convenience the *Sephardim* conduct *hoshanot* immediately after *Hallel* as part of *Shakharit*.

Circling, a symbol of perfection and completion and part of Sukkot, Hoshanah Rabbah, and Simkhat Torah celebrations, is popular in other Jewish ceremonies (for example, when the bride circles the groom seven times in a traditional wedding) and art. In folk beliefs, a "magic ring" could keep out bad spirits. Among the Jews, it was believed that one could gain God's favor by setting an object off within a circle. The concept was made famous by the righteous Honi, "The Circle Maker," who would draw a ring around himself and refuse to budge until God had granted his requests. Ingathering suggests collecting within the protective circle of our arms. We draw the *lulav* and *etrog* back to us almost in a circling motion, creating an insular, secure space enveloping God's spirit within it.

Bible Selections

While the Torah readings consist of the straightforward festival laws, commandments, and sacrifices (Leviticus 23; Numbers 29; Exodus 33), the *haftarot* provide colorful glimpses of Sukkot celebration future and past.

Zekhariah 14, read on the first day, describes the festival at the time when all nations of the world will gather in Jerusalem to praise God together. Their acknowledgment that He is the supreme king will indicate acceptance of one moral standard and bring universal peace. On the second day we read I Kings 8:1–21, describing the dedication of Solomon's Temple, which took place during Sukkot. Ezekiel 38, read on the intermediate Sabbath, previews the war of Gog and Magog—by tradition to take place during the season of Sukkot—from which Israel will emerge victorious in the messianic era.

Ecclesiastes

Also on this Shabbat, we read *Kohelet* (Ecclesiastes), the scroll especially assigned to the holiday. Popularly known thanks to the Byrds' hit song, "Turn! Turn! Turn!" which uses its verses "For every thing, there is a season . . . ," the book is attributed to King Solomon. Solomon was at a different point in his life when he penned this from when he wrote the sensual Song of Songs we read on Pesakh. He is much older, near the end of his life, and philosophical about what life has meant. Having explored every experience open to him, physical and spiritual, uplifting and degrading, having chased gratifying pleasures and maintained a moral highroad, he warns that anything not done in service to God is "vanity of vanities, all is vanity" (1:2).

Contrasting the two continually opposed facets of life, good and evil, material and spiritual, and expressing the range of human mood, Ecclesiastes is a treatise on what brings permanent joy, not the fleeting pleasures of the body but devotion to something much greater than the self. Solomon concludes with the message "The end of the matter, all having been heard, fear God and keep His commandments; for this applies to all mankind" (12:13).

At the time of our greatest material abundance, when we might mistakenly applaud our self-sufficiency, Solomon reminds us that there is nothing new under the sun, that things of this world are temporary and can be fleeting, that true happiness comes in being content with what we have and recognizing the source of whatever that is. The lesson eloquently complements the meaning of the *sukkah*.

Beating the Willows

Although Hoshanah Rabbah, on the seventh day of Sukkot, is part of *khol hamoed*, it seems to have greater status because of the synagogue service. Since the day has been seen from the Middle Ages as a "Yom Kippur *Katan*" (little Yom Kippur), when the annual judgment verdict is delivered, it is approached as the last opportunity for those who have not yet completed their repentance. (It certainly cannot be said that Judaism does not give us every last chance to fulfill our obligations!) That's why we see and hear similarities to the Day of Atonement: the Torah scrolls wear white vestments, the cantor wears a *kittel*, candles may be lit in the synagogue, the plaintive chants of Yom Kippur embrace our prayers, we say the verses of the Days of Awe—"remember us for life"—and conclude with the same passages used to end Yom Kippur. Some congregations also insert *shofar* blasts during the service.

Unlike the other days of Sukkot, when we remove one scroll from the Ark and make one procession encircling the *bimah*, on Hoshanah Rabbah all the scrolls are removed from the Ark and seven processions, each one accompanied by the recitation of a *hoshanah*, are made. After each *hoshanah* we recite a scriptural verse related to one of seven *sefirot* (part of the kabbalistic system representing qualities of God): kindness (Psalms 89:3), strength (Psalms 89:14), splendor (Micah 7:20), triumph (Psalms 16:11), glory (Psalms 8:2), foundation (Psalms 145:17), and kingship (Zekhariah 14:9). These correspond to the attributes of the heavenly visitors to the *sukkah* and the qualities attributed by David to God (I Chronicles 29:11), to which our circuits correspond and through which we hope to gain God's favor.

The seven circuits represent the seven heavens that separate God from the earth, which we want to pierce with our supplications. They also stand for the seven times Joshua's army marched around Jericho. I Kings 17:1 says that because of the rebuilding of the city against God's will and Joshua's decree, Israel was punished with years of drought. Therefore, on Hoshanah Rabbah, when we pray for dew and rain—mentioned seven times in Torah as blessings—we appropriately remember that drought and consequent famine resulted from disobeying God's commandments. In addition, the crumbling walls symbolize the collapse of the walls of our transgressions. In one tradition, a scroll is returned to the Ark after each circuit.

It has long been the custom to stay up all night on Hoshanah Rabbah to meditate, study, and read holy books. Many congregations read Deuteronomy in its entirety, because it summarizes all the laws and warnings found in Torah. (Some read all five books to make up for any failure to review the weekly portions and translation during the previous year [per Talmud's requirement].) Others recite the Thirteen Attributes from the Days of Awe services.

Since King David is the honored *ushpiz* on this day, Psalms, attributed to his authorship, is read (in some places punctuated by *shofar* blasts at the conclusion of each of its five books). Kabbalists in particular recall David, who is said to have remained awake, except for a short nap, every night. Concentrating on *Tikkun* (improvement) *Leil* (for the night of) Hoshanah Rabbah, a compilation of selections from Deuteronomy, Psalms and *Zohar*, the kabbalists attempt to "unite" the darkness of night with the light of day.

As on Shavuot, synagogues and Jewish institutions (such as Hillels) often arrange special study sessions and serve coffee and cake to participants. After the late-night learning, traditional men often go to the *mikvah* for a ritual bath.

Procedure

For the processions, the knotted rings holding the leaves of the *lulav* together are usually removed so that they wave more freely in expression of joy.

Following the *hoshanah* prayers, we put down the four species, take up willow branches, and beat them on the ground or against a chair while reciting a passage asking for forgiveness, dew, and rain. According to ritual law, the bundle needs to be beat only five times, but many people continue thrashing away until most of the leaves are gone. Women and children also participate in this ritual. Since it is a custom continued only through the force of folk tradition, and not a biblical commandment or rabbinic ordinance, no blessing accompanies the action.

The same calendar alteration that ensured that Yom Kippur will never fall immediately before or after a Shabbat also ensures that Hoshanah Rabbah cannot fall on the Sabbath, when the beating ritual cannot not take place (since we are not supposed to hurt or destroy plants).

Reform congregations treat the seventh day of Sukkot no differently than any other part of *khol hamoed* and with no special Hoshanah Rabbah services or rituals.

Shemini Atzeret

Just as Sukkot gives us a transitional period between the Days of Awe and our normal routines, the last day of the festival, Shemini Atzeret, or the Eighth Day of Solemn Assembly, the day we are held back to extend the party with God, eases us out of the transience of the *sukkah*.

As a separate holiday in its own right, also referred to as *Shemini Khag* (festival) *Ha'atzeret*, the eighth day is honored with the lighting of candles and reciting the festival *kiddush*. Common practice is to do *kiddush* and eat in the *sukkah* in the evening and morning, but not to recite the blessing for dwelling in the *sukkah* or to take up the four species. (In Israel, where Shemini Atzeret clearly follows Sukkot, the *sukkah* is not used at all.) At the conclusion of the last meal we recite the blessing for leaving the *sukkah* (see "Dwelling in the *Sukkah*" earlier in this chapter).

Prayer for Rain

The distinct feature of the day is recitation of the prayer for rain so that the earth will be able to produce in the coming year. It is not said earlier during Sukkot, which marks the beginning of the rainy season in Israel, because we do not want rain to prevent us from dwelling in the *sukkah* or to interfere with our enjoyment of doing so.

From the beginning of Shemini Atzeret until the first day of Pesakh, we insert a phrase in the second benediction of the *Amidah*: "who causes the wind to blow and the rain to fall" (*mashiv haruakh u'morid hageshem*). However, the full prayer for rain, except for on the holiday itself, is not included in the ninth benediction of the *Amidah* until the seventh day of the month of *Markheshvan* in Israel, and on December 5 in the Diaspora, based on the rabbinic calculation on the Gregorian calendar of the start of the winter weather (the difference in dates in and outside of Israel has to do with the needs for rain in both places). Saying the prayer was delayed beyond Shemini Atzeret in recognition that the pilgrims needed time to return home before the seasonal rains began.

In the synagogue, the prayer for rain (analogous to the prayer for dew recited on the first day of Pesakh) is said during the *khazzan's* repetition of the *Mussaf Amidah*. He wears a *kittel*, the Ark is opened, and the congregation stands. In asking God to send rain to the earth, we remind Him of the merits of the patriarchs, Moses and Aaron and specific connections they had with water, as well as the Twelve Tribes who crossed the parted waters and for whom God sweetened bitter water in the desert. We ask that the rain be for a blessing, life, and plenty.

Saying the prayer outside Israel heightens our awareness of our connection to the Land and the Jews who live there, reminding us that our destiny is joined with that of our homeland.

Yizkor

As on the last day of the other pilgrimage festivals (as well as Yom Kippur), the service in memory of the deceased is part of the day's observance (except among the majority of Reform congregations, which include it only at Pesakh and Yom Kippur [for more information on the service, see chapter on Pesakh]).

Simkhat Torah

Next to Purim, the Jewish calendar offers no abandon like the Rejoicing of the Torah. If you are going to go to an Orthodox *shul* any day of the year, this is the one. You will be pulled into the uplifting atmosphere and get a glimpse of what religious joy means.

One of the names given to our sacred writings to express the feeling is "Bride," to which Israel is wedded. This is the perfect image for Simkhat Torah, whose celebrations take on the symbolism and rituals of a marriage feast. If you have ever been to a traditional Jewish wedding, you'll understand the comparison. An exuberant expression of the Jewish people's love for our holy book, it is a day full of exceptions to the usual restrictions for the sake of celebration, such as reading Torah after nightfall and indulging in liquor.

Like all festivals, it begins with candlelighting at

home, with *shehekheyanu*; prior to the evening meal, *kiddush* and *motzi* are recited (see "Dwelling in the *Sukkah*" for the *brakhot*). Since there is no biblical reference for Simkhat Torah, a holiday developed in the Middle Ages, liturgically it is regarded as a second day of Shemini Atzeret—with the addition of special ceremonies surrounding the completion of the annual cycle of Torah readings.

The celebration begins with responsive reading of a set of verses taken from various parts of *Tanakh*, the *Atah Hareita* (You Have Been Shown). In many congregations, the privilege of deciding who gets to recite verses is auctioned. The purchaser says the first section, then distributes the honors among other members.

The Ark is opened and all Torah scrolls are removed. So that the Ark will not be empty, some congregations place a Bible or candle inside, symbolizing the Torah. The scrolls are distributed to the first group of people to be honored (in traditional synagogues, the *Kohanim* and *Levi'im*, but any categories can be used: scholars, donors, *shul* volunteers, longtime members, newcomers).

Led by the Torah-bearers, congregants parade around the synagogue. In liberal settings, women and girls participate in the processions, called *hakafot* (circuits), adapted from the ancient Temple *lulav* ritual. In traditional settings the procession passes the women's section to give women the chance to kiss the Torah as it passes. (Out of respect, it is customary for both men and women to not touch the Torah directly, but to bring the spine of a *siddur* or edge of a *tallit* or handkerchief to the scroll and then touch it to the lips.) Since the eighteenth century, children have marched along behind the adults, like a little army, carrying their paper flags. Today, it is also common for children to carry miniature or stuffed versions of the Torah.

For each *hakafah* short verses are chanted responsively asking God to give us success and save us now. When a circuit has been completed, the leader breaks out in song, and dance circles form around those with the Torah scrolls, whirling, stomping, and kicking in spirited *khasidi* or folk dances to Yiddish, Hebrew, and Israeli songs. Those who do not join the dancing sing and clap.

At some arbitrary time, the scrolls are passed to the next group of people who will carry them, and another *hakafah* around the sanctuary begins. To avoid getting tired out before the end of the seventh circuit and its attendant dancing, some congregations insert a short *devar Torah* (homiletic lesson) about midway through the proceedings to give people a chance to rest. On one or more circuits, or after the Torah reading, it is customary in most congregations to sing the traditional "*Sisu v'Simkhu*" (Rejoice and be Glad [with the Torah]). During the *hakafot*, you might hear hundreds of the more than eight hundred *piyyutim* written for the holiday, in Ladino, Aramaic, Yiddish, Judeo-Arabic, and Hebrew—more than for any other festival. Since the celebration is meant to be participatory, an attempt is made to give everyone who wants it the chance to carry a Torah before the end of the evening.

At the conclusion of the *hakafot*, all Torah scrolls but one are returned to the *Aron Hakodesh*. Although reading from the Torah in synagogue at night is usually prohibited, it was deemed improper to have the *Sifrei Torah* out of the Ark without using them at all. So on Simkhat Torah night, we read from the final portion of Deuteronomy, containing Moses' farewell, stopping before the end of the book (33:26).

The next day, the *hakafot* again take place. When finished, the necessary scrolls are kept out of the Ark for an extended Torah-reading ceremony. First, Deuteronomy 33:1–26 is read, with *aliyot* given to as many men who want them. (In very large congregations, the crowd splits into manageable groups, each around its own Torah scroll.)

At the end of each *aliyah*, the honoree customarily pledges a *tzedakah* contribution, then makes a *kiddush* over wine or liquor, which has been set out in the rear of the sanctuary or just outside it, along with cake, fruit, herring, and perhaps gefilte fish and taffy apples. The custom of celebrating with joyous feasting at the completion of the cycle of Torah reading (called *siyyum*) is based on King Solomon's experience: When he awoke from the dream in which God had endowed him with the wisdom of Torah, he offered sacrifices at the Temple and then prepared a feast for all his servants in gratitude (I Kings 3:15).

Since in the joyful abandonment of the day it is not unusual for people to celebrate a little too strenuously, the *Kohanim* are exempt from the service called *dukhan* (literally "platform," the place where the priests stood in the Temple, and where the *Kohanim* stand in the synagogue to give the priestly blessing), as they might have difficulty concentrating on any duty other than rejoicing of the law. Sometimes they *dukhan* during the repetition of the *Shakharit Amidah*, instead of that of *Mussaf*, the usual place, before the feasting and celebration have disturbed the solemn atmosphere necessary for the blessing.

Once the adults have been called to Torah, "all the lads" (*kol hanearim*), boys under the age of *bar mitzvah*, are called up together. In a ritual based on Jacob's blessing of his grandchildren (Genesis 48:8–20), an esteemed adult spreads a prayer shawl over their heads and pronounces the *aliyah* blessing, which the boys repeat word for word.

The person honored with reading the blessings for the last verses, Deuteronomy 33:27–34:12, is called *Khattan Torah*, Groom of the Law. (In some places he is actually a newlywed, in others an esteemed member of the congregation or someone who has paid for the honor.) At the conclusion of the reading, which is the end of Torah, the congregation calls out *khazak, khazak venitkhazek!* (be strong, be strong and let us be strengthened), the exclamation made whenever a book of Khumash has been completed.

Hagbah (raising the scroll before the congregation following a Torah reading) is done in a special way. Instead of lifting with the left roller in the left hand and the right roller in the right, the person crosses his hands to take the opposite roller in each hand and uncrosses them when he raises the scroll so it is reversed, with the writing facing the congregation (instead of facing the *hagbah*, as usual). This symbolizes turning of the Torah back to its beginning and reminds us of the expression "Turn [the Torah] over and over for everything is in it" (*Pirkei Avot*). The congregation rises with the scroll and chants the phrase used whenever the Torah is presented following a reading, "*Zot haTorah, shesahm Moshe lifnei b'nei Yisrael al pi Adonai b'yad Moshe*" (This is the Torah Moses placed before the children of Israel by the command of God through Moses' hand.)

As at an *uf-ruf*, the calling of a groom-to-be to Torah on the Shabbat before his wedding, the *Khattan Torah* is pelted with candies (in some places nuts and raisins) representing the sweetness of scripture.

From the second scroll, the Creation account is read (Genesis 1:1–2:3) after blessings recited by *Khattan Bereshit*, Groom of the Beginning, another honoree. The entire congregation recites the verse "*Vay'hi erev, vay'hi voker*" (it was evening, it was morning) for each day, then it is recited by the reader. At the sixth day, the congregation continues reading through the verses for the seventh day. Some congregations spread a *tallit* over the bridegrooms. (The full Torah portion of *Bereshit* [in the beginning] is read on the Shabbat following the festival.)

The *haftarah*, Joshua 1, picks up the story of Israel following Moses' death. Just as we turn again to life, immediately starting the Torah reading cycle again with the birth of the world and humanity, the account of our history continues as the mantle of leadership is passed to Moses' successor, who leads us to the next stage in our development. Going from the end to the beginning without hesitation shows our ongoing devotion to Torah, a sort of annual renewal of vows.

Some congregations take advantage of Simkhat Torah as a time of joyful affirmation of the *mitzvah* of Torah study by holding special consecration ceremonies for children entering religious school for the first time. It is customary to give the children something sweet, so they associate learning with the pleasurable taste (a custom also on Shavuot). Mini Torah scrolls might also be given. (Reform congregations often hold their consecrations on the Sabbath during Sukkot.)

Conclusion

As on all festivals, the brief ceremony marking the transition between sacred and ordinary time, *Havdalah*, is performed, either following the *Ma'ariv* service in synagogue or at home after nightfall. On a weeknight, only the blessings over wine and separation are made. If the departure of the festival coincides with the close of Shabbat, we recite the full *Havdalah*, including the blessings over spices and fire (see chapter on Pesakh).

Isru Khag

Although our festival has already been extended for an extra day, Isru Khag, the day following the extension, like the day after Pesakh and Shavuot, is another occasion when the holiday is held back so we can sustain its spirit and carry it with us into the work week. Unmarked in the Diaspora except for the omission of penitential prayers and the prohibition of fasting, in Israel boisterous celebration marks the occasion (see Customs).

FOR FURTHER READING

Fabricant, Rabbi Isaac. *A Guide to Succoth.* London: Jewish Chronicle Publications, 1958.

Components of the various synagogue services during the week of Sukkot are detailed.

Succos—Its Significance, Laws and Prayers. Ed. by Rabbi Nosson Scherman and Rabbi Meir Zlotowitz. Brooklyn: Mesorah Publications, 1969.

This is a compact alternative to a *siddur* for the full text of all the blessings needed for the holidays. In addition, explanations are provided for key phrases in the prayers.

WHERE DO WE BEGIN?— PREPARATION

Ritual

A *midrash* tells us that God gave Israel the days between Yom Kippur and Sukkot as a special gift, a time when the nation is considered pure, having just emerged from judgment. Presumably, being preoccupied with obtaining a *lulav* and *etrog* and building the *sukkah* would keep one out of trouble.

To earn extra "*mitzvah* points" during the Ten Days of Repentance, Jews traditionally prepared the four species then. (Today, synagogues complete orders for them prior to the Day of Atonement.) Some people use the time to begin to get their booths ready. If it has not been begun earlier, starting construction of the *sukkah* immediately following Yom Kippur services is particularly meritorious.

Seizing that moment has practical advantage: It is not only in Israel that the holiday coincides with the rainy season. You cannot count on good weather at the last minute. Obviously, you will want to obtain the supplies needed, or purchase a pre-fab model, well before the construction date. If you want to get branches for *s'khakh* from your parks department, early inquiries would be prudent.

The same holds true for extending invitations if you plan to host meals in your *sukkah*. Particularly in communities where many families have booths, schedules for sharing meals are established in the weeks prior to the holiday. That is also the time to engage the children in making decorations for the *sukkah*.

Spiritual

A *khasidic* anecdote reminds us that not all advance work for Sukkot is material: A member of his sect wanted a special benediction from the Dizekover rabbi that he would obtain a regal palm branch, a flawless citron, and a lovely myrtle and willow in order to observe the holiday. The rabbi informed him, "What you require is an honest mind, a generous heart, and a meek spirit. Once you have acquired these, then you can seek and find an extraordinary *lulav* and *etrog*."

WHAT ARE WE SUPPOSED TO DO?— *HALAKHAH*

Festival Laws

All the laws of festivals that apply to the pilgrimages and to Rosh Hashanah, and the *khol hamoed* laws in effect for Pesakh, govern Sukkot (see "*Halakhah*" in chapter on Pesakh).

Tzedakah

We are obligated to increase charity the day before Sukkot. Providing for the poor and others in need is inherent in celebration of the festival.

Constructing the *Sukkah*

Walls

The shelter should have four walls, though theoretically two and part of a third will qualify it. (The regulations about minimum widths and areas of opening of an incomplete wall are technical and should be reviewed with an authority.) If you do not have enough materials for four full walls, it is preferable to make three that are finished. Already existing walls, like sides of a house or fence, may be used. A permanent part of a house—such as a porch or attic room— may be used if the roof is removable.

Any material is acceptable, as long as it will withstand a normal wind and prevent candles from being extinguished. If you use cloth for the walls, it must be tied down so it will not flap in the wind.

Size

The minimum height of the walls is approximately three feet (traditionally ten *tefakhim*, which different authorities designated as being between three and three and three-eighths inches each). The structure must be at least twenty-six inches long and twenty-six inches wide, an area sufficient to accommodate the head and major portion of one's body and a table.

The walls may not be higher than thirty feet (twenty cubits, each about eighteen inches). If the walls of the *sukkah* are too high, when you sit inside the booth you would tend not to notice the *s'khah* and would therefore be unaware that you are in a *sukkah* and not concentrating on its significance. Tall walls also cast shadows inside the structure, and any shade is supposed to be provided by the covering.

Covering

The *s'khakh* must be composed of materials that grow from the earth and have been detached from it. Straw, cornstalks, bamboo reeds (as long as they are not in bundles of more than twenty-five pieces), and narrow wood beams are all acceptable. The material should be organic and unprocessed and not susceptible to ritual impurity (metals, leather, and food-stuffs may not be used). You are not supposed to use boards or beams wider than sixteen inches, even if stood up on their narrowest sides, because they resemble those used for a house roof or ceiling.

More decorative leafy tree branches are used whenever possible. They must last for the duration of the holiday without becoming dried and brown. Branches whose leaves continually drop or are ill-smelling are not appropriate.

The *s'khakh* should be spaced evenly with no gaping holes or openings wider than eleven and a half inches. It should provide more shade than sun and allow you to see the stars at night and should not prevent rain from falling into the booth.

Just as a *sukkah* may not be built under a tree whose branches reach over it, it may not be built under a permanent overhang that extends over it more than six feet. An area of a *sukkah* under a shorter overhang does not count as part of the booth, so no one should sit there.

Since the element that makes the booth a *sukkah* is the *s'khakh*, it should be put on last. If you leave a booth standing from one year to another, the *s'khakh* has to be replaced. Check with a local rabbinic authority about the particulars.

Decoration

Any decorative ornaments, like the *sukkah* itself, are considered dedicated for sacred purpose for the duration of the festival, and therefore may not be removed, even if they fall down, or used for any other purpose. Not even a splinter of wood from a wall can be taken for a toothpick. (For the same reason, once the holiday has ended, the *sukkah* is to be treated with respect, carefully stored for the next year, or burned. It should not simply be discarded.)

Dwelling in the *Sukkah*

Fulfilling the Mitzvah

During the seven days of the festival, you are to regard the *sukkah* as your principal abode and your house as just a temporary residence. Any activity you normally do at home—eat, drink, sleep, spend leisure time—should be done in the *sukkah*. Since it is a sanctified space, time spent in it should be devoted to study of Torah and matters of sanctity, rather than to idle talk. In keeping with honoring the space, the finest tableware should be brought into it and dirty dishes removed as soon as a meal is finished.

The essential aspects of dwelling, the ones most detailed in the laws, concern eating and sleeping. Since there are numerous technicalities regarding what constitutes a snack, a meal, and a nap, consult a detailed guide or an authority.

Eating

In general, you may not eat a meal outside the *sukkah*. While outside it is permissible to have any amount of beverages and fruit, vegetables, bread, or cake up to the volume equivalent of an egg, taking all sustenance inside is commendable.

The exemption for weather (see below) does not hold for the first night of the festival, when the obligation to eat in the *sukkah* is more stringent than it is during the rest of the week. Some authorities say a piece of bread at least the volume of an olive (*k'zayit*) must be eaten in the *sukkah* despite heavy rain. Because of dispute on the matter, no blessing is made.

You should wait an hour or two (some postpone a meal until as late as midnight) in the hope that the rain will cease. If it does not, or the presence of guests or young children precludes waiting, make *kiddush* in the *sukkah*, don't recite the *ushpizin*, eat the minimum amount required, and finish the meal indoors. In case of inclement weather on the second night, you may do *kiddush* and have the meal in the house, then go into the *sukkah* and eat the minimum amount.

If the light goes out in your *sukkah* on Shabbat, when it may not be relit, and one is on in the house, you should eat there (unless you can eat in a neighbor's *sukkah*).

Sleeping

Original law forbade even a nap outside the *sukkah*. It was relaxed in recognition of weather conditions in northern latitudes. If it is too cold to sleep outside, you may sleep in the comfort of your permanent home. (The pious, especially in warmer climates, make every effort to sleep in the *sukkah*.)

Exemptions

In certain conditions or situations, you are excused from the obligation to dwell in the *sukkah*. Except for discomfort, however, it is considered meritorious to transcend the excuse and observe the *mitzvah* (though you do so without saying the blessing). It is also commendable to do something to remind yourself of the holiday if you cannot be in a *sukkah*, such as including Torah discussion at your meals.

If dwelling in the *sukkah* causes physical distress (if you are bothered by wind, flies, or bees), or if it is raining heavily, you are excused. Sickness (even a headache) exempts you from the obligation. (A sick person's attendant is also exempted if s/he is needed by the patient.) If women and young children fulfill the obligation to eat in the *sukkah*, they recite the benedictions. Any other exempt person who remains in the *sukkah* despite discomfort is not to recite a blessing.

If you are away from home during the holiday you do not have to take meals or sleep in a *sukkah*. But if you have the opportunity to have a meal in a *sukkah*, you should take advantage of it.

The bride, groom, and wedding party are exempt for the traditional seven days of celebration following the wedding. This is because the *sukkah* is not the most comfortable setting for a couple's wedding night, and because one kind of joy (wedding) should not be mixed with another (festival).

If you are engaged in performing another *mitzvah*, such as Torah study, redeeming captives, or visiting your teacher, you are excused from the *mitzvah* of *sukkah*.

Brakhot

The benediction for sitting in the *sukkah* is recited only if you will perform a function requiring you to be in it—such as eating a meal. The benediction does not have to be said before each meal if you remain in the *sukkah* between one meal and another, if you leave it for only a short period of time, or if you are just visiting someone. If you forget to say the blessing before you start eating, you may say it anytime during the meal.

Selecting the Four Species

In order to perform the ritual and say the *brakhot*, you need to have all four species. If some of your four species are invalid, and no kosher set is available on loan in your vicinity, then you should use what you have but not make a *brakhah*. Don't substitute species other than those identified. Details of the validity of the species, and the differences in what is acceptable the first two days and the rest of the week, need to be reviewed with an authority.

Etrog

The *pittam* (tip) must be intact. The species of *etrog* that naturally grows without a *pittam* is acceptable, but one that is the result of grafting (lemon and citron) is not. It should be at least the size of an egg (a smaller one is considered unripe and therefore not yet a fruit); there is no maximum size, but you need to be able to hold it in your hand. The fruit is valid even if half of it is scarred and if it is perforated, as long as no part of it is missing. (Many people prefer *etrogim* that are completely free of spots.)

Leaves

The other species should be fresh and green. If you will choose your own, check a detailed guide regarding specific characteristics such as shape and composition. The palm should be about fifteen inches long and four inches longer than the other twigs, each of which should be ten to eleven inches long.

The *lulav* is to be tied in three places with palm fronds. (Some consider the point where the myrtle and willows are attached as one of the points, and therefore tie it in two more places up the shaft. Others place three rings above the holder.) The top four inches are to be left untied so the leaves rustle when the *lulav* is shaken.

Using the Four Species

Ownership

On the first day (or first two days in the Diaspora) of the festival, the *lulav* and *etrog* you use must belong to you. You may use those of another person if s/he gives them to you as a gift (with the understanding that you will return them). Since a minor is not empowered to transfer ownership, you may not use the four species of a child, and for the same reason if a child will be using another's s/he should be the last to do so. On intermediate days, since the *mitzvah* is performed only in commemoration of the Temple and not by commandment or ordinance, you may borrow the *lulav* and *etrog* without acquiring ownership. Synagogue sets bought with public funds are considered jointly owned property.

Women

Although women are exempt from the obligation of the four species, they have accepted it on themselves and may recite the *brakhah*.

Taking Up

There is disagreement as to whether left-handed people reverse the order of picking up the four species (taking the *lulav* in the left hand, *etrog* in the right); majority holds that they do not. Nothing should create a barrier between the hands and the four species, so it is appropriate to remove *tefillin* straps and rings.

The *mitzvah* should be fulfilled only during daytime, after sunrise. If you must leave home before that time, you may take up the species as long as it is after dawn (seventy-two minutes before sunrise). It is prohibited to eat beforehand, but you may have a snack if necessary. Also, if the four species won't be available in the morning (in case you do not have your own), do not defer the meal until noon because it is forbidden to fast on a festival or the intermediate days.

Simkhat Torah

It is a *mitzvah* to participate in the Torah procession honoring completion and beginning of the reading cycle, for it symbolizes the observance of the *mitzvah* of continual Torah study.

FOR FURTHER READING

Succos—Its Significance, Laws and Prayers. Ed. by Rabbi Nosson Scherman and Rabbi Meir Zlotowitz. Brooklyn: Mesorah Publications, 1969.

Explication of the laws, including some of their more technical aspects, is presented in contemporary, easily understood terms. Illustrations of the four species are included.

WHAT OTHER THINGS DO PEOPLE DO?— CUSTOMS

Other Times and Places

Four Species

From ancient times, the *lulav* and *etrog* have been treated with reverence. Men sometimes undertook difficult journeys during the Middle Ages to obtain *etrogim*, and Jews have always been willing to spend beyond their means for the choicest ones. Because of the high cost, several people would often form partnerships in order to merit in ownership, if only partial. This created the necessity of having a messenger ferry it among the co-owners, at home and at different synagogues, so that each could take up the four species. Sometimes one *etrog* sufficed for an entire community. Among the Judeo-Spanish, the honor of providing the four species for a congregation was auctioned; sometimes a set was purchased exclusively for the women to use.

The *etrogim* of Corfu, renowned for their beauty, were particularly prized and sought after (leading to the Eastern European expression "a girl like a Corfu *etrog*"), until rumors that they were the result of grafting led to their being avoided.

To protect the *etrog*—particularly to ensure that the *pittam* remained intact—containers were adapted to hold it and carry it to synagogue. The custom of using sugar bowls and candy or soap dishes of silver, wood, and glass led to the creation of boxes specifically for the fruit. Centuries of folk art have left us with incredible versions made of wood, pottery, and silver, some elaborately shaped or decorated. (One of the earliest surviving containers is from late seventeenth-century Germany, and other examples are family treasures or parts of museum collections.)

The Moroccans decorated their *lulavim* with colorful silk ribbons and protected the tips with decorative caps. The Judeo-Spanish placed seven rings along the top third of the *lulav* so that one could be removed on each circuit on Hoshanah Rabbah.

Once the holiday ended, children often turned the *lulav* leaves into braided rings and bracelets. Many communities would save the *lulav* and/or willows. They were kept upright in flower pots all year as a charm for good health for the family or, by the *Sephardim*, above the door lintel. This was based on the biblical instruction to "take a cluster of hyssop and use it to dip the blood of the Passover sacrifice on the doorpost" (Exodus 12:22). Many used them before Pesakh to light the fire for baking *matzah* or burning *khametz*. The *lulav* leaves sometimes replaced the feather for the *khametz* search.

In Europe, the *aravot* were treated with dignity and placed on top of the *Aron Hakodesh*. In several *Sephardi* communities, the *aravot* were beaten lightly on the backs of household members as a good omen for fertility or health (a custom shared by many cultures). Some people marched around with them as they burned. Moroccan Jews used them to fuel a fire for broiling meat that was considered a remedy for barren women.

Most of the superstitious customs regarding conception and childbirth revolved around the *etrog*. According to tradition, the *etrog*, not the apple, was the Garden of Eden's "forbidden fruit." So it was viewed in folk medicine as a substance for facilitating birth.

Talmudic legend asserts that one who eats an *etrog* will have fragrant children, so it became customary for women to bite the *pittam* off the *etrog* after Hoshanah Rabbah services (when the *etrog* no longer has ritual value). The act demonstrated that they had resisted the temptation to eat the fruit throughout the holiday. Eastern European Jews believed that a pregnant woman who bit off the citron's tip would give birth to a male (fostered by a popular German legend that Princess Louise did so with the prescribed accompanying supplication and gave birth to the boy

who later became Frederick William IV, King of Prussia). The *pittam* was placed under the pillow of a woman in labor in the belief that it would alleviate her pain.

Others used the *etrog* for *Havdalah* until it was dried. Filled with cloves, it lasted longer and provided a sweet way to revive the faint during the following year's Yom Kippur services. After the festival many collected the citrons and made jelly for Tu B'Shevat.

Building the Sukkah

For Eastern European Jews, the *sukkah* became a symbol of the destroyed Temple (based on Amos 9:11, promising to "raise up the *sukkah* of David," understood as the Temple, at the time of the Messiah). Following the biblical commandment to build the altar without using tools of metal—considered instruments of war—they constructed their *sukkot* without the use of nails, emphasizing its representation of peace. The wealthy commissioned folk artists to paint murals on their *sukkah* walls. (A magnificent example, the Fischach *Sukkah* from nineteenth-century Germany, depicting scenes from the Bible and local culture, is in the Israel Museum in Jerusalem.)

It was common to convert a room in a house (such as attic space) or a storage shed into a *sukkah* by having a roof that could be raised and lowered by means of hinges or a pulley. *S'khakh* was placed over the opening for the duration of the festival. In the Middle Ages, communal *sukkot* were built to accommodate travelers.

Decorating the Sukkah

The Jews in Europe and Russia sprinkled fine sand on the ground of the *sukkah*, perhaps in remembrance of the desert journey the festival commemorates. Hollowed out eggs decorated with paper or feathers became birds. Strings of cranberries or plums were used to resemble the grapes gathered in the valley of Eshkol in Canaan when representatives of the Twelve Tribes were sent to explore the Land (Numbers 13:23). The Judeo-Spanish decorated with circular or six-pointed baked pastries.

In some communities, a light was kindled each night in honor of the particular *ushpiz* of the day; others lit seven candles every night, for all seven distinguished guests. In Calcutta, a Bible in the corner of the *sukkah* was opened each night to a section on the life of the heavenly guest. Moroccans also studied the appropriate sections of *Zohar*.

In Israel, in order for those in the defense forces to

be able to observe the holiday, *sukkot* are constructed on navy boats or put on wheels and carried to field units, even during times of combat. The Lubavitch *khasidim* do the same with their "*Sukkah*mobile," visiting schools, hospitals, public institutions, and shopping centers. They distribute brochures describing the traditions of the holiday and invite people to bless the *lulav* and *etrog*.

Use of the Sukkah

Even before it became popular to include great women of Israel among the honored guests each night, North African Jewish women went into the *sukkah* during the day to welcome the matriarch Rachel.

In Salonika, the first days of the holiday were devoted to family visiting. The men and children made the rounds, while the women stayed home to receive guests. They served a "sweet table," a tray containing a jar of preserves with a water chaser and exotic citrus fruits. Adults were given traditional gifts of eggs made brown by boiling them with onion skins, and children received apples. In addition to inviting friends to join them in the *sukkah*, Moroccans also sent gifts of fancy foods.

A napkin hung in front of a Jerusalem *sukkah* entrance indicated a meal was in progress and guests could come in to partake of it.

In predominantly Jewish neighborhoods, it is still customary to "tour" *sukkot*, sometimes on the initial days to make *kiddush* with wine and cake. In Israel, where you see *sukkot* on balconies, rooftops, squares of land in front of buildings, and municipal settings —creating a scene out of Nehemiah (8:16–18)—the army and individual cities often run contests for the most beautiful.

Worship

If a Syrian Jew were prevented from attending synagogue due to illness, and he recited *hoshanot* at home, he placed a *Tanakh* on a table or chair and walked around it with the *lulav* and *etrog* to fulfill the *mitzvah* of the *hakafot*.

On the evening of the second day of Sukkot, pious Eastern European Jews had their version of the *Simkhat Beit Hashoavah*. They lit candles and lamps throughout the synagogue and used the money raised by auctioning honors to pay for apples and brandy consumed by the participants.

Today in religious communities, and throughout the city of Jerusalem, *Simkhat Beit Hashoavah* celebrations are often held on one of the intermediate nights and are like big parties, with *klezmer* groups (traditional Eastern European street music), singing, dancing, and food and drink. Often the fifteen *Shir Hamalot* (Song of Ascents, Psalms 120–134) are recited, as was done in the Temple.

Hoshanah Rabbah Symbols and Superstitions

The custom of staying up all night to apply oneself to Torah study developed because of belief that at precisely midnight, the heavens open and if one uttered a wish at that very moment, it would be fulfilled. It was also believed by common folk in the Middle Ages that your shadow cast by the moon on this night indicated the verdict you had received on Yom Kippur: If it were headless, you would die during the coming year, unless you repented, in which case punishment would be reduced to an illness.

Despite the solemnity imposed on the day for inducing rain, it was a time for pranks and frivolity, especially in Oriental Jewish communities (Yemen, Persia, India, Bukhara). Children playfully hit passersby with palm leaves, and adults grabbed *lulavim* and *etrogim* from children, threw water on each other, or tossed one another into lakes or streams.

Introducing a Boy

On Simkhat Torah in Cochin (India), the six-year-old boy of a leading family chanted a portion of the prophets to mark his entry into the group of those allowed to read from the holy books for the congregation. All the men of the synagogue then blessed him, and his female cousins gave him gifts. After services, the family hosted a feast for the community.

In Yemen, a boy was introduced to the community and blessed by them on the first Simkhat Torah of his life. The same custom was followed in Morocco, where the boy's father presented a magnificent candle to the synagogue, which would then be lit on each significant occasion in the boy's life.

Rejoicing with the Torah

In Babylon in the tenth century and later in Italy, North Africa, and Provence, Simkhat Torah observance included elegies for Moses, whose death is recorded in the day's Torah portion. These mournful tunes gave way to brighter songs and hymns once the *hakafot* were instituted.

In Moroccan and Afghani synagogues the walls were almost completely covered with textiles, plaques, and flowers. In Jerusalem and Oriental countries, the Bridegrooms of the Law and the Beginning sat on thrones under canopies of silk or a lavishly decorated *khupah* in the sanctuary's center. Jasmine wreaths and candles added to the aura of gaity in Cochin. The Bridegrooms were symbolically crowned with wreaths of myrtle (the plant used in ancient Judea in bridal processions) or, as begun in thirteenth-century Spain, with the actual crown from the Torah scroll. Sometimes it was placed on the head of every man called to the Torah and on children's heads. In other places, special hats adorned with bells were used.

In Vienna—where Simkhat Torah services were so popular that people lined up early and often had to be turned away—the *khatanim* wore top hats and tails in the regal ceremonial processions, led by the beadle in a Turkish fez.

Torah scrolls, the truly honored members of the party, were themselves specially adorned, sometimes in vestments made by the women of the community, flower or myrtle wreaths, or gold or silver crowns (even before they were used as regular ornaments). The Afghani Jews set up their *Sifrei Torah* in a pyramid on the lectern and covered it with silk cloths. One scroll was placed in Elijah's Chair, around which everyone danced.

Eastern European synagogues added the auction of honors for special Torah portions throughout the year to those for Simkhat Torah in order to generate their operating expenses for the next twelve months. In Amsterdam, congregations voted on who was to receive honors. Those who had been married during the previous year received them in some locales.

Children carried flags with cored apples that held candles lit to symbolize the Torah's light. This custom may have developed from the abolished practice of burning *sukkot*, which led to carrying torches into the synagogue. When judged too dangerous, the torches were replaced by the small candles.

The congregation showered the bridegrooms with candy and other sweets (gathered up afterward by the children), and they in turn made feasts for the congregation. In medieval Worms, children too young to attend synagogue were showered with fruits and sweets at home. (A non-Jewish woman stipulated in her will that the fruit from her garden be provided for the Jewish children on Simkhat Torah until the Messiah arrived.) In Mediterranean countries, guests were sprinkled with fragrant sprays. Congregations in Italy, Netherlands, and England, singing and carrying banners and torches, carried the bridegrooms home. The Italian wives were known as Brides of the Law and the Beginning. Their festivities were so extravagant in the eighteenth-century that the community had to issue *takanot* (edicts for communal benefit) to restrict the ostentation and expenditure.

Gunpowder salvos and bonfires, which encouraged leaping and dancing, were often part of *Ashkenazi* celebration in Central and Eastern Europe. Many well-known *khasidic* melodies developed from the enthusiastic rejoicing in the streets and courtyards.

In Israel, congregations join in massive dancing processions to the Western Wall, behind Torah scrolls under canopies, each like a bride being led under her *khupah* to the marriage ceremony.

Post-Holiday

Those who had the custom of fasting on the Monday, Thursday, and Monday after the extended pilgrimage festivals to compensate for any excesses of imbibing and feasting in the previous days waited until *Kheshvan* to do so. While the fast (called *bet, hei, bet,* the Hebrew letters designating the first and fifth days of the week on which those observing it abstained) should have immediately followed the close of Sukkot, since the month of *Tishrei* is totally devoted to rejoicing because of all its holidays, it was postponed until the following month, *Kheshvan*.

In Salonika, public games on *motzi* (the exit of) Simkhat Torah were held in the courtyard of the host bridegroom, preceding his banquet for the community. In Israel, expanded versions have turned into the institution of *Hakafot Shniyot* (Second Circuits). At Liberty Bell Park, Mea Shearim and other locations in Jerusalem, and in other spots around the country (like the Florentine quarter in Tel Aviv and on army bases), people come together by the thousands and tens of thousands for a continuation of the joyous frenzy. While the rest of the Jewish world is just getting into Simkhat Torah, the Israelis—secular and religious alike—joined by tourists, honor different ethnic groups, professions, and communities as each, with its characteristic dress, music, and dancing, is called on to lead a procession.

FOR FURTHER READING

Chagall, Bella. "The Rejoicing of the Torah." In BL, pp. 106–114.

The author reminisces about the postsynagogue celebrations of her childhood in Vitebsk, Russia.

"Sukkot and Simkhat Torah in Many Lands." In Sukkot and Simhat Torah HA, pp. 179–256.

Essays describing Simkhat Torah celebrations in Sholom Aleichem's Kasrielevky, Eastern Europe, Salonika, and Israel give a sense of what it is like to observe the holiday in communities where being Jewish is a dominating aspect of life.

Greeting

"*Gut yom tov*" (Yiddish) and "*khag samei'akh*" (Hebrew), "happy holiday," are appropriate on Sukkot and Simkhat Torah. During *khol hamoed*, "*a guten yom tov*" (Yiddish) or "*mo'adim l'simkhah*," "a good or joyous holiday," is also exchanged. Some people continue to wish others Yom Kippur's "*gemar tov*" ("be sealed for good") through the seventh day of Sukkot, since repentance and therefore the chance to avert a bad verdict are possible until then. On Hoshanah Rabbah, people traditionally have wished each other "*piktah tovah*," "a good note," referring to the judgment to be issued that day. The *Sephardim* continue their greetings of the new year, "*tizkeh leshanim*" ("may you merit long life"), rejoined with "*tizkeh vetikhyeh veta'arikh yomim*" ("may you merit, live, and have length of days").

Dress

Shabbat clothes are appropriate for the *yom tovim*.

WHAT IS THERE TO EAT?— TRADITIONAL FOODS

No one dish or menu is associated with Sukkot, although foods harvested in the fall, as you would expect, are generally used. In ancient times these included figs, dates, pomegranates, apricots, squash, romaine lettuce, onions, barley, and wheat. For Eastern Europeans, plentiful cabbage, cucumbers, sweet potatoes, and apples were turned into stuffed cabbage, pickles, *tzimmes*, and strudel.

Cabbage dishes are popular on Simkhat Torah in some communities, since the Hebrew word for cabbage, *k'ruv*, means "cherub," an allusion to the angels carved on the Ark of the Covenant (Exodus 25:18–22). For Berliners, the cabbage dish *vasser kal* was eaten on Hoshanah Rabbah because of the hymn *Kol Mevasser* (Announcing Voice) recited as the willows were beaten.

In America, many of the same dishes popular for Thanksgiving appear first on the Sukkot table. Casseroles, which retain their heat from the kitchen to the *sukkah*, are popular, as are stuffed vegetables (perhaps "being stuffed" indicating abundance).

Throughout the holiday, bread is dipped in honey, as for Rosh Hashanah, for a sweet year. *Khallot* on Hoshanah Rabbah take on the symbolic shapes of the earlier holiday (circular, and ladder-shaped), and are also shaped into keys, for opening the heavenly gates, and hands, for receiving the Divine decree. As for other holidays, which encompass symbolic beatings and concealment (the *makkot* and unknown verdict of Yom Kippur; the effigies of Haman and hiddenness of God on Purim), *kreplakh* (dough pockets filled with meat and completely sealed) are the most traditional menu component on Hoshanah Rabbah. After morning services, some people serve a festive meal that features *kreplakh*, nuts, and carrots cut in rounds (representing wealth).

DO YOU HEAR MUSIC?—SONGS TO SING

Most of the songs associated with this festival are those traditional for the *hakafot*, particularly of Simkhat Torah. They include folktunes and numerous *khasidi niggunim* (melodies), among them "*Yom Tov Lanu*" (Our Holiday), about celebration of Sukkot, "*Sisu V'Simkhu*" (Rejoice and Be Happy), expressing our feeling for Torah, and "*Mipi El*" (From the Mouth of God), a song of appreciation that accompanies the Simkhat Torah circuits.

"*Lamah Sukkah Zu?*" (Why this *Sukkah*?), a folk song, is a child's request for his father to explain the rituals of the holiday. Folk songs and more recently created Israeli tunes are widely used in Simkhat Torah celebrations. One of the most appropriate is the lively "*U'shavtem Mayim*" (You Shall Draw Water), Isaiah's promise of joyful salvation, known by thousands of Jewish youth group and summer camp veterans who learned not just the song but the dance that accompanies it. You'll be able to learn the simple tune for the refrain of the *Hoshanot* during the services.

FOR FURTHER READING

High Holidays and Sukkot Melodies. Cedarhurst, NY: Board of Jewish Education of Greater New York and Tara Publications.

There is an accompanying cassette tape for the booklet of traditional tunes for the fall holidays, whose words are transliterated into English.

WHAT TALES ARE TOLD?— STORIES TO READ

A number of poems for this holiday season convey simple ideas and images about the ritual items and observances, making them appropriate for children. Israel Zangwill described a *sukkah* in his poem "A Tabernacle Thought." Hayyim Nahman Bialik wondered about the dreams of the moonlit *lulav* and *etrog* in "Foreigners," and their fate following the holiday in "Elegy on the *Etrog* and *Lulav*." In the equally brief "Beating the Willow" he describes the noise and passion surrounding the Hoshanah Rabbah thrashings. Saul Tchernichovsky's "*Sukkah*" tells how his father built and his mother decorated the booth, and "*Hakkafot*" describes the synagogue scene during the processions with the Torah (all included in *The Sukkot and Simkhat Torah Anthology*; see Appendix C).

The celebration of the last set of fall holidays provided rich material for Sholom Aleichem and other writers who recreate scenes and sentiments in traditional homes.

FOR FURTHER READING

Folktales

"The Death of Moses—An Ethiopian Tale." In CT, pp. 167–169.

In this very different account of the end of Moses' life, the great leader is most cooperative with God's last order.

"Moses Resists His Fate," "Only a Glimpse of the Promised Land," and "A Kiss of the Shekhina." In CT, pp. 158–164.

Together these three brief stories portray Moses' last moments on Earth. Fantastic in their presentation of the great leader as obstinate in the face of God's last command to him, they are moving and spiritually uplifting.

Other Stories

Agnon, Samuel Joseph. "The Story of the Melody." In *Agnon's Twenty-One Stories*. New York: Schocken Books, 1990, pp. 22–24; and Sukkot and Simhat Torah HA, pp. 295–297.

As the congregation is rapt with Raphael's chant during the Simkhat Torah celebration, an accident between the candle on a young woman's flag and the eligible young man's robe becomes the basis for a match.

Aleichem, Sholom. "The Dead Citron." In HT, pp. 69–85; and Sukkot and Simhat Torah HA, pp. 273–279.

Moshe Yankel, a clerk, was determined to have his own *etrog* one year, but his mischievous son and a clumsy carpenter thwart his dreams.

———. "The Merrymakers—Sketches of Disappearing Types." In FT, pp. 550–559.

Simple people are transformed by their revelry on Simkhat Torah and provide welcome entertainment for the town.

———. "The Miracle of Hoshanah Rabbah." In FT, pp. 228–238.

A Jew, a priest, a runaway locomotive, and Aleichem's amusing turns of phrase and characterizations make for a wonderful story about the meaning of faith on Hoshanah Rabbah.

———. "Really a Sukkah." In HT, pp. 3–16.

Despite enduring difficult times, neighbors who share a *sukkah* are glad to be Jews.

"Because of a Little Sukkah." In TS, pp. 204–207.

The idea of the *sukkah* as God's protection takes on special meaning for a refusenik wanted by the KGB.

Samuel, Maurice, based on the story by I. L. Peretz. "Between Two Cliffs." In *Prince of the Ghetto*. New York: Alfred A. Knopf, 1948, pp. 235–239; and Sukkot and Simhat Torah HA, pp. 291–295.

Two rabbis, one a *khasid*, the other an opponent of the *khasidi* movement, cannot understand each other's approach to the Torah: one arid and scholarly, the other soulful and joyous.

Sayer, Abraham. "Whose Sukkah?" In Sukkot and Simhat Torah HA, pp. 322–327.

Reb Samson is able to remain happy even after his glass *sukkah* is destroyed, because he understands the real meaning and goal of the *sukkah* and living in it.

Weilerstein, Sadie Rose. "How K'tonton Prayed for Rain." In KT, pp. 81–85.

The thumb-sized boy realizes how much more important it is that Israel receive rain than he enjoy clear weather. Ages 3–8.

———. "How K'Tonton Rejoiced and Was Merry on Simkhat Torah." In KT, pp. 86–89.

Despite his tiny size, K'tonton gets his wish to participate in the Torah procession. Ages 3–8.

Books

Adler, David A. *The House on the Roof*. New York: Bonim Books, 1976.

Based on a historic occurrence that inspired a folktale, this updated version concerns an old man and the crusty landlady who wants the shack he has constructed on top of her building removed. Ages 5–9.

Gellman, Ellie. *Tamar's Sukkah*. Rockville, MD: Kar-Ben Copies, 1988.

Successive friends keep contributing parts to the *sukkah* in Tamar's yard until it is perfect. Ages 5–8.

Lebovies, Aydel. *The Wind and the Sukkah*. Brooklyn: Merkos L'Inyonei Chinuch, 1982.

When a big wind blows wood, *s'khakh*, and *lulav* for a *sukkah* into the backyard of someone who never had one, his neighbors insist he keep the materials so that he can observe the holiday, too. Ages 4–8.

Schram, Peninnah. *The Big Sukkah*. Rockville, MD: Kar-Ben Copies, 1986.

Adapted from the Yiddish story, the book tells how poor Berel, who has the tiniest house in the village, figures out a way to create a *sukkah* large enough to accommodate all the relatives who host him and his family on all the other holidays. Ages 4–7.

Singer, Isaac Bashevis. *A Tale of Three Wishes*. New York: Farrar Straus Giroux, 1975.

After staying up to wait for the sky to open on Hoshanah Rabbah, three children think they have wasted their wishes. An old man tells them how to achieve what they really want. Ages 7–11.

Youdovin, Susan Schaalman. *Why Does It Always Rain on Sukkot?* Niles, IL: Albert Whitman & Company, 1990.

This charming story tells how every holiday was given its ritual item in heaven. Each year, Sukkot remembers how he felt when he thought everything had been assigned and there was nothing left for him. Ages 5–9.

KHANUKAH

Khanukah (khahn' new kah): Rededication of the Temple. Observed on *Kislev 25–Tevet 2** (late fall— early winter; November–December).

Khanukah, a postbiblical holiday, marks a historic victory over enemies—internal as well as external— who tried to obliterate Judaism in the Jewish home- land during the Second Temple era. Rather than com- memorating the military triumph that secured Jewish autonomy, the festival instead celebrates the reaffir- mation and persistence of our religious heritage. Also known as the "Feast of Lights" for its main ritual, it is a joyous eight-day family event that holds strik- ing messages for the modern age.

---

*Since *Kislev* can have either twenty-nine or thirty days, the last day of Khanukah can fall on the second or third of *Tevet*.

ORIGINS: WHY WE CELEBRATE KHANUKAH

WHERE DID IT ALL BEGIN?— HISTORIC FOUNDATION

The Events Behind the Holiday

In 168 B.C.E., the ruler of the Syrian kingdom, Antiochus Epiphanes IV, stepped up his campaign to quash Judaism so that all subjects in his vast empire—which included the Land of Israel—would share the same culture and worship the same gods. He marched into Jerusalem, vandalized the Temple, erected an idol on the altar, and desecrated its holiness with the blood of swine. Decreeing that studying Torah, observing the Sabbath, and circumcising Jewish boys were punishable by death, he sent Syrian overseers and soldiers to villages throughout Judea to enforce the edicts and force Jews to engage in idol worship.

When the Syrian soldiers reached Modin (about twelve miles northwest of the capital), they demanded that the local leader, Mattathias the *Kohein* (a member of the priestly class), be an example to his people by sacrificing a pig on a portable pagan altar. The elder refused and killed not only the Jew who stepped forward to do the Syrian's bidding but also the king's representative. With the rallying cry "Whoever is for God, follow me!" Mattathias and his five sons (Jonathan, Simon, Judah, Eleazar, and Yokhanan) fled to the hills and caves of the wooded Judean wilderness.

Joined by a ragtag army of others like them, simple farmers dedicated to the laws of Moses, armed only with spears, bows and arrows, and rocks from the terrain, the Maccabees, as Mattathias' sons, particularly Judah, came to be known, fought a guerilla war against the well-trained, well-equipped, seemingly endless forces of the mercenary Syrian army. In three years, the Maccabees cleared the way back to the Temple mount, which they reclaimed. They cleaned the Temple and dismantled the defiled altar and constructed a new one in its place. Three years to the day after Antiochus' mad rampage (*Kislev* 25, 165 B.C.E.), the Maccabees held a dedication (*khanukah*) of the Temple with proper sacrifice, rekindling of the golden *menorah*, and eight days of celebration and praise to God. Legal Jewish worship had been reestablished.

That is the history-based story which has been told —with the addition of one element—in homes and Hebrew schools for generations to explain why we celebrate this holiday.

The Complete Picture

The full story takes a little longer to tell, because it begins more than a century earlier and continues for more than one hundred years after the Maccabees retook the Temple. And it is more complex than the children's version of the good Jews against the bad Greeks. While the Maccabees battled an outside oppressor, they also struggled against enemies among their own people. Syria's turn—from initially granting the Jews favored status to attempting to completely obliterate Torah, Temple worship, and all vestiges of Judaism—might never have happened without the complicity of Jews all too eager to become more Greek (the culture of the Syrians) than the Greeks.

By the time of the Maccabees, the Jews of the Holy Land had endured foreign rule for hundreds of years, under Babylon, then Persia, then Alexander the Great's Asia-to-Africa empire. As Greece met the East under the Macedonian, a highly accomplished culture encompassing art, literature, science, and philosophy developed, an ancient Enlightenment. Called Hellenism, it soon supplanted many traditional ways of life and pagan religions.

When Alexander died after just a decade on the throne, his kingdom was divided into thirds, each ruled by the head of a Grecian (Hellenic) dynasty. Palestine, that tiny diamond of territory between major land masses and political aspirations, was caught between the Syrian Seleucids (ruling the territory that also included Mesopotamia and Persia) and the Egyptian Ptolemies.

At the end of the third century B.C.E., Syria won control of the territory from Egypt. In 176 B.C.E., Antiochus IV ascended the throne. Calling himself Epiphanes, god manifest, he claimed to be Zeus' embodiment on Earth. (Others at the time called him Epimanes, "madman.") The Temple priests and upper-class Jews of Jerusalem, realizing that in his trading empire their power was dependent on commerce, wanted their city to have the status and economic benefits of other Hellenistic metropolises throughout the Seleucid domain. To qualify, they had to adopt a Greek constitution.

This was the beginning of an internal power struggle that ignited the rebellion. By bribing Antiochus, always in need of money to finance his military forays, the Hellenizers were able to buy the position of high priest—who was supposed to be the paragon of Jewish holiness—for men who were successively more sympathetic to Greek culture.

The influences and allures of Hellenism were so strong that the dedicated priests began to abandon their Temple responsibilities in favor of the gymnasium (symbol of Greek emphasis on physical perfection, the scene of naked competition between athletes). Among the aristocracy, Greek fashion, manners, and names proliferated. Men who wanted to hide their distinctness subjected themselves to painful operations to reverse their circumcisions, and self-expression, science, and external beauty were preferred over morality, spirtuality, and inner truth.

By their choices, the community's leadership condoned the erosion of Jewish values. They also sent a strong message to Antiochus that the Jews themselves wanted to forsake their ancient heritage for modern Hellenism.

There were people who remained faithful to Jewish life, the Pietists (or *khasidim*, unrelated to the eighteenth-century Eastern European movement). But since they believed that the situation in Judea was God's justified punishment for Israel's transgressions, they counted on their own repentance to spur God to redeem them. For the most part, they remained passive, until Menelaus, not even in direct line for the hereditary position (only descendants of Aaron were eligible [Numbers 18:1]), was made *Kohein Gadol*. When a false rumor spread that Antiochus had been killed in his war against Egypt, Menelaus' more moderate predecessor Jason and his followers forced the pretender to flee.

When he learned what had transpired in Jerusalem, the enraged Antiochus invaded the city, ordered a massacre of his enemies, desecrated the Temple, and outlawed Judaism outright. After having to abandon his aspirations for Egypt in the face of an ascendant Rome, he had realized that the only way to secure his kingdom was by unifying the diverse peoples under his rule.

The attempt to eliminate what distinguished them from others, to get them to forsake the one Ruler they recognized above all others, presented the Jews with three choices. They could acquiesce and fully become Hellenes, as many preferred to do. They could die for their religious beliefs, as another large number did. Or they could fight back, a choice that Antiochus, motivated by political expediency rather than by anti-Semitism, and one not presented by any other population, never anticipated.

From the beginning, the revolt was a minority guerilla campaign. As Mattathias' initial act of resistance demonstrated, it was directed both at the Syrians and at the Hellenists. Going through the countryside destroying pagan altars and circumcising boys who had not ritually been brought into the covenant, Mattathias and his followers were not fighting for each Jew to make his or her own religious choices but for the nation of Israel to be able to obey God.

On his deathbed, Mattathias designated his son Judah to be in charge of the resistance. He became known as the Maccabee, or Judas Maccabeus, usually translated as "hammer" (*mahkehbet*, מקבת) and interpreted as designating the hammerlike blows his attacks inflicted on the enemy. Some historians have suggested it was actually a reflection of Judah's appearance, his "hammerhead," since it was common practice in Hellenistic circles to name people according to physical characteristics. More likely, particularly because of the preferred spelling of Maccabee in Hebrew (מכבי), it was an acronym, either for *Mattayahu Kohein Ben Yokhanan* (Mattathias the Priest, son of Yokhanan), by which his sons perpetuated their father's name, or for the phrase *Me Khamokhah B'Elim Adonai* (Who is like You among the Mighty, O Lord [Exodus 15:11]), the phrase under which Judah went into battle.

The Conflict Continues

A year after the Maccabees' triumph at the Temple, the Hellenists still refused to give up their fight. Displeased that the "old-fashioned" Jews were once again in religious power, and that Torah law had been reinstated in Judea, they repeatedly invited the Seleucids to send more troops. Political maneuverings in Syria on more than one occasion saved the Maccabees by frightening the Syrian commanders home after hurried peace negotiations with Judah to protect their personal positions. Yet the war dragged on for a generation. Eleazar died in the battle against Nicanor and his elephants, then three more of Mattathias' sons lost their lives, including the seemingly invincible Judah.

In 142 B.C.E., Simon, the last surviver of the Maccabee brothers, was recognized as high priest and political leader by his own people. He severed bonds of allegiance to the Syrian rulers, got the Greek garrison out of Jerusalem, and began to mint his own coins, the first ever by a Jewish state. (The British Museum in London has the world's largest collection of them.) He was succeeded by his son John Hyrcanus, who established the Hasmonean Dynasty. (The term first introduced in Talmud may have been Mattathias' family name, from his grandfather, Simon Hasmonai, or a designation meaning prince, possibly related to the position of priesthood.)

Taking control of the kingship violated the people's trust because it transgressed Torah: The Bible stipulates (Genesis 49:10) that the kingship should always rest in the tribe of *Yehudah* (descendants of Jacob's son Judah), as it did once David's line was established. It was to be separated from the priesthood, which comes out of the tribe of *Levi* (from which Aaron descended [Numbers 3:6–9]), to balance the secular and the spiritual. The Hasmoneans, though *Kohanim* of the tribe of *Levi*, were not in line for the high priesthood or for political leadership, which they usurped.

What began in glory ended in ignominy. The nine Hasmonean rulers to be recognized by the Roman Senate engaged in the same political intrigues, self-aggrandizement, and bloodshed as the previous regime. When two brothers who were not eligible claimed the kingship, they called on a representative of Rome to arbitrate. Foolishly repeating the mistake of the Hellenized Jews, the contending brothers opened the door to the Roman conquest, which ended their rule (when Herod killed the last of them) after just 103 years—and ended Jewish sovereignty in Israel for almost two thousand years.

The Hasmoneans' early triumphs were soon shadowed by their corruption. Due to the unpopularity of its founders, Khanukah itself came to be largely ignored within a few decades after its origins. Then when Rome's crushing power began to be felt in Palestine, the people recognized in Khanukah a message of hope that new Maccabees would rise and independence would be restored. The holiday came to be seen in an entirely different light.

The Written Record

Although Khanukah is the only important festival in the Jewish calendar not to be mentioned anywhere in the Hebrew Bible (before the events surrounding the holiday occurred, the Hebrew canon had been closed to all future texts), it is also the only important premodern festival for which there are definitive historical records.

Within twenty years of the reclamation of the Temple, The First Book of Maccabees was written. Possibly based on historical records of the Hellenistic period and the authority of an eyewitness, it chronicles the events from the rise of Antiochus Epiphanes through Hasmonean rule. Evincing great pride in the Maccabees' accomplishments, it stresses that they fought "for God," so that they could carry out His plan for a just world. The original Hebrew manuscript, later lost, was soon translated into Greek for the large Jewish populations living in Hellenic centers.

In describing the purification of the Temple, I Maccabees calls the occasion the "dedication [*khanukah*] of the altar" (4:59). Judah and his brothers, and the entire congregation of Israel, decreed that these days should be kept with gladness and praise at their due season, year after year, for eight days from the twenty-fifth of the month of *Kislev* (I Maccabees 4:52–59).

The Second Book of Maccabees, written decades later, confirms much of the action of the previous book. Based on a Greek volume by a Hellenized Jew, Jason of Cyrene, it opens with letters reminding Jews in Egypt to celebrate "the new festival" (II Maccabees 10:1–8). This suggests it was written to persuade people who were ignoring the holiday to observe it.

Unrestrained in its support of the by then unpopular founders, the book reflects Jewish spiritual beliefs current at the time, beliefs that developed out of the concept of choosing death over apostasy. Containing mystical references, it records cases of pious Jews who chose to die rather than submit to the Syrians: Mothers knowing they would be slain and their murdered infants hung around their necks circumcised their sons anyway (II Maccabees 6:10). The revered ninety-year-old scribe Eleazar chose martyrdom rather than eating, or even pretending to eat, pork (II Maccabees 6:18–31). A celebrated mother (referred to in Talmud as Miriam, in Josephus by the more commonly accepted identification Hannah) encouraged the expression of unfaltering faith in God as she was forced to watch her seven sons, one by one, be barbarically tortured to death for refusing to bow to an idol, and then she killed herself (II Maccabees 7).

In this version of events, the celebration initiated by Judah is called the purification festival (2:16–18) and is described as a second Sukkot, possibly because the Maccabees had missed the festival earlier that year while fighting in the wilderness. They also modeled their celebration on the previous Temple dedication, which had occurred at the harvest festival (I Kings 8:2, 65; Nehemiah 8:14–18). For that reason, they carried *lulavim* and recited *Hallel*.

The Roman-Jewish historian Flavius Josephus used I Maccabees as a resource for his first-century account of the period in *Jewish Antiquities* but makes his own contribution to the annual commemoration. Recounting that the dedication was celebrated with feasting, "splendid" sacrifices, songs of praise to God, and the playing of harps, he mentions a newly popular form of observance: kindling lights, especially torches. In fact, he introduces a new designation for the holiday, *Khag Haorim* (Festival of Lights), which he tentatively tries to explain as representative of the glow of freedom that lit up Jewish life.

The Books of Maccabees were lost to the Jews until recently, when they were translated into the original Hebrew for Jewish use, and into other languages, from the versions retained by the Church in its Old Testament. However, their story, of sorts, was kept alive in the Scroll of Antiochus (also called the Scroll of the Hasmoneans). Modeled after the Scroll of Esther, the rabbinic work was written in Aramaic, later translated into Hebrew, and meant to be read in synagogue during the eight-day celebration. That custom, practiced mostly in the Middle Ages, has long since been discontinued except in some *Sephardi* communities.

A legendary account incorporating various tales popular among the Jews centuries after the actual events, and inconsistent in sequence and details with the Books of Maccabees, it largely reflects the political situation, rabbinical antimilitary attitude, and spiritual orientation of Judaism expressed at the time of its origin, probably shortly after the destruction of the Second Temple. These currents and its account of the miracle of oil—that added element in the traditional Khanukah story—were incorporated into the Talmud some two hundred to three hundred years later.

The Talmudic Tradition

Unlike I and II Maccabees, the Talmud barely touches on the armed struggle, never mentions the word Maccabee, and of the leading rebels, names only Mattathias. The *Mishnah* (on which Talmud commentary is based) makes no reference whatsoever to Khanukah, and the few relevant passages in the commentaries begin "What is Khanukah?" (*Mai Khanukah?*) as though its significance had been forgotten. The response redirected the holiday.

The rabbis said that when they reclaimed the Temple, the Hasmoneans found a single cruse of pure oil still bearing the unbroken seal of the high priest. Although only enough to last one day, it miraculously burned eight days, the amount of time needed to secure a new supply of oil to keep the *menorah* lit. In the following year, the holiday, to be observed with songs and praises, was ordained, a distinction that presented Khanukah as a rabbinic, and not Hasmonean, proclamation.

This curious bit of revisionism has logical bases. By the time Yehudah Hanasi compiled the Mishnah (second century), the Hasmoneans had been discredited. As a descendant of the Davidic dynasty, from which all future rulers of Israel were to come, Hanasi was particularly sensitive to the Hasmoneans' having trampled his family's rights.

There was another reason for his failure to mention the rebels: Rome already dominated Palestine, and Hanasi was the first sage in decades to maintain a decent relationship with that power. It would have been grossly irresponsible to discuss the Jewish overthrow of any oppressive foreign rule, a red flag of rebelliousness that would have instigated terrible consequences for the Jews.

So because of political considerations, the rabbis limited their discussion of the holiday, which had enjoyed a resurgence for nationalistic reasons, to explaining the relatively new kindling custom. On the most basic level, it represented the relighting of the *menorah* in the reclaimed Temple. However, by the time the talmudic rabbis wrote, the attempts to overthrow Rome's yoke had failed miserably. Sovereignty, the Temple, and altar sacrifice were gone. The story of the miracle of oil, which may have originated as an embellishment on the initial dedication account, helped them shift attention away from the physical world—in which the Jews had lost so much—to the spiritual and give the holiday a purely religious interpretation. Rather than being tied to the Temple and its ritual objects, Khanukah came to symbolize the continuity of the distinct Jewish way of life. The lights represented Jewish spirituality.

The form of observance may have actually evolved from the practice of using lighted torches during Sukkot's *Simkhat Beit Hashoavah* celebrations or carrying lighted torches in the streets of Jerusalem during the harvest festival. (According to *midrash*, when Judah and his men reclaimed the Temple, the *menorah* was missing. But they found eight iron rods, into which they made grooves to hold oil and wicks, and kindled them.) Later, like much observance, the lighting moved from the public domain into the home. Despite the prominence of lights, the "Festival of Lights" around this time was formally named "Festival of Dedication" (Khanukah).

Some secular scholars believe that lighting flames in connection with Khanukah reflected winter solstice festivals, such as the one celebrated in Greek pagan culture, in which ancient people lit bonfires and held torchlight processions to encourage the return of the sun. (Khanukah arrives at the end of both lunar and solar cycles, a particularly dark time, because the moon is waning toward the close of the month of *Kislev*, and Earth is farthest away from the sun.)

However, there is no question that the symbolism of fire and light were well rooted in Judaism, from God's first words in the Torah ("Let there be light" [Genesis 1:3]), to the comparison of Torah to light (including the Aramaic word, *Oraisa*, meaning "source of light"), to God's manifestation as the Burning Bush, to the Temple *menorah*. All were symbols of God, a fire that does not consume but provides illumination.

Modern Times

When the Torah academies of Babylon opened in the third century, the lighting practice spread to the Diaspora; however, until the last century, Khanukah remained a secondary festival in much of the world. Then Zionism appeared as a major force. While the notion of the miracle of oil had come into disfavor with the rationalism of the Enlightenment, the Maccabees became models of the heroic Jew willing and able to fight for his rights. The initial miracle, of the few against the many, the weak against the strong, gave the Zionists and early settlers in Palestine hope.

Throughout the Holocaust, the Jews—saving bits of butter to fuel small flames held in hollowed potatoes—continued to thank God for the miracle of Khanukah, believing, as had the Jews under Rome, that another miracle was possible. Even if individuals died, they believed the Jewish people, as always, would survive. In 1948, the chances of the new Israelis were likened to those of the Maccabees at the beginning of their struggle. Today, the Jewish state observes Khanukah as a national patriotic holiday. The term *Maccabee* has come to mean physical prowess and serves as the name of several sports endeavors including Israel's Olympics (Maccabiah).

Khanukah also enjoyed a resurgence in America, although this is due mainly to its close proximity to Christmas rather than to appreciation of Khanukah's significance. In a spirit of fairness, public schools often added Khanukah to their holiday season celebrations, and that reminded families to light *menorot* at home. Popular with assimilated Jews as well as the observant, for many it has come to be seen as "a Jewish Christmas." Consequently, although celebrated out of proportion to its place on the Jewish calendar (especially when compared to the overshadowed biblically ordained holidays Shavuot and Sukkot), it is too often diminished by the very culture-borrowing the holiday's founders fought.

FOR FURTHER READING

For Adults

Chanukah—Its History, Observance and Significance. Ed. by Rabbi Nosson Sherman and Rabbi Meir Zlotowitz. Brooklyn: Mesorah Publications, 1989, pp. 33–66.

The easily read, easy-to-follow detailed history surrounding Khanukah includes the intriguing intricacies of the political machinations that affected Jewish life.

Fast, Howard. *My Glorious Brothers*. Boston: Little Brown & Company, 1948.

This historical novel brings the personalities of the Maccabees and the Land of Israel to life. Told by Simon as he tries to understand and explain what drove the Jews, and, in a small part, by a representative of the Roman Senate, it illustrates what set the Jews apart from all other peoples and is an interesting and, at times, moving story.

The First Book of Maccabees. Ed. by Solomon Zeitlin. Translated by Sidney Tesche. New York: Harper &

Brothers, for Dropsie College for Hebrew and Cognate Learning, 1950.

Detailed explanations of the ancient world and the situation in Judea sets up the apocryphal book, a translation into English (with facing Greek) made for the Jewish reader. (The Second Book of Maccabees, published in 1954, is also available.)

Grayzel, Solomon. "Hanukkah and Its History." In Hanukkah HA, pp. 3–26.

The essay provides a well-written historical background of Khanukah.

"Megillat Antiochus/Scroll of Hashmoneans." In *Daily Prayer Book*. Ed. by Philip Birnbaum. New York: Hebrew Publishing Company, 1977, pp. 713–724.

The text of the scroll read in synagogues during the Middle Ages appears in Hebrew and in English.

For Children

Feder, Harriet K. *Judah Who Always Said "No!"* Rockville, MD: Kar-Ben Copies, 1990.

Judah was negative throughout childhood, and through each step of the Greeks' demands, until his refusal to agree made him victorious. Ages 5–9.

Koralek, Jerry. *Hanukkah, The Festival of Lights.* New York: Lothrop, Lee & Shepard Books, 1990.

Illustrated in epic style, this is an all-around beautiful presentation of the Khanukah story. Ages 5–9.

Zwerin, Raymond A. and Audrey Friedman Marcus. *Like a Maccabee.* New York: UAHC Press, 1991.

This simple yet lovely telling of the Khanukah story intersperses definitions of what being a Maccabee means with questions to let the young reader determine if he or she is like a Maccabee. Vibrant illustrations form stage scenes for the action of the story. Ages 3–6.

WHAT DOES IT MEAN?— RELIGIOUS IMPORTANCE

Had there not been a Maccabean revolt, there would not be a Jewish religion. That struggle—the first ever in the world fought for the right of a people to follow its spiritual conscience—saved Judaism and transformed it into a system able to survive through millennia of turmoil.

National and Individual Self-Preservation

The Maccabean age marks the first time that people were willing to sacrifice their lives for what they believed. *Mesirat hanefesh* (self-sacrifice, or literally "handing over the soul"), also called *Kiddush Hashem* (sanctification of God's name), was seen as the highest form of service to God by those who continued to follow His laws.

Giving some significance to their brutal deaths, this new concept in religious commitment became a model for Jews throughout history, particularly in the Middle Ages. During the Roman persecutions, Crusades, Inquisition, pogroms, and the Holocaust, victims died believing they were giving up their lives for a higher purpose.

Unlike the way other religions interpreted the idea, Judaism never considered the death a value in itself. Relinquishing life for religious idealism is not for God's sake—a lesson we learn in the Rosh Hashanah story of the near sacrifice of Isaac— but for the sake of continuity and the strength of the community.

While this form of resistance may have been viewed as a laudable alternative to accepting the demands of the Syrians, in the end it could serve no practical purpose for the Maccabees because it would only lead to extinction. As related in Maccabees (I, 2:32–34; II, 6:11), a group of khasidi men, women, and children was trapped in a cave by the enemy on the Sabbath. Offering no resistance because it was a holy day, they all perished. On hearing of this tragic encounter, Mattathias declared that from then on, the Jews were to defend themselves, even if it meant violating Sabbath law.

His ruling reflected the position of the Pharisees, one that had positive ramifications for the future of Judaism. They believed that sages had the right and duty to interpret the law. Unlike the Sadducees, who took Torah literally and based Jewish service solely on the Temple sacrificial rites, the Pharisees understood that Torah was meant to be humanly explained, and that study and prayer were also avenues to God. Without their leadership, Judaism, instead of being a vibrant, creative influence, would have ended when the Temple was destroyed.

With this approach the rabbis later formalized Mattathias' ruling based on the commandment "You shall observe my statutes and laws that a man shall live by them" [Deuteronomy 30:16], understood to imply "and not die by them." Protecting one's life was a higher value than keeping the Sabbath and almost every other commandment. The rabbis limited the circumstances under which one should, and is permitted to, die in sanctification of God's name to three: idolatry, murder, and certain sexual abominations.

Miracles and Man

Consistent with exercising authority regarding *mitzvot*, the Maccabees rejected the postprophecy idea that only God could vanquish Israel's enemies and restore the Temple. After they took matters into their own hands, acting on behalf of God and according to His laws, the miracle occurred: Judah's outnumbered, outlawed band of guerillas defeated the professional army of Antiochus.

Though a minority of the Jews, the Maccabees and their followers were able to succeed because they unified not only the extreme right wing (the Pietists who adhered to the laws and wanted to wait for supernatural relief) but the left wing as well (the Hellenists, who saw no harm in updating their lives with the fashionable ways of the Greeks, initially not realizing that they posed any threat to their own culture). Together they achieved something outside all normal expectations by acting under the Maccabee standard, or *nes*, "Who is like You among the mighty, O God?"

The Hebrew word *nes* (sign) also means miracle. The "great miracle happened there" because when we follow common guidelines and pursue common goals, we are given the power to create extraordinary results. (If we could forge a coalition between the most religious and the most religiously lax, between the traditionalists and the liberal interpreters today, wouldn't we consider it a miracle?!)

The Maccabees witnessed the miracle of oil because at the darkest moment of Jewish history, when it looked as though Judaism would be extinguished, they themselves searched and found the fuel necessary to keep the lamp lit. As a rabbinic parable interprets it, the undiminished oil was Mattathias himself. In his home, in his soul, the spirit of Judaism continued to burn. He turned the light on the Jews, he ignited their drive to search their souls, where they found the strength and desire to perpetuate their religious tradition. That provided enough fuel for the flames of the *menorah*, the presence of God among human beings, to continue.

Judaism emerged strengthened, not by withdrawing from the world but by joining the religious fervor of the Pietists with the positive elements of the competing culture (such as sophisticated patterns of reasoning, science, artistic accomplishment). The integration prepared it to better withstand repeated blows from outside forces and opened avenues through which we are able to share our vision and work toward fulfilling our mission. (It was during the Hellenistic period that the Bible was translated into Greek by seventy-two Jewish scholars, giving the world the *Septuagint*, the basis for Judeo-Christian culture and American democracy.)

An Eternal Light to the Nations

The strongest image and metaphor of Khanukah, and of Judaism, is light. All Jewish, and world, history is the struggle to maintain light against the force of darkness, a struggle between the sparks of creativity and the fires of destruction, between the shadows of evil and the radiance of human goodness, being in the dark of ignorance and seeing the light of truth.

The Torah, which illuminates the path that will allow us to enjoy the most enlightened life, is wisdom's light (Proverbs 6:23). The soul, which provides the vision to make the right choices, is inner light (Proverbs 20:27). When we follow them, in fulfillment of our mission, the Jewish people is a "light to the nations" (Isaiah 49:6).

In the world conquered by Hellenism, only two nations were able to retain their identities: Rome, with its military power, and Israel, with its spiritual purpose. When the Jews prevailed, they did not commemorate their success in battle; fighting was only a means to an end. Instead, they celebrated the rekindling of the lights of the *menorah* to express recommitment to their religious ideals.

The term *khanukah* had been in use long before the Maccabees. Completion of the First Temple (1 Kings 9:63; Psalms 30:1) and the wall enclosing the city of Jerusalem (Nehemiah 12:27) were both *khanukot*. Based on grammatical structure in scripture, the sages termed completion of the Tabernacle in the wilderness (Exodus 39:32) and its erection for the first time (Numbers 7:1) as dedications as well.

Since the Tabernacle actually represented the universe, with its roof as heaven and its *menorah* lights as the fixtures of the firmament, the sages also called the Creation of heaven and Earth (Genesis 2:1) a *khanukah*, as they did the prophet Isaiah's reference to the final redemption, when the sun will shine seven times brighter than usual (30:26). Through those designations, they made the Maccabean rededication part of that continuum that began on the first day of the world and projected to its last.

Each *khanukah*, in its way, was aimed at widening the circle of light in the world. Primordial light dispelled the darkness of chaos. The sun, moon, and stars illuminated the earth, making human life and history possible. The seven-branched *menorah* placed outside the entrance to the Shrine where God's presence resided represented spiritual light in the Tabernacle and in the universe.

Made from a single piece of gold, the purest firmest metal, the *menorah* suggested resoluteness and permanence. Yet created in the form of flowering branches, it implied growth. Within an unyielding framework, the Jewish moral tradition, Judaism was to become a great influence in lightening the burdens of the world.

Its fire, like Israel's moral example, was to be kept aglow constantly (Exodus 24:1–4). After the Temple —said to give light to the whole world—replaced the Tabernacle, and then was destroyed, rebuilt, and defiled, relighting the *menorah* each time signified that the Jews wanted to continue carrying the torch. *We* would be a flame of spirituality, countering the darkness of ignorance and evil, shining the light of Judaism's justice, a vision of the brilliance human existence can achieve.

WHAT DOES IT MEAN TO US?— PERSONAL SIGNIFICANCE

Our tradition includes several moving stories about men lost in a forest or blinding snowstorm who, because they catch a glimpse of a flickering Khanukah candle in a distant window, are able to find their way home. It is so easy for us, especially in our media-saturated world, to get lost in the images and messages of the society around us and, like the Hellenists in Judah Maccabee's day, to be seduced by their superficial appeal. Khanukah candles can be guiding lights helping us "find our way home," back to our history, our values, our spiritual source.

The same candle that shines like a beacon to someone lost in the dark outside in the house casts an intimate circle of light that draws the family around it. You can use this glimmer of spirituality as more than a prelude to presents and potato pancakes. Yes, these are nice ways to enhance enjoyment of the holiday and should certainly be employed to get children's attention and generate some excitement for them.

But, remembering what this holiday is all about, you can light a fire inside your family members. It is no accident that we observe this holiday within the embrace of family, the most important element in the transmission of Jewish values and tradition. Khanukah (from the same root as *khinukh*, meaning "education") is all about the perpetuation of that tradition; the Maccabees fought not just for the principle of religious freedom but to be able to live a full Jewish life unencumbered by the negative influences of an alien culture and the allures of easily assimilating into it.

We follow the declaration "Hear O Israel" (the *Shema*) by reciting the commandment to love God and take His laws to heart. The very next phrase instructs "Teach them diligently to your children" (Deuteronomy 6:7). Every Jew, not just our religious leaders, is supposed to share in our heritage and be knowledgeable about it. Although we are legendary for our emphasis on education, and vastly overrepresented (population percentage-wise) among those who hold advanced academic and professional degrees, too many of us are ignorant of our own religious culture.

If we want our children not to be swallowed up by the values (or lack of them) of our secular society, we have to give them a sense of belonging to Judaism and the Jewish people that is positive and relevant. The process has to start with the parent. The best Jewish day school cannot do its job if what is learned there is not reinforced at home and built on the Jewish identity shaped there.

As we know, sometimes to our chagrin, children learn most readily through example. The Talmud says that one who is careful about lighting Khanukah candles will merit children who are *talmidei khakhumim*, wise students. The sages looked on kindling the *menorah* as a model for behavior and also indicative that one was keeping a Jewish home in general, and thereby teaching his/her children about Judaism and Jewish values. Even if lighting the *menorah* is all you do, it is a good first step. The challenge is to prolong the glow of Khanukah light beyond the second or third of *Tevet*.

If Jewish survival is a priority for you (What are the chances your children or grandchildren will be Jewish, that they will intermarry? How would you feel if they did?), you might start by evaluating what you are doing to keep Judaism alive in your own home. (These are not questions pondered by most Jews in Western societies today. But in view of the fact that our numbers are falling, intermarriage rising, identification waning, and formal Jewish education failing, they are questions that demand consideration.) Do the choices you make support how you feel about Judaism and its continuity? (Is Friday night for family Shabbat dinners or for school sports competitions? Is it more important that your children attend band, dance, hockey, cheerleading, or drama practice than Hebrew school? Is money more readily allocated for a new television or new outfits than for construction materials for a *sukkah*? Is it preferable to support the local art museum, symphony, or dance company rather than the local agency for Jewish education? Do the stories you share, the songs you sing, the words you use, the videos you watch, the rituals you observe include Jewish ones? When it comes to choices between Jewish and non-Jewish activities or items, are they negotiable?) Do you realize the probable ramifications of those choices, and are those the results you want?

We cannot expect our children to choose to be Jewish (and later be able to raise Jewish children) if it is not integral in their lives. (Try a little experiment. Ask your children to use five words to describe themselves. See where Jewish shows up on their lists. See if it shows up at all.) They must share enough of our common culture to feel that they belong to the Jewish people and know enough about what it means to be able to evaluate their religion against others. Many young people who investigate different faiths and get involved with cults are spiritually hungry. But in most cases it does not even occur to them to check out what Judaism has to say in answer to their questions. Exposed to it only superficially, or experiencing it as burdensome, they have no idea of its depth, wisdom, or joy.

You can give the riches of Judaism to yourself and your children by enlightening your lives through education at home (following the holiday cycle goes a long way in establishing a Jewish identity) and in the community, where many programs, for all ages and families, are available. There will be more, and better ones, as Jewish communities throughout the country grapple with the problems created by the double-edged sword of tolerance in our society: acceptance and assimilation.

You start Khanukah with one small flame, the observance of one holiday, doing one *mitzvah*, imparting one piece of information. It lights only the area immediately around it. Yet as our rabbis say, and as those men lost in the forest or snow would agree, "a little light dispels much darkness." It is a beginning, like a penlight or match that allows us to put ourselves on the right country path. Fire has the incredible quality of being able to give itself away without at all being diminished. As long as it is fueled, it continues to grow; it takes only a spark to ignite a million-acre blaze. All you have to do is light the first match.

For Further Reading

Herzl, Theodor. "The Menorah." In *Hanukkah, The Feast of Lights.* Ed. by Emily Solis-Cohen, Jr. Philadelphia: The Jewish Publication Society of America, 1947, pp. 279–282.

After years of allowing Khanukah to pass unobserved, the founder of the Zionist movement came to recognize that devotion to ancient Jewish tradition, not assimilation into surrounding cultures, was the only route to salvation and decided to expose his children to the beautiful commemoration. This essay is still timely.

TRADITIONS: HOW WE CELEBRATE KHANUKAH

What Do We Use?— Ritual Items

Menorah/Khanukiah

Though commonly called a *menorah*, the candelabra used to hold the Khanukah lights is properly referred to as a *khanukiah* (particularly by Orthodox Jews who reserve *menorah* for the lampstand that stood in the Temple). Anything that will hold the oil and wicks or candles can be used, even a row of small glasses, jars, or other receptacles.

Originally, individual oil lamps ordinarily used for

illumination sufficed, but gradually creative interpretation led to a limitless variety of *khanukiot*, both for hanging on doorposts or walls (these contained upright backs) or for sitting on windowsills or tables (equipped with flat bottoms or legs).

Among Judaica collections in synagogues, museums, and private homes are those of clay, porcelain, tin, silver, and brass, embellished with historic and decorative symbols and forms (including images drawn from the Maccabean struggle, scripture, wildlife, and the crests of nobles under whom European Jews received protection). By the Middle Ages the talmudic injunction against making *khanukiot* to resemble the original seven-branched Temple *menorah* (to preserve its sacred status) was ignored, and eight- and nine-branched versions developed. Today, Judaica artists continue to create new designs, both whimsical and graceful.

A *khanukiah* can be made at home or purchased from a Jewish supplies store or catalogue. Candles (forty-four to a box, the total you need for all eight days) are also available from a supplies store or catalogue and can often be found in grocery, stationery, and drug stores. Many *khanukiot* that normally take candles can be converted for oil by inserting into the candle wells small glass bulbs that are available (along with the wicks) where *menorot* are sold. Any oil you use for cooking can be put into the *menorah*.

Dreidel

Though not necessary for observance of Khanukah, the *dreidel*, spinning top, is a traditional part of the celebration. Used in a game of chance played after the candles are lit, the *dreidel* has a Hebrew letter on each of its four sides. The *nun* (נ), *gimmel* (ג), *hei* (ה), and *shin* (ש) represent the phrase *Nes gadol hayah sham*, "A great miracle happened there." In Israel, a *pei* (פ) replaces the *shin*, signifying *po* (here). The spinning tops used to be carved of wood or made of lead (often by young boys who poured metal, obtained from melting spoons, into homemade molds). Collectable pieces, some fashioned of silver and crystal, are available. Inexpensive wood and plastic models for play, which come in a variety of shapes and sizes, are widely displayed in Jewish and general stores during the Khanukah season.

How Do We Show We Celebrate?— Observance

Khanukah belongs to the family. Full of images and activities that particularly appeal to children, the festival is centered around a home ceremony that brings members together eight nights in succession for lightheartedness, warmth, and appreciation of the Jewish heritage whose survival is being celebrated.

Kindling Preparation

Since shortly after the destruction of the Temple, the centerpiece of Khanukah observance has been kindling the Khanukah lights. The rabbis determined that we kindle these lights to publicize the miracle (*pirsum hanes*) that occurred. For that reason, the *khanukiah* is supposed to be seen from the street.

Originally it was placed on the left doorpost outside the home, opposite the *mezuzzah* on the right, to surround anyone standing in the doorway with spirituality. Today it is more common to place the lampstand in or near a window so that it will be clearly visible from outside (some even say that since the lights are mainly directed to those of the household, the *menorah* can be placed anywhere in the home). In Israel and in some Jewish neighborhoods in the Diaspora, you can still see specially made outdoor lamps. Some reconstructed houses in the old city of Jerusalem have niches for them in the walls next to the doorways.

The candles are placed in the *menorah* from right to left, the number corresponding to the night of the holiday, beginning with one and adding a single taper or wick each night through the eighth. In addition, an extra candle, or *shammash* (servant), which is used to kindle the others, is placed in the *menorah* every night.

One *menorah* may be, and usually is, lit for the entire family, although it has been the custom, and a good learning experience for children, particularly among the devout for each member of the family to kindle his or her own. The glow from the extra candles, especially on the last night of the festival, is a gorgeous sight.

Traditionally, the lighting takes place after nightfall, when stars appear, so that the flames will be most noticeable to people returning home from work and shopping. But you can light any time during the night as long as there are still people awake to see the flames.

Kindling Ceremony

Benedictions

On the first night, the person who will light the candles (it can be any member of the household, and it is a good idea to involve children) lights the *shammash* and, while holding it, recites three blessings.

(The *shammash* does not count as one of the candles being sanctified. Actually, a match could be used to light all the Khanukah candles, but since the Middle Ages, the *shammash* has been customary. Originally it was added as a precaution against violating the law that prohibits using the Khanukah candles as a source of light for any activity. If one read by the candles' light, or otherwise utilized the *menorah*'s illumination, it was considered that the light had come from the *shammash* rather than the sanctified flames. In time, it was used to kindle the others and given the name "servant.") Many families chant the blessings to a special tune, which you can learn from a book or recording of melodies for the holiday.

בָּרוּךְ אַתָּה, יהוה אֱלֹהֵינוּ, מֶלֶךְ הָעוֹלָם, אֲשֶׁר קִדְּשָׁנוּ בְּמִצְוֹתָיו, וְצִוָּנוּ לְהַדְלִיק נֵר שֶׁל חֲנֻכָּה.

Barukh Atah, Adonai Eloheinu, Melekh Haolam, asher kidshanu b'mitzvotav, v'tzivanu l'hadlik neir shel Khanukah.[*]

Blessed are You, O Lord Our God, King of the Universe, Who has sanctified us with His commandments and commanded us to kindle the lights of Khanukah.

---

[*]Some, particularly the Judeo-Spanish, use the wording *ner Khanukah* (Khanukah light), implying that the light is exclusively for the *mitzvah* of kindling, rather than *ner shel Khanukah*, which implies that the light is being used otherwise.

בָּרוּךְ אַתָּה, יהוה אֱלֹהֵינוּ, מֶלֶךְ הָעוֹלָם, שֶׁעָשָׂה נִסִּים לַאֲבוֹתֵינוּ, בַּיָּמִים הָהֵם בַּזְּמַן הַזֶּה.

Barukh Atah, Adonai Eloheinu, Melekh Haolam, she'asah nisim l'avoteinu, b'yamim haheim baz'man hazeh.

Blessed are You, Lord our God, King of the Universe, Who made miracles for our forefathers in those days at this time.

בָּרוּךְ אַתָּה, יהוה אֱלֹהֵינוּ, מֶלֶךְ הָעוֹלָם, שֶׁהֶחֱיָנוּ, וְקִיְּמָנוּ, וְהִגִּיעָנוּ לַזְּמַן הַזֶּה.

Barukh Atah, Adonai Eloheinu, Melekh Haolam, shehekheyanu, v'kiyamanu, v'higgiyanu lazman hazeh.

Blessed are You, Lord our God, King of the Universe, Who has kept us alive, sustained us, and brought us to this season.

The second blessing, commemorating great miracles performed for our ancestors, is said at just one other occasion of the year, prior to reading the Purim *Megillah*. The *shehekheyanu*, used at milestone occasions such as arriving at a holiday, is omitted on subsequent days (unless for some reason you don't say it the first night, in which case you may say it on another evening, but only once during the holiday because "arrival at this season" refers to its onset).

Lighting

The candles are lit from left to right, in reverse order from the way they were placed in the *menorah*, so that the last candle put in is the first one kindled. The *shammash* is placed into its holder and allowed to burn with the other candles.

Originally, there was disagreement as to how the candles were to be arranged. One of the great schools of learning of talmudic times, that of Shammai, asserted that on the first night, eight candles should be lit, and be diminished by one each subsequent night. This arrangement reflected the observance of Sukkot, when fewer sacrifices were brought on each successive day. It also demonstrated a pessimistic attitude, implying that life in the absence of the Temple was a lesser experience, that the glory of Jewish life was in the past, that holiness among Jews and in the world was fading.

Fortunately, the sages ruled in favor of the suggestion of the School of Hillel, that we start with one and build up each day. The progression moves us from faint illumination in the darkness to light, from little hope in the present to faith in the future, an expression of expectation that our holiness, the impact we can have in the world, can and will increase.

Follow-Up Songs

While the kindling is being done, it is customary to sing "*Hanerot Hallalu*" (These Lights), to remind us that the lights are sacred, used only to express our thanks for the miracles and not for any other purpose. Based on a Talmud text, the original passage consisted of thirty-six words (there are minor variations between the *Ashkenazim*, *Sephardim*, and various *khasidim*), reflecting the thirty-six candles we light during the holiday (not including the *shammashim*) and reminiscent of the thirty-six righteous people said to exist in each generation, on whose merit the world continues.

The *Ashkenazim* and some *Sephardim* follow with "*Maoz Tzur*" (Rock, or literally fortress, of My Salvation), the thirteenth-century liturgical poem sung to a medieval German hymn. Recalling the downfalls and rededications of Israel throughout her history, and expressing hope for the restoration of the Temple, it became Khanukah's theme song.

The *Sephardim* recite Psalm 30 since it was composed by King David to be used when his son Solomon dedicated the First Temple. It was said by the Maccabees at their dedication and is almost universally associated with the Khanukah festival. Its imagery of an individual saved from danger alludes to Jewish national life.

FOR FURTHER READING

Hanukah Melodies. Cedarhurst, NY: Board of Jewish Education of Greater New York and Tara Publications, 1981.

The compact booklet contains the candlelighting tunes, traditional follow-up songs, and other folksongs standard for the holiday. A companion cassette tape is available.

FOR FURTHER EXPLORATION

Chanukah Live: The World Celebrates Chanukah Together.

Brought to you by the same people who bring municipal *menorot* to our cities, this is a one-hour record of the live worldwide celebration of Khanukah orchestrated on December 1, 1991, when satellite broadcast linked candlelighting ceremonies at Lubavitch World Headquarters in Brooklyn, the Western Wall in Israel, the Eiffel Tower in Paris, Red Square in Moscow, and the White House in Washington. The documentary, which covers the singing and dancing that followed each ceremony, allows you to share the holiday with Jews all over the world.

Games

Although Khanukah was never considered sacred time when work is forbidden, no work is to be done for a half hour after the *menorah* is lit in order that we appreciate the flames and what they represent. It became traditional for people freed from the normal routines of household chores and study to pass the time in a variety of games, particularly playing cards and the Khanukah favorite, *dreidel*.

Origin

Legend has it that the spinning top game (called *sevivon* in Hebrew, meaning "spin") developed at the time of the Maccabees as a cover: The Syrians killed any Jews caught studying Torah. Those who risked their lives to learn kept tops within reach and would play when soldiers approached so as to appear innocent. The markings we know were added later.

The letters, and probably the game itself, were adapted from those on the *dreidel* (from the German *dreihen*, "to spin") popular in medieval Germany. "N" stood for *nicht* (nothing), "G" for *gantz* (all), "H" for *halb* (half), and "S" for *shtel* (put), forming instructions for play. Though transformed into Hebrew, the letters retained their meaning.

The Rules

Each player (up to five people is optimum) puts an agreed-upon amount of small objects—pennies, nuts, jelly beans—into the common pot. All take turns spinning. If the *dreidel* lands on *nun* (נ), the player takes nothing, *gimmel* (ג), s/he takes all, *hei* (ה), s/he takes half, and *shin* (ש), s/he puts a predetermined amount into the pot. When the pot is empty, everyone antes up again. The game ends when one person has everything, or after a set number of rounds or amount of time.

You can also play by awarding points for each letter, according to their values in Hebrew. *Nun* = fifty, *gimmel* = three, *hei* = five, and *shin* = three hundred. The first to reach one thousand, or some other goal, wins.

Parties and Events

Jewish communal organizations, synagogues, and families often host parties with special emphasis on activities for children. Candlelighting, eating *latkes*, songfests, sporting events, and torch relays modeled after the annual event in Israel often take place during the season.

Gifts and *Gelt*

Before the influence of commercialized Christmas made it a widespread custom, particularly in America, to give gifts during Khanukah, sometimes on all eight nights, children received Khanukah *gelt* ("money," in Yiddish).

Possibly in commemoration of the coins minted by the first Hasmonean ruler, the practice grew out of the custom of providing gifts to support poor yeshivah students and teachers, an appropriate response to the Hellenists' attempt to obliterate Judaism by destroying Jewish texts and outlawing Jewish learning. It became common to give money to the children who in seventeenth-century Poland distributed the money to teachers. Often it was a way of rewarding them for past studies and encouraging them to learn more.

Today, some grandparents still give money, but more often only symbolic packets of foil-covered chocolate coins are handed out while presents of all sorts are more common. To keep gift-giving within reason, some families exchange gifts only on one night, limit the number of major gifts, or designate different nights for different givers: one for parents to children, one for grandparents to children, one for children to parents, one for siblings to each other, and so on.

The important thing to remember about exchanging gifts is that it be done in the distinct spirit of Khanukah. The holiday originated, after all, as a result of the attempt to eliminate our tradition, when Jewish texts were burned, Jewish learning was a crime, and Jewish people were murdered for showing allegiance to their religion. Therefore, items that promote Jewish learning, such as books, video- and audiotapes, and games, and excursions to places or events of Jewish interest, are most appropriate. Also, a portion of any money received, either as *gelt* or from gambling at cards or *dreidel*, is customarily given as *tzedakah*. (In some families, each child chooses one of his or her toys, new or old, to donate to poor children or to a hospital.)

The Khanukah—
Christmas Disconnection

It has become far too common for Jewish families to bring Christmas customs into their homes, whether in the form of extravagant gift-giving (sometimes even moved from the eight days beginning *Kislev* 25 to December 25!), decorations, family parties on Christmas Day, or caroling get-togethers.

Such things are usually done under the mistaken impression that Christmas is not a religious holiday. It is not surprising that Jews uneducated in our own rich tradition are misled by the season's commercialization and because our society has so broadly embraced the occasion as to make it a national holiday.

This does nothing to change the fact that Christmas—meaning Christ's Mass—is a celebration of the birth of the man Christians believe to be the Messiah. With all due respect to the millions of people who accept this theology, the concept is anathema to Judaism. In addition, Jews have suffered horrendously through two thousand years of anti-Semitic persecutions often perpetuated in Jesus' name or by beliefs attributed to his inspiration.

So no matter how anyone tries to justify substitutes for or supplements to our own winter holiday, they are totally inappropriate. (A Christmas tree by any other name—like "Khanukah bush"—is still a Christmas tree—and like its ornaments, mistletoe, wreaths, and even the exchange of gifts, it is symbolic of aspects of the man and his life being celebrated [in this case, the cross on which he was crucified and his immortality through resurrection].)

Treating a religious occasion as a secular event does not change its intrinsic identity. And diverting attention from what in Judaism is attractive and valuable robs our children of an opportunity to learn about and be proud of positive aspects of their own religion. It also destroys the message of the festival: The Maccabean Khanukah resulted from the struggle (without which there would never have been a Christianity) against adopting the customs of other people, against the Jews' becoming indistinguishable and undistinguished from those around us. When Khanukah is not an isolated incidence of Jewish observance but kept in the perspective of an incredibly rich schedule of opportunities for celebration throughout the Jewish calendar, it no longer has to be viewed as being in competition with someone else's holiday.

(Maybe if your children have built and decorated a *sukkah*, festooning it with greenery, garlands, fruit, and ornaments, or have adorned the house with flowers and branches for Shavuot, they won't feel that they are missing anything. Celebrating Khanukah when everyone around them is celebrating Christmas also helps youngsters believe in themselves and their own choices. Seeing that they do not have to follow their peers can give them strength when they face other decisions they are often pressured to make.)

FOR FURTHER READING

Gittelsohn, Roland B. "The Menorah or the Tree?" In Hanukkah HA, pp. 122–124.

Mincing no words, the author details the symbolism of Christmas and its ornamentation and provides an intelligent explanation of why Christmas and Khanukah should not be mingled.

Sussman, Susan. *There's No Such Thing as a Khanukah Bush, Sandy Goldstein.* Niles, IL: Albert Whitman & Company, 1983.

The pain and frustration of feeling different and left out because of the pressures on a Jewish child at Christmas, particularly when not all Jews "stick together," are explored. Unfortunately, the book solves Sandy's difficulty by allowing her to experience someone else's Christmas party, rather than by reinforcing what Khanukah and Judaism have to offer. Ages 8–11.

Synagogue

While the ritual of Khanukah takes place exclusively at home (except for communal lighting ceremonies), there is some recognition of the holiday in the house of worship.

Menorah

Since the Middle Ages, when transients often slept in the synagogue, communities have lit *menorot* there. Usually placed on the southern wall, the location of the golden *menorah* in the Temple, it is lit before *Ma'ariv* to be seen by people coming home from work. For those who attend services, it does not substitute for lighting at home. It has also become customary for the *khanukiah* to be kindled before *Shakharit* in the morning, without the blessings, to remind people how many candles are to be lit that day.

Prayer

The services are the same as on ordinary weekdays, with two additions. *Hallel* is chanted daily, because each day has a distinct nature as continuance of the miracle of the oil, and Khanukah itself, as a celebration of independence, warrants the thanksgiving. During the *Amidah*, we insert the paragraph *Al Hanisim* (For the Miracles), which summarizes the story of the Maccabees and thanks God for delivering us.

Torah Reading

The portions of the Torah, read on every day of Khanukah, connect this commemoration of dedication with the initial dedication of the Shrine in the wilderness, when the heads of the Twelve Tribes of Israel brought offerings. On the first day of Khanukah we read about the offering of the first tribe, on the second day the offering of the second, and so on, until the last day, when we read about the offerings of the last five tribes and the verse about lighting the *menorah* (Numbers 7–8:4).

On the Shabbat of Khanukah, in addition to the regular Torah portion and the passage from Numbers, we read a special *haftarah*. (Some scholars believe the custom of reading prophetic portions began during the Maccabean era, when Antiochus forbade Torah but not *Nevi'im*. It was also during this time that the rabbis, to inspire the people and make education accessible to the masses, extended the *Hockheil* custom by dividing the Torah into portions to be read on Shabbat over the course of the year, as well as Mondays and Thursdays when people came into town for market.)

Zekhariah 2:14–4:7 presents the image of a *menorah* kept lit by a flow of unending oil from an unseen source. Written three hundred years before the Maccabean revolt, it supported the rabbis' tradition of stressing the miracle of the oil over the military offensive, particularly with its famous summary phrase, "Not by might, nor by power, but by My spirit—said the Lord of Hosts" (4:6). It clearly places the emphasis on dedication to Jewish ideals, instructing that only through spiritual replenishment will Judaism and the Jewish nation triumph.

When a second Shabbat falls during the week of Khanukah, we read the *haftarah* describing the preparation of ornaments and implements for the dedication of Solomon's temple, the second "*khanukah*" (I Kings 7:40–51).

Tevet 10

If you are keeping track of all special days in the Jewish calendar, the next follows Khanukah by one week. Commemorating the day that Babylonian King Nebukhadnezzar began his siege of Jerusalem, which paved the way for the destruction of the Temple and the first exile, *Tevet* 10 is a minor fast day (for more information, see chapter on Tisha B'Av).

WHERE DO WE BEGIN?—PREPARATION

Aside from making sure you have the appropriate supplies—*menorah* (cleaned from last year's residue of wax and carbon!), candles or wicks and oil, potatoes if you will be making the traditional delicacy *latkes*, *dreidels* and any gifts or coins you intend to distribute—there is little that must be done in advance.

However, families that enjoy decorating the house for the holiday begin getting ready several weeks early. Happy Khanukah signs, paper chains, cut-outs of holiday symbols, and so on can be purchased at a Jewish supply store or made at home or school in advance. (The idea is not to compete with the lawn displays, blinking lights, and rooftop ornaments of non-Jewish neighbors, but to create a festive atmosphere that will enhance the Jewish spirit of the holiday.)

Extended families often get together for kindling the lights, a meal, singing, games, and gift exchanges one night during the week (the fifth candle was traditional, but today the most convenient night is chosen). Obviously, if you attend or host such a gathering, you will need to allow time to shop and cook.

WHAT ARE WE SUPPOSED TO DO?— *HALAKHAH*

A number of *halakhot* pertaining to the main observance of Khanukah have changed over the years because of shifts in lifestyle and living conditions since the time the laws were written and codified.

Suitable *Khanukiot*

The lamp used for Khanukah must be dedicated to the use of kindling lights for this holiday and must be distinct from any other source of illumination in the house. Although the original vessels were the clay oil lamps in common use, the post-talmudic sages disapproved of pottery *menorot* (unless cleaned every night), favoring metal or glass, which did not become soiled and unsightly after used just once. In other words, the holiday is to be honored with an attractive lamp.

Anything that holds the flames will do, as long as the lights are all at the same level, the wicks remain separate to make distinct flames, the flame of one candle does not melt the wax of another, and the *shammash* sits at a different height, or off to the side, from the other lights.

Ever since the invention of the incandescent bulb, the question of whether an electric menorah may be used has generated debate. Their reasons differ, but authorities on *halakhah* do not sanction their use for other than decorative purposes. According to some, since the *khanukiah* is modeled on the Temple *menorah*, fuel and wick must be used. Others explain that at the time it is lit, the lamp is supposed to contain enough fuel to burn for the prescribed amount of time. (If it doesn't, it must be extinguished and relit.) An electric lamp does not store the required amount of current but continually draws it from an outside source. Also, turning it on may be an indirect, rather than the required direct, action. Merely twisting a bulb in its socket does not fulfill the spirit of kindling lights.

Making Kindling a Priority

Maimonides ruled that even one supported by charity should borrow, beg, or sell a garment in order to purchase oil and a lamp and be able to kindle Khanukah lights. That is because of each household's contribution to publicizing the miracle.

If you must choose between lights for the holiday or for the Sabbath, provide the latter as a matter of domestic peace and comfort. (At the time this ruling was made, Sabbath lights were often the only illumination in a home.) But between Khanukah lights and wine for Sabbath *kiddush*, the lights take precedence.

Positioning the *Menorah*

Maimonides asserted that we be diligent in performing the "exceedingly precious" *mitzvah* of lighting the Khanukah lamp because it promotes recognition of the miracle and is a way of praising God for it. Originally, the *halakhah* stipulated that the *menorah* be hung on the doorpost so that anyone passing by saw it, and it had the added benefit of encouraging observance in Jewish neighborhoods, where everyone would know whether or not a family had complied.

When hostility from non-Jewish neighbors made it dangerous for Jews to openly observe the holiday, the rabbis ruled that the *menorah* could be lit inside. Today publicizing the miracle is primarily directed at those in the home who, often more than passersby, need to be reminded of the Maccabees' miracle. So the *menorah* may be placed anywhere. Still, when possible, the kindling is preferably done near a window facing the street or the entryway, if the flames will not be extinguished when the door is opened.

Fuel

If you use oil, that from olives is preferred. The original Khanukah cruse contained olive oil, which provides a clear light (although not necessary, the clarity enhances the *mitzvah*). A *midrash* gives an additional basis, comparing Israel to the olive because of its by-product: All liquids mingle with one another, except oil. Likewise, Israel remains separate in following God's laws. Using olive oil for Khanukah reminds us of the distinctness by which Israel has survived and for which the Maccabees fought.

Lighting the Lights

Obligation

Both men and women are bound to the *mitzvah* of kindling. A man, woman, or religiously mature (twelve years for a girl, thirteen for a boy) youth can light on behalf of the entire household.

Time

Once the time for lighting has arrived, you may not eat, drink, perform work, or study until the *menorah* has been kindled. The rule of lighting at nightfall, when the stars appear, was made so that the last pedestrians coming home from the marketplace would see the flames. Since our routines are less tied to natural light today, the *menorah* may be kindled any time people are still outside or are awake in the household. If you light the candles after everyone in your home has gone to sleep, and there is no one on the streets, you do not recite the blessings.

On *Erev* Shabbat, the *menorah* is kindled before Sabbath candles, more than an hour before nightfall. (Once the latter are kindled, no additional fire can be made.) In order to comply with the *halakhah* that at least one of the Khanukah candles burns a minimum of thirty minutes after the sun goes down, you need to use thinner wicks or bigger candles. Following Shabbat, the synagogue *menorah* is lit prior to *Havdalah*. At home, it can be kindled either before or after *Havdalah*.

Benedictions

Since tradition requires that performance of a *mitzvah* be preceded by the recitation of a *brakhah*, all three blessings (two on all but the first night) must be recited prior to kindling any lights. The first blessing uses the phrase "Who has commanded us to kindle" even though lighting Khanukah lamps was not directly instructed by God in the Torah. Deuteronomy 17:11 was interpreted to mean that the sages had the authority to make rulings to which we are to adhere. As Maimonides presented it, the implication of the blessing is "Who has sanctified us with His commandments, having commanded us to heed the sages who have instructed us to kindle. . . ." (The Khanukah candlelighting *brakhah* became the format for all subsequent kindling benedictions.)

Duration

Although the candles are supposed to burn for a minimum of thirty minutes, most authorities agree that the *mitzvah* is fulfilled once the lights are lit. For that reason, you do not have to relight them if they become extinguished or if they do not burn the full half hour (as long as the amount of fuel necessary for thirty minutes of burning is present). If they are relit, the blessings are not repeated.

If the lamp is still burning after people have left the streets, you may extinguish it. Any oil left over can be added to and used the next day. Any oil left on the eighth day should be burned so that it is not used for purposes other than the sacred one for which it was designated.

Once lit, the *menorah* is not to be moved until the flames have been extinguished, so as not to appear that the light is serving a purpose other than expressing thanks to God.

Travel

When you are away from home, if someone in your household kindles a *menorah* on your behalf, it is not necessary for you to light one yourself. If one is not being lit for you, and you are unable to light your own, you can be a partner in someone else's home if you share the expense of the oil. Otherwise, if you see the flames of another person's *menorah*, you recite the second blessing and the *shehekheyanu*. (The existence of portable *khanukiot* in Judaica collections, some cleverly installed in cigarette and other travel cases, testifies that wayfarers made provisions to fulfill the *mitzvah* of the occasion.)

Work

There are no restrictions on work during the week of Khanukah.

Mourning

Since Khanukah is a festival, fasting and funeral eulogies, except for a scholar, are prohibited. Outward signs of sadness are to be avoided.

Tzedakah

Charity should be donated during the holiday, especially to support those who study Torah.

FOR FURTHER READING

Chanukah—Its History, Observance and Significance.
Ed. by Rabbi Nosson Scherman and Rabbi Meir
Zlotowitz. Brooklyn: Mesorah Publications, 1989,
pp. 112–119.
The detailed laws of the holiday are presented very
clearly in laypersons' language.

WHAT OTHER THINGS DO PEOPLE DO?— CUSTOMS

Other Times and Places

Festivities

Khanukah has been a week punctuated by parties, a
feeling of relaxation and optimism even in the most
oppressive external circumstances. In the spirit of
pride and hope, Eastern European Jews often closed
their shops early and devoted their evenings to so-
cializing and annual concerts. The restriction against
using the light of the candles for any purpose, and
the fact that they are to be enjoyed, provided the
luxury of leisure time not often available to previous
generations. With this free time, forms of entertainment not generally indulged in became popular
Khanukah pastimes. The fifth night, when the youngsters received their *gelt*, was often set aside for family get-togethers.

Though Khanukah was traditionally the time for
rabbis to visit small villages to teach Torah and inspire people to obey God throughout the year, even
study was interrupted once candles were lit. *Yeshivah* students instead engaged in talmudic riddles
and *gematria* arithmetic puzzles whose answers were
numbers totalling forty-four (for the number of candles consumed in the *menorah*). Prohibitions against
gambling were relaxed for *dreidel*, chess, checkers,
dominoes, and card games like *kvitlakh*, played with
a set of thirty-one numbered and artfully decorated
cards representing the kings the Israelites fought on
their entrance to Canaan. (The rabbis usually forbade
gambling because they considered the transfer of
"unearned" funds robbery. At Khanukah it was sanc-
tioned as being in the spirit of the season; some
viewed the games as contests of wit, and often the
winnings were donated to *tzedakah*.)

Children in Yemen received coins every day of
Khanukah, with which they bought small bags of
sugar with a pinch of red coloring, used to make a
Khanukah "wine." Every night they took their drinks
to the home of a different one of their friends, whose

mother had cooked up a peas and lentils treat. In
Eastern Europe, the holiday dish was *kugel* and often
roast goose or duck with dumplings. The Moroccans
served couscous and rooster. Many *Sephardim* had
the custom, on the last night, of roasting nuts and
seeds on a large tray for the children, who grabbed
handfuls for immediate gratification and to take to
school the next day.

Honoring Women

Among the *Sephardim*, the nights toward the end of
the festival had special connotations. The Tunisians
called Rosh Khodesh *Tevet* (the sixth or seventh
candle, depending on whether *Kislev* was twenty-
nine or thirty days long) "New Moon of the Daughters," when parents gave gifts to their girls and
grooms gave to their brides. A bride's father then
hosted a feast for friends and relatives of both families.

The seventh night was widely dedicated to Jewish women, in commemoration of the contributions
they made to the Maccabees' victory (and all of Jewish history). In special gatherings, the women recalled that by decree, maidens on their wedding
nights first had to surrender to the Syrian governor
and retold the stories of Hannah and Judith (from the
apocryphal Book of Judith). A beautiful widow,
Judith (in Hebrew, *Yehudit*, meaning "Jewess"), used
her physical charms and quick mind to best the captain of the enemy. After convincing Holofernes that
she was aligning with his side, she fed him salty
cheese to make him drink an excess of wine. Once
he fell into an intoxicated sleep, she decapitated him
and left his headless body to frighten his men, who
retreated. (Although set in the Babylonian period, the
Book of Judith is thought to have originated at the
time of the Maccabees. Medieval Hebrew versions
understood the story in the context of the Hasmonean revolt.)

In remembrance, the women ate cheese dishes,
sang, danced, received special blessings, and sometimes embraced the Torah scrolls in the synagogue. Often they took a vacation from all household
chores on that day, and often for the entire Khanukah
week.

Some European communities dedicated the eighth
night to Judith, when her story was read in Yiddish.
Called *zot* (literally "this is," but implying this is the
essence, the culmination, of) Khanukah, alluding to
the day's scriptural portion dealing with the dedication of the Tabernacle (Numbers 7:84), it was a day
for giving charity, telling stories about Jewish heroes,
and enjoying elaborate meals.

Candles and Kindling

When the Jews of Antioch (Syria) received their candles from Jerusalem, they sang praises to them, then sold them publicly in the synagogue to raise money for their religious school. If a congregation had a beadle (also known as a *shammash*), he would send each family a decorative taper to use in lighting their *menorot*, for which he was financially rewarded. Children received candles as gifts, each in the shape of a hand with the fingers upright, to protect them against the "evil eye."

The ancestors of Aleppo's Jews wandered for months following their expulsion from Spain in 1492 before being allowed to settle in Syria during the Khanukah season of that year. In thanks, they lit an extra candle for finding a country willing to accept them and began the lasting custom of having two *shammashim*. They also light twelve oil lamps in the synagogue, in memory of the gifts of the heads of Israel's tribes during the Tabernacle dedication in the wilderness.

Yemenite children make their own *menorot* of clay; the Tunisian children decorate theirs with flowers and receive coins called flower money.

The Jews of Aden dressed in blue and attended afternoon services together. Upon returning to their homes, they kindled their doorpost *khanukiot* at the same time, lighting up the entire community. In Venice, Jewish families rode through the canals in their gondolas, serenading at every home that had a *menorah* in the window or doorway.

Today, *menorot* are seen in public squares all over the world, as the Lubavitch *khasidim* continue their campaign to remind Jews to rededicate themselves to their tradition.

Tending to the Needy

In many communities, particularly among the *Sephardim*, providing for those in need took special forms. The Judeo-Spanish called the Sabbath that fell during the festival Shabbat *Khalbasha* (clothing the poor). The rabbi expounded on the importance of providing garments for the needy, which were later brought to the synagogue and distributed during Rosh Khodesh *Tevet* (at the end of Khanukah). Whenever a person in need would approach someone and quote from the Torah portion that usually falls during Khanukah, "*Shuvu shivru lanu mei'at okhel*" (Go again, buy us a little food [Genesis 43:2]), he would be given food or money.

The children of Damascas, and *Sephardi* children in Israel sometimes accompanied by teachers, went through their communities reciting the same phrase

to collect food or money. On the eighth day of the festival, with the help of rabbis, the children used the donated food to prepare three banquets: one for the poor, one for their teachers, and one for themselves.

Leaders of the Jewish community in Turkey visited the affluent to collect money for the poor, distributing *latkes* from the platters they carried to each contributor. The Bukharans baked coins into cakes for their needy relatives and teachers.

Children of the poor Persian Jews went door to door for contributions. In return for a gift, they burned a piece of grass to ward off the "evil eye."

In the Land of the Maccabees

In Israel, of course, Khanukah is a national holiday and one with special meaning. Not only did the Maccabean victory and rededication miracle take place there 2,100 years ago, but the conditions of the struggle for survival were repeated as the modern state came into being. During the holiday period, when new buildings (like the Tel Aviv Museum) and settlements (particularly strategic *nakhal* ["take possession"; a special army unit] *kibbutzim*) are traditionally dedicated, *menorot* crown public buildings. Prior to the start of school vacation, which coincides with Khanukah, the curriculum is devoted to the holiday and its history. Families, schools, organizations, hotels, and *kibbutzim* hold gatherings, parties, dances, and other special events.

This is also the time in Israel for meetings and conferences, especially on the subject of education, and for touring the country. *Sephardim* in Jerusalem visit the grave of Simon the Just, the last high priest before Hellenization tainted the position, and children climb the hills to pick a white flower studded with red dots called Blood of the Maccabees.

On *Khag Hamakkabim* (Festival of the Maccabees, as it is called in Israel), members of the Maccabi sports movement gather at the ancient Maccabee catacombs in Modin, the starting point for a reenactment of their triumphant march into Jerusalem. Torches are lit from a bonfire to begin the Freedom Torch Relay. Runners pass their torches on to successors at predetermined positions, who carry them to towns and cities throughout the country. On reaching Jerusalem, the torch is used to kindle a *menorah* at the president's residence during a public ceremony and is then carried to Mount Zion, where another is lit in memory of Holocaust victims. (Torches, extinguished en route and relit in New York, have also been sent to America to symbolize the Israel–Diaspora connection.)

Other processions, races, and outdoor celebrations are held for Israeli teens. By providing meals and gifts at old age homes and hospitals, and sponsoring activities at army posts and absorption centers (where new immigrants are prepared to enter Israeli society), the Israelis continue a Khanukah tradition of community service.

FOR FURTHER READING

The Book of Judith. Ed. by Solomon Zeitlin. Trans. by Morton S. Enslin. Philadelphia: E. J. Brill, Leiden, for Dropsie University, 1972.

The text of the apocryphal book translated into English for Jewish use is supplemented with explanatory material.

Chagall, Bella. "The Hanukkah Lamp," "Hanukkah Money," and "The Fifth Light." In BL, pp. 122–153.

These magical reminiscences of Vitebsk, Russia, are told through the eyes, heart, and mind of a child.

"Hanukkah in Many Lands." In Hanukkah HA, pp. 151–204.

Essays about observance of the holiday in Frankfurt, London, Lithuanian ghetto, Eastern European towns, nineteenth-century America, New York, World War II fighting arenas, concentration camps, and Israel provide colorful, detailed pictures of how the holiday has been viewed and celebrated at home and in public by children and adults.

Sussman, Susan. *Hanukkah: Eight Lights Around the World.* Niles, IL: Albert Whitman & Company, 1988.

After summarizing the story behind the holiday, the book provides a glimpse into the celebrations of eight contemporary families reflecting the different circumstances and customs of their surroundings. A thread of eternity in the common last word of each section connects the pictures of Israel, Mexico, Argentina, America, France, India, Morocco, and the Soviet Union.

Greetings

On this holiday, it is appropriate to say either "*khag samei'akh*" ("happy holiday" in Hebrew) or "*gut yom tov*" (the Yiddish version).

WHAT IS THERE TO EAT?— TRADITIONAL FOODS

The fact that feasting is not part of ordained Khanukah observance (the Syrians wanted spiritual sub-ordination, not physical annihilation) has never stopped people from indulging in at least one festive meal in honor of the occasion. Those who recite psalms and songs of thanksgiving elevate these repasts to the status of *mitzvah* banquets, but most people are content to concentrate on the special dishes that have become intimately associated with the holiday.

Latkes

It is not unusual to hear people wax ecstatic about this crispy concoction, the simple potato pancake, a mix of grated potatoes, onion, egg, and a pinch of flour or *matzah* meal. (According to a folk proverb, Khanukah's *latkes* teach us that we cannot live by miracles alone. The fourteenth-century Italian Jewish writer Kalonymous ben Kalonymous wrote a poem extolling them.)

The Khanukah connection has nothing to do with the potato and everything to do with the oil in which it is fried—to commemorate the miraculous oil used to rededicate the Temple. A more complex connection links the Hebrew words for the Hamoneans (*Hashmonayim*), oil (*shemen*), and eight (*shemoneh*), the number which symbolizes completion of a holy task and elevation above the mundane Earth (circumcision of a Jewish boy and sacrifice of firstborn animals in the Temple take place on the eighth day; the dedication of the Temple itself lasted eight days).

Although many families swear by the *latkes* of their mother or grandmother, recipes found in virtually any Jewish cookbook and typically in Jewish publications in the weeks prior to the holiday are remarkably similar. Perfectly delicious plain, *latkes* are usually eaten with sour cream or, preferably, applesauce. Oriental Jews add sugar and sesame seeds to theirs, and a wide variety of vegetables serve as the main ingredient in place of potato.

In Israel, *latkes*, called *levivot* in Hebrew, are supplanted in popularity by *sufganiot*, jelly doughnuts. Other communities developed their own variations of the oil-fried food for Khanukah, such as tempura-style vegetables and fruits, *fritto misto* in Rome, and deep-fried sweets dipped in honey or sugar in Greece and Iran.

Cheese Dishes

Latkes may have developed from the custom of eating cheese pancakes in honor of Judith when Eastern European Jews had to substitute what was most available to them, potatoes, for the unattainable cottage cheese. Among some people, it is still customary to eat various cheese dishes. In addition to using them to trick Holofernes, Judith had taken dairy food with her to his encampment so that she could continue to scrupulously follow Jewish dietary laws. Eating cheese dishes on Khanukah also commemorates this commitment.

FOR FURTHER READING

Drucker, Malka. *Grandma's Latkes*. San Diego: Harcourt Brace Jovanovich, 1992.

Grandma passes on the tradition to the next generation by teaching her granddaughter Molly how to make the potato pancakes and why we eat them. Her recipe is included at the end of the book, which is illustrated with hand-painted woodcuts. Ages 4–8.

Hirsch, Marilyn. *Potato Pancakes All Around*. Philadelphia: The Jewish Publication Society of America, 1982.

A peddler has a special recipe for making *latkes*—and keeping everyone in a family happy. A synopsis of the holiday and the recipe for the book's "best ever *latkes*" follow the story, based on a folktale. Ages 3–8.

Wikler, Madeline, and Judyth Groner. *Miracle Meals: Eight Nights of Food & Fun for Chanukah*. Rockville, MD: Kar-Ben Copies, 1987.

The story of the holiday and information about lighting candles are followed by recipes for soups, *latkes*, dairy and meat dishes, desserts, and fun foods, and Khanukah parties and games. Ages 3–10.

DO YOU HEAR MUSIC?—SONGS TO SING

Starting with psalms at the Maccabees' dedication of the Temple, singing has always attended Khanukah festivities. Unfortunately, often the only song anyone knows is the banal "I Have a Little *Dreidel*" (known to practically everyone, Jewish or not, since it is the one token Khanukah tune included in public school Christmas programs). We have better examples than that, a repertoire of folk songs in Yiddish and Hebrew.

Aside from the musical theme of the holiday, "*Maoz Tzur*," the most traditional include "*Mi Yimalel*?" (Who Can Retell?), a tribute to the brave Maccabees who led Israel to redeem itself; "*Y'me Khanukah*" or "*Oy Khanukah*" or "*Erev Khanukah*," describing the way the holiday is celebrated; and "*Levivot*" (*Latkes*), in appreciation of the holiday deli-

cacy. Frederick Mendelsohn wrote "*Neirot Dolkim*" (Burning Candles) in honor of the glow on the street created by candles in the windows; Handel's "See the Conqu'ring Hero Comes" from his oratorio *Judah Maccabeus* has been adapted into Hebrew as "*Hineh Bo*"; and the composer Debbie Friedman, who writes new music for old liturgy and scriptural passages, has created a wonderfully upbeat version of the Zekhariah verse read on Shabbat Khanukah, "Not By Might, Not By Power."

There are numerous recordings of Khanukah music to help you and your children learn the tunes for the blessings and holiday songs.

FOR FURTHER READING

Friedman, Debbie. *Not By Might, Not By Power*. New York: Transcontinental Music Publications, 1980.

Traditional songs for the holiday are given new life with Friedman's wonderful music.

Songs of Chanukah. Compiled by Jeanne Modesut. Boston: Little Brown and Company, 1992.

Beautifully illustrated with pictures of sweet-looking mice or rabbits, each glowing with light, the book explains each song or relates it to some aspect of the holiday. Though small, this is a nice book for the family to gather around together.

WHAT TALES ARE TOLD?—STORIES TO READ

Both the history of the holiday, with its drama and heroic themes, and its celebration, reflecting the security of family and the carefreeness of childhood, have been captured in the poems, essays, and stories of some of our most beloved writers.

The most eminent modern Hebrew poet, Hayyim Nakhum Bialik, a leader of the Hebrew literary renaissance, presented the pleasantness of the festival in "For Khanukah" and "My *Dreidel*." He also used the positive image of the Maccabees to express disgust at the cowardly Jews who hid helplessly during the Kishinev pogrom (in "City of Slaughter"). Another of our esteemed poets, Saul Tchernichovsky, expressed the same sentiments in "A Night in Khanukah." The poem bitterly scorns ghetto residents who had lost the legacy of the Maccabean spirit.

Emma Lazarus (whose "The New Colossus" adorns the base of the Statue of Liberty) celebrates the Maccabean victory in "The Banner of the Jew" and "The Feast of Lights"; the Hebrew poet and

Yiddish novelist Zalman Shneour wrote "Khanukah Candles" and the Israeli poet Natan Alterman "It Happened on Khanukah." (All the above are included in *The Hanukkah Anthology*; see Appendix C.)

For Theodor Herzl, the image of the Maccabee was an inspiration and a promise of how the Jews would return to self-determination and strength, as expressed in his essay "The *Menorah*" and writings about his vision of the Jewish state.

Henry Wadsworth Longfellow, the nineteenth-century epic poet, portrayed the conflict between Judaism and Hellenism in his five-act tragedy *Judah Maccabeus*. Others have created fictional accounts of episodes in the Maccabean revolt against the Syrians, such as Howard Fast in his novel *My Glorious Brothers*, parts of which are excerpted in *The Hanukkah Anthology*.

Stories and books for this holiday are full of family togetherness, one generation helping or teaching another, gathering to celebrate and solve problems, reflecting the warmth and values of the occasion and providing models for your own observance.

FOR FURTHER READING

For Adults

Steinberg, Milton. *As A Driven Leaf*. Northvale, NJ: Jason Aronson, 1987.

This novel is based on the life of the second-century sage, Rabbi Elisha ben Abuyah, who renounced Judaism because he thought the logic of the Greek system would answer his doubts—only to find tragedy. Though it takes place after the time of the Maccabees, it shows how Hellenism invaded the traditional beliefs of the Jews, and is a classic about the conflict between Jewish faith and Greek philosophy.

Folktales

"Judith and Holofernes," "The Legend of the Septuagint," "The Death of Nicanor," and "Miriam bat Tanhum and Her Seven Sons." In CT, pp. 280–285 and 330–331.

Each is a brief telling of a story connected with Khanukah and the conflict between Judaism and Hellenism.

"The Law is Not in Heaven." In CT, pp. 305–307.

Based on a talmudic account, this is the classic story used to prove that sages have the last word in interpreting Torah.

Other Stories

Aleichem, Sholom. "Hanukkah Money." In FT, pp. 183–199; Hanukkah HA, pp. 244–253, and other collections; and published as a picture book (New York: Greenwillow Books, 1978).

This cheerful description from a child's viewpoint is full of colorful details of the food, characters, and excitement that accompany the receipt of holiday *gelt* at home and at the homes of relatives. Ages 10–14.

"Five." In Hanukkah HA, pp. 351–355.

Despite the disagreement of all around him, when a *kibbutz* member lights the *menorah* on the water tower on the fifth night of the festival, he unknowingly averts a tragedy. Ages 11–14.

Frishman, David. "The Last Hour." In Hanukkah HA, pp. 232–239.

The experiences of a young boy on the day before the Syrian edicts against Judaism go into effect make him realize what he will miss. Ages 11–14.

Jafe, Leonard. "Bee-utiful Candles." In Hanukkah HA, pp. 307–313.

When the teeny Pitzel-land is left without candles the day before Khanukah, a little boy figures out how to get wax so the mini-people can make candles themselves. This is a lightweight but amusing story. Ages 4–8.

"The Light of a Small Candle Shines in Valley Forge." In TS, pp. 237–239.

Lighting a candle during the Revolutionary War, a soldier inspires George Washington, who understands the relationship between his fight and that of the Maccabees. Ages 11–14.

"A Mitzvah Gives Life." In TS, pp. 240–242.

A follower of the Baal Shem Tov gains strength from saying the Khanukah blessings, learning that the commandment to kindle lights the Jewish soul.

Paver, Chaver. "The Pan of Oil." In Hanukkah HA, pp. 328–330.

A grateful man commemorates the Khanukah light whose beacon saved his life years earlier. Ages 9–13.

Peretz, Isaac Loeb. "The Little Hanukkah Lamp." In Hanukkah HA, pp. 253–257.

Shlomo-Zalman turns his back on tradition once he strikes it rich, but when he loses everything, an old *menorah* symbolizes his return to Judaism. Ages 11–14.

Weilerstein, Sadie Rose. "K'tonton Takes a Ride on a Runaway Dreidel." In KT, pp. 27–31.

As a result of his Khanukah travels, the thumb-sized youngster gets to fulfill a plan to add coins to his JNF *tzedakah* box for land in Israel. Ages 4–7.

Books

Backman, Aidel. *One Night, One Hanukkah Night.* Philadelphia: The Jewish Publication Society of America, 1990.

In simple rhythmic text, and illustrations portraying a modern house and a scene of Palestine or a *shtetl*, the book shows how traditions are passed from generation to generation. For each night, a different aspect of the holiday is portrayed, in the present day, in Zaidy and Bubby's day, or at the time of the Maccabees. Ages 3–6.

Cohen, Floreva G. *A Hanukkiyah for Dina.* New York: Board of Jewish Education of Greater New York, 1980.

Little Dina wants to be like everyone else in the family and have her own *menorah.* Her grandfather helps her make one like his poor family had when he was a boy. Ages 3–8.

Goldin, Barbara Diamond. *A Hanukkah Tale—Just Enough is Plenty.* New York: Viking Kestrel, New York, 1988.

A charming story of a poor famiy in a small village in Poland who may not have one kopek left after all the preparations for Khanukah and the peddler who entertains and rewards them. Ages 3–8.

Levine, Arthur A. *All the Lights in the Night.* New York: Tambourine Books, 1991.

Two boys escaping from their *shtetl* to join an older brother in Palestine draw strength from the Khanukah candles they light on the run. Beautifully illustrated, the book is based on the true story of the author's grandfather. Ages 6–10.

Manishkin, Fran. *Latkes and Applesauce, A Hanukkah Story.* New York: Scholastic, 1990.

A family's kindness to two stray animals is repaid when they run out of food during a storm that lasts throughout Khanukah. The wonderful illustrations portray a village long ago and far away. Ages 5–9.

Rosenfeld, Dina. *A Chanukah Story for Night Number Three.* Brooklyn: Hachal Publishing, 1989.

Matisyohu Dov Ber Chaim Tavi, whose birthday is on the third night of Khanukah, has a fun, rhymed adventure on his way to making the biggest *latke* ever. This book is sure to appeal to young children and the adults who read it to them. Ages 3–9.

Schram, Peninnah, and Steven M. Rosman. *Eight Tales for Eight Nights, Stories for Chanukah.* Northvale, NJ: Jason Aronson, 1990.

These lovely stories, meant to inspire families to share their reminiscences between generations, reflect the customs and traditions in different countries and centuries. From poignant to humorous, featuring ordinary and extraordinary people, they express the meaning and power of the lights. Background on the holiday and songs and blessings are included. Ages 7–11.

Sidon, Ephraim. *The Animated Menorah: Travels on a Space Dreidel.* London: Scopus Films, 1986.

On each night of Khanukah (told in eight brief stories), a *dreidel* spaceship transports Danny and Judy to the time of the Maccabees or other scenes of persecution against the Jews, where they learn about fighting for religious freedom. All ages.

Singer, Isaac Bashevis. *The Power of Light.* New York: Farrar, Straus, Giroux, 1980.

The eight moving stories of miracles and visitations support the lessons of the holiday. Ages 8–12.

Wurtzel, Yehuda and Sarah Wurtzel. *Lights: A Fable About Hanukah.* Chappaqua, NY: Rossel Books, 1984.

The full-length storybook version of the animated children's program tells of one light—the Jewish spirit—that refused to be extinguished during the Greek oppression. With humor and drama, expressing hope and joy, it shows how the Jews were drawn to the pleasures of the Hellenistic world and later had to struggle to restore light once it was curtailed. This is a thoughtful and effective telling of the story and what it means. Ages 6 and up.

Videotapes

Chanukah at Bubbe's

Puppets enact the history of Khanukah, narrated by Bubbe (grandma). The award-winning forty-minute show features original music, including "Be Yourself," about the importance of religious freedom.

Lights: A Fable About Hanukah

The original version of the book listed above is deservedly highly acclaimed. In twenty-eight minutes, it presents the message of the holiday beautifully.

Lovely Butterfly—Chanukah

In the award-winning Israeli program, puppets and human friends use songs and stories to present the traditions and celebration of the holiday in twenty-four minutes. This *"Parpar Nechmad"* tape has been made in English.

Shalom Sesame—Chanukah

The Sesame Street puppets and celebrity friends visit the Maccabees' birthplace, play *"Dreidel* of Fortune" with hostess Lavana White, and see the famous torch relay race. It is a typical Sesame Street mix of animation, song, puppets, and comedy.

OF ADDITIONAL INTEREST

Music

In the 1700s, Frederick, Prince of Wales, commissioned George Frideric Handel to create a composition to commemorate the Duke of Cumberland's triumphant return from battle in Scotland. The result was the oratorio *Judah Maccabeus*, with a libretto by a Greek scholar based on I Maccabees and *Jewish Antiquities*, first performed in 1747.

In Israel

It is possible to visit a working village from the Second Temple period, reconstructed near Moshav Shilat (about ten miles east of Lod), which portrays what everyday life was like for the people who lived at the time of the Maccabees. Their actual birthplace, Modin, is nearby. Other sites in Israel important in the story of the Maccabees—such as locales of major battles—are identified by Aryeh Dean Cohen in his article "A Hanukka Tour," in *Hadassah* magazine (December 1987, pages 44–50).

TU B'SHEVAT

Tu B'Shevat (too' beh shvaht'): New Year of the Trees. Observed on *Shevat* 15 (mid-winter, January–February).

The minor holiday Tu B'Shevat has been transformed over the centuries probably more than any other holiday on the Jewish calendar. From an agricultural technicality it has become a celebration of national ideals. For generations it was observed mainly by spiritual Jewish sects and Hebrew school students, but recently adults have recognized the relevance of its messages about Zionism and environmentalism.

ORIGINS: WHY WE CELEBRATE TU B'SHEVAT

WHERE DID IT ALL BEGIN?— HISTORIC FOUNDATION

An Agricultural Necessity

The fifteenth of *Shevat* became a special day because of a commandment in the Torah. The law (Deuteronomy 14:22) instructed Jewish farmers to contribute ten percent of the fruit from their orchards to the Temple to help support the priesthood. The way the commandment is phrased, "you must take a tithe . . . year after year," suggested to the sages that the fruit offered had to have grown in a specific year. The problem was, how were they to determine when the growth started and in that way know which fruit to count?

They decided to designate the date that fruit began to flower as the new year. By then the soil had soaked up the winter rain water and was ready to nourish new growth.

After some arguing between the people of the plains and valleys of the geographically diverse Israel (who saw the almond trees blossom around the first of *Shevat*) and the people of the hills and mountains (where flowers did not appear until the fifteenth), the latter date was accepted. Since then the New Year of the Trees—in Hebrew called *Rosh* (head) *Hashanah* (of the year) *La* (of the) *Ilanot* (trees)—has been celebrated on *Shevat* 15.

We know the holiday as Tu B'Shevat, in accordance with a system in which each letter of the Hebrew alphabet represents a number. T (*tet*, ט) is nine, and V (*vov*, ו, which also functions as a vowel that can have an "oh," or, in this case, "oo," sound) is six. Together they make fifteen. *B'Shevat* means "of (the month of) *Shevat*," the tenth month of the Jewish year that starts with *Nissan*, the month of Passover. Outside the Holy Land, the holiday is also called *Khamishah Asar* (the fifteenth) *B'Shevat*.

Post-Temple Tu B'Shevat

The date started to assume the character of a holiday after the Second Temple was destroyed and the Jews were exiled from Israel for two thousand years. From its origins as the simple distinction between one fruit-growing season and the next, Tu B'Shevat became a powerful symbol.

Even though the soil of Israel was no longer under their feet, the Jews considered it central to their national self-image. Their thoughts and prayers throughout the year were full of desire connected with the Land, and Tu B'Shevat gave them a special opportunity to display their longing to return to it and make it productive again. To recognize the day, they indulged in the luxury of eating fruit grown in Israel.

But it was the kabbalists who originated the celebration of the tree. Centuries after the exile began, these Jewish mystics living in the northern Israeli city of Safed focused on the symbolism of the tree as life, an image as old as the story of Creation (Genesis 2:9). They understood "the new year of the tree" to be the New Year of *the* Tree, the Tree of Life. And the Tree of Life, they said, was actually a symbol of God, whose roots in the heavens carry nourishment, or energy, to the branches extending to Earth. So the kabbalists embraced Tu B'Shevat as rejoicing for renewal and growth not just of trees but of the entire universe.

With their typical life-affirming exuberance, they designed a special service in honor of the day, modeled somewhat on the *seder* for Passover. It included eating fruits that grow in *Eretz Yisrael*, drinking four glasses of wine, and reading from *Tanakh*, Talmud, and *Zohar*.

The original sixteenth-century Tu B'Shevat liturgy, expanded with poems and rituals, spread from Safed to *Sephardi* communities in Europe, North Africa, and Asia and was eventually published in 1753 in Salonica, Greece, as *Pri Eitz Hadar* (Fruit of the Goodly Tree). It became customary for Jews throughout the world to eat fifteen kinds of fruit from trees, the number being for the date of the observance.

In Modern Times

When the Jews of Europe began to establish agricultural settlements in what was then Palestine in the late nineteenth century, they were fulfilling the dream of Jews for almost two thousand years before them. As they reclaimed the Land long celebrated by Tu B'Shevat, and revived Jewish life on it, the holiday was again transformed.

The Jewish National Fund (*Keren Kayemet LeYisrael*, established in 1901 to collect money to buy property in Palestine) arranged highly spirited annual Tu B'Shevat tree-planting ceremonies. In a procession with marching bands and banners, thousands of people carrying young trees sang and danced on their way to the hillsides. (Today, almost one-seventh of the entire population of the State of Israel goes to the countryside to plant saplings.)

Outside Israel, the day was often devoted to activities centered on the geography and produce of the land. Palestine Day, as it was known in America, was celebrated with parties, songs, games, and stories at school, synagogue, and home.

Many *Sephardim*, particularly Turks, Moroccans, and Iraqis, continued to conduct Tu B'Shevat *sedarim* throughout the centuries. During the 1980s, small groups of American Jews looking for meaningful rituals discovered the oriental tradition and have adopted, and adapted, the ceremony for their families and communities.

For Further Reading

Cohen, Robert L. "The February Seder." In *Hadassah*. February 1988, pp. 46–51.

The article, illustrated with reproductions of wonderful pieces of art, details the revival of interest in the holiday and development of modern *haggadot*. If you have access to a good reference library that would have the article, it's worth reading.

What Does It Mean?— Religious Importance

At first glance, Tu B'Shevat may seem to lack religious underpinnings. It is not an obligation commanded by the Torah. And it does not commemorate an event of national significance demonstrating the involvement of God in human, and particularly Jewish, history. Yet this minor folk festival embraces two ideals central to Judaism: the primacy of the Land of Israel, and the irrevocable partnership between God and the people of Israel.

Primacy of the Land

Early in the saga of the Jews, God guaranteed that the descendants of Abraham would inherit a certain area of the Middle East (Genesis 12:7). This covenant was repeated with the patriarchs Isaac and Jacob, and with Moses (Genesis 15:7–21; 26:3; 35:12; Exodus 3:8).

As the property promised to them by God himself, the Land was inherently holy. *Eretz Yisrael*, as it became known, indicated not just a geographic destination but an emotional homeland and a spiritual grounding as well.

Here Jews could express themselves with no restrictions and could openly show their devotion to God. This was the only place in the world where all 613 *mitzvot* apply, and the only place where all could be fulfilled (see chapters on Yom Ha'atzmaut and Tisha B'Av).

The Jews who went into exile felt that along with their political base they had lost their spiritual center. Israel was not just the place where they lived but where God resided with them. The Holy of Holies, the innermost chamber of the Temple, was God's special abode on Earth, the resting place of the *Shekhinah*, His spirit. When His home was destroyed and the Jews scattered to other nations, they could no longer be as close to Him. Their generations of longing to return was partly a yearning to end the estrangement from God.

Partnership with the Landowner

According to the Talmud, "When the Holy One, Blessed be He, created the first man, He took him to all the trees of Paradise, and told him: 'See my works, how handsome and fine they are: everything I have created was created for you. Make sure not to spoil and destroy My world, because what you spoil—no one can repair'" (*Kohelet Rabbah* 7:13).

The practice of tithing, the original reason behind Tu B'Shevat, is supposed to remind us to recognize the real "owner" of the Land; even though we work on it, even though it supports us with food and other products, it does not really belong to us. The Jews were made sovereign in the Land so they could be its caretakers, acting as God's representatives on Earth.

This concept—that Jews act in partnership with God—is central to Jewish tradition. All notions of Paradise aside, the earth is deliberately incomplete and imperfect. The purpose of Jewish existence is to perfect the world according to God's commandments.

The process, *tikkun olam*, means bringing the morality of Torah law to others by behaving morally ourselves. Tu B'Shevat draws attention to some of the ways we act in concert with God, the first environmentalist. When we show appreciation for the things the earth produces, we also show our recognition that we are responsible for its well-being. When we plant trees, we express our thanks to those who prepared for us in the past, and our concern for those who will come after us. In however small a way, we are contributing to the re-creation of the world as it existed at the very beginning, as it is supposed to be, with all things living in perfect balance.

FOR FURTHER READING

Insights about the special nature of the Land, and the special relationship between the Jews and Israel throughout history, are presented in:

Ausubel, Nathan. *The Book of Jewish Knowledge*. New York: Crown Publishers, 1964, pp. 143–144.

"*Eretz Yisrael.*" In *Encyclopedia Talmudica*. Vol. 1. Ed. by Rabbi Shlomo Josef Zevin. Translated by Rabbi David B. Klein. Jerusalem: Talmudic Encyclopedia Institute, 1978.

Kitov, Eliyahu. *The Book of Our Heritage*. Trans. by Nathan Bulman. New York: 'A' Publishers, 1968, pp. 352–357.

WHAT DOES IT MEAN TO US?— PERSONAL SIGNIFICANCE

Just when the world seems its bleakest, in those dreary days of midwinter, along comes Tu B'Shevat and reminds us that, even if we cannot yet see it, a change in nature is about to occur. Marking a transition in stages of growth for trees, this holiday can be a turning point for us, too.

Many of us, at some time, experience what might be called "psychological winters." Like hibernating animals, we limit or eliminate our involvement with life. We become complacent, sluggish, pessimistic, ineffectual, maybe even bored or depressed. This internal climate may be, but often is not, a reaction to the weather outside.

Tu B'Shevat does two things. It assures us by example that new possibilities exist when they seem to be least viable and may even be invisible. It also tells us it's time to wake up, to throw off the inhibiting blanket and experience psychological and physical renewal. Like the trees beginning to draw on stored energy and nutrients to send out new shoots and fruit, we must summon our inner strengths to emerge from a stagnant period.

A new beginning holds great potential for growth. Tu B'Shevat is a time for us to take steps that will help us and our families grow toward meeting our potentials.

TRADITIONS: HOW WE CELEBRATE TU B'SHEVAT

WHAT DO WE USE?—RITUAL ITEMS

Haggadah

If you choose to observe the holiday by hosting a Tu B'Shevat *seder*, you will need a text for the service. The original version developed by the kabbalists of Safed, based on the Passover *haggadah*, is an anthology of readings about trees and the Land of Israel from scripture, commentaries on it and the standard work of Jewish mysticism (*Zohar*), and blessings for ritual foods and wine. You can create your own version, which can include songs, history, stories, questions, and devices that will engage children and other participants.

FOR FURTHER READING

For Adults

Tu Beshvat: A Mystical Seder for the New Year of the Trees. Ed. by Yehoshua Bergman. Jerusalem: Diaspora Yeshivah.

Based on the original kabbalists' *seder*, this *haggadah* is published both in English and Hebrew versions. (Available from the Yeshivah, P.O. Box 6426, Jerusalem, Israel, for an $18 donation plus postage.)

Fisher, Rabbi Adam. *Seder Tu Bishevat—The Festival of Trees.* New York: Central Conference of American Rabbis Press, 1989.

The *haggadah* contains two *sedarim*, one for teens and adults and one for children, full of stories, songs, and blessings.

For Children

Appleman, Harlene Winnick, and Jane Sherwin Shapiro. *A Seder for Tu B'Shevat.* Rockville, MD: Kar-Ben Copies, 1984.

This charming *haggadah* for children is easy to use and nicely illustrated.

How Do We Show We Celebrate?—Observance

Eating Fruit

Since leaving Palestine, Jews throughout the world have maintained connections with the Land on Tu B'Shevat by eating fruits produced there.

For the kabbalists, this symbolic gesture causes tremendous spiritual ramifications. According to their explanation, every piece of fruit, the parent generation, holds the seed of the next generation, in other words, the potential for new life. If, when we eat the fruit, which releases the seed, we do so in a holy way, with proper blessing and gratitude, then we are helping God to renew nature, and the flow of life continues.

Today, with Israel's agricultural richness and exports, we have many choices for Tu B'Shevat feasting, in addition to the dried figs, dates, raisins, and carob of previous generations. Oranges, avocados, bananas, pomegranates, olives, and almonds are wonderful staples for Tu B'Shevat meals, either in their natural forms or as recipe ingredients.

Planting Trees

The Meaning of Trees

In the Jewish scheme of the world, trees have always occupied a key and revered role. According to the Creation story, seedbearing plants and fruit trees were put on the Earth before any other living thing (Genesis 1:11–12). In other words, the first thing God did once He had firm land was to plant trees!

The Tree of Life, which He placed at the heart of the Garden of Eden, became a symbol of Jewish existence, a core value of individual and communal living: continuity.

The Talmud sages held wonderfully imaginative discussions about trees in life and legend. They believed that mankind, which they often compared to trees, owes its existence to them and should treat them with special recognition. Serious consequences would result from destroying a tree. The Torah (itself called a Tree of Life [Proverbs 3:18]) prohibits the destruction of fruit trees, even in times of war (Deuteronomy 20:19–20), and to prevent the loss of Israel's natural forests, the sages prohibited the Jews from allowing goats to graze freely. Today in Israel, anyone who wants to destroy a tree must apply for a license, even if the tree is on his or her own property.

Adding a Tree to the Environment

Rabbi Yokhanan ben Zakkai, who lived in Jerusalem when it was being sacked by the Romans, cleverly taught the priority of planting. "If you should be holding a sapling in your hand when they tell you the Messiah has arrived," he advised, "first plant the sapling, then go out and greet him."

Planting a tree—a concrete, practical act—has represented hope since ancient times. On Tu B'Shevat in Palestine, trees were planted for children born during the previous year: for a boy, a cedar, with the wish that the child would grow to be tall and upright; for a girl, a cypress, which was graceful and fragrant. Later, branches from the cypress and cedar of a bride and groom were used to make the *khupah* (canopy) for their wedding ceremony. The planting was associated with two of the most important times in an individual's life, birth and marriage, two occasions when we concentrate on the possibilities for the future. So powerful is this connection that even in the Theriesenstadt concentration camp, children planted a tree.

Planting was also considered a way to create eternity. As the Talmud relates, the righteous man Honi once encountered a man planting a carob tree. "How long will it take to bear fruit?" he inquired. "About seventy years," the man replied. "Do you think you will live long enough to taste its fruits?" The man explained, "I have found ready-grown carob trees in the world. As my forefathers planted them for me, so I plant for my children."

As a result of the Jewish National Fund (JNF) reforestation projects in Israel, the land once desert now supports successful farming endeavors, and millions of trees cover the hills. Visitors to Israel, on Tu B'Shevat or at other times, can participate in the Plant a Tree with Your Own Hands Program. A popular alternative is to purchase tree certificates, through local and national JNF and Hadassah offices.

Each inexpensive certificate represents one tree planted in Israel in memory or honor of an individual or on a special occasion. (Only large plantings, not individual trees, are actually designated on site, as shown in JNF's entertaining and informative videotape, *Grandpa's Tree*.) Outside Israel, symbolic plantings are often done for the holiday, with trees planted in one's yard or community, or houseplants started from seeds, particularly parsley, which will sprout in time for Passover.

FOR FURTHER EXPLORATION

The *JNF Education Department* produces copies of a prayer used in Israel when trees are planted there. It can be adapted for other tree planting ceremonies. (Available from 114 East 32nd Street, New York, NY 10016; 1-800-542-8733.)

The *National Arbor Day Foundation* offers tree planting instructions and other educational and membership information. (Available from 211 North 12th Street, Suite 501, Lincoln, NB 68508; 402-474-5655.)

Readings

The kabbalists introduced the idea of reading relevant texts during their Tu B'Shevat *seder*. A meaningful scriptural passage (such as the traditional ones listed below) or a poem or commentary recited prior to eating a particular fruit can add new dimension to holiday observance.

FOR FURTHER READING

The order below follows the passages' appearance in the Bible.

Genesis 1:11–18
These verses in the first chapter of the first book of the Bible describe how trees and plants were created.

Leviticus 26:3–18; Deuteronomy 8:1–10
In the third and fifth books of Torah, the promise of abundance as reward for keeping the commandments is made.

Ezekiel 1
The prophet uses the parable of the spreading vine to describe the people of Israel.

Amos 9:13–15
The prophet uses images of fruitful vineyards to represent Israel restored to the Land.

Psalms 104:10–16
The psalmist praises trees and other things that grow from the earth.

Job 14:7–9
In this book in the Writings section of the Bible, the man who loses everything for no reason other than the will of God contrasts his lot with that of a tree, which can be renewed.

Song of Songs
This magnificent poem, with its incredibly rich imagery incorporating the fruits of Israel, provides some great Tu B'Shevat material.

Tzedakah

During the service for Yom Kippur, we repeatedly say the phrase "but [repentance and prayer and] *tzedakah* annul the evil decree." We mean that through things we do to help others we can alter for the better the scales of justice being weighed on our behalf.

On Tu B'Shevat, the decree concerns trees: tradition states that as the beginning of their growth cycle, it is a day of judgment for them. Therefore, our efforts for trees are warranted.

As a festival, and particularly one so closely associated with eating, Tu B'Shevat also calls for *tzedakah* for those who cannot afford to purchase fruit. The *Sephardim* of the sixteenth century, while observing the holiday with their intricate ceremony, also established the *Ma-ot Perot* (Fruit Fund) to provide fruit for the poor. In some places, it became traditional to give ninety-one coins, to correspond to the numerical value of the Hebrew word *ilan* (אילן), meaning "tree": *aleph* (א), one; *yud* (י), ten; *lamed* (ל), thirty; *nun* (ן), fifty.

Today it is appropriate to contribute to a local *Ma-ot Perot* or *Ma-ot Khitim* (wheat fund), which provides food for needy Jews for holidays and Sabbath; a synagogue *tzedakah* box, whose contents go to the needy; a food pantry or food drive; or to a national or international organization such as MAZON, A Jewish Response to Hunger (2940 Westwood Boulevard, Suite 7, Los Angeles, CA 90064). MAZON, whose name means food in Hebrew, serves as an umbrella organization to collect and distribute money for food to groups throughout the world. It encourages donors to contribute three percent of the amount spent on food for a *simkhah* (joyous event, such as a *brit*, *bar mitzvah*, or Tu B'Shevat *seder*).

Tu B'Shevat *Seder*

There are probably as many variations of the Tu B'Shevat *seder* as there are people who conduct them.

All, however, share three major themes: appreciation of the Land of Israel as the fruitful Jewish homeland; rejoicing at the continuity of life from generation to generation—for us as individual Jews, as a people, and as a nation restored to our own country; and recognition of our responsibility to provide for others through conservation and contributions.

The *seder* designed by the kabbalists was an opportunity to worship and study, with participants sometimes staying up the entire night in celebration. First they created the proper environment, covering tables with white cloths adorned with flowers and fragrant branches. Also on the tables were lit candles and pitchers of red and white wine.

They opened the *seder* by reading thirteen biblical passages about the produce of the Land of Israel. Then they studied a section of Talmud (like the tractate *Zeraim*, "seeds," which deals with agriculture) and part of *Zohar*, following with prayers that their eating of fruit would bring strength and abundance for trees. This pattern continued, interspersed with drinking wine and eating fruit that had been properly blessed. The wine progressed from pure white (representing dormancy in winter) to pure red (life in bloom), with shades in between (for stages of thaw and new growth).

They ate the fruits in groupings, one following each cup of wine. Some kabbalists chose thirty different fruits, ten in each of three categories representing different levels of creation and types of personalities: externally protected but internally giving (having inedible peels, or thick skinned, including pomegranate, walnut, almond, pine nut, chestnut, hazelnut, coconut, Brazil nut, pistachio, and pecan); superficially sweet but unavailable at the core (having inedible pits, or hard hearted, including olive, date, cherry, jujube, persimmon, apricot, peach, loquat, plum, and hackberry), accessible both at the surface and inwardly (totally edible, or full of goodness, including grape, fig, apple, *etrog*, carob, lemon, pear, raspberry, blueberry, and quince). Some also highlighted the seven species that grow in Israel (Deuteronomy 8:7–9): wheat, barley, grape/raisin, fig, pomegranate, olive, date.

Using the traditional Tu B'Shevat *haggadah* as a model, the service has been altered since its origins and continues to be given new expression today. Four questions (designed, like those in the Passover *haggadah*, as devices to draw children and other participants into the explanation of why the commemoration is important); history and customs of the holiday; readings and songs around a theme such as conservation or feeding the hungry; symbolic tree plantings and collecting money or food for *tzedakah* have all been incorporated into modern versions. The *seder* is done either with tastes of foods from just the seven species, from the three kabbalistic categories, or from all four groups, or with a full meal of dishes using the traditional fruits and nuts paced throughout the ritual.

FOR FURTHER READING

See *haggadot* suggested under "Ritual Items" earlier in this chapter.

WHERE DO WE BEGIN?—PREPARATION

The rabbis provided no guidelines about getting ready for Tu B'Shevat on the personal level, in the home or in the community. Taking thirty days to learn the whys and ways of the holiday certainly can't hurt. Depending on how you choose to celebrate, however, preparing might require no more than adding a few items to your grocery shopping list. Give yourself a few months if you want to write your own *haggadah* and at least several weeks to organize a *seder*.

WHAT ARE WE SUPPOSED TO DO?— *HALAKHAH*

For the most part, the laws connected with Tu B'Shevat do not apply for the majority of Jews today. Anyone concerned about following religious law, though, should be aware of a few restrictions.

Fasting

In the tenth century, Rabbeinu Gershom Meir Hagolah designated Tu B'Shevat a festival and, therefore, a day of rejoicing. In its honor, no one is to do anything that would be inconsistent with celebration. Consequently, delivering a funeral oration or proclaiming a public fast are prohibited. So is individual fasting: if a wedding takes place on the fifteenth of *Shevat*, even the bride and groom who would normally not take food from sunrise until after the ceremony do not abstain from eating.

Prayer

In keeping with the joyous aura of Tu B'Shevat, the daily service is modified to eliminate prayers that

Blessed are You, Lord our God, King of the Universe, and are then followed by the appropriate completing phrase, as follows.

Drinking grape wine or grape juice:

בּוֹרֵא פְּרִי הַגָּפֶן.

borei pri hageffen.

Who creates fruit of the vine.

Eating tree-grown fruit:

בּוֹרֵא פְּרִי הָעֵץ.

borei pri ha'eitz.

Who creates fruit of the tree.

Eating produce grown directly from the earth:

בּוֹרֵא פְּרִי הָאֲדָמָה.

borei pri ha'adamah.

Who creates fruit of the earth.

Eating fruits of a new season (counted from the previous Rosh Hashanah) for the first time:

שֶׁהֶחֱיָנוּ, וְקִיְּמָנוּ, וְהִגִּיעָנוּ לַזְּמַן הַזֶּה.

shehehkeyanu, v'kiyamanu, v'higgiyanu lazman hazeh.

Who has kept us alive, sustained us, and brought us to this season.

Smelling fragrant edible fruit or nuts:

הַנּוֹתֵן רֵיחַ טוֹב בַּפֵּרוֹת.

hanotein rei'akh tov b'perot.

Who places a good aroma into fruits.

Smelling fragrant shrubs and trees or their flowers:

בּוֹרֵא עֲצֵי בְשָׂמִים.

borei otzei v'sameem.

Who creates fragrant trees.

Smelling fragrant herbs, grasses, or flowers:

בּוֹרֵא עִשְׂבֵי בְשָׂמִים.

would dampen the spirit of the day, which are omitted on all festival days (see "*Halakhah*" in chapter on Pesakh).

Agriculture

The remaining *halakhot* related to Tu B'Shevat concern plants and fruits that grow in Israel and regulations regarding the tithing of them. Even though the Temple and priesthood responsibilities no longer exist, we are still required to set aside portions of Israel-grown grain, fruits, and vegetables we plan to eat. If you are concerned about when and how to do this, consult a rabbinic authority and become familiar with the distinctions before going to Israel or eating produce grown in Israel.

Blessings

A number of *brakhot* (blessings) cover occasions on which we see, smell, or taste fruits, fruit trees, and other plants. All of the blessings begin with:

בָּרוּךְ אַתָּה, יְהֹוָה אֱלֹהֵינוּ, מֶלֶךְ הָעוֹלָם,

Barukh Atah, Adonai Eloheinu Melekh Haolam,

borei isvay v'sameem.

Who creates fragrant herbage.

Seeing exceptionally beautiful people, trees, or fields:

שֶׁכָּכָה לוֹ בָּעוֹלָמוֹ.

shecakhah lo ha'olamo.

Who has such in His universe.

On seeing fruit trees in bloom during spring (recited only once each year):

שֶׁלֹּא חִסַּר בָּעוֹלָמוֹ דָּבָר, וּבָרָא בוֹ בְּרִיּוֹת טוֹבוֹת וְאִילָנוֹת טוֹבִים, לְהַנּוֹת בָּהֶם בְּנֵי אָדָם.

shelo khisar ba'olamo davar, uvarah vo b'riyot tovot v'ilanot tovim, l'hanot bahem b'nei adam.

for nothing is lacking in His universe, and He created in it good creatures and good trees, to cause mankind pleasure with them.

After you have consumed fruit, wine, or a grain product, it is appropriate to recite a short blessing for the specific item, and then a follow-up paragraph. It is a wonderful summation of the spirit and aspirations expressed in the celebration of Tu B'Shevat.

For fruit:

עַל הָעֵץ וְעַל פְּרִי הָעֵץ.

al ha'eitz v'al pri ha'eitz

for the tree and the fruit of the tree

For wine:

עַל הַגֶּפֶן וְעַל פְּרִי הַגֶּפֶן.

al hageffen v'al pri hageffen

for the vine and the fruit of the vine

For grain products:

עַל הַמִּחְיָה וְעַל הַכַּלְכָּלָה.

al hamikhyah v'al hacalcalah

for nourishment and sustenance

וְעַל תְּנוּבַת הַשָּׂדֶה, וְעַל אֶרֶץ חֶמְדָּה טוֹבָה וּרְחָבָה שֶׁרָצִיתָ וְהִנְחַלְתָּ לַאֲבוֹתֵינוּ, לֶאֱכֹל מִפִּרְיָהּ וְלִשְׂבּוֹעַ מִטּוּבָהּ. רַחֵם נָא, יהוה אֱלֹהֵינוּ, עַל יִשְׂרָאֵל עַמֶּךָ, וְעַל יְרוּשָׁלַיִם עִירֶךָ, וְעַל צִיּוֹן מִשְׁכַּן כְּבוֹדֶךָ, וְעַל

מִזְבְּחֶךָ וְעַל הֵיכָלֶךָ. וּבְנֵה יְרוּשָׁלַיִם עִיר הַקֹּדֶשׁ בִּמְהֵרָה בְיָמֵינוּ, וְהַעֲלֵינוּ לְתוֹכָהּ, וְשַׂמְּחֵנוּ בְּבִנְיָנָהּ, וְנֹאכַל מִפִּרְיָהּ, וְנִשְׂבַּע מִטּוּבָהּ, וּנְבָרֶכְךָ עָלֶיהָ בִּקְדֻשָּׁה וּבְטָהֳרָה, כִּי אַתָּה יהוה טוֹב וּמֵטִיב לַכֹּל, וְנוֹדֶה לְךָ עַל הָאָרֶץ וְעַל הַמִּחְיָה / וְעַל פְּרִי הַגֶּפֶן / וְעַל הַפֵּרוֹת. בָּרוּךְ אַתָּה יהוה, עַל הָאָרֶץ וְעַל הַמִּחְיָה / הַגֶּפֶן / הַפֵּרוֹת.*

*פֵּרוֹתֶיהָ

v'al t'nuvaht ha'sadeh, v'al eretz khemdah tovah urkhavah, sherahtzitah v'hinkhalta la'avoteinu, le'ekhol mipiryah v'lisbo'ah mituvah. Rakhem na, Adonai Eloheinu, al Yisrael amekhah, v'al Yerushalayim irekha, v'al Tzion mishkahn k'vodekhah, v'al mizbakhakhah v'al heikhalekhah. U'b'nei Yerushalayim ir hakodesh b'miheirah b'yameinu, v'ha'aleinu l'tokhah, v'samkheinu b'vinyanah v'nokhal mipiryah, v'nisbah mituvah, u'n'varekhekhah aleha bik'dushah u'v'taharah. Ki Atah Adonai tov umeitiv la'kol, v'nodeh l'khah al ha'aretz v'al hamikhyah/v'al pri hagaffen/v'al hapeirot.* Barukh Atah Adonai, al ha'aretz v'al hamikhyah/pri hagaffen/hapeirot.*

and for the produce of the field, for the desirable, good, and spacious Land that You were pleased to give our forefathers as a heritage, to eat of its fruit and to be satisfied with its goodness. Have mercy, Lord our God, on Israel, Your people, on Jerusalem, Your city, and on Zion, the resting place of Your glory, upon Your altar and upon Your Temple. Rebuild Jerusalem, the city of holiness, speedily and in our days. Bring us up into it and gladden us in its rebuilding and let us eat from its fruit and be satisfied with its goodness and bless You upon it in holiness and purity. For You, O Lord, are good and do good to all and we thank You for the Land and for the [after grain:] nourishment/ [after wine:] fruit of the vine/ [after fruit:] fruit.* Blessed are You, O Lord, for the Land and for the nourishment/fruit of the vine/fruit.*

---

*If the fruit grew in *Eretz Yisrael*, substitute "its fruit"/ "peirotekhah."

WHAT OTHER THINGS DO PEOPLE DO?— CUSTOMS

Other Times and Places

Creativity in connection with Tu B'Shevat did not stop with the kabbalists' *seder*. Colorful practices for eating, distributing, collecting, and even trying to influence fate with fruit developed, largely in *Sephardi* communities.

Fruitful Superstitions

Hoping to affect nature, the Kurdistani Jews placed sweet fruits, like raisins, in rings around trees, then prayed for an abundant fruit season. Some barren women, similarly believing in the power of sympathetic magic, would plant raisins and candy near trees or embrace trees at night, praying for fertility and many children. Young girls eligible for marriage were "wedded" to trees in a mock wedding ceremony. If shortly after buds were found on the tree to which one was "married," she knew her turn would soon arrive. (In Salonica, it was believed that the trees themselves embrace on Tu B'Shevat, and anyone seeing them do so would have his/her wish fulfilled.)

Fruit Feasts

Persian Jews climbed onto their neighbors' roofs and lowered empty baskets into the houses through the chimneys. The baskets would be sent back laden with fruit. Some designed rituals, called *Las Frutas* (The Feast of Fruits), that were even more elaborate than the *seder*. One custom of the day was to give children bags of fruit (*balsas de frutas*) to be worn as pendants around their necks. Although in Bucharia and Kurdistan the holiday was known as "the day of eating the seven species," the Jews there actually ate thirty different types of fruit. (The Indian Jews counted fifty!)

The wealthy of villages of some countries, like Morocco, hosted lavish feasts for all the residents at which as many as one hundred different kinds of fruit, nuts, and vegetables were eaten—or they would invite all the townspeople into their homes and fill their hats with fruit. In Morocco, this home feast was often preceded by a banquet in the synagogue after *Ma'ariv*. During the day on the fifteenth, the children would visit relatives to fill their sacks with gifts of fruit.

The *Ashkenazim*, much less colorful by comparison, recognized the day primarily by eating fruits that gave them a connection with Israel (perhaps from an ornamental dish, such as the nineteenth-century Austrian hand-painted ceramic Tu B'Shevat plate now in the collection of the Israel Museum in Jerusalem). The wealthy would eat dates, raisins, figs, and occasionally, a costly orange—a splurge even for them. Others would have *bokser* (Yiddish for "carob"), which grew in great abundance and was therefore less expensive. (When fresh, it is chewy and tastes faintly like the date. After it's been off the tree for awhile—which is how the Diaspora Jews eat it—it loses much of its appeal.)

After their Hebrew lessons in the *kheder*, the children would give up bags of fruit brought from home, the contents of which would all be mixed and redivided so that rich and poor alike would share the same sweets. American Hebrew schools distributed bags of the same types of fruits to their students, an observance that continues today.

According to the tradition of the *khasidim*, God decides the fate of trees and their fruits on Tu B'Shevat. Therefore, they pray that God will grant a beautiful *etrog* for the next Sukkot, and following the fall festival, they make preserves of the citrus fruit to eat on Tu B'Shevat.

Greetings

When speaking with or meeting someone on Tu B'Shevat, the appropriate phrase is *"khag samei'akh,"* meaning "happy holiday" in Hebrew. Many American Jews who are descendants of Yiddish-speaking Europeans use the expression *"gut yom tov."*

Dress

In keeping with the spirit of rejoicing, clothing normally worn for attending synagogue or participating in a special occasion is appropriate. *Khasidi* rabbis sometimes wore their *yom tov* clothes in honor of the festival.

WHAT IS THERE TO EAT?— TRADITIONAL FOODS

Since there are no customary dishes for Tu B'Shevat, all dishes that use the fruits and nuts traditionally eaten on this day are appropriate.

FOR FURTHER READING

If you use the cookbooks listed in Appendix C, keep in mind that often the best recipes for Tu B'Shevat are found outside the sections for the holiday. So browse and be alert for dishes whose names include Tu B'Shevat ingredients.

DO YOU HEAR MUSIC?—SONGS TO SING

Several children's songs written specifically for Tu B'Shevat are popular in Israel and among American Hebrew school students. The most typical is probably *"Hashekeidiyah"* (The Almond Tree), since the subject, the first tree to blossom as spring approaches, is the symbol of the holiday. Other songs dealing with trees, planting, harvesting, and the landscape of Israel, drawn from scripture and developed by the Israeli pioneers, are also popular for this day. Among those familiar to generations of Israelis and American Jewish youth group and summer camp participants are "*Artzah Aleinu*" (Our Land); "*Eitan Bamidbar*" (A Cedar in the Desert); "*Eitz Khayim*" (Tree of Life), which we sing when the Torah is returned to the *Aron Hakodesh* after being read; "*Eitz Rimon*" (Pomegranate Tree); "*Eitzei Zeitim Omdim*" (The Olive Trees Are Standing); "*Nad Ilan*" (The Tree is Swaying); "*Nirtzanim Niru*" (Buds Are Seen); "*El Ginot Egoz*" (To The Nut Garden), from Song of Songs; "*Eretz Zavat Khalav*" (Land of Milk and Honey), Torah's description of the Land of Israel; "*Tzaddik Katamar*" (The Righteous Shall Bloom), from Psalms, describing the people of Israel; and "*Veyashav Ish*" (Every Man Shall Sit . . .), the prophetic version of everyone being at peace under his fig tree or vine at the time of the Messiah. The Yiddish lullaby "Raisins and Almonds" was also often sung among the Eastern European Jews.

For Further Reading

Tu B'Shevat and Purim Melodies. Cedarhurst, NY: Board of Jewish Education of Greater New York and Tara Publications.

Words and music for some holiday songs are included in the booklet, which has a companion cassette tape.

What Tales Are Told?— Stories to Read

While the Jewish world's literary luminaries did not choose this holiday as subject matter, there are Tu B'Shevat folktales based on talmudic references, stories from Eastern Europe collected in Jewish anthologies, and some wonderful books which portray holiday observance in past decades and relate Tu B'Shevat themes appropriate for any day or age.

For Further Reading

Folktales

Calisch, Edith Lindeman. "The Blessing of the Tree." In *Fairy Tales from Grandfather's Big Book: Jewish Legends of Old Retold for Young People.* New York: Behrman House, 1949, pp. 75–81.

With a charming and eternal lesson about the gifts of trees, this tale is based on a parable from Talmud.

"Honi and the Carob Tree." In CT, pp. 294–295.

The story is drawn from the talmudic records about the deeds of the Jewish Johnny Appleseed.

Other Stories

Bryant, Sarah. "The Pine Tree's Needles." In *More World Over Stories.* Ed. by Ezekiel Schloss and Morris Epstein. New York: Bloch Publishing Company, 1968, pp. 45–47.

Just in time for Tu B'Shevat, a pine tree learns that he's best off just the way he is.

Kranzler, Gershon. "The New Year of the Trees." In *Jewish Youth Companion.* Brooklyn: Merkos L'Inyonei Chinuch, Brooklyn, 1957, pp. 114–116.

A poor frustrated teacher in a small European village gains new insight and inspiration from the trees on Tu B'Shevat.

Levinger, Elma Ehrlich. "The New Year of the Trees." In *Tales Old and New.* New York: Bloch Publishing Company, 1926, pp. 93–95.

This short tale shows the observance of Tu B'Shevat from the point of view of trees.

Myrim. "The Revolt of the Trees." In *More World Over Stories* (see above).

The Tree of Life sets things straight when nonfruit-bearing trees decide to boycott the Tu B'Shevat celebration because they are not mentioned in the story of Creation.

Weilerstein, Sadie Rose. "How K'tonton Sent His Tree a Shanah Tovah." In KT, pp. 36–41.

After K'tonton finally figures out how to get a special holiday message to the tree that was planted in Israel when he was born, he receives a surprise response. Ages 3–8.

———. "A Tree for Michael." In *Little New Angel.* Philadelphia: The Jewish Publication Society of America, Philadelphia, 1947, pp. 27–38.

When baby Michael arrives, his big sisters agonize over what to get their new brother. The story provides a lovely overview on Tu B'Shevat and what it means. Ages 3–8.

Books

Ganz, Yaffa. *The Tree that Grew.* New York: Feldheim Publishers, New York, 1987.

A young boy gets a second chance, and learns how to give one to a tree, after he takes a little too much from it. Ages 7–9.

Gershator, Phillis. *Honi and His Magic Circle.* Philadelphia: The Jewish Publication Society of America, 1979.

This is a picturebook version of the tales based on Talmud. Ages 5–10.

Rosenfeld, Dina Herman. *A Tree Full of Mitzvos.* Brooklyn: Merkos L'Inyonei Chinuch, 1985.

A maple tree wants to do *mitzvot* just like the family that lives next to him. Ages 5–8.

Ross, Betty Ann. *Dates as Sweet as Honey.* New York: Board of Jewish Education of Greater New York, 1982.

This picturebook tells how American and Israeli children celebrate Tu B'Shevat and includes a refrain that teaches the seven species. For preschoolers.

The following books are often read on Tu B'Shevat because they share the themes and messages of the holiday:

Cherry, Lynn. *The Great Kapok Tree: A Tale of the Amazon Rain Forest.* New York: Harcourt Brace Jovanovich, 1990.

Kellogg, Steven. *Johnny Appleseed: A Tall Tale Retold.* New York: Morrow Junior Books, 1988.

Seuss, Dr. *The Lorax.* New York: Random House, 1971.

Silverstein, Shel. *The Giving Tree.* New York: Harper & Row, 1964.

PURIM

Purim (poo'-reem): Victory over would-be annihilator. Observed on *Adar* **14 or 15** (between winter and spring; March).

Purim, the last festival of the biblical holiday calendar, is the most boisterously observed occasion of the year. Jews throughout history recognized that the Purim saga not only records a near-tragedy in Persia long ago but tells the story of Jews living in a non-Jewish environment—in any place and time. While not ignoring its religious significance, the Jews chose to celebrate the triumph in fabulous secular style.

ORIGINS: WHY WE CELEBRATE PURIM

WHERE DID IT ALL BEGIN?— HISTORIC FOUNDATION

The Recorded Story

Approximately 2,500 years ago, the modest young Esther, who was Jewish, married the Persian King Ahasuerus, a non-Jew. This allowed her, along with her righteous uncle Mordecai, to avert a plot by Haman, the king's Jew-hating advisor, to kill the Jewish people. Recorded in the Book of Esther in the *Ketuvim* (Writings) section of the Bible, the events of their struggle include elements of comedy, tragedy, intrigue, and seeming coincidences.

The account begins at the time that King Ahasuerus had just consolidated his rule over the Persian Empire of 127 provinces. He celebrated with almost six months of banquets for the provincial potentates and then a week of feasting for the residents of the capital, Shushan. The comfortable Jewish community there was well represented and actively participated in the Persian frivolities.

When his Queen Vashti refused to appear during the party at his command—either out of modesty (one explanation is that the king wanted her to dance naked to entertain the guests who had been drinking for a week), vanity (the sanitized Hebrew school version says she did not want to be seen with an unsightly blemish that erupted on her face), or because she was a political adversary (her supposed lineage as the granddaughter of the Babylonian King Nebukhadnezzar gave her her own power base)— the king heeded his advisors' counsel to kill her.

This left Ahasuerus without a wife. At the urging of his advisors, once more, he held a beauty contest throughout the land in order to find a new queen. The king chose Esther (as she was known in Persian circles, or Hadassah, to her Jewish friends). At the advice of her Uncle Mordecai, who had raised her, she did not reveal her Jewish identity.

Shortly after Esther became queen, Mordecai, sitting as usual at the palace gate so he could keep tabs on his niece, overheard two of the king's servants plotting Ahasuerus' assassination. He reported the scheme to Esther, who told the king on Mordecai's behalf. After the plotters were punished, the incident was recorded in the king's chronicles, then promptly forgotten.

Meanwhile, Ahasuerus elevated one of his advisors, Haman, to the position of chief minister. The egotistical Haman couldn't contain his rage when Mordecai refused to bow down to him, and decided to kill not only that obviously observant Jew but all the Jews of the empire, even those who considered themselves more Persian than Jewish.

After casting lots (*pur* is Persian for "lot"; *purim* is its Hebreicized plural) to determine the most auspicious day for the genocide, he sought the king's approval using an argument typical of anti-Semites: that the Jews were dispersed throughout the realm, followed their own laws rather than the king's, and were not to be tolerated (Esther 3:8).

Considered alternately a buffoon, for his drunkenness and easy sway by his advisors, and a closet anti-Semite all too eager to approve Haman's plan, Ahasuerus gave his chief minister the authority to immediately dispatch a letter to all provinces calling on the citizens to arm and prepare to massacre every Jew on the thirteenth day of the twelfth month.

When Mordecai learned what was happening, he donned sackcloth and ashes and began to mourn. Esther, on hearing of the reason for her uncle's behavior, at first denied his urging to plead with the king. He advised her not to expect that she alone would be safe, just because she lived in the king's house. So she rallied to her tradition, praying and fasting for three days after asking that the Jewish community support her by acting likewise. Then she bolstered her courage and visited the king uninvited —a forwardness punishable by death—won his favor and requested that he and Haman come to a special banquet she was preparing just for the two of them.

At the banquet, she again sidestepped the king's offer to give her practically anything, and requested once more that the two most powerful men in Persia attend another private dinner party. Haman's euphoria at his exalted position and treatment was ruined when he bumped into the unyielding Mordecai outside the palace. Haman couldn't wait for the day of the planned massacre to get rid of his mortal enemy, so at the urging of his wife Zeresh and advisors, he erected a huge gallows in his yard. Then he ran back to the palace to request the king's permission to hang Mordecai the next morning.

That night the king had trouble sleeping; he didn't know why his dear wife was conducting these tête-à-têt-à-têtes as though he and Haman were equals. In his restlessness, the king called for the Book of Chronicles to be read to him and discovered that Mordecai never had been rewarded for disclosing the assassination attempt. When the king asked for his input as to how a man should be honored, Haman (who had been conveniently hanging around in the courtyard), assuming the king planned to reward *him*, suggested that the lucky gentleman be adorned in the king's robes and the king's crown, paraded through the streets on the king's horse, and proclaimed as the king's honoree.

Haman was understandably reluctant when he learned that he was to do all he had described for the hated Mordecai. And the suspicious king was none too pleased with his own situation either: His supposed right-hand man seemed to be too close to Queen Esther and suggested that someone other than the king wear the royal crown. Also, according to his solution to the Jewish problem, Haman would destroy the very man who had saved the king's life.

At the second banquet, which followed Haman's humiliation at having to lead the elevated Mordecai through the streets, Esther finally revealed herself, identified the evil plotter, and pleaded for her people. Haman was ordered to be hanged. Since by Persian law a decree could not simply be rescinded, a new letter was sent to the provinces to supersede the first. It allowed the Jews to arm and fight back to defend themselves. On the predetermined day, they killed those who tried to destroy them. Mordecai received Haman's position, and he and Esther wrote letters proclaiming the day after the fighting stopped an occasion for celebration by all Jews in every generation to come.

FOR FURTHER READING

For All

Esther in any Jewish Bible

The Book of Esther also appears in numerous editions of the Five Scrolls (along with Ruth, Lamentations, Song of Songs, and Ecclesiastes) and on its own.

For Children

ArtScroll Youth Megillah. Ed. by Rabbi Avie Gold. Trans. and Commentary by Rabbi Nosson Scherman with Rabbi Meir Zlotowitz. Brooklyn: Mesorah Publications, 1988.

With clear language, complete discussion, summary phrases, and colorful illustrations, this is a good version to use with children. Taking a traditional approach to the miracle of Purim, along with the *Megillah* text, it provides historical context, the laws of the holiday, and *midrash*. Ages 7–12.

Davis, Linda. *A Purim Story*. New York: Feldheim Publishers, 1968.

This simple retelling of the story of Purim uses cartoonish illustrations and funny expressions effective in making children laugh. Ages 5–8.

de Paola, Tomie. *Queen Esther—A Bible Story Book*. San Francisco: Harper and Row, 1986.

A less wordy telling of the Purim tale, the book provides two backdrop pages in the center, puppets to cut out, instructions for performing a puppet show, and a page for a child to draw his or her own banquet scene. Ages 4–8.

Feder, Harriet K. *It Happened in Shushan*. Rockville, MD: Kar-Ben Copies, 1988.

Using pictographs for key people and places, this is a humorous original telling of the Purim story. Ages 3–7.

Also see *My Very Own Megillah* (Saypol and Wikler) in Appendix C.

The Historical Context

No historical evidence has been found to support the details, or even the main events, of Esther's story. Many secular scholars doubt that it did take place or even could have occurred. They regard it as an adaptation of a nature myth (designed to legitimize the Jewish celebration of their neighbors' pagan festivities); a veiled and re-situated account of the Maccabean defeat of the Syrian General Nicanor (which occurred a few hundred years later than the backdrop to Purim [see chapter on Khanukah]); or a fancifully exaggerated version of an averted plan to destroy the monotheistic Jews, possibly during the reign of Persia's polytheistic Xerxes II (485–465 B.C.E.) or Ataxerxes II (403–358 B.C.E.), both of whom have been identified as Ahasuerus.

The rabbis, of course, have their own speculations, presented in talmudic discussion and *midrash* as fact. They say Ahasuerus' reign coincided with the anticipated fulfillment of a prophesy made by Jeremiah. While all but the weakest Jews were being driven from the kingdom of Judah around the beginning of the sixth century B.C.E., the prophet foresaw that after seventy years of exile, the soon-to-be destroyed Temple would be rebuilt and the Jews restored to their homeland (Jeremiah 25:11–12). The prediction worried rulers like Ahasuerus, because they realized that their own power would be threatened by a renewed Israel.

The third year of Ahasuerus' reign, when all those banquets took place, was, according to the rabbis, the date he calculated as the end of the seven-decade expulsion. Since the Jews didn't seem to be going anywhere, the king thought that the prophesy had been wrong, that the threat to him was gone, and that the Jews would remain his loyal subjects. (He had simply miscalculated the beginning and end dates of the seventy-year period.)

When the Jews participated in his royal party, explain the rabbis, they were celebrating their own permanent estrangement from the Land of Israel, and doing it in the style of their hosts. (Tradition holds that goblets used at the banquet were actually the holy vessels stolen from the Temple when it was destroyed by Nebukhadnezzar in 586 B.C.E., bad enough for the pagans but unconscionable for the Jews.) Abandoning their belief in redemption, and many of the Torah ways of life, they readily chose assimilation—repeatedly warned against in Torah and by the prophets—and, in the process, invited annihilation.

FOR FURTHER READING

Bloch, Abraham P. *The Biblical and Historical Background of the Jewish Holy Days*. New York: Ktav Publishing House, 1978, pp. 74–99.

Using references from the Hebrew Bible and talmudic discussion, the author tries to historically identify and date the characters and events of the Purim story. A summary of the holiday's observance is included.

Nissan, Mindel. *The Complete Festival Series*. Brooklyn: Merkos L'Inyonei Chinuch, 1967, pp. 33–80.

"The Complete Story of *Purim*" incorporates rabbinic explanations and *midrash* with the Book of Esther to present the full action along with background explanations, character motivations, and so on.

Weinbach, Mendel. *127 Insights into Megillas Esther*. Southfield, MI: Targum Press, 1990.

Going step by step through the story of Esther, the author presents the *midrashim* that round it out and explain much of the action. Quotes and citations from rabbinical writings are given in Hebrew and English. Large type and separate layout of each element make it easy to read.

A True and Eternal Story

History's Proof

Whether or not the events leading up to Purim happened just as they are presented in the Book of Esther, whether one reads the book as history, romance, political intrigue, myth, or farce, its story is absolutely true. It presents an account of the enduring experience of the Jew living in others' lands, not the first nor the last time enemies have plotted, or will plot, our destruction, either physical or spiritual.

In the days of oppression that occurred in the years following the Purim events for Jews in other lands—Maccabees against Syria (see chapter on Khanukah), the Great Revolt and Bar Kokhba Rebellion against Rome (see chapters on Lag B'Omer and Tisha B'Av), and the ensuing wanderings in hostile nations—the messages of Purim provided comfort to the Jews in their predicament. They supported the idea that God was still with them, and therefore fostered the belief that eventually they would prevail.

The notion of "Purim" became so entwined with the idea of God's role in Jewish destiny that Jews in danger of destruction by natural disasters or individual or communal persecution marked their escapes by establishing their own "Purims." The *Encyclopedia Judaica* lists more than one hundred—with intriguing names like Plum Jam Purim, Curtain Purim, and Purim de las Bombas—that were celebrated by the communities or families of Jews saved from execution, freed from prison, rescued from massacre, and redeemed in numerous other ways, observed on the anniversaries of their rescues. Often written documents prepared as scrolls, with the same format as the Book of Esther, were created to record the events and later read amid joyful celebration by the descendants of those who had been saved.

The theme of the Jews' ultimate victory over injustice was supported by the rabbis' broadened interpretation of Purim as part of Israel's eternal battle against Amalek. Amalek was the tribe that attacked the just-liberated Israelites of the Exodus as they wandered weakly in the desert (Exodus 11:14–16). In the Torah, God insists that we be continually vigilant in doing away with Amalek. The struggle started with the tribe's ancestor Esau (also known as Edom), who fought from before birth with his twin brother Jacob (also known as Israel), whose sons became the founders of the Twelve Tribes (Genesis 25:23–28:20).

Centuries later, King Saul, a descendant of Jacob's son Benjamin, came up against the Amalekites, descendants of Esau, led by King Agog. (Through the prophet Samuel, Saul was instructed to kill Agog and his family and not take any spoils [Samuel 15:3]. Saul's failure to obey cost him the kingship.)

The Amalekites showed up again in the form of Haman (identified as an Agagite, descendant of Agog [Esther 3:1]) and his sons, pitted against Mordecai, identified as a descendant of Benjamin (Esther 2:5).

Modern Evidence

Whether or not one accepts the national genealogy by which students of medieval history claim Germany evolved from Edom, only Holocaust revisionists would argue that the Nazis were not the embodiment of the depraved evil represented by Amalek and Haman. The Nazis themselves recognized the connection. In Poland, Hitler ordered synagogues closed for the entire day of Purim and prohibited the reading of the Book of Esther. Secular journalists wrote that the story of Purim foreshadowed the end of Hitler, who himself said in a 1944 speech that if the Nazis went down in defeat, the Jews would celebrate a second triumphant Purim. Indeed, on October 16, 1946, ten Nazis were hanged at Nuremberg, the fulfillment of Esther's image of the ten sons of Haman hanged again, as she had requested in Persia (Esther 9:13). As reported in news publications of that day, on his way to the gallows, Julius Streicher shouted "Purim Fest, 1946!"

The sages declared that even after the Messiah arrives, Purim alone would remain a holiday to be observed by all the world. As long as the Jews remain faithful to our God and our people (and history has proven that even when we try to abandon them we are brought back, brutally, if necessary), we can never be eradicated from the Earth, as Torah promises. And there will rise up Hamans who will plot to destroy us, because our beliefs are a denial of and an affront to their claims to absolute power—and history has also proven this. Therefore, we will always have reason to celebrate, not only our temporary victories but our ultimate indestructibility. When Amalek is finally eradicated, in the time of Messiah, the Book of Esther will testify to the long fight.

FOR FURTHER READING

"Frankfurt Purim, 1614." In TS, pp. 280–284.

In detailing the "special" Frankfurt Purim commemorating the downfall of a Haman of the late Middle Ages, the story provides a picture of what life was like for Jews in that time.

Kramer, William Mordecai. "Purim Plum Jam." In Purim HA, pp. 286–290.

Another "special Purim," based on an incident that occurred in 1731, marks the salvation of a family nearly ruined by a false accusation.

Praeger, Dennis, and Rabbi Joseph Telushkin. *Why the Jews? The Reason for Antisemitism*. New York: Simon and Schuster, 1983.

The authors explain why, no matter what positions the Jews have held in societies, no matter what they have done throughout history, hatred of them has persisted. Practical—if sometimes radical—ways of dealing with this unique prejudice are suggested.

"Purim, Buchenwald, 1943." In TS, pp. 298–301.

Demonstrating the indomitability of the Jewish spirit, despite incredible force and mortal danger, concentration camp prisoner Nakhum finds a way for the Jews of Buchenwald to read the *Megillah*.

Acceptance into Canon

While ordinary people readily adopted Purim, the sages were more reserved in their recognition of Esther's account. First, they had to contend with the principle that the Law of Moses is complete, that nothing in the way of observance is to be added to or taken from it. Second, the Book of Esther contained not one mention of God. In addition, it ordained a method of celebrating, encouraging drinking and revelry, totally out of keeping with traditional Jewish behavior.

Just after the Second Temple was destroyed, the sages (largely as a result of the persuasiveness of Rabbi Akiva) decided to include Esther as part of the Hebrew Bible. They found support in the book of Deuteronomy (32:18): "*Anokhi haster astir*—I will hide my face on that day." They understood *astir* (hidden) as a pun on Esther and connected it to the fact that God is not revealed in the Book of Esther.

An entire tractate of the Talmud, *Megillah* records the arguments for and against accepting the Book of Esther and elaborates on its events and characters. It states that the text we know was edited and canonized between the fifth and fourth centuries B.C.E. by the Men of the Great Assembly (the central authority on Jewish matters), of which Mordecai was a member, based on the letters written by him and Esther. They ordained the *mitzvah* of reading it at first as an informal retelling of the story. Prior to the destruction of the Second Temple, even before Esther had been accepted as a sacred text, selected portions were read on days chosen to coincide with gatherings, such as market days for farmers.

By the end of the second century, the book was being read publicly on Purim morning. The rituals associated with the holiday today were formally established during the following century. Throughout the Middle Ages, special foods and entertainments developed to add to the gaity of the occasion, with masquerades and parodies being especially popular means of reflecting the themes and turnabouts in the Purim story.

Kabbalists of the sixteenth century regarded this holiday so highly that they connected it to the day considered the holiest of the year, Yom Kippur—or, in its formal biblical name, *Yom Hakippurim*, a day like Purim. Both holidays share the use of lots (cast to determine the day to kill the Jews, to choose *Azazel*, the symbolic scapegoat); the notions of fate and providence; the power of prayer to avert negative outcomes; and the role of self-transformation in producing desired outcomes.

WHAT DOES IT MEAN?— RELIGIOUS IMPORTANCE

God's Role in History

The absence of any reference to God is one of the most striking features of the Book of Esther, making it unique among Bible texts. It is also the element that strengthens the book's value, because it helps us recognize and relate to God in a world in which His presence seems to elude us.

This is the opposite of the way things were when the Jewish people was created. At our birth (which we celebrated twelve months ago at the beginning of the Jewish holiday cycle, with Pesakh, a commemoration of our redemption *from* exile), the Jews needed constant assurances—signs and wonders— that the God who had led them into the perilous wilderness was still among them. They were like infants who know only what is before their eyes, but which, when out of sight, might as well not exist. By the time we reach Purim (the end of the festival year, and a commemoration of our redemption *in* exile), there are no more obvious signs, wonders, and prophets showing us God's involvement in our lives.

Having been thrown off the Land as punishment for not following Torah, the Jews who experienced Haman's original oppression would naturally wonder whether the promise of the ultimate redemption was still in effect. Purim resoundingly says "it is!" The message is that although God's presence is not obvious, He has not absented Himself. The fact that He is not recognized at a specific place—like the Tabernacle in the desert or the Temple in Jerusalem—is supposed to reassure us that He is anywhere and everywhere.

The little twists of the Purim story, the seeming coincidences, can be read as God's intervention. In essence, this indirect indication of His lasting protection provided the Jews with a national will to live.

Countering Evil

One of the hallmarks of Purim is our raging against Amalek/Haman. The original attack by Amalek against the former Egyptian slaves came from behind, when they were starving and exhausted (Deuteronomy 25:18). And it came immediately after they expressed doubts—despite everything He had done for them—as to whether or not God was still providing protection (Exodus 11:14–16).

This is a paradigm of Jewish history. Amalek (Haman, Antiochus, Hitler) arises when we are weak, when our defenses are down. When there is dissension within our own community, when we are scattered and assimilated (like the Persian Jews), when we stray from the commandments that define and defend us as Jews, when we lose faith in our mission and disavow our relationship with God, we invite Amalek. For what is absolute depravity but godlessness? What threatens to eliminate us, we who are supposed to be a kingdom of priests, is our own denial of our responsibilities: If we do not live as Jews, upholding the moral standards that are supposed to light the way for all nations, then we cease to exist.

Living as Jews in Exile

Logic and world history tell us that the conquered Jews should have adopted the customs and standards of those among whom they were forced to live. Instead, as Purim instructs, they saved themselves *not* by "fitting in" with the surrounding populations but by maintaining their values and way of life. The philosophy they developed to compensate for their generally miserable situation embraced the belief that their difference was positive, that they had a system of life worth protecting, and they had somewhere to go with it.

Their design of the commemoration of Purim for all generations developed out of this attitude. It provides guidelines on how to live as Jews—how to preserve ourselves—in the Diaspora.

The custom of giving gifts to friends, and especially to the poor, along with praying and fasting together, teaches us the importance of unity and community. We are responsible for each other and working together we can accomplish miracles.

Retelling the story of Purim instructs us to learn not only the Book of Esther but all the books of Torah. They tell us who we are, where we came from, where we are going—and, most important, how to get there.

The self-transformation of Esther, and the Jewish community of Persia, illustrates the importance of recognizing the influences of other cultures, including subtle economic and social pressures, which interfere with our spiritual values and can make us blind to political realities. At the same time, the Book of Esther clearly shows that it is not necessary to abandon Judaism for professional or political advancement, or vice versa. One can be both a loyal citizen *and* a practicing Jew.

WHAT DOES IT MEAN TO US?— PERSONAL SIGNIFICANCE

While the Purim saga warns us about the consequences of abandoning our religion, it also teaches that it is never too late to return to the faith and strength of our heritage. Although the rabbis go to great lengths to explain how Esther continued to live according to Jewish law, it can be argued instead that she was as assimilated as her Persian Jewish friends. Being an orphan indicates that she was cut off from

her past. She used her Persian name. And she intermarried—the most visible symbol of assimilation. Yet she summoned the courage to do something that threatened her own comfortable situation because it had the potential of saving thousands of fellow Jews.

The actions of one person—in this case Esther's interceding with the king—eventually solved a critical problem. The message to us is that each individual, regardless of where s/he might seem to be in terms of commitment to the community, can make a difference in fighting against what could destroy us.

In our day, assimilation rather than anti-Semitism is the greatest threat to Jewish survival. And our greatest weapon against it, one of the ways the Book of Esther instructs us to safeguard our Judaism while living in exile, is through education. The dignity and pride in being Jewish, which sustained the Jews through decades of oppression and millennia of uprootedness, came through their knowledge of who and what they were, their understanding and appreciation of their special way of life. It gave them the tools, with or without God's direct intervention, to take matters of redemption into their own hands.

On Purim we celebrate our ultimate, if seemingly unnatural, invincibility. We are about to start another year marking the progression of the Jewish people through time and space. What better time could there be for you to assess what you are doing to contribute to the survival of the Jewish family, community, and people? What each of us does can determine whether or not another Jew, and his/her children or grandchildren, will be Jewish.

A Jewish maxim instructs that to save one life is to save the entire world, for who knows where that one saved person and his/her actions will lead. Exposing someone to the richness of Judaism could be considered saving a life. (We are instructed to "live" by following Torah.) This doesn't mean changing your whole lifestyle. It doesn't mean having to become an Orthodox Jew. It means knowing enough to answer the questions "What does it mean to be Jewish? Why is it important to be Jewish?"

What you learn yourself, what you teach your children—and the *way* you teach them—and how you extend yourself to fellow Jews will determine what they know and how they feel about Judaism and being Jewish. (How about inviting an uninvolved friend to a Purim feast, or making sure that someone who knows nothing about it receives a *shalakh mannes* package [see "Observance"] just to prompt questions?) This is a great time to plan and implement things you can do, for yourself, for children, and others, to give all of you the opportunity to be part of Jewish destiny, part of what the Purim saga demonstrates is an eternal endeavor.

TRADITIONS: HOW WE CELEBRATE PURIM

WHAT DO WE USE?—RITUAL ITEMS

Megillah

Originally, the story of Esther was written on one long strip of pieced-together animal skins that formed a scroll. Based on the Hebrew word for roll (*galah*), it is called a *megillah*. (The other scrolls of the Bible—Ruth, Lamentations, etc.—also took this form and are called *megillot*.) The person who reads the Purim saga aloud publicly on the holiday must do so from a scroll (just as the Torah reading is done from the Torah scrolls, and not from a printed *Khumash*).

Few if any individual members of congregations have their own *Megillot*. Painstakingly written by hand, and often illuminated or housed in decorative holders, they are treasured heirlooms and Judaic collectibles. It is more common for people attending the service to use a book form of the *Megillat Esther*. Synagogues generally provide copies.

Gragger

Formerly made of wood and often intricately designed and carved, the noisemaker used during the synagogue reading of the *Megillah* is an inexpensive metal toy today. As you grasp the handle and whirl the gadget around, the toothed wheel inside hits against a tongue to make a grating sound. If you have a special noisemaker at home, you may bring it to the service; otherwise, the synagogue usually distributes *graggers*.

HOW DO WE SHOW WE CELEBRATE?—OBSERVANCE

Meaningful Frivolity

It is no wonder that Purim is the most raucous, fun-filled holiday of the Jewish year: it represents the promise that Jews will always, in the end, triumph over our oppressors. It celebrates the unrestrained joy in survival over death, and in the process, mimics the topsy-turvy nature of the Purim story's events.

Just to be sure it would always be distinct from the non-Jewish festivities also celebrated as secular carnivals, study and doing things for others were incorporated into observance to give the holiday a spiritual dimension.

Megillah Reading

The synagogue reading of the *Megillah* is like no other service you've ever seen in a house of worship. It starts solemnly enough: Just before the reading begins, a *makhazit hashekel* (half *shekel*) collection is made for the needy. Then the *Megillah* is unrolled, each section to be folded as it is read to resemble the letters (*iggerot*) that were sent to the Jews in all of Persia's provinces. The person to read the *Megillah*, hoping he is worthy, blesses God and expresses thanks for the miracles of Purim and says the *shehekheyanu*, grateful for being alive.

Then the fun begins. While the content and message are to be taken seriously, the delivery is not. Congregants, especially children, create an electric atmosphere as they anticipate the first of fifty-four mentions of the name of the evil Haman. Because of the Torah's commandment to blot out Amalek (Deuteronomy 25:19), it is part of the *Megillah* reading ritual for the name of Haman (and in some congregations the naming of his sons) to be met with all manner of eradication methods—banging on the seats, stomping the floor, twirling deafening *graggers*, blowing horns. (In some communities, only the six times that the text uses the villain's full name, "Haman the son of Hammedatha the Agagite," generates the loud response.)

In keeping with the party atmosphere produced by the noisemaking, the reader may take on different voices for the various characters, or speed through the text trying to trip up the children as they strain to hear "Haman" (hah-mahn´ in Hebrew). Communities use differing melodies for the *Megillah*, some borrowing sections from other holiday liturgies and even popular tunes of the day, particularly for the four verses chanted by the entire congregation dealing with Mordecai's origins and triumph (2:5, 8:15, 8:16, 10:3). Some place special emphasis on verse 6:1, about the king's sleepless night, for this point marks the beginning of the Jews' salvation, and the *trop* (cantillation) of Lamentations (see chapter on Tisha B'Av) is used for verse 2:6 because both deal with the destruction of Jerusalem.

The blessing following the *Megillah* reading praises God for having fought for us, avenged us, and punished our enemies. A special prayer, *Shoshanat Ya'akov* (Rose of Jacob, understood as the Jewish people), gives the highlights of the Purim story in terms of curses on the villains and praises for the heroes. A special reference to Kharvonah, who alerted the king that Haman had already erected the gallows—thereby providing a convenient way for him to be immediately executed—reminds us of our debt to righteous gentiles.

While most people today attend readings of the *Megillah* on the evening of *Adar* 13, it is the *Adar* 14 morning reading that is commanded.

The Purim *Seudah*

Esther and Mordecai proclaimed that Purim was a time of feasting and merrymaking (9:17, 22). This ordinance developed into the special Purim meal, or *seudah*, which takes place during daylight hours on the holiday. It is a most appropriate way to commemorate our success against a decree to physically destroy us, since it gives pleasure to the body.

As a secular meal, it does not include a *kiddush* (blessing over wine), except perhaps for a nonsense parody version, but nonetheless encourages partaking of plenty of wine. In fact, the most notable feature of the Purim *seudah* is the injunction, uncharacteristic among Jews, to drink until you don't know (*ad lo yoda*) the difference between *barukh Mordekhai v'arur Haman* (blessed be Mordecai and cursed be Haman).

This is not an invitation to drink uncontrollably but a way to recognize your limit. Once you reach the point of confusion, stop. (You *are* responsible for any damage caused by merrymaking and intoxication!) You are not supposed to get rip-roaring drunk on Purim, but happily tipsy. Not only does wine add to frivolity, it highlights the theme of drinking, and how

it helped create the miracle, throughout the Purim story. The saga opens with a series of wine-infused banquets (1:1-9), Esther's coronation is celebrated with a banquet (2:18), the Jews' fate is sealed with a banquet between Ahasuerus and Haman (3:15), Esther hosts two banquets for the king and Haman (5:6, 6:7), and the book ends with the Jews celebrating and agreeing to annually celebrate with feasts (9:17-19).

But why imbibe *ad lo yodah*? It seems to be a very strange notion in a religion that stresses remembering and making choices between different values. The formula may have been derived from a liturgical poem of talmudic times whose alternate verses ended "cursed . . ." and "blessed. . . ." Only one who was sober could keep the rhymes straight. Another possibility is that since the *gematria* (numerical value) of both phrases is 502, the two equal each other, and when you're drunk you can no longer prove this.

The "same" means that God is to be praised equally for Haman's downfall (cursed be Haman) and Mordecai's elevation (blessed be Mordecai). Wine, according to Jewish thought, takes us away from petty distractions and gives us greater spiritual awareness. Under its influence, even when we can no longer distinguish the two benefits, we should continue praising God and His protection of us.

Portions to Friends

The *Megillah* tells us to celebrate Purim by sending gifts to friends—*mishlo'akh manot* (the sending of portions [9:19, 22], often called *shalakh mannes* in Yiddish). The gift-giving serves as an expression of brotherly love and unity, which is our strongest defense against threats to our sprirtual and physical survival. The portions (which traditionally were made up of kosher food) also serve as symbolic compensation for the participation of Shushan's Jews in the non-kosher banquet of the king. Since *mishlo'akh manot* is a commandment, it is actually proper *not* to thank the giver (although it does not hurt to acknowledge that a package has in fact been received). It is particularly nice to provide *mishlo'akh manot* to people in nursing homes. Since the instruction is to "send," it is traditional to have the packages delivered (in Jewish neighborhoods this is often done by children), and it is appropriate to tip the messengers.

Tzedakah

The same passage of the *Megillah* also expressly states that we are to make presents to the poor (*matanos lo'evyonim*). In the past, it was common to give gifts of food, or to directly provide money to those in need. Today the donations are made less personally, through contributions to an organization such as a local Jewish food fund or through a synagogue.

This cornerstone of Jewish life is one of the critical elements that sets us apart from Amalek, who attacks the weak, while we do whatever we can to help them stand on their own. It also fosters unity, making us worthy of protection and redemption. You can give Purim *tzedakah* any time prior to the holiday.

Merrymaking

Purim became a time to make fun of everything, even those things considered most sacred: holy text, religious leaders, prayers. Jesters and musicians, lighthearted songs, dressing in costume, and pranks enliven the day. Today, costume parties and carnivals, with games like Dunk Haman, Pin the Crown on Esther, *Hamantaschen* Toss, and a variety of other games of skill and chance, are held by Hebrew schools, youth groups, Jewish community centers, and synagogues for and by children and teenagers.

For Further Reading

See *Building a Jewish Life/Purim* (Grishaver) in Appendix C.

Where Do We Begin?—Preparation

A talmudic saying reminds us "when *Adar* begins, joy is increased," for in this month Purim, the Hashmonean victory over the Syrian General Nicanor, the day of the order to rebuild the walls of Jerusalem, and a miraculous escape of sages from their enemies all took place. (In Galicia in the eighteenth and nineteenth centuries, *Adar* wall tablets called *misheniknas*, after the initial word of the saying, were popular.) A positive upbeat month, *Adar* leads into preparing for Pesakh.

The personal preparations for Purim for the most part center on secular activities, while the religious preparations are communal in nature.

Synagogue Service

Adar starts a cycle of special Torah selections, *arba* (four) *parshiot* (sections), read in the synagogue on the Sabbaths between the end of winter and the beginning of spring. Two directly relate to Purim.

Shabbat Shekalim

The first special Sabbath is named for the Torah commandment requiring each male more than twenty years of age to contribute a half *shekel* to the Temple before the first day of the month of *Nissan* (Exodus 30:13–15). The money was used to pay for sacrifices that were offered on behalf of the community. Since as of the first of *Nissan* only new *shekalim* could be used to buy the animals, reminding people of the obligation on the first Shabbat of *Adar* gave them a month to fulfill it. The reading, done in addition to the regular Torah portion, consists of the first six verses of *Ki Thisa* (Exodus 30:11–16) pertaining to the *mitzvah*, and a special *haftarah* (II Kings 11:17–12:17) on the subject. The collection was set for Purim since attendance was traditionally high on that date.

Fulfillment of the *mitzvah* continued even after the Temple no longer stood, the money going to support institutions in the Land of Israel. Three mentions of the term *makhazit hashekel* in the commandment led to the custom of using three coins. It also became commonplace for a silver dollar or packet of coins to be placed on the collection plate so that even the poor could seem to be giving the full amount required: They would put down some coins, "borrow" the silver dollar or packet, and then put it back, as though it were their gift.

This Purim collection of *shekelim* holds special significance as a reminder of the 10,000 talents of silver Haman offered King Ahasuerus to pay for the destruction of the Jews (Esther 3:9). It symbolizes our redeeming ourselves, particularly through the giving of *tzedakah*.

Shabbat Zakhor

The Sabbath preceding Purim, "Shabbat of Remembrance," sets the stage for the Purim tale. We must read its particular extra portion (Deuteronomy 25:17–19) accompanied by its *haftarah* (I Samuel 15:2) once a year. This is because twelve months is the period of time after which we generally forget things; it defines the period of mourning for a deceased loved one and identifies when an abandoned object is considered ownerless. Since the *parshah* commands us to remember the deeds of Amalek and erase his memory, the Sabbath preceding Purim is the most appropriate occasion for reading it.

The purpose of the *parshah*, which is to be heard by both men and women, is to warn us of the consequences of not eliminating what threatens to destroy us. What we must blot out is the vestige of Amalek (evil); what we must not forget is our own Jewishness (moral responsibility). The week before we will hear about how the assimilated Jews of Persia were almost eliminated, we are being warned not to so identify with the society around us that we lose our unique identity and mission.

Personal

Costumes

You'll want to give yourself ample time to prepare costumes for children who will be attending Purim parties or carnivals or want to dress up for the *Megillah* reading.

Ta'anit *Esther*

A day of fasting from sunrise to sunset is supposed to be observed on the day before Purim (*Adar* 13). It ostensibly commemorates the fast Mordecai and Esther endured, which Esther instituted among all the Jews, prior to her visit to the king (Esther 4:16). In keeping with Judaism's system of measure-for-measure reward and punishment, it is the flip side of feasting in celebration of Purim's outcome: denying pleasure to the body appropriately atones for the transgressions committed by the Jews when they shamelessly indulged their bodies during King Ahasuerus' banquet. Fasting was also commonly practiced among Jews whenever they prepared for battle (as with the Persians who had been instructed to massacre them), in remembrance that their strength and victory would come from God.

The fast on *Adar* 13 became the custom well after other observances were adopted for Purim, possibly as an adaptation of the periodic Monday and Thursday fasts the Jews followed. While it carries less obligation than the fasts ordained in *Tanakh* and others in Talmud, some, particularly the Persian (Iranian) Jews, have kept it as faithfully, reciting special *selikhot* (penitential) prayers and selections of Torah recited on all other fast days.

Home

The number and elaborateness of the *mishlo'akh manot* gifts you plan to send to friends will determine how much time you need to assemble them. Some people send simple packages—particularly if they send many—that may consist of one or two *hamantaschen* and a few pieces of candy or a piece of fruit together in a plastic sandwich bag. Others use bakery boxes lined with colored tissue paper, wicker baskets, Purim containers available in Judaica stores, decorative gift bags, or baskets made of construction paper, and fill them with packets of dried fruit, candy, bottles of wine or juice, hardy fresh fruit like oranges, and/or an assortment of baked goods (the *Sephardim* include *baklava* and other pastries made with paper-thin dough, sugar, and ground nuts).

Additional time will be needed for cooking, baking, and setting up the house if you will be hosting a Purim *seudah*.

WHAT ARE WE SUPPOSED TO DO?— *HALAKHAH*

When We Celebrate

The date of Purim, *Adar* 14, commemorates the day after the fighting took place in the Persian Empire. As the *Megillah* tells us, fighting continued in the Fortress Shushan for two days, not ending until the fourteenth of *Adar* (Esther 9:18). Therefore, the rabbis ruled that Shushan Purim was to be celebrated by inhabitants of walled cities on *Adar* 15. To avoid the disappearance of this recognition were Shushan ever to lose its Jewish population, they decreed that any city that had had walls at the time of Joshua would keep Shushan Purim on *Adar* 15, as Jerusalem does today. Outside walled cities, Shushan Purim is treated as a half holiday, marked mainly by the prohibition of fasting and eulogies constant for all festival days.

In a city where it is unknown whether it had been walled in Joshua's day—like Jaffa, Acco, Safed, Tiberius, and Lud—the *Megillah* is read on both days, but on the fifteenth only at night and without the blessings.

A slight complication occurs during the Jewish leap year, when there are two months of *Adar*. Since Purim and the special days that come earlier in the month lead to Pesakh, *Adar* II was designated as Purim's month. This was so the redemption of Esther and the Jews of Persia would be temporally related to the redemption of Moses and the Israelites of Egypt, bringing the Jewish festival year full circle. However, so as not to "slight" the days that would have been the holiday, the 14 and 15 of *Adar* I are considered minor festivals, called Purim and Shushan Purim *Katan* (or "little"). They share a joyful mood and prohibition of activities related to mourning.

The day of Purim never falls on Shabbat, but Shushan Purim on occasion does. When that occurs, the *Megillah* is read Thursday night and Friday morning; gifts are sent to the poor on Friday and the Purim *seudah* is held and *mishlo'akh manot* sent to friends on Sunday.

If Purim begins on Saturday night, the *Megillah* is read after *Havdalah*.

Megillah

Every man, woman, and child is commanded to hear the reading of the *Megillah* in its entirety, at night and especially during the day. The evening reading of convenience, which does not fulfill the *mitzvah*, can be done any time between nightfall and sunrise. The obligatory *Megillah* reading, which usually takes place on the morning of *Adar* 14 (15 for walled cities), can be done anytime between sunrise and sunset.

The Temple priests had to set aside their duties, and even someone engaged in studying Torah must take a break to listen to the reading. Only burying the dead takes precedence. Women, who are generally exempt from the positive duties of Jewish law specified for fixed times, must be present at the *Megillah* reading, since Purim commemorates the salvation of the Jews through the actions of a woman. And since the obligation regarding hearing the *Megillah* is the same for a woman as for a man, some authorities say she may be the one to read it aloud, even to a congregation of men (as long as she is technically proficient).

If no synagogue *minyan*—preferable for the reading—is present, the *Megillah* must be read individually. Before the reading, you can eat or drink only if you are sick. It is prohibited to recite the *Megillah* by heart. Verses 2:5, 8:15, 8:16, and 10:3 are read aloud by the congregation, then repeated by the reader. At the words "*B'lailah hahu*" ("that night" [6:1]), the reader should raise his voice to emphasize the turning point of the story; at "*ha'iggeret hazot*" ("those letters" [8:9]) he should shake the *Megillah*. The names of the ten sons (9:7–9) should be read in one breath, from "*Khameish meiot ish*" to "*aseret*" ("five hundred men . . . the ten" [9:6–10]), since they were hanged at the same time. An early ruling allowed for the *Megillah* to be read in any language understood by the community, but later it was determined that it must be read in Hebrew.

Since you are supposed to hear every single word, which is difficult in the general atmosphere in the synagogue on Purim, you should have your own copy of the *Megillah* and say each word to yourself.

The scroll from which the story is read to the congregation must be created according to rules as stringent as those for preparing a Torah scroll or liturgical work: sewn parchment skins attached with dried sinews, to form one scroll, written in Assyrian (square form) letters with ink, following lined rules incised into the skins.

Gifts of Food

To fulfill the *mitzvah* of *shalakh manot*, you must give at least two portions (two different types of food, or one kind of food fixed two different ways) to one friend. The food must be ready to eat without requiring the recipient to do any preparatory work. Even the poor who receive *tzedakah* must send portions; if they cannot afford to do so, they must at least arrange to exchange with a friend.

The person receiving a gift that fulfills the obligation of *mishlo'akh manot* must be acquainted with you. Though it is traditional to send *manot* through a messenger, it is not required, but the gift is to be given during the day of Purim.

Gifts to the Poor

Every male and female must give food or money to the poor—the equivalent needed for a minimal Purim meal for at least two people. The recipient need not be aware of the identity of the donor and may use the money for purposes other than paying for a Purim meal. If you cannot give donations directly to those in need, make a contribution to an organization that will appropriately distribute the money. If there is no one to give to immediately, set aside money, clearly designated as Purim *tzedakah*, to be given at a later date. If you do not have the means to present a lavish meal, give more than one *shalakh manot* package *and* give to the poor, first priority is to provide for the needy.

Torah Reading/Prayer

During the *Shakharit* synagogue service on Purim, three passages from Exodus 17 recounting the attack of the Amalekites against the Israelites are read. The service also includes Psalm 22 (according to tradition, the prayer offered by Esther after her three-day fast, in preparation for her visit to the king), and some recite Psalm 83 (beseeching God to not be aloof but to deal with His—Israel's—enemies). The *Amidah* of the three daily services and the *Birkat Hamazon* include *Al Hanissim* (we thank You for the miracles), the prayer that gives a concise account of Purim and the miraculous salvation. *Hallel* is not said, however, since the Jews remained under foreign dominion, and the *Megillah* itself serves as praise of God. Prayers normally omitted on festival days (see "*Halakhah*" in Chapter on Pesakh) are also omitted on Purim.

Purim Feast

Feasting on Purim is obligatory and encompasses both eating and drinking. The Book of Esther uses *mishteh* to describe the celebrations, a word derived from the root of *shoteh*, meaning "drinking," which led to all the miracles of the holiday.

Since the *Megillah* refers to future celebration of Purim as *days* of rejoicing (9:22), the religious obligation of the *seudah* is that it take place during the day after the *Minkhah* service (or before midday on *Erev* Shabbat so as not to interfere with the Shabbat evening meal). Candles should be lit, since light accompanies joy, and Torah, considered light by the Jews, should be studied prior to eating ("The Jews enjoyed light" [Esther 8:16]). The festive meal includes bread and meat—but not in the form of a sandwich—and wine to the degree that your thinking becomes clouded and you cannot tell the difference between "blessed be Mordecai" and "cursed be Haman." If imbibing makes you sick, it is permissible to drink just a little more than normal, or to fall asleep, because when asleep you cannot "tell the difference." It is preferable not to eat alone, and only under extenuating circumstances are you permitted to leave your family on Purim.

Work and Celebration

While it is permissible to work on Purim, all unnecessary labor, that which is not related to supporting others or avoiding loss, is prohibited. Creative work is not. Most authorities allow weddings to take place on Purim, but many prefer that they be scheduled for other times according to the idea that no joy should be intermixed with another.

Mourning

If you are sitting *shivah* when Purim occurs, you continue to observe the laws of mourning. While you should not partake in festivity, you should also not diminish the joy of the community. For that reason, you are not obligated to display the signs of grief publicly (you may wear leather shoes and sit on a chair), for these acts are seen by others. You may either assemble a *minyan* for prayer and the reading of the *Megillah* at home, or pray at home and then attend the synagogue to hear the *Megillah* read. It is appropriate to send modest portions to friends, but unless s/he is poor, or one of only two Jews in a community, a mourner should not receive gifts (but his/her spouse may).

It is forbidden to deliver a funeral address on *Adar* 14 and 15, since they are festival days.

FOR FURTHER READING

Purim—Its Observance and Significance. Ed. by Rabbi Nosson Scherman and Rabbi Meir Zlotowitz. Brooklyn, NY: Mesorah Publications, 1991.

The laws and customs of the holiday (along with background, explanations, and insights into it and its observance) are covered in concise contemporary language. This book is part of the acclaimed ArtScroll series.

WHAT OTHER THINGS DO PEOPLE DO?— CUSTOMS

The level of excitement generated by Purim seems more consistent with a just-won victory than the commemoration of an ancient event. And that is how the celebrants often felt; even though the post-Persian Jews had not yet been released from their "Hamans," Esther's story provided such a powerful model that they believed in a similar outcome and celebrated as though it had already been accomplished. For one day, they forgot their dreary, precarious lives and, in throwing off all discipline, which allowed them great creativity and humorous self-expression, felt that they had some control over their own fates.

Other Times and Places

Rehanging Haman

One of the earliest Purim customs developed in Babylonia and Persia during the talmudic era: beating and burning Haman in effigy. Spirited shrieking, singing, and jumping through hoops suspended above the fire accompanied the symbolic destruction of the enemy.

Although fifth-century Christians, likening Haman on the gallows to Jesus on the cross, prohibited such public celebration of Purim as a mockery of their savior, the Jews continued, often inviting violent attacks as a result. The effigies were particularly popular in Italy during the Middle Ages. Prior to being set ablaze on a pyre the effigy was part of a sports tournament. It was elevated to trumpet blasts and shouts of "*Ira!*" (vengeance), and Jewish fathers on horseback and their sons on foot, using nuts as pellets and wooden sticks as lances, raced through the streets and attacked the representational puppets.

The Jews of Caucasus avoided their non-Jewish neighbors' wrath by holding their ritual in the home. When a husband returned from synagogue, he found a piece of wood his wife had blackened in the kitchen stove. "What is it?" he asked. "It is Haman!" the wife replied. The husband then screamed that it had to be burned, kicked the wood, and threw it into the fire.

In eighteenth-century Frankfurt, a miniature house of wax containing figures of Haman, his wife Zeresh, and two guards was placed on the reader's desk in the synagogue and lit as the *Megillah* reading began. This, too, disturbed the Christians, who therefore outlawed the ceremony. (The Yemenite Jews perhaps avoided censure by simply using ten candles at the evening and morning services.)

Megillah

Persian children spent the weeks before Purim writing out the Book of Esther in proper block letters, then took their finished versions of the *Megillah* to the public reading. Instead of going to synagogue, many would gather at the site believed to be the burial place of Mordecai and Esther in Hamadan. The Jews of that city, located in southwest Persia, believe it was the biblical Shushan.

Since the name of God does not appear in the Book of Esther, artists felt free to illustrate it, and it became the only biblical book whose text is ornamented with gold leaf, miniatures, and decorative borders. Customs arose in writing of the text itself: The names of Haman's sons were placed on ten lines, one directly under the one above, and the *vov* (ו, "and") before the last name was elongated to resemble the gallows on which they were all hanged. *Sephardi* Jews presented engraved *Megillah* scrolls to bridegrooms (in Yemen it was the grooms who paid for the privilege of reading the story to the congregation). When the Jews moved to Eastern Europe, it became more popular

to create elaborate cases in which the scrolls were held. There are substantial examples of illuminated *Megillot* and of carved wood and silver Purim scroll containers, from the sixteenth century on, in Jewish museum and private collections.

When ancient congregations heard "Haman," they whispered "cursed be Haman and cursed be his offspring," a practice continued by the Austrian Jews in the Middle Ages, who whispered "*zekher tzaddik liverahkhah*" (may the memory of the righteous be a blessing) after Mordecai's name and "*shem reheim yirkav*" (may the name of the wicked rot, based on Proverbs 10:7). The practice may have been related to the *seudah* drinking custom. In some communities, the eradication of Amalek was accomplished by erasing the name, which had been written on paper. (In Yemen, where noisemakers were forbidden as inappropriate in a solemn synagogue setting, upon returning from the service the head of a house would write "Haman" on paper with ink, and then wash it off in a cup of water.) Over time, the method of following the commandment became less and less reserved. In Venice, hand clapping drowned out the sound of Haman's name. Others did away with Haman by stomping out his name written on the soles of their shoes. Children in medieval Europe drew pictures of the villain on two stones or pieces of wood and knocked them together.

The *gragger* we associate with Purim developed in the thirteenth and fourteenth centuries in Germany and France, where people made their own, some of them quite elaborate. The grinding noisemakers spread throughout Europe. In his diary, Samuel Pepys recorded that he was almost deafened when he visited a London synagogue in the 1600s. In the following century, the Board of Trustees of the Spanish Portuguese congregation in that city apparently lost sight of the *Megillah*'s warning against the dangers of assimilation and were so wary of being negatively viewed by their quietly worshipful non-Jewish neighbors that they promised to evict anyone making a disturbance in the synagogue. The community leaders in Posen, Poland, also prohibited the use of *graggers* in the synagogue in order to preserve decorum.

In Egypt, the decision to limit beating and stomping to the naming of Haman's ten sons at the end of the story was for practical purposes: to avoid dragging out the reading and the confusion of continual interruptions.

Special Foods

The Italians made a poppy-seed-filled pastry known as *orecchie de'aman* (Haman's ears), after the former

European custom of cutting off the ears of a criminal before he was hanged. In Western Europe, another poppy-seed cookie, *mohn plaetzen*, was popular. Some communities baked special cookies bearing the names of Vashti and Zeresh, which allowed the Jews to "devour" their enemies; marzipan and almond cookies were standard *Sephardi* treats. A special Purim *khallah* called *keylitsh*, exceptionally large, braided to represent long ropes used to hang Haman, and sometimes decorated with raisins, accompanied the *seudah*.

In the Balkans, the Jews had a sweet *pita de'susam* (Shushan), red jellied candies, and halva. The Moroccan Jews baked little cakes and bread in a special form for each child—a ladder, representing ascent for Jews, descent for Haman; birds (from the same passage that inspires *khallah* shapes for the Days of Awe, Isaiah 31:5, likening God's protection to birds flying), other images drawn from Talmud, and characters of the Book of Esther. These sweets and other cakes and honey were sold throughout the day of Purim by merchants of Marrakesh, who set up special booths in the streets.

Non-Jews in Middle Eastern countries began to call Purim *id al sukar*—sugar festival—for all the items fashioned out of sugar by confectioners: *megillot*, inkpots, pens, clocks, cups, books, the Messiah on a donkey (as illustrated in Bella Chagall's reminiscence, "Purim Gifts"). Some school principals would commission a large Haman-like doll, paid for with contributions from the students. It would be hung in the doorway of the school, like an edible *piñata*, where the children would hit it with a small stick as they entered, until it fell apart and they could gather up the pieces to eat.

For many, it became popular to serve turkey for the *seudah*. In Russian, turkey, considered the most foolish of fowl, translates to "cock of India." The Book of Esther tells us that Ahasuerus' kingdom included India, but even more appropriate, he was somewhat of a turkey himself. The Jews of thirteenth-century Provence preferred goose and chicken, and later the Italians ate all kinds of fowl, along with pancakes, macaroni, and jellies. (An Italian parody designates twenty-four dishes, all fowl, supposedly set down by Moses at Sinai as the Purim menu.)

Masks, Masques, and Masquerades

In general, Purim is one holiday that the *Ashkenazim* celebrated with as much, if not more, color and abandon as their Oriental cousins. This was probably due to their exposure to Carnivale and Mardi Gras, held around the same time of year, in the Catholic countries they inhabited. Just as the church had reworked the pagan new year and Roman bacchanalian feasts widely practiced so that they would be religiously acceptable, the Jews transformed the popular pre-Lenten celebrations to fit their religious values.

Costumes

Although masquerading did not become part of Purim until the Middle Ages, the *Megillah* sets the precedent for it. First, there is Esther's name, which lays the foundation of hiddenness, which a costume and mask accomplish for one's identity. Then there's a series of costume changes in her story: The Jewish maiden puts on the robes of a Persian queen; Mordecai and Esther change into sackcloth. Later Mordecai dresses up in the king's garments. And the roles change: Haman goes from elevated minister to servant of Mordecai to hanged traitor, the king from condemner to pardoner of the Jews, and Esther from assimilated Jew (masquerading as a non-Jew) to Persian queen to heroine of her people.

Originally, the European Jews may have simply donned peasant's clothes to avoid anti-Semitic attacks that occurred periodically over hundreds of years at this season. Masks may have helped them feel uninhibited as they danced around foolishly and engaged in silly pranks like flour throwing, ghetto donkey rides, and street games. Gradually the costumes became more elaborate and focused, portraying biblical characters. The celebrants paraded through the streets, going house to house, performing and demanding wine. Masked children would knock on doors singing "*Heint iz Purim, Morgan iz aus, Gist mir a dreier und waft mikh araus*" (Today is Purim, Tomorrow is gone, Give me a penny [or *kopek, groshen, hamantasch*, etc., depending on time and place] and throw me out). Although some rabbis disapproved, men and women were even permitted to wear each other's clothing, a transgression normally strictly prohibited.

Entertainment

Sometimes a Purim King, and later the Purim Rabbi, would lead the entertainment and serve refreshments to townspeople. By the 1800s, Purim had become known in Europe as the Day of Students because the yeshivah boys would dress up and go house to house mocking their rabbis, teachers, community leaders, and great Jewish personages in the tradition of parodies extending back several hundred years.

Kalonymous ben Kalonymous of Rome may have started the grand heritage with the *Massekhet Purim* (tractate of *Purim*), the oldest and best known parody. Based on the format and method of talmudic discussion, it expounds on the nature of this holiday with great wit. Other parodies—some written by such illustrious Jewish poets as Solomon Ibn Gabirol (1021–1069), Abraham ibn Ezra (1092–1187), and Judah Halevi (1080–1142)—were spin-offs of synagogue liturgy and popular songs of the day. Wine and the effects its excesses produce were well exploited in these humorous works. (Recently, the tradition has continued with college campus debates pitting the contributions to world peace of the *hamantasch* against those of the *latke*.)

The revelers, accompanied by a *Klezmer* group (traditional Eastern European street musicians, whose name is a contraction suggesting both music and musician), would act as troubadours and minstrels, performing their improvisations and set pieces in home after home with goodhearted levity. (In Amsterdam in the early 1800s, the humorous songs composed for the holiday were circulated prior to Purim in a special publication so everyone could become familiar with them.)

The people enthusiastically welcomed these *Purimspiels* (Purim plays), which developed into biting satires on life. The plays provided an opportunity for the Jews to vent their feelings and express control over the outcome of their situations. Spreading throughout Poland, Russia, Lithuania, Galicia, Romania, and Western Europe, they became so popular that they were performed in theaters for large audiences. In 1713 Frankfurt, the Jewish leaders thought the humor so shocking and obscene that they prohibited further performances. In other communities, however, an entire two-week theater season revolved around Purim. Plays such as *Ahasuerosspiel*, *David and Goliath*, and *The Sale of Joseph* were so popular that even Christians attended the shows, some of which continued in Eastern Europe until the turn of the twentieth century.

In 1912, the pioneers in Palestine organized the first Purim carnival in the first all-Jewish city in the modern world, Tel Aviv. Named *Adloyodah* ("Until you don't know"), it has developed into a two-day festival of parades, street decorations and theater, a children's pageant, Queen Esther election, sports carnival, masquerade balls, and throngs crowding around the Great Synagogue to hear the reading of the *Megillah*.

Gifts

Another kind of performing evolved around the exchanging of *mishlo'akh manot*—when people had to carefully consider what to send to whom to ensure that friends honored each other with gifts of equal value—as amusingly detailed in Sholom Aleichem's story, "Two Shalachmones, or A Purim Scandal." In the eighteenth and nineteenth centuries special plates, often made of pewter and engraved or embossed with lines or scenes from the *Megillah*, were used to transport one's food gifts to friends.

Sometimes gifts of coins were given to children. Because it was customary to send Christian servants to solicit donations for those in need, the Jews in France and Provence started the practice of giving gifts to the non-Jews as well.

Providing money for the poor during Purim probably reached its height in Western Europe and America in the mid-1800s to early 1900s, when Purim balls were held for charity. The Queen Esther Society and the Purim Association of New York, both founded in the latter half of the nineteenth century, sponsored such events for a number of years. (Hadassah, the Women's Zionist Organization named for the heroine of the Purim story, which has done so much to help Israel and Jews in need, was founded on the holiday in 1912.)

Judeo-Spanish communities didn't wait for Purim to show their generosity. On Shabbat *Zakhor*, called Shabbat *de Foulares* (derived from the Portuguese word for gift), the women created a special pastry representing the hanging of Haman. On this day, also known as Shabbat *Hakallot* (Sabbath of the Brides), in-laws in particular sent trays of new clothing, to round out the trousseau, to a bride (a woman was considered a bride during the first year of marriage) in return for the trays of sweets delivered to them.

FOR FURTHER READING

Chagall, Bella. "Purim Gifts." In BL, pp. 162–174.

The little girl Bella details the excitement, disappointment, and joy connected with sending and receiving figurines made of sugar for Purim in her native Vitebsk, Russia.

Greetings

Yiddish-speaking Jews wish each other "*gut Purim*," the phrase sung by *Purimspieler*s when they entered a home to perform. They also wish each other "*freilikhen* (joyous) *Purim*." Another traditional greeting of the season is "Happy Purim and kosher Pesakh." In Israel, "*khag samei'akh*" or "*Purim samei'akh*" (happy holiday or happy Purim) is said.

Dress

It is customary to wear Sabbath or holiday clothes for the *Megillah* reading. Many synagogues also encourage children to come dressed in their Purim costumes. It has become commonplace for them to pretend to be all kinds of characters and figures from popular culture (drawn from cartoons, secular books, television programs). Since this is a Jewish holiday, it is appropriate to choose costumes drawn out of our own rich culture and heritage. You don't have to be limited to the preponderance of Esthers, Mordecais, Hamans, and Ahasueruses. Biblical characters; people important in Jewish history; famous Jewish writers, musicians, scientists, and rabbis; and objects that have significance to us—*tzedakah* box, Torah, *kiddush* cup, *Megillah*, even a *hamantaschen*, bagel, or *khallah*—are effective costume subjects. There are many ways to be glamorous, scary, messy, or silly—and still be Jewish.

WHAT IS THERE TO EAT?— TRADITIONAL FOODS

Since Rashi (the eleventh-century Torah commentator, considered one of Judaism's greatest teachers) said that Haman was hanged on the third day of Passover, on Purim Eastern European Jews in the Middle Ages ate *matzah* balls and *fritlekh*, a small thin cracker resembling *matzah*. Fortunately, much more appetizing treats were developed for the holiday.

Hamantaschen

The delicacy most readily identified with Purim is *hamantaschen* ("Haman's pockets"), a three-cornered pastry traditionally filled with a honey and poppy-seed mixture. First mentioned in an eleventh-century poem by Abraham ibn Ezra, it was probably an adaptation of a German dessert called *mohntaschen* (*mohn* means "poppy seeds," *taschen* means "pockets"), whose name with slight alteration yielded Haman and whose shape was associated with the tricornered hat said to have been worn by him. (Others claim that the three sides represent the three patriarchs, Abraham, Isaac, and Jacob, by whose merit the Jews were able to succeed against their enemy.) Later it became customary to fill the pastry with prune jam, to commemorate the rescue of eighteenth-century Bohemian Jews when a plum merchant was wrongly accused of murder. Just about any filling is used today (chocolate, apple-cinnamon, apricot preserves, nuts), but poppy seed and prune jam remain the most authentic.

Other Specialties

For some reason, it became a custom to eat *kreplakh*, dough filled with chopped meat, on days when beating occurs. On Purim, the *kreplakh*, and versions of it developed in other countries, carry additional meaning, since the filling is completely concealed within the dough, suggesting the aspects of hiddenness of the Purim story.

Some people eat chickpeas, according to a tradition that says they were all Esther ate in order to keep *kashrut* in the palace. (A variation is cooked and salted beans.) In Morocco on Purim morning, the Jews eat a dairy couscous cooked in butter and milk (*berkuls*), and many have a special breakfast, *seudah shel Haman* or *kebura diHaman*, during which everyone mocks the villain.

DO YOU HEAR MUSIC?—SONGS TO SING

The joyousness expressed during the *Megillah* reading carried over into the home, and along with parodies and *Purimspiels*, songs became part of the celebrations. In the sixteenth and seventeenth centuries, Jews composed folksongs expressing the happiness of the day, describing revenge on Haman, extolling Esther and Mordecai, and focusing on sending gifts and enjoying *hamantaschen*. Pioneers in Palestine in the late nineteenth century dealt with Purim themes as well as the carnival atmosphere in their folksongs. Some were original, others Yiddish poems translated to fit new melodies, or parodies of Yiddish folksongs. And in America, words were often written to the tunes of folk songs, nursery rhymes, or simple popular tunes like "It Ain't Gonna Rain No More," "Polly Wolly Doodle," "Farmer in the Dell," "Bicycle Built for Two," and "Ten Little Indians."

Among the songs most well-known for the holiday are the khasidi folktunes "*Shoshanat Yaakov*" and "*Mishenikhnas Adar*" (about joy increasing during the month); the children's Yiddish celebratory "*Heint Iz Purim*" and "*Hop, Mein Hamantaschen!*" "*A Gitn* (a good) *Purim*" in Yiddish, and "*Khag* (holiday of) *Purim*" in Hebrew express the fun of the celebration. "*Utzu Etza*," a traditional Hebrew folktune (Form Your Plot), is a short affirmation that it will fail because God is with us.

Among the songs best known to American children are the amusing "In Shu- Shu- Shushan Long Ago" and "Once There Was a Wicked Wicked Man."

FOR FURTHER READING

Tu B'Shevat and Purim Melodies. Cedarhurst, NY: Board of Jewish Education of Greater New York and Tara Publications.

Some of the traditional songs, with words transliterated into English, are included in this compact booklet. A companion tape is available.

WHAT TALES ARE TOLD?— STORIES TO READ

Celebrated writers, Jewish and non-Jewish, have been attracted by the color, romance, and drama of Esther's story and the customs it inspired. Yehuda Halevi reveals the plot against the Jews in the conversation presented in his twelfth-century poem "The Banquet of Esther." Perhaps the first drama authored by Jews, *Esther*, by Solomon Usque and Lazaro Gratiam, published in Spain in 1567, deals with the Purim saga. Jean Baptiste Racine, the well-known dramatist of seventeeth-century France, later wrote a play by the same name.

The revival of the Hebrew language in the 1800s generated numerous poems, short stories, and plays to add to the oversupply of Purim books produced a century earlier, and later, the Nobel-Prize–winning Israeli writer Samuel J. Agnon and the beloved Sholom Aleichem were among those who also wrote about Purim celebration.

FOR FURTHER READING

Folktales

"Good Purim, Good Purim." In CT, pp. 528–530, and TS, pp. 294-297.

A poor water carrier of Kozenitz finds wonderful rewards when he learns to properly experience the mood of the day.

"The Jewish People Had Light, Gladness, Joy and Honor." In TS, pp. 275–279.

When a wicked duke, a descendant of Haman, prohibits the Jews of medieval Worms from celebrating Purim, Mordecai pays him a nighttime visit and again saves his people.

von Sacher Masoch, Leopold. "Haman and Esther in Poland." In Purim HA, pp. 290–298.

A Purim prankster plays the role of Elijah to answer the needs of a poor humble girl and her blind father. The sweet story gives a picture of Eastern European Jewish life in the nineteenth century.

Other Stories

Aleichem, Sholom. "The Goldspinners." In HT, pp. 86–108.

Told with his usual lighthearted humor, Aleichem describes how Naftali and his wife and children, with each of their talents and attributes, make money on Purim as messenger, *Purimspieler*, baker, and *gragger* maker. The story includes a short excerpt of a Purim play.

———. "The Purim Feast." In FT, pp. 627–634.

Told from the point of view of a child, Aleichem's description of the preparations and outcome of a Purim *seudah* at a rich uncle's home is especially amusing for its characterizations.

———. "Two Shalachmones, or a Purim Scandal." In FT, pp. 580–590.

Messengers sent with plates of *shalakh mannes* cause long-lasting repercussions when they decide to sample the treats. The story humorously illustrates a social custom taken too seriously.

Garvey, Robert. "The Sound of the Greggers." In *More World Over Stories*. Ed. by Ezekiel Schloss and Morris Epstein. New York: Bloch Publishing Company, 1968, pp. 91–94.

When thunderous noise reaches the heavenly congregation listening to the *Megillah* reading, Elijah goes to investigate and discovers that the children swinging their noisemakers are trying to eradicate all kinds of prejudice.

Weilerstein, Sadie Rose. "How K'tonton Masqueraded on Purim." In KT, pp. 42–48.

When the mischievous thumb-sized boy gets mixed up in his mother's *hamantaschen* filling, he takes an unexpected trip and entertains his sick neighbor. Ages 3–8.

Books

Goldin, Barbara Diamond. *Cakes and Miracles—A Purim Tale*. New York: Viking Press, 1991.

A blind boy wants to help his mother prepare for Purim. A vision he has in a dream provides him guidance and results in a surprise for his village. Beautifully written, the book includes the history of the holiday and recipes for *hamantaschen*. Ages 5–10.

Schul, Yuri. *The Purim Goat*. New York: Four Winds Press, 1980.

A ten-year-old boy who lives in a *shtetl* with his mother finds a way to make their goat worth keeping just in time for Purim. Holiday songs sung at the time are included. Ages 8–10.

Sidon, Ephraim. *The Animated Megillah*. London: Scopus Films, 1986.

Part of a series of "Animated" books for Jewish

holidays and Israel, this one, like the others, uses photographs of colorful sculpted clay models to bring to life the goings on in Shushan that are being investigated by modern-day characters Judy and Danny, who travel back in time. Ages 6–10.

Silverman, Maida. *Festival of Esther—The Story of Purim Retold*. New York: Simon and Schuster, 1979.

A beautifully illustrated version of the *Megillah*, it tells the tale, explains traditions of the holiday, provides a *hamantaschen* recipe, and supplies the words and music for a popular Purim song. Ages 5–8.

Of Additional Interest

Music

George Frideric Handel wrote two oratoria based on the Purim saga, *Esther* and *Haman and Mordecai*. Several other versions of the *Megillah*'s story have also been set to music: the overture to Franz Grillparzer's *Esther*, the dramatic *Esther Queen of Persia* by A. W. Binder, and Darius Milhaud's opera *Esther de Carpentras*, which moves the story to Provence for the updated context of a threat from the bishop.

Art

The story of Esther has inspired artists for more than 1700 years. Murals in the third-century Dura Europus synagogue show Mordecai's triumphant ride through Shushan on the king's horse and Ahasuerus and Esther on their thrones. (The latter subject may have been chosen for political reasons, as Dura, once part of Persia, was ruled by the Romans at the time the synagogue was built. The Jews, hoping for a return to the previous jurisdiction, presented an idealized Ahasuerus.)

European church leaders later likened Esther's modesty, courage, and self-sacrifice to similar qualities of Mary, and the Jewish queen's intercession with Ahasuerus on behalf of the Jews with Mary's intercession with God on behalf of mankind. Consequently, scenes from the Book of Esther were created for churches by Renaissance artists such as Botticelli, Tintoretto, Reubens, and Rembrandt, whose paintings of climactic points in the story are included among the holdings of the Rijksmuseum in Amsterdam and the Hermitage in Leningrad.

At that time, it was customary in aristocratic Italian families for the mother to give a bridal chest to her daughter. Called a *cassone*, it was adorned with an appropriate myth or biblical scene, those from Esther being particularly popular because they glorified feminine virtues. Among extant panels from the *cassoni* are those attributed to the school or workshop of Botticelli, showing Esther on her way to the palace, Mordecai's triumph, and the elevation of Esther.

APPENDIX A: HOLIDAY PREPARATION CALENDAR

Even though the festival calendar begins with *Nissan*, *Adar* is listed first because preparation for Pesakh starts at the beginning of that month. *Adar* II occurs only in Jewish leap years (see Appendix B to determine when they fall). In all other years, the "holidays" listed under *Adar* are omitted, and everything indicated for *Adar* II occurs in the regular month of *Adar*. With the exception of getting rid of *khametz* and the Fast of the Firstborn for Pesakh, and Yom Hazik-karon for Yom Ha'atzmaut, preparatory steps and special Torah readings are not given for specific dates but are placed in general time relationship to the holidays they precede or follow.

Bracketed listings under holidays are for specially designated days no longer observed as holy days, but on which adjustments are made in the liturgy and expressions of mourning are prohibited.

Month		Holiday	Preparation	Special Shabbat
Adar				
	14	Purim Katan		
	15	Shushan Purim Katan		
Adar II			Pesakh	*Shekalim*
				Zakhor
	13	Ta'anit Esther		
	14	Purim		
	15	Shushan Purim		
				Parah
Nissan				
				Hagadol
	13		Search for *khametz*	
	14		Fast of firstborn	
			Burn/sell *khametz*	
		First Seder		
	15	Pesakh First Day		
	16	Pesakh Second Day Sefirah Day 1	Shavuot	

Month		Holiday	Preparation	Special Shabbat
Nissan		Pesakh Khol Hamoed	(Shavuot)	
	21	Pesakh Seventh Day		
	22	Pesakh Eighth Day; Yizkor		
	23	[Isru Khag Pesakh]		
	28	Yom Hashoah		
Iyar	4		Yom Hazikkaron	
	5	Yom Ha'atzmaut		
	14	[Pesakh Sheni]		
	18	Lag B'Omer		
	28	Yom Yerushalayim		
Sivan	6		Tikkun Leil Shavuot	
		Shavuot		
	7	Shavuot; Yizkor		
	8	[Isru Khag Shavuot]		
Tammuz				
	17	Fast of 17 *Tammuz*	Tisha B'Av ("Three Weeks")	
Av	9	Tisha B'Av		*Khazon*
				Nakhamu
	15	[Tu B'Av]		
Elul			Days Of Awe	
			Plant tulip bulbs for Yom Hashoah	
			Selikhot	
	29		Hatarat Hanedarim	
Tishrei	1	Rosh Hashanah		
	2	Rosh Hashanah		
	3	Tzom Gedaliah		
				Shuvah
	9		Kapparot	
	10	Yom Kippur		
			Sukkot	
	15	Sukkot		

Month		Holiday	Preparation	Special Shabbat
Tishrei	16	Sukkot		
		Khol Hamoed Sukkot		
	21	Hoshanah Rabbah		
	22	Shemini Atzeret; Yizkor		
	23	Simkhat Torah		
	24	[Isru Khag Sukkot]	___Make *etrog* jam for Tu B'Shevat ___Save *Lulav* for Pesakh *khametz* search	
Khesvan				
Kislev			___Get Khanukah supplies	
	25	Khanukah - 1		
	26	2		
	27	3		
	28	4		
	29	5		
	[30]	[6]		
Tevet	1	6 or 7	___Order yellow *yahrtzite* candles for Yom Hashoah	
	2	7 or 8		
	[3]	[8]		
	10	Fast of 10 *Tevet*		
Shevat			___Get Tu B'Shevat supplies	*Shirah*
	15	Tu B'Shevat	___Plant parsley for Pesakh	
Adar	14	Purim Katan		
	15	Shushan Purim Katan		
Adar (II)			___Pesakh	*Shekalim*
			___Purim	
				Zakhor
	13	Ta'anit Esther		
	14	Purim		
	15	Shushan Purim		

APPENDIX B:
TWENTY-FIVE-YEAR
JEWISH CALENDAR

The date listed is the first day of the holiday; remember that all Jewish holidays begin the previous evening. When Yom Ha'atzmaut falls on a Friday or Saturday, observance is moved to the Thursday immediately preceding. Likewise, when the Fast of Esther falls on Saturday, it is observed the previous Thursday. In any of these cases, the date of observance is marked with an asterisk (*). When Tisha B'Av or any of the fasts connected with it coincides with Saturday, it is observed on Sunday. When that is the case, the date of observance is marked with a plus sign (+). (No standard ruling has been issued as yet for when Yom Hashoah or Yom Yerushalayim falls on a Saturday; in those cases, the Chief Rabbinate of Israel makes a decision at the time the coincidence occurs.) Leap years are indicated by the pound symbol (#) and the *shmittah* (sabbatical) by the equal sign (=).

	1995/1996	1996/1997#	1997/1998	1998/1999	1999/2000#	2000/2001=	2001=/2002	2002/2003#	2003/2004	2004/2005#	2005/2006#	2006/2007	2007/2008#=
Pesakh *Nissan 15–22*	Sun, Apr 16	Thu, Apr 4	Tue, Apr 22	Sat, Apr 11	Thu, Apr 1	Thu, Apr 20	Sun, Apr 8	Thu, Mar 28	Thu, Apr 17	Tue, Apr 6	Sun, Apr 24	Thu, Apr 13	Tue, Apr 3
Yom Hashoah *Nissan 27*	Thu, Apr 27	Tue, Apr 16	Sun, May 4	Thu, Apr 23	Tue, Apr 13	Tue, May 2	Fri, Apr 20	Tue, Apr 9	Tue, Apr 29	Sun, Apr 18	Fri, May 6	Tue, Apr 25	Sun, Apr 15
Yom Ha'atzmaut *Iyar 5*	Thu, May 4*	Wed, Apr 24	Mon, May 12	Thu, May 1*	Wed, Apr 21	Wed, May 10	Thu, Apr 26*	Wed, Apr 17	Wed, May 7	Mon, Apr 26	Thu, May 12*	Wed, May 3	Mon, Apr 23
Lag B'Omer *Iyar 18*	Thu, May 18	Tue, May 7	Sun, May 25	Thu, May 14	Tue, May 4	Tue, May 23	Fri, May 11	Tue, Apr 30	Tue, May 20	Sun, May 9	Fri, May 27	Tue, May 16	Sun, May 6
Yom Yerushalayim *Iyar 28*	Sun, May 28	Fri, May 17	Wed, Jun 4	Sun, May 24	Fri, May 14	Fri, Jun 2	Mon, May 21	Fri, May 10	Fri, May 30	Wed, May 19	Mon, Jun 6	Fri, May 26	Wed, May 16
Shavuot *Sivan 6–7*	Sun, Jun 4	Fri, May 24	Wed, Jun 11	Sun, May 31	Fri, May 21	Fri, Jun 9	Mon, May 28	Fri, May 17	Fri, Jun 6	Wed, May 26	Mon, Jun 13	Fri, Jun 2	Wed, May 23
17 Tammuz	Sun, Jul 16	Thu, Jul 4	Tue, Jul 22	Sun, Jul 12+	Thu, Jul 1	Thu, Jul 20	Sun, Jul 8	Thu, Jun 27	Thu, Jul 17	Tue, Jul 6	Sun, Jul 24	Thu, Jul 13	Tue, Jul 3
Tisha B'Av *Av 9*	Sun, Aug 6	Thu, Jul 25	Tue, Aug 12	Sun, Aug 2+	Thu, Jul 22	Thu, Aug 10	Sun, Jul 29	Thu, Jul 18	Thu, Aug 7	Tue, Jul 27	Sun, Aug 14	Thu, Aug 3	Tue, Jul 24
Rosh Hashanah *Tishrei 1–2*	Mon, Sep 25	Sat, Sep 14	Thu, Oct 1	Mon, Sep 21	Sat, Sep 11	Sat, Sep 30	Tue, Sep 18	Sat, Sep 7	Sat, Sep 27	Thu, Sep 16	Tue, Oct 4	Sat, Sep 23	Thu, Sep 13
Fast of Gedaliah *Tishrei 3*	Wed, Sep 27	Mon, Sep 16	Sun, Oct 6+	Wed, Sep 23	Mon, Sep 13	Mon, Oct 2	Thu, Sep 20	Mon, Sep 9	Mon, Sep 29	Sun, Sep 19+	Thu, Oct 6	Mon, Sep 25	Sun, Sep 16+
Yom Kippur *Tishrei 10*	Wed, Oct 4	Mon, Sep 23	Sat, Oct 11	Wed, Sep 30	Mon, Sep 20	Mon, Oct 9	Thu, Sep 27	Mon, Sep 16	Mon, Oct 6	Sat, Sep 25	Thu, Oct 13	Mon, Oct 2	Sat, Sep 22
Sukkot *Tishrei 15–22*	Mon, Oct 9	Sat, Sep 28	Thu, Oct 16	Mon, Oct 5	Sat, Sep 25	Sat, Oct 14	Tue, Oct 2	Sat, Sep 21	Sat, Oct 11	Thu, Sep 30	Tue, Oct 18	Sat, Oct 7	Thu, Sept 27
Hoshanah Rabbah *Tishrei 21*	Sun, Oct 15	Fri, Oct 4	Wed, Oct 22	Sun, Oct 11	Fri, Oct 1	Fri, Oct 20	Mon, Oct 8	Fri, Sep 27	Fri, Oct 17	Wed, Oct 6	Mon, Oct 24	Fri, Oct 13	Wed, Oct 3
Shemini Atzeret *Tishrei 22*	Mon, Oct 16	Sat, Oct 5	Thu, Oct 23	Mon, Oct 12	Sat, Oct 2	Sat, Oct 21	Tue, Oct 9	Sat, Sep 28	Sat, Oct 18	Thu, Oct 7	Tue, Oct 25	Sat, Oct 14	Thu, Oct 4
Simkhat Torah *Tishrei 23*	Tue, Oct 17	Sun, Oct 6	Fri, Oct 24	Tue, Oct 13	Sun, Oct 3	Sun, Oct 22	Wed, Oct 10	Sun, Sep 29	Sun, Oct 19	Fri, Oct 8	Wed, Oct 26	Sun, Oct 15	Fri, Oct 5
Khanukah *Kislev 25–Tevet 2 or 3*	Mon, Dec 18	Fri, Dec 6	Wed, Dec 24	Mon, Dec 14	Sat, Dec 4	Fri, Dec 22	Mon, Dec 10	Sat, Nov 30	Sat, Dec 20	Wed, Dec 8	Mon, Dec 25	Sat, Dec 16	Wed, Dec 5
10 Tevet	Tue, Jan 2	Fri, Dec 21	Thu, Jan 8	Tue, Dec 29	Sun, Dec 19	Fri, Jan 5	Tue, Dec 25	Mon, Dec 15	Sun, Jan 4	Wed, Dec 22	Tue, Jan 10	Sun, Dec 31	Wed, Dec 19
Tu B'Shevat *Shevat 15*	Mon, Feb 5	Thu, Jan 23	Wed, Feb 11	Mon, Feb 1	Sat, Jan 22	Thu, Feb 8	Mon, Jan 28	Sat, Jan 18	Sat, Feb 7	Tue, Jan 25	Mon, Feb 13	Sat, Feb 3	Tue, Jan 22
Ta'anit Esther *Adar 13*	Mon, Mar 4	Thu, Mar 18*	Wed, Mar 11	Mon, Mar 1	Mon, Mar 20	Thu, Mar 8	Mon, Feb 25	Mon, Mar 17	Thu, Mar 4*	Thu, Mar 24	Mon, Mar 13	Thu, Mar 1*	Thu, Mar 20
Purim *Adar 14*	Tue, Mar 5	Sun, Mar 23	Thu, Mar 12	Tue, Mar 2	Tue, Mar 21	Fri, Mar 9	Tue, Feb 26	Tue, Mar 18	Sun, Mar 7	Fri, Mar 25	Tue, Mar 14	Sun, Mar 4	Fri, Mar 21
Shushan Purim *Adar 15*	Wed, Mar 6	Mon, Mar 24	Fri, Mar 13	Wed, Mar 3	Wed, Mar 22	Sun, Mar 10	Wed, Feb 27	Wed, Mar 19	Mon, Mar 8	Sat, Mar 26	Wed, Mar 15	Mon, Mar 5	Sat, Mar 22

	2008*/2009	2009/2010	2010/2011#	2011/2012	2012/2013	2013/2014#	2014/2015=	2015*/2016#	2016/2017	2017/2018	2018/2019#	2019/2020
Pesakh *Nissan 15–22*	Sun, Apr 20	Thu, Apr 9	Tue, Mar 30	Tue, Apr 19	Sat, Apr 7	Tue, Mar 26	Tue, Apr 15	Sat, Apr 4	Sat, Apr 23	Tue, Apr 11	Sat, Mar 31	Sat, Apr 20
Yom Hashoah *Nissan 27*	Fri, May 2	Tue, Apr 21	Sun, Apr 11	Sun, May 1	Thu, Apr 19	Sun, Apr 7	Sun, Apr 27	Thu, Apr 16	Thu, May 5	Sun, Apr 23	Thu, Apr 12	Thu, May 2
Yom Ha'atzmaut *Iyar 5*	Thu, May 8*	Wed, Apr 29	Mon, Apr 19	Mon, May 9	Thu, Apr 26*	Mon, Apr 15	Mon, May 5	Thu, Apr 23*	Thu, May 12*	Mon, May 1	Thu, Apr 20*	Thu, May 9*
Lag B'Omer *Iyar 18*	Fri, May 23	Tue, May 12	Sun, May 2	Sun, May 22	Thu, May 10	Sun, Apr 28	Sun, May 18	Thu, May 7	Thu, May 26	Sun, May 14	Thu, May 3	Thu, May 23
Yom Yerushalayim *Iyar 28*	Mon, Jun 1	Fri, May 22	Wed, May 12	Wed, Jun 1	Sun, May 20	Wed, May 8	Wed, May 28	Sun, May 17	Sun, Jun 5	Wed, May 24	Sun, May 13	Sun, Jun 2
Shavuot *Sivan 6–7*	Mon, Jun 9	Fri, May 29	Wed, May 19	Wed, Jun 8	Sun, May 27	Wed, May 15	Wed, Jun 4	Sun, May 24	Sun, Jun 12	Wed, May 31	Sun, May 20	Sun, Jun 9
17 Tammuz	Sun, Jul 20	Thu, Jul 9	Tue, Jun 29	Tue, Jul 19	Sun, Jul 8+	Tue, Jun 25	Tue, Jul 15	Sun, Jul 5+	Sun, Jul 24+	Tue, Jul 11	Sun, Jul 1+	Sun, Jul 21+
Tisha B'Av *Av 9*	Sun, Aug 10	Thu, Jul 30	Tue, Jul 20	Tue, Aug 9	Sun, Jul 29+	Tue, Jul 16	Tue, Aug 5	Sun, Jul 26+	Sun, Aug 14+	Tue, Aug 1	Sun, Jul 22+	Sun, Aug 11+
Rosh Hashanah *Tishrei 1–2*	Tue, Sep 30	Sat, Sep 19	Thu, Sep 9	Thu, Sep 29	Mon, Sep 17	Thu, Sep 5	Thu, Sep 25	Mon, Sep 14	Mon, Oct 3	Thu, Sep 21	Mon, Sep 10	Mon, Sep 30
Fast of Gedaliah *Tishrei 3*	Thu, Oct 2	Mon, Sep 21	Sun, Sep 12+	Sun, Oct 2*	Wed, Sep 19	Sun, Sep 8+	Sun, Sep 28+	Wed, Sep 16	Wed, Oct 5	Sun, Sep 24+	Wed, Sep 12	Wed, Oct 2
Yom Kippur *Tishrei 10*	Thu, Oct 9	Mon, Sep 28	Sat, Sep 18	Sat, Oct 8	Wed, Sep 26	Sat, Sep 14	Sat, Oct 4	Wed, Sep 23	Wed, Oct 12	Sat, Sep 30	Wed, Sep 19	Wed, Oct 9
Sukkot *Tishrei 15–22*	Tue, Oct 14	Sat, Oct 3	Thu, Sep 23	Thu, Oct 13	Mon, Oct 1	Thu, Sep 19	Thu, Oct 9	Mon, Sep 28	Mon, Oct 17	Thu, Oct 5	Mon, Sep 24	Mon, Oct 14
Hoshanah Rabbae *Tishrei 21*	Mon, Oct 20	Fri, Oct 9	Wed, Sep 29	Wed, Oct 19	Sun, Oct 7	Wed, Sep 25	Wed, Oct 15	Sun, Oct 4	Sun, Oct 23	Wed, Oct 11	Sun, Sep 30	Sun, Oct 20
Shemini Atzeret *Tishrei 22*	Tue, Oct 21	Sat, Oct 10	Thu, Sep 30	Thu, Oct 20	Mon, Oct 8	Thu, Sep 26	Thu, Oct 16	Mon, Oct 5	Mon, Oct 24	Thu, Oct 12	Mon, Oct 1	Mon, Oct 21
Simkhat Torah *Tishrei 23*	Wed, Oct 22	Sun, Oct 11	Fri, Oct 1	Fri, Oct 21	Tue, Oct 9	Fri, Sep 27	Fri, Oct 17	Tue, Oct 6	Tue, Oct 25	Fri, Oct 13	Tue, Oct 2	Tue, Oct 22
Khanukah *Kislev 25–Tevet 2 or 3*	Mon, Dec 22	Sat, Dec 12	Thu, Dec 2	Wed, Dec 21	Sun, Dec 9	Thu, Nov 28	Wed, Dec 17	Mon, Dec 7	Sun, Dec 25	Wed, Dec 20	Mon, Dec 3	Mon, Dec 23
10 Tevet	Tue, Jan 6	Sun, Dec 27	Fri, Dec 17	Thu, Jan 5	Sun, Dec 23	Fri, Dec 13	Thu, Jan 1	Tue, Dec 22	Sun, Jan 8	Thu, Dec 28	Tue, Dec 18	Tue, Jan 7
Tu B'Shevat *Shevat 15*	Mon, Feb 9	Sat, Jan 30	Thu, Jan 20	Wed, Feb 8	Sat, Jan 26	Thu, Jan 16	Wed, Feb 4	Mon, Jan 25	Sat, Feb 11	Wed, Jan 31	Mon, Jan 21	Mon, Feb 10
Ta'anit Esther *Adar 13*	Mon, Mar 9	Thu, Feb 25*	Thu, Mar 17*	Wed, Mar 7	Thu, Feb 21*	Thu, Mar 13*	Wed, Mar 4	Wed, Mar 23	Thu, Mar 9*	Wed, Feb 28	Wed, Mar 20	Mon, Mar 9
Purim *Adar 14*	Tue, Mar 10	Sun, Feb 28	Sun, Mar 20	Thu, Mar 8	Sun, Feb 24	Sun, Mar 16	Thu, Mar 5	Thu, Mar 24	Sun, Mar 12	Thu, Mar 1	Thu, Mar 21	Tue, Mar 10
Shushan Purim *Adar 15*	Wed, Mar 11	Mon, Mar 1	Mon, Mar 21	Fri, Mar 9	Mon, Feb 25	Mon, Mar 17	Fri, Mar 6	Fri, Mar 25	Mon, Mar 13	Fri, Mar 2	Fri, Mar 22	Wed, Mar 11

APPENDIX C:
ADDITIONAL RESOURCES

The annotated bibliographies throughout the book are for materials that deal with individual holidays or specific aspects of them. The following are comprehensive anthologies, series, or collections covering multiple holidays that may be of additional interest or use.

On the Holidays

In various ways, the following can support your overall understanding of the Jewish year and deepen your knowledge about particular aspects of the holidays. The selections for children include widely recognized collections and series, each of which covers a number of our festivals and commemorative days.

For Adults—General Holiday Information

ArtScroll. Brooklyn: Mesorah Publications.

Highly respected and widely used, the books in the far-ranging ArtScroll library include separate volumes on the holidays (covering history, laws, liturgy, and observance for each, based on talmudic and traditional sources), special texts used for them (such as *Akdamus*, *Aseres Hadibros*, and *Pirkei Avos* for Shavuot), the five *megillot*, festival *halakhah*, and much more. If you are looking for texts for use on a holiday, or additional background from a traditional viewpoint, these can be very useful.

Basic Principles of Chabad Chassidic Philosophy: Holiday Series. Brooklyn: Sichos in English.

For those searching for more depth and spirituality in holiday celebration, this may be just the thing. Four sets of cassettes cover the spiritual dimensions of the holidays (Rosh Hashanah, Yom Kippur, and Sukkot; Sukkot, Simkhat Torah, Khanukah, and Purim; Passover and Days of the *Omer*; and Shavuot, Tisha B'Av, and the month of *Elul*). Presented on an introductory level, they relate the messages of each to everyday situations through intellectual study of

Torah and the human mind (Available from 788 Eastern Parkway, Brooklyn, NY 11213; 718-778-5436).

The Hanukkah Anthology; The Passover Anthology; The Purim Anthology; The Rosh Hashanah Anthology; The Shavuot Anthology; The Sukkot and Simhat Torah Anthology; The Yom Kippur Anthology. Ed. by Philip Goodman. Philadelphia: The Jewish Publication Society of America, 1949–1992.

Each of these volumes is a wonderful resource for parents and children, rabbis and educators, laypeople and professionals, presenting a broad array of material—biblical and historical narratives; talmudic references; essays on liturgy, law, music, art, culinary traditions, worldwide customs, reminiscences of celebrations in foreign lands and trying times; explanations of a holiday's themes, and literary selections for children and adults. Information particular to a given commemoration is included in the book devoted to that holiday—such as the development of the Rosh Hashanah greeting card, Purim pranks, dances for Simkhat Torah, and so on. Some of the selections tend to go into scholarly detail, and there is sometimes repetition between essays since these are collections of writings. Still, by their sheer comprehensiveness these books have much to recommend them and are especially attractive if you want to learn more about a particular aspect of a holiday.

Ginsburg, Marvell. *Teaching Holidays to Young Jewish Children*. Chicago: Board of Jewish Education of Metropolitan Chicago, 1991.

Although designed as a manual for teachers, this guide can be very useful for parents as well. Holiday themes, learning goals, games, discussion topics, field trips, and other activities—for preschoolers and kindergarten-age children—are delineated. There are also lists of books, recordings, and songs to use. This is a valuable resource, because it helps you identify what messages to convey to your three-to five-year-old, and suggests numerous ways to get them across. (Available from the Board of Jewish

Education of Metropolitan Chicago, 618 South Michigan Avenue, Chicago, IL 60605; 312-427-5570.)

Greenberg, Irving. *The Jewish Way: Living the Holidays.* New York: Summit Books, 1988.

This warm, insightful, inspiring book is not only about living the holidays but about Judaism as a living, evolving religion. Greenberg demonstrates the interrelatedness of holidays, their recurring themes, and our destiny and gives the special days in our year renewed relevance for today and tomorrow.

For Adults— Holiday Insights and Inspiration

Blech, Rabbi Benjamin. *More Secrets of Hebrew Words: Holy Days and Happy Days.* Northvale, NJ: Jason Aronson, 1993.

Looking at *gematria*, acronyms, roots, and words within words provides insights into words and concepts connected with holidays to give new layers of meaning to observance and themes. This is a fascinating educational and entertaining supplement to an understanding of the holidays.

Chagall, Bella. *Burning Lights.* New York: Schocken Books, 1988.

The charming reminiscences of holiday celebrations in pre-Revolution Vitebsk, Russia, are told from a child's point of view. They lovingly express all the wonder, magic, and excitement home observance can hold. The author's husband, artist Marc Chagall, provided pen and ink illustrations.

Zevin, Rabbi Shlomo Yosef. *Treasury of Chassidic Tales on the Festivals.* Brooklyn: Mesorah Publications, 1983.

This book is for anyone interested in the mystical/spiritual experiences of *khasidi* leaders and the inspirational vignettes they told.

For Adults—*Halakhah*

Appel, Gersion. *The Concise Code of Jewish Law—A Guide to Prayer and Religious Observance in the Daily Life of the Jew* (Vol. 1), *A Guide to Prayer and Religious Observance on the Sabbath* (Vol 2). New York: Ktav Publishing House, 1977.

Organized by subject, this is a clearly written and easily comprehensible practical guide to *halakhah.* Included is an explanation of *melakhah* and a breakdown of the principal classes of labor forbidden on Sabbath (and festivals).

Fried, Rav Yerachmiel O. *Yom Tov Sheni Kehilchaso/ The Second Day of Yom Tov in Israel and Abroad.* Southfield, MI: Targum/Feldheim, 1990.

With clear, concise explanations, the book clarifies the differences between the first and second days of *yom tov* in Israel and in the Diaspora and gives the laws governing Israelis outside their country on a holiday and Diaspora Jews in Israel.

For Children

The Best of Olomeinu. Comp. by Rabbi Yaakov Fruchter. Ed. by Rabbi Nosson Scherman. Brooklyn: Mesorah Publications, 1981–1984.

Stories that appeared in the popular magazine for Orthodox children over a forty-year period have been compiled into seven volumes, each grouped around a season, holiday, or Shabbat. Recommended by the Jewish Book Council, the stories treat Jewish subjects in the context of mystery, history, or fantasy and reflect the experiences of Jews in all times and places. Ages 10–14.

Drucker, Malka. *A Jewish Holiday ABC.* San Diego: Harcourt Brace Jovanovich, 1992.

Colorful and interesting collages and colored pencil illustrations accompany sentences containing not only a holiday word but information about its role. The addition of a paragraph on each holiday, and a glossary, makes the book particularly useful. Ages 3–7.

Fisher, Adam. *My Jewish Year—Celebrating Our Holidays.* West Orange, NJ: Behrman House, 1993.

This is a beautiful and exciting introduction to holidays that combines the emotions surrounding their celebration with the traditions of observance. Engagingly laid out around photographic images and color illustrations, ritual, history, and legend make the holidays integral to the young readers' lives. Relevance for today is stressed, and activities get children directly involved with key aspects of holiday observance. It includes almost every holiday of the calendar (fasts, Lag B'Omer, and Yom Yerushalayim are omitted) and Shabbat. Ages 7–9.

Grishaver, Joel Lurie. *Building a Jewish Life/Haggadah; Hanukkah; Passover; Purim; Rosh Hashanah and Yom Kippur; Sukkot and Simhat Torah.* Los Angeles: Torah Aura Publications, 1987–1989.

Directed at children, written for parents and teachers (additional information for both, plus vocabulary lists and three or four lesson plans for classroom, follow the main text), the books explain the concepts of a holiday in terms to which children can relate. Each volume is somewhat different in format and may include history, a story—perhaps in the form of a modern *midrash*—and learning activities. Combinations of photography and cartoonish drawings show actual observances or put today's children in historic settings with amusing result. The texts are based on tradition and traditional sources so closely that the only clue that they were produced with a "liberal" orientation is the explanation of *mitzvah* provided for parents in the supplementary material. Overall, the books are meant to encourage a partnership in family education, providing a bridge between classroom learning and home observance. Ages 7–8. (A coordinated series of activity books for the same holidays is available for younger children, ages 5–6.)

Home Start Play and Learn Magazine for Kids and Parents to Share. Ed. by Dr. Hyman Chanover. West Orange, NJ: Behrman House, 1979.

This critically acclaimed series is designed to support classroom learning with coordinated story and activity books and cassette tapes for home use. Informative and entertaining, they explain what each holiday means and how it is celebrated, with stories, arts and crafts, masks, finger puppets, puzzles, and recipes. A set including fall holidays, Khanukah, Passover, and Purim is available for ages 3–5; the set for ages 6–7 also includes Shavuot (and Shabbat). This is one of the few resources available for very young children. Ages preschool–7.

Rouss, Sylvia. *Fun with Jewish Holiday Rhymes*. New York: UAHC Press, 1992.

Rhymes and movement activities, some with places to insert a child's name, teach Judaic symbols and concepts. It is a fun approach to learning. Ages 3–6.

Saypol, Judyth, and Madeline Wikler. *All About Hanukkah; My Very Own Haggadah; Megillah; Rosh Hashanah; Shavuot; Simchat Torah, Sukkot; Yom Kippur*. Rockville, MD: Kar-Ben Copies, 1974–1988.

Each of the slim books in this popular series is full of lovingly presented information adapted for the young child: stories, prayers, projects, themes, objects used, activities. Contents vary by holiday to reflect its main and most relevant aspects for the audience. Ages 5–10.

Weilerstein, Sadie Rose. *The Adventures of K'tonton*. New York: Women's League for Conservative Judaism, 1964.

K'tonton is a little Jewish boy, no bigger than a thumb. His amusing and heart-warming adventures —almost all of which take place on holidays—teach holiday themes and traditions and Jewish values. This has been a classic for decades. Ages 3–8.

Prayer Books

Each of the movements (Orthodox, Conservative, Reform, Reconstructionist) has its own *siddurim*, which you can find at any Jewish library or bookstore. Several include special readings on key themes in Judaism or services for the modern commemorative days. The prayer books listed below reflect the Orthodox tradition and were selected because they are the only ones that provide commentary on services, prayers, and observance.

The Complete ArtScroll Siddur. Trans. and Commentary by Rabbi Nosson Scherman. Brooklyn: Mesorah Publications, 1984.

The operative word in the title of this prayer book is complete. For weekday, Sabbath, and festival use at home and in synagogue, it includes the full text of daily and special services, blessings for a variety of situations, the rituals connected with holidays, texts of the prophetic readings for special Sabbaths, Torah readings for the holidays, *halakhot* of prayers, the Book of Psalms, and prayers said for a sick person. What makes the volume so useful is its explanation of the prayers—their development and significance —and rituals. The book is particularly helpful for people learning to pray because it gives full instructions— when to stand and sit, bow and straighten, read silently or with the congregation, and so on. *Ashkenazi* and *Sephardi* versions are available.

The Complete Metsudah Siddur. Trans. and Commentary by Rabbi Avrohom Davis. Metsudah Publications, 1990.

The major advantage of this version is its linear layout, matching short Hebrew and English phrases side by side so that you can follow in the Hebrew and at the same time read the English meaning. The commentary is not as extensive as that in the ArtScroll edition.

The NCSY Bencher—A Book of Prayer and Song. Ed. and Trans. by David M. L. Olivestone. New York: National Conference of Synagogue Youth/Union of Jewish Congregations of America, 1983.

If you have ever been to an Orthodox wedding or *bar mitzvah*, you may have seen copies of this book on the tables (characteristically enhanced with a cover bearing the names of the bride and groom or *bar mitzvah* boy and the date of the happy occasion). Provided so that guests may participate in the grace after meals, it is a handy little book to have at home for ushering in holidays. Candlelighting, *kiddush*, *Birkat Hamazon*, and *Havdalah*, as well as blessings for numerous occasions and a selection of songs, are included. Everything is transliterated.

Cookbooks

Next to books, food is probably the one item for which the Jews are known. (You can tell an occasion is a Jewish one by the type and amount of food served.) There seems to be a recent proliferation of Jewish holiday and kosher cookbooks, some of them aimed at adapting traditional recipes for the health conscious. Part of the fun of using them is reading the customs, history, and personal anecdotes and reminiscences that often accompany the recipes.

For Adults

Angel, Gilda. *Sephardic Holiday Cooking: Recipes and Traditions*. Mt. Vernon, NY: Decalogue Books, 1986.

This is a great introduction to authentic *Sephardi* cooking, full of vignettes about the holiday customs and how they differ from those of the *Ashkenazim*, commentary on dishes and seasonal ingredients, complete menus, and more than two hundred recipes, in English and Ladino.

Locke, Norton. *The Land of Milk and Honey, A Cooking Book/An Epicurean Tour of Israel with a History of Foods in the Holy Land*. Fort Lauderdale: Ashley Publishing Co., 1992.

With this fun and fascinating book you can serve what Abraham did for Rosh Hashanah and what Saul did for Sukkot. Following a brief overview of the holidays with a summary of foods historically associated with them, it explains the various foodstuffs used in biblical times. Liberally peppered with quotes from scripture, the text covers the culinary tradition of Jews in Israel, based on Torah and historical records going back as far as 2500 B.C.E. You'll find recipes for every holiday (measurements, utensils, and so on are adapted for the modern cook). One drawback of the book is its organization (or lack of it) for the first section, pre-Roman recipes. Those for post-Roman dishes (which, unlike the first, contain almost no commentary and only a few quotations) are arranged by course (there are fifty soups alone!), but you still have to flip through the pages to find appropriate dishes for a given occasion. With the wealth and variety of information interspersed, you almost don't mind. (One note: The book refers to the New Testament, but from the standpoint of history, not religion. It takes a decidedly Jewish view. If in doubt, check out the epilogue.)

Machlin, Edda Servi. *The Classic Cuisine of the Italian Jews, Traditional Recipes and Menus and a Memoir of a Vanished Way of Life*. New York: Everest House Publishers, 1981.

The reminiscences of the author about her medieval Tuscan hometown, Pitigliano, includes the preparations and celebrations surrounding the holidays. Descriptions of each festival and suggested menus introduce the recipes, which are arranged by course and annotated with anecdotes and vignettes. This is a loving look at a luscious cuisine.

Nathan, Joan. *The Jewish Holiday Kitchen*. New York: Schocken Books, 1988.

Easy to follow, the book is enhanced with short explanations of ancient food traditions, Jewish holidays, the life cycle, *kashrut*, and the development of Jewish food customs, with scriptural and literary quotes. Recipes, introduced with personalized background information or anecdotes about their origins, are arranged by holiday, but do not be limited to specific sections or the suggested holiday menus in selecting appropriate dishes or planning meals.

Prince, Francine. *Francine Prince's New Jewish Cuisine*. New York: G. P. Putman's Sons, 1991.

The 175 recipes for everyday and special occasions have been updated to eliminate excess fat, cholesterol, and salt while retaining the tradition and taste of long-time holiday favorites. Included are an overview of holidays and Jewish food customs and laws and lists of dishes suggested for each holiday. Recipes are arranged by course.

Zeidler, Judy. *The Gourmet Jewish Cook*. New York: William Morrow and Company, 1988.

Here are updated and elegant versions of old standards and new ideas based on traditional food customs. Sections defined by holiday include suggested menus and reflect a range of ethnic and modern international cuisines. There are some fabulous recipes here. Again, do not be limited to the particular holiday divisions in choosing dishes for a particular festival.

For Children

The Animated Children's Kosher Holiday Cookbook. Ed. by Yaacov Peterseil and Rivka Demsky. Efrat, Israel: Ohr Torah Institutions, 1991.

Arranged by holiday, with an introduction by Rabbi Shlomo Riskin that beautifully explains *kashrut* and its value in Jewish life, the chapters begin with the basic *mitzvot* of a holiday, its customs and symbols. Recipes are broken down into lists of ingredients, lists of utensils, and numbered steps. Riddles, gems of history, great rabbis' comments about food, and cartoonish illustrations are sprinkled throughout.

Nathan, Joan. *The Children's Jewish Holiday Kitchen*. New York: Schocken Books, 1987.

The explanations and vignettes provide information that could be relayed to children but are not presented for them to read themselves. Each recipe gives lists of ingredients and equipment, and then steps are identified to be performed by the child alone, adult alone, or both.

Songbooks

Like folktales, traditional Jewish songs show up in a multitude of collections, so you'll want to check any to which you have access.

Friedman, Debbie. *The Best of Debbie Friedman*. Cedarhurst, NY: TARA Publications, 1987.

Known for her concerts and work with children, contemporary musician Debbie Friedman has brought bright, soul-touching new melodies to traditional liturgy, scriptural verses, folksongs, and blessings. Included are blessings, "Not by Might, Not by Power" (Khanukah), "*Im Tirtzu*" (Yom Ha'atzmaut), "*Ani Ma'amin*" (Yom Hashoah), and "*Eitz Khayim*" (Shavuot). (There are complementary recordings to go with them: "And The Youth Shall See Visions," the Shavuot service; "Not By Might, Not By Power," for Khanukah; and "*Ani Ma'amim*," a selection of songs for the spring holidays.)

Holidays in Song. Comp., Arr., and Ed. by Velvel Paternak. Cedarhurst, NY: Tara Publications, 1985.

Organized by holiday, the book includes traditional folktunes, well-known parts of liturgy, and melodies for blessings. All Hebrew is transliterated, and English translation is provided.

Siddur in Song. 100 Prayerbook Melodies. Comp., Ed., and Arr. by Velvel Pasternak. Cedarhurst, NY: Tara Publications, 1986.

Tunes for weekday, Sabbath, Rosh Khodesh, Torah reading, *Hallel*, and *Mussaf* services and some special tunes for holidays are included. A companion tape is available.

The Songs We Sing. Selected and Ed. by Harry Coopersmith. New York: The United Synagogue Commission on Jewish Education, 1950.

If you are going to have only one book of Jewish songs in your home, this is probably it, for its sheer comprehensiveness. There are liturgical selections from all the major holidays, folksongs, Israeli work, folk and dance songs, Yiddish classics, cantillations for reading scripture, prayer motifs, and the tunes for the major blessings.

General Reference

There's always the *Encyclopedia Judaica* and any number of books on specific subjects to consult for additional background information on any aspect of a holiday. The following are good comprehensive resources.

The Book of Legends (Sefer Ha-aggadah)—Legends from the Talmud and Midrash. Ed. by Hayim Nahman Bialik and Yehoshua Ravnitsky. Trans. by William G. Braude. New York: Schocken Books, 1992.

First published in 1908–1911, this classic anthology of rabbinic literature arranges entries according to theme. Many of the folktales you'll find in collections of Jewish legends (like *The Classic Tales* and *Time for My Soul* frequently cited in this book) are drawn from the sources contained here. If you're interested in material that supplements the Torah and is the authentic basis for so many of the stories told about our history, sages, and beliefs, this book makes it easily accessible.

Telushkin, Rabbi Joseph. *Jewish Literacy: The Most Important Things to Know About the Jewish Religion, Its People and Its History*. New York: William Morrow and Company, 1991.

This wonderful book belongs in every Jewish home. It is made up of entries limited to a few pages each that can be read straight through for an overview of our history and life or consulted individually for information on specific subjects. Its engaging style—full of warmth, wit, and anecdote—perfectly reflects the nature of Judaism and Jewish life and makes it a resource you will want to pick up again and again.

Craft Books

Once you know the symbols and meaning of a holiday, you can adapt any creative hobby to make decorations and ritual items for it. Specific ideas and instructions are presented in several books devoted to arts and crafts for the Jewish year.

Becker, Joyce. *Jewish Holiday Crafts*. New York: Bonim Books, 1977.

The projects suggested cover a variety of craft forms and make extensive use of readily available household materials. There are some nice suggestions here, all fully explained with illustrated instructions.

Sharon, Ruth. *Arts and Crafts the Year Round*. Vol. 1. New York: United Synagogue Commission of Jewish Education, 1965.

Very popular with teachers, this two-volume work goes beyond the mundane with its wide variety of ideas for each holiday and all age groups. Materials and fully illustrated instructions are provided for each ritual, decorative, or practical item. Most of the holidays are covered in Volume 1, while Volume 2 covers months, Rosh Khodesh, Israel, Tisha B'Av, and miscellaneous nonholiday subjects.

Mail Order

The following resources are listed for two reasons: For people who do not have access to Jewish books and ritual items locally, catalogues provide an easy solution. In addition, companies that specialize in books, videos, and recordings help keep you apprised of new titles. You will find other companies in ads or listings that regularly appear in Jewish periodicals.

America's Jewish Bookstore, 1-800-Judaism, The Catalog for a Jewish Lifestyle. 2028 Murray Avenue, Pittsburgh, PA 15217-9946; 1-800-583-2476.

Representing a broad range of publishers of all denominational movements, this company offers classic and contemporary books for children and adults.

Ergo Media Inc., 668 Front Street, P.O. 2037, Teaneck, NJ 07666; 1-800-695-3746.

This is a source for Jewish videocassettes. Theatrical releases, music (Yiddish, holiday, Israeli folk and popular), holiday cooking demonstrations, Jewish communities around the world, yearbooks, history, holiday observance, and holiday-related themes, for adults and children, are available.

Hamakor Judaica, Inc.—The Source for Everything Jewish, P.O. Box 48836, Niles, IL 60714-0836; 1-800-426-2567.

Books, videos, musical recordings, and ritual items

—holiday and everyday—in a variety of styles and price ranges can be ordered. Full-color catalogues are produced several times a year, highlighting selections for upcoming holidays.

The Jewish Book Club, 834 N. 12th Street, Allentown, PA 18102.

Twice a month, members receive the *Jewish Book News*, which includes author interviews, in-depth introductions to featured books, and an extensive list of available titles at discount. Membership is free, and there is no obligation to make any purchases. It's a great way to keep informed of books of Judaic interest.

Nefesh Ami—Soul of My People, P.O. Box 651, Hicksville, NY 11801; 516-933-2660.

Specializing in music, this company offers a tremendous selection of cassettes, compact discs, music videos, and books. It also sells videos (including those about holidays produced for children) and some books.

Sisu Home Entertainment, Inc., The Source for Israeli Video and Music, 20 West 38th Street, Suite 402, New York, NY 10018; 212-768-2197.

There are quite a few holiday-themed videos and holiday song videos, classical music selections, history videos that have holiday themes, and tapes on Israel in the vast collection offered by this company.

Tara Publications, 29 Derby Avenue, Cedarhurst, NY 11516, 516-295-2290.

Books, cassettes, and compact discs in English, Yiddish, and Hebrew, covering classics, contemporary music, and holiday themes, include a selection of *Sephardi–Ladino* recordings.

GLOSSARY

The pronunciations given are for the Hebrew rendition of words or phrases. The Yiddish (which is also the Americanized version), if significantly different, is also given. Explanations of holiday names and words particular to one holiday are covered in the appropriate chapter.

Aggadah (ah'-gah-dah'): legend or folklore; from the *aggadata*, the nonlegal discussions of Talmud.

Ahavat Yisrael (ah-hah-vaht' yis-roh-eil'): love of Israel, denoting the feeling of one Jew toward all others and unity within the nation.

Akeidah (ah-kay-dah'; Yiddish: uh-kay'-duh): "binding"; the biblical account of Abraham's test of loyalty when God asked him to sacrifice his son Isaac (Genesis 22) (during the preparation for which Isaac was bound with rope).

Aliyah (ah-lee-ah'; Yiddish: ah-lee'-yuh): "ascent"; the honor given to one called to "go up" to recite the blessings before and after a section of Torah verses is read; also immigration to Israel, since moving to the Holy Land is considered an elevation; plural: *aliyot*.

Amidah (ah-mee'-dah): the central prayer of all services, recited while standing (*amad*, to stand); also referred to as the Silent Devotion, since it is said to oneself, and as *Shemoneh Esreih* (Eighteen), for the number of benedictions it originally contained (now nineteen).

Arba Kanfote (ahr-bah' kahn-fote'; Yiddish: ahr'-buh kahn'-fus): "four corners"; the undergarment worn by religious Jewish males that has ritual fringes (*tzitzit*) at each of its corners (Numbers 15:39), as a reminder of the commandments; also called *tallit* (garment) *katan* (small).

Aron Hakodesh (ah-rone' hah-koe'-desh): "holy Ark"; the enclosure on the eastern wall of a synagogue in which the Torah scrolls are housed.

Ashkenazi (ash-ken-ah-zee'; Yiddish: ahsh-ken-ahz'-ee): a Jew from West, Central, or Eastern Europe or one descended from Jews of this region, and the customs and liturgy of Jews from this region; from the Hebrew word for Germany (*Ashkenaz*), which was the center of European Jewish life; plural: *Ashkenazim*.

Atzeret (aht-tzer'-rette; Yiddish: aht-tzeh'-ress): solemn assembly; the last day of Pesakh and Sukkot as designated in Torah, and the talmudic designation for Shavuot as the conclusion of Pesakh.

Bar Mitzvah (bahr mitz'-vah): "son of commandment"; a Jewish male of thirteen years or older, and the coming of age ceremony in which he participates signifying that he is taking on the responsibilities of living by Torah; for females, called *bat* (daughter [of]) *mitzvah* and held at age twelve among the Orthodox.

Bimah (bee'-muh): "platform"; raised floor in the synagogue from where the service is conducted and the Torah read.

Birkat Hamazon (beer-kaht' hah-mah-zone'; Yiddish: beer'-khus hah-mah'-zun): "blessing for the food"; grace said after any meal at which bread has been blessed and eaten.

Blood Libel: malicious lies fabricated since the twelfth century claiming that Jews kill Christians and use their blood for making *matzah* for Passover; used to incite deadly riots and pogroms against Jews.

Brakhah (brah-khah'; Yiddish: bruh'-khuh): blessing; prayer of praise or gratitude, from *barukh*, praised or blessed; plural: *brakhot*.

Brit (brit; Yiddish: bris): covenant; circumcision of a Jewish male at the age of eight days to bring him into the covenant of the Jewish people; formally *brit milah* (covenant of circumcision).

Diaspora: Greek for dispersion, indicating the place outside the Land of Israel where Jews live and their situation there.

Eretz Yisrael (eh'-rehtz yis-roe-ail'): the Land of Israel.

Erev (eh'-rehv): evening; the start of the Jewish day and therefore the beginning of every Jewish holiday; used to designate the daytime prior to the start of a holiday or Shabbat (for instance, all of Friday is called *Erev* Shabbat).

Eruv Tavshilin (eh'-roov tahv-she-lin'; Yiddish: eh'-ruhv tahv-she'-lin): Aramaic for "mixture of cooked foods"; a ritual that allows us to cook for the Sabbath on a holiday when the Sabbath immediately follows the holiday.

Etrog (et'-roag; Yiddish: es'-rug): citron; lemon-like fruit considered a symbol of beauty and perfection, used as a ritual item on Sukkot; plural: *etrogim*.

Five Scrolls: Song of Songs (*Shir Hashirim*), Ruth (*Rut*), Lamentations (*Eikhah*), Ecclesiastes (*Kohelet*), and Esther (*Esteir*); part of the Writings section of the Hebrew Bible and each assigned for reading on a festival with which it has some thematic or historic connection.

Gabbai (gah'-bie): the synagogue treasurer or caretaker; one who keeps order during services.

Galut (gah-loot'; Yiddish: gul'lus): exile; the situation of the Jewish people outside of the Jewish homeland and before the final redemption; related to *geulah* (redemption) and *Go'al Yisrael* (Redeemer of Israel).

Gaon (gah-ohn'; Yiddish: g-own or goon): eminence, excellence, genius; the title of the heads of the Babylonian talmudic academies between the sixth and eleventh centuries and title of respect for other exceptional leaders/scholars (such as the Vilna Gaon); plural: *gaonim*.

Gemara (gah-mah-rah'; Yiddish: guh-moor'-uh): collected commentaries and elaborations on the *Mishnah*.

Gematria (geh-mah'-tree-ah): system of deriving deeper meaning from Jewish text through the numerical values assigned to letters and words.

Gemillut Khasadim (guh-mee'-loot khah-sah-dim'; Yiddish: g-mee'-loose khah-suh'-dim): acts of lovingkindness; one of the pillars, according to Jewish tradition, on which the world stands, along with Torah and Divine service.

Genizah (geh-nee'-zuh): storage place for damaged or unused scripture and other Jewish texts that may not be discarded or destroyed.

Golem (goe'-lum): legendary clay automaton created by Rabbi Yehudah Lavi of Prague in the mid-seventeenth century to protect the community against attacks instigated by blood libels.

Haftarah (hahf-toh-rah'; Yiddish: hahf-taw'-ruh): "conclusion"; selection from the prophets read after the Torah portion on Sabbath, holidays, and fast days; plural: *haftarot*.

Haggadah (hah-gah-dah'; Yiddish: huh-guh'-duh): "narration, telling"; printed version of the Passover *seder* service, a collection of scripture, literary selections, and songs; from the verb *l'haggid*, "to tell"; plural: *haggadot*.

Hakafot (hah-kah-fote'; Yiddish: hah-kaw'-fes): "circuits"; the circlings around the inside of the sanctuary or outdoors made by congregants carrying the Torah and dancing behind it on Simkhat Torah; singular: *hakafah*.

Halakhah (hah-lah-khah'; Yiddish: huh-luh'-khuh): body of Jewish law according to which a Jew is supposed to live; a combination of Torah commandments and the rabbinic interpretation of them; from the same root as "to go" and "ways"; plural: *halakhot*.

Hallel (hah'-lail): "praise"; Psalms 113–118 chanted on festivals.

Hatarat Nedarim (hah-tah'raht neh-dah-rim'): annulment of vows, customarily done on *Erev* Rosh Hashanah.

Havdalah (hahv-dah-lah'; Yiddish: hahv-duh'-luh): "separation"; the prayer and ritual recited at the close of every Shabbat and festival day to make a distinction between sacred and ordinary time.

Hillula (hih-loo'-lah): Aramaic for "celebration"; originally used to designate wedding festivities, later applied to the *yahrtzite* of a famous rabbi or scholar, whose soul wed with God; particularly used among *Sephardim* for pilgrimages to the burial sites of great scholars.

Hoshanah (hoe-shah'-nah): "please save us," a contraction of *hoshiah nah*; series of supplications made during processions around the synagogue on Sukkot and Hoshanah Rabbah; plural: *hoshanot*.

Isru Khag (iss'-roo khahg'): "to bind the festival"; the day following the pilgrimage festivals, specially designated so that we will carry the mood of the holiday into our everyday lives.

Jubilee: the fiftieth year, when all land is returned to its original owners; a precept of the social justice system ordained by Judaism; in Hebrew called *yovel*.

Kabbalah (kah-bah-lah'; Yiddish: k-buh'-luh): Jewish mysticism, from the Hebrew verb *likabeil*, to receive (as in receiving understanding); system designed to uncover the secrets of the universe and God dating back to the earliest studies of Torah; see also **Zohar**.

Kaddish (kah-deesh'; Yiddish: kah'-dish): "sanctification"; prayer marking the end of a section of a service; one version is recited by mourners during the eleven months following the death of a parent.

Karet (kah'-rette; Yiddish: kohr'-ess): excision from the community; biblically ordained punishment for refusing to identify with the Jewish people, specifically by purposely not participating in the Passover sacrifice and not undergoing circumcision.

Kasher/Kashrut (kah-shair', kash-root'; Yiddish: kah'-sher; kash'-ruse): ritually fit for use (from the same root as the words for honest and wholesome); kosher; the system of Jewish dietary laws.

Ketubah (keh-too'-bah; Yiddish: k-soo'-buh): marriage contract.

Khabad (khah-bahd'): a sect of *khasidim* originally from the town of Lubavitch who use the acronym standing for the levels of intellectual approach to Torah study: *Khokhmah* (wisdom), *Binah* (understanding), and *Das* (knowledge); the *khasidim* most active in educational outreach among Jews.

Khag (khahg): festival; descriptive word and, in biblical terms, often part of the name of holidays (*Khag Hamatzot, Khag Hakatsir,* etc.).

Khallah (khah-lah'; Yiddish: khal'-luh): the loaf of bread, usually braided, used for Shabbat and festivals; plural: *khallot.*

Khametz (khah-maitz'; Yiddish: khuh'-mitz): leaven; substances that are leavened or could become leavened and are totally prohibited to Jews during Passover.

Khasidim (khah-see-deem'; Yiddish: khah-see'-dum): "the pious"; adherents of the religious revolutionaries of the early 1700s who, under the leadership of Baal Shem Tov (Master of the Good Name) reacted against the stress on Talmud scholarship that had made Judaism stale and formal by emphasizing meditation, communion with God, and spiritual joy to bring the religion back to the masses; they gradually put more stress on learning and today are on the conservative end of Judaism.

Khazzan (khah-zahn'; Yiddish: khah'-zun): cantor; one who leads prayers in the synagogue.

Kheder (khay'-dehr): "room"; the traditional Jewish school for young boys in Europe and later America.

Khesbone Hanefesh (khesh'-bone hah-neh'-fesh): "accounting of the soul"; the personal evaluation done around Rosh Hashanah.

Khet (khait): error or wrongdoing, from the archery term meaning "to miss the mark"; used to designate our shortcomings during the Days of Awe.

Khol Hamoed (khole' hah-moe'-aid): intermediate festival days, those between the first two and last two days of Pesakh and Sukkot.

Khumash (khuh-mahsh'; Yiddish: khuh'-mush): the printed version of the Torah, from the word *khameish,* "five," for the Five Books of Moses.

Khupah (khuh-pah'; Yiddish: khuh'-puh): wedding canopy.

Khurban (khur-bahn'; Yiddish: khor'-bun): destruction by fire; refers to the destruction of Jerusalem in 586 B.C.E. and 70 C.E. and sometimes to the Holocaust.

Kibbutz (kee-bootz'): communal farm in Israel.

Kiddush (kee-doosh'; Yiddish: kid'-dish): "sanctification"; prayer sanctifying Sabbath and festivals, usually chanted over a cup of wine.

Kinot (kee-note'; Yiddish: kee'-nus): "elegies," the poems recited on Tisha B'Av; sometimes used to refer to the book of Lamentations in rabbinic literature; singular: *kinah.*

Kippah (kee-pah'; Yiddish: kee'-puh): skullcap, worn by men when praying or by traditional men as a sign of commitment to Jewish law; called *yarmulke* in Yiddish.

Kitniyot (kit'-nee-yote'; Yiddish: kit'-nee-us): legumes, specifically rice, millet, peas, beans, peanuts, corn, and buckwheat, which *Ashkenazim* are prohibited from using on Pesakh but are permissible for *Sephardim.*

Kittel (kit'l): white robe reminiscent of the Temple priests' vestments worn over regular garments by men for the Passover *seder,* on Rosh Hashanah, and Yom Kippur, by the groom on his wedding day, and a father at his son's *brit,* to represent mercy, purity, and mortality.

Klal Yisrael (klal' yis-roe-ail'): all of Israel; an expression of the unity and indivisibility of the Jewish people.

Kohein (koe'-hein): priest of the Temple; descendant of the tribe of *Levi* who served in the Temple; *Kohein Gadol* was the high priest, a descendant of Aaron (the first high priest) and member of one of the three categories of Jews, along with *Levi,* a descendant of the tribe of *Levi* who served as priests in the

Temple, and *Yisraeli*, an ordinary Israelite; plural: *Kohanim* (*Levi'im*, *Yisraelim*).

Lukhot Habrit (loo-khote' hah-brit'; Yiddish: lukh'-os hah-brees'): tablets of the covenant; the stones on which the Ten Commandments were engraved.

Lulav (loo'-lahv): palm leaf; the ritual item used for Sukkot consisting of palm, myrtle, and willow leaves.

Ma'ariv (mah'-reev): "from *erev*"; evening prayer service.

Maftir (mahf'-teer): concluding Torah verses, the last verses (or *parshah*) of any weekly or holiday Torah reading; also used to designate the person called to the Torah for that *parshah*, "one who concludes," because he generally reads the *haftarah* ("conclusion").

Mah Nishtanah (mah' nish-tah-nah'; Yiddish: mah nish-tah'-nuh): "why is this different?" the first phrase of and designation for the "Four Questions" recited at the Passover *seder*.

Makhzor (mahkh-zur'; Yiddish: makh'-zoor): "cycle," the prayer book for the holy days and festivals throughout the year; also applied to the festival liturgies in which poems specific to each holiday are included.

Ma'ot Khitim/Perot (mah'-ote khee'-tim/pay-rote'; Yiddish: mah'-os khee'-tim/pay'-ros): fund for wheat/fruit; community collections to provide food for the poor on Passover and Tu B'Shevat, respectively.

Marranos: hidden Jews of Spanish-Portuguese descent who renounced Judaism during the fifteenth-century Inquisition to save themselves but continued to observe Jewish practices in secret.

Matan Torah (mah-tan' toe-rah'; Yiddish: mah'-ten toe'-ruh): giving of the Torah during the Revelation at Mount Sinai.

Matzah (maht-zah'; Yiddish: maht'-zuh): unleavened bread made from water and flour in less than eighteen minutes, eaten during Passover; referred to as *shmurah* (guarded) if every step of the process from the time the wheat was reaped has been supervised; *ashirah* (rich) if made with other ingredients such as fruit juice or eggs; plural: *matzot*.

Megillah (meh-gee-lah'; Yiddish: meh-gill'-uh): scroll; from the word for "to roll"; the parchment strips on which certain books of the Bible were recorded; especially used to designate the Book of Esther; plural: *megillot*.

Menorah (meh-noh-rah'; Yiddish: meh-noh'-ruh): candelabra; the seven-branched lamp used in the Temple and, popularly but incorrectly, the eight-branched lamp used for the lighting of Khanukah candles (properly called a *khanukiyah*); plural: *menorot*.

Mezzuzah (meh-zoo-zah'; Yiddish: meh-zuz'-uh): "doorpost"; a piece of parchment containing parts of the *Shema* (Deuteronomy 6:4–9; 11:13–21) encased and affixed to the doorpost of a Jewish home.

Midrash (mih'-drash): the part of Talmud that consists of rabbinic interpretation of the Torah in the form of homilies, parables, and allegories that derive ethical and spiritual lessons from scripture; related to the word *d'rash* for "to investigate" or "to lecture."

Mikvah (mick-vah'; Yiddish: mick'-veh): ritual bath.

Minkhah (min-khah'; Yiddish: min'-khuh): afternoon prayer service.

Minyan (min-yahn'; Yiddish: min'-yun): group of ten people (by tradition men) needed in order to conduct a public prayer service.

Mishnah (mish-nah'; Yiddish: mish'-nuh): Code of Oral Law, the official recorded version of the laws, decisions, opinions, and ethical teachings transmitted orally by religious authorities for generations after the giving of the Torah and compiled in written form in the third century.

Mitzvah (mitz-vah'; Yiddish: mitz'-vuh): any of the commandments given in Torah governing virtually every aspect of a Jew's life; often popularly mistranslated as "good deed"; plural: *mitzvot*.

Moshiakh (mah-shee'-akh): "anointed one" derived from *mashakh*, "to anoint"; the term used for Messiah.

Motzi (moe'-tzi): bringing out; the blessing said over bread at the beginning of the meal (bread that is brought forth, or taken out of the earth); also used to designate the end of the Sabbath (*motzi* Shabbat) or festivals.

Mussaf (moo'-sahf): "addition"; the extra prayer service read on Sabbaths, festivals, and new moons.

Nevi'im (nehv-ee-eem'; Yiddish: n-vee'-im): prophets; the section of the Hebrew Bible containing the prophetic writings.

Omer (oh'-mehr): measure of grain, usually identified as a sheaf; the period of time marking the progress of the barley harvest from the second day of Pesakh through Shavuot, during which every day is counted.

Oriental: Jews from Middle Eastern and Asian communities such as Yemen, Ethiopia, Soviet Georgia, Bukhara, Cochin, India, and Persia, often grouped with *Sephardim*.

Parshah (par'-shah): "section"; a grouping of verses from a Torah reading, a set part of the *sidrah*; plural: *parshiot*.

Pesakh (peh'-sahkh): "paschal," referring to the lamb offered on the night of the Exodus and its commemoration, the holiday of Passover.

Pharisees: fathers of rabbinic Judaism who believed in extrapolating from Torah according to Oral Law, and that study and proper behavior were just as valid in serving God as Temple sacrifice.

Pidyon Haben (pid-yahn' hah-ben'; Yiddish: pid'-dyun huh-ben'): redemption of the (firstborn) son; a ceremony on the thirty-first day after the birth of a firstborn male child, in which the father pays a *kohein* five *shekalim* (today, five dollars in coins), as was done in Temple times, to release the child from the obligation of being dedicated to God and of serving the priests (Exodus 13:1–2, Numbers 18:16).

Piyyut (pee-yoot'): Greek for liturgical poem; major part of liturgies for festivals; plural: *piyyutim*.

Rosh Khodesh (roesh' khoe'-desh): "head of the month"; the one or two days that mark the beginning of each new month.

Sabbatical: the seventh year in which the land in Israel is given complete rest, debts are forgiven, and slaves released (Leviticus 25:2–4; Deuteronomy 15:1); in Hebrew called *shmittah*.

Sabra: term for a native-born Israeli, from the fruit of the cactus plant of the same name, which has a hard prickly outside but is sweet inside.

Sadducee: member of the aristocracy connected with the priesthood in Second Temple days who believed in a literal interpretation of Torah and in the supremacy of sacrifice as the way to serve God.

Seder (say'-dir): order; refers to the order of service and in particular to the home ceremony conducted on the first two evenings of Pesakh; plural: *sedarim*.

Sefer (say'-fehr): book; plural: *sifrei* (used when referring to multiple Torah scrolls, *Sifrei Torah*).

Sefirah (s-fee-rah'; Yiddish: s-fee'-ruh): counting; the forty-nine days between Pesakh and Shavuot during which the *omer* is counted, a period for self-improvement and spiritual elevation; also, one of the ten spheres that make up the world in *kabbalah*'s view; plural: *sefirot*.

Selikhot (s-lee-khote'; Yiddish: slikh'-us): "forgiveness"; series of penitential prayers recited in the week prior to Rosh Hashanah and at other times when repentance is made.

Sephardi (s-phahr-dee'; Yiddish: s-phahr'-dee): a Jew descended from those expelled from Spain or Portugal in 1492, predominantly those who settled in Arab countries, and their customs and liturgy; from the Hebrew word for Spain (*Sepharad*); often used to refer to all non-*Ashkenazi* Jews (also see **Oriental**); plural: *Sephardim*.

Seudah (soo-dah'; Yiddish: soo'-duh): a festive meal, required as part of holiday or Shabbat observance, especially the meal eaten as part of Purim celebration; *seudah mafseket*, the meal that "interrupts," immediately precedes a fast; *seudat mitzvah* refers to the special meal following fulfillment of a commandment at a joyous occasion (*brit, bar mitzvah,* wedding, *siyyum*); *shalosh seudot* (often garbled as "shallushu-dus") is the third meal of Shabbat, served on Saturday afternoon / evening.

Shabbat (shah-baht'; Yiddish: shah'-bus): Sabbath; to stop work, rest.

Shakharit (shah-khah-reet'; Yiddish: shakh'-ris): morning prayer service, from one of the words for morning, *shakhar*.

Shalosh Regalim (shah-loesh' reh-gah-leem'): "three pilgrimages," the festivals when all Israelite men were required to go to the Temple in Jerusalem with seasonal offerings, Pesakh, Shavuot, and Sukkot.

Shammash (shah-mahsh'; Yiddish: shahm'-us): servant; the auxiliary candle used to light the flames of the Khanukah *menorah*; in European synagogues, the sexton.

Shehekheyanu (sheh-heh-kheh-yah'-noo): "Who has kept us alive"; prayer of gratitude and celebration recited at the arrival of a holiday or when something is experienced for the first time during a Jewish year (e.g., new fruit eaten, new garment worn, major accomplishment made).

Shekhinah (sheh-khee'-nah): Divine Presence in the world; God's feminine nature.

Shem Hameforash (shem' hah-meh-foh'-rash): "Explicit Name"; the ineffable Name of God, pronounced only by the high priest at the Temple during the *Avodah* service on Yom Kippur.

Shema (sheh-mah'): "hear," from "Hear O Israel, the Lord our God the Lord is One"; central creed of Judaism, the declaration of faith in One God, said in daily prayers, prior to retiring for the night and, if possible, just before death; the biblical passages Deuteronomy 6:4–9, 11:13–21, and Numbers 15:37–41.

Shmittah (shmee'-tah): see **Sabbatical.**

Shirah (sheer'-ah): "song"; Exodus 15:1–18, the song sung by the Israelites after they left Egypt, "Song of the Sea"; part of daily services, read on the Sabbath when we reach that section of Torah, on the seventh day of Passover commemorating the crossing of the Reed Sea, and on special Sabbaths.

Shivah (shiv'-uh): week-long mourning observed by the deceased's immediate family; from same root as seven (*sheva*), for the seven days of the period.

Shoah (show'-ah): modern Hebrew word for the Holocaust, meaning devastation, ruin; often *Hashoah* (The Holocaust).

Shofar (show-fahr'; Yiddish: show'fer): ram's horn instrument used to call the nation together since earliest times and a main ritual item of Rosh Hashanah.

Shul (Yiddish: shool): modest place of worship, a small synagogue.

Siddur (see-duhr'; Yiddish: sid'-der): prayer book; indicating the order (*seder*) of service; plural: *siddurim*.

Sidra (sid'-ruh): portion of Torah read on Sabbath or a festival; plural: *sidrot*.

Simkhah (sim-khah'; Yiddish: sim'-khuh): "joy," feeling generated by a holiday; also, a happy occasion, such as a *brit*, *bar mitzvah*, or wedding.

Siyyum (see'-yoom): "conclusion"; celebration marking the conclusion of study of a tractate of Talmud, three tractates of *mishnayot* (sections of *Mishnah*) with commentary, or a book of *Tanakh* with commentary.

Streimel (strie'-mul): fur-trimmed hat worn by certain sects of *khasidim* for Shabbat, festivals, and other joyous occasions.

Sukkah (soo-kah'; Yiddish: sook'-uh): booth; structure in which a Jew lives during the holiday of Sukkot; plural: *sukkot*.

Ta'anit (tah-ah-neet'): fast; as in Fast of Esther or Fast of the Firstborn.

Tallit (tah-leet'; Yiddish: tahl'-lis): "garment"; prayer shawl with ritual fringes (*tzitzit*) on each corner as a reminder of the commandments; plural: *talleisim*; see also **Arba Kanfote.**

Talmud (tahl'-mood): collection of books embodying collected Jewish wisdom: *Mishnah*, *Gemara*, and *Midrash*, developed in two versions, the Babylonian and Jerusalem, by the sages of the academies.

Tanakh (tah-nahkh'): acronym for the entire Hebrew Bible, made up of the initials of each part, Torah (Five Books of Moses), Nevi'im (Prophets) and Ketuvim (Writings).

Tefillah (teh-fee'-lah): prayer.

Tefillin (teh-fih'-lin): phylacteries, or prayer accessories, consisting of two small leather boxes containing parchment strips on which the text of Exodus 13:1–10, 11–16, and Deuteronomy 6:4–9, 11:13–21 (*Shema*), has been written, attached with leather strips—one box on the left arm and the other on the forehead (Deuteronomy 11:18)—during morning prayer.

Tehillim (teh-hih'-lim): psalms.

Teshuvah (t-shoo'-vuh): "turn, return"; make repentance by turning away from bad and turning toward good and God's commandments; also indicates one who has come back to a Jewish way of life, *ba'al*, or for a female *ba'alat* (master [of]) *teshuvah*.

Tikkun (tee-koon'): repair or improvement; the study session on the night of Pesakh, Shavuot, or Hoshanah Rabbah or the collection of scriptural, talmudic, and literary passages that are studied during it.

Tikkun Olam (tee-koon' oh-lahm'): perfection of the world; the Jewish mission on Earth and basis for social action agendas.

Torah (toe-rah'; Yiddish: toe'-ruh): "teaching"; the Five Books of Moses; also referred to as *Torah Sheh Bikhtav* (Written Torah) and by non-Jews as Old Testament; any insight or instruction derived from the study of classic Jewish text; the scroll containing the Hebrew text of the five books, also referred to as *Sefer Torah*.

Torah Sheh B'al Peh (toe-rah' sheh b'ahl peh'): Oral Law or Oral Tradition, the body of explanations believed by Orthodox Jews to have been given at Mount Sinai along with the written law that allowed for understanding of Torah's intent and for interpretation in accordance with changing conditions in the world.

Treif (trayf):   ritually unfit; nonkosher food.

Twelve Tribes: The descendants of the sons of Jacob who became the Jewish people: Reuben, Simeon, Levi, Judah, Issachar, Zevulun, Dan, Gad, Naftali, Asher, Joseph (represented by his sons, Ephraim and Menassah), and Benjamin.

Tzaddik (tzah-deek'; Yiddish: tzah'-dik):   a righteous person; plural: *tzaddikim.*

Tzedakah (tzeh-dah'-kah; Yiddish: tzu-duh'-kuh): "justice"; from the same root as *tzaddik*, "just" or "virtuous"; contribution to help those less fortunate (commonly called charity), and in that way create a just balance in the world.

Yahrtzite (yahr'-tzite; Yiddish: yor'-tzite):   memorial; anniversary of death; describes the memorial candles burned on occasions when the deceased are recalled.

Yamim Nora'im: (yah-meem' noh-rah'-yim): "Days of Awe":   Rosh Hashanah, Yom Kippur, and the days in between.

Yeshivah (yeh-shee-vah'; Yiddish: yeh-shee'-vuh): academy devoted mainly to the study of Talmud and rabbinic commentary; plural: *yeshivot.*

Yetzer Harah (yay'-tzir hah-rah'):   evil inclination in human nature.

Yetzer Hatov (yay'-tzir hah-tove'):   good inclination in human nature.

Yetziat Mitzrayim (yeh-tzi'-yaht mitz-rah'-yim): departure from Egypt; the Exodus.

Yishuv (yee-shoov'):   "settlement"; the Jewish colony in pre-State Palestine.

Yizkor (yiz-kohr'; Yiddish: yis'-kir):   "May [God] remember"; memorial service held on the last day of pilgrimage festivals and Yom Kippur.

Yom Tov (yome' tove; Yiddish: yum' tof and often mispronounced as yun'-tif):   "good day"; holiday.

Yovel (yoe'-vell):   see **Jubilee**.

Zeman (z-mahn'):   time or season; used for pilgrimage festivals as *Zeman Kheiruteinu* (Season of Our Freedom, Pesakh), *Zeman Matan Torateinu* (Season of Giving of Our Torah, Shavuot) and *Zeman Simkhateinu* (Season of Our Rejoicing, Sukkot).

Zohar (zoe'-hahr):   "brilliant, splendid light"; the central work of *kabbalah.*

INDEX

INDEX

ABOUT THE AUTHOR

Lesli Koppelman Ross received a master's degree from New York University. A writer and artist, her photographs and feature-length articles have appeared in national consumer magazines, newspapers, and trade publications, including *Cosmopolitan*, *Redbook*, the *New York Post*, and *Hadassah* magazine. Her sculptural works are shown in gallery exhibitions in various cities. She has devoted herself to Jewish communal life, serving as an officer for several organizations. Recently, she has focused her service energies on Ethiopian Jewry and Jewish education. Mrs. Ross resides in Chicago with her husband, Jordon.

This innovative how-to guide and reference book on the Jewish holidays provides a well-rounded foundation for both knowledge and action. Unlike many books of its kind, *Celebrate! The Complete Jewish Holidays Handbook* is nondenominational and comprehensive in approach. The author includes the historical development, religious importance, and personal significance of each Jewish holy day in a way that is useful to both beginners and those well versed in Jewish practice. The richness and depth of Jewish tradition, with a full range of information on why and how to celebrate, is presented in a lively, warm, and user-friendly manner.

"Celebrate! is a book for all generations. From grandparents to preschoolers, this compendium of Jewish holidays has something for everyone—history, religion, prayers, songs, books to read, games to play, food to serve, with answers to nearly every question one might have on how these holidays got started, why we celebrate them, what they mean to us personally, and how to enrich our lives by singing and reading and even watching movies built around the Jewish calendar of holiday celebrations.

"What is unique about *Celebrate!* is that it includes not only the traditional holidays but also takes us into the present with chapters on Yom Hashoah—commemorating the Holocaust, Yom Ha'atzmaut—Independence Day, and Yom Yerushalayim—Jerusalem Day.

"It is a book to read and reread, to savor and study, to taste and take joy in the truth and the beauty of the holidays it celebrates. It is a perfect *bar* and *bat mitzvah* gift, wedding gift, or even a gift for a newborn, who may begin to enjoy it at the age of three. It is scholarship made luminous."

—Ruth Gruber
Author of *Raquela: A Woman of Israel*

"Written with passion, insight, and chock full of information, this handbook is a marvel of organization and accessibility. The sections for each holiday on historic background, religious importance, and personal significance (including the contemporary holidays of Yom Hashoah, Yom Ha'atzmaut, and Yom Yerushalayim) provide meaning and guidance to those who seek to fully celebrate the life and heritage of the Jewish people."

—Rabbi Nathan Laufer
Vice President, Wexner Heritage Foundation

"Lesli Koppelman Ross's book *Celebrate!* is charmingly written, packed with information, and remarkably informative. There is nothing quite like it on the market. It will deepen the knowledge of Jewish holidays among Jews who already observe them, while teaching and touching Jews eager to integrate family observances into their lives."

—Rabbi Joseph Telushkin
Author of *Jewish Literacy*

Jason Aronson Inc.
230 Livingston Street
Northvale, New Jersey
07647

No. 9 Hampstead West
224 Iverson Road
West Hampstead, London
NW6 2HL England

Cover photo by Bill Aron

Cover design by Judith M. Reitsema

1-56821-154-6